D1615556

The Making of the Transport and General
Workers' Union:

The Emergence of the Labour Movement 1870–1922

THE NEW WORLD UNITES WITH THE OLD WORLD TO HELP THE DOCK LABOURER

JUSTICE · AM · NOT · I · A · MAN · HUMANITY · AND · A · BROTHER

DOCK STRIKE 1889

AFTER NOVEMBER · 4 · 1889
DOCK · LABOURERS
TO · BE · PAID · 6d · PER · HOUR
OVERTIME 8d
CONTRACT & PIECE
WORK
MEN · PAID · AS
BALANCE · DIVIDED
EQUALLY

WE · STRIKE · FOR BREAD FOR STARVING WIVES & CHILDREN

THE · UNIVERSAL · BROTHERHOOD · OF · LABOUR · WE · SECURE

BY · UNION

HOMES WHERE DECENCY IS POSSIBLE AND FOR · OUR MANHOOD

INASMUCH AS YE DID IT UNTO ONE OF THE LEAST OF THESE MY BRETHREN YE DID IT UNTO ME

OUR · RIGHTS

IN · COMMEMORATION · OF · THE · GREAT · STRIKE · SEPTr · 1889

THE HISTORY OF THE TRANSPORT AND GENERAL WORKERS' UNION

VOLUME I

The Making of the Transport and General
Workers' Union:

The Emergence of the Labour Movement
1870–1922

Part I

1870–1911: From Forerunners to Federation

Ken Coates and Tony Topham

Basil Blackwell

First published 1991

Basil Blackwell Ltd
108 Cowley Road, Oxford, OX4 1JF, UK

Basil Blackwell, Inc.
3 Cambridge Center
Cambridge, Massachusetts 02142, USA

British Library Cataloguing in Publication Data
A CIP catalogue record for this book is available from the British Library.

Library of Congress Cataloging in Publication Data
Coates, Ken.
The history of the Transport and General Workers' Union / Ken Coates and Tony Topham.
p.   cm.
Includes bibliographical references and index.
Contents: v. 1. The making of the Transport and General Workers' Union:
The emergence of the labour movement, 1870–1922 (2 pts.)
ISBN 0–631–17964–X (v. 1, pt. 1)
1. Transport and General Workers' Union (Great Britain) – History.
2. Labor movement – Great Britain – History. I. Topham, Tony.
II. Title.
HD6668.T73T73   1991
331.88′11388′0941–dc20   90–1277
CIP

Typeset in 10.5 on 12pt Ehrhardt
by Hope Services (Abingdon) Ltd
Printed in Great Britain by T. J. Press Ltd, Padstow, Cornwall

To the memory of the pioneers who dreamed of One Big Union, and to the success of their heirs, the members of the Transport and General Workers' Union.

Contents

List of Illustrations

List of Figures

List of Tables

List of Acronyms

AATVW	Amalgamated Association of Tramway and Vehicle Workers (shortened form: AAT)
ADM	Annual Delegate Meeting
AEU	Amalgamated Engineering Union
AFL	American Federation of Labour
AGC	Annual General Council (of the NTWF)
AMWU	Amalgamated Marine Workers' Union
APEX	Association of Professional, Executive, Clerical and Computer Staff
ASE	Amalgamated Society of Engineers
ASLEF	Amalgamated Society of Locomotive Engineers and Firemen
ASRS	Amalgamated Society of Railway Servants
AS of WL & B	Amalgamated Society of Watermen, Lightermen and Bargemen
AUCE	Amalgamated Union of Co-operative Employees
BSP	British Socialist Party
BSU	British Seafarers' Union
CAWU	Clerical and Administrative Workers' Union
CGT	Confédération Générale du Travail
CPGB	Communist Party of Great Britain
CRC	Cardiff Railway Company
CTU	Coal Trimmers' Union
DWRGLU	Dock, Wharf, Riverside and General Labourers' (later Workers') Union
DWRGWU	*see above*
EC	Executive Council/Committee
F & EC	Finance and Emergency Committee (of the TGWU)
GEC	General Executive Council (of the TGWU)
GFTU	General Federation of Trade Unions

GLNC	General Labourers' National Council
GMBATU	General, Municipal, Boilermakers' and Allied Trades Union
ILP	Independent Labour Party
ITF	International Transport Workers' Federation
ITGWU	Irish Transport and General Workers' Union
IWW	Industrial Workers of the World
LCC	London County Council
LDCMU	Liverpool and District Carters' and Motormen's Union
LMSA	London Master Stevedores' Association
LPL	Labour Protection League
LPULVW	London and Provincial Union of Licensed Vehicle Workers (shortened form: LPU)
LRC	Labour Representation Committee
MEA	Municipal Employees' Association
NAC	National Administrative Council (of the ILP)
NACWU	National Amalgamated Coal Workers' Union
NALU	National Amalgamated Labourers' Union
NAUL	National Amalgamated Union of Labour
NDL	National Democratic League
N of ET & TA	North of England Trimmers' and Teemers' Association
NFGW	National Federation of General Workers
NFLA	National Free Labour Association
NFWW	National Federation of Women Workers
NIC	National Industrial Council
NJIC	National Joint Industrial Council (shortened form: JIC)
NMB	National Maritime Board
NSFU	National Seamen's and Firemen's Union
NTWF	National Transport Workers' Federation (shortened form: TWF)
NUDAW	National Union of Distributive and Allied Workers
NUDL	National Union of Dock Labourers
NUDWSS	National Union of Docks, Wharves and Shipping Staffs
NUGMW	National Union of General and Municipal Workers
NUGW	National Union of General Workers
NUR	National Union of Railwaymen
NUVW	National Union of Vehicle Workers
PEC	Provisional Executive Committee (of the TGWU)
PLA	Port of London Authority
PLC	Port Labour Committee
PLP	Parliamentary Labour Party
RCA	Railway Clerks' Association
SDF	Social Democratic Federation
SSLPL	South Side Labour Protection League
SSTA	Short Sea Traders' Association

TA	Triple Alliance
TGWU	Transport and General Workers' Union
TUC	Trades Union Congress
UCS	Upper Clyde Shipbuilders
ULC	United Labour Council
UOGL	United Order of General Labourers
URTU	United Road Transport Union
USDAW	Union of Shop, Distributive and Allied Workers
UVW	United Vehicle Workers
WU	Workers' Union

Foreword

No one before has written a comprehensive history of the TGWU. There have been many special studies and some key biographies, making up many thousands of words, some in important works. But I believe that this double volume is the beginning of a major book because it starts out with a sort of pre-history, with the 1870s and the period running up to the great dock strike of 1889 – the 'Dockers' Tanner Strike', as we have come to know it from history passed down through dockers' families.

This background history had to be done, so that we can start to understand how the 'One Big Union' amalgamation of 1922 actually came into being. In looking back into our real origins, the authors have found a lot more, some of it controversial, some of it potentially of great value in helping the union chart its way through the final decade of the twentieth century, after bitter and difficult times in recent years for trade unionism right across the world. Their book shows how TGWU origins lie deep in Labour history and class development in our country. Indeed, part of the title of this work tries to capture the point that the emergence of the TGWU has been central to the whole character of the British Labour movement and its socialist aspirations.

The authors have tabled some clear challenges, in the best spirit of debate and searching for the truth. Our formal co-operation with their work has been 'warts and all', to coin a phrase that probably hasn't been put like that in the minutes. It was given in the spirit that our movement deserves candour, straightforward argument and analysis. Have no doubt, we have got these from the authors. I have every confidence that they will carry on in the same way as they approach more recent times in further volumes.

Their narrative includes the familiar heroes, some new ones, and some villains against whom our predecessors struggled hard. In a sense, the TGWU was never born – it was made by hard labour, by incessant struggle, a monumental achievement that was at risk time and again. The authors have argued strongly for the essential continuity of the movement for amalgamation from the 1870s, through the great dock strike and up until the Leamington Conference of 1921. They argue that the unskilled workers who built the general labourers' unions were people of invention and imagination, setting trends with new forms of organization and policy and strategy for the whole Labour movement. That is a different picture to the common one of the unskilled labourers somehow 'catching up' with the pre-existing craft-union traditions, and then taking their due place in an established Labour movement. What these workers did was revolutionize this very movement, not least in its political aspirations, seen in the creation of the ILP and the Labour Party and the turn away from dependence on the Liberals; and also in their willingness to join with pioneer socialist thinkers and agitators when others sought respectable incorporation.

The labourers fashioned the unique multi-industrial structure of the eventual TGWU, going beyond federation to organizational unity, but keeping the proper autonomy of trade-group interests against a divisive sectionalism. They consistently demanded recognition and institutionalized bargaining machinery from employers and the state, long before they were achieved, amidst competing pressures for immediate gains in wages and conditions, the heady temptations of utopian independence, and moderation and subordination to the employers. The distinct strategy of securing independent trade unionism through joint regulation remains a strength to this day, a feature of mainstream trade unionism that politicians too often ignore in their attacks on trade-union power.

The authors portray leaders who were quick in the field of building international trade unionism, especially in the transport industries, as a power-base for spreading their influence. Their 'new unionism' gave birth to the movement for independent labour representation, with the two dockers' unions and the Amalgamated Society of Railway Servants jointly convening the first union conference for forming labour's own political party.

Above all, the authors show how the pioneers were people of vision, capable of setting big targets and sustaining them in bad times as well as good. So it is a story of big thinking, rooted in bread-and-butter organization, professional skills and political vision, in committed energy and incessant hard work.

It is a long time back, but it may be the case that some of the problems we face in the British trade-union movement today are not so far removed from those covered in this first part of our history, least of all in the battle between the new unionism of today's TGWU and the various types of new realism espoused by some other trade unions.

We have been looking to extend our base by organizing amongst the new army of part-time and temporary workers, the so called 'periphery' of the modern labour market, now totalling around a quarter of all workers. We have carried this and other important messages into the Labour Party at a time when there is a strong current of opinion in favour of a historic loosening of those very ties which came into being in the period which this history covers. We are seeking major mergers and looking to new kinds of links with European unions, below the formal levels already in existence, so that trade-union solidarity can be developed, and common demands can be formulated, as close as possible to the factories and offices, as our economies become more deeply integrated. We have kept our focus wide, helping South Africa's oppressed workers to form their unions, and championing opposition to obscene militarism, when others have counselled a narrower focus on the immediate interests of employees, whatever they may be, and assuming that it is actually possible to separate the industrial and the political so neatly.

For organizations like ours, it has always made sense to examine where we have been, before asking where it is best to go now. I sense the end of a period and the opening of a new one. Not the end of working-class struggle and organization; not the end of broad socialist aspiration; not the end of opposition to market forces and social domination by powerful classes who control and own the core capital of our societies; not the end of struggling against injustice and privileges secured through daily control of our societies, often by subtle, but sometimes brutal means; not the end of independent trade unionism, rooted in workplace democracy, and its replacement by a carefully controlled system run by anonymous backroom committees and murmuring manipulators. No, I sense a renewal of emphasis on public interest, commonwealth and community, and on human decency undertaken as a social obligation. A new and clear sense of what democracy is for ordinary people now that the Cold War competition about freedom is behind us.

I sense that a new era of international Labour movement organization is near, most obviously in Europe and in what is fast becoming greater Europe. If there is to be a meaningful socialist political party for the Europe of the future, then it must surely find its power and democracy in partnership with an extended trade unionism. And I sense that the terrible burden of military expenditure in advanced and less-developed countries alike will be overturned – if future generations play their politics correctly – by forces committed to overcoming the vast problem of world poverty and the ecological threat.

As usual, there is much to be done. That is in the essential spirit of the TGWU, as friends and foes alike know. But I make a direct appeal, again in our best traditions, for time to be found by even the most active of our members to study this story closely. For, have no doubt, as you follow this first part of our common history – a leading history for the whole of working-class organization in Britain and internationally – I am confident that you will draw energy and commitment from reading about the battles that were fought in the early days. In many respects things are overwhelmingly better today than then: that is what we have helped substantially to achieve. But in other respects we cannot relax our guard. Nor can we safely carry on fighting unless we know our place in history and look to take its lessons on board.

Someone else will write a Foreword to later sections of this history. For my part, I am pleased that the first full history of the whole of the TGWU was started during my period of office as General Secretary. I take comfort that the terms of reference have been wide and free, and that the first instalment has turned out as neither the authors nor the union originally expected. We looked forward to having our story told with the focus on the great amalgamation, but I think we already have a lot more than that in the challenges presented from this crucial foundation period in the history of our whole Labour movement. The implications for the subsequent periods could be large. But for the moment, let it suffice that our sort of history requires that we respond in future action, making new history as we read the old.

Ron Todd
General Secretary, TGWU
September 1990

Acknowledgements

Since the Transport and General Workers' Union is the largest trade union in modern Britain, those adult-education tutors who teach trade-union students are prone to meet a large number of TGWU members in their classes. Both in extra-mural work and in courses organized by the union itself, we became very much aware of a gap in our reading lists: there was no history of our biggest union.

We began to nurture the idea that we might try to fill this gap, and for many years we mulled it over with officers and members of the union. Our first and most abiding debt of gratitude therefore lies with the members and officers of the union who have encouraged us and taught us far more than they realize. We must begin with Ron Todd, who saw the need for this study and gave us every possible support. His Executive and its national officers were encouraged to help us, and indeed they did so, unstintingly. Ron Todd very keenly followed our progress in the cellars of Transport House and all the other archives. He combined patience with understanding and sympathy, and his reactions were shared by very many of his staff. Our debt to him and his team is immense, and we shall not be able to repay it until we have carried this absorbing story forward into recent times.

We are very grateful indeed to the Leverhulme Trust, which made a research grant available to Nottingham University in order to sustain this work over three years.

Professor Michael Stephens, at the time director of Nottingham University's Adult Education Department, and Kenneth Lawson, his deputy director, gave every possible support to the project, and were an unfailing source of good advice and practical assistance.

Rita Maskery, secretary to the project, worked ceaselessly in typing and retyping the text as it grew, and in transcribing innumerable interviews. She was a model of patience and skill.

In Transport House, and beyond, Regan Scott, the Union's national secretary for education and research, a true collaborator and colleague, has been, and continues to be, our essential 'anchorman', guiding us through the accumulated records housed there, always prompting new thought and opening avenues of research and enquiry. He has given freely of his time in a busy schedule of union duties, and offered his own extensive knowledge and experience of the union at all times, as well as making us welcome and comfortable in our work in the union's archives and library. The central office staff, in the library and in Trade Group and other departments, have responded warmly to the lead given by Regan, and by Ray Collins, the union's administrative officer, in smoothing our way through the records and the cellars.

Academic and library staffs in Nottingham and Hull Universities have provided continuous support, facilities and advice. On our visits to the Modern Records Centre at Warwick University, which houses an important archive on the TGWU, and the Bevin Papers, we have benefited from the expert advice and service of Richard Storey and Alistair Tough. Similar services were afforded us in the John Rylands Library in Manchester, and at the National Museum of Labour History.

Gordon Phillips and Paul Smith very kindly loaned copies of their important theses, and Arthur Marsh allowed us access to his joint manuscript (with Victoria Ryan) of the now published history of the Seamen's Union. Bruce Spencer, lecturer in Trade Union Studies at Leeds University, undertook enquiries for us in Region 9 of the union, and we have had the benefit of John Saville's advice: he provided access to important sources and his expertise on labour history was always available to us. Ted Gillett, historian of Hull, culled his files of press reports in our aid.

Professor Tsuzuki went to great efforts to provide us with access to chapters of his important new work on the life of Tom Mann. Graham Stevenson, at the time a trade-group secretary in the union's Region 5, has written a comprehensive account of trade unionism in Derbyshire, and we are most grateful for the loan of his manuscript.

We wish also to thank all who read and commented on drafts of chapters and sections, including Ken Fleet, Michael Barratt Brown, John Hughes, the late Steve Bodington, Walt Greendale, Tom Watkinson, Michael Somerton, Daniel Vulliamy, Denis Mayhew, Geoff Brown and Brian Barker.

We must place David Howell, Professor of Politics at Manchester University, in a special category. He undertook a systematic reading of the whole text, when it had reached an advanced stage of preparation, following which we spent two fascinating days with him as he led us through his corrections, comments and appraisal. We learned so much, and we are very grateful.

Geoff Stuttard, now retired from a lifetime of teaching on trade-union day-release for London University's Extra-mural Department, and a colleague in many TGWU schools and in trade-union studies publication, invited us to give three 'progress reports' to his London seminar series on Industrial Relations. We derived much valuable advice, as well as enthusiastic encouragement, from him and his groups. Their selfless identification with our work became important to us. Rodney Mace supplied us with details of the career of Cardinal Manning's father.

Before his death, Frank Cousins gave us several extended interviews: his insights have been of great value. Jack Jones has given us a preliminary interview, has made texts and records available to us, and has been warmly supportive of our work. We shall have occasion to record an even greater debt to him, and to his generation of the union, when our projected study down to recent times is complete.

The same is true of a large number of retired and senior union leaders and officers, whose interviews, documentary loans and advice have already helped our understanding of the structure and traditions of the union, and pointed us on our way into Volume II. These include Moss Evans, Tim O'Leary, Bill Lindley, the late Bill Jones, Stan Pemberton, Walt Greendale, Sid Easton, Eddie Roberts, the late Bob Edwards, Alex Kitson, Sid Forty and Jack Ashwell.

A further source which overlaps this, and subsequent work, has been the archive of the Communist Party, where Francis King has been an expert and helpful guide. We also received valuable help from Noreen Branson of the Labour Research Department.

We wish to make collective acknowledgement of all those authors on whose published work and theses we have drawn so freely and so gratefully. Our debt to them will be evident in our text and footnotes.

At the outset of the project, we published appeals in the press and in the *Record* asking for memories and documents held by private individuals and retired members. Among union members and others who kindly wrote to us, often sending books and papers, some of which were of very great interest, are the following: Mrs W. J. Barnshaw, Mrs R. Bannister, Bertie Bassett, E. J. Brawn, J. K. Cochrane, Fred Cole, J. E. Constantine, F. G. Deacon, Douglas Dean, J. R. Foskett, Mike Gibbons, Bill Gillman, W. Howard, G. Johnson, Vic Kerviel, J. K. Leathwood, Les Nichols, Allan Parfitt, W. T. Parsons, D. Payne, Bill Punt, H. W. Pusey, Mrs A. Roots, Mrs G. Sinclair, Gavan Smith, R. H. Thomas, Sir Robert Thomas, Harry Tindell, Reg Weller, P. R. Whili, Albert Wyman.

Tony Topham wishes to add his personal thanks to Monica Hare and Tony Eyles of the Foundation for Communication for the Disabled, and to Mike Portus, Sally Hubbard, Brian Charles and Dave Tuck of the Disablement Advisory Service, for their invaluable technical and advisory services to him.

Finally, we thank René Olivieri, Tim Goodfellow and Jane Robertson of Basil Blackwell for their great labours in seeing the work through all stages of its publication, and Brenda Thomson for her thorough, sympathetic, and immensely helpful work on this very large text, as our copy-editor. Our grateful thanks are also due to Colin Hutchens and Valerie Mendes, who read the proofs, and to Sarah Ereira, who compiled the index.

Whatever errors remain after the helpful scrutiny of colleagues and friends will, we hope, be corrected by our critics, of whom we anticipate no shortage.

Ken Coates, Matlock
Tony Topham, Hull
November 1990

The authors and publishers are indebted to the following for permission to quote from copyright material:

Lord Askwith and John Murray (Publishers) Ltd (Lord Askwith, *Industrial Problems and Disputes*); the London School of Economics and Political Science (Beatrice Webb, *My Apprenticeship*, and Sidney and Beatrice Webb, *The History of Trade Unionism*); H. C. G. Mathew, R. I. McKibbin, J. A. Kay, J. M. Roberts, G. A. Holmes and the Longman Group (*The English Historical Review*, vol. XCI, 1976); Harvester Wheatsheaf (C. J. Wrigley, *A History of British Industrial Relations*, vol. II); Lawrence and Wishart (Yvonne Kapp, *Eleanor Marx*, vol. II: *The Crowded Years*); Oxford University Press, (H. A. Clegg, Alan Fox and A. F. Thompson, *A History of British Trade Unions since 1889*, vol. I: *1889–1910*; H. A. Clegg, *A History of British Trade Unions since 1889*, vol. II: *1911–1933*; Gordon Phillips and Noel Whiteside, *Casual Labour*; and C. H. Feinstein and S. Pollard, *Studies in Capital Formation in the United Kingdom, 1750–1920*); Cambridge University Press, (B. R. Mitchell, *Abstract of British Historical Statistics*); and the Trustees of the Yorkshire Bulletin of Economic and Social Research (Sydney Pollard, 'Trade Unions and the Labour Market, 1870–1914', vol. 17, no. 1, May 1965).

Introduction

When he returned from climbing Mount Everest, Sir Edmund Hillary was asked why he had done it. 'Because it was there,' he is said to have answered. It was perhaps in something of the same frame of mind that we embarked upon the project of preparing a history of the Transport and General Workers' Union. Unkind people will tell us, as indeed they told Sir Edmund, that this involved no small degree of folly. However, no one can deny that it also reveals a certain commitment.

We began our trek when the union was nearing its centenary, by most conventional reckoning. Towering over the industrial scene, for years it had been Britain's largest trade union. As it reached its ninetieth birthday, in 1979, it produced a colourful poster to commemorate itself. It said:

> There is a TGWU member in almost every family in Britain. They are the people who make our cars, drive the lorries, load and unload ships, keep the buses and taxis running, work in the power stations, build the motorways, operate vital oil, food processing, chemical, rubber and engineering plants. They are the lighthouse keepers, coachbuilders, tugboatmen, trawlermen, civil aviation workers, office workers, supervisors and managers, laundry and canteen staffs. They are the men and women whose skill and expertise keeps Britain going.

At that time, there were 2 million of these people.

A truly vast effort of human organization had brought them together, joining their individual powers into a real collective strength, and enabling them, together, to dominate the industrial and political landscapes. But while lesser mountain ranges of big unions had all been scaled, often in histories of great complexity and detail, and, indeed, while dozens of smaller hillocks had been extensively mapped and chronicled, this one major peak had inspired no comprehensive history. Its presence had become unavoidable. It represented an enduring and yet innovative influence, and this fact was necessarily reflected in a vast literature. A library of monographs raked over this and that face of the great ascent, explored the screes of particular strikes and disputes, and charted their institutional effects. Here and there major biographies had left pitons to help us over formidable cliffs.

But although much good work existed when we began, we have no doubt that the hitherto neglected archives of the union will still provoke much more. There are many important lessons to be drawn from all the detail which remains in them. None the less, we think that the time was overripe for an effort to see the processes which created our union, as a whole, in their interrelationships. Even in the errors of such an attempt, others will learn things of value.

Neither of us has been a professional historian. Both of us regret this, for we have had to learn painfully what practised scholars could have achieved with much greater ease. Our experience was won as partisans of the trade-union movement, and although both of us have spent most of our working lives learning from trade unionists, as adult educationists, we come, initially, from different disciplines.

For this reason, when we began we thought that we should start our story in 1922, when the new Transport and General Workers' Union was finally born, and carry on through a series of phases which we thought we understood until we reached the recent past. Of course, we knew of a body of writings about what we saw as the 'prehistory' of the union, which we thought to subsume in a preliminary chapter. The more we discovered, however, the more questions we found to need exploration. Our focus moved inexorably further back. Soon we began to joke with one another about the fact that our book was going to resemble Laurence Sterne's immortal *Tristram Shandy*, whose hero takes a hundred pages to get himself born. In fact, Sterne was present at what we now know to have been a very easy parturition, because our own subject has involved us in one volume of two fat books of nearly a thousand pages before its umbilicus has at last been tied.

It is comforting to know that at least one very distinguished historian has acknowledged similar problems. John King Fairbank, the American authority on China, tells us candidly that

> I had two years by the tail, and both were pulling me back to earlier times. In my observation this regression in time is typical . . . would-be modernists have wound up as medievalists. The rule seems to be, if you want to study the mid-period of a century, begin at the end of it and let the problems lead you back. *Never* try to begin at the beginning. Historical research progresses backward, not forward.[1]

Our reverse progression took us to the London docks in 1889, and then beyond that, to the rudimentary organizations of the 1870s. The reasoning behind this is not abstruse, and we think that it will be accepted when we come to unravel the events in the docks in the 1950s and 1970s. Books may start or finish wherever their authors take the whim, but the events which shape the choices which people feel it sensible to make, and which close those options into apparent inevitabilities, are subject to no such caprice.

Inevitably, this appreciation involves us in argument about the framework of periods into which we have been led. Starting back from the formation of the great general unions in the 1920s, we were led by a continuous thread directly to the impulses of 'new unionism', following the upheavals among allegedly unskilled workers in the late 1880s. Of course, this was not at all a new perception, although it has had distinguished challengers in recent years. We believe that our narrative will largely reinforce the case of an older generation of historians, although not without some important cavils. We also believe that the forgotten voices which have been reawoken in these pages will speak not only for a different past, but perhaps also for a different future.

The goals of trade-union democracy have never been simply external targets. Unions have always known that, for the dispossessed to change the world, they first must change themselves. Always their creative drive has involved the dynamism of self-reliance and, within whatever collective space they have been able to win, they have always asserted their commitment to self-development, self-realization and, quite literally, self-government. So, the idea of 'One Big Union', which was proclaimed with such fervour as all the potential constituents of the Transport and General Workers' Union began to ballot for amalgamation, may be traced back over all the setbacks and defeats not only to the high days of the great strikes of 1911, but on through to its germ of 'general' organization, back to 1889 and then further behind.

As a goal, One Big Union was a means of defence for those whose jobs were otherwise in jeopardy from the competition of unorganized labour. It was an agency for reform, in that it could bargain from strength. It was a school in which men and women could learn those skills and techniques which could offer them some rudiments of authority and control over their own toil. It was a university, in which they could generate new aspirations, political programmes, a new charter for the recovery of power over the machines and capital which were dominating their lives. Indeed, it was a way of life.

This way of life was once widely celebrated as the pursuit of industrial democracy. It was never confined to the ritual dimensions of Westminster. In the high years of Labour advance after the First World War, our narrative traces the developments of the transport workers' programme for a comprehensive Board of Communications, to administer publicly owned ports, road, rail, sea and air transport, postal and telephone services. But this conception was formed in the struggle for joint control, with employers and the state, of the crisis-torn war-transport industries. And behind this shaping movement, tracing back the influences which made it possible, we find ourselves eavesdropping on the Royal Commissioners of 1892, reacting in a state of shock, bemused, to the claims of Ben Tillett for municipal ownership of the Port of London, and the plans of Tom Mann for the reconstruction of the whole port area. Moreover, we hear there a succession of dock workers extolling the merits of trade-union control over all these processes.

One Big Union was never far removed from the ideals of workers' control and self-management. It was also never narrowly confined. Its tributaries lead us to the Knights of Labour in the United States, to the anarcho-syndicalists of France, to Australia and New Zealand.

But if we have been led backwards in time and outwards in space, our narrative has to follow the calendar, and to register firmly the spirit of the places on which it depends. A great man once told us that the universal *is* the particular, and it is in the particular lives of these, our people, that we have been moved to search for whatever universal meanings can be found.

Maybe we are too close to our subjects fully to appreciate some current ideas about what constitutes history, and maybe this makes us over-empirical. The feel of poverty and oppression tends to render its victims prone to a certain pragmatism, and even we, as mere observers, cannot claim immunity from this process. Certainly we have tried to create a narrative which actually relates what happened, and which seeks to explain why people reacted as they did. But while our people lived by bread, they never lived by bread alone. Many of them went without, not because they must, but because they were proud and honest enough to hope that the world could be different. Today this is an unfashionable belief, but tomorrow, we think, it might be more widely shared. Objectivity asks us to consider indices of earnings, inflation and productivity. But it also compels us to seek to discover what kinds of people the subjugated workers had it in themselves to be, and what thoughts and aspirations they could nurture in pursuit of their freedom.

Where the modern systems-theorists do engage us is in the attempt to comprehend how far the real choices of living people are determined by the social inheritance in which they are locked.

Imperial Britain gave birth to a socialist rebellion, which directly fostered the young trade-union activists who began to organize the poor – hitherto unorganizable – masses of uneducated and relatively 'unskilled' labourers. Had we been drafting a brief synopsis of the story we have tried to tell, we would have sought to identify a point of juncture where this happened.

The late nineteenth century found the metropolis in a condition which fell a long way short of democracy, and not only in industry. Many working people lacked votes. Women were all disenfranchised. Plural votes gave advantage to the business community and graduates. Access to the levers of power within most nation states was formally closed to many people who might be thinking of joining the new trade unions. At the same time, the world was rapidly shrinking, as innovations in shipping, together with the extension of railways, made communication between working people a much easier and more normal occurrence. Transport workers, in particular, might range freely across a very much wider world than that imagined by their grandparents. True, wherever they went, they would be liable to find some similarities in the conditions of life.

The battle for democracy has been widely represented as a unilinear process, because in one country after another Chartists and suffragettes demanded a widening of the franchise, popular upheavals insisted upon the vote, strikes and demonstrations mounted in great waves in protest against exclusion from the political process. But the aspiration for democracy during these turmoils might plausibly have been led in either of two directions. Yes, perhaps nation states might have been compelled to yield a general suffrage. But also, perhaps the growing identification of allegiances to class and occupation might have burst through national integuments, and created new institutions for democratic representation, on an international scale. Not only the socialists, but also the new unionists, including such conservative leaders as the seamen's Havelock Wilson, laboured with all their powers to achieve precisely this. Even in 1911 Wilson called the British seamen to strike under the banner of the Seamen's and Firemen's International Movement.[2] After the event, it is easy to efface from the mind the alternative choices, because it is quite evident that trade unionism, like socialism, was led into reconciliation with strictly national spaces. However, the notion of internationalist democracy died hard, if it ever died at all.

Today, the internationalization of capital has become so comprehensive that trade unions have been compelled to reassert priorities for transnational linkages. Nation states in Western Europe have been similarly compelled to seek new forms of association, culminating in a headlong rush towards a federal order. The extent of global problems, both economic and environmental, is encouraging a new globalism in radical thinking, including the thinking of trade unions. Accordingly, traditions which have been submerged over very many years of nationalist ascendancy suddenly seem to acquire a bright new relevance, even if they had previously been perceived as the rosy fingers of a false dawn.

Of course, the trade unionists of the late nineteenth century were reacting to a socialist message which had been spelt out almost half a century before. In the *Communist Manifesto*, Marx identified the modern bourgeoisie as the product of 'a series of revolutions in the modes of production and of exchange'. The bourgeoisie has 'put an end to all

feudal, patriarchal, idyllic relations'. It has not severed feudal ties, but
replaced them with 'callous "cash payment"' . . .

Yet this same bourgeoisie

> cannot exist without constantly revolutionizing the instruments of produc-
> tion, and thereby the relations of production, and with them the whole
> relations of society . . . all fixed, fast frozen relations . . . are swept away . . .
> all that is privileged and established melts into air . . . the need of a
> constantly expanding market for its products chases the bourgeoisie over
> the whole surface of the globe. It must get a footing everywhere, settle
> everywhere, establish connections everywhere.

To have seen the cosmopolitan force of capitalism in 1848 was no
mean achievement. It might have been thought an audacious perception
in 1889, and it is not at all an accident that workers in communication
saw it first. But to fail to see it today, in the era of gigantic multinational
corporations, is to fall over one's own feet. Unfortunately, in some
Labour movements there is a propensity to do just that. The unexpected
longevity of capitalism has left its revolutionary propensities undiminished, and the advent of the transnational corporation has radically
impacted on the nation state itself. In the 1990s all but the most powerful
states feel themselves to be mere contenders for influence in a world of
major forces, in which great companies commonly outweigh governments and united nations.

Addressing himself to the working class, Marx gave us the immortal
phrase, 'The working men have no country. We cannot take from them
what they have not got.' He followed this with a prescription which has
often been seen as containing a contradiction: 'Since the proletariat must
first of all acquire political supremacy, must rise to be the leading class of
the nation, must constitute itself *the* nation, it is, so far, itself national
though not in the bourgeois sense of the word.'

Had the workers refused the advice of Marx, it is conceivable that it
might have remained true that 'national differences and antagonisms
between peoples are daily more and more vanishing' because of the
growth of commerce and the corrosive solvent of the world market. But
in fact, the struggle of the proletariat to 'acquire political supremacy' was
precisely, as Marx himself said, the struggle to win 'the battle for
democracy'. When that battle confined its scope within the nation, then,
to the extent that it succeeded, its partial victors gained a stake in the
nation. They won representation in its Parliament, and even designated
some of the ministers in its governments. More fundamentally, closer to
their daily experience, they won important powers over local administrations. And, more important still, influencing all their perceptions of their
rightful status in society, they won recognition and representation in
institutional frameworks for collective bargaining.

Work-people in one country might run in front of their opposite numbers in another. The struggle for democracy, like economic growth, has always been uneven. Its gains have always been particular. By slow degrees, these gains led to a general presumption that social democracies might be established separately, in one country after another. The nation had become an aspiration for the subject class within it.

This book may be seen as a detailed study of how this happened. Other volumes will be needed to trace the story of this one trade union down to our own times, when the ideal of One Big Union is already beginning to reappear, with some urgency, as an international aspiration.

Notes

1   J. K. Fairbank, *Trade and Diplomacy on the China Coast* (Stanford University Press, 1969), pp. vii–xii; cited in A. G. Frank, 'A Theoretical Introduction to Five Thousand Years of World System History', *Review*, vol. XIII, no. 2 (Fernand Braudel Center, Binghamton, New York, spring 1990), pp. 162–3.
2   In Hull, Southampton, the Bristol Channel and on the Mersey, the strike banners all carried the same inscription: 'War is Declared: Strike Hard for Home and Liberty!' (A. P. Lloyd, 'The Influence of Syndicalism on the Hull and Manchester Dock Strikes of 1911', unpublished MA thesis, Warwick University, 1973, pp. 25–6).

PART I

1870–1911

From Forerunners to Federation

I

The Earliest Forerunners

I

Introduction

Fourteen trade unions came together in the amalgamation of 1 January 1922 to form the Transport and General Workers' Union. Waterfront workers had taken the initiative and provided the drive to integration: to the new union's estimated total membership of 350,000, they contributed a core component.[1]

The 1889 London dock strike has commonly been regarded as the starting-point of the TGWU story, and no one can doubt its impact. The courage of those who took part, the sheer verve of their leaders, the widespread support that was aroused all insist that it is entirely proper to celebrate it. But recent historical research has documented substantial organization amongst dock workers long before that great event. Nearly two decades of struggle against overwhelming difficulties left permanent influences behind them to colour and influence the new unionism. The breakthrough of 1889 was real enough, but it was not a total break with what had gone before.

Although there are scattered records of spasmodic local stoppages by dockers in earlier times, historians have found little or no trace of stable trade-union organization amongst waterfront workers before the 1870s, with the notable exception of the guild-inspired Society of London Watermen and Lightermen, which had pre-industrial origins. In the conditions of that time 'stability' was difficult to achieve, but the idea of trade-union organization commonly took root and survived, even when particular organizations were unable to keep going. People remembered. Children listened to their parents. Once lit, the torch was passed from hand to hand, and from one generation to the next. It is therefore necessary to begin our account of the origins of the TGWU with the rise of waterfront unionism from the 1870s. What kind of world was it in which these long unorganized people began to try to join forces with one another?

Boom and Slump

In the years after 1870, powerful though it remained, Britain was losing its dominant position in the world economy. German and American rivals pressed harder and harder, and Britain's industrial lead was coming to an end. The global economy of these decades was uneven, and the British economy was less buoyant than in the past. Growth continued, but at a slower pace. The Russian economist N. D. Kondratieff[2] later identified a series of 'long waves' in the world's capitalist economy going back to the French Revolution, in addition to the generally recognized ups and downs of the business cycle. From 1789 to 1814, he suggested, there was an upswing of twenty-five years, followed by a decline to 1849, a period of thirty-five years. The first cycle therefore lasted for sixty years. The second wave 'begins in 1848 and ends in 1873, lasting twenty-four years . . . the decline of the second wave begins in 1873 and ends in 1896, a period of twenty-three years. The length of the second wave is forty-seven years'.[3] The third wave (1896–1945) will occupy us throughout most of this volume and for a good part of the next. The down-wave of Kondratieff's second major period was widely recognized by British historians, and was frequently referred to as 'the Great Depression'. This term has recently been questioned, but in spite of innovations the period was certainly a difficult one, even in Britain with all its earlier advantages as the frontrunner. Productivity began to lag. Within the global long waves, the curve of activity bumped up and down in a succession of lesser cyclical slumps. These appear to differ, depending on how one looks at them: the movement of industrial output gives one picture, and that of foreign trade another. Michael Barratt Brown has tabulated the relevant figures for the period, using these two variables, and juxtaposing them against the pattern of innovation (see table 1.1).[4]

During the slump years, unemployment rose, output commonly fell, and times were hard. For the poorest people they brought not only relative distress, but real hunger. In between there were recurrent recoveries and upturns, which were periods of more optimistic activity. Throughout the nineteenth century unemployment relief was unknown, so that each of the downturns spelt privation for many and widespread social tumult.[5] But the upturns were times in which labour could often answer back.

Not very far into the downturn, in 1876, Queen Victoria assumed the title of Empress of India. Before her death, she was to add 5 million more

Table 1.1 Boom and Slump, 1848–1921

Boom or Slump	Years	Industrial Output Index (1880=100)	Foreign Trade Volume Index	Industrial Changes and Foreign-Trade Developments
Boom	1848–53	39–52	25–37	Electric telegraph and
Slump	1854–5	52–51	36–34	railway building in Europe
Boom	1856–60	51–63	41–49	and USA. New machine
Slump	1861–2	60–58	48	tools make the UK the 'workshop of the world'.
Boom	1863–74	61–92	49–81	US Civil War and European
Slump	1875–9	91–85	84–91	war. Iron and steel development and US railway boom.
Boom	1880–3	100–110	100–111	Shipbuilding boom, iron
Slump	1884–6	104–101	108–109	ships and agricultural
Boom	1887–91	106–122	114–180	machinery and markets in
Slump	1892–3	116–113	128–125	Canada, Australia and South America.
Boom	1894–9	120–142	134–160	UK development of electric
Slump	1900–4	142–141	160–175	power. Tramways and house-building boom. Russian, Japanese and African markets grow.
Boom	1905–7	151–160	182–198	Internal combustion engine.
Slump	1908–9	152–154	187–193	Naval and arms race. Oil and
Boom	1910–13	159–184	203–232	the Near East market. Rapid growth of US industry.
War	1914–18	173–149	200–127	US and Japanese arms
Boom	1919–20	163–168	169–187	booms – iron, steel,
Slump	1921	105	153	chemicals, motors – challenging UK trade.

Note: In both indices the first figure gives the proportion of 1880 levels in the first year of boom or slump, the second figure the proportion for the last year.
Sources: B. R. Mitchell and P. Deane, Abstract of British Historical Statistics (Cambridge University Press, 1962), pp. 271–2 and 282–3; Ernest Mandel, Marxist Economic Theory (Merlin Press, 1968), pp. 359–60.

square miles and 90 million additional souls to her domains. Thus she died as sovereign of 13 million square miles and 370 million people, most of whom were Indians. Stamps bearing her portrait franked the mails in Shanghai and Vancouver, in Lagos and Calcutta, all across Africa and Asia. Missionaries flocked around the globe to spread Victorian morality, and where they were not prudently broiled or otherwise seen off by the indigenous populations, they were commonly followed by trade, the flag and the imperial armies. Rows and rows of streets in England's burgeoning towns took on the names of distant, exotic places, commemorating the victories of Birmingham technology over the courage of a hundred resistance movements. The riches of the new dominions were not spread about among the English poor, however, and London's East End, like many northern slums, festered and sweltered in squalor, vice and distress. Domestic poverty was widespread and growing, and civil turbulence was not far beneath the ordered surface. In Ireland trouble brewed and stewed.

Just as Britain was losing its industrial pre-eminence, so too the end of the age when Britannia ruled the waves was approaching. Europeans and North Americans entered into hot competition for territories in Africa and Asia. Excluding the unlimited Sahara, the French gathered 3.5 million African square miles and a population of 40 million to their own empire. Belgium and Germany grabbed 1 million square miles apiece, with 30 and 17 million Africans, respectively, resident in their new colonies. Portugal joined the plunder. The Americans seized a chain of former Spanish outposts across the Pacific and dominated the Caribbean. Everyone chipped away at China, in the last throes of the decline of her classic empire. The Russians joined in this process, spreading to the ocean boundary and pushing down to Manchuria. This was the age of imperialism, and it was to culminate in global collision, mayhem and catastrophe. Before that, it was savagely to distort the politics of Europe, and colour the attitudes of even the poorest wage-slaves in the great imperial centres.

The Glamour of Trade . . .

British ports, which handled the trade of the largest empire and stowed and unloaded the new vessels which carried that trade, were the first point of contact with this rapidly changing world.

Henry Mayhew had published his *London Labour and the London Poor* two decades earlier, in 1851. It was crisp reading, and even today provides an inexhaustible mine for historians in search of a graphic vignette or sweeping phrase. Here is his description of the London docks, then spread across 90 acres of St George, Shadwell and Wapping.

As you enter the dock the sight of the forest of masts in the distance, and the tall chimneys vomiting clouds of black smoke, and the many coloured flags flying in the air, has a most peculiar effect . . . Along the quay you see, now men with their faces blue with indigo, and now gaugers, with their long brass-tipped rule dripping with spirit from the cask they have been probing. Then will come a group of flaxen-haired sailors chattering

German; and next a black sailor, with a cotton handkerchief twisted turban-like round his head. Presently a blue-smocked butcher, with fresh meat, and a bunch of cabbages in the tray on his shoulder; and shortly afterwards a mate, with green paroquets in a wooden cage. Here you will see sitting on a bench a sorrowful woman, with new bright cooking tins at her feet, telling you she is an emigrant preparing for her voyage. As you pass along this quay the air is pungent with tobacco; on that it overpowers you with the fumes of rum; then you are nearly sickened with the stench of hides, and huge bins of horns; and shortly afterwards the atmosphere is fragrant with coffee and spice. Nearly everywhere you meet stacks of cork, or else yellow bins of sulphur, or lead-coloured copper-ore. As you enter this warehouse, the flooring is sticky, as if it had been newly tarred, with the sugar that has leaked through the casks . . . Here you sniff the fumes of the wine, and there the peculiar fungus-smell of dry rot; then the jumble of sounds as you pass along the dock blends in anything but sweet concord.[6]

It is not surprising that Mayhew was so powerfully impressed by the sensuous images of the import trade. But, of course, it all had to balance with the outflow of manufactures, textiles, coal and machines. These export trades were more the business of the Mersey and the Humber than that of the capital. All this merchandise had to be carried to the quays, and from the time of Mayhew's description down to the years after the great London dock strike, all the long-haul work was done by railway. Once goods had arrived in depots, they would then enter the short-haul system: they would be put in carts and drawn through crowded thoroughfares by horses. Otherwise, railways and ships were the Victorian means of transport. But, needless to say, carterage was the most labour-intensive of these operations. At the same time, it was a greater problem for would-be labour organizers. For prospective trade unionists, the closer co-operative division of labour between railwaymen and seamen made it much easier for them to associate than it was for the carters, who were living in an older world, altogether more fragmented.

Speed of transit meant that all Mayhew's exotic products could be funnelled out to customers with little delay. Storage costs were cut, as ease of access to regular supplies meant that provincial traders could coast along on very meagre stocks. Money circulated faster as trade increased its tempo. The railways, with trade, promoted the growth of towns and the migration of peoples. The scale of expansion was phenomenal, but understandable in modern terms if we compare it with that of twentieth-century urbanization in South America. Between 1801 and 1901, London's population multiplied five times, from 957,000 to 4,536,000. Liverpool's increased ninefold, from 82,000 to 704,000. Hull's went up eight times, from 30,000 to 240,000. Scotland's largest port, Glasgow, exceeded all these: it registered a tenfold growth, from 77,000 to 776,000. The principal Welsh port, Cardiff, however, grew by eighty times, from 2,000 to 164,000. Concentration called and pushed the rural population to move. At the same time, ocean transport was stimulated and its technologies improved. By 1838 the first purely steam crossing of the Atlantic had been made in nineteen days. As engines developed, so new screw propulsions came to displace the paddle wheel. A gigantic growth of port capacity followed. In 1820, London handled 777,858 tons of imports. The figure rose to 4,089,366 in 1870, and to 10,000,000 in 1901. The Mersey took 4,500,000 tons of shipping in 1848; by 1908, it received 16,000,000 tons. Glasgow doubled its harbour area in the last quarter of the nineteenth century, and the dock area of Hull almost trebled between 1863 and 1885.[7]

While Mayhew wrote, 3 per cent of cargoes were mechanically propelled. By 1861 the figure had become 10 per cent. It was to pass the halfway mark in 1883, and before the First World War it reached 91 per cent. The growth of empire locked these advances into place. Sail could not pass the Suez Canal, so that after 1869 steam ruled the Eastern trade.

. . . and the Reality of Toil

All these developments were the spectacular evidence of progress. But what of the people who earned their living in this upheaval and turmoil? Once again, let us start with Mayhew:

> He who wishes to behold one of the most extraordinary and least-known scenes of this metropolis, should wend his way to the London Dock gates at half-past seven in the morning. There he will see congregated within the principal entrance masses of men of all grades, looks and kinds . . .
>
> Presently you know, by the stream pouring through the gates and the rush towards particular spots, that the 'calling foremen' have made their appearance. Then begins the scuffling and scrambling forth of countless hands high in the air, to catch the eye of him whose voice may give them work. As the foreman calls from a book of names, some men jump up on the backs of the others, so as to lift themselves high above the rest, and attract the notice of him who hires them. All are shouting. Some cry aloud his surname, some his christian name, others call out their own names, to remind him that they are there. Now the appeal is made in Irish blarney – now in broken English. Indeed, it is a sight to sadden the most callous, to see thousands of men struggling for only one day's hire; the scuffle being made the fiercer by the knowledge that hundreds out of the number there assembled must be left to idle the day out in want. To look in the faces of that hungry crowd is to see a sight that must be ever remembered. Some are smiling to the foreman to coax him into remembrance of them; others, with their protruding eyes, eager to snatch at the hoped-for pass. For weeks many have gone there, and gone through the same struggle – the

same cries; and have gone away, after all, without the work they had screamed for.[8]

This description of the savage ritual of the call-on was to lose none of its force in succeeding years. The social scientists of the 1880s and 1890s registered the same shock. The press of casual labourers demanding work simply grew and grew, as the railways brought more and more people to the port cities, and successive immigrations either were added to the crowds or ousted existing workers from other trades to join the scramble for work in their place. It was a scene that would have been recognized by port workers right up to the 1960s.

For Mayhew, the scrimmage was made even more dreadful by an understanding of its object, which was employment in conditions of utter inhumanity:

> The work may be divided into three classes.
> 1. Wheel-work, or that which is moved by the muscles of the legs and weight of the body; 2. jigger, or winch-work, or that which is moved by the muscles of the arm. In each of these the labourer is stationary; but in the truck work, which forms the third class, the labourer has to travel over a space of ground greater or less in proportion to the distance which the goods have to be removed.
> The wheel-work is performed somewhat on the system of the treadwheel, with the exception that the force is applied inside instead of outside the wheel. From six to eight men enter a wooden cylinder or drum, upon which are nailed battens, and the men laying hold of the ropes commence treading the wheel round . . . The wheel is generally about sixteen feet in diameter and eight to nine feet broad; and the six or eight men treading within it, will lift from sixteen to eighteen hundred weight, and often a ton, forty times in an hour, an average of twenty-seven feet high. Other men will get out a cargo of from 800 to 900 casks of wine, each cask averaging about five hundred weight, and being lifted about eighteen feet, in a day and a half. At trucking each man is said to go on an average thirty miles a-day, and two-thirds of that time he is moving one and a half hundredweight at six miles and a-half per hour.[9]

The pay for such a day's work, Mayhew tells us, would be 2s. 6d.; and for those men not hired until the afternoon, the hourly rate would be 4d.

These conditions were a continuing affliction, impeding port workers in their efforts to organize, not only during the movements of the trade cycle in the 1870s but on through to the great strike of 1889 and beyond it well into the twentieth century.

As a young man, Ben Tillett, who figures very largely in the chapters which follow, felt real shame about working on the docks. 'So real was the stigma', he wrote 'that [we] concealed the nature of our occupation from our family as well as our friends.'[10] A contractor would describe his employees as 'dock rats'. In his memoirs, Tillett claimed to have originated the term 'docker'; if this be true, we can count it as the first of many steps he took towards affirming the human status and dignity of his members. The brutal indignity of the call-on goes far to explain these attitudes. 'Coats, flesh and even ears were torn off. The strong literally threw themselves over the heads of their fellows and battled . . . through the kicking, punching, cursing crowds to the rails of the "cage" which held them like rats – mad human rats who saw food in the ticket.'[11]

An Observant Participant

Tillett saw the life of the dockers from inside. During the 1880s, more and more witnesses followed in Mayhew's footsteps to see it from outside.

In 1886 Beatrice Potter (the future Beatrice Webb) took up work as a researcher in Charles Booth's team at the Charity Organization Society, which had begun a sustained investigation of London poverty. Early the next year she was assigned to the study of the docks. Bare statistics were not enough for her: 'I want local colouring; a clear description of the various methods of employing men, of types of character of men employed, and where they live. Must realise the "waiting at the gates", and find out for myself'.[12]

This was a classic definition of the role of 'participant observer', to which Beatrice applied herself with great zeal. Morning after morning she reported at the dock gates and watched the often brutal struggle for work. She also observed 'the leisurely unloading of sailing vessels, compared to the swift discharge of steamers.'[13] Day after day the entries in her diary record an undiminished sense of shock. Her experiences were digested into an essay on dock life in East London, which was immediately published in *Nineteenth Century*. Beatrice was dissatisfied with this essay, but it was to prove more than capable of extending her own sense of outrage to a much wider circle. At the same time, her prescriptions for reform were also strongly canvassed.

Writing about the behaviour of 'the lowest class of casual labourers', she expressed a mixture of fascination and distress in her contribution to Booth's final research:

> These men hang about for the 'odd hour' work, or one day in the seven. They live on stimulants and tobacco, varied with bread and tea and salt fish. Their passion is gambling. Sections of them are hereditary casuals; a larger portion drift from other trades. They have a constitutional hatred to regularity and forethought, and a need for paltry excitement. They are late risers, sharp-witted talkers, and, above all, they have that agreeable tolerance for their own and each other's vices which seems characteristic of a purely leisure class, whether it lies at the top or the bottom of society.

But if we compare them with their brothers and sisters in the London Club and West-end drawing-room we must admit that in one respect they are strikingly superior. The stern reality of ever-pressing starvation draws all together. Communism is a necessity of their life: they share all with one another, and as a class they are quixotically generous. It is this virtue and the courage with which they face privation that lend a charm to life among them.[14]

The shock of dockland, red in tooth and claw, of course registered more than a disapproval of poverty and deprivation. The conditions of the dockers went along with radically different attitudes. Dock work was different. Subject to irregular movements of trade, as well as to the other variables we have already discussed, it was strangely pre-industrial in the challenges it posed to normal notions of factory discipline, the rule of the clock and the ordered regularity of work which had become ingrained in Victorian social organization.

Accidents Were Not an Accident

Dock life in London in the declining years of the nineteenth century was hell, and getting worse. In January 1888 the *East London Observer* carried a report of the death of a dock worker, who was discovered in his last minutes at the kerbside. James Butler, who was forty-five, was found by a carman who had seen him sitting by the road, 'apparently very ill'. He was wheeled on a barrow to the London Hospital, where he was found to have died of heart failure. 'At one time deceased was a very strong man, but lately he had become weak', testified his brother at the inquest.[15] True, the weather at the time was bad. That same January, during a fog, numbers of dockers were drowned. Had they 'belonged to a better class of society', reported the *East End News*, 'the clamour . . . would have changed the insouciance of the dock authorities into active measures for the prevention of a similar recurrence but –

> "rattle his bones over the stones
> He's only a docky whom nobody owns".'[16]

Casualties, fatal and otherwise, were by no means confined to the Port of London. The man who was to lead Liverpool's dockers, James Sexton, recorded the story of the accident which disfigured him for life. He got the chance to work over Christmas, on 24 and 25 December, and he was overjoyed, because double-time payments would ensure that his family could celebrate, albeit a day late.

> In the early hours of the morning an incompetent man at the winch and a defective hook on the end of the rope-fall caused me to be struck in the face with a whole sling of bags of grain which broke loose, and I was hurled into the hold of the barge to which the cargo was being transferred

. . . my face struck the keelson of the barge. My right cheekbone was smashed, my right eye forced out of the socket, and my skull was slightly fractured. But such happenings were too common to be allowed to interfere with work, especially when a rush job like this was being tackled, so I was just hoisted out of the hold and laid in the shed whilst my mates carried on.

I was left there for two hours whilst somebody hunted up a cab – no ambulances were stationed at the docks in those days – and this exposure on a bitter winter's night caused such serious complications that I was detained in hospital for nearly two months, with my head packed in ice for most of the time.

This happened in 1881, immediately after the passing of the Employers' Liability Act, of which I knew nothing – not even of its existence – until I heard about it from one of my workmates . . . who visited me in hospital seven weeks after my admission. He . . . imparted to me something of his belief that I was entitled to compensation under [the Act]. The resident surgeon, who happened to be near, asked my mate for particulars of what had happened. Two days later he told me he thought I was well enough to risk a visit to my employers. He played the part of the good Samaritan so far as to hire a cab and go with me for an interview which did not seem so alluring now.

The boss met the statement of my case with a blunt denial of any liability on his part and raised a second line of defence by pointing out that even if he were liable, I had no claim, as he ought to have had notice of the accident within six weeks of its occurrence. The best he could be induced to do was to say that when I was physically fit he would see what possibility there was of finding some light work for me.

The consequence was that when I got back I was offered a lad's job – driving a winch, with one and six-pence a day less than I had been accustomed to as a 'casual labourer' (when I could get any casual labouring to do!). However, total starvation was the only alternative, so, propelled by the devil of dire necessity, and with the thought of my wife before me, I took it on. I had a broken week, and at the end of it, on reckoning up my time, I found I had earned fifteen shillings. When I crawled round to the pay table to draw that magnificent sum, all that my wife and I would have to live on until another pay day came round, I was 'docked' half a crown for the fare for the cab that had taken me to hospital.[17]

II

Trade Unions in the 1870s

How could men endure such things without resistance? The answer is that they did resist, at every moment when the possibility presented itself. Between 1863 and 1874, industrial output grew by 50 per cent and export volume by 65 per cent (see table 1.1). Here was opportunity.

The three principal ports, London, Liverpool and Hull, all experienced strikes and attempts at trade-union organization on the docks in the

1870s. All of these were of local or at best regional dimensions, although all were influenced by national economic conditions and by national trade-union responses to them. That is why, in order to understand what was happening in our sector, we need also to understand the main features of trade unionism as a whole during these formative years of dockers' organization.

In 1871 the population of England and Wales was 22.7 million, and of Scotland and Ireland 3.4 and 5.4 million respectively. Of these people taken together, 8.2 million men and 3.2 million women were employed. The proportion of people in trade unions was very small, and figures are in any case inaccurate, since no attempt at official counts was made until 1886; but the Webbs calculated a total membership of under 143,000. By 1881 the population had grown to about 35 million for the entire British Isles, and employment had reached 12.7 million. During the decade, trade unionism had expanded to 266,000. What kinds of organizations were involved?

The great 'amalgamated' societies of craftsmen, categorized as the 'New Model' unions in the Webbs' classic *History of Trade Unionism*, had dominated the scene in the 1850s and 1860s: in 1868 they had, along with miners and cotton workers, made up the bulk of membership in the affiliates which formed the Trades Union Congress in 1868. Their leaders had also been the grouping with whom Karl Marx had built the International Working Men's Association, the First International, in 1864. This was the trade unionism which, through the agency of the TUC's Parliamentary Committee, was to campaign successfully for an acceptable legal status, which Parliament finally granted in the Acts of 1871 and 1875. In that year the TUC's secretary, George Howell, declared that 'the legislation with respect to Trade Unions was then so perfect that the natural time had run for the existence of Trade Union Congresses so far as Parliamentary action was concerned'.[18]

Yet the rather complacent craft societies began to lose their dominance over the movement as trade unionism experienced a substantial phase of growth in the early 1870s. Stable non-craft organization already existed in cotton, where, however, it remained localized; and in mining, where it took on national proportions in the 1860s. Two miners' unions could, after spectacular growth in 1873, claim 100,000 members each. Both of them organized all grades of workers. More akin to the cotton unions, where organization was not only local but mainly confined to the skilled operatives, were the unions in iron and steel.

New sections of the working population, however, participated in the sharp increase of union membership in the prosperous years of the early 1870s. They included gasworkers, who formed an East End Union in 1872; London's builders' labourers, who formed their General Amalgamated Labourers' Union in the same year; agricultural labourers, led

by Joseph Arch, whose National Union of 1872 reached a turbulent peak
with membership of 100,000 in only eighteen months; and railwaymen,
whose Amalgamated Society of Railway Servants dates from 1871. In
their efforts to engage hitherto unorganized occupations and industries,
all these bodies anticipated the 'new unionism' of the 1880s. In addition,
some, such as the agricultural and railway workers, aspired to *national*
organization. They were also frequently touched and inspired by the
national movement for the nine-hour day, which was accompanied by
large and successful strike actions.

In structure and general aspirations, however, they made no dramatic
break with the older unions of the skilled workers, and sometimes, as in
the case of the railway servants, they depended for encouragement,
strategies, and even finance, on middle-class sympathizers. Nevertheless,
the union upsurge of these years was substantial, even on the Webbs'
calculation quoted above. Others claim a much greater representation at
the beginning of the decade, and a sharp rise immediately afterwards,
from a total membership of 199,000 in 1866, to 735,000 in 1873.[19]
Some of the new organizations were destroyed and most were seriously
squeezed in the acute depression of the later 1870s; or again, after partial
recovery in 1881–3, by the severe slump of 1887. But vestigial
organizations often survived, to reach into and to qualify the 'newness' of
the new unionism of the 1880s. Perhaps more important, their members
survived, having learned from hurtful experience which only reinforced
their efforts when the time became ripe.

Activist farmworkers were victimized and driven for survival to seek
work in the towns, where many of them became carters, since their skill
with horses was the most saleable asset they could bring to the urban
labour market. How many of these displaced people were later involved
in the recruitment of carters, cab-drivers and other transport workers to
the experimental new organizations which began to develop?

None of the standard trade-union histories which describe this period
pays any sustained attention to dock workers' organization or strikes in
the 1870s.[20] It has been left to a later generation of labour historians to
remedy this omission, and to show that, in London, Liverpool and Hull,
at least, the dockers participated fully in the ferment of the 1870s.[21]

Dock Unions: Sectionalism and Casualism

Out of a total employed population of 11.4 million in 1871, 600,000
worked in transport. Their numbers had risen to 900,000 by 1881.

For much of the nineteenth century the London docks were
characterized by the fragmented organization of cargo-handling. Small-
scale capital dominated many branches of the industry. Different firms
specialized in particular operations. Thus there were separate entities in

lighterage, in stevedoring (which was originally the separately organized function of loading ships, as distinct from unloading, but which later came to include all shipboard work, as distinct from work on the quayside and in warehousing). Separate trades, such as tea, timber, coal- and corn-handling, were also owned or operated by distinct enterprises. These subdivisions had to be reflected in the labour force engaged in them. Far from 'dockers' being an undifferentiated mass of interchange- able labour-atoms acting according to textbook notions of individualism, the regular core of port workers formed discrete, highly specialized groups. These developed strong bonds of loyalty and local pride, which in turn could lead to intimate relationships with individual specialist employers.

Nor was this the end of the complicated process, since the division of functions took different forms in the enclosed docks and on the riverside wharves, whilst still other traditions prevailed on the river in the lighterage and watermen's trades. This fragmentation was common to all the main ports of the country, although it was more marked in London than elsewhere. The distinction between shipboard and quayside work, giving rise to the sectionalism of the stevedores, was particularly marked in the capital. There, craft exclusiveness, reaching back to memories of the guild status of the Thames lightermen, and bolstered by the high proportion of 'over-side' transhipment to and from lighters and barges, was also most marked. This is not to say that sectionalism was confined to London: as we shall see, it created problems in the other ports too; but it was most deep-seated in London.

Moreover, the older view of Victorian dock work as an occupation dominated by its casual nature remains broadly true, even after recent historical research has emphasized the complex reality summarized here. There were two elements to the dockers' poverty and insecurity. One was that, even amongst the core of workers who pursued the work regularly, there was a permanent over-supply. This arose partly to suit the port employers' widely fluctuating demands for labour. Their operations were dependent upon tides, weather, seasons and the state of trade. The problem was reinforced by the specialisms we have described, which were rendered even more inflexible by the tendency of dockers, even when short of work, to look for employment only in their immediate neighbourhood. Geographical immobility was thus added to occupational specialization. In the 1870s, the waterfront workers overcame many of these divisions in their early drive for unionization, but as the upturn of trade receded, old sectionalism reasserted itself in the ensuing depression.

At the same time, what stability there had been in the division of labour became more liable to disruption by new types of employers and the growth of capital concentration in the ports. The shipping companies themselves, swollen in size by the need to finance larger steamships and transcontinental refrigeration[22] moved into handling their own cargoes, as did bulk-handling flour-milling and cement companies. The ship- and port-owners developed new docks to take the larger, deeper draft ships down the estuary at Tilbury, 26 miles from the port of London. These developments destabilized the sectional unions which emerged from the growth of the 1870s, and drove them either to attempt more open methods of association or, working against such adaptation, to turn in on themselves in self-defence.

The other element in the casual nature of port employment was the fact that non-regular workers surrounded the docks, and at certain seasons, or when a general depression closed other jobs and laid them off, would present themselves at the dock gates for hire. This happened, for example, with the gasworkers of the East End during the summer months, when employment in the gasworks was slack, and with agricultural labourers during the winter. Without the protection of all-inclusive unionism, and with casual hiring occurring several times a day, the dock workers' vulnerability from all these causes was of course extreme. This was a longstanding problem. We have evidence of its extent as far back as 1844, when Henry Mayhew estimated the London docks' maximum employment figures at 3,012, while its minimum need for labour was 1,189. At St Katharine's Dock, the jobs available varied between 1,713 and 515, while there was a fluctuation between 4,000 and 1,300 at the East and West India Docks.[23]

London Forerunners

The first record of modern trade unionism in the Port of London is in 1871, a year in which the port employers chose to impose wage cuts. The dockers responded: clergymen conducted their first protest meetings and urged an appeal to public conscience. ('The poor cannot strike,' they advised.) But the dockers won the support of Patrick Hennessey, an Irish tailor and trade unionist, and of Charles Keen, an activist in the First International. Both men were involved in the Land and Labour League, which had been formed in 1869 following a decision of the Basle Congress of the First International in favour of land nationalization. George Eccarius, a friend of Karl Marx, and Martin Boon, a follower of the Chartist Bronterre O'Brien, were the first joint secretaries of this League, and the founding treasurer was John Weston, the Owenite.[24] If the Land and Labour League thus looked back to the Chartist preoccupation with access to the land, which was becoming less and less appropriate to a fully industrial society, it none the less offered a link to a developed organizational experience.[25]

In December 1871 Hennessey and Keen helped the dockers to form the Labour Protection League (LPL). At first, there was only poor support from the general dockers, the biggest stimulus being to the stevedores, who had set up five branches and recruited 3,000 members by 1872. Enrolment followed on the wharves, involving corn-porters and then general labourers. Building and engineering labourers, dustmen, slopmen and scavengers also joined its ranks, which added up to 30,000 by October 1872.

Sectional strikes in different parts of the port won wage increases – mostly to 5*d.* an hour. The objective of the 'tanner' was canvassed – seventeen years before its realization in the great strike. Mass unionism had arrived, and its day was celebrated in an East End demonstration of 20,000 people, complete with bands and banners.

But problems arose in the government of the LPL. Its leaders were not subject to membership control, for its growth had been too rapid to allow for the careful creation of any adequate central representative machinery; there was no co-ordination between the fifty branches. Later in the 1870s its leaders evolved into a rather conservative clique, and were ousted from office. Even in the upsurge, some groups preferred to form sectional unions of their own, such as the lightermen and the coal-whippers. Separatism was also evident within the LPL as corn-porters and others formed occupational, rather than local branches. Their aim was the preservation of job control; port-level solidarity was secondary to that purpose. The bulk of the union's funds remained in the branches, which were largely self-governing.[26] The Executive Committee had a very weak constitutional position. Efforts were made to overcome this by the appointment of district delegates with powers to visit and inspect branches, but with no powers to sanction strikes.

The recession of the later 1870s wore away the LPL. Such an experience was not uncommon for trade unions at that time. The leaders attempted an early form of federation, and at a conference of the LPL, the Carmen's Union, the Lightermen and Watermen, and the Railway Servants, a loose alliance with a joint Executive Committee was formed to co-ordinate industrial action. Entitled the Amalgamated Labour Union, there is no evidence of its having been effective.

A lock-out at the Millwall Docks in 1876 drained the LPL's funds and reduced its membership to about 2,000. By the 1880s it was further reduced to just six branches, five of which were of stevedores on the North Bank, the other of corn-porters on the South.

These two sectional survivals from the London dockers' struggles of the 1870s made significant contributions later on – the corn-porters in London, and the stevedores ultimately in three major ports. It is reasonable to say that 'mass unionism on the London waterfront began in 1872',[27] and that the LPL was more than ephemeral. But when the Labour Protection League changed its name to the Amalgamated Stevedores' Labour Protection League, the corn-porters' branch opted for secession and revived as the South Side Labour Protection League in the great movement of 1889. It was ultimately absorbed into the TGWU in 1922. The stevedores, on the other hand, kept up a sectional organization down to very recent times. This was strong enough to frustrate the objective of dockers' unity. Moreover, London dockers' unionism in the 1870s was local in its ambitions, and this distinguishes it sharply from the new unions which were to come at the end of the next decade. Many years later those local and sectional bodies were to try to recruit further afield. But we shall consider this change in their style, after the Second World War, in volume II.

Stevedores: a Sectional Model

The stevedores' now separate organization was the most lasting result of the movement of the 1870s. As export shipboard workers, they had a measure of mobility throughout the docks of the north side. Most worked for small master-stevedoring companies, in whose ambit the very smallness of scale fostered a marked occupational identity. Such employers were relatively weak in any dispute, and wages of 6s. a day (of nine hours) were possible, with 1s. an hour overtime. More, the masters recognized the union, something which the big shipping companies resisted until the First World War. Union stevedores, whilst not enforcing a closed shop, obtained preference of employment, and calling-on rules were elaborated and accepted by the masters. Union cards were inspected at the call-on, providing a sanction against arrears and ensuring membership stability. In return, the employer derived real benefits, as the union promoted order and maintained a high quality of work. This is therefore an example of closed, craft-like unionism which consciously restricted entry – so much so that the death-rate amongst members regulated the rate of entry, with stevedores' sons having preference. No one under the age of eighteen was admitted unless he was a stevedore's son, in which case he would join at one-quarter of the standard entrance fee. Adult entrants had to have a background of shipwork, and many were ex-sailors. Even so, the union sometimes closed its book to all except sons of members. Ben Tillett, although a former seaman, was refused admission when he arrived in the Port of London from Bristol. The stevedores also had a large Irish membership, which helped to cement group solidarity at a time when the Irish question was becoming an urgent issue.

The stevedores' closed society suffered from inflexibility in the face of technical and structural change, a defect inherent in this kind of unionism. Coming into existence in the last days of the sailing ship, it failed to adapt as the new oceangoing steamers, owned and run by large-scale companies, took over. The change brought with it the building of new docks, including that at Tilbury, remote from the stevedores' established controls. The big shipping companies defied the union's rules and controls, hiring non-unionists in the docks which they operated with their own stevedoring businesses. The union faced the classic choice of closed unions in this situation: either to amend and dilute its restrictions on entry in order to recruit the workers in the new companies and locations, or to preserve its working rules by accepting a reduced sphere of influence confined to its existing territory. It chose the latter, more cautious, defensive option with consequences which were to mark port unionism deep into the twentieth century. These go a long way towards explaining the problematic management of dockers' unionism at key moments in the TGWU's history. But the immediate consequence was that non-unionism emerged during the 1880s in the new docks and in the employ of the big shipping companies, and a new, less rigid United Stevedores' Union was formed to cater for them. The original five-branch union stayed within its limited horizons, remaining isolated also from the labour movement on general questions of trade unionism and politics, preferring to foster a tight, status-conscious social life within its fraternity and community.

The Workmen's Elite: Lightermen

The organization of lightermen in the Port of London dates back to Elizabethan times, when it took the form of a liveried company. (They were originally 'watermen', but usage of this term declined as passenger trade on the river dwindled.) They were the elite of all labour in the port, with a formal apprenticeship system. The guild system, in which journeymen could expect to make the transition to become masters in their turn, gave way to wage-earning capitalist employment relations with increased scales of operation, and the masters broke with the apprenticeship system in the mid-nineteenth century. The result was that the wage-workers formed the Amalgamated Society of Watermen and Lightermen in 1872, thus joining the general wave of unionization of the period. Although its formation was stimulated by a wage dispute, for a long time it remained heavily preoccupied with the defence of the apprenticeship system in order to perpetuate the elite status of its members.

Some picture of the ancient traditions of the watermen is recorded in the memoirs of Harry Gosling, who was to become the founding president of the TGWU. Gosling was the great-grandson of a Thames waterman who owned several barges, in addition to his 'dumb craft', the chief of which was a clipper called the *Effort*, moored in the Surrey docks to receive merchandise which was bound for Ramsgate, Margate, Herne Bay, 'and sometimes to Chatham and Sheerness'.[28]

At the age of fourteen, Gosling himself was bound apprentice for seven years at a ceremony in the hall of the Watermen's Company, St Mary-at-Hill, in a room 'practically unaltered since 1785'.

My father and I arrived at the court on the day I was to be bound, and were ushered in by a uniformed beadle who used to act as a kind of river policeman, a modernised type of those who in earlier days impressed men for service in the Navy . . . Under the flags of the Watermen's Company, in a high-backed state chair, sat the Master of the court, wearing a heavy chain of office . . . on the wall hung a great oil painting of the Judgement of Solomon . . .[29]

The beadle solemnly proclaimed that William Gosling wished to bind his son apprentice for seven years. Then the master of the court asked the boy whether he was willing to be bound, and after he and his father had made the appropriate avowals, indentures were signed, 'and copies handed to us both'. The terms were tough. Each apprentice swore

to learn his Art, and with him (after the manner of an Apprentice) to dwell and serve upon the river of Thames from the Day of the Date hereof until the full End and Term of seven years from thence next following, to be fully complete and ended; during which Term the said Apprentice his said Master faithfully shall serve as aforesaid, his Secrets keep, his lawful Commandments everywhere gladly do; He shall not waste the Goods of the said Master, nor lend them unlawfully to any; He shall not commit Fornication, nor contract Matrimony within the said Term; He shall not play at Cards, Dice, Tables nor any other unlawful games whereby his said Master may have any loss. With his own Goods or others during the said Term, without License of his said Master he shall not buy nor sell; He shall not haunt Taverns nor Play Houses, nor absent himself from his Master's service Day nor Night, unlawfully, but in all things as a faithful Apprentice he shall behave himself towards his said Master and all his during the said Term.[30]

In return for all this the master also undertook certain responsibilities: 'He his said Apprentice in the Same Art, which he useth, by the best means that he can, shall teach and instruct, or cause to be taught and instructed, feeding unto the said Apprentice Meat, Drink, Apparel, Lodging, and all other necessaries according to the custom of the City of London.[31]

The whole induction ceremony was dauntingly conducted and, at the end, young Gosling was issued with a tract entitled *The Honest Waterman*, an inspirational account of the life of Thomas Mann, a saint among Thames watermen. The virtues of Thomas Mann were abundant, but deferent to a fault:

He (the Honest Waterman) was a very early riser, and would often do nearly a day's work before the other people were up in the morning; and then he was so very honest in never asking more than his fare, and so very civil, and his boat and his person always so clean and neat and comfortable, that I suppose he had generally more fares than other watermen . . . His constitution being excellent, his attention unceasing, and his deportment invariably correct, business of course increased, and he never by intemperance abused the good health by which he had been blessed . . . Not only in his youth, but when far advanced in years, it was commonly his custom to row as if matched against time, and after rowing twenty or thirty miles he would row in to the Irongate Stairs by the Tower in the lively spirited manner in which he set out. He made a point, however of never rowing for a wager, and was never known to lay a bet of any kind . . . When discussions on the subject of parliamentary reform were so generally held as often to come under the notice of our watermen, he would calmly endeavour to inculcate just and moderate sentiments or change the discourse, by showing the much greater importance of self-reformation . . . His charity was so universal, so constantly and daily practised that the detail of it would be as monotonous as it was unceasing, and he died worth something under three thousand pounds.[32]

'It was', wrote the future leader of the transport workers, somewhat wryly, 'with this bright beacon shining ahead that I emerged into the everyday life of the river on June 13th, 1875'.[33]

As evidence of the attitudes of Gosling's workmates, we should note that they excluded from membership of their organization a new labour force, the bargemen, which arose as the enclosed docks and the canal system were developed. These workers did not have a licence to work on the Thames tidal waters and were, for this reason, ostracized by the Lightermen's Union.

The lightermen's clannishness [and] isolation . . . were common to all waterside groupings, although perhaps not to the same exaggerated extent. Waterside unionism was essentially defensive and restrictive in character. This was so whatever the trade, the port or even the country. In a casual, overstocked labour market such a form of organisation followed inevitably from the uncertainty of employment. The 'new unionists' of 1889 were to find that this was the framework within which they had to work. Expansive gospels of general unionism carried little weight on the waterfront.[34]

This thesis is overstated: the new unionism strove against sectionalism for good pragmatic reasons. But it was a long, hard struggle, in which sectional unions often played a retarding role but sometimes provided checks and balances against over-powerful bureaucracy in the more inclusive organization.

Liverpool Dockers

The history of trade unionism on the Liverpool docks has been overshadowed by the focus upon London and the great strike of 1889.

Since the 1970s, however, Liverpool has found its historian, Eric Taplin, who has provided accounts to parallel the local studies of London produced by John Lovell.[35] Taplin is able to demonstrate that important activity, including unionism and major strikes, were features of Liverpool's history as they were of London's. These reached climactic proportions in the 1870s.

The economics and labour relations of the Liverpool docks had much in common with those of London. The same picture emerges of a core workforce of experienced, specialized and relatively immobile dockers, employed by a variety of bosses: master-stevedores, master-porters, some owned by shipowners and some engaged under contracts, the shipowners themselves who did their own stevedoring and porterage, and the Mersey Docks and Harbour Board, owner of the port, which had its own (smaller) labour force. As in all the ports of the major trading nations, an upheaval in scale and modes of operation was surging through the last quarter of the nineteenth century, as steam replaced sail and big capitalist shipping companies in consequence began displacing the small capital of the 'master' cargo-handling firm.

Taplin is as concerned as Lovell to dispel the legend of the dockworker as uncouth and unskilled. He also rejects the idea that port employment was wholly casual.

> most dock workers looked to the docks as their sole source of employment, frequently within a narrow range of docks. Thus the majority were known by their employers and would receive preference in employment over those less well known . . . The genuine floating labourer who drifted into the docks in search of work would be taken on only if the supply of experienced, known dockers was fully employed . . . the inexperienced worker was slow, inefficient, and a danger, for the job required considerable physical stamina allied to a knack of handling and moving heavy weights. Such expertise could not be picked up in a matter of days but was the result of many years' experience.[36]

Strikes in the port have been traced back to the 1850s, and occurred also in 1866. In the early 1870s Liverpool shared in both the general trade boom and in the wave of unionization. A minor strike in one dock in 1870 led to the brief appearance of a 'rudimentary' trade union, the Steamboat Labourers' Friendly Burial Society. In 1872 the nine-hours' movement swept through the city, involving carters, omnibus workers, shop assistants, rag-pickers and many others. Two middle-class sympathizers, William Simpson and James Samuelson, businessmen active in Liverpool's Liberal politics, emerged as spokesmen for the unskilled, one advocating 'moral force' and mediation, the other encouraging 'New Model' unionism, friendly-society methods, conciliation and arbitration.[37]

On the docks, pay claims, strikes and deputations from the men led by

Simpson and Samuelson rained down on the employers throughout 1872. Many of them were successful. Another ephemeral union was formed – the Liverpool North End Steamship Dock Labourers' Friendly Burial Society. Its innocuous name misled, for in addition to friendly benefits it submitted claims to the employers that only society members be engaged as foremen and that society men would not work with non-members. These views were wholly unacceptable to the employers and remained so for forty years. A strike called in support of the claims failed and the society is not heard of again. Within a year the wave of disputes petered out, as the boom was succeeded by a trade recession in 1873–4. Defensive strikes on a local scale did occur in 1876 and 1877, showing that the will to resist worsening conditions was present.

The general character of all the dockers' activity of this decade was, here as well, its persistent sectionalism. Cotton-porters, provision- and grain-warehouse porters, in seeking parity of wages with general dock labourers, acted in isolation from each other. The spread of improved wages from dock to dock was haphazard and uneven. This reflected the immobility of the workforce, which, as in London, was accustomed to seek employment only at a dock, or a group of docks, where the men were known. The prevalent sectionalism also accounts for the failure of the 1870s movement to produce a stable and lasting trade union.

Rivalries and jealousies were reflected in the small and transient societies which appeared, confined to either the North End or the South End Docks. Eric Taplin comments that

A further divisive factor resulted from religious differences among the dock workers. A large proportion of Liverpool dockers were Irish Catholics. The recruitment of Irish labour was not a peculiarity of Merseyside but it took an acute form in that no other large urban area in nineteenth century England was so divided between Catholics and Protestants. It entered into most aspects of Liverpool's business, political and social life and the docks were no exception. Broadly the Protestant dockers were to be found at the south end docks, the Catholics at the north end. It is, however, no more than a rough generalisation as there were substantial enclaves of Protestants at the Bootle end of the docks and Catholic groups at the Toxteth end. Although the line of docks from south to north was unbroken, in practice there was a sharp labour division between the two. South end labourers rarely sought work at the Bootle end or vice versa . . . The walking time from the north end to the south end, different types of job specialism, smaller docks at the south end, different types of vessels, different types of employers all played their part, but the division between Catholics and Protestants may have been one feature . . . an undercurrent of petty argument and recrimination . . . weakened unified action but in the event of a major conflict the labourers acted together and religious differences were subsumed for the more important immediate issue at stake.[38]

Taplin also finds that the absence of strong local trade unionism outside the docks – a reflection of the frail manufacturing sector in the city, which rendered the Liverpool Trades Council a weak reed – were factors helping to explain why the dockers' organizations were so ephemeral. Further, and related to this, was their dependence upon their patron Simpson, a philanthropic middle-class extrovert who rigidly discouraged self-help through unionization. In London the dockers freed themselves from similar tutelage at an early stage, and had the benefit of leadership from Hennessey and Keen, who although not dockers were trade unionists and political radicals.

Sectionalism in Liverpool, however, did not give rise to the permanent division between stevedore and docker which rooted itself in London. The explanation seems to be that Liverpool was, at an earlier date than London, dominated by the major shipping companies to which both stevedores and dockers looked for employment. Quayside and shipboard workers thus had more mutual affinities than in the capital. The same was true, as we shall see, of Hull. When trade unionism became permanently established in the northern ports, the fragmentation of the workers into groups and specialisms, although it created obstacles to unity, was less deeply entrenched than the institutionalized segregations in London. After the formation of the TGWU, of course, the London stevedores found themselves the magnet for all subsequent dissaffections, including the provincial ones, which plagued the general union for generations.

The Mersey Struck

After the recession of the mid-1870s, Liverpool docks exploded in mass strike action in 1879. The whole docks complex came to a standstill in a dispute that lasted three weeks and involved the seamen as well as the dockers. The spark was a planned and announced wage cut, concerted by all the port employers. It was enforced at first at the North End, where the dockers struck, to be followed in sympathy by the South End – an act of solidarity without precedent in the port. The seamen joined the stoppage with their own grievances, and by that stage no fewer than 35,000 were on strike. The leaders, though still including Simpson and Samuelson, now counted rank-and-file dockers in their numbers. The strike occasioned some violence, and the artisan-dominated Trades Council withheld its support. The numbers out of work because of the stoppage reached 60,000. Blacklegs were imported from Hull and elsewhere, but they refused to work when they understood the situation. There was large-scale police mobilization and troops were also drafted into the port. After three weeks the dockers capitulated.

Yet, amazingly, the dockers regrouped their forces, formed unions in both Liverpool and Birkenhead,[39] and renewed their effort to advance wage claims. The two unions formed a joint committee and presented a single claim for the restoration of previous wages. At arbitration the union case prevailed, following which triumph the dockers' union sought vainly to persuade the employers to establish a Board of Conciliation. The wage settlements of the 1880s in Liverpool remained unchanged until 1915, when a war bonus was added.

But three unions emerged from this conflict: the two dockers' organizations and one of the seamen. Their success followed recourse to arbitration in 1879–80, a move reflecting their defeat in the previous year's strike, and the continuing influence of Samuelson and Simpson. The unions created at that time were modelled on artisans' methods, and they did not survive the later depression of the 1880s. But the movement was not a purely local event, for Hull too saw a serious dock strike in 1879.

During the depression years of the 1880s, the American Knights of Labour carried on some clandestine work on the Liverpool docks, in which the young James Sexton was involved. The Knights of Labour had been founded in the United States in 1869 by a group of garment workers led by Uriah Stevens. Because they were convinced that trade unions were handicapped in a prejudiced environment, they 'imitated capital' by organizing in secret. The society was not referred to by name, but was usually called 'the Five Stars'. The result was slow growth: eighty assemblies by 1875 and 52,000 members in 1883. But by 1886, secrecy set aside, membership rocketed to more than 700,000. By then the union had already crossed the Atlantic to Liverpool; later it was also to appear elsewhere. The Knights' organization harked back to Robert Owen and the Grand National Consolidated Union of the 1830s in Britain. 'An injury to one is an injury to all,' they proclaimed. The union was open to all races, to men and women equally, and to skilled and unskilled workers. Only bankers, lawyers, traders in alcoholic liquors, and stockbrokers were excluded. Terence V. Powderly, Stevens's successor, was a pioneer of the concept of 'One Big Union', including all who laboured. This idea later found room enough to grow in Liverpool.

Meantime the Liverpool Union of Stevedores, Labourers and Quay Porters played a large part in relief work for destitute port workers. Neither this organization nor the Knights survived for long, and the Birkenhead union also failed, leaving the Mersey with no dockers' unions at all. The seamen's union formed in 1879 disappeared from the records after 1880.[40]

The Third Port: Hull's Dockers

The third great estuarial port of the industrial revolution was Hull, whose merchant class had already between the sixteenth and eighteenth centuries built a thriving network of trade with northern Europe, to which was added, in the nineteenth century, intercontinental trade, including imperial raw-material imports and the vast exports of the new industries of West Yorkshire and the Midlands. This growth sparked a huge population explosion – from 28,000 in 1801 to 122,000 in 1871. In the last quarter of the century the population again more than doubled, reaching 240,000 in 1901. By the mid-century the transport trades engaged 23 per cent of the male working population, and the complex of docks, largely augmented by investment from the railway companies – eager to create trade and cargo movements from the industrial heartlands – grew until it eventually extended over 7 miles of the north bank of the Humber, completely dwarfing the pre-industrial harbour at the mouth of the river Hull.

Alongside the docks grew up a range of industries for handling and processing the raw materials which formed a large proportion of Hull's trade: cement, flour-milling, seed-crushing, animal feedstuffs, chemicals, timber storage and processing, warehousing, and paint and dyestuffs. All were characterized by the same heavy manual-labour needs as were required on the docks. To this extent Hull was typical of other ports. Its relative isolation from other urban and industrial centres also left it surrounded by a hinterland of arable, and therefore labour-intensive, agriculture. The Hull employers drew on these sources of casual and seasonal labour, which rose to an immigrant flood during the agricultural depression of the 1870s and onwards. This workforce added to the sizeable migration from Ireland, which became as large, proportionately, as that into London and Liverpool. The Irish often arrived as 'navvies', to dig out the new docks, and stayed on to become dockers.

Although, therefore, Hull provides another classic case of a pool of casual, 'unskilled' labour for the tasks of cargo-handling, the student of the period, Raymond Brown, is as concerned as Lovell in London and Taplin in Liverpool to dispel the stereotypical picture.

> There has usually been a tendency to think of the dockers as a homogeneous group of men with common aims and ideals shaped by their environment of mean living conditions, low and irregular pay, casual employment, and unskilled work which they or anyone else with reasonable strength could do ... This is much too simplified, and dockers have very properly always regarded themselves as in some measure specialists ... There was a tendency to emphasise the social rank of, say, a deal carrier as opposed to a lumper or a raff-yard labourer although all were involved in the same sort of work, namely carrying timber. This insistence upon the slightest difference in skill and experience of one group of dock workers as against any other was, of course, to add to the more obvious problems of union organisation.[41]

Hull's skilled workers, who dominated the Trades Council, took their full part in the national nine-hours' movement in the early 1870s. Their example was quickly followed by raff-yard labourers (timber-porters) on the Hull docks, and by dockers in Grimsby, on the south bank of the Humber. Several new unions appeared: Grocers' Assistants, Chemists' Assistants, and Hairdressers, calling for reduced shop hours. The following year, marine firemen on both banks struck for improved pay and conditions, and in the important adjacent agricultural districts trade unionism was spreading rapidly in rhythm with Joseph Arch's national movement. The Hull Labourers' Union and the Hull Dockside Labourers' Union were formed at this time. The Dockside Union drew up rules to limit working hours, which it submitted to the employers along with a wage claim.

A port-wide strike was staged in support of these demands, and during it the quays were 'almost at a standstill'. The strike collapsed at the end of three weeks, after an influx of blacklegs: seamen and farm workers from Lincolnshire. Some of these rural immigrants were subsequently enrolled by the Lincolnshire Labourers' League, which claimed to have 700 members in Hull in 1873.

There were further dock strikes in 1872 and 1877, and again in 1879. Throughout this period, and also through the 1880s, a local Dock Labourers' Union continued in existence. Local unions of seamen and ships' firemen also came and went, and conducted a series of strikes. The year 1881 was climactic in Hull's trade-union history, as wave after wave of strikes swept through both skilled and unskilled trades, and a reconstituted Trades Council now included dockers' and seamen's representatives. Amongst the major strikes was one by the dockers, who demanded that the basic wage of 5d. an hour be raised to 6d. – another move anticipating the cause of the men of 1889 in London. Despite the records of previous unionism on the docks, this strike threw up an evident need for concerted leadership, and a Hull Labour League was formed, which, as well as assuming responsibility for the conduct of the strike, intended to work for the amalgamation of dockers, seamen and firemen. Although all three groups were on strike together, in the midst of the dispute the seamen announced the formation of their own Hull Seamen's Union. Fighting between dockers, blacklegs and police was followed by serious arson on the dock estates, but after three weeks the dockers returned to work at the old rates, as did the seamen. (A section of the firemen gained a rise of 1s.) 'But the real significance of the strike is that the three unions which took part did not break up at its conclusion and they were all existing strongly in 1889.'[42]

The end of the period before the 1889 explosion in Hull was marked by a symbolic occasion when the trade and friendly societies clubbed together in 1886 to provide a farewell dinner to honour the local Tory leader A. K. Rollitt, who had played a role in the labour disputes of the preceding years similar to that of the 'outside' sympathizers in London and Liverpool. The next generation of leaders acknowledged by Hull's labourers were to be quite different. They were no longer outside philanthropists, but national, working-class representatives.

Political Action: Samuel Plimsoll

We have seen how, during the 1870s and early 1880s, port unions in key areas rose and fell with the state of trade. Echoing G. D. H. Cole, we would claim that checks on the industrial plane tended to stimulate political campaigning and vice versa. This process can be clearly seen at work in the movement to defend seamen from unsafe ships and mercenary shipowners.

Samuel Plimsoll was elected as Liberal MP for Derby in 1868, and from the moment of his adoption he styled himself 'the sailors' friend'. For certain, seamen needed friends in the 1870s. The most elementary safety provisions were not simply neglected, but commonly deliberately flouted in order to profit from insurance claims on lost ships and cargoes. Between 1867 and 1882 more than 1,600 sailors perished in collisions; 519 passengers went down with them. But 31,768 crewmen and 5,468 passengers were drowned from other causes. Between 1874 and 1885, 251 steamers foundered, as did 1,657 sailing ships, with a total death-roll of 12,494. Nearly 40,000 deaths in sixteen years, a large proportion of which were due to negligence, and far too many to criminal exploitation of insurances: here was a classic example of Victorian values, fully operational.

The statistics by themselves are too cruel to be understood. George Howell, the TUC's secretary, illuminates them with a single illustration. Visiting Plimsoll at home one day, he found his host was distraught, collapsed on a couch. He rallied himself, and read aloud to Howell a letter he had just received from a new widow. Her husband's ship had gone down with all hands. The man had expected that this would happen: the ship, he knew, was a 'coffin ship'. His wife had begged him not to go, but he had asked, 'What am I to do? If I refuse, there is no other berth.' He hoped against hope that the hulk might struggle through. But on the night he sailed, he sent home his best clothes, his watch and everything of value that he had been carrying. 'His wife knew it,' wrote Howell. 'It was his farewell . . . She, with her two young children, never saw him again.' Howell was shattered. Silent, he blinked back the tears from his eyes. Thinking that his visitor was wanting in feeling, Plimsoll looked up impatiently and saw the distress written plainly all over him. From that moment, the two men shared a bond of commitment which never wavered.[43]

Plimsoll collected a massive dossier about the deployment of unseaworthy ships; about undermanning, overloading, misloading and over-insurance. In spite of every possible litigation, his charges held water. Plimsoll demanded – and, after making a great fuss, got – a Royal Commission to consider his heartbreaking allegations.

At the Leeds TUC in 1873 copies of Plimsoll's book *Our Seamen* were distributed, and George Howell was invited to organize a 'workmen's committee' to lobby for the establishment of an appopriate inquiry.[44] Howell secured the support of Lord Shaftesbury and other peers, and that of his fellow trade unionist George Odger. Behind this team, say the Webbs, he enlisted 'practically the whole force of the trade union movement'.[45] Throughout 1873 a sustained campaign of mass meetings spread throughout the country, from Newcastle-upon-Tyne down to Plymouth, and from Cardiff to Greenock. All major ports were covered, as well as dozens of lesser centres. A great meeting took place in Whitby. The main cities held large rallies. A pamphlet, *Ship Ahoy!*, was distributed in huge numbers. In 1873 the Royal Commission was set up, and it reported in August the following year. Meanwhile, Plimsoll introduced Bills for a Merchant Shipping Survey in 1873, and again in 1874. Both were defeated. After the General Election of 1874, a third Bill was brought in in 1875, only to be abandoned in a great parliamentary scene. At last, in 1876, the Merchant Shipping Act made it through to the statute book. Without doubt, that agitation had its influence on waterfront trade unions. The Webbs record that 'the powerful Shipping Trades Council of Liverpool . . . which played an important part in Samuel Plimsoll's agitation . . . was broken up in 1880 by [a] quarrel' between constituent unions.[46]

Soon, however, trade-union political campaigning was to take on new, direct forms, which would ultimately transform the relationships between philanthropists and their intended beneficiaries. This began during the upsurge of waterfront unions but unlike them political action on behalf of waterfront workers could not be restrained by downturns in the economy, or by the retreat or even collapse of trade-union organizations. Indeed, it came to a head during the middle years of the decade, while such unions as survived along the docks were in greater trouble.

The Quarries Also Stir

Distanced from the ports, but connected with them by their trade, was another rugged group of workers in the great slate mines of Wales. Events during the 1870s and 1880s led them eventually to become the core of the Transport and General Workers' Union in North Wales in 1923. How did they embark on such a road?

The North Wales Quarrymen's Union was founded in 1874. The industry had enjoyed a boom until 1879, and membership reached 8,000 out of a possible 14,000.[47] Powerful bonds united the communities of this region, who maintained the Welsh language and had no use for

English either in their work or in their union meetings.[48] Immigration was negligible in statistical terms, with the result that social organization was close and homogeneous. (Few Irish had settled in North Wales, despite its nearness; some English professionals joined the town populations, but usually these were people apart, maintaining their own culture and identity.)

The quarries belonged to the super-rich landowners. Lord Penrhyn ensconced himself in a massive castle, as if he were a feudal baron. He employed 2,500 men in Bethesda, and as late as 1899 the Penrhyn quarries earned him a profit of £133,000, which he added to his rental income of between £60,000 and £70,000. In 1869 George William Duff Assheton-Smith inherited 36,000 acres and the Dinorwic quarries, which brought him more than his annual rental income of £42,000.[49]

The intermediaries who managed the quarries, however, were often English. The men distrusted them, the more so because many could not speak Welsh, and lacked all practical skills.

> Slate-quarrying was a Welsh-speaking industry . . . consequently the whole terminology of the craft was Welsh[50] and it seemed impossible to the men that it could be practised in English. John Williams, a quarryman, recalled in 1942 how an English manager visiting his quarry saw a man smoking, and asked, 'Do you allow this idleness?' The accompanying agent explained that the man was, in fact, studying the rock as well as smoking. This episode, concluded Williams, proved that 'a quarry cannot be worked in English'.[51] A hundred years earlier, in the 1840s, a David Jones had sung:

> > In workplaces here in Wales
> > See Englishmen interfering;
> > But you must get Welshmen to break the stone,
> > For the rock does not understand English.[52]

> 'The English element', explained Robert Parry to the annual conference of the union in May 1882, 'was . . . very damaging to the success of the quarrymen.'[53] Few present would not have nodded in agreement.[54, 55]

In 1874 the mock-baronial owners and their imported managers confronted an untried trade union which, however, could rely on two advantages – the temporary boom in trade, and the resources of a close community culture as well as the bonds of class. Assheton-Smith's managers at Dinorwic tried to crush the new organization in April by refusing work to those of its members who refused to resign. Only eleven men chose this option; 2,200 loyal unionists were locked out. Within five weeks they had won their point. The contagion spread next to the workers in the Bethesda quarries of Lord Penrhyn who, having already given support to their brethren in Dinorwic, went on to call for higher wages themselves, together with revisions in their contracts. The dispute was a bitter one, but most of the union's programme was conceded in September. However, the local managers (those English-men) flouted the new terms, provoking a fresh strike. Three managers were dismissed and replaced. This was an astonishing demonstration of the union's power. It was in the aftermath of the drama that the union's membership rose to more than 8,000 in 1878.

The gains were shortlived. The boom gave way to a slump in the following year: it lasted until the late 1890s, and 'the union came perilously close to extinction.'[56] Membership slid to under 3,500. But it survived, and the triumph of 1874 had created an indelible trade-union tradition on which to draw in the turbulent years which lay ahead.

III

Out Into the Open

The sum of these experiences seems perfectly clear. Port labour was not easy to organize, but it operated under conditions which made trade unionism seem necessary to increasing numbers of workers. Other groups of allegedly 'unskilled' people shared this dilemma. As the first unions formed ranks, they commonly encountered fierce opposition from employers. That opposition led the dockers, and many other groups in the 1870s, into much more frequent strikes, which were used as a means of developing organization. The 1870s witnessed the first of a series of 'strike waves' which accompanied – indeed promoted – the spread of trade unionism to wider and wider sections of the working class right through to the 1920s. An early statistician of strikes wrote in 1880 of strikes as 'a disease, and a very grave disease [which] shows no sign of having run its course', whilst George Howell, reviewing the 1870s, spoke of 'a period of strike epidemics'.[57]

Trade upturns made association a practical option, increasingly inevitable. Downturns sometimes smashed, and always greatly enfeebled, the new associations, just as they commonly eroded union support in other industries and trades. Employers had not yet learned to live with organized labour. But as the idea took hold, trade unionism became a continuing commitment, more and more rooted among workers even when it was difficult, if not impossible, to proclaim it openly. This is why the semi-clandestine Knights of Labour put out its links in the Liverpool docks, having traversed the Atlantic to do so. By the late 1880s the Knights had discarded secrecy in America and were leading mass struggles. And at that point in Britain, the hour of new unionism, out in the open and defiant, had finally come.

Notes

1   We shall analyse the composition of the membership fully in vol. II. It is indicative of the immense structural changes through which the TGWU has lived that in December 1986 the membership of its Docks, Waterways and Fishing Trade Group had shrunk to just 28,000 out of a total of 1.4 million.

2   Writing in 1926, while the TGWU was consolidating its merged ranks, and trying to cope with the tumult of the General Strike, Kondratieff stimulated a very active debate. But his diagnosis of capitalism's trajectory did not commend him to Soviet leaders. He was arrested in 1930 and figured in the show trial of the mythical Peasant Labour Party. Subsequently he was deployed as a 'witness' in the equally rigged trial of the Menshevik 'conspiracy' a year later. He was finally rehabilitated in 1987.

3   N. D. Kondratieff, 'The Long Waves in Economic Life', *Lloyds Bank Review* no. 129, (1978), pp. 41 and 42.

4   Michael Barratt Brown, *What Economics is About* (Weidenfeld and Nicolson, 1970), pp. 170–1.

5   There is an extensive discussion among economists about 'long waves'. See in particular Ernest Mandel, *Long Waves of Capitalist Development* (Cambridge University Press, 1980), and the same author's *The Second Slump* (New Left Books, 1978). But although the empirical evidence for the existence of long waves is very strong, it is much more difficult to explain them satisfactorily. The most important recent attempt to do so is to be found in Joshua Goldstein, *Long Cycles* (Yale University Press, 1988). This provides a comprehensive summary of the debate, together with a careful analysis of the evidence. See also James E. Cronin, 'Stages, Cycles and Insurgencies: The Economics of Unrest', in T. Hopkins and I. Wallerstein (eds), *Processes of the World System* (Sage, 1980), where the author identifies the Kondratieff long wave as an influence upon those patterns of labour unrest in Britain with which we shall be concerned throughout this book. The three great strike waves of pre-war Britain occurred in 1871–3, 1889–90 and 1911–13.

6   Henry Mayhew, *Mayhew's London: Selections from London Labour and the London Poor*, ed. Peter Quennell (Pilot Press, 1949), pp. 544–5.

7   H. J. Dyos and D. H. Aldcroft, *British Transport: An Economic Survey from the Seventeenth Century to the Twentieth* (Leicester University Press, 1969), pp. 247–55.

8   Mayhew, *Mayhew's London*, pp. 545–7. Dennis Mayhew, coincidentally a namesake of the London chronicler, joined the Hull dock labour force in 1951, a century after Henry Mayhew wrote. He became a member of the unofficial Port Workers' Committees on the Hull docks in the 1950s and 1960s, and a student in Hull day-release extra-mural classes. When he read this chapter for us, he commented that the nineteenth-century Mayhew's description of the 'call-on' could readily have been taken as a description of the scene on Hull's docks in the 1950s.

9   Ibid.

10 Ben Tillett, *A Brief History of the Dockers' Union* (Twentieth Century Press, 1910), p. 89.

11 Ibid., p. 12.

12 Beatrice Webb, Diary, May 1887, in *My Apprenticeship*, vol. II (Penguin, 1938), p. 345.

13 Ibid., p. 345.

14 Ibid., p. 486.

15 W. J. Fishman, *East End, 1888* (Duckworth, 1988), p. 16.

16 Ibid.

17 James Sexton, *Sir James Sexton, Agitator: the Life of the Dockers' MP* (Faber and Faber, 1936), pp. 74–6. It is a further indication of the neglect of safety standards at that time that winch-driving, regarded by a twentieth-century docker as a highly responsible and adult post, should then have been 'a lad's job'.

18 Henry Pelling, *A History of British Trade Unionism* (Penguin, 1963), p. 76.

19 The figures are given in G. D. H. Cole, *An Introduction to Trade Unionism* (Allen and Unwin, 1953), appendix 1, p. 289. The source is not disclosed, and all other historians commence comparable statistical series in the 1890s. '1892 is the first year adequately covered by official statistics of trade union membership' (H. A. Clegg, Alan Fox and A. F. Thompson, *A History of British Trade Unions since 1889*, vol. I: *1889–1910* (Oxford University Press, 1964), p. 1). Pelling, *History of British Trade Unionism*, p. 261, commences his series with the 1893 membership of 1,559,000. These statistics were first compiled following the appointment of John Burnett as Labour correspondent to the Board of Trade in 1886 – itself a highly significant moment, since he had been the president of the Nine-hours' League, and a leading member of his Tyneside branch of the Amalgamated Society of Engineers, who had published an account of the nine-hours' strike in that region. In 1875 he was elected general secretary of the ASE, on the death of William Allen. He was promoted to chief Labour correspondent at the Board of Trade when it established its Labour Department in 1893 (see Sydney and Beatrice Webb, *The History of Trade Unionism* (1894; WEA edn, 1912), p. 300).

20 Histories consulted include Pelling, *History of British Trade Unionism*; Clegg, Fox and Thompson, *History of British Trade Unions since 1889*, vol. I; Webb, *History of Trade Unionism*; G. D. H. Cole, *A Short History of the British Working Class Movement*, vol. III (Allen and Unwin, 1927).

21 See John Lovell, *Stevedores and Dockers: a Study of Trade Unionism in the Port of London, 1870–1914* (Macmillan, 1969); E. L. Taplin, *Liverpool Dockers and Seamen, 1870–1890* (University of Hull, 1974); Raymond Brown, *Waterfront Organisation in Hull, 1870–1900* (University of Hull, 1972). The account of the three ports' histories through the pre-1889 years presented here draws heavily on these three studies.

22 Refrigeration was introduced by Sir Alfred Haslam of Derby in 1880 to bring mutton from Australia and New Zealand. It caught on very quickly. By the time of the First World War there were more than 200 insulated steamers in the British merchant fleet alone. (See Adam Kirkaldy and A. D. Evans, *The History and Economics of Transport* (Pitman, 1927), pp. 309ff.)

23 Henry Mayhew, *London Labour and the London Poor*, vol. III; cited in Gordon Phillips and Noel Whiteside, *Casual Labour: The Unemployment Question in the Port Transport Industry, 1880–1970* (Oxford University Press, 1985), p. 22.

24 Weston lives on as the partner addressed by Marx in his famous pamphlet *Wage-Labour and Capital*, prepared during the heyday of the International Working Men's Association.

25 See Henry Collins, 'The English Branches of the First International', in Asa Briggs and John Saville (eds), *Essays in Labour History* (Macmillan, 1960), pp. 247ff. See also Henry Collins and C. Abramsky, *Karl Marx and the British Labour Movement* (Macmillan, 1965).

26 'The central government of the League must have found itself in a situation similar to that described by James Sexton . . . In his autobiography he recounts how when he took over the leadership of the Liverpool union in 1893, he found himself at the head of what was virtually a federation of "almost innumerable small clubs and societies all hostile to each other"' (Lovell, *Stevedores and Dockers*, p. 71).

27 Ibid., p. 91.

28 Harry Gosling, *Up and Down Stream* (Methuen, 1927), p. 1.

29 Ibid., p. 16.

30 Ibid., pp. 17–18.

31 Ibid.

32 Ibid., pp. 18–19.

33 Ibid., p. 19.

34 Lovell, *Stevedores and Dockers*, p. 73.

35 Taplin, *Liverpool Dockers and Seamen*.

36 Ibid., p. 10.

37 Ibid., pp. 19–20. See also entries for both men in J. M. Bellamy and J. Saville (eds), *Dictionary of Labour Biography*, vol. II (Macmillan, 1974).

38 Taplin, *Liverpool Dockers and Seamen*, pp. 10–11. See also P. J. Waller, *Democracy and Sectarianism: A Political and Social History of Liverpool, 1868–1939* (Liverpool University Press, 1981), pp. 509–10 and 511.

39 They were called the Birkenhead Amalgamated Dock Labourers' Union and Benefit Society, and the Liverpool Union of Stevedores, Labourers and Quay Porters.

40 The Liverpool unions of this period do not seem, even in their heyday, to have achieved mass membership. The Liverpool stevedores' and dockers' union's best year was 1881 when its membership was a mere 403 (Eric Taplin, *The Dockers' Union: A Study of the National Union of Dock Labourers, 1889–1922* (Leicester University Press, 1986), p. 26.)

41 Raymond Brown, *Waterfront Organisation in Hull*, pp. 8–9.

42 Ibid., p. 32.

43 See George Howell, *Labour Legislation, Labour Movements, and Labour Leaders* (Fisher Unwin, 1905), p. 266.

44 Ibid., chapter XVIII.

45 Webb, *History of Trade Unionism*, p. 370.

46 Ibid., p. 354.

47 R. Merfyn Jones, *The North Wales Quarrymen, 1874–1922* (University of Wales, 1981), p. 106.

48 Ibid., pp. 57ff.
49 Ibid., pp. 11–12.
50 Some words were originally English, for example *rybelwrs*, derived from 'rubbelers'; and some English terms were used – the classification of slate sizes according to the noble hierarchy (e.g. duchesses) – but most quarry words were Welsh. For a glossary see Emyr Jones, *Canrif y Chwarelwr* (Gwasg Gee, 1963).
51 John Williams, 'Atgofion chwarelwr', *Y Llenor* (winter 1942), pp. 129–35.
52 British Museum, *Welsh Songs 1767–1870* (n.d.), p. 69.
53 *Y Genedl Gymreig*, 24 May 1882.
54 The feeling was mutual: 'these Welshmen', wrote E. A. Young in 1900, 'are so childish and ignorant'.
55 R. Merfyn Jones, 'Y chwarelwyr: the slate quarrymen of North Wales', in Raphael Samuel (ed.), *Miners, Quarrymen and Saltworkers* (Routledge and Kegan Paul, 1977), pp. 123–4.
56 Jones, *The North Wales Quarrymen*, p. 107.
57 James E. Cronin, 'Strikes and Power in Britain, 1870–1920', in Leopold H. Haimson and Charles Tilly (eds), *Strikes, Wars and Revolutions in an International Perspective* (Cambridge University Press, 1989), pp. 80–1.
    The statistician was G. P. Bevan, whose study for the Royal Statistical Society in March 1880 included tabular data indicating a tenfold increase in numbers of strikes between 1870 and 1872, which was sustained through most of the following years to 1879 (ibid., p. 82). Cronin suggests that 'beneath the considerable variation over time in the incidence and scale of strikes there was a fundamental continuity to strike movements before 1914. What united these several outbursts of conflict was a broad effort to enrol ever larger sections of the workforce into stable unions. This *de facto* objective seems, in retrospect, to have overshadowed issues of wages, hours, working conditions, and job control, however important these may have been at the moment or in specific conditions . . . the early 1870s probably were years when strikes became the dominant form of workers' collective activity' (ibid., pp. 81–3). What follows in our subsequent chapters certainly upholds this thesis.

2

The New Socialists, and the Way to a New Unionism

I

Educating a Militant

Tom Mann was twenty-four years old in 1880.[1] His father was a colliery clerk at the Victoria pit near Coventry, and at the age of nine Tom went to work down the mine. Four years later, a fire forced the permanent closure of the pit, and the family was compelled to move to Birmingham in search of work. There, when he was fifteen, Tom was apprenticed to a firm of toolmakers. His chosen new vocation entailed a standard sixty-hour, six-day week, but 'frequently we were called upon to work overtime, usually two hours of an evening.'[2] A year later, in 1871, the engineers' 'society' negotiated the establishment of a nine-hour day.[3] For Tom this was a true liberation. Characteristically, he began to use his new free time to gain some access to the world of letters, from which he had been kept apart: 'Three evenings a week for five years I attended classes . . . In addition I attended a Bible class one evening a week.'[4]

Tom Mann was growing up to be a skilled man, but also, thanks to the 'society', an educated man. He was never to forget that, in the agitation for shorter hours, the trade union had given him the key to learning. Younger children were more fortunate than the teenagers of Tom's generation: they were able to benefit from compulsory, if minimal, schooling as a result of the 1870 Elementary Education Act. Through the last decades of the nineteenth century, therefore, literate working people were becoming more and more common, and it is unsurprising that they began to find interesting things to read.[5] Tom Mann read Henry George,[6] took keenly to his message about land reform and briefly found employment in the United States in 1883 while hoping to meet fellow disciples.[7] On returning to London he graduated from George's radical influence to that of the economic historian Thorold Rogers, whose *Six Centuries of Work and Wages* gave powerful historical authority for the idea of an eight-hour working day: 'The artisan who is demanding at this time an eight hours' day in the building trades is simply striving to recover what his ancestor worked for four or five centuries ago'.[8] And, he asked, were not the cathedrals better built than modern industrial towns?

In 1884 it was a short step from the study of Thorold Rogers to that of Karl Marx, who had pointed out that new inventions were not deployed in order to save the time of working people. A searing chapter on the length of the working day appears in *Capital*.[9] 'A horse . . . can only work from day to day, eight hours', Marx insists, but machinery ensures that there is a continuously applied pressure to lengthen the working day for people. The longer machines are operated, the sooner their investment costs can be recovered.[10] It was not strange that this message gripped Tom Mann, and soon enrolled him as a reader of *Justice*, the journal of the new Marxian Social Democratic Federation (SDF), whose Battersea branch Mann quickly joined.[11] John Burns, then also a colleague in the ASE, belonged to the same branch. Among the regular speakers at Battersea Park Gates and other local meeting places were Henry Mayers Hyndman and H. H. Champion. Hyndman, a wealthy stockbroker, cut an imposing and even lordly figure, resplendent in top hat and whiskers. He was the first well-known English publicist to popularize some of Marx's ideas although he did not improve his stock with the master by plagiarizing him without acknowledgement.[12] Champion was formerly an artillery officer, and the proprietor of a print-shop. 'He approved', wrote Mann in his *Memoirs*, 'my ardent advocacy of the eight-hour day, and urged me to write a pamphlet on the subject which he would print'.[13]

This was the first blow in a campaign which was to lead the doctrinaires of the socialist movement into a direct relationship with trade unionists, and with many thousands of working people as yet unorganized.

'Isms' and Schisms

The socialists were not a united force. All their groups fizzed with argument, and not only on matters of high theory. When Tom Mann outlined his ideas about the eight-hour day at the Battersea SDF branch, he met vigorous opposition from his friend Burns, who believed that the 'time had long passed for such trivial reforms'; it would be a better notion, thought Burns, 'to seize the whole of the means of production and wipe out the capitalists altogether'.[14] Battersea plumped overwhelmingly for the Burns prospectus. Yet not many years were to pass before both groups in this controversy were working side by side in the struggle for the very 'palliatives' that Tom Mann was pursuing.

At the end of 1884 William Morris, the most famous member of the SDF, led a breakaway Socialist League opposed to electoral dealing.[15] Some of the members of this distinguished group opposed all parliamentary action on principle, while others were concerned only to build sufficient strength to act independently, eschewing compromises and pacts with established political parties. With Morris went Eleanor Marx, the daughter of Karl, who was to play a major part in the upsurge of trade unionism.[16] She was soon to part company with the Socialist League, however.

Remaining with the parent body was a key group of young workers: Harry Quelch, who was to become a leader of the dock workers on London's South Bank;[17] Will Thorne, the gasworker who was tutored by Eleanor Marx in reading and writing;[18] James MacDonald, who was to become secretary of the London Trades Council. George Lansbury joined in 1892; he was to become leader of the Labour Party in the early 1930s. A later recruit was Ernest Bevin.

Unions and the Vote

In Britain in 1880 the large majority of adults, and all women, were voteless; the suffrage extended to less than 3 million men only.[19] A man in middle years might have childhood memories of the People's Charter; no one younger could recall those days, but all had spent their lives under a political system in which voting was a middle-class perquisite, shared by only a minority of labour 'aristocrats'.

From the beginning of the 1880s, the argument for independent political organization of the working-class movement began to gather force and influence. Friedrich Engels drafted a series of articles which appeared in the *Labour Standard* in 1881.[20] Even the restricted extension of the franchise of 1867, which added some 1 million male voters to the electoral register, mostly in urban constituencies, had been inadequately grasped by the trade unions, wrote Engels. Now, with a mounting agitation for wider democracy throughout the civilized world, it was clear that 'in England, where the industrial and agricultural working class forms the immense majority of the people, democracy means the dominion of the working class, neither more nor less.'[21]

But while other socialists were either impatient or contemptuous of the unions, for Engels they were the very foundation of any alternative politics. Whilst consistently arguing for a socialist goal ('there is no real redemption for the working class until it becomes the owner of all the means of work'), he did not share the view of such converts as Burns that all lesser objectives were merely 'palliatives'. On the contrary, he argued that without trade-union action 'the labourer does not even receive what is due to him according to the rules of the wages system. It is only with the fear of the Trade Unions before his eyes that the capitalist can be made to part with the full market value of his labourer's power.'[22]

Even with the 1867 electoral rules, Engels believed it quite possible to secure the election of forty or fifty working-class Members of Parliament. Instead, development was very slow, and those Labour Members who were elected up to this time invariably enjoyed the patronage of the Liberal Party.[23] The reason for this was more to do with arithmetic than pessimism, because the absolute numbers of workers with votes mattered less in Britain than their distribution in the wider population. (We return to this question in chapter 7.) It was precisely in that 'pool of stagnant misery', London's East End, that Engels's followers were to arouse a real challenge to this state of affairs. And this particular political response was to depend on the effort to extend trade-union powers to the 'numberless' trades outside their remit. Of course, the further extension of the vote in 1884 imposed its own discipline on the established parties. Now they had to pay attention to all kinds of people whose wishes might never have been given a thought in earlier days. That is why, in Eric Hobsbawm's judgement, 'the 1880s and 1890s, far more than the earlier years, are the real heyday of "Liberal–Labourism"'.[24]

For the Liberal Party, these were difficult times. They needed the votes of working people newly enfranchised, but their constituency included big employers who had no desire to see trade unions forming among the dispossessed. Around these great fish were many minnows, such as the small shopkeepers who feared and detested the uppity lower ranks.

II

Labour and the Liberals

In the beginning of this phase, however, these polarities were by no means clear to those who were to suffer them. While the old parties were seeking to attract supporters among recently enfranchised voters, so the newly awoken spirits of formerly excluded people were, at first, often disposed to look for support among existing establishments. A notable example was provided by Ben Tillett, who, when he set out to create a trade union among his tea coopers on the London docks, actively sought assistance from prominent Liberals. We shall turn to this episode in chapter 3. Tillett's 'conversion' to socialism was to follow the dramatic lessons of the experience through which he lived, and it was to become so influential that he has often since been represented as a born revolutionary. But of course his politics were not congenital: he grew into them,[25] and a more natural evolution than that which followed his exploration of the scope and limits of liberal radicalism could hardly be found in East London during the late 1880s. Tillett learned new ideas quickly. Others were not so quick to adapt.

Standing on the brink of a wider franchise on the eve of the 1884 Act, the infant workers' movement faced a natural division. There were those who sought to increase their influence by cultivating Liberal sponsorship or support; others, meanwhile, with Engels, were looking for means of gathering independent scope, without which it would be impossible to go beyond partial, ameliorative demands to the 'abolition of the wages system itself'.

The Political Economy of Labour: Shorter Hours

For this second group, no demand could possibly have greater relevance than the simple call for the reduction of working time. Marx, writing decades earlier, had celebrated the victory of the ten-hours' movement in 1848 as the 'first great victory of the political economy of labour over the political economy of capital'.[26] In another work which was not to see the light of day until many years after his death, he had written: 'the true economy is economy of labour time'.[27] Quite obviously, this had direct appeal for the exploited wage-slaves who toiled for wretchedly long hours in the sweatshops of London. The great release felt by Tom Mann and his brother engineers with the nine-hours' victory could represent, for all these abject victims of Victorian values, a tremendous promise of freedom. At the same time, with the expansion of the franchise, there could be no proposal more calculated to prise apart likely independent Labour voters from the long hegemony of the Liberal Party. Liberal capitalists might be willing to accept many things, but most of them were hardly enthusiastic for a diminution of the hours of work. Like their Conservative colleagues, they had laid out good money on machines and plant, and they wanted to get it back quickly. Shortening the burden of labour would not help this. By mobilizing and demonstrating for an eight-hour day, Tom Mann and his colleagues were simultaneously recruiting their army, and beginning to separate it from the adversary.

This campaign was to grow continuously, and the demand for a legal restriction of hours, joined to that for a statutory minimum wage, was to attract widespread and committed support.[28] By the end of the decade it had become an international commitment, and the platform of the original May Day demonstrations.[29]

But these years were not marked only by the extension of the franchise, and a concomitant political agitation. The new voters were not as numerous as all that, and even by the end of the century, the total electorate numbered only a little more than 6.7 million. The vote was extended to 58 per cent of adult males, but they made up only 27 per cent of the adult population. Certainly the working class could now find space in the parliamentary struggle, although there were large and intractable obstacles.

Meanwhile, the position of old-style trade unionism was less than rosy. A slight economic upturn followed the slump at the end of the 1870s, but by 1884 shipbuilding was in deep crisis and the Boilermakers' Society reported widespread destitution in the yards.

Two years later, reported the Webbs, James Mawdsley of the Lancashire Cotton Spinners' Union told an International Congress that workers in Britain were suffering great privation:

> Wages had fallen, and there was a great number of unemployed . . . Flax mills were being closed every day . . . all the building trades were in a bad position . . . iron foundries were in difficulties, and one third of the shipwrights were without work . . . Steam engine makers were also slack . . . the depression affecting the great leading trades was felt in a thousand and one occupations.[30]

Mawdsley, a confirmed moderate, felt that there was no way out within the present state of society:

> He did not understand their socialism; he had not studied it as perhaps he ought to have done. The workmen of England were not so advanced as the workmen of the Continent. Nevertheless they, at least, possessed one clear conception: they realised that the actual producers did not obtain their share of the wealth they created.[31]

Yet official trade unionism, squeezed between declining resources and expanding obligations, seemed less and less credible as an effective opposition, let alone defence. The old leaders were intellectually in thrall not only to the established parties, but, more damagingly, to *laissez-faire* philosophy. (There were among them many Liberals, together with not a few Conservatives. Of course, *laissez-faire* as a philosophy was easy to endorse, but as a practice it might often give trouble to a Labour representative.) Neither on the political nor on the industrial plane could this hold out any reasonable prospects of advance for the poorest workers in the sweated trades.[32]

Criticizing the Old Unions

For the unorganized workers, this framework was distinctly unappealing. But even for the organized it was a stimulus to dissent and, in the end, rebellion. After all, Burns and Mann, who were both uninhibited critics of the old trade-union order, were themselves products of the

Amalgamated Society of Engineers, and among the new generation of craftsmen there were numerous audacious spirits who found it easy to respond to such clarion appeals as this justly famous outcry from Tom Mann:

> How long, how long, will you be content with the present half-hearted policy of your Unions? I readily grant that good work has been done in the past by the Unions, but, in Heaven's name, what good purpose are they serving now? All of them have large numbers out of employment even when their particular trade is busy. None of the important societies have any policy other than that of endeavouring to keep wages from falling. The true Unionist policy of *aggression* seems entirely lost sight of: in fact the average Unionist of today is a man with a fossilised intellect, either hopelessly apathetic, or supporting a policy that plays directly into the hands of the capitalist exploiter . . . I take my share of the work of the Trade Union to which I belong: but I candidly confess that unless it shows more vigour at the present time [1886], I shall be compelled to take the view – against my will – that to continue to spend time over the ordinary squabble-investigating, do-nothing, policy will be an unjustifiable waste of one's energies. I am sure there are thousands of others in my state of mind.[33]

John Burns, speaking from within the same craft union, developed a specific criticism of the mutual insurance methods of the old unions. Writing in *Justice* in 1887, he said:

> constituted as it is Unionism carries within itself the source of its own dissolution . . . Their reckless assumption of the duties and responsibilities that only the State or whole community can discharge, in the nature of sick and super-annuation benefits, at the instance of the middle class, is crushing out the larger Unions by taxing their members to an unbearable extent. This so cripples them that the fear of being unable to discharge their friendly society liabilities often makes them submit to encroachments by the masters without protest. The result of this is that all of them have ceased to be Unions for maintaining the rights of labour, and have degenerated into mere middle and upper class rate-reducing institutions.[34]

Mobilizing the Unemployed

The socialists had an analysis of economic crisis and of the debility of working-class institutions, but they had more: they were full of youthful fire and audacity. A major agitation against unemployment was set in motion.

London during the winter of 1885–6 was so cold that in February 1886 outdoor work became nearly impossible. The depression had already struck home, and this was now joined by bitter weather, driving distress in the docks and on the building sites beyond endurance. Throughout East London, hunger ruled. On 8 February a rally against unemployment, called by the Fair Trade League, was the subject of organized heckling by the SDF, who led part of the crowd out of Trafalgar Square in protest at Tory manipulation of the issue of jobs. On the way to Hyde Park, some clubmen in Pall Mall jeered at the demonstrators, who replied with a volley of stones. Soon a full-scale riot was raging through the West End, with breakages everywhere and sporadic looting of shops. The SDF leaders realized that things were beyond control, and they withdrew. But the angry crowd did not disband, and looting began in earnest. Carriages were overturned in Hyde Park, and their owners were levied a toll in money and jewels.

The result was a mood of hysteria among the well-to-do. Fog on ensuing days only intensified the jitters. 'Not since 1832', writes Gareth Stedman Jones in a graphic account of this turmoil, 'had private property in London been so disturbed'.[35]

Burns was indicted for sedition, and his answer to the charge, *The Man with the Red Flag* (published as a penny tract), served only to widen his influence.[36] By 13 November 1887 the unemployed were ready to join with the radical left in a huge rumpus in Trafalgar Square, and both Burns and his parliamentary comrade Cunninghame Graham were sent to prison for six weeks for breaking through a police cordon.[37] Far from discouraging his supporters, this punishment did not prevent them from electing Burns to the London County Council in January 1889.

As this agitation developed, it was accompanied by new political initiatives. In 1886 the Trades Union Congress had resolved to respond to the post-reform successes of 1885 by founding a Labour Electoral Committee, even while seeking not to break its protective association with the Liberal Party. George Howell claimed sixty-nine beneficial statutes between 1868 and 1889, enacted as a result of the interactions between Labour and the established parties.[38] The following year the committee changed its name, styling itself 'Association', and claiming to emulate the Irish in becoming the 'centre of the National Labour Party'.[39] H. H. Champion, tired of the wrangles in the SDF, sought to use this association for more independent purposes and was soon joined by Burns and Mann, and then by Eleanor Marx and her husband Edward Aveling after their secession from the Socialist League. Champion began to publish a newspaper called the *Labour Elector*, which became the voice of the eight-hours' movement.[40] Soon, after heavy intervention from the dominant Liberal faction of the Labour Electoral Association had failed to dissuade Keir Hardie from contesting the Mid-Lanark by-election against a Liberal barrister, Champion's journal was to provide the core of a campaign not only for Hardie himself (he lost very damagingly) but for the principle of truly *independent* Labour representation.[41]

The Pedagogy of the Oppressed

The pedagogy of this campaign was direct and practical. It dealt in simple issues, and it kept on about them. For example, in the course of an agitation to enforce a law restricting juvenile hours to seventy-four per week, a famous scandal about conditions of work came to light in the Northwich alkali plant of Brunner, Mond and Co. 'The head of the firm was a Member of Parliament, being reported to be an advanced Radical and a keen sympathiser with the poor'.[42] The *Labour Elector* published a succession of devastating exposures of appalling standards. Handling red-hot lime for twelve hours at a stretch using only wheelbarrows; exposure to alkaline poisoning which affected the hair, blackened the gums and caused the teeth to fall out; gassing by soda fumes: a range of such dreadful practices turned out to be 'normal' operating standards in this enlightened firm which yielded a 49 per cent dividend to its philanthropic shareholders.

. The mechanics worked a customary nine-hour day; but the most vulnerable workers – those who actually manufactured the most noxious substances – found themselves not only doing regular twelve-hour shifts, but also reporting seven days a week. Champion duly recorded these facts, and was promptly served with a writ for libel which could have destroyed his newspaper. He refused to withdraw and resolutely carried on his offensive, while Tom Mann stepped in to secure the evidence to answer a lawsuit. Mann's account is still richly appropriate to everyone who wishes to understand the resource and courage of those who had taken up the fight for honest trade unionism:

> I decided to apply for a job as labourer, and dressed the part. Since caution was necessary, I adopted the name of 'Joe Miller'. I learned the customary time and place of taking on, etc., and applied. The second morning I was started as a general labourer, and put with a gang emptying trucks of slack. I was not on the 'process' but on general works, so I was liable to be moved about to any rough job; also, I had meal hours. I was 'posted' as to what departments to take stock of, etc., and in about ten days I had all the confirmatory detail required. Just at this time a public meeting was advertised a few miles distant chiefly political in character, really to serve the political interests of the head of the firm. I had now left the firm as an employee, and attended the meeting where eulogies of the firm were indulged in largely. When question time came I took part in a manner that caused some consternation; but very few knew me by sight, and not more than two knew me by my own name. Suffice it to say that in a few months all legal proceedings against the *Labour Elector* were suspended, and the eight-hour day was established at the works of Messers. Brunner, Mond & Co., Cheshire.[43]

This was some achievement, and it had a sequel. A few weeks after the inauguration of the eight-hour day, Mann received an invitation to attend a meeting to be held by the employees of the firm in a schoolroom adjacent to the works.

The meeting was to celebrate the inauguaration of the eight-hour day, which had resulted in starting one-third more men. The letter inviting my attendance referred to various other advantages of the change, now that the men had some leisure. I accepted gladly, and I duly presented myself at the committee room a little while before the appointed hour. Not more than one on that committee had an inkling that the 'Joe Miller' who had taken part in the public meeting of some weeks earlier, and who had made comments upon the firm, was really Tom Mann. One member of the committee was a trade union official who, doubtless, knew me by reputation; but he had never seen me before except at the public meeting previously referred to, and he had not appreciated the part I had taken in it. His astonishment when he realized that 'Joe Miller' was none other than Tom Mann was so pronounced that it took him some time to get over it.[44]

But all these initiatives, the exposés, the thousands of meetings, the demonstrations and police charges, the pamphlets and the electoral thrusts, all were building a new kind of awareness, a new questioning, and an unprecedented courage. Masses of people, toiling in dank sweatshops and living in sunless slums, were only waiting for a glimpse of hope.

The first great flash in London was·lit in Bow, at Bryant and May's match factory.[45] Here the workers, most of them very young women, finally rose up against dreadful health risks and poverty wages. In June 1888, at a Fabian meeting called to discuss female labour with Clementine Black, the first woman to join the factory inspectors, H. H. Champion produced the first spark. Lighting his pipe at the end of the lecture, he flourished the match. Were the Fabians aware of Bryant and May's dividends? These ran at 20 per cent. Bryant and May were also, of course, strong supporters of the Liberal Party.[46] Their employees could not vote, and neither were their dividends very large:

Girls who filled the coils were paid a shilling for one hundred coils, those who cut the matches down got twopence-three-farthings the 'duck' [three gross of small boxes or two-and-a-half gross large]. The wax taper makers earned about ten or twelve shillings a week. Wax box fillers got five shillings per hundred frames, and packers got one and ninepence per hundred gross of boxes wrapped.

These wages were low enough, but the girls complained that they rarely saw the whole of their money. You could be fined for dropping matches, fined for answering back, fined for having dirty feet, fined for leaving burnt matches on a bench. The fines varied from threepence to a shilling. The girls engaged in making the phosphorus matches complained less about

the fines than of the risk of getting what they called 'phossy-jaw'. This was
a necrosis of the jaw which often set in because the girls' hands became
infected with phosphorus through handling the freshly made matches.
Phosphorus got on to the benches, and as the girls brought their dinner to
work and had nowhere to eat it except the workrooms, the food itself was
often contaminated.[47]

Phosphorus poisoning creates terrible debility, sometimes rotting the
entire lower face. 'Bryant & May admitted that between 1880 and 1900,
51 employees contracted the disease and nine died from it.'[48]

But the immediate grievance of the girls was very different. There are
some grounds for believing that, contrary to the report of Ann Stafford,
health hazards were, to far too great an extent, seen as part of the
'natural' order of things. When Annie Besant, hot with anger from the
Fabian meeting, presented herself at the factory gate and offered to write
down their grievances, she was immediately assailed with the story of 'the
statue'. A statue of William Gladstone had been erected in the factory
forecourt as a monument to the employers' loyalty. But the girls had been
told to subscribe to it, had contributions docked from their wages, and
were compelled to take an unpaid holiday for the unveiling. They
rebelled, throwing rocks, and mobbing the statue, cursing it and
screaming, 'and some girls twined their arms round it and cut themselves
so that their blood dripped onto its stony plinth.'[49]

Mrs Besant's exposure was carried in *The Link*, a little weekly
newspaper which she edited. The revelations produced threats of
litigation by the directors and a solid strike of all the girls. The leaders
were Alice France, Kate Slater, Mary Driscol, Jane Wakeling and Eliza
Martin: their names are preserved in the company's files, and their
picture was reproduced in Annie Besant's *Autobiography* (see plate 1);[50]
but nothing else is known about them.[51] To maintain spirits and gain
publicity, a march was arranged on 11 July to meet MPs at a committee
room in the House of Commons:

Mrs. Besant gave Mr. Cunninghame Graham a list of the girls who had
been fined in the past six weeks. He at once asked:
    'Any other stoppages?'
    The girls spoke up: 'Yes, we have to pay for paint for the matchboxes,
and also for brushes.'
    The two Members of Parliament asked them all sorts of questions, and
'they showed sharp wits, directness and frankness in answering'.
    Then a little girl, aged fifteen and earning four shillings a week, pulled
off her shawl and displayed her nearly bald head; she had lost her hair, she
said, through carrying boxes on her head. The sight of this little girl seems
to have made an immediate impression on the hard-headed MPs and
reporters. Of all the girls there she probably had the least real grievance;
her plight was so much less pitiable than that of the girls who contracted

'phossy-jaw'. And yet there was something about her baldness so painful to the eye that it stirred uneasy consciences.[52]

Not only did the matchgirls win: their example shocked the comfortable, who learned the fates which Royal Jubilee London was offering its poor. More significantly, the girls' action inspired fellow sufferers who knew only too well the bitterness of semi-starvation and of subjugation. Now, at last, they could also see hope, and with it came the will to struggle against intolerable inhumanity.

Notes

1   Tom Mann, *Memoirs* (1923, reissued McGibbon and Kee, 1967), p. 9.
2   Ibid., p. 4.
3   J. B. Jeffreys, *The Story of the Engineers* (Lawrence and Wishart, 1945), pp. 79ff. See also E. Allen et al., *The North East Engineers' Strikes of 1871* (Frank Graham, 1971), pp. 98ff.
4   Mann, *Memoirs*, pp. 5–6.
5   Their reading matter is set in its context in Raymond Williams, *The Long Revolution* (Chatto and Windus, 1961), pp. 156–213.
6   Henry George, *Progress and Poverty* (Dent, n.d.). In *The History of Trade Unionism* (1894; WEA edn, 1912), pp. 375–6, Sidney and Beatrice Webb wrote: 'If we had to assign to any one event the starting of the new current of thought, we should name the wide circulation in Great Britain of Henry George's *Progress and Poverty* during the years 1880–82. The optimistic and aggressive tone of the book, in marked contrast with the complacent quietism into which the English working-class movement had sunk, and for the force of the popularisation of the economic Theory of Rent, sounded the dominant note alike of the "New Unionism" and of the British Socialist Movement.'
    George proposed to appropriate all land rents by taxation, and abolish all other taxes. In the United States as well as in Britain this was a popular call among the trade unions, who persuaded him to run for Mayor of New York in 1886. He would probably have won if the votes had been counted properly (*Encyclopaedia of the Social Sciences* (Macmillan, 1938), vol. VI, p. 635).
7   Mann, *Memoirs*, p. 21. He found only one fellow disciple during his trip to the USA, and that was a Scotsman.
8   J. E. Thorold Rogers, *Six Centuries of Work and Wages* (Swan Sonnenschein, 1884), p. 542.
9   Karl Marx, *Capital* (Dona Torr edn, Allen and Unwin, 1946), p. 215.
10 Ibid., chapter X, pp. 214ff.
11 Mann, *Memoirs*, p. 25. The early days of the Social Democratic Federation are described in A. L. Morton and George Tate, *The British Labour Movement, 1770–1920* (Lawrence and Wishart, 1956), pp. 166ff. See also H. W. Lee and E. Archbold, *Social Democracy in Britain* (Social Democratic Federation, 1935).

12 Franz Mehring, *Karl Marx* (Allen and Unwin, 1951), pp. 525–6.

13 Mann, *Memoirs*, p. 27.

14 Ibid., p. 44.

15 Its manifesto, published in January 1885, is given in full in Yvonne Kapp, *Eleanor Marx: The Crowded Years, 1884–1898* (Lawrence and Wishart, 1976), pp. 63ff.

16 See Chushichi Tsuzuki, *The Life of Eleanor Marx* (Oxford University Press, 1967), pp. 127ff.

17 Quelch's activities are reported in Lee and Archbold, *Social Democracy in Britain*. Some of his statements on behalf of the dockers are reproduced in J. T. Ward and W. H. Fraser, *Workers and Employers* (Macmillan, 1980), pp. 122 and 130.

18 This relationship has been differently reported. Olga Meier, in her notes to *The Daughters of Karl Marx: Family Correspondence, 1866–1898* (Penguin, 1984), p. 221, says that Eleanor taught Thorne to read and write. Giles and Lisanne Radice, in *Will Thorne, Constructive Militant* (Allen and Unwin, 1974), p. 25, say that she taught him 'to write correctly'.

19 In addition to its restrictive scope, the 1867 Reform Act remained far short of democratic standards. As D. L. Keir put it in his *Constitutional History of Modern Britain* (A. and C. Black, 1943), pp. 466 and 470–1: 'The reform of 1867 had made an immensely larger addition to the electorate than the Act had intended. Even so, the process of change was far from being arrested at the point now reached. The new democracy in the first place had to emancipate itself from the coercion and bribery still prevalent in the electoral system. Secondly, defects in the method of registration, which impeded many voters from establishing their qualification, had to be eliminated. Thirdly, the electoral franchise itself had to be made simpler and more uniform, and the qualification lowered. Finally, the discrepancies between population and representation which the redistribution of 1868 had served rather to emphasize than to cure still called for remedy.'

Bribery was indeed widespread, and Keir documents only the more sensational cases. Registration was incredibly complex: 'Alike in the boroughs and the counties a variety of different qualifications existed. In the former, besides a surviving remnant of ancient-right franchises, there were both the £10 occupancy qualification of 1832 and the householder and lodger franchises of 1867. In the latter, besides a substantial proportion of ancient-right voters, amounting to a fifth of the aggregate county electorate, and those qualified by the various franchises introduced in 1832 and modified in 1867, there were also those qualified by the new £12 rateable value franchise created in the latter year. These complications were perhaps less effective in stimulating the demand for reform than the anomaly that the franchise was notably less democratic in the counties than in the boroughs.'

The struggle for the extension of the franchise was to continue; not until 1928 was an adult suffrage established, and even this was marred by plural voting, which remained in force until 1948. The problem of unequal representation arises again in chapter 7.

20 Reprinted in Friedrich Engels, *The British Labour Movement* (Lawrence and Wishart, 1936).

21   Ibid., p. 34.
22   Ibid., p. 14.
23   Cf. Ross H. Martin, *TUC: The Growth of a Pressure Group* (Oxford University Press, 1980), chapter 3, 'The Politics of Deference'.
24   Eric J. Hobsbawm, *Labour's Turning Point, 1880–1900, History in the Making*, vol. III (Lawrence and Wishart, 1948), p. xvii.
25   The evidence for this has been documented by Jonathan Schneer, *Ben Tillett: Portrait of a Labour Leader* (Croom Helm, 1982), chapter 2, pp. 24–38. In greater detail, the same author covers the same ground in 'Ben Tillett's Conversion to Independent Labour Politics', *Radical History Review*, 24 (fall 1980), pp. 42–65.
26   Karl Marx, *Address to the Inaugural Meeting of the International Working Men's Association*, Marx–Engels Selected Works, vol. I (Lawrence and Wishart, 1942), p. 347.
27   Karl Marx, *Gründrisse: Foundations of the Critique of Political Economy* (Penguin, 1973).
28   Morton and Tate, *The British Labour Movement*, pp. 187ff.; Kapp, *Eleanor Marx*, pp. 389ff.; Mann, *Memoirs*, chapter IV.
29   Kapp, *Eleanor Marx*, pp. 368ff.
30   Webb, *History of Trade Unionism*, p. 379.
31   Subsequently it became crystal clear that Mawdsley 'did not understand their socialism': he finished his political career not even as a Liberal, but as an active Conservative.
32   Not that this appreciation came easily, either to trade unionists or to non-unionists. Other issues, especially that of the Irish question, ensured that Liberal influence over working people, and radical opinion, remained a hardy growth for a long time. But it was always disengaged from the core social issues, to which only a committed fringe of the party made any sustained contribution.
33   Tom Mann, *What a Compulsory Eight-hour Day Means to the Workers* (1886; reissued Pluto Press, 1972), pp. 22–3. Introducing this text, Richard Hyman highlights its 'flaws', and judges Mann to have been completely wanting in revolutionary consistency. After all, was it not inconsistent to 'appeal for a major legislative initiative' without considering 'at all the question of the class character of the state'? That Mann was engaged in a political struggle, as well as in a series of industrial engagements, seems not to weigh in this judgement. True, Friedrich Engels made several waspish comments about Mann, and these were collected in the introduction to Mann's *Memoirs* (Ken Coates, 1967), but on this issue of substance, Engels gave total support to Mann's initiatives.
34   Webb, *History of Trade Unionism*, p. 385.
35   Gareth Stedman Jones, *Outcast London* (Penguin Books, 1971), p. 292.
36   Webb, *History of Trade Unionism*, p. 374.
37   Ibid.; and G. D. H. Cole, *John Burns*, Fabian Biographical Series; reprinted in Michael Katanka, *Radicals, Reformers and Socialists* (Charles Knight, 1973), pp. 163ff.
38   Martin, *TUC: The Growth of a Pressure Group*, pp. 28ff.
39   Morton and Tate, *The British Labour Movement*, pp. 179–84.
40   Ibid., p. 182.

41   Kenneth O. Morgan, *Keir Hardie, Radical and Socialist* (Weidenfeld and Nicolson, 1975), chapter 2.
42   Mann, *Memoirs*, p. 54.
43   Ibid., p. 57.
44   Ibid.
45   Ann Stafford, *A Match to Fire the Thames* (Hodder and Stoughton, 1961).
46   Champion could have learned about this scandal from Tom Mann's pamphlet, *What a Compulsory Eight-hour Day Means to the Workers*, which he had published himself only eighteen months earlier.
47   Stafford, *A Match to Fire the Thames*, p. 66.
48   David Keys, 'Statue to Strike that Lit the Way for Unions', *Independent*, 12 October 1988.
49   Stafford, *A Match to Fire the Thames*, p. 67.
50   Annie Besant, *An Autobiography* (Fisher Unwin, 1908), facing p. 336. See also the photograph facing p. 338.
51   An exhibition was organized in 1988 by the archives department of Hackney Public Libraries. This was reported in the *Independent*, 12 October 1988.
52   Stafford, *A Match to Fire the Thames*, pp. 74–5.

3

The Great London Dock Strike

I

A Centenary

There is magic in numbers. The year 1889 was the first centenary of the great French Revolution. 'Scientific' though they may have been, the early socialists were as impressed as anybody else by round figures. H. M. Hyndman thought that the Revolution would echo along the years:

> Noble Robert Owen, seventy years ago perceived 'the utter impossibility of succeeding in permanently improving the condition of our population by any half-measures'. We see the same truth if possible yet more clearly now. But the revolution which in his day was unprepared is now ripe and ready . . .[1]

Warming to this theme, he later named the date:

> Let our mission be to help to band together the workers of the world for the great class struggle against their exploiters. No better date could be chosen for the establishment of such international action on a sound basis than the year 1889, which the classes look forward to with trembling and the masses with hope. I advocate no hasty outbreak, no premature and violent attempt on the part of the people to realise the full Social-Democratic programme. But I do say that from this time onwards we, as the Social-Democratic Labour Party of Great Britain, should make every effort to bear our part in the celebration by the international proletariat of the First Centenary of the great French Revolution, and thus to prepare for a complete International Social Revolution before the end of the century.[2]

The time arrived. To begin with, things were quiet.

'Terrible Dreams'

That summer, during a prosperous interlude in the long recession, work was brisk in the London docks. The dock companies' directors were away on holiday in, amongst other places, Russia and Cornwall.

Ben Tillett,[3] secretary of the recently formed Tea Operatives' and General Labourers' Union and himself a dock worker in London, was reflecting on the lessons of a disastrous strike recently concluded at the Tilbury dock. He had begun what he called a 'hole-and-corner' trade-union agitation in the depth of the 1880s depression. The tea coopers' tiny organization had in the beginning met with sympathy from some of the interested outsiders to whom Tillett appealed. Samuel Montagu, later Lord Swaythling, sent a donation of £5, and Professor Stewart, MP, wrote in praise of 'combination'; but the London Trades Council blew cold, in spite of initial encouraging words from George Howell and George Odger. When the employers brought in farm labourers as blacklegs, the Tilbury strike collapsed. Tillett knew that, to succeed, his small union needed a more general scope. In the aftermath of defeat he wrote:

> The brutal condition of our class, the squalor and misery of their homes and lives, is a bitter proof of how terribly it is used. How long the aristocracy of labour will hold aloof, how long our mistaken philanthropists will ply with impracticable charity, how long the world will be dead to the wants and wrongs of a neglected class of unorganised labour – and that only so because of the general indifference – I cannot tell; but this must be patent to all, that unless combination on constitutional grounds is encouraged, the country will have to face a graver danger than bludgeons will be able to suppress.[4]

Tillett had other problems. Bogus unions, little short of criminal conspiracies, abounded. His meetings were disrupted and even broken up by hired bullies. He himself was assaulted and badly beaten. Insults and intimidation were rife. Stones and 'filthy refuse' were thrown at union organizers. Tillett was not easily dissuaded. He drew strength from the adult-education movement, which influenced him in ways that were never intended by its initiators. In the days after the Tilbury defeat, he attended a lecture by Cosmo Gordon Lang (later Archbishop of Canterbury), during one of his visits to the Bethnal Green Settlement of Oxford University; the subject was 'The Strategy and Tactics of Napoleon'. As a result, Tillett found his mind engaged on the problem of conquering the world of shipping. Setting off for work in the foggy London mornings, he chewed through all the problems of creating 'a colossal picketing system', neutralizing every wharf in the docks. His minuscule organization was an embryo, but because he could imagine its growth, 'I saw how the Thames might and would be made idle . . . a thousand million pounds of financial power brought to a standstill. These were my dreams, my terrible dreams.'[5]

With these great issues boiling in his head, he would walk the 20 miles from the East End to Tilbury, where the rate was 4*d*. an hour. Sometimes he would be disengaged after thirty minutes, with 2*d*., because of the rain. In 1888 the strike for 5*d*. an hour at Tilbury collapsed disastrously. Tillett's exertions during the strike led to the first of his many physical breakdowns; when he recovered he came back to a Tea Operatives' Union reduced to less than half of its initial enrolment, although the precise numbers involved are a matter of dispute.[6] What is not in doubt is that the union was small: the maximum claim was that it enrolled 2,400 people; hostile witnesses put the figure as low as 300.

Little wonder that the solid craftsmen of the London Trades Council thought that organization of mere 'casuals' was a quixotic labour.

Help at Hand

Fortunately, Tillett had other moral resources upon which to draw. He had already befriended Tom Mann and John Burns, and was drawn to Annie Besant by the example she set in her intervention in the matchgirls' dispute. He had also come to know and work alongside Will Thorne, with his gasworkers' union.

In 1882 Will Thorne had walked to London from Birmingham after various abortive efforts to organize a trade union of gasworkers in the Midlands. An old friend who had been employed with him at Saltley helped him to get a job with the Gas, Light and Coke Company in its works at Beckton in the East End. In 1884 he settled in Canning Town, joined the Social Democratic Federation, signed the pledge and began the work of proselytizing for a gasworkers' union. As a socialist activist, he soon found himself presiding over Tom Mann's meetings, marching through the West End in the demonstrations against unemployment and joining forces with Ben Tillett in his little union.

On the last day of March 1889, a Sunday and 'a lovely sunny morning', all Thorne's canvassing at Beckton bore fruit: 2,500 workers attended a mass meeting to announce to the world their decision to form an organization, the Gasworkers' and General Labourers' Union. The title was highly significant – the first moment of general, new unionism. Thorne, Tillett and William Byford were elected to a provisional committee and charged with drawing up rules. Thorne made a powerful speech: 'I pledge my word that, if you will stand firm and don't waver, within six months we will claim and win the eight-hour day, a six-day week, and the abolition of the present slave-driving methods . . .'[7]

The gasworkers did stand firm, and their union began to shape itself.

A delegate meeting held that May launched a ballot for the new general secretaryship, in which both Thorne and Tillett stood for the office. Thorne won a large majority, with over 2,000 votes. Tillett took his defeat with good grace, since he had always had reservations about leaving his dockers in order to represent the gasmen. As things turned out, the dockers were to rally to trade unionism within three months. But before then, on 11 July 1889, the London gasworkers had achieved their famous and peaceful victory with the establishment of the eight-hour day.

As well as being able to call on other trade unionists for support, Tillett had got to know Cardinal Henry Manning, Archbishop of Westminster and head of the Roman Catholic Church in England. More than half the dock workers in London were Irish or of Irish extraction, and the Cardinal was a major influence among them. He was also an astute and sympathetic listener, and he took to Ben Tillett as father to son. Tillett wrote:

> In that time, I met with the kindliest and greatest man it has been my good fortune to encounter, Cardinal Manning. In my despair and pessimism I had sought advice from him. I was discouraged and in doubt about the future. 'Hope deferred maketh the heart sick.' It was deferred hope which brought about my sickness of heart, and the consciousness of the futility of my endeavours . . . left me in a thoroughly discouraged state of mind. What the Cardinal told me was of the sternest, simplest, and most practical character, couched in the tersest terms . . . Its essential message was that if a thing was worth doing at all it was worth doing well, whether it brought success or failure. A commonplace and a platitude perhaps, but it was for me not merely a slogan but an inspiration. As I recall the numberless people who have offered me advice in the different stages of my career, I think that Cardinal Manning's influenced me most.[8]

II

The Worm Turns

On 12 August 1889, two members of Tillett's union came to him with the request that support should be given to a dispute at the South West India Dock concerning the sailing ship *Lady Armstrong*. Tillett's shock was evident:

> I could hardly believe my ears. Months of heart-breaking effort and organisation amongst the poverty-stricken and dispirited dock workers had not encouraged me to expect any such manifestation. Had the worm indeed turned? Was it possible to strike with men who shivered with hunger and cold, bullied and intimidated by the petty tyrants who took a delight in the brutalities of the 'call-on'?[9]

The spark which fired the ensuing strike was a local argument about the distribution of the 'plus' – the bonus paid on tonnage for particular jobs. This was a much-hated system, since the basis of its calculation was concealed from the men; Tillett himself had called it 'systematic robbery'. In this case the initial contention was about a piece-rate of ½*d*. an hour, but once the dispute had broken out, it provided a platform for the thousand other cries from the victims of the dock world. It was agreed to present the employers with a comprehensive programme of demands. These included not only the famous 'dockers' tanner' (the raising of the base-rate from 5*d*. to 6*d*. an hour), but also the end of both the contract and plus systems. The dockers also insisted on a minimum of four hours' work, a reduction in the number of call-ons to two each day, and an overtime rate of 8*d*. an hour.[10]

Tillett tried to restrain any action on the *Lady Armstrong* until the employers had replied, but impatience ran away with the men. Within forty-eight hours they had walked out and the strike was spreading rapidly. Tillett did not instantly turn for help to Cardinal Manning. Instead, by telegram, he summoned Tom Mann and John Burns to his aid.

Enter Tom Mann . . .

Mann appeared within a few hours on the same day – 14 August – that the men walked out. As a result of the battle which followed, he and Tillett were to become lifelong friends. Their love for one another survived intense political differences, and a worldwide split in the socialist movement. Tillett was later to describe Mann as 'a giant, a power'. Will Thorne spoke of him as 'a streak of human quicksilver, here, there, and everywhere, commanding, pleading, cajoling, enthusing'. When, half a century later, death parted the two dockers' leaders, Tillett delivered a valediction of haunting beauty. None who heard it ever forgot it.

Initially, John Burns had been cautious. But by Friday, the 16th, he had committed himself and was leading a demonstration of 6,000 men. Burns was very well known in the docks, not only as the recently elected socialist county councillor, but also as a stump-orator at the gates. He had helped form a branch of the Gasworkers' Union at Vauxhall, and so he had friends in Thorne's union as well. In addition to these qualifications, in 1887 he had himself put in a brief spell as a docker. Burns had a genius for publicity. He was a natural leader for these demonstrations, and, wearing a straw hat which enabled the constabulary to identify him as the responsible chief marshal, he became a highly visible symbol. The hat passed into legend. Its material remains vanished when it was thrown overboard during a celebratory boat trip on the Thames, after the great victory.

. . . and Other Reinforcements

The strike was quickly reinforced by the invaluable official support of the two stevedores' unions, who had no immediate grievance of their own but who felt 'our duty is to support our poorer brothers'. Tom McCarthy, secretary of the Amalgamated Stevedores' Labour Protection League, became a key leader on the Strike Committee.

In addition to the stevedores, the lightermen joined the movement. The Seamen's and Firemen's Union, formed in 1887, committed itself in support. In the first days of the strike, Will Thorne thought of trying to recruit the men from the docks directly into his own gasworkers' ranks, but, after flirting with a bid to lead the conflict himself, he decided against the idea and threw his weight wholeheartedly behind Tillett's union. All, it seemed, were now happy to work within this new convergence of forces. Tillett had assembled a strong team, and he himself rapidly put aside his initial doubts and surprise. This, he saw, was to be an historic movement. Within days it was clear that the strike would indeed encompass the whole port. No section held back; at its height, 100,000 workers were involved, and the army of pickets numbered 15–16,000.[11]

So it was that between 14 and 22 August, the entire port stopped. Initially there were two Strike Committees, of the Stevedores' and of the Tea Operatives' Unions. Soon, however, they were merged into a single body, much to the benefit of the dockers, who lacked the administrative skills and experience of the stevedores. The South Side, with its separate Labour Protection League, proved difficult to co-ordinate, and later Tom Mann was sent there to organize and to raise morale. Outstanding sectional claims were advanced there, from corn-porters, deal-carriers, stevedores, trimmers, weighers, warehousemen, granary workers and steamship workers.

A Pageant of the Oppressed

The noise of the daily marches of dockers and their families, with their bands and banners, filled all the streets of the city. Converging on Hyde Park, the marchers attracted huge crowds to listen to Tillett and his colleagues – above all to Burns. The two contemporary historians of the strike, Llewellyn Smith and Vaughan Nash, have left us a vivid picture of this carnival of the most downtrodden people of the capital, which reflected all the complexity of East London society.

First came a posse of police, behind whom the marshals of the procession, with axes and scarves, reserved a clear space for the leaders. With them sometimes walked Superintendent Forster, a familiar figure in the strike. His solicitude for the comfort and passage of his convoy was unmistakable, and the man in the straw hat [Burns] at his side, deep in consultation, might have been a brother officer in plain clothes. Next came a brass band of the stevedores, following which streamed the multitude whose calling lay at the docks and riverside. Such finery as they boasted in the way of flags and banners had been lent by friendly and trade societies, and this gave the procession the appearance of a great church parade or demonstration of foresters. There were burly stevedores, lightermen, ships' painters, sailors and firemen, riggers, scrapers, engineers, ship-wrights, permanent men got up respectably, preferables cleaned up to look like permanents, and unmistakable casuals with vari-coloured patches on their faded greenish garments: Foresters and Sons of the Phoenix in gaudy scarves: Doggett's prize winners, a stalwart battalion of watermen marching proudly in long scarlet cloaks, pink stockings, and velvet caps, with huge pewter badges on their breasts, like decorated amphibious huntsmen: coalies in wagons fishing aggressively for coppers with bags tied to the end of poles, a brother coalie in effigy attached as figure-head to one of their vehicles, placarded with the announcement that he wouldn't go a step higher up the ladder on which he sprawled till the docker got his tanner: skiffs mounted on wheels manned by stolid watermen: ballast heavers laboriously winding and tipping an empty basket, Father Neptune on his car in tinsel crown and flowing locks, surrounded by his suite, – Britannia in a Union Jack skirt, the doctor in a faultless hat . . . and the barber brandishing a huge razor, ready for the victims of the equator on the other side of the car. Emblems quaint and pathetic were carried in the ranks, the docker's cat and the sweater's cat, the docker's dinner and the sweater's dinner, the docker's baby and the sweater's baby, diminutive and ample, respectively: Sir Hardwood (a gentleman understood to be connected with the Joint Committee), attired in mortar board, gown and mask, gravely saluted the bystanders and bowed low in front of Dock House. The bass dressers, locked out for forming a union, brought up the rear, carrying their bass brooms like lictors.

Such was the strike procession. It had its moods – was merry on some days, taciturn on others, laughed at the Dock House sometimes, howled at it at others, but it never lost command over itself or caused serious anxiety to its leaders or to the citizens of London.[12] (See plate 5.)

'Sir Hardwood' was in fact generally understood to represent the chief dock director, C. M. Norwood. He was also given a harsher character-ization: the dockers referred to him as 'Jack the Ripper', who was at the time vividly present in the minds of all East Enders. The *Star* newspaper said of him: 'He is in appearance the very embodiment of the insolence of capitalism. He is stout, well-fed and arrogant.'

The pageant was compelling, but its significance was even more moving for the old men who remembered the legendary years of

Chartism. One of these was George Julian Harney, who was still young enough, at seventy-one years of age, to compose a memorable description for the *Newcastle Chronicle*:

> The strike has recalled the memory of other great labour struggles . . . But all strikes, turn-outs and lock-outs of the past must pale their ineffectual fires in presence of the great revolt at the East End of London . . . Not since the high and palmy days of Chartism have I witnessed any movement corresponding in importance and interest to the great strike of 1889. How poor and paltry in comparison, appear the make-believe Caucus-manufactured 'movements' of recent years . . . Whatever the immediate issue, the strikers have 'felt their strength and made it felt' and it is safe to predict that this will not be the last revolt of the East End.[13]

These public rallies owed much to the experience of the earlier socialist demonstrations against unemployment. They enabled sympathetic journalists to generate over the condition of the dockers a public sense of shame without precedent in the history of labour struggles. The ground had been cleared for this understanding presentation by the social studies of the London poor, and of dockers' conditions specifically, carried out by Charles Booth and Beatrice Webb, and by the Fabian and Social Democratic Federation agitations during the preceding years. In the end (after an initial humanitarian lapse) *The Times* was the only major newspaper to oppose the strike.

A major influence was the newly founded evening newspaper, the *Star*, created by T. P. O'Connor, Irish Home Rule MP. O'Connor was to be the only Irish Nationalist member to hold a seat at Westminster on the votes of a constituency in England.[14] He sat for Liverpool Scotland from 1885 to 1929, and represented a massive concentration of port workers throughout that time. But in 1888 he had opened the *Star* with the assistance of H. W. Massingham, as much as for the radical as for the Irish cause. His first article in it was composed 'in a white heat', and it made a very firm commitment: 'The charwoman that lives in St. Giles, the seamstress that is sweated in Whitechapel, the labourer that stands begging for work outside the dockyard gate in St. George's-in-the-East – these are the persons by whose condition we shall judge the policy of the present political parties . . .'[15]

The judgement was a forthright one. The new paper was innovative in style: short, punchy articles, many crossheads and bold typography, strong coverage of items of popular interest – all features which were soon to become staple components of mass-circulation newspapers.[16] Yet, unlike its successors, O'Connor's *Star* was truly a radical journal. It began with a circulation of 140,000, and levelled at 130,000. George Bernard Shaw was among the first contributors, but he resigned because he thought socialist affairs were inadequately treated. Even so, he was to return as music critic, replacing a fellow socialist, Belfort Bax, at his own request.[17] Engels's letters are full of references to the *Star*: he clearly found it more sympathetic and perhaps more important a forum than did Shaw.[18] Be that as it may, the dock strike was a perfect issue for such a newspaper, and it campaigned ceaselessly to present the dockers' case.[19]

Tillett was familiar with the socialist agitation of the day. Its activists had already shown their readiness to leave their drawing rooms and studies in order to help the struggles of people who were trying to league themselves into unions. Annie Besant of the Fabians and Herbert Burrows of the SDF had both given selfless help, without seeking to impose direction, in the 1888 Tilbury strike.

The alliance which gathered round the dockers to organize the vast enterprise of the 1889 upheaval comprised people from every part of the new spectrum of radical socialist thought in the capital.[20]

Prominent among them were H. H. Champion and Eleanor Marx. Harry Quelch had been elected to the secretaryship of the South Side Labour Protection League. He was a controversialist and, in spite of his unsparing polemics about the weakness of trade unionism, he made an important mark administering a part of the old, decentralized, job-oriented London port unionism. Will Crooks, the cooper, had been conducting his 'college' of regular agitational meetings at the dock gates. His lectures were Socratic. The students argued back, and his answers were down to earth and spiced with Cockney wit. He 'gave both day and night to the dockers', wrote his biographer.[21]

Pickets and Strike-breakers

Harry Orbell, president of Tillett's union, played a role which could fairly be called heroic, out of the limelight, in organizing the strike and the picketing at Tilbury docks, 26 miles from the main port. When he was assigned this job, Orbell was diffident. 'I don't think I can do it, Ben', he said.[22] But he did. More, he maintained some loyal union men on the job as 'blacklegs', and their intelligence ensured that the union could intervene effectively when, as was expected, the company brought in outside strike-breakers. A group of labourers was imported from Liverpool, having been untruthfully informed that the strike was finished. Once in place, the employers tried to persuade them to stay on by alleging that the union would 'skin them alive' if they caught up with them. No, we 'will take you by the hand', Orbell wrote to them. That weekend they took the train home, paying their own fares. Harry's pickets provided a friendly protective escort.[23]

On another occasion, getting wind of a carriage-load of blacklegs due at the docks, Orbell mustered some four hundred men, and started with them in procession, nominally to Gray's, near Tilbury – for he was closely watched by the agents of the company – but making a detour, they worked round, with lowered banners to the north gate of the dock, where the men concealed themselves under the embankment. As the train drew near and slowed down, the men started up and wanted to push it back into the station. There was no occasion for this, however, as twenty-seven of the men came out on getting Orbell's message, for the crowd of dockers made it clear that they had been inveigled there under false pretences. The Tilbury men boast that they succeeded in detecting and frustrating an ingenious device of the company for passing blacklegs through the gates. It was found that a large number of individuals, with black coats and bags, and sticks, were daily entering and leaving the docks. The company, so the story runs, had dressed up the labourers in this fashion, hoping that they would run the gauntlet of the pickets without notice. To the dismay of the black-coated blacklegs, and of the dock officials, an effigy, inscribed 'the new docker', and correctly attired with bag and stick was hoisted up to a prominent place. Thus the new dockers were check-mated.[24]

Overall, picketing was organized by Tom Mann. This crucial responsibility kept him largely out of the attention of the newspapers, but it was absolutely vital to the solidarity of the resistance. The sum of £1,200 was expended by the strike fund on picket duties and banner carriers.[25] But, for this incredibly modest amount, at least 15,000 men were organized under 'picket foremen' to patrol the rivers, police the railway stations from which invariably blacklegs might arrive, and, of course, control the docks. At the Albert and Victoria Docks the pickets were paid in food tickets. Often women would be encouraged to enter the wharves, ostensibly to take in lunches. Then they would 'fairly nag' the blacklegs to leave.[26]

The pickets on night duty at Tilbury received 9d. each; by day they were relieved every two or three hours, and did their turn gratuitously. About one thousand dockers were out at Tilbury and two thousand of their allies, not reckoning the women, or the Chinamen who were locked up in Gray's police station for refusing to coal their steamer. 'Daddy' Rooark, the second in command at Tilbury, a stevedore from head-quarters, said of the Tilbury strikers that he never knew such men – they were as good as gold.[27]

If such efforts largely contained the threat of imported strike-breakers, they did not succeed in breaking down skill barriers, and the division between 'old' and 'new' unions. Even if Mann and Burns had a wide following in the Amalgamated Society of Engineers, their influence was not enough to bring about solidarity on the Commercial Docks, where three engine-men of the ASE kept the cranes running in spite of all efforts to persuade them to stop.[28]

The employers found this blockade intolerable. Norwood maintained a consistent volley of anguished letters, badgering the Home Secretary,

Henry Matthews. As a result, the Metropolitan Fire Brigade was kept on constant alert to inhibit fictitious arson attempts. The police were pushed to send 2,000 constables for the same reason.

> John Burns gave them a great welcome; he said he was glad they had been taken away from the hard duties of the West End to come to the East End, where he could promise them they would have nothing to do. He liked to have them there; they were friends; and he knew every one of them would drop a tanner into the collecting boxes on the sly.[29]

The Role of Tom Mann

Smith and Nash, in their vivid chronicle of events, appreciated the less flamboyant style of Tom Mann, who took over the responsibility for organizing with the South Side strikers once the picketing had been regulated and rendered lethally effective.

> [Tom Mann] supplied an element in the councils of the strike leaders in which otherwise they would have been weak. He was the eyes of the strike, always ready to see where there was necessary work to be done, and to set to work to do it. Strong and wiry, and capable of great physical endurance, and withal cool-headed and quietly energetic, he applied himself to the details of organization, which frequently carry with them the success or failure of a movement, and yet are so often over-looked by those who are great at beating the big drum. When occasion required, however, he would beat the big drum as well as any, and with all these qualities he combined an unswerving loyalty to his comrades, and an absence of all attempt to gain credit for himself, which are only too rarely met with in the history of labour movements.[30]

Mann himself unselfconsciously corroborates this view in his *Memoirs*:

> I can honestly say that I cared nothing at all for the public meetings, whether on Tower Hill or elsewhere, or for what was thought of the fight by the public. I concentrated on the work of organization and was indifferent to outside opinion. I had been at it about three weeks, and was now dealing specially with the south side of the Thames. One day I realised that my boots had become so worn out that I must get others or go barefoot (we always had long marches, and I invariably marched with the crowd). I slipped away from the marching column as soon as I noticed a boot shop. Hastily buying a pair of boots, I put them on and hurried to catch up with the crowd. When we reached Sayes Court, Deptford, I spoke as usual . . . A few days later, we were marching again along the thoroughfare where I had bought the boots. My eye lighted on the shop window and to my amazement I noticed my name on a card . . . to my still greater astonishment . . . the card bearing my name was on the pair of old boots I had shed a few days before: The writing on the card ran: 'The

boots worn by Tom Mann during the long marches in the Dock Strike'. I
was positively flabbergasted to think that importance of any kind could
attach to such articles or to me . . .

   I . . . felt so completely a part of everything that was taking place, that I
had left work, home, and all else and paid no regard to anything other than
the fight I was in.[31]

Liberal Support

Others besides the socialists were also to rally round. Liberals often
helped. As we have seen, the Liberal Party needed to worry about votes,
because a wider franchise meant that hitherto unheard interests now
required consideration. But many Liberals were moved by the experience of the strike, and gave open-hearted support. The Roman Catholic
Church was also concerned, because a core constituency within its flock
was directly involved.

Sydney Buxton (later Sir Sydney, later still the Earl Buxton), the
radical Liberal MP for Poplar, who was to become Postmaster-General
in Sir Henry Campbell-Bannerman's first ministry of 1905, befriended
the strikers from the outset. Tillett had written to him enlisting his
support before the strike, as part of his long-term strategy for the Tea
Operatives' Union. When the strike broke out, Buxton cut short his
holiday and returned to London to speak at the mass strike rallies. He sat
on the Conciliation Committee which sought a solution to the strike, and
when the men repudiated its first recommended terms, he stuck by
them, refusing to play the middleman or to seek a broker's role. He
worked in close partnership with Cardinal Manning in the search for a
peace formula, and did indeed produce one proposal for compromise
which proved unacceptable to the men and their leaders. When Tillett
and Mann showed their embarrassment, however, Buxton loyally
withheld his public endorsement of the offer. His 'fidelity as a mediator
was as heroic as [Manning's]', and he 'never lost the confidence of the
men, as the Cardinal so nearly did'.[32]

After the strike, Buxton remarked: 'For my part I have never been so
proud of being an Englishman and a Londoner, as during the past few
weeks. Fancy 100,000 hungry men in the streets with nothing to do from
morning to night, and never a row of any sort or kind, never so much as
an apple taken from an old woman's stall.'[33] If this was obviously a
spontaneous and unaffected tribute, behind it ran the still-fresh memory
of the far from tranquil events of two years earlier, which had terrified
the respectable classes. Riot was still a live memory in London.

Smith and Nash believed that Buxton 'was largely instrumental in
bringing about' the eventual settlement of the 1889 strike. Moreover, he
raised a fund of £2,300, 'which was chiefly applied to helping the families

of the strikers in the Poplar district. Mr. and Mrs. Buxton worked unremittingly, distributing in all some 100,000 meals and grocery tickets'.[34] To set this contribution in context, we should note that a total of £21,396 was paid to tradesmen for redeeming food tickets issued by the Strike Committee from several centres. This commissariat took a lot of organizing. At the beginning of the dispute, 4,000 men besieged the picketing headquarters asking for money, and it was Tom Mann who braced himself at the door of Wroote's Coffee House, his back to one jamb, and his foot against the other, to pass each claimant in, one by one, to receive his ticket. Chatting affably with the crowd, he rapidly cooled the temper of the occasion. But at the end of the day he had lost the skin off his back. Immediately afterwards the distribution was decentralized, so that stewards could recognize their own local strikers, and thus restrict payment to those entitled to it.

The Clergy Lend a Hand

Tillett also records the important contribution, in raising funds and offering encouragement, of the clergy of the East End, notably the Oxford House and Toynbee Hall clerics, who were often Christian socialists.[35] At the climax of the strike the mediating role of Cardinal Manning became crucial. His interest in the dispute, and his effectiveness in it – greatly enhanced by his influence with the preponderantly Irish Catholic dockers[36] – never detracted from the friendly personal relationship he had established with Tillett and Mann, in spite of their distinctive appeal to his own flock.[37] Manning left a brief summary of his part in the difficult to-ing and fro-ing of the negotiations, passed on to us by his biographer:

> On 5th September Miss Harkness came to me from the leaders of the strike to tell me that the coal heavers who had returned to work would strike again at noon the next day, if the dock directors did not grant the demands of their men. If the coal supply had failed, the railroads and the gas factories would have been affected. I went at once to the Home Office; both Secretary and Under Secretary were out of London. I went to the Mansion House; the lord mayor was in Scotland. But I found the deputy lord mayor and the second chief of police. We went together to the directors. They received us courteously but nothing came of it. This was Friday. The lord mayor and the bishop of London came to town. Saturday we met the leaders of the strike at the Mansion House, and drew up terms to be laid before the men, i.e. 6d. from January. We waited for an answer till ten o'clock. No answer was ever given. But next morning, Sunday, appeared a manifesto repudiating terms, negotiations and negotiators. In the afternoon in Hyde Park the meeting passed a resolution, accepting the terms, to begin on 1 October. This the directors rejected, and next,

Monday, the leaders met at the Mansion House, and it was arranged that Mr. Buxton and I should meet the strike committee at Poplar next day, Tuesday. We did so at 5 o'clock, in the Wade Street Schools. The conference lasted three and a half hours. About sixty-five men were present. For two hours there was little hope. I had proposed that the difference of time between then and 1 January should be split, fixing 4 November. Gradually a change came, and Mr. Champion moved a resolution adopting my proposal and empowering me to treat with the directors. This was at last carried by twenty-eight to fifteen, nineteen Surrey men not voting, their demand being distinct from the north.

Next day, Wednesday, we saw the directors. The lord mayor, by telegram, empowered me to urge the proposition of the men upon the directors. They gave no definite answer. We saw Mr. Norwood in private, and things seemed more favourable. The directors said they were bound in honour not to come in, until the wharfingers, and lightermen, and Surrey men came in.

The next days were spent in dealing with the two first, but until Saturday we could not get an agreement. It was five o'clock before the lightermen gave in, and six o'clock before the directors signed.

The strike then ended.

The lightermen then came to the Mansion House to thank us and to shake hands.[38]

Feeding the Families

During the period when the strike was just beginning to attract support from outside, the *Star* had reported that 'Cardinal Manning and the Salvation Army' shared the credit for feeding the hungry, clothing the naked, and visiting the sick.

But the real story of the funding of the stoppage depends on forces far apart from the Liberal and Catholic influences on London's docklands. Of course, Church funds could be applied directly to the relief of distress, and would not necessarily pass through the hands of the Strike Committee, so that their full extent cannot be calculated. But the evidence we have shows very clearly that the main support came from elsewhere.

At the end of August, the flow of British relief funds was desperately short of the amount needed to sustain the action. Close at hand though they were, the Church and the Liberals had by then made relatively scant financial contributions. The problem of blackleg labour was ominous, and there were rumours of the diversion of ships to other ports. The general trades of London had withheld all but financial support, and negotiations with the employers were in deadlock. The men and their families were hungry.

In these critical circumstances Tom Mann felt that new initiatives were vital. He proposed that a call be made for a general sympathy strike of the whole of the London trades. What became the famous 'no-work' manifesto was hurriedly drawn up and signed by the Strike Committee. Tillett, completely exhausted, returning to his bed after long hours convincing the Wapping dockers not to return to work, was persuaded to sign without fully realizing the significance of what he was doing. Fortuitously, on the very same day, the first meeting of the dockers of Brisbane had been summoned to organize practical support for London. They immediately sent a telegram to communicate the good news. Australian funds began to arrive soon after, and they came in a flood. Beyond doubt this was providential for the dockers.

A General Strike?

The manifesto, dated 29 August, was issued from the strike headquarters at the Wade's Arms. It read, in part: 'We now solemnly appeal to the workers in London of all grades and of every calling to refuse to go to work on Monday next unless the directors have before noon on Saturday, 31st August, officially informed this committee that the moderate demands of the dock labourers have been fully and finally conceded'. Once he had time to weigh up this attempt to call a general stoppage, over the heads of the cautious leaders of the other unions, Ben Tillett was deeply troubled. He rightly doubted whether such an appeal could be heard. If it failed, it would certainly alienate the established union officers and isolate the dockers. Engels shared Tillett's view, on wider grounds. He wrote at once to Eleanor Marx, asking her to oppose 'such a desperate game', because it would foreclose the support of the 'great mass of the bourgeoisie who all hate the dock monopolists'.[39] In some anguish, the call was withdrawn and its possible effect was thus never tested.

Notwithstanding the prudent influence of Eleanor Marx, masses of unorganized workers from outside the docks did nevertheless flock to join the dockers' marches and so promote their own disputes:

> As soon as it became obvious that the Strike was not merely a local dispute, but would be carried on with courage and energy and on a very large scale, numberless trades threw in their lot with the Strikers, abandoned their work, and joined the processions. Men who had been working for years with every appearance of being resigned to their lot suddenly discovered that they too had grievances, and must have an increase of wages or reduction of hours. So rapidly did the discontent spread that the Committee were seriously hampered by the applications to them for advice, encouragement, and assistance by workmen whose precipitate action hindered rather than helped the Dockers' cause ... it is certain that a very large number of East London workmen, who took occasion by the hand and demanded a higher wage, obtained it after

stopping work for a few hours, as an indirect result of the Dock Labourers' action. Nor can it be doubted that amongst such men the principles of Trade Unionism will find countless adherents, and that in the next few months the lessons they have learnt will bear fruit in a great increase of organisation amongst them. The Committee were obliged to refuse to assist such Strikers, since it was obvious that the funds with which they were entrusted were meant by the donors exclusively for the benefit of the Dock Labourers. On dozens of occasions we were obliged to advise men who came to tell us of their intention to come out on strike, to refrain from doing so unless they were prepared to fight their own battle alone. At last it became necessary to publish a manifesto warning the discontented that if they came out on strike without the authority of the Committee, they must do so at their own risk.[40]

But, of course, none of this uprush of action among the East End poor would have engaged the older unions in supporting strikes. The level of their sympathy was not negligible, but we can measure it in cash. Checkmated in efforts to spread the strike, only new monies could sustain the dockers in what was becoming unendable hardship.

Funding the Strike

The final balance sheet of the strike fund covering the period from 14 August to 16 November, showed that out of a total income of £46,499, the 'colonies' remitted £30,423,[41] whilst from all sources in Britain came £16,075. Trade unions gave something over £4,000: the 'public generally' remitted by letter and otherwise £10,661. Of this, £6,723 was collected by the *Star*. Street-box collections yielded £1,039.[42] Without the Australians, the outcome would have been completely different. But with their help, the strikers held out and won. Within two years the Australian waterfronts were themselves in tumult. The defeat of the maritime strike of 1890 has been seen as the turning-point in Australian labour history. After it, political action and the establishment of arbitration became a priority for most trade unionists.[43] None the less, the London dockers were fondly remembered. Cardinal Manning's portrait still decorated at least one Labour Hall in Australia in the late 1960s, where Tom Mann is similarly and widely commemorated.

III

Recognizing a New Power

The strike lasted from 12 August until 14 September. The strikers' demands, we should recall, had been for an increase in the hourly rate from 5*d*. to 6*d*., the ending of contract work and the plus system, and for taking-on times to be limited to two per day for a minimum of four hours' work. The settlement finally agreed conceded the hourly 6*d*., and 8*d*. per hour overtime (defined as from 6 p.m. to 8 a.m.). It established 2*s*. – i.e. four hours at time rates – as a minimum wage for any call-on. The contract system was converted to piece-work, and the surplus was to be equally divided amongst the gangs under the joint supervision of both company and dockers' representatives. These people, in negotiating the price for their jobs, acquired a role which would later be familiar throughout industry as that of the shop stewards.

During the strike, the Tea Operatives' Union rose in numbers from a few hundred to 18,000. Immediately following the strike, it was reorganized as the Dock, Wharf, Riverside and General Labourers' Union (DWRGLU), and by the end of November had grown to 30,000 members. Branches were set up in Bristol, Southampton, South Wales and Hull, as well as in Rotterdam and Amsterdam, Ipswich, Harwich, Gloucester and the Medway ports. But it was the leadership of the London men which officered the new union. Tom Mann was elected president, Tillett continued as secretary, and Tom McCarthy and Harry Orbell were appointed organizers.

That these leaders understood that the strike settlement must be vigilantly defended and generalized in all its ports is evident in the rules of the new union. Rule 1 established its name. Rule 2 fixed its objects to be:

1   To control the system of boy labour.
2   To abolish the present system of sub-contracts.
3   To regulate hours of hiring.
4   To enforce a minimum of four hours. (Minimum rate of pay to be 6*d*. per hour ordinary, and 8*d*. per hour overtime.) Working in stream 7*d*. ordinary, and 9*d*. overtime.
5   To establish a general fund for the protection of trade interests, for the recovery of compensation in cases of accidents, and for the provision of a 10*s*. weekly payment to members on strike.
6   To abolish extra work and overtime.
7   To establish a labour bureau.

Contributions were fixed at 2*d*. per week, with an entrance fee of 2*s*. 6*d*., and a quarterly charge of 4*d*. for management expenses. It is noticeable that the only money benefit at the outset was strike pay. The real incentive to join the union was, however, the recognition of its card by the employers, who granted work preference to members.

Central Power and Sectional Division

The constitution of the union centralized power in the hands of its executive, which was appointed by a Delegates' Council comprising two representatives from each branch. (Branches had a maximum of 500 members, and were grouped under District Committees, which could appoint paid secretaries.) The National Executive had nine members, presided over by Tom Mann. It collected *all* the funds received by the branches, and decided on *all* disbursements. It held the authority to sanction strike action. (In constitutional matters the Delegates' Council functioned as an ultimate court of appeal.)

Tom Mann undoubtedly had great influence on this centralized constitution. Lovell speaks of his policies as being

> sweeping and sometimes high-handed. As an outsider, and an impulsive one at that, he occasionally encountered the most ferocious opposition from port workers and on one occasion he told Burns that he was forced to carry a revolver to protect himself. Nevertheless his personality was such an engaging one that he won in the end the whole-hearted support of his members.[44]

It is improbable that Mann's need for weapons stemmed from any need to defend himself from ordinary port workers, but it would be a very probable precaution when confronting the professional strike-breakers. But Lovell is right about Mann's influence: so great was it that when he resigned for a short time in 1892, it was feared that the organization would break up.

Lovell contrasts the centralizing initiative of Mann, whose motivations were 'his passionate concern for downtrodden labour generally', with the approach of Harry Quelch, the South Side's Labour Protection League leader. Both had come from the SDF, but Quelch followed and embodied the traditions of the 1870s dock unionism, localized, sectional and autonomous.

Waterfront trade unionism in London remained divided after the great strike, between the new union, the South Side Labour Protection League, the Stevedores, the Watermen and Lightermen, and numerous smaller sectional bodies such as the Non-Freemen's Society, the Ballast Heavers' Society, and the Coal Porters' Winchmen's Association. Among these, the Amalgamated Stevedores' Labour Protection League and its general secretary Tom McCarthy had played a key part in the strike. Their branch headquarters at the Wade's Arms had been the main organizing centre. McCarthy had always held a wider view of waterfront unionism than was expressed in the separatism of the stevedores, and had supported Tillett's organizing efforts in the Tea Operatives' Union for months before the strike. It will be recalled that the second union formed by the stevedores in the 1870s, the United Stevedores' Union, had also supported the strike. In 1890, overcoming a history of mutual tension, the two stevedores' unions merged in the Amalgamated Stevedores' Labour Protection League. This step, whilst an advance on their previous division, none the less represented a solidification of their shared sectionalism in the face of Tillett and Mann's new union, and was in this sense a retreat from the outward-looking commitment of McCarthy.

The perpetuation of the old corn-porters' branch in the Surrey docks as the South Side Labour Protection League (SSLPL), further entrenched divisions in the port. The great strike was a fillip to the LPL, which added 'South Side' to its name in 1889 and modelled itself deliberately on the 1872 union. It remained separate from the Dockers' Union (as we shall henceforth refer to the DWRGLU) until the amalgamation of 1922, when it brought its 2,500 members into the TGWU.

Following the strike, partial attempts were made in London to overcome these divisions. The Wade's Arms Strike Committee was used as the basis for a United Labour Council (ULC). Most of the smaller occupational unions joined, as did the seamen, but not the Dockers' Union or the SSLPL. In staying out of the ULC, the Dockers' Union hoped, by its numerical dominance, to absorb the smaller unions in the port. In pursuit of this objective, in 1890 it formed its own federation with the seamen and the SSLPL, and in September 1891, as we shall see, it merged this federation with the ULC of the smaller unions. These initiatives demonstrate that there were strong currents flowing for wider forms of unity in London's dockland, and that the formation of the Dockers' Union was never likely to be the last word on the structure of waterfront unionism.

IV

Evaluation

How then should we evaluate the great dock strike? Before it, as Engels wrote to Edward Bernstein while it was still running its course:

> the East End was bogged down in passive poverty. Lack of resistance on the part of those broken by starvation, of those who had given up all hope was its salient feature. Anyone who got into it was physically and morally lost. Then last year came the successful strike of the match girls. And now this gigantic strike of the lowest of the outcasts, the dock labourers – not of the steady, strong, experienced, comparatively well-paid and regularly employed ones, but of those whom chance has dumped on the docks, those who are always down on their luck, who have not managed to get along in any other trade, people who have become professional starvelings, a mass of broken-down humanity who are drifting towards total ruination,

for whom one might inscribe on the gates of the docks the words of Dante: Lasciate ogni speranza voi che entrate! ['Abandon hope, all ye who enter here!'] And this host of utterly despondent men . . . this motley crowd thrown together by chance and changing daily in composition has managed to unite 40,000 strong, to maintain discipline and to strike fear into the hearts of the mighty dock companies.[45]

It is easy to share Engels's exultation:

> How glad I am to have lived to see this day! If this stratum can be organised, that is a fact of great import. However the strike may end . . . with the dock labourers the lowest stratum of East End workers enters the movement and then the upper strata must follow their example. The East End contains the greatest number of common labourers in England, of people whose work requires no skill or almost none. If these sections of the proletariat, which until now have been treated with contempt by the Trade Unions of the skilled workers, organise in London, this will serve as an example for the provinces.[46]

At the same time the novelist Olive Schreiner was staying in London. She wrote to the poet Edward Carpenter, who had inspired Annie Besant:

> Isn't the strike splendid. You ought to see the East End now. The strange earnest look in the people's faces, that sort of wide-eyed look. You look straight into their faces and their eyes look back at you; they are possessed with a large idea. It's very wonderful. I went yesterday to the place where the Salvation Army are giving away tiny packets of tea. About 500 men were there . . . waiting. The serious, silent, elated atmosphere, the look in the face of the most drunken old man was wonderful. I think I never felt so full of hope as yesterday.[47]

Another witness who was deeply moved was eighteen years old at the time. Soon he was canvassing in Whitechapel, discovering the depths of its squalor and misery. 'I was appalled by what I saw,' he wrote in his memoirs. 'The contrast between what I was seeing day by day, and what I found when I returned home . . . to our too opulent household, upset my equanimity altogether'. Thus it was that Herbert Samuel, future leader of the Liberal Party, go-between in the General Strike of 1926, and Home Secretary in the National Government of Ramsay MacDonald, came to write his youthful manifesto against those who rode in 'glittering carriages' in Hyde Park:

> All these callous, unthinking folk live on, unmoved, untouched by any thought of those millions, whom in contempt they unite to form the collective masses . . . The masses! – what a tale in one word. To be one of them – what a hopeless, endless fate; what a stifling of impossible

ambition, still-birth of ideals . . . And what are they, dull, short-visioned, who see not the ground shaking beneath their very feet, and angry voices, quiet, marvellously refraining yet, that are soon to rise, in ever-swelling clamour. Short-lived was the warning of a hundred years ago* . . . Let there be but one bad King, one unscrupulous minister, and down will crumble your monarchy and your upper classes. May it be well led, our English revolution . . . Have you ever thought – upper classes, of a humble workman's daily life, its sorrows, its hardships . . .[48]

In time, Lord Samuel learned how to bring his views into somewhat closer conformity with the forces of order. Others proved less adaptable.

Yet adaptation there was, and it did not take all that long. Only a few months later, the same Engels who had welcomed the 'example' of the strike was bemoaning the respectability of the new leaders of these outcasts of London. Burns, he told F. A. Sorge on 7 December 1889, was 'secretly prouder of his popularity with Cardinal Manning . . . than of his popularity with his own class'. Champion had intrigued with the bourgeoisie. 'Even Tom Mann . . . the finest of them, is fond of mentioning that he will be lunching with the Lord Mayor'. Hope sprang eternal with Engels, though: 'It will not help the bourgeoisie much if they do succeed in enticing some of the leaders into their toils. By that time the movement will have become strong enough to overcome this sort of thing'.[49] None the less, 'If one compares this with the French, one sees what a revolution is good for, after all'.[50]

Engels had been right first time. A new constituency had announced itself. Its potential power could not be disputed.

Yet the established order had indeed noticed what was going on. The Liberal Party had a suitably ambivalent structure, and a division of forces which could connect with even the most intransigent rebels. Shortly Tom Mann was to find himself serving on a Royal Commission. This was not to prove fatal, either to him or his supporters. But in due time, the 'man in the straw hat', John Burns, was to arrive in a Liberal Cabinet. Generations of socialists have seen this simply as an apostasy. So it was: but was it not also the beginning of a great process of deliberate incorporation, in which trade-union militancy was to become simultaneously a protest against and a bid for a place in established society?

Recognition: the Magic Word

Everything turns on what happens when a hitherto unorganized section of people obtains 'recognition'. With hindsight, recognition may appear to be the first step to 'incorporation'. Certainly once class divisions are not only intuited but also organized, it becomes possible to devise

* The French Revolution of 1789.

structures for regulating and controlling their interconnection. This is the basis for all the various institutions which have since been described as 'corporatist'. To look at the problem in the light of its resolution is signally to misunderstand it in its origin.

For the leaders of the dock workers in 1889, things appeared in a very different light. They had been part of a momentous upheaval. Most of them had stepped into the waterfront arena from outside. Burns and Mann were highly skilled engineers, with a long tradition of craft unionism behind them, even where they rejected it. Champion and Eleanor Marx, and a small host of others, whose influence was vital in the conduct of the strike, were highly qualified professional people acting in the interest of the socialist movement, seeking to proselytize. The skilled workers on the waterfront itself carried an immense burden, and without Tom McCarthy and his supporters no rebellion would have been possible. Lastly, there were those who could truly be identified with the hitherto unorganizable 'dock rats': most notably, Ben Tillett himself.

The mutinous workforce had few points of community reference. Ill- and often impermanently housed migrants, refugees from different forms of oppression and poverty, they were less tractable to permanent organization than any other group which had hitherto atttempted it. Before 1889, and since, there have been innumerable explosions of rage among oppressed populations, which have given rise to a few days or weeks of ferocious combat, only to be followed by the restoration of 'order', and the rebirth of apathy, quiescence and hopelessness.

In the United States, during the great days of the Industrial Workers of the World (IWW) from 1910 to 1922, city-wide stoppages of work could be organized – even up to the point of physical battles – as the union message spread. But once a year had elapsed, the IWW could often muster the merest handful of members among those once 'vanguard' populations. (The military image in such cases is almost appropriate.) In short, nothing could guarantee the continued association of the London dock workers once their claims had been satisfied. Organizing on the day was one thing: organizing a continuous presence was quite another.

But then the concept of recognition comes into play. If the employer 'recognizes' the association of port workers, he does far more than agree to deal with a group of workers' representatives. Now the members of that group can recognize their own collective identity through his opposing eyes. Their personal separateness is overcome, not only by their own efforts to join together but by the concession of collective status on the part of the adversary. If the adversary, in his own newly perceived weakness, seeks to associate himself with others of his class, so much the better: this means that the realities of class have now entered into the formal structure of social relations, so that the words describing it take on a new and deeper meaning.

Long before the complete transformation of our vocabulary, however, we may expect the intervention of a third party. If the state intervenes, whether to 'hold the ring' or for some more direct engagement to uphold its rule, this too may easily offer the prospect of recognition. Class relationships, in short, are built through interaction, and are not simply self-ascribed. Recognition is one of the boundaries evolved in interaction, and becomes a major determinant in the development of trade-union organization.

The events of 1889 were crucial in this process. In them was born a persistent effort, which would survive brutal countermeasures. Recognition could be withdrawn, but the will to establish it could not be cancelled so easily. Its effect would bring vast changes in industrial life, and a transforming influence in politics.

This is an argument about which much was to be heard for almost 100 years afterwards. On the day after victory, the situation was differently perceived.

What, after all, had happened to the people of dockland? They had been pushed to the outermost fringes of rejection by Victorian society. Crowded a dozen at a time into squalid tenement rooms, exhausted, starved, forced to fight one another for a few hours' work which commonly they were too enfeebled to perform: these wraiths had joined forces, recovered strength in their solidarity, and, at last, won. Their message had gone round the world. They had got their sixpence; but more, they had regained their self-respect, and with it their human powers, by daring to rebel. The evolution of 'dock rats' into 'new unionists' turned whole lifetimes of personal subjection and defeat into a wild joy of collective triumph. Could this inspire further victories? Would the union continue? Might it, indeed, become the foundation for all the wider changes in the political order which had seemed so necessary to all those who had rallied to give help? By the time of the opening of the dock strike, Parliament was old, but modern democracy was waiting to be born. At the end of that strike, its healthy embryo was beginning to grow, and nothing would ever be the same again.

Notes

1 *Justice*, 18 July 1885; cited in Sidney and Beatrice Webb, *The History of Trade Unionism* (1894; WEA edn, 1912), pp. 410–11.
2 Ibid., 6 August 1887.
3 Benjamin Tillett (1860–1947), born in Bristol, ran away from home as a child, joined a circus, then entered the navy at the age of thirteen, where he learned to read and write. He transferred to the merchant marines in 1876 and gravitated to London's East End, seeking work on the docks, in 1885.
4 *Justice*, 24 November 1888; quoted in Jonathan Schneer, *Ben Tillett: Portrait of a Labour Leader* (Croom Helm, 1982).

5   Ben Tillett, *Memories and Reflections* (John Long, 1931), pp. 112–13.

6   John Lovell, *Stevedores and Dockers: a Study of Trade Unionism in the Port of London, 1870–1914* (Macmillan, 1969), p. 97, puts the membership at a maximum of 800 and a minimum of 300, and gives two sources, one of which is Tillett's *Memories and Reflections* (p. 113). But this is inaccurate, and Tillett gives no such figures. He does, indeed, speak of a 'tiny' union (p. 118), 'my own feeble union' (p. 110) and 'our small union' (p. 112). But the only figure we can trace to Tillett himself is 2,400, which is the membership he claimed on 20 November 1888, during cross-examination at the Select Committee on the Sweating System, (Second Reports, p. 111, Parliamentary Papers, 1888, V, XXI). Lovell's second reference is to George Howell, *Trade Unionism New and Old* (Methuen, 1891; 3rd edn, rev. to 1990), p. 153. In fact this reference is to a markedly hostile source, as we shall see when we examine the controversy which gave rise to this report. Of course, the boasted 2,400 might have been a propaganda exaggeration. But in July 1887 Tillett invited MPs and other public figures to an open meeting of 2–3,000 dockers (*Memories and Reflections*, p. 99). Perhaps this is connected with his claim during the Select Committee hearings? In any event, Colonel George Raymond Birt, manager of the Milwall docks, strongly contested Tillett's estimate of the number of dock workers in London, but made no attempt to challenge his statement about union membership. (Tillett said there were 100,000 dockers in London; Birt put the number at an absolute maximum of 75,000.)

7   Yvonne Kapp, *The Air of Freedom: The Birth of the New Unionism* (Lawrence and Wishart, 1989), p. 53. While this book offers an incomparable story of the day-by-day struggles of the gasworkers, for an analysis of the social and technological context of their union it is still necessary to go to Eric J. Hobsbawm's remarkable work, *Labouring Men* (Weidenfeld and Nicolson, 1968), pp. 158–203.

8   Tillett, *Memories and Reflections*, p. 119.

9   Ibid., p. 91.

10 Tillett claimed in retrospect that this programme represented the first challenge to the whole casual system of employment (*Memories and Reflections*, p. 120).

11 The figure of 100,000 workers is Tillett's, supported by Jonathan Schneer, *Ben Tillett*, p. 42. The estimates of picket numbers given here are higher than those of Ann Stafford and other historians.

12 Llewellyn Smith and Vaughan Nash, *The Story of the Dockers' Strike* (Fisher Unwin, 1890), p. 84.

13 Eric J. Hobsbawm, *Labour's Turning Point, 1880–1900*, History in the Making, vol. III (Lawrence and Wishart, 1948), pp. 85–6.

14 F. W. S. Craig, *Minor Parties at British Parliamentary Elections, 1885–1974* (Macmillan, 1975), p. 47, gives details of all contests.

15 T. P. O'Connor, *Memoirs of an Old Parliamentarian*, vol. II (Ernest Benn, 1929), p. 255.

16 Cf. Raymond Williams, *The Long Revolution* (Chatto and Windus, 1961), pp. 198ff.

17 G. B. Shaw, *Collected Letters, 1874–1897*, vol. I (Max Reinhardt, 1965), pp. 183ff.

18 Friedrich Engels, Paul and Laura Lafargue, *Correspondence* (Foreign Languages Publishing House, Moscow, n.d.), vol. II, pp. 239–57, 260–8 and 402; vol. III, pp. 78–82 and 92.

19 Ann Stafford, *A Match to Fire the Thames*, makes extensive use of *Star* reports. This gives a clear impression of the scale of the newspaper's coverage and commitment.

20 Their principal press officer was H. H. Champion. From him, at strike headquarters, the regular newspaper journalists received daily briefings and releases. Eleanor Marx worked 'unceasingly, literally night and day, at our headquarters' (Tillett, *Memories and Reflections*, p. 135) as minute-secretary, counsellor and treasurer. She had already helped greatly in the formation of the Gasworkers' Union during the previous year. Her work earned deeply affectionate tributes in the subsequent memoirs of both Tillett and Mann, who remembered, in their old age, how much they gained from her sparkling intellect and her great force of character. Alas, they also had to record how much they had been moved by her tragic fate. There is copious evidence of the frequency of the meetings attended jointly by Eleanor Marx and Tom Mann during the 1880s in the correspondence of Eleanor, in Olga Meier (ed.), *The Daughters of Karl Marx: Family Correspondence, 1866–1898* (Penguin, 1984), part four, pp. 163–219.

21 George Haw, *From Workhouse to Westminster* (Dalton, n.d.), p. 68.

22 Ann Stafford, *A Match to Fire the Thames* (Hodder and Stoughton, 1961), p. 106.

23 Ibid., p. 117.

24 Smith and Nash, *The Story of the Dockers' Strike*, pp. 104–5.

25 Not £12,000, as Stafford erroneously reports (*A Match to Fire the Thames*, p. 116).

26 Stafford, *A Match to Fire the Thames*, p. 116.

27 Smith and Nash, *The Story of the Dockers' Strike*, p. 105.

28 Friedrich Engels, letter to H. Schluter, 11 January 1890, in *Karl Marx and Frederick Engels on Britain* (Foreign Languages Publishing House, Moscow, 1953), pp. 523–4.

29 Stafford, *A Match to Fire the Thames*, p. 119.

30 Dona Torr, *Tom Mann and His Times*, vol. I: *1856–1890* (Lawrence and Wishart, 1956), pp. 295–6.

31 Ibid., p. 296.

32 Stafford, *A Match to Fire the Thames*, p. 198.

33 Ibid., p. 142.

34 Smith and Nash, *The Story of the Dockers' Strike*, p. 97.

35 Alan Fox analyses the role of these groups in the evolution of the British system of industrial relations in his *History and Heritage: The Social Origins of the British Industrial Relations System* (Allen and Unwin, 1985), pp. 235–55.

36 John Lovell reports that the close-knit, kinship-dominated trades and trade unionism of the Port of London, produced by the Irish immigrants, were more marked in the South Side Labour Protection League (SSLPL), and the Stevedores' Union, than amongst the dock labourers who constituted Tillett's union and who later formed the membership of the DWRGLU. He ascribes the father–son succession practices specifically to the Irish: 'In the London dock area of the 1890s the story was told of a foreman named

Donovan, who was said to have taken on 57 Donovans for work one day, and was only stopped by the men threatening him with violence if he took on any more relations! Tom McCarthy, himself London Irish, recorded that "they collared the corn portering and the stevedoring and being very clannish have kept it in their families ever since. Thus the second generation of Irish got the pick of the work"' 'The Irish and the London Dockers', *Bulletin of the Society for the Study of Labour History*, no. 35 (autumn 1977), pp. 16–17.

This was precisely the kind of unionism which rejected, and was rejected by, the new unionism which arose out of the London dock strike. Yet we need not follow Lovell in supposing that the Irish – who may well have established this pattern in the SSLPL and the stevedores' unions – necessarily *invented* it: the much older and indigenous practice of the Thames lightermen existed to set an example of clannishness.

37 Tom Mann, *Memoirs* (1923; reissued MacGibbon and Kee, 1967), p. 85, wrote, 'As the Cardinal had been so closely identified with the wind-up negotiations of the dock strike, he maintained his interest in the welfare of the dockers, and on a number of occasions he wrote asking me to call on him to tell him how matters were developing. I have before commented upon his wonderful features, and upon the ultra-refined manner that always characterized him. He was perfectly natural, and simple, and I was entirely at ease with him'.

38 E. S. Purcell, *Life of Cardinal Manning* (1896; 2nd edn, 2 vols, 1985), vol. II, pp. 662–3.

39 Engels and Lafargue, *Correspondence*, vol. II, p. 317.

40 H. H. Champion, *The Great Dock Strike in London: August 1889* (Swan Sonnenschein, 1890), p. 169.

41 P. F. Donovan has analysed the Australian contributions to the dockers' fund ('Australia and the Great London Dock Strike, 1889', *Journal of the Australian Society for the Study of Labour History*, no. 23 (November 1972), pp. 17–26). He shows that there was very widespread support for the strikers, involving extensive middle-class contributions. Not only the unions, but the overwhelming majority of the Australian press, took part in a truly massive campaign. Donovan reports, however, that 'an analysis of the subscription lists that were published [in Australia] suggests that the total was nearer £37,000' than the £30,000 recorded in the British accounts. Donovan offers the following breakdown:

Queensland	£2,135 9s 2d
New South Wales	£8,386 5s 7d
Victoria	£22,569 5s 4d
South Australia	£3,073 9s 9d
	£36,164 9s 10d

These figures are based on reports in the *Brisbane Courier*, *Sydney Morning Herald*, Melbourne *Age*, and Adelaide *Observer* between 24 September and 24 October 1889. In addition, the Tasmanian government had sent £500 to the dockers by 11 September, and the New Zealand unions had each forwarded £200. This 'means that the total from the Australasian colonies must have stood at least at £37,064 9s. 10d. The probability is that the final total was even greater than this'. The dockers' balance sheet (*The Great Dock Labourers' Strike, 1889, Manifesto and Statement of Accounts* (Green and McAllan, 1889)) carries a note to the items recording 'colonial' contributions, explaining that certain sums had been sent directly to the Lord Mayor of London for the relief of 'distress' during the strike, without passing through the hands of the Strike Committee. These, of course, were unrecorded in the dockers' accounts. It thus appears that the Lord Mayor handled a minimum of £7,000 from Australia, in addition to whatever was collected in London or the rest of Britain.

Not all these monies reflected the appeal of solidarity, however. Various other motives intruded. They have been discussed and analysed by Humphrey McQueen, *A New Britannia* (3rd edn, Penguin (Australia), 1986), pp. 221 and 259.

42 See Smith and Nash, *The Story of the Dockers' Strike* appendix E, pp. 186–7.
43 'The great turning point in the history of Australian labour was undoubtedly the maritime strike . . . in 1890 . . . The effect of . . . defeat was to galvanise into life the hitherto latent idea that voting power carried with it not only the choice of the Parliamentary representative, but also of the work he was expected to do . . .' (W. G. Spence, *Australia's Awakening* (1909), pp. 94 and 185). See the discussion of this claim by June Philipp and Jean O'Connor in *Historical Studies*, second series, (Melbourne University Press, 1967), pp. 126–50.
44 Lovell, *Stevedores and Dockers*, p. 115.
45 Engels, letter to Edward Bernstein, 22 August 1889, in *Karl Marx and Frederick Engels on Britain*, pp. 520–1.
46 Ibid., p. 521.
47 Cited in Chushichi Tsuzuki, *Edward Carpenter, 1844–1929* (Cambridge University Press, 1980), p. 90.
48 The Rt Hon. Viscount Samuel, *Memoirs* (Cresset Press, 1945), p. 7.
49 *Karl Marx and Frederick Engels on Britain*, p. 523.
50 Ibid.

4

The New Unionism Arrives

I

Nothing Succeeds Like . . .

If we say that the dock strike was to become the symbol of an uprising of the poorest workers, we are saying that it was not an isolated event. It was by no means the first event of its kind: but it happened in London, at the centre of a national media network, under the noses of national political spokesmen. That London poverty was merely a concentrated example of nationwide deprivation meant only that the news of the uprising of the London poor electrified the slums of the North, and the dockside tenements of ports all around the country. Equally, it inspired the conscientious middle classes, the active Christians, and that part of the intelligentsia that was already beginning to think about socialist ideas. Unions had already been forming during the earlier months of economic upturn, and their further mushrooming could only be encouraged by the dockers' success. Indeed, in the minds of its beholders that success grew to assume almost mythic proportions. The prosperity of the affluent classes in late Victorian England was constantly reproached by the squalor and destitution they engendered all around them. Any challenge to this polarity was bound to arouse wide moral support, and so stiffen the will to resistance. As hopes rose, so the stature of the dockers' heroes rose with them.

Havelock Wilson, the seamen's leader, wrote:

> Demonstrations became very frequent. Every branch of a union felt it must have a banner. The silk industry and the painters had quite a boom in trade . . . everyone's portrait had to be painted on the banners. The national men (that is to say, the leaders of national importance) had first

place, such men as John Burns, Tom Mann, Ben Tillett, Will Thorne and myself.[1]

In fact these were remarkable men, but they were plainly incapable of fulfilling the legendary tasks which were to be laid upon them. Having been set to long hours of work in early childhood, each was responsible for his own education, and even if rich experience was a fine instructor, none the less there were bound to be important gaps in learning. To a great extent the social and strategic goals of such leaders had to be formed in reaction to the heaving flux of events. It was necessary to think on one's feet.

And for all the great men whose pictures were carried in procession, there were hundreds of others whose role was equally indispensable. A giant wave of unionization broke over the country in the years between 1888 and 1890. People who had previously been thought incapable of organization were suddenly in the forefront of turbulent trade-union actions. Of these struggles, those concerned with the seamen and with dock workers outside London are closest to our concern. But others were also very significant.

The Seamen

A loosely federated union of seamen had existed as far back as 1851, with branches in thirty ports. It won some concessions from the shipping companies, but, having no central government, it collapsed in 1860.[2] The seamen had formed a number of local associations in the 1870s, mirroring the state of unionism in dockland at that time. Having been a member of one such union in the North-east, Havelock Wilson formed the National Amalgamated Union of Sailors and Firemen in 1887.[3] In 1889 the seamen struck for wage increases in all the principal ports. In most cases they were successful. These stoppages ranged over the first six months of the year, thus preceding the dock strike.[4] By the time the dockers were out, the seamen had formed forty-five branches nationwide.

The National Union of Dock Labourers

In Glasgow, two craft unionists, the compositor McHugh and the engineer McGhee, formed the National Union of Dock Labour in February 1889, and rapidly spread its recruitment to Liverpool. Soon they had reached out to other ports in the North-west and throughout Scotland. Glasgow dockers joined in strike action with the seamen in that port in June, following an appeal for support from Havelock Wilson, who urged them to form a dock-workers' union which could then federate

with his seamen's organization. The new union did not have the impetus
that was afforded to London by the great strike. After the collapse of the
seamen's strike in Glasgow it led a shadowy existence, and owed much of
its survival to the skill and persistence of McHugh, its first general
secretary, and McGhee, its first president. McHugh was a personal
friend and follower of Henry George, a supporter of the Scottish
crofters' Highlands agitation, and already a well-known Scottish radical.
McGhee had similarly close relations with Henry George, and with
Michael Davitt, the Irish land-reformer. He had participated in the
Knights of Labour agitation in the Midlands in 1887, on behalf of the
nail- and chain-makers, and the Knights had nominated him to organize
in Glasgow. However, he acted independently of them in the NUDL,
and worked as a commercial traveller whilst serving the dockers. These
two leaders shared the advantage – in dockland – of Irish origins. They
were also committed to Irish Nationalism. Their adherence to Georgeism
drew no less popular support from the people, many of whom had
desperate experience or memories of injustice in the severance of their
families from the land.

The full title of their union became the National Union of Dock
Labourers in Great Britain and Ireland. Its national aspirations were new
to dockland: its specific remit to organize across the Irish Sea had a
special significance, with consequences which were to reach far into the
twentieth century. Glasgow dockers had a spasmodic record of unionism
going back to the 1850s, and one small body continued to challenge the
monopoly of the NUDL for some years. Before 1889 had passed,
organizers had established the new union in Belfast and, most
significantly, Liverpool. Derry, Dundee and Leith followed quickly
behind. In Liverpool a strike was provoked during the course of the
London strike, 'deliberately inspired . . . by the employers, who hoped to
stamp out the union before it attained its full strength, before we
ourselves, indeed, could realize the full measure of our strength',
reported James Sexton, who joined the union at once, even though he
had already been victimized and was forced to earn his living as a coal
merchant outside the docks.[5] He bankrupted his new business giving aid
to the strikers.

The Birth of Ca'canny

A three-week strike for higher pay in the Glasgow docks in 1889
collapsed because the employers made ruthless use of blackleg labour.
The inefficiency of the substituted workforce was highlighted by the
union, and the employers responded by declaring themselves well
satisfied with it: whereupon McHugh seized his opportunity. The
dockers returned to work, and McHugh advised them that if the

employers were satisfied with incompetent cheap labour, and unwilling to pay for work of better quality, then it would be a mistake to give them more than the value of their offered rewards. He told the workers:

> We have seen them [the blackleg farm workers], we have seen that they don't know how to walk on a boat, that they have dropped half the stuff they carried: in short that two of them can't do the work of one of us . . . Work like the farmworkers worked. Only it happened that several times they fell into the water: it is useless for you to do the same![6]

In this way, McHugh invented the tactic of 'ca'canny'. The Glasgow employers were soon driven to appeal for normal work effort, and to get it they conceded the wage increase which strike action had failed to win. Ca'canny thus became an official expedient of the NUDL. It emphasized amongst other things that dock labour was *not* unskilled, and this undoubtedly must have initially contributed to that self-confidence and sense of pride which are important ingredients in developing loyal commitment to trade unionism.

The union's first Annual Report elevated this tactic to a philosophy, based on a reading of contemporary political economy, the law of value and price; in simple terms, 'you get what you pay for'. After invoking the classical economist W. S. Jevons in support, the report concluded: 'If employers of labour or purchasers of goods refuse to pay for the genuine article they must be content with veneer and shoddy'.

The NUDL made the claim to be 'the pioneer organisation of what is called the new Unionism' in its executive report of December 1892. This challenge to the hegemony of the Dockers' Union was often to be repeated in the years down to the 1922 amalgamation. Yet the NUDL, which certainly competed with its London-based rival in the ports (particularly, in its later years, in those of the Humber), never sought members beyond the waterfront: unlike the dockers' organization, it never aspired to be a general union.

In the matter of ca'canny, however, it was a pioneer, and the practice soon spread unofficially to the London docks. There the Dockers' Union Executive, nursing its newly won recognition, met it with scant enthusiasm. Within months of the great strike it put out a 'Manifesto urging members of the Union to work Energetically'. It began:

> Fellow members, – complaints have been made by the Dock Directors that the men are not working as energetically and heartily as in times past, and in consequence they are not only put to a very considerable expense, but very serious delays are brought about in the departure of vessels.
> The Union will, of course, at all times and places, protect its members against anything in the nature of nigger-driving [sic], but we regret to know that at some of the docks the men are not working with that hearty goodwill and efficiency that is necessary to make our position strong . . .

We therefore most earnestly appeal to all our members . . . to work in a smart and workman-like manner.[7]

The Webbs, in *Industrial Democracy*, sternly disapproved of ca'canny. Tom Mann's was of course the presidential signature on the Dockers' Union manifesto, and Ben Tillett subsequently opposed the adoption of such working practices by the International Federation of Ship, Dock and River Workers in 1896. It is clearly therefore mistaken to see ca'canny as a 'method' of the new unionism: and even in the NUDL it was not carried on by James Sexton, the successor to McHugh and McGhee. In his memoirs, he described it as a 'boomerang'.[8] For all that, the call to work to rule, to husband energy, to deliver only the effort for which one was being paid, was to recur over and over again, and to be denounced over and over again. Sometimes people who called its genie out of the bottle were the same people who tried to persuade it back in again. Sometimes, indeed, they succeeded in the beginning, only to fail in the end. Yet ca'canny does tend to emerge during times in which employer recognition and bargaining relations are of secondary concern, or simply unobtainable. It sat uneasily with the general, mass-union ambitions of the new unions, and only tended to recur when these ambitions were frustrated by employer recalcitrance.

Organizing Liverpool

The NUDL's rise in Liverpool, in the climate of trade expansion and the aftermath of the London strike, was rapid. Ben Tillett made an early visit, and newspapers were reporting anything between 10,000 and 18,000 members by March 1890. The union was able to sweep aside the rival Knights of Labour, which had established a Bootle branch in 1885 with the active participation of James Sexton, then thirty-three years old. Sexton's parents were both Irish, and he records that the family inherited memories of 'the pitch-cap and the gibbet . . . the certain fate of any priest caught celebrating Mass', which had been the British rulers' revenge for the Irish Rebellion of 1798:

> The story of those days was handed on to the children of all who endured their agony . . . and engendered in the mind of every Irishman and every Irishwoman who heard it hatred – bitter and boundless hatred – of everything connected with the Briton and the British. That, so far as my mind was concerned, was my principal political and spiritual inheritance.[9]

Sexton tells of his early activity as an agitator, which culminated in his helping to form the Knights of Labour branch. 'We met like conspirators hatching a second Guy Fawkes plot, gathering together in a gloomy cellar with only the flickering half-lights given by tallow candles thrust into the necks of pop bottles'.[10] The picture, and the analogy with the Catholic gunpowder plot, are revealing, for Cardinal Manning, as we have seen, had determined to identify his Church with the cause of labour, especially that of the unskilled, and to this end he had given active encouragement to the Knights. Thus the cause of Irish Nationalism, reinforced by the folk memory of an oppressed and persecuted Church and embodied in the person of the 'saintly old priest' of London, was harnessed in the cause of trade unionism. That it did not stagnate in the clandestine and sectarian forms adopted in Bootle, but was swept up in the powerful current of new unionism, deliberately open and public, is a testimony to the force of that upheaval. But the impetus, the tradition, of the Irish Catholic stream were fused into the new flood to provide much of its vital dynamism. Manning's intervention in London can now be seen as the most public manifestation of a consistent policy, which reached to the heart of the international Catholic Church in the years to come. The famous papal encyclical, *Rerum Novarum* of 1891, which determined Church initiatives in the promotion of confessional trade unionism throughout Europe and beyond, were 'to some extent' the work of Cardinal Manning.[11] Forty years later, *Quadregesimo Anno*, promulgated by Pius XI, was to continue in the same vein.

Manning was hated and feared by the conservative, property-owning wing of his church, who regarded him as a traitor to his class – for his father had been a director of one dock company and his brother of another.[12] But like the papal edict which followed the dock strike, Manning's influence recognized the corporate interest and status of labour, whilst explicitly opposing any transformation of its power from negative protection to positive initiative. His influence on labour extended, and was indeed at its greatest, in the American circles of Henry George and the Knights of Labour. An Italian cardinal wrote of him: 'Manning, living as he did in the midst of the independent and tenacious English people, did not hesitate to put himself at the head of Christian "Socialism"'.[13] The influence reaches down through the union's later history, notably in the docks. Tim O'Leary, London–Wapping Irish Catholic, presided over the docks section of the TGWU throughout the 1950s and 1960s, his faith arming him for his running war against the communists and other dissidents in dockland. A Hull docks officer, appearing before the resolutely secular leadership of Jack Jones and Bill Jones in 1966 to plead his case against dismissal, held up two books, the Bible and the union Rule Book, and declared that he had lived his whole life by these two infallible guides.

The 'Button' Strike

The docks of Liverpool flared up in mass strike action in 1890. At first McHugh and McGhee sought to contain it – they certainly did not promote or call it. The demands were many and varied: wage increases were called for; hours of work and meal breaks were issues; but the most common demand was for union control of work, which in the NUDL took the form of a dockers' coat-lapel button to be displayed by members, who should receive preference at the call-ons. The union also drew up port working rules, which it sought to negotiate with the employers. In these ways, the union aimed to gain control of the strike, which had begun in a spontaneous manner. The larger employers, formed into the Employers' Labour Association, resisted union recognition and insisted on their right to employ non-union labour. The smaller employers, independent of this association, were prepared to make concessions. The union's official policy was to settle and return to work in these cases, but the men rejected this advice in the name of solidarity. After three weeks, the strikers could hold out no longer, and McHugh called on Michael Davitt's services as mediator. He achieved little, and the terms of settlement were a victory for the big employers. Union members had to agree to work with non-unionists, and could wear their union buttons at the call-stand but not at work.

Yet the union itself survived without discredit, although it remained heir to many sectional and occupational divisions in the port, and in spite of the fact that relations with the seamen's union, which had not supported the strike, had become strained. 'By the end of the dock strike sectionalism at all levels was as prominent as ever. To eliminate the "caste" system endemic to the docks would clearly be a task of heroic proportions'.[14]

For Liverpool, as elsewhere, after the events of 1889 there followed a period of guerrilla war between union and employers, with victory going to the employers, who successfully reneged on their agreement that the union button could be worn at the call-on, which had made recognition instant. Initially, the button had been a powerful weapon in the union's struggle to win members and enforce preference of employment. Cunard set the employers' pace by banning the button, followed widely by other firms. McHugh's response was to enjoin permanent ca'canny on the men, but this failed to prevent a decline of 50 per cent in membership after the ban.

McHugh also sought wider union alliances. There were abortive proposals for an alliance with the seamen, for affiliation with the Miners' Federation, and for a federation with the Tyneside and National Labourers' Union, which had docker members in the North-east. (It was the NUDL which rejected this particular link.)

In 1892 Richard McGhee opened a widespread recruitment campaign
for an Ulster Labourers' Union, aimed mainly at rural labourers and
built around a strike at a waterworks scheme in Lurgan, where labourers
did not even receive the 15s. a week which had been agreed. In England
the same work would be rewarded by £1, or 1 guinea, a week. The
connection between 'the low pay of agricultural labourers in neighbouring
counties and the rates for unskilled labour in the city [was] well
understood' by the NUDL organizers, writes the Belfast historian John
Gray.[15]

After Tillett's 1890 visit to Liverpool, he claimed that his Dockers'
Union could shortly expect 'an addition of 30,000 members from
Liverpool and district'. In fact, such a departure was never contemplated
by McHugh, who held together a union of 25,000 members, half of them
on the Mersey, and the rest in thirty-four other branches.

Although Tillett's overtures in Liverpool had no success, meeting as
they did a union with origins outside London, a strong Celtic loyalty and
national aspirations, his recruitment tours of the English east, south and
south-west coasts and South Wales were accorded enthusiastic responses.
A line drawn across the map from mid-Wales to north of the Humber,
then to its south and east outlined Tillett territory, whilst to the north and
west of it lay the NUDL ports, with the exception of the North-east (the
Tyne), where indigenous unions for dockers and labourers grew up
independently of either of them.

Organizing the Humber

In Hull the effects of the London dock strike were felt before the year
was out. Tillett visited the port on 5 December 1889 and addressed a
mass meeting. The local press found him 'a most reasonable man', and
the dockers abandoned their former local union for his card. The
shipping magnate and dock employer Charles Henry Wilson granted
wage increases and union recognition without industrial pressure. By
September 1890 the Dockers' Union had 12,000 members and thirty-
one branches in Hull, and by December it was a 100 per cent union port,
Tillett's pride and joy, the best-organized port in the land. The dockers'
delegates outnumbered all others on the Hull Trades Council. Wilson's
attitude was crucial to this success, his pro-union stance being unique
amongst the port employers. He told the men that 'they ought to be very
proud of the success they had attained by taking the management of their
own affairs into their own hands', though advising them simultaneously
to 'act with moderation'.[16] An early skirmish with the newly formed
Shipping Federation's Free Labour Bureau, involving the dockers in
blacking a non-union ship, resulted in an isolated victory over the anti-
union cause in the port at that time, many Hull employers following

Wilson's lead in deciding that the counterforce of 'free labour' was unnecessary. Three years later, it was to be a very different story.

A succession of campaigns based on Hull sought to reach out to farmworkers in the region. Tom Mann toured north Lincolnshire early in 1891, speaking to 'a largely attended' meeting at Binbrook, and to other gatherings in Market Rasen, Brigg and Normanby. 'Some half a dozen branches will be formed in the course of a week', reported the *Eastern Morning News*.[17] This tour was the subject of a meeting in Hull, where 'the large audience' received the news of its successes with enthusiasm. By 1892 eleven agricultural branches of the Dockers' Union from this one region were listed in its Annual Report. Two others may have belonged to Lincolnshire, but may have been located in other regions.[18] They did not last for long, quickly disappearing from subsequent Reports.

In shipping, Havelock Wilson's union smoothed out differences with a locally based Humberside seamen's union to achieve high levels of organization. Will Thorne visited Hull in January 1890 and negotiated the merger of a local gasworkers' union with his own, though membership before and after this move remained modest. Thorne launched a drive for recruitment in both town and port, clashing with the Dockers' Union. The National Labour Federation, from its Tyneside base, also founded general worker branches in Hull in 1889. Other local unions were formed that year and through 1890, for tramwaymen, carters, furniture workers and shop assistants. But the dockers dominated the town and applied a policy of not working with non-unionists. The *Hull News* reported that 'the blackleg is about a non-entity in Hull docks'. The extension of this policy to a refusal to work with *any* labour apart from members of the Dockers' Union provoked an outcry from other unions, however, threatening the harmony of the local trade-union scene. The Hull dockers' euphoria was set against a national background of mounting employer attacks on the union. But 'dismal reports' from elsewhere failed to discourage the 'union bastion' of Hull: 'At this particular point of time [the end of 1890] for an unskilled unionist, Hull must have been one of the better places in Britain in which to work'.[19]

. . . and Bristol

In Bristol, the London dock strike produced an immediate response. The local gasworkers' union (formed in 1888 and merged with Thorne's union in 1889) organized a march to raise funds for the London dockers. They followed this with a spectacular and hugely successful strike of their own, which ended in excited and delighted proclamations of the triumph of the poor over the rich. The dock workers followed with a spontaneous strike, which quickly won the 'tanner' for them, together with 8*d*. overtime rates. Altogether 2,300 dockers were involved, one-third of whom were employed by Bristol Corporation, which had developed and owned the port installations. On 26 October, Tillett, Thorne and Mann addressed a victory rally of 15,000: 'The new unions, the bootworkers, and the bricklayers provided the bulk of the procession, the socialists the bulk of the platform party'.[20]

Just as was happening throughout the country, the success of gas- and dock workers triggered off a wave of disputes in many unskilled Bristol trades during 1889. Amongst these were oil-cake millers, sawyers, cotton operatives, tobacco workers, carters, warehousemen, scavengers, brush-makers, hatters, tailoresses, cigar- and pipe-makers, oil- and colour-mixers and charcoal workers. Being non-unionized, their efforts were co-ordinated by a Strike Organization Committee dominated by socialist activists: 'The socialists were important in the success of new unionism in Bristol'.[21]

All the new unions registered membership gains, the Dockers' Union reporting 2,544 members in March 1890. Whilst the gasworkers and the seamen quickly adopted a policy of support for a conciliation and arbitration scheme in the city, the dockers held back from it until 1892.

A Sectional Success

In the South Wales ports, it was a rather different story, for two local unions were formed in the wave of new unionism. These were the Cardiff, Penarth and Barry Coal Trimmers' Association, established in 1888, and the National Amalgamated Labourers' Union of Great Britain and Ireland, which was founded in Swansea in 1888 and reached Cardiff in 1889. The former was an exclusive, closed union, rejecting general aims, confining itself to regular workers and their foremen. Whilst paying death and accident benefit, it made no provision for strike pay. Coal exporting was an important element of the Cardiff docks business, and the trimmers were specialists. Their job was to 'trim', or level, the cargo of coal in the ships' holds after it had been tipped from the quayside into a heap on the floor of the hold. For this purpose they used their own shovels, which were large with pointed ends. To fill the corners and extremities of the hold, the trimmers were often forced to work on their stomachs, and clearly required great physical prowess, as well as the knack which comes of experience and tradition. They evolved an elite status. Since they were difficult to replace, it paid the employers to develop good, stable relationships with them, and so they could command high differentials over general dock-labourers' pay. Their mode of unionism reflected all of these characteristics, and did not square with the general methods and objectives of new unionism. The work was hazardous, with the continuing dangers of gas and possible explosions; much of the effort of the union was concerned with safety and ventilation. These issues were highlighted when the union appeared before the Royal Commission on Labour in 1892, but several examples of union action to improve working conditions were also recorded. The Cardiff, Penarth and Barry Coal Trimmers' Association maintained its exclusiveness for eighty years; its entry into the TGWU was delayed until 1968. By this time, it had become one of the six smallest unions in the TUC, but its traditions were so well established that the TGWU welcomed it into the ranks by printing a full-colour photo of its expensive and richly coloured banner in a subsequent Annual Report.

General Unions in Wales [22]

The Trimmers' Union was in part protected against the encroachments of the Dockers' Union through the controls exercised by their foremen, who deducted union dues from the men's pay. Many trimmers would have preferred membership of the Dockers' Union, and some in fact held membership in both organizations. In Newport, the trimmers and tippers initially joined the Dockers' Union, and throughout the South Wales ports there was frequent inter-union conflict, leading eventually to a mutual recognition agreement between them.

The National Amalgamated Labourers' Union (NALU) was formed in Cardiff by an official of the Seamen's Union. This is yet another example of the formative influence exerted by seamen over new union evolution. NALU enrolled several classes of general labour, including dockers. It quickly spread to other South Wales ports, and immediately won wage increases. It was a hybrid form of union: whilst having a strike fund, its leaders eschewed militancy, and its rules provided for several other cash benefits, including grants to members travelling in search of work. Its officials were elected by its Annual General Meeting.

Despite the prior existence of these two unions, the Dockers' Union opened a Cardiff branch in November 1889. Its first recruits were general labourers, including those at Spillers' Flour Mill; the dockers enrolled when Tillett came to the port later in the month. In 1890 they won a substantial wage increase without a strike. Union members at the Graigola Fuel Company did strike – successfully – and also won an advance. Patent-fuel production was an important industry in Cardiff, and its organization in the dockers' ranks reinforced the idea that general organization could be both practicable and effective.

Thereafter, Tillett and Mann argued for conciliation and arbitration boards in the locality, and for the avoidance of strikes. They sought recognition agreements, and work preference for members, to be achieved by card-checks by foremen members at the call-on. Despite the leadership's pacific method, the dockers struck more than once in 1890 in protest at the hire of non-unionists.

In Swansea the growth of the Dockers' Union to a membership of 4,650 in November 1890 was achieved in part at the expense of the National Amalgamated Labourers' Union. Most port workers transferred: they had seen the gains won by the new union, but they were also aware that it refused to recognize the NALU card. In the hinterland of Swansea, the Dockers' Union organized copper, chemical and steel-tube workers, Harry Orbell and Tom McCarthy being frequent visitors. Wage increases were obtained in all these industries, in the case of the copper workers through arbitration. In Newport, the Dockers' Union had less success against the NALU in the docks, but in the Gwent valleys behind the port it established branches in the steel industry. At the height of its initial burst of success, before the employers' counterattack, the Dockers' Union had 6,000 members in Swansea, 3,000 in Cardiff and 800 in Newport. The union claimed 57,000 members nationally in 1890.

The National Amalgamated Union of Labour

On Tyneside, a series of attempts at organizing the labourers began in February 1889, producing the Tyneside (quickly renamed the National) Amalgamated Union of Labour (NAUL), with membership in the docks, shipyards and sundry other industries, and the National Labour Federation, with similar coverage.

The Cabmen Follow On

The example of new unionism was not lost upon workers in the capital city's road-transport systems. Both in the cab trade and amongst bus and tramway workers, trade-union organization and strike action were soon to follow the dockers' 1889 victory.

The nineteenth-century London cab trade was turbulent, and trade-union organization comparatively unstable. There had been strikes as early as 1853, then in 1867 and again in 1868. In 1894 one cabby claimed that he had been a member of eight different cab unions in thirty-four years. The cabmen suffered from a number of oppressive conditions peculiar to their trade. The London police authority was responsible for issuing licences, which were necessary either to own or to hire out a cab. Separate licences were needed to operate as a cab-driver. Police returns in 1890 showed that there were 11,700 licensed cabs but over 15,000 licensed drivers. In addition, the cabbies complained of 'butterflies' – illegal, summer-season drivers who infiltrated the trade.

This situation led to chronic destructive competition between the drivers. Most operated under a 'hire-and-reward' system, paying a daily hire-charge to cab-owners, who could therefore rack up this charge to cabbies desperate to secure a cab. There were 3,599 cab-owners in the capital, of whom 2,500 owned only a single vehicle (plus the necessary horse and equipment); 450 of them owned more than five cabs, and a dominant handful of companies owned up to 400. Unregulated, competitive and individualistic, the system forced cabbies into excessive hours of work to earn even a pittance over and above the daily hire-charge and their other expenses, including stable charges and the licence fee.

Their work brought them under constant harrassment by the police; cabstands were few and ill defined, so that cabbies were regularly summoned for 'loitering'. The railway companies withheld permission for ordinary cabbies to ply for customers on their mainline station forecourts, thus preserving their monopoly for a fleet of railway-owned cabs. The London streets were overcrowded with horse-drawn vehicles, private and public, passenger and freight, and the accident rate was high. Acrimonious disputes between passengers and cabbies were an everyday occurrence, as fares, tips and waiting times were contested at the journey's end; these conflicts led with distressing regularity to the courts, and to costly and demoralizing petty litigation.

What stirred the cabbies' accumulated sense of grievance and fed a special form of class consciousness was the character of their customers – the London rich, both the aristocratic and the bourgeois. The cabby, in an age of mass domestic servitude, was regarded as an extension of the feudal system which prevailed 'upstairs and downstairs' in the households of the prosperous; and he was expected to behave with the deference of a vassal towards m'Lord and m'Lady, whilst accepting without complaint whatever manners they displayed towards him. He was by turns insulted and patronized as a simple, potentially villainous, but vaguely romantic character of London life, known sentimentally as the 'gondolier of the London streets'. He, his vehicle and his horse provided the colourful background for the adventures of Conan Doyle's contemporary hero, Sherlock Holmes. In 1890 the 'gondolier' was labouring, under a heap of grievances, for anything up to twenty hours a day, and he had had enough.

When in 1890 the Prince of Wales joined a charitable party of peers, judges and diplomats in a charade depicting – in grossly patronizing terms – the cabbies' way of life, one of those pilloried sent a protest to the *Star*:

> Ah! Noble sirs and princes, what to you
> The bitter work of working lives, whose rue
> You do but dream of in your festal halls,
> Where mirth runs riot and fat plenty stalls.

You come amongst us with your oily speech,
And eat a banquet in pretence to reach
Those dull, dreary deeps in which we moil,
Some false and foolish patronage of toil.

Back to your places sirs, whilst we keep ours,
We do not play, like you, through God's stern hours;
So keep your idle pity – we'll have none;
There's nought in common twixt us; Get you gone.[23]

The cabmen established their Metropolitan Cab Drivers' Trade
Union in 1890, and by October of that year, at a mass meeting in the
early hours of the morning, heard from a Mr Walter Drummond of the
Dockers' Union a speech in praise of their initiative, which had brought
1,000 into membership already, and was still drawing fifty new members
a week. The principal grievance they set out to redress was the hire-
charge of 16s. a day, which Drummond characterized as 'sweating'.
Their programme also sought to reduce the number of licences issued,
to secure the designation of adequate numbers of cabstands, and to
break the railway-cab monopoly at stations. In addition, they wanted the
issue of licences to be taken from the police and managed by the London
County Council.

Drummond told the rally that, just as the dockers had won £300,000
in increased wages, so 12,000 London cabmen could, by similar united
action, win £150,000 by forcing a reduction of 1s 6d. a day in the hire-
charge. 'The meeting ended shortly before 5 a.m.'[24]

Organization, and the further elaboration of a programme, continued
through the following months until, in March 1891, the union was busy
pressing the Royal Commission on Labour to hear its grievances, and
had prevailed upon the most famous member of the LCC, John Burns, to
address a mass rally in Hyde Park on Good Friday. Burns rose to the
occasion; the 'Season' was beginning, the moment was right. The call for
strike action was taken up immediately, on 3 April, by the cabbies of the
Shrewsbury and Talbot Cab Company, owners of 400 cabs, the first of
whose proprietors was none other than Lord Shrewsbury himself. The
strike was in resistance to a proposed 1s. increase in the hire-charge.

The company's several yards were vigorously picketed, and washers,
horse-keepers, yardmen and other employees were thrown out of work.
The directors refused to meet the union. They put out a statement
justifying the increase on the grounds of the superiority of their rubber-
tyred cabs, with which any competent cabmen could, they claimed, earn a
living (The 'S and T' was itself the proprietor of a subsidiary rubber-tyre-
making company!) The employers' intransigence was carried to the
extreme: the company began to sell off its horses by public auction. At
first the union interpreted this as an intimidatory bluff, assuring the
members that only old horses were being weeded out. But by the end of

May it was evident that the 'S and T' had indeed gone out of business, being content for the future to hire out its cabs to other, horse-owning, companies. On 30 May the *Star* commented sardonically:

> Of course, a company the individual members of which for the most part derive their incomes from ground rents and other agrarian iniquities; and who, as much for pastime as for profit, come down from their high estate to compete with legitimate traders, can readily close the shop when their sweating practices are objected to. Therefore the Shrewsbury company has, in part at least, disappeared – a benefit for which the other proprietors are indebted to the men.

But the withdrawal of the 'S and T' did not subvert the strike, which surged, wave on wave, from one company to the next. Pickets moved in on a company, the union presented its demand for a reduction in the hire-charge, the proprietors vainly set up an association and a defence fund, but one by one they negotiated the required reduction, following which the union allowed a resumption of work and moved on to the next target.

For sixteen weeks, into early August, this tidal action was sustained, cheered along by marches, rallies and speeches. John Burns, chief spokesman for the strikers, was reported to have 'worked like a Trojan night and day, in meetings in halls and in the open, and the wholehearted way in which he has thrown himself into the struggle has been both a help and a source of inspiration to the cause.'[25] At one meeting, held outside the St Pancras Station arches, Burns addressed the rally from the top of a hansom cab.

From spring through the summer, the pressure was all on the proprietors to yield, for the Season, with its high-society events – Ascot, Epsom, the Eton and Harrow and MCC matches, the balls and garden parties – was the most lucrative time of the year for their trade. Public sympathy swung towards the strikers, as the press gave their grievances extensive and sympathetic coverage. The radical *Star* was prominent, but the *St James Gazette* was not far behind in its coverage.

The Metropolitan Union did not consist entirely of John Burns and Dockers' Union sympathizers. During the strike, membership rose to 4,000. With it rose income. The union's president, John Beasley, was probably a cabman, but its treasurer was a Mr W. Everitt, the proprietor of the Guardsman Coffee House in Buckingham Palace Road. There the union had its headquarters, its 'business-like' offices, and its executive meetings. The address itself intrigued the *Star*: '. . . almost within smelling distance of the Royal Stables themselves!'[26]

On 7 August Burns presided over a wind-up meeting of the strikers. He reported that up to 2,500 cabmen had been on strike during the previous four months, but never more than 300 at any one time. Thirty-five different companies had been visited by the action, and the hire-charge reduced by between 1s. 6d. and 3s. a day. The cabmen had largely helped themselves to this victory; the accounts of the Strike Committee and Mr Everitt showed that donations of £3,480 had been received by collections from the public, but also £3,400 from cabmen themselves, helped by only £70 from 'other unions'. One of the biggest cheers at the wind-up meeting greeted the announcement that Mr Sydney Buxton, MP, had intervened with the judges to secure twenty-one days' remission of sentence on three cabmen pickets sentenced for 'initimidation'.

After the strike, the Metropolitan Union turned to its campaign for the regulation of the cabmen's trade by the LCC. The union expired in 1894, but continuity was hardly broken, for the London Cab Drivers' Union set up shop immediately afterwards, in the heat of a four-week strike. In turn, this body was transmuted into the London and Provincial Union of Licensed Vehicle Workers in 1913, extending its recruitment into the bus and tram industries. Before the First World War, it earned the nickname the 'Red Button Union', because of its consistent militancy and its radical syndicalist politics.

So began an experience and a tradition which reaches down from the 1891 strike almost to the present day. In 1987, we interviewed the veteran trade unionist Sid Easton, whose family's knowledge of the London cab trade, including his father's experiences, reaches back to the Edwardian period. Sid Easton had been an active communist, working at one time as chauffeur and bodyguard to the late Harry Pollitt, general secretary of the British Communist Party, and he served on the TGWU executive during the 1970s. He recalled his experience behind the wheel before the Second World War:

> except for the occasional wedding or Christmas time, the only people who could afford to ride in cabs were the rich folk. You then came into contact with the worst elements of capitalism directly. I mean, if you work in a factory, you are one of many, you know there is an employer, [but] it's a thing, a company. But when you get a man or a woman who has no thought about cost, merely about your behaviour towards them, it changes your regard for them, whether your forelock is long enough for you to pull or not. And I believe that was the reason why we had something in excess of 120 members of the London cab section members of the Communist Party, which was a higher figure by ratio than in almost any other industry.

Tramwaymen and Busmen

The London County Tramway and Omnibus Employees' Trade Union was formed in 1889, under the presidency of Thomas Sutherst, a young barrister.[27] One of its initiators was William Collison, who will reappear in our story in a more sinister guise, following his quarrel with the busmen.[28] In June 1891 between 8,000 and 10,000 London busmen struck, ostensibly for a twelve-hour day, but in fact more because of the introduction of tickets, which controlled the conductor's returns. These had hitherto been based on a highly informal system, in which the companies got that proportion of the fares which could be sustained by custom. This tradition dated back to the coaching system and was tolerated by the London General Omnibus Company, the largest undertaking, until the retirement of its managing director in February. His successor imposed ticket machines, alongside a wage increase of 1s. a day for drivers and 6d. for conductors in compensation for lost perquisites.

The tram and busmen were expected to buy their own uniforms and to contribute to an accident-repair fund. They perceived their status, like the cabmen's, as being more akin to vehicle hirers than employees, and saw in the imposition of ticketing a severe change of status. Their strike received the enthusiastic endorsement of the Metropolitan Cab Drivers' Union. Mutual support, to curtail unregulated competition and excessive working time, made every kind of sense to passenger carriers of all modes of transport in the metropolis. They carried the members of the most prosperous ruling class in the world, as well as, increasingly, a new mass public which was creating heavy demand.

Sutherst argued for municipalization of the omnibus industry and for reduced hours: 'The county council should buy up the whole of the tram lines and the rolling stock, and lease them out to companies who should be under their control, and the control of the men as well.'[29] Workers would be entitled to seats on the board, and after making interest payments, profits would be 'divided between the ratepayers and the men'. This was the system applied in Huddersfield, 'with admirable effect'.

In spite of Sutherst's advocacy, the tramway and omnibusmen did not maintain the impetus of their new union. Their strike resulted in an ostensible victory in that shorter hours were conceded, alongside pay cuts; but the workday was soon extended piecemeal as union members traded their new-found leisure for more pay.[30]

The Gasworkers

In London itself, of course, the gasworkers had set the example of new unionism, ahead of the dockers, with their successful campaign for the eight-hour day in 1889, and with the formation of the Gasworkers and General Labourers' Union. Will Thorne maintained his leadership of this organization, whose rules were drafted by Eleanor Marx.

Eric Hobsbawm has drawn attention to the special features of the gas industry at that time, which help to explain the relative ease with which the union established and maintained itself through all the vicissitudes which fell upon less stable organizations, such as the dockers. The gas industry enjoyed monopoly status, and depended upon a body of workers who had real technical skills. Its technology remained constant at a time of large expansion of domestic demand for its product. Commonly it was organized under public, municipal ownership or control; hence it was exposed to public and consumer opinion. For these reasons, 'unlike so many other unions of the 1889 vintage, the gasworkers were never effectively dislodged from the positions they occupied then'.[31]

In Birmingham the Amalgamated Society of Gas-workers and Brickmakers dated also from 1889. We should add to this list two latecomers to the role-call of the principal new unions: the Workers' Union of 1898 and the National Federation of Women Workers of 1906. But these arose out of developments which will receive attention later.

II

Results: Quantity and Quality

What, then, was the overall result of this novel explosion? From the great London dock strike through to its early successes in other ports, from the pioneering work in the gas industry, and amongst general labour in a multitude of industries over a wide area – within two short years the reach of labour organization had been extended further than anyone before had imagined to be possible. The membership of the six principal new unions in 1890 totalled some 326,000; their affiliation figures to the TUC in that year are shown in table 4.1.

Table 4.1 *Membership of New Unions, 1890*

Dock, Wharf, Riverside and General Labourers' Union	56,000
National Union of Dock Labourers	50,000
National Amalgamated Union of Sailors and Firemen	60,000
National Union of Gasworkers and General Labourers	60,000
National Amalgamated Union of Labour	40,000
National Labour Federation	60,000

Source: TUC Reports

London labourers' hourly rate of pay averaged 5½d. in 1881 and 6d. in 1891, whilst the index of food prices had fallen in the same period from 140 to 109 – (1900 = 100). These gains rode on the back of the trade cycle: industrial production (1880 = 100) from a trough of 101 in 1886 climbed to a peak of 122 in 1891; it was to collapse to 113 in 1893. Unemployment stood at 9.6 per cent in 1886 and fell to 6 per cent in 1891. Productivity (1850 = 100) rose from 159 to 186 between 1886 and

1891.[32] In all these quantitative economic respects, the years with which we are concerned here were auspicious ones. But the new unionism involved more than statistical growth of membership: it also signified a qualitative, moral change.

The London dock strike occupies a special place in trade-union history not only because it was a spectacular, public upheaval, but because it happened when and where it did. London was the capital. It could focus metropolitan comment and attention, and thus appeal to every province. That the London industrial scene was so out of phase with the provinces could mean only that *this* movement would exert a singularly powerful influence. London disputes were necessarily rare, exceptional; their impact could energize others far afield. The extension of the franchise had created political uncertainties of great complexity. The cumulative results of the growth of poverty in urban concentrations were bursting into the consciousness of people who were themselves comfortably secure. The increase in literacy and in the media serving it ensured that communication was instant and effective.

It is this social context which explains why the dockers' initiative is widely taken as the founding moment and symbol of new unionism. This was what made possible a deliberate rejection of older models and of various attempts to depart from the norms of pre-existing unions. The young men of 1889 aimed at the creation of a new type of organization. A number of characteristics are associated with this aim: modern historians accept none of them without argument, but all would accept that new unions involved at least five innovations, even if some were less significant than others, or less consistently practised. They were:

1   The organization of workers deemed to be 'unskilled'.
2   The recruitment of members from a wide range of industries and occupations, which is to say that, commonly although not always, they were open, general unions.
3   The commitment to be 'fighting unions', charging low subscriptions, avoiding heavy friendly-society benefits, and using their funds primarily for strike pay.
4   Militancy.
5   Political radicalism, often embracing socialism and questioning the older unions' adherence to the Liberal Party.

To these five generally accepted qualities we would add:

6   They made space for the organization of women, and indeed the whole movement drew an example from the matchgirls' strike (see chapter 2). Other unions, like the Boot and Shoe Operatives' Union and the cotton unions, did this. But women workers in general trades were to offer a special challenge to union organizers.

Helpers from Outside

The seventh innovation is both a weakness and a strength. Of all the qualities which marked the new unions, perhaps the most remarkable was the extent to which outside helpers could be assimilated into their structures, providing a whole range of specialized services and skills. We have already seen how skilled engineers like Burns and Mann stepped into the roles of spokesman and organizer during the dock strike, and how Champion furnished the new Dockers' Union – as well as the Gasworkers' Union – with their press office during disputes and with an 'official journal' in the shape of the *Labour Elector* immediately afterwards. In the same way, Eleanor Marx gave crucial assistance to both dockers and gasworkers and helped organize the women at the Silvertown rubber works during their strike in 1889. But these were the stars of the socialist movement, and all eyes were upon them in 1889. Outside London the story followed the same trends, but often the volunteers were not socialists, or at any rate not seen as socialists. The Birmingham Amalgamated Society of Gas-workers and Brickmakers was organized by the Lib.–Lab. City Councillors Eli Bloor and Allan Granger;[33] Bloor was a glassworker and Granger a printer. James Bartley, a journalist on the *Workman's Times* and a socialist, carried this same union to the Bradford area with the active help of the trades council. In 1888 E. R. Pease became the first secretary of the National Labour Federation in Tyneside, before he took over the same office in the Fabian Society.

When the London omnibus companies were organized during their strike in June 1891, their first spokesman, as we have seen, was the barrister Thomas Sutherst, who soon stepped aside to assume an advisory role. (His testimony at the Royal Commission on Labour took place some months later.) Sutherst was joined in the work of creating a permanent union by a nominee of the London Trades Council, Fred Hammill, an engineer, who was paid a monthly wage of £10 to establish an organization for the busmen.[34] Hammill had been the socialist candidate for the secretaryship of the Trades Council in 1890, during a heated controversy about the commitment (or lack of commitment) of the incumbent, George Shipton, to the dockers' cause in the great strike. Trades Councils took similar action in many parts of the country, with the result that many skilled men became involved in the disputes of their hitherto unorganized colleagues.

If it is not surprising that inexperienced workers should welcome help during the time that they found themselves actually out on strike, it remains true that similar assistance was frequently needed for considerable periods afterwards in order to establish and stabilize the habits of organization. Thus in September 1889 the Rev. John William Lewis, curate of Bow, became the chairman of two branches of the Dockers' Union for the first year of its existence; he remained chairman of one branch for a further year. If he taught his members something about the rules of procedure, they also contributed to his education.

Questioned in 1892 by the Royal Commissioner, Michael Austin, about how far the conditions of dockworkers had altered since the strike, Lewis replied, 'No doubt it was on the whole very much worse than it is now.' 'Therefore the Union has improved the conditions of the men?' 'I believe it has. It is, however, a long and slow work, and one cannot expect very much in the course of two years.'[35] The curate of Bow had learned his lessons well, because he not only defended the achievements of his dockers, but went on to embrace the aim of general membership. Indeed, he informed the Commission that 'every man throughout the country . . . should join a trades union'. 'You would have no non-unionists?' responded Lord Derby, incredulously. 'None at all anywhere,' came the firm response.[36]

Centralizing

Although Tom Mann is rightly credited with many of the innovative features of the Dockers' Union, Ben Tillett was also driving in the same direction, in respect both of the centralization of executive power – initially for 'fighting' purposes – and in seeking the widest possible national scope for his organization. These strategies stemmed from his own experiences in London. The Tilbury strike in 1888 had been defeated by the use of blackleg labour from the farms; in the immediate recruiting drive after the great strike, therefore, the union's efforts to recruit in agriculture and among general labourers around the ports was a conscious policy. Moreover, Tillett had sought to hold central control of union funds even in the days of his Tea Operatives' Union, with the object of preventing autonomous branch strikes from dissipating them. Tillett's policy was further determined by his own sceptical opinion of his members' wisdom in their use of trade-union powers. An article in the *Labour Elector* after the 1889 strike expressed this attitude:

> Today it [the Dockers' Union] is numerically the strongest trade organization in the metropolis. But the 18,000 men who have flocked to it are ignorant of the rudiments of trade unionism, are flushed with their sudden success, and are unaware that unless their society is at once thoroughly and closely organized every advantage they have gained must inevitably be taken from them in a few years – perhaps a few months.[37]

Tillett's and Mann's drive for centralization caused much ill-feeling amongst the London membership. The roots of twentieth-century conflict between Ernest Bevin, and later Arthur Deakin, and their docks' membership, may indeed lie in the origins of London dockers' unionism. Harry Quelch's opinion was that the authoritarian tendencies of the new union leadership guaranteed the continued existence of his own South Side Labour Protection League.

The expansion of the union outside London is reflected in the organizing tours undertaken by the leaders. Immediately following the London settlement, Tillett set off for Hull, Gloucester, Bristol, Sharpness, Southampton, Ipswich, Liverpool, Harwich amongst other ports, whilst Tom McCarthy and Harry Orbell covered still more. Sixty-three new branches were formed in the first quarter of 1890 – an unprecedented and truly astonishing achievement. Yet after the initial enthusiasm, some of the provincial members also found the dominance of the London leadership irksome.[38] At times the resentment exploded, as we shall see when we examine the events at Southampton in chapter 5.

The leadership's concern for central control was dictated by anxiety to conserve funds, and to ensure stability and longevity for their new creation. It was an outlook shared by Burns, Tillett and Mann, and was sharply reinforced by the downturn in the trade cycle which began in late 1890. This goes some way to explain how, in South Wales and elsewhere, the initially militant new-union leaders could become the pioneer advocates of conciliation and arbitration. The simplistic view of the new unions solely as a proto-revolutionary development – for which many of Tillett's own fiery utterances have been responsible – obviously required drastic amendment, which it received with interest from the Labour historians of the 1960s and 1970s. But there is a case for believing that these modern accounts have bent the stick too far.

The Long View

Both Tillett and Mann held a long view of the prospects for political action offered by the new unionism. Both had lengthy and uninterrupted careers, in which the militant industrial phases of 1889–90 and 1910–14 have naturally attracted most attention in popular history and myth. They never doubted that they had created something new in 1889, but they also never hesitated to act to preserve it from collapse when circumstances – particularly those created by the ebb and flow of the trade cycle – required prudent, conservationist policies.

But in the ups and the downs alike, a core requirement of the new unions was that of recognition. Centralization helped. Recognition ensured that the hitherto unorganized masses saw their leaders' perceptions of their own role reflected back in the responses of their adversaries.

The Webbs were soon to identify three main trade-union methods:

mutual insurance, collective bargaining and legal enactment. Downgrading the importance of mutual insurance was not perhaps the central defining characteristic of the new unions, and an extensive literature shows how, at different times, new unions were willing to return for this piece of forgotten baggage, which in varying degrees was found to contain useful elements.

This should not inhibit us from registering what was really going on: the upgrading of collective bargaining and legal enactment. In different ways, both methods extended the crucial principle of recognition. Recognition for bargaining purposes may surely be a means of regulating conflict; but it is also a powerful reinforcement of labour solidarity, since it compels employers to define the social world in the same terms as does the trade union. Wages, hours and conditions – all the most important dimensions of life at work – owe their shape to a collective process. Even if he hates it, the participating employer has sanctioned it. The organized working class thus draws strength from its adversaries, even when it is under attack. Political reform involves a wider social recognition of the same divisions. New unionists, then, ceased to be 'the poor', atomized, rejected, starved. In becoming 'the union', their strength went beyond the scope of their actual organization. Organization could be beaten back, and even temporarily extinguished; but to the extent that society recognized it, the union could burst back into full flame whenever social pressures passed a certain point.

The 'Old' Unions Take Umbrage

The new unionists were instantly assailed by the old. The most concerted onslaught came from George Howell, who raised a whole series of objections to the new doctrines, most of which were codified in a sour little book, *Trade Unionism New and Old*, first published in 1891.[39] In it he attacked the new unions' drive for the closed shop, their 'needless public display', their quest for legislative rather than self-reliant friendly-society protections, and their overreadiness to support strikes. Howell did have his own loyalties, which he was not shy to affirm: 'In its old age, even in its ruins, perchance, the old trade unionism is not unlike some of the old medieval structures, worthy of veneration by reason of its age and its present uses'.[40]

From such a gothic standpoint, it is not surprising that Howell found the more rudimentary and functional organizations of dockers, seamen and carters indecorous and uncouth. 'In all the earlier battles of trade unionism', he wrote, 'the fighting garrison had this advantage, they were fighting an attacking or besieging army from without . . . [now] the attacks come from within'.[41]

From this point of view, the new leaders were all much the same: their distinguishing trait 'has been, and is, their persistent, cowardly and calumnious attacks upon the old leaders'. Such criticisms, said Howell, had brought about various early retirements and resignations: 'There is . . . scarcely a secretary of long standing who has not had to endure abuse, misrepresentation, and calumny from some of the new leaders or their satellites'. Worse, the Labour Members in Parliament have received 'the extreme violence of the abuse'.[42]

'The culmination of vulgar abuse', Howell went on, 'was reached at the Liverpool Trade Union Congress . . . According to one "leader", tall hats and black coats and also the size and stature of the delegates from the old days, were indications of a frightful state of decay, in the policy and management of the old trade unionism'.[43]

John Burns was the culprit in this once-famous case. After the Congress he had recorded his impression of the difference between the old and new unionists, and had registered the striking fact that the craftsmen's representatives were physically taller, more robust and more comfortable in every aspect of their appearance than the representatives of the dockers and transport workers. Such an observation can hardly, in itself, be interpreted as derogatory, although it is evident that the trade-union establishment found it so. It was intended as a sociological observation, and indeed as such it was acute.

Some societies upheld codes of conduct on dress, even incorporating them in rules. The Phoenix Society of Compositors excluded from its meetings all those members who were improperly dressed: correct attire was a tall hat and evening dress.[44] This rule cut two ways. To those above the line, it registered that deference which cannot be surpassed, since imitation is the ultimate in flattery. To those below, it revealed a chasm of separation: no entry into this artisan universe could be afforded to those too poor to wear the uniform. With such badges of rank went a set of attitudes. Harry Quelch raged against them:

Can there be anything more exasperating than to hear a skilled artisan, who ought to know that the whole of society is living on the labour of himself and his mates, skilled and unskilled, talking of his home as 'not bad for a working man', his set of books as 'quite creditable for a working man', his children as 'a good-looking lot of kids for a working man', and so on? You never hear this abominable servile cant in any other country. Nor before the old Chartist movement died down was it nearly so common here. The systematic and degrading respect for their 'betters', inculcated into the workers from their childhood upwards, tells its tale in after years.[45]

Burns, who provoked such disapproval among the craftsmen, was himself a craftsman engineer, and no doubt it was his intermediate status as someone identified as a public spokesman of the dockers, many of whose own leaders were far from able to afford to dress in the approved

TUC manner, which made him sensitive to the differences which he recorded.[46] More understandable than the objections to Burns's article, perhaps, is the resentment of the craftsmen over the uninhibited behaviour of the new delegates, prone as they were to heckle or even interrupt ceremonial speeches. 'The loud voice, impatient gestures, persistent interruptions,' thought Howell, rendered the 1890 TUC 'sad and pitiful to behold'.[47]

Secondly, the old-union men objected very strongly to the doctrine that the new organizations should be 'fighting machines'.[48] Howell saw the friendly-society benefits of the old unions as a factor in their self-reliance, and deeply resented any effort to downplay them, let alone manage without them.

But, thirdly, Howell especially objected to the antagonism of the new unions to non-union workers. 'It was reserved for the recent development of the new trade unionism to systematically revert to terrorism, and brute force, to compel non-union hands to leave their employment'.[49] Such infractions, he alleged, accompanied the dock strikes in London, Liverpool, Cardiff, Southampton and other places; the strikes of gas-stokers in South London, Manchester and elsewhere; and various outbreaks of industrial action by the seamen.

Picketing, he went on to argue, gave full scope to this coercive trend.[50] Therefore he was entirely scandalized when the TUC, following the experiences of the dock strikes, instructed their Parliamentary Committee to seek the entire repeal of the clause of the Conspiracy Act of 1875 'making picketing illegal'. At the same Congress, there was a move to abolish Clause 7 of the Conspiracy and Protection of Property Act, as being dangerous to the liberties of the working classes. This clause outlawed 'watching and besetting', and interference with tools, as well as violence or intimidation. That the Congress should record this prohibition as being capable of repressive interpretation was a scandal to some of its elder members. They were even more distressed when the same delegates voted to censure the Irish Constabulary for shadowing participants in a tailors' strike in Derry. The Congress, alleged Howell, now approved of 'shadowing' when it was employed by trade unionists against strike-breakers, but disapproved of it when the Constabulary employed it against trade unionists.

In the same vein, Howell inveighed against 'popular demonstrations'.[51] Parades cost money, which should be laid up for strike benefit, he thought. Yet the dockers' parades had raised far more money than they could ever have put by, even if their membership had in fact been far higher than the 300 (out of 100,000) which he alleged in the same tract.

'The new unionists have also a weakness for federations', he continued. They believe that a grouping 'of weak societies will supply . . . aggressive strength'.[52] All this is a foible, and if general *amalgamation* were achieved it would level down and crush emulation, undermining skill and personal character.

Had Howell's admonitions been heeded, no attempt to organize the so-called 'unskilled' could ever have got off the ground. Of course, general organization could not be easily or quickly achieved: but the goal imposed itself as the only constructive response to the free-for-all that brought masses of starvelings and displaced people to fight for a few hours' labour at the dock gates. Picketing was not a principle, but an expedient. It could provide temporary support, but only if behind it lay an appeal to wider solidarity. Mere force could always provoke answering, and more lethal force.

Mann and Tillett Reply

Howell's books had been preceded in June 1890 by an article in *Murray's Magazine*, written by George Shipton of the London Trades Council land and entitled 'Trades Unionism: The Old and the New'. Tom Mann, from his presidential position in the Dockers' Union, joined with Ben Tillett in responding in a penny pamphlet entitled *The 'New' Trades Unionism – A Reply to Mr. George Shipton*. In it their 'long view' is clearly discernible:

> Many of those who are identified with the 'new' trades unionism have been connected with their own trade societies for many years past, and it was a continual source of bitter grief to them that so much poverty should exist amongst workers of all sections, but especially among the unskilled and unorganized, and that the old Societies should be so utterly callous to this poverty as not to make any special exertion to alter matters for the better . . .
>
> The methods adopted by us of determining a change in our present industrial system, are on a strictly trade-union basis. All our public utterances, all our talks to our members, have been directed towards cultivating a sturdy spirit of independence, and instilling a deep sense of responsibility. In fact we have been at pains to discredit appeals to the legislature, contending that the political machine will fall into our hands as a matter of course, so soon as the educational work has been done in our labour organizations. We are convinced that not until Parliament is an integral part of the workers, representing and responsible to industrial toilers, shall we be able to effect any reform by its means . . .
>
> The statement that the 'new' trade unionists look to Governments and legislation, is bunkum: The keynote is to organize first, and take action in the most effective way, so soon as organization warrants action, instead of specially looking to Government. The lesson is being thoroughly well taught and learned that we must look to ourselves alone, though this, of course, does not preclude us from exercising our rights of citizenship.
>
> It is quite true that most of the newly formed unions pay contributions

for trade purposes only, leaving sick and funeral benefits to be dealt with by sick and insurance societies. The work of the trade unionist is primarily to obtain such a re-adjustment of conditions between employers and employed as shall secure to the latter a better share of the wealth they produce, in the form of reduced working hours and higher wages, and our experience has taught us that many of the older unions are very reluctant to engage in a labour struggle, no matter how great the necessity, because they are hemmed in by sick and funeral claims, so that to a large extent they have lost their true characteristic of being fighting organizations, and the sooner they revert to their original programme the better for the well-being of the working masses . . .

Our ideal is a Co-operative Commonwealth. This we believe will be reached by honest effort in various directions, chief among which will be the efforts of the trade unionists: and while striving for the ideal, we are glad to know that we need not wait for years before further advantages can be obtained, but that by discreet conduct on our part, we can be continually gaining some advantage for one or other section of the workers.

While in the heat of this polemic Mann was anxious to refute the 'bunkum' of overreliance on legislation, he and the wave of new-unionist delegates to the 1890 TUC congress in Liverpool led the successful fight for the adoption of an eight-hours' Bill as a campaigning demand of the whole movement. This was not inconsistent: what is clear from the pamphlet is Mann's understanding of the need to 'walk on two legs'; and also that, of the three classic modes of trade-union action delineated by the Webbs – mutual insurance, collective bargaining and legislation – the new unionism discarded the first as an encumbering constraint, adopting collective bargaining as the immediately available method, viewing legislation as a vital support and ultimately as an element in a *socialist* strategy.

If Tom Mann would not subordinate trade unionism to state intervention, he was not, in the 1890s, willing to walk away from any possible source of help. This explains why for a long time he kept some very elevated company indeed. Because hundreds of strikes had erupted during 1889 and the following year, the Conservative government of Lord Salisbury announced that it intended to probe the causes of this unprecedented unrest. On 21 April 1891 it duly appointed a Royal Commission on Labour.

The Royal Commission

The Commission was constituted under the chairmanship of Spencer Compton Cavendish, Marquess of Hartington, soon to inherit the dukedom of Devonshire. Its terms of reference were to 'enquire into . . .

the relations between employers and employed', to examine the combinations of both sides, and 'the conditions of labour which have been raised during the recent trade disputes'. The Commission was charged to report on proposals for legislation which might 'be directed to the remedy of any evils that may be disclosed'.

It laboured on for nearly three years, into the succeeding Liberal administration, Gladstone's fourth, and beyond it after the old man withdrew in favour of Lord Rosebery in March 1894.

The Royal Commission was, wrote Beatrice Webb, 'a gigantic fraud . . . made up of a little knot of dialecticians plus a carefully picked parcel of variegated Labour men, and the rest landlords or capitalists, pure and simple'.[53] The Labour men were Thomas Burt and William Abraham, Liberal MPs from the Northumberland and South Wales coalfields respectively; the Irish typographical worker, Michael Austin; Henry Tait of the Scottish Railwaymen, who had been involved in an epic strike which was extensively raked over in the Commission's hearings; the Darlington Ironworker, Edward Trow; the Conservative leader of the Lancashire Cotton Spinners, James Mawdsley; and Tom Mann, still, of course, president of the Dockers' Union. Mann accepted the appointment after consulting his union and the London Trades Council. He held it 'during their pleasure' as he put it. He found the work 'interesting . . . but [was, in the end] unable to point to any legislative measures as a direct result' of his three years' stint.[54] By the time the Commission reported, the Liberal government was in decline and hastening towards an early General Election, which it was to lose. Tom Mann had used the proceedings to table his appeal for an eight-hour day, 'by trade and local option', and to advocate measures to 'dockise the river Thames' under a unified port authority. He advocated improved facilities by cutting a canal across the loop from Limehouse to Blackwall, thus providing space for 9½ miles of 'scientifically arranged warehouses, to which any vessel could get right up'.[55]

Whatever might have been the intention of the Salisbury administration, or of the Liberals, in establishing the Royal Commission, as it continued its long and extensively documented hearings, the results were largely rhetorical. Among the final paperwork was a minority report written by Sidney Webb and signed by Mann (who initiated the project), Mawdsley, Austin and Mabon (Abraham). Beatrice Webb wrote whimsically about the efforts which brought about a joint report from such widely different sectors of the trade-union movement:

This report was produced at yesterday's sitting of the Commission (the *Westminster Gazette* of March 16, 1894, reports), and it created (says the *Manchester Guardian*) almost as much consternation as if a bomb had been exploded in Westminster Hall. The Duke of Devonshire was clearly unprepared for it. It altered the whole situation so far as his draft recommendations were concerned, and he suggested that the Commission should have time to consider the new report, for which purpose he then adjourned the Commission until after Easter. The minority report, it is reported, will propose among other matters a legal eight-hour day, with certain limitations, the amendment of the Factory Acts in the direction of the abolition of home work, the relief of the unemployed by empowering Boards of Guardians to acquire land and to till it by the labour of persons temporarily unemployed, the improvement of the lot of the dock labourers and other casual workers, and the amelioration of the condition of the agricultural labourer. The same report will also express regret that the nationalisation of the land cannot be dealt with. These questions bristle with opportunities for controversy, and it will not be possible to conclude the work of the Commission by the end of the month. It is expected that five members of the Commission at least will subscribe to this report.

Apparently Mawdsley was under no delusion about the authorship of the report. When a number of the majority of the Royal Commission observed with a sneer that the signatories had obviously not written the report, Mawdsley answered sharply: 'Certainly not: nor has the Duke or any of you written the majority report. The only distinction between us and you is that you have paid your man, and we have been sharp enough to get it done without payment, and better done too'. On the close of the Commission, Mawdsley insisted on the three Labour members, Tom Mann, Michael Austin and himself, signing a formal letter of thanks to Sidney Webb for enabling them 'to submit a report which we believe will prove to be of great value to the cause of Labour in the future, also in some sense a guide to the industrial and political policy to be endorsed by the workers'.[56]

Tom Mann sat on the Commission, so his interventions were of a special kind. But his colleagues could, and did, appear as witnesses. A whole procession of port workers gave testimony.

Municipality versus State

Tillett's own programme was laid out before the Royal Commission at an early stage.[57] He first called for regulation of labour to prevent the exploitation of young people and to prevent strain and injury. He then argued what was to become the classic new-unionist case for municipal-ization of dock plant and installations, and 'an absolute popular control of the docks'. This entailed the exclusion of subcontracting middlemen. The state should legislate for and finance local-authority ownership and control, buying out existing owners over twenty-five years at the gross rateable values of their properties. The development of democratic local-government machinery was creating the possibility of decentralized state economic intervention, through a variety of 'enabling' measures which did not impose identical responses to problems, but called forth local initiative and inventiveness. In seeing these opportunities, the new unions were developing, with great prescience, an important agency of reform.[58]

Lord Derby immediately counterattacked. First he raised the question: 'You said that the docks were to be worked on the principle of employing the largest number possible?' If that principle were applied, 'would they pay very well?' Tillett replied:

I think so. Why I would say so is this, that we are quite prepared to admit of the most effective machinery being brought into use, and the best class of labour procured providing that the result of that class of labour's efforts went to support their fellows, and the municipal powers generally. At the present moment, every advantage in the direction of effective machinery and effective labour goes into the pocket of the private owner of the company. Under the other control it would go for the general benefit.[59]

But would it 'be cheaper to employ, say, 12 men where you now employ 10?' asked Lord Derby. 'It would be cheaper to the municipality, but not . . . to the private employer,' said Tillett. And at this point he began to invoke the principle of social costs: 'the municipal power would be responsible as much for the poverty of the community as for the wealth of the community . . . [while the] employer is not responsible for the poverty of the community . . . [if the municipality gave] men employment in one direction, they would not have to give them charity in another.'

But, came the inevitable response, is this not turning the docks into a system of outdoor relief? Tillett thought not, but could easily overcome overmanning problems in municipal docks if the state could be persuaded to co-operate with local bodies in establishing municipal workshops

to find employment, to provide means of technical education for youths and for men, if they so desire, to provide them all with the necessaries of life, providing them with work; and I would go so far as to say that the man who would not work should not eat . . .

I would say that the Government recognises the necessity of teaching their convicts trades; they understand it, I believe, as the best means of giving the men a fair start in life and allowing them to be honest. If we could get the State to recognise the poor man as it does the convict, to recognise the incapable man as it does the convict and the criminal, if we could get the State to further that idea and to increase the facilities to give every man a chance to learn a trade, then I think one of the most serious labour problems would be grappled with.[60]

Tillett's workshops would, he said as he warmed to his theme, be locally and democratically administered. They would 'select their own officials', maintain access to the accounts and operate under local or district control. This prospectus was no more appealing to the Royal Commission's majority than it was to Margaret Thatcher's administration when it was revived by the Greater London Council and the Greater London Enterprise Board nearly a century later. But in the effort to combine public enterprise with decentralized initiative, it showed a bold imagination which was unfortunately missing when later Labour leaders began to blueprint the idea of the public corporation which was, for long years, to be synonymous with socialism in Britain. Tillett's successors in the TGWU were to become notable among the critics of this model and of its architect, Herbert Morrison.

But this was not all that Tillett had to tell the Royal Commission. He went on to outline a comprehensive framework for industrial relations, which involved far-reaching national proposals.

To deal with labour unrest and to avoid the ill-effects of disputes, Tillett proposed an integrated package of governmental initiatives: 'There should be a ministry of labour; a state board of arbitration; and the men should be bound as well as the employers by any suggestion that the board might make.'[61] The functions of a Ministry of Labour would involve data-collection and the appointment of inspectors to enforce relevant legislation on safety, equipment maintenance and the proper working of shifts.

Government presence in industrial relations was a novel idea, even though Arbitration Acts in 1867 and again in 1872 had made provision for voluntary conciliation. There was no organizational basis for the enforcement of any but the most limited legislation. Neither the government nor the civil service had disposed of any cadre for dealing with labour matters before 1886. After an agitation by Charles Bradlaugh, a Bureau of Labour Statistics was established to inquire into organization, pay and spending patterns of working people. But by the early 1890s all this added up to the most rudimentary provision. Tillett's proposals, therefore, amounted to a comprehensive reform.

Sidney Webb and Tom Mann also ventilated the idea that a Labour Department could arbitrate in industrial disputes. There were differences in the details of their proposals. Tillett wished his arbitrators to be empowered to issue legally binding awards, equally applicable to both parties. Sidney Webb suggested that arbitrators should work by appealing to public opinion: they should inquire into the reasons for disputes and publish their findings. Tom Mann thought that mediation should be organized by a central board with national coverage, and should offer a last court of appeal to which voluntary arbitration boards might have recourse. Mann's proposal was a sensitive compromise. It did not seek final arbitration lightly, but provided for the agreed regulation of disagreements, wherever this was possible.

Not long after the Royal Commission had concluded its work, Sidney and Beatrice Webb published their lectures at the London School of

Economics under the title *Industrial Democracy*. They showed that compulsory arbitration was by no means a popular demand among many established trade unions. It would, they said, amount to the state regulation of wages, and would no longer be restricted to 'the patching up of a quarrel between capitalists and workmen'.[62]

The pressure of unnumbered casual workers undoubtedly confirmed Ben Tillett in his pursuit of the social regulation of both wages and employment. Similar pressures were at work on the other side of the world. In 1894, an Arbitration Court was established in New Zealand, and by 1896 arbitration had spread from New South Wales (1892) through South Australia (1894) to Victoria (1896). The working of this style of government intervention naturally interested the dockers' leaders, and it is not an accident that both Tillett and Mann were to be found in Australia and New Zealand within the next few years.

The Case for General Unions

Both Tillett and Mann went out to study the effects of the new system. That they drew different and opposed conclusions was to counterpoint the union agenda during the next great upsurge of transport workers a generation later.

Among the other first-generation new-union leaders, Will Thorne also saw clearly the necessity for the new organizations to be all-grade, all-industry, general unions. He went before the Royal Commission in 1892: 'If we should confine ourselves to one particular industry, such as gasworkers alone, and if those other people in various parts of the country are let go unorganised, then, if we had a dispute with any of the gas companies, these men would be brought up to be put in our places'.[63]

Thorne, Burns and Mann had all, as we have seen, been members of the Social Democratic Federation, which had this to say on the question of trade unionism:

> The real emancipation of labour can only be effected by the solemn binding together of millions of human beings in a federation as wide as the civilised world . . . The day has gone by for the efforts of isolated trades . . . Nothing is to be gained for the workers as a class without the complete organisation of labourers of all grades, skilled and unskilled . . . We appeal therefore earnestly to the skilled artisans of all trades, Unionists and non-Unionists alike, to make common cause with their unskilled brethren, and with us Social-Democrats, so that the workers may themselves take hold of the means of production, and organise a Co-operative Commonwealth for themselves and their colleagues.[64]

Thorne's union, whose original preamble to its rules had reflected 'the language of the old unionism', changed it to that of 'the class war' in

1892, when it decided to admit 'every kind of "unskilled" labour . . . on an equal footing'. Eleanor Marx had a hand in this important amendment.[65]

The naming of the new unions reflected, with noticeable consistency, the notion of 'general' unionism. The most famous cases, of the dockers and the gasworkers, added 'and General Labourers' to their titles from the outset. The move away from local to national scope was reflected in other cases. Thus, as we have seen, the Tyneside Labour Union soon became the National Amalgamated Union of Labour, a similar South Wales body soon called itself the National Amalgamated Labourers' Union of Great Britain and Ireland, and the Lancashire Labour Amalgamation became the British Labour Amalgamation.

Of the new unions founded in the late 1880s, only the Sailors and Firemen were untouched by socialist thinking amongst the leadership, and only they and the Glasgow-originated, Liverpool-dominated National Union of Dock Labourers of Great Britain and Ireland sought no recruits outside their original industrial base. Even so, Havelock Wilson had envisaged a federation between his union and the National Union of Dock Labourers in Glasgow in its initial phase. It is true that McHugh and McGhee were Georgeites, not Marxists of the SDF, but both they and Sexton, who succeeded to their leadership, were followers of some brand of socialist thought, since Sexton's and McGhee's membership of the Knights of Labour brought them in touch with an order which 'had an ambitious programme of social and political amelioration . . . [which] may be compared with the grandiose schemes of trade unionism in Owen's day rather than with the cautious and exclusive societies of Gompers's American Federation of Labour, or the British Trades Union Congress before the advent of "new unionism".'[66]

Sexton's instinct to move into politics from his trade-union base was evident from his earliest days of activity, pre-dating the Liverpool strike of 1889 and his entry into new unionism. Following an initial campaign against jerry-building in the city and related corruption on the Liverpool City Council's Health and General Purposes Committee, he recalled in his memoirs:

> From that time onwards some of us banded together to wage open and unceasing war on the jerry-building crew . . . We fought municipal election after municipal election on purely labour principles in the teeth of my old enemies the Unholy Alliance of the official Irish and Liberals, to whom another Unholy Alliance was now attached – that of the Liberal and Tory jerry-builders.[67]

(Sexton maintained that some of his fellow Irishmen, having won council seats, became involved in the corruption.)

In pursuing municipal Labour politics, Sexton was committing himself to a strategy which was also followed by the Gasworkers' Union, which sought council seats where the municipalities owned the gasworks. Later this course was taken by such waterfront leaders as Harry Gosling, the London lighterman, who became a prominent member of the London County Council, as John Burns had done before him. Later again, in the twentieth century, Sexton, Tillett and Gosling, like their opposite numbers Thorne and Clynes of the Gasworkers' Union, were to combine high union office with parliamentary careers. Tom Mann was never elected, although he stood several times on the ticket of the Independent Labour Party. As early as 1890 he was offered, anonymously through his lawyer, a grant of £2 a week to present a candidature.

New Unions Seen By Others

If these were the politics and the strategies of the leaderships of the new unions, we can turn now to discuss the responses of other parties – the contemporary historians, the radical sympathizers and mediators, and the employers.

But we should begin with the workers who were involved – the members of the new unions. The evidence lies in the statistics: here was spectacular, almost overnight, growth. Quite simply, in the years 1889 and 1890, previously unorganized workers – whole sections of the Victorian underclass of the poorest employees – flocked to the new organizations in their hundred of thousands. This, at the very least, demonstrates a felt need on their part for association and action. They were responding to, and at the same time encouraging, the initiative of a new type of leader. This had been for some time the age of working-class autodidacts, who won their influence on the basis of their own studies. Now the new ideas of socialism helped such men to evolve a deliberate strategy of trade unionism. It was the interaction between such leaders and the mass of members and potential members that produced new unionism. Significantly, those members were largely indifferent to the structure of the unions which emerged. Often, indeed, they sought to break through occupational and industrial boundaries in their eagerness for inclusive forms of organization. Thus the Glasgow dockers initially sought to be enrolled by the Sailors' and Firemen's Union; the Welsh dockers transferred in large numbers from a local to a national union; and, also in Wales, many groups in hinterland industries joined up. In Hull the dockers promptly abandoned their earlier local union for Tillett's new national one, and, as we have seen, agricultural workers joined in from Lincolnshire and East Yorkshire. Inland transport trades such as the carters, usually displaced from the land and closely associated with the docks, made members for the Dockers' Union. The tramway-men were often distanced from this process, having a more separate industrial conception of their identity, and they created their own unions. But at this point neither road-passenger transport nor commercial road haulage was a mass, labour-intensive industry in its own right, the railways still dominating in both passenger and freight traffic. The carters and hauliers who were drawn in to the Dockers' Union were those working alongside the union's founders on the dock and in its immediately surrounding warehouses and markets. Comprehensive statistics of vehicles in use exist from 1904. In that year, there were a mere 5,000 buses, coaches and taxis, 4,000 goods vehicles and 7,000 tramcars, compared to 75,000, 101,000 and 13,000 in 1920.[68]

We should also note that Sexton and his fellow trade unionists readily abandoned the clandestinity of the Knights of Labour (the equivalent in Liverpool of Tillett's 'hole-and-corner' Tea Operatives' Union before the great strike in London) in favour of the open, bands-and-banner-waving public demonstrations of the new unions, which so scandalized the decorous old unionists like George Howell.

Sectionalism and Generalism

Of course, not all the old sectionalisms gave way before the new upsurge, particularly in London. We have seen that the stevedores, although swept along in the generous wave of sympathetic action which characterized the great strike, preserved their separate identity thereafter. Striking testimony to the tug-of-war between sectional and general impulses is given by Harry Gosling of the London Lightermen's Union, the very embodiment of craftlike organization in the port. In his memoirs he recalls:

> We, too, benefited enormously by 1889: it practically revolutionised our industrial outlook. All through their history skilled rivermen had been craft unionists out and out. Even in my early days a riverman was a craftsman, and that only . . . But now, after 1889, for the first time these same skilled rivermen began to feel a half-conscious groping, an urge . . . towards a new group life for themselves. Somehow it came to them, vaguely at first and helplessly, that they could no longer stand each craft for itself, but that all the men engaged in waterside transport work – seamen, dockers, carters, lightermen, coal-porters or whoever they might be – fundamentally belonged together as members of one body and must assert themselves as such. And this new idea was an immense triumph, though it took fully twenty years before it matured, and the first live federation of transport workers came into existence . . . Even the strong impulse they received in 1889 did not convert them to the forward policy of more active groups of workers, and it took years of propaganda before they could be persuaded to join forces with other organisations . . . At times I admit I used to get rather impatient with this attitude, and I remember saying to Tom Mann

once in my early days as a trade union official: 'Well, shall I leave them, and come along with the others?' . . . 'No' he said, 'stay where you are, and bring them along with you'. Strangely sober advice from one who has always been branded as an extremist.[69]

Gosling of course followed the advice and, as the only president successively of the National Transport Workers' Federation from its inception in 1910, and then of the newly formed Transport and General Workers' Union, had the satisfaction of 'bringing them along' into the 1922 amalgamation – which he even then saw as simply a further stage in the long march towards total unity. At the TGWU Rules Conference in 1921, which prepared the way for formal amalgamation the following year, in his presidential peroration he spoke thus of unfulfilled hopes: 'But this was the beginning: they had to get an alliance with the railwaymen and then get towards the point when one card would represent trade unionism'.[70] These words were greeted with applause – they echoed what Ernest Bevin had said earlier in the proceedings. One is tempted to add: strangely revolutionary hopes from those who have always been praised as moderates!

In a later volume, we shall see that the tug-of-war between general and craft unionism for the London lightermen was not finally resolved in 1922. Nevertheless, we can legitimately take this case as symbolic of a force, an impetus towards wider and wider association, which ebbed and flowed in the decades succeeding the formation of the Dockers' Union, not only down to 1922 but beyond it to the present day.

This logic was to assert itself again and again. True, immediately following the first triumphs, new unionism shrank back into dependence on more stable employment groups outside the casual docks industry. In an era of unregulated boom and slump, the wider the association, the more prone it was to instability of membership and allegiance. A period of decline, retrenchment and caution was to follow, covering almost two decades from 1891 to 1910. Yet when revival came, it immediately promoted the trend to federation, universally seen by the participants as a prelude to amalgamation.

That this was a resumption of previous tendencies is seen in the federation of the 1870s – of London dockers, carmen, watermen, lightermen and railway servants' unions; in the formation of the United Labour Council arising from the Joint Strike Committee which ran the great strike of 1889; and in the federation formed by the Dockers' Union, the Sailors' and Firemen's Union and the South Side Labour Protection League in London in 1891. This is the record for London alone. The federal process is also very marked in the North-east and in Hull (to take just two more examples) at the height of the first wave of new unionism. Finally, we have already noticed that the NUDL, too, sought wider alliances in 1889–90.

III

Academic Appraisals

What did contemporary opinion outside the ranks of the new unions make of the phenomenon? The most weighty, and subsequently influential, account comes to us from Sidney and Beatrice Webb, the first edition of whose *History of Trade Unionism* was completed in 1894. It benefits not only from the all-round scholarship of the authors, but also from the specific social studies which Beatrice Webb had undertaken in London's dockland for the studies of Charles Booth.

It is from the Webbs that the first attempt to identify the character of the new unions comes. They point to the common features of low subscriptions and concentration on a single benefit – strike pay. They recognize the tendency to general recruitment – what they call 'comprehensive membership' – and to the concomitant emergence of federations, and also of new Trades Councils, together with the formation of local joint committees of unions in kindred trades, all of which are part of a general 'sinking of rivalries'. They demonstrate the link between socialist propaganda of the previous decade and the leadership of the new unions. They relate this to the conflict between the 'old' and the 'new' unionism and to the triumph, even within the old, of the new unionists' call for the legal limitation of the hours of labour, as the engineers, the carpenters and the London Trades Council (including its secretary George Shipton) became the converts who helped to secure its adoption by the 1890 TUC Congress. They cite John Burns's résumé of that formative Congress. 'Out of . . . sixty resolutions', he declared, 'forty-five were nothing more or less than direct appeals to the State and Municipalities of this country to do for the workman what Trades Unionism, "Old" and New", has proved itself incapable of doing'.[71] They show that this impulse was already, by 1894, producing 'Collectivist victories on the London School Board and County Council, the steady growth of municipal activity and the increasing influence exercised by working-men members of representative bodies'.[72]

The Webbs acknowledged that they were too close to the events 'to estimate the precise character of the new movement itself'. Yet they offered an historical appraisal based on a comparison between new unionism and its only preceding counterpart in Labour history, the Owenite wave of the 1830s, in which mass enrolment in a trade union with large social goals took place – in a matter of months – with similar explosive force to that of 1889. The Webbs continue:

> But however strongly the outward features of the wave of 1889–90 may remind the student of those of 1833–4, the characteristics peculiar to the

new movement significantly measure the extent of the advance, both in social theory and social methods, made by the wage-earners in the two intervening generations. Time and experience alone will show how far the empirical Socialism of the Trade Unionist of to-day, with its eclectic opportunism, its preference for municipal collectivism, its cautious adaptation of existing social structure, may safely be pronounced superior in practicability to the revolutionary and universal Communism of Robert Owen . . . To the great majority of the Trade Unionists the theories of the leaders at either date did but embody a vague aspiration after a more equitable social order. The practical difference – the difference reflected in the character and the temper of the men attracted to the two movements, and of the attitude of the public towards them – is the difference of method and immediate action. Robert Owen . . . despised and rejected political action . . . In this disdain of all existing organisations, and the suddenness of the complete 'social revolution' which it contemplated, the Owenism of 1833–4 found . . . an echo in much of the Socialist propaganda of 1884–9. The leaders of the New Unionists, on the contrary, sought to bring into the ranks of existing organisations – the Trade Union, the Municipality, or the State – great masses of unorganised workers who had hitherto been either absolutely outside the pale, or inert elements within it. They aimed, not at superseding existing social structures, but at capturing them all in the interests of wage-earners. Above all, they sought to teach the great masses of undisciplined workers how to apply their newly acquired political power so as to obtain, in a perfectly constitutional manner, whatever changes in legislation or administration they desired . . . To Robert Owen, whose path was blocked on the political line by the disfranchisement of five out of six of the adult male population, open voting under intimidation, corrupt close corporations in the towns and a Whig oligarchy at the centre, the idea of relying on the constitutional instrument of the polling-booth must have appeared no less chimerical than his own programme appears today. The New Unionists of 1889–90, on the other hand, found ready for their use an extensive and all-embracing Democratic social structure, which it was impossible to destroy, and would have been foolish to attempt to ignore.[73]

Despite a substantial attempt at a 'revisionist' version of the import of new unionism, which has appeared in our own times at the hands of H. A. Clegg, Alan Fox and A. F. Thompson, supported by John Lovell,[74] the Webbs' assessment, made so close to the events, still has a loud ring of truth. The traditional view has in fact been reinforced by some important subsequent historical studies, including the recent spate of regional histories on which we have drawn. Of twentieth-century historians, Eric Hobsbawm's findings mostly serve to underscore the Webbs' version. He finds that:

The theory in the mind of the founders of the general unions (and of their predecessors), was fairly simple. The 'labourer', mobile, helpless, shifting from one trade to another, was incapable of using the orthodox tactics of craft unionism. Possessing 'merely the general value of labour' he could not, like the 'skilled man', buttress a certain scarcity value by various restrictive methods, thus 'keeping up his price'. His only chance therefore was to recruit into one gigantic union all those who could possibly blackleg on him – in the last analysis every 'unskilled' man, woman or juvenile in the country: and thus to create a vast closed shop.[75]

Hobsbawm also insists that:

the large national and regional 'general' unions of 1889 were the offspring of a marriage between the class unionism of the socialists and the more modest plans of the unskilled themselves. (The only general union with a really national network, the Gas-workers, secured this largely through the help of local socialist groups.) The expansion of the early 1870s, in other respects an important – and neglected – forerunner of the 'New Unionism', produced unions of a far more sectional type.[76]

The Liberal Sympathizers

There was another, contemporary, view of the new unionism which was as influential in ruling-class circles and in particular in Whitehall as was that of the Webbs in the Labour movement. It was also sympathetic, welcoming of the new movement, but sought to harness it in the interests of social peace and class harmony. It is embodied in the work and writings of Llewellyn Smith and Vaughan Nash, of Sydney Buxton, Lord Askwith, and Cardinal Manning. It has been given modern appraisals by Gareth Stedman Jones, Roger Davidson and by Alan Fox.[77]

Hubert Llewellyn Smith (later Sir Hubert), was only twenty-five years old in 1889, when he co-authored the first account of the great dock strike. Of middle-class Quaker extraction, he joined the New Oxford Movement of enlightened liberalism, nourished at Balliol College, Oxford, by the philosophers Benjamin Jowett and T. H. Green. He was patronized by the Webbs, and gravitated to the study of East End poverty through Toynbee Hall. He became a university extension lecturer, and a researcher for the Booth inquiries. He espoused the cause of new unionism, helped to publicize the plight of the matchgirls, worked for agricultural trade unionism in 1890, and with John Burns co-ordinated picketing in the London bus strike of 1891. He became Commissioner of Labour at the Board of Trade in 1893, Controller-General from 1903, and Permanent Secretary from 1907 to 1919. He was one of the archetypal figures (George Askwith being the other), representing a continuous strand of enlightened liberalism, which, in pursuit of the preservation and reinforcement of ruling-class hegemony, sought to encourage state–employer–trade-union relations, in particular through the leaderships of the new unions.[78] Smith's co-author of the first history of the London dock strike, Vaughan Nash, became secretary of the Cabinet Reconstruction Committee concerned with post-war social policies in 1916.

These two draw an unexpected lesson from the success of the London dock strike. They predict and hope that it will transform the casual labour force into a disciplined, regular workforce, free of the encumbrance of

the loafer, the cadger, the failure of the industrial race – the members of 'Class B' of Mr. Charles Booth's hierarchy of social classes. [This subclass will] find another door closed against them, and in many cases the last door to employment . . . the difficulty which the loafer will find in competing with the higher class labourer under the new regime will be the exact measure of the success of the strike. Hitherto, all these grades of labour have jostled each other at the dock gates, and the standard of life of the lowest has set the standard of all. Now they will be more sharply divided . . . The problem of dealing with the dregs of London will thus loom up before us more urgent than in times gone by, but it will be simplified by a change which will make it impossible, or at least unpardonable, to mix up the problem, which is essentially one of the treatment of social disease, with the radically different question of the claims of labour.[79]

Sydney Buxton, in his introduction to Smith and Nash's history, reinforces the point: 'in the past, the Docks have formed a "gigantic system of out-door relief" – a huge pauperising agency, planted in the heart of London; a centre from which have been recklessly recruited the ranks of unskilled labour in the Metropolis'. He rejoices that the 'labour question', the 'condition-of-the-people question', has been placed so forcefully before public attention by the dock strike. It is not difficult to sympathize with his enthusiasm: like Smith, he had been working away in obscurity on that very question in his constituency to no avail, and now, suddenly, his constituents had achieved dramatic publicity for themselves.

Buxton's other expectation and hope was that the settlement would be followed by the generalization of the spirit and practice of conciliation and arbitration boards, which he notes were common in many industries in the North, but hitherto unknown in London and in dockland: 'Thus, the formation of a strong Trades Union tends on both sides to bring about that which is the most desirable of all ends, in disputes between labour and capital; a permanent and recognised Board of Conciliation; a Board that shall consist partly of masters, partly of men, with, perhaps, an impartial outsider as final arbitrator'.[80]

Askwith, in his monumental study, *Industrial Problems and Disputes*, also links the dock strike with the spread of conciliation:

It was then too, that efforts at conciliation were found not to be without result, a belief fostered by the closing of the long six weeks' coal dispute in the Midlands, under the chairmanship of Lord Rosebery, in 1893; the national agreement established, through the Board of Trade, in the Boot and Shoe trade in 1895; and the reference of the North-Eastern Railway dispute to Sir Henry James in the same year. The dockers' strike, it seems to me . . . marked a great epoch in the relations of Capital and Labour.[81]

Askwith was writing long after the event, and was able to put the earlier optimism of the social engineers such as Smith and Buxton into a somewhat bitter perspective, as he pointed to the unsolved problems of casualism in the docks industry of the twentieth century, and to his own frustrations at the hands of the dock employers over years of conciliation in the industry.

Not only was the settlement of 1889 inadequate to solve the structural problems of port labour: it was a failure in material terms as well. Pay, conditions and the new call-on system were soon undermined. The power of the Dockers' Union to secure preference of employment for the union ticket lasted just fourteen months through the continued trade boom. As trade turned down, the employers took the opportunity to break the men's dependence on union-preferred hiring by introducing a measure of 'decasualization' which switched dependence to a system of preference lists operated by the companies, through their co-ordinated Joint Docks Committee, which amalgamated the separate dock systems. To the existing 'permanent' men, the companies added the categories A-, B- and C-men. The A-men got some of the 'perms' conditions, but not sick pay or pensions; B-men were registered, with a ticket, but moved up and down the preference list according to their attendance records and performance. C-men were engaged only when all A- and B-men had work. Booth found that 'whatever has been gained by the men on the "B" list has been lost by those on the "C" list and outsiders . . . ultimately they must surely decrease in number if less and less work is offered to them, but the process is a painful one and some of the distress from lack of employment in East London . . . is probably attributable to this cause'.[82] Stedman Jones comments: 'The casual poor had played a full part in the strike of 1889, but for them at least, the experience of victory had been vicarious'.[83]

A Temporary Settlement?

This sobering picture, of the dockers divided by employer devices which were to play so prominent a part in labour relations and trade unionism in the industry for the next eighty years, and which preface the full-scale assault on new unionism by the Shipping Federation in the 1890s, is perhaps the point at which to close this review of the first phase of new unionism, poised on the eve of its greatest trials.

In 1889, the employers were divided. Mr. Norwood, their spokesman in London, represented intransigence. So did the large shipping companies in Liverpool. The railway company in South Wales adopted similar attitudes. But in all ports there were significant bodies of smaller employers willing to compromise and offer concessions and recognition, and this, as we have seen, was true of a genuine shipping magnate in Hull. In the next phase, the employers presented a united, fighting front, and a pre-planned strategy. Conciliation was no part of it: it was to be outright battle, red in tooth and claw.

Notes

1   Havelock Wilson, *My Stormy Voyage Through Life*, vol. I (Co-operative Printing Society, 1925), p. 176.
2   Havelock Wilson's evidence to the Royal Commission on Labour, 1892, Minutes of Evidence, Group B, Vol. I, Qs. 9176–88.
3   See Arthur Marsh and Victoria Ryan, *The Seamen: A History of the National Union of Seamen, 1887–1987* (Malthouse, 1989).
4   The Board of Trade recorded 40,000 days lost in each of two major shipping disputes in 1889, making them larger than the Board's figure for the London dock strike (H. A. Clegg, Alan Fox and A. F. Thompson, *A History of British Trade Unions Since 1889*, vol. I: *1889–1910* (Oxford University Press, 1964), p. 55.
5   James Sexton, *Sir James Sexton, Agitator: the Life of the Dockers' MP* (Faber and Faber, 1936), p. 94.
6   Geoff Brown, *Sabotage: A Study in Industrial Conflict* (Spokesman Books, 1977), p. 6.
7   Reprinted in an appendix to Llewellyn Smith and Vaughan Nash, *The Story of the Dockers' Strike* (Fisher Unwin, 1890), p. 190. For ca'canny in Glasgow, see Brown, *Sabotage*, pp. 3–8.
8   Sexton, *Sir James Sexton, Agitator*, p. 104. Sexton thought that 'the policy had some success for a time', but because it backfired 'it was eventually abandoned'.
9   Ibid., p. 18.
10 Ibid., p. 80.
11 Vincent Alan McClelland, *Cardinal Manning: His Public Life and Influence, 1865–92* (Oxford University Press, 1962), p. 141.
12 Manning's father, William (1763–1835), was a West India merchant with large plantations on the West Indian island of St Kitts. He was a founder member of the West India Dock Company in 1797, which was the first wet dock built outside the control of the City and of existing labour customs. He was an MP, Governor of the Bank of England, married twice and fathered seven children. He was bankrupted in 1831. (Information supplied by Rodney Mace.)
13 McClelland, *Cardinal Manning*, p. 149.
14 Eric Taplin, *Liverpool Dockers and Seamen, 1870–1890* (University of Hull, 1974), p. 38.

15 John Gray, *City in Revolt: James Larkin and the Belfast Dock Strike of 1907* (Blackstaff Press, 1985), p. 5.

16 See Raymond Brown, *Waterfront Organisation in Hull*.

17 7 February 1891.

18 Cf. Rex C. Russell, *The 'Revolt of the Field' in Lincolnshire* (Lincolnshire County Council Committee, National Union of Agricultural Workers, 1956), pp. 152–4.

19 Quotations in this passage are from Raymond Brown, *Waterfront Organisation in Hull, 1870–1900* (University of Hull, 1974), pp. 50–1.

20 Brian Atkinson, *Trade Unions in Bristol* (Bristol Branch, Historical Association, University of Bristol, 1982), p. 9.

21 Ibid., p. 10.

22 This section draws upon Phillip J. Leng, *The Welsh Dockers* (G. W. & A. Hesketh, 1981), pp. 13–34.

23 The *Star*, May 1891.

24 *Evening Standard*, 3 October 1890.

25 The *Star*, 30 May 1891.

26 Ibid.

27 Sutherst's evidence to the Royal Commission on Labour, Minutes of Evidence, Group B, Vol. II, Qs. 743–17, 197.

28 See William Collison, *The Apostle of Free Labour* (Hurst and Blackett, 1913), pp. 24–37.

29 Royal Commission on Labour, 1892, IUP, p. 508.

30 See Kenneth Fuller, *Radical Aristocrats* (Lawrence and Wishart, 1985), pp. 22–3.

31 Eric J. Hobsbawm, *Labouring Men* (Weidenfeld and Nicolson, 1968), chapter 9: 'British Gas-workers, 1873–1914', pp. 158–79.

32 These statistics were supplied by Michael Barratt Brown.

33 Clegg, Fox and Thompson, *History of British Trade Unions*, vol. I, p. 65.

34 George Tate, *The London Trades Council, 1860–1950: A History* (Lawrence and Wishart, 1950), p. 73.

35 Royal Commission on Labour, Minutes of Evidence, Group B, Vol. II, Qs. 13,169–13,170.

36 Ibid., Qs. 13,037–13,038.

37 Quoted in Jonathan Schneer, *Ben Tillett: Portrait of a Labour Leader* (Croom Helm, 1982), p. 47.

38 Ibid., pp. 48–9.

39 George Howell, *Trade Unionism New and Old* (Methuen, 1891; 3rd edn rev. 1900).

40 Ibid., p. 131.

41 Ibid., p. 133.

42 Ibid., pp. 134–5.

43 Ibid., p. 136.

44 Zigmunt Bauman, *Between Class and Élite: The Evolution of the British Labour Movement, a Sociological Study* (Manchester University Press, 1972), p. 73.

45 H. M. Hyndman, *Further Reminiscences* (Macmillan, 1912), pp. 249–50.

46 See Ben Tillett, *Memories and Reflections* (John Long, 1931), p. 93: 'John Burns . . . felt entitled to jibe at the delegates to the Trades Union Congress because so many of them looked like respectable City gentlemen; wore very

good coats, large watch-chains and high hats; and in many cases were of . . .
splendid build and proportion . . . When I became the organiser of a union,
I fell far short of these sartorial standards.'

47 Howell, *Trade Unionism New and Old*, pp. 136–7.
48 Ibid., pp. 137–9.
49 Ibid., p. 139–42.
50 Ibid., pp. 142–8.
51 Ibid., p. 224.
52 Ibid., p. 225.
53 Beatrice Webb, *Our Partnership* (Longman, 1948), pp. 40–1.
54 Tom Mann, *Memoirs* (1923; reissued MacGibbon and Kee, 1967), p. 75; also Tate, *The London Trades Council*, pp. 80ff.
55 Mann, *Memoirs*, p. 78.
56 Webb, *Our Partnership*, p. 41.
57 Royal Commission on Labour, Minutes of Evidence, Group B, 3 July 1891, p. 142.
58 This was to be developed, with great panache, by the Greater London Council and its offshoots – especially the Greater London Enterprise Board – during its last years of existence. No doubt this is one of the reasons why a Conservative administration under Margaret Thatcher resolved to do away with the GLC.
59 Royal Commission on Labour, Minutes of Evidence, Group B, Vol. I, Q. 3582.
60 Ibid., Q. 3594.
61 Ibid., Q. 3615.
62 Sidney and Beatrice Webb, *Industrial Democracy* (1897; reissued Longman Green, 1926), p. 245.
63 Quoted in Hobsbawm, *Labouring Men*, p. 181.
64 From the manifesto of the Social Democratic Federation to the Trade Unions, September 1884; quoted in Sidney and Beatrice Webb, *The History of Trade Unionism* (1894; WEA edn, 1912), p. 396.
65 See Clegg, Fox and Thompson, *History of British Trade Unions*, vol. I, p. 92.
66 Henry Pelling, 'The Knights of Labour in Britain, 1880–1901', *Economic History Review*, second series, vol. IX (1956), pp. 313–31.
67 Sexton, *Sir James Sexton, Agitator*, p. 92.
68 B. R. Mitchell and P. Deane, *Abstract of British Historical Statistics* (Cambridge University Press, 1962), p. 230.
69 Harry Gosling, *Up and Down Stream* (Methuen, 1927), pp. 144–5.
70 TGWU *Record*, vol. I, no. 3 (October 1921), pp. 22–3.
71 Webb, *History of Trade Unionism*, p. 395.
72 Ibid., p. 399.
73 Ibid., p. 404.
74 In Clegg, Fox and Thompson, *History of British Trade Unions*, vol. I, chapter 2; and John Lovell, *Stevedores and Dockers: a Study of Trade Unionism in the Port of London, 1870–1914* (Macmillan, 1969), *passim*. See also Lovell, 'The New Unions', *Bulletin of the Society for the Study of Labour History*, no. 36 (winter 1977), pp. 15–16, in which he makes his own comments on the large controversy amongst historians on the significance of the new unionism: 'There are those who see 1889 as the great watershed or turning

point in the history of British labour, and there are those who play down the significance of the new unionist phase and suggest that the periods 1872–4 and 1910–14 were no less important than 1889–92. This paper subscribes to the latter viewpoint'.

The separation of 1889 from the 1910–14 period, as though the latter was a fresh phase with no roots in the new unions, is, it seems to us, erroneous. It leads to a 'playing down' of the new unions by isolating what is really their first phase, and then focusing upon all their subsequent and subsidiary errors and reverses. Thus, after tracing the severe collapse of membership in the 1890s, Lovell declares that 'The impact of the new unions upon the composition of the total movement was thus a fleeting one', a truly astounding judgement. In what looks like an attempt to correct it, he concedes their subsequent growth after 1910, which 'made a lasting impact upon the composition of the movement'. Recognizing the contradiction between the two statements, he seeks escape by (i) putting quotation marks – 'new' unions – around that term *only* when referring to the later stage of revival; and (ii) finding it 'worth noting, however, that the most remarkable gains in membership after 1910 were made by an organisation that was not of 1889 vintage, namely the Workers' Union founded in 1898'. To which we must respond: (a) the Workers' Union was founded in a very personal campaign by Tom Mann, one of the fathers of new unionism, on new union lines, as a socialist, class union; (b) its growth up to 1914, the period chosen by Lovell for comparison, was in industries and occupations untouched by the Dockers' Union, much of it in virgin territory; (c) the Workers' Union, struggling with difficulties more acute than those facing the ultimate product of new unionism – the TGWU – in 1929 was taken over by that union, thus completing a process which was surely inherent in its logic and history.

Lovell's solid achievement in his history of trade unionism in the London docks demands recognition. But this assessment of the broad sweep of events is more questionable.

Clegg, Fox and Thompson express a similar view, in seeking to make final judgements on the new unions on the basis of their first few years' existence. This is reflected in the timespans into which their volumes were divided. It seems to us that the proper periodization is to regard the late 1880s as the beginning of a process of change in trade-union structure and method which was consummated only in the 1920s, with the formation of the two large general unions, the ASE's transformation into the AEU, and the rewriting of the TUC's constitution. Between the two dates lies the equally formative creation – initiated (as we shall see) by new-union influence – of the Labour Party. Clegg, Fox and Thompson, as also Lovell, seek to minimize the role of socialist ideas and of socialists in the formation and evolution of the new unions, even asserting that they played 'no role' in the formation of the NUDL! They give polemical support to their approach by preferring to rely on the opinion of Tillett's greatest enemy, the self-styled 'apostle of free labour', Collison, who called him a 'sybarite; a voluptuary with the hide of an agitator', rather than to make a sober appraisal of his undoubtedly considerable contribution to trade-union history. Fortunately, we now have the biography of Tillett, 'warts and all', by Ben Schneer, to fill the gap.

The dismissal of the 'newness' in the new unions attempted by these four authors is, it seems to us, refuted by the record. For an informed and critical review of the Clegg, Fox and Thompson volume, see Eric J. Hobsbawm, 'Trade Union History', Essays in Bibliography and Criticism, LVIII, *Economic History Review*, second series, vol. XX, no. 2 (August 1967), pp. 358–64.

75 Hobsbawm, *Labouring Men*, p. 181.
76 Ibid., p. 182.
77 Gareth Stedman Jones, 'Working Class Culture and Working Class Politics in London, 1870–1900', *Journal of Social History*, vol. 7, no. 4 (1974), pp. 460–508, Roger Davidson, *Whitehall and the Labour Problem in Late Victorian and Edwardian Britain* (Croom Helm, 1985) and Alan Fox, *History and Heritage: The Social Origins of the British Industrial Relations System* (Allen and Unwin, 1985).
78 R. Davidson, 'Llewellyn Smith, the Labour Department and Government Growth', in G. Sutherland (ed.), *Studies in the Growth of Nineteenth Century Government* (Routledge and Kegan Paul, 1972).
79 Smith and Nash, *The Story of the Dockers' Strike*, pp. 164–5.
80 Ibid., p. 10.
81 Lord Askwith, *Industrial Problems and Disputes* (John Murray, 1920), p. 74.
82 Booth's evidence to the Royal Commission on Labour, 1892, quoted in Gareth Stedman Jones, *Outcast London* (Penguin, 1971), p. 319.
83 Ibid.

5

Defeat: Defence and Defiance

I

Up Like a Rocket – Down Like the Stick

The explosive uprush of new unionism between 1889 and 1891 was without precedent. In spite of what followed, this was a formative event. In the short run, no one doubted this.[1] Membership of the TUC increased by 80 per cent between 1888 and 1890[2] and there were some 2,400 strikes and 11 million man-days lost between 1889 and 1890. The implosion that followed so swiftly was, however, almost as dramatic, leading some modern historians to question the long-term influences of the upsurge.

By 1893 one-third of the new membership had been lost. The London dockers, who had affiliated 56,000 members to the 1890 TUC, were down to 22,913 by 1892 and dwindled to 10,000 in 1896. Thereafter their union recovered to 13,879 by 1900. The NUDL peaked at 50,000 in 1890, then slumped to 8,463 by 1892, with a recovery to 11,697 in 1896 and 13,388 in 1900. The National Labour Federation, which claimed 60,000 members in 1890, was dissolved in 1894 following heavy costs incurred during the previous year's Hull dock strike.[3] The Seamen's Union was also bankrupted and dissolved after its membership declined from 78,000 in 1891 to only 5,000 in 1894. It was immediately reformed with a new title – the National Amalgamated Sailors' and Firemen's Union became the National Sailors' and Firemen's Union, with strong central control of its funds incorporated in its revised rules. Havelock Wilson's office was changed from secretary to president, but he retained all his powers.[4] The NUDL's Executive Reports record thirty-eight branches in existence in 1891, of which five were on the Mersey, seven in Scotland and fourteen in Ireland. By 1895 there were only twenty-five branches, of which five were on the Mersey, three in

Scotland and four in Ireland. In 1918 branch numbers were back to thirty-six, although Ireland's recovery was minimal, and Hull appears for the first time with five branches.[5]

Beyond the immediate environment of the docks and shipping, many unions which originated in inland transport in the upswing of 1889–90 recorded membership losses of similar proportions. The London Carmen's Trade Union, formed in 1888, lost 4,000 of its original 6,000 members by 1892; its surviving 2,000 represented only 5 per cent of the carmen of the capital at that date.[6] Between 1892 and 1893, the Amalgamated Carters, Lurrymen and Motormen's Association fell from 4,000 to 2,500. The new-union wave undoubtedly stimulated unionization in haulage and road-passenger transport, but it was overwhelmingly sectional and, above all, local. Thus we have such organizations as the Wigan and District Carters and Lurrymen's Association, and the Blackburn and District Tramway Workers' Union. Over a dozen attempts at the unionization of London cabmen have been traced to these years.

The mortality rate amongst new unions of this type was staggering. They were, in the main, 'new' only in the literal sense. Using Marsh and Ryan's invaluable data, we find that, amongst carters and horsemen six unions date from before 1889, whilst twenty-six originate in the expansionary period following 1889. Of these thirty-two unions, twelve were defunct by 1911, unable to participate in the next phase of growth. Of cab, tram and omnibus unions, eight were formed between 1870 and 1888, and thirty-one in or after 1889. Of these, twenty-eight had disappeared by 1911.

If local and sectional unions were still the norm in road transport, they were also widespread in dockland. Twenty-six began life between 1870 and 1888, and no fewer than forty-six in or after 1889. All of forty-four of these had died by 1911. It should be said that in these figures a union which is known to have merged with another and thus to have lost its name and separate existence is not counted amongst those which failed. Information on transfers of allegiance, of course, are normally not documented, so we cannot be sure that the collapse of an organization necessarily involved the loss of its members to the trade-union movement.

Three transport-related unions are, of course, in a distinct category of their own: that which began life as the Tea Operatives' and General Labourers' Union of Great Britain and Ireland; the National Amalgamated Labourers' Union; and the National Amalgamated Union of Labour. Each of these was to endure, in spite of all tribulations. All three had an occupational and local origin, in the London docks, South Wales ports, and among Tyneside unskilled shipyard workers. All expressed in their titles an aspiration to general unionism, reaching beyond their waterside origins. None of them was extinguished in the collapse of the

1890s. The NALU survived, never more than 3,500 strong, as a rival to the Dockers' Union in South Wales, until it joined the TGWU amalgamation of 1922. The NAUL, a much larger body with the bulk of its members in the North-east, was one of the three unions to found the General and Municipal Workers in 1924 (taking its Tyneside dock members with it), along with the other prototypical new union, the Gasworkers', and the Municipal Employees' Association. The Gasworkers' Union, the most substantial of these, exhibited some of the volatility of the transport-based unions in the 1890s, but not to the same degree. It affiliated 60,000 to the 1890 TUC, and reported 36,108 members in 1892, 29,730 in 1896 and 47,979 in 1900.[7] Gas supply always had to be organized with a more stable workforce than that which scrambled for jobs at the dock gates, but improvements in technology reinforced the need for a consistent work organization.

We might add to this list a fourth, marginally general, transport union – the South Side Labour Protection League. It reached a membership of 5,000 after the 1889 strike, but stagnated thereafter. It certainly survived to participate in the amalgamation of 1922. Although it had a branch of labourers at the Woolwich Arsenal, and one of Engineers' Helpers at Deptford, it was predominantly an 'old' sectional union.

How, then, should we account for the substantial collapse of the new unions' membership between 1890 and the middle of that decade? Three types of explanation have been offered, based on respectively, the movements of the trade cycle; the changing structure and technologies of transport and general trades; and the policies of employers and the state towards trade unionism.

The Trade Cycle

In the overall economy there were short-cycle recoveries at the beginning and the end of the 1880s. The great explosion of new unionism occurred during the second of these upturns. Yet the impact of trade cycles both on the labour market and on the prospects for trade unionism have never been simple.[8] Hobsbawm has pointed to the growth of tonnage passing through the London docks between 1878 and 1888, at a time when key skilled groups such as lightermen were actually falling in number, as a major contributory factor in any explanation of the great strike of 1889. The more general conditions of trade revival in the years 1887 to 1891 may then be invoked to account for the release of a nationwide explosion of visible discontent among general labourers which coincided with the dock strike. In those years the volume of foreign trade rose. Indexed at 1880 = 100, 1887 showed 114, and 1891, 130. During the whole decade there was a shipbuilding boom, and a great growth in the production and export of farm machinery.

By 1892 depression had resumed its course. It was pushed on its way by a famous scandal at the beginning of the decade: the Baring crisis.[9] The nadir of decline was reached in the middle of the decade: thereafter an economic upswing became evident, gathering strength until 1901–2. The established evidence has been tabulated by Clegg, Fox and Thompson, as shown in table 5.1.

Table 5.1   *Trade Union Membership, Strikes and the Trade Cycle,*
1889–1910

Year	Total Union Membership (000s)	Number of stoppages beginning in year	Total working days lost by all stoppages in progress during year (000s)	Average retail prices (1850 = 100)	Average money wages (1850 = 100)	Percentage unemployed
1889	679	1,211	3,730	91	156	2.1
1890	871	1,040	7,473	91	163	2.1
1891	1,109	906	6,809	92	163	3.5
1892	1,576	700	17,248	92	162	6.3
1893	1,559	599	30,439	89	162	7.5
1894	1,530	903	9,506	87	162	6.9
1895	1,504	728	5,701	84	162	5.8
1896	1,608	906	3,565	83	163	3.3
1897	1,731	848	10,327	86	166	3.3
1898	1,752	695	15,257	87	167	2.8
1899	1,911	710	2,503	86	172	2.0
1900	2,022	633	3,088	89	179	2.5
1901	2,025	631	4,130	90	179	3.3
1902	2,013	432	3,438	91	176	4.0
1903	1,994	380	2,320	92	174	4.7
1904	1,967	346	1,464	93	173	6.0
1905	1,997	349	2,368	92	174	5.0
1906	2,210	479	3,019	92	176	3.6
1907	2,513	585	2,148	95	182	3.7
1908	2,485	389	10,785	97	181	7.8
1909	2,477	422	2,687	97	179	7.7
1910	2,565	521	9,867	98	179.5	4.7

Source: H. A. Clegg, Alan Fox and A. F. Thompson, *A History of British Trade Unions since 1889*, Vol. I: *1889–1910* (Clarendon Press, 1964), p. 489.

(Reproduced by permission of Oxford University Press.)

These swings correlate well with the specific trends of the major new unions' membership given above, as well as with the movement of steamship prices, specific to the fortunes of the port industries (see figs 5.1 and 5.2). They also accord with the tramp shipping freight rates for the period (see table 5.2).

Table 5.2   *Index of Tramp Shipping Freight Rates, 1869–1900*

1869 = 100
1886 = 59
1887 = 65
1888 = 76
1889 = 75
1890 = 64
1891 = 63
1892 = 55
1893 = 60
1894 = 58
1895 = 56
1896 = 56
1897 = 56
1898 = 68
1899 = 65
1900 = 76

Source: L. Isserlis, cited in B. R. Mitchell, *Abstract of British Historical Statistics* (Cambridge University Press, 1962), p. 224.

(Reproduced by permission of Cambridge University Press.)

The imprint of the pattern of boom and slump on the waterside labour market was considerably more marked than it was in industry generally, because of the sensitivity of foreign trade to that cycle, and – overwhelmingly – because of the dominance of the casual-hiring system. By contrast, although the gas industry suffered seasonal fluctuations of demand, it experienced neither the full impact of trade swings nor the rigours of casual employment. The relative stability of the Gasworkers' Union through the 1890s, noted above, is largely explained by this.

Changing Technologies

The major technological change affecting the port industry at this time was the displacement of sailing ships by steamships. This was of course a long, if inexorable, process. It experienced no particular moments of intensity, so it does not help explain the rapid shifts in the fortunes of the new waterside unions. Certainly the conversion to steam was in full swing over the period 1889–95 (see table 5.3).

The changeover did not lead to economy in the use of labour in the

Fig. 5.1 Steamship prices, £ per net registered ton, present estimate, Cairncross's, and Gray's series, 1850–1920

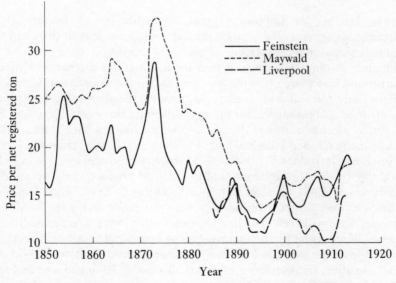

Fig. 5.2 Steamship prices, £ per net registered ton, present estimate, Maywald's series, and prices paid by Liverpool shipowners, 1850–1913

Source: Charles H. Feinstein and Sydney Pollard (eds), *Studies in Capital Formation in the United Kingdom, 1750–1920* (Oxford University Press, 1988), p. 343. (Reproduced by permission of Oxford University Press.)

Table 5.3   *The Conversion from Sail to Steam, 1878–1915*

	Sailing Ships		Steamships	
	No.	000 tons	No.	000 tons
1878	21,058	4,239	4,826	2,316
1888	15,025	3,114	6,871	4,350
1889	14,640	3,041	7,139	4,718
1890	14,181	2,936	7,410	5,043
1891	13,823	2,972	7,720	5,307
1892	13,578	3,080	7,950	5,565
1893	13,239	3,038	8,088	5,740
1894	12,943	2,987	8,263	5,969
1895	12,617	2,867	8,386	6,122
1900	10,773	2,096	9,209	7,208
1905	10,059	1,671	10,522	9,065
1910	9,090	1,113	12,000	10,443
1915	8,019	779	12,771	11,650

Source: B. R. Mitchell, *Abstract of British Historical Statistics* (Cambridge University Press, Cambridge, 1962), pp. 218–19.

(Reproduced by permission of Cambridge University Press.)

ports, but it did impose a great intensification of labour effort. Steamships represented a much greater capital investment than had the sailing ships they displaced. This fact compelled their owners to schedule minimum periods in port for loading and discharge. Quicker turnround was more effective use of an expensive investment. Competition – between sail and steam, and between the shipping companies – intensified this pressure. But the intensification was not achieved, in the main, by mechanization of the labour process. In a few special trades, like grain-discharge and coal-handling, elevators and steam-driven machinery were being introduced at this time. Elsewhere productivity grew in sweat and toil, by greater exploitation of the manual processes and by allotting more work-gangs to each ship and hatchway.[10] True, some technical advances were under way; but they were not about easing the burden of labour. Steam-driven winches on board ship were a new, additional means of speeding up the manual-labour process of transferring cargoes to and from the ship's hold. There remained, through all this period and for long after, an abundance of cheap, disposable labour to hire and fire, to maim and discard. There was simply no incentive for employers to rationalize on labour use, or to cut down the potential dock labour force. The difficulties encountered, even by skilled groups such as stevedores, in maintaining closed and restricted entry to their jobs, reinforced this employer indifference, which was indeed aggravated by the depression of the early 1890s.

The Employers' Counterattack

The pressure for greater work intensity was redoubled as, after the prosperous years of the late 1880s, the squeeze on prices and profits in the fiercely competitive shipping business resumed. Spurred by competition, the industry gave a classic response: the strong ate the weak. Larger and larger units of ownership emerged, leading to oligopoly. In 1889 the figure who symbolized opposition to the new union during the great London strike was Mr Norwood. He stood for the purely local, fragmented capital as a member of the Joint Committee of London dock companies, wharfingers and stevedoring contractors. Within two years, labour policy had fallen under the domination of the great shipping magnates, who, although often based in the major provincial ports of Liverpool, Hull and Southampton, represented the new, internationally orientated concentrations of maritime capital. Even in London the dock companies after 1889 moved to hand over their cargo-handling function increasingly to the shipowners.

In all ports, regardless of their peculiarities, the combination of trade-cycle downswing and competitive pressures ensured that the employers' tolerance of the new unions would be shortlived. The force of new unionism was to be confronted by the counterforce of a fighting, militant, anti-union employers' organization: the Shipping Federation, formed just twelve months after the 1889 strike. Its purpose was to break the recently created union controls by the forcible introduction of what it called 'free labour', but which was really quite simply non-union labour. This process was not confined to the waterfront, but it achieved its most open and brutal expression there.

'Formal organisations of employers', reported the Royal Commission on Labour in 1894, 'usually make their appearance at a later date than those of the workmen and arise for purposes of joint resistance, when individual employers find themselves too weak to cope with the growing strength of trade unions.'[11] The historian Elie Halevy was impressed with this judgement, even though he had no illusions about employer pacifism in the years following the birth of the new unionism. By 1892, he reported, there were seventy associations of employers, a dozen of which had been formed since the beginning of the decade. The oldest local association originated in 1865. The first National Federation had been brought together in 1873 'in consequence of the extraordinary development, oppressive action, far reaching but openly avowed designs, and elaborate organization of the trade unions'.[12] It had withered away after a few years, but its revival was proposed amongst employers in the early 1890s, once the agenda of the new unions had made itself understood in the boardrooms:

Already there were many districts completely industrialised, where the employers' sole resource, when the union had declared war upon them, was to introduce labour from outside. They found such labour in the eastern counties – Norfolk and Suffolk – where trade unionism hardly existed. They found it in Ireland which for a century past had furnished British capitalism with the 'reserve army', to use Marx's phrase, which it needed. The new hands thus engaged were brought by railway and taken to barracks where they were confined, out of reach of the strikers' persuasions and threats, so long as they worked . . . but was it impossible to improve on this makeshift? The employers . . . were asking themselves whether it would not be worthwhile to form from the ranks of non-unionist labour, a permanent 'reserve', a 'reserve' in the strict sense, ready to give their assistance the moment they were called up.[13]

The state, and the press, would need to adopt new roles appropriate to the reinforcement of this strategy if it were to succeed. *Laissez-faire* had to be reaffirmed in Labour affairs. In its cause, the judiciary would be required to remove the limited legal supports afforded to strikes and picketing. The police and military would need to be deployed to protect the free labourers and harass the pickets. Newspapers, in which shipping magnates acquired large interests, could usefully assist in turning the sympathy engendered during the great London strike into anti-union, anti-socialist alarm. It is this consciously chosen line of march which, more than any other factor, determined the experience of the new unions during their first decade of existence, including their sharp turn to political action.

Honeymoon in London

In the London docks, the reorganized Dockers' Union's first task after the strike was to secure its control over the labour supply – in other words, to enforce a closed shop. The blacklegs who were in place after the strike were paid off with a week's wages by the union itself, and then allowed to join the union and take their turn as casuals at the call-on. The majority of the 1,100 treated thus prudently disappeared from the waterside. The companies actually facilitated this process, and at least two managers/directors symbolized their support by joining the union themselves. The union's card became 'the only passport to work',[14] and enrolled not only the permanent and casual labourers, but also many officials and foremen. Yet some foremen, conscious of their ambiguous role, formed their own union; they also had grievances, which they felt required separate representation. Of this honeymoon period, Smith and Nash enthuse: 'It is greatly to the credit of the Companies that they have so heartily recognised and encouraged the Union'.[15]

The problem of the casual docker – the irregularity of work and income – was not of course solved by the settlement of the strike. By the standards of unskilled labour, the dockers did regard their hourly rates as high, but 'tolerably steady employment' was as remote as before. Harry Quelch, the leader of the South Side Labour Protection League, thought that in 1891 25 per cent of dockers earned £1 a week, 25 per cent earned 5s., and 50 per cent earned less than 5s.[16] Joseph Falvy of the Rotherhithe and Bermondsey corn-porters thought that of the 2–3,000 corn-porters involved, only 20 per cent put in a full week's work, and that many did not average one full day per week.[17] Tom McCarthy, in his evidence to the Royal Commission on Labour in 1891, thought that 6 per cent had permanent, year-long work, 10 per cent got ten months' work, 12 per cent averaged eight months, 16 per cent worked only six months, 20 per cent got four months, while 36 per cent found three or fewer months' work in a year. McCarthy also estimated that the average improvement in earnings flowing from the strike and unionization was about 4s. a week.

At this time – 1891 – the employers still engaged a majority of union members, according to several witnesses before the Royal Commission. But they did so with growing reluctance, and were beginning a long-drawn-out process of cutting back on the dockers' gains. Joseph Falvy was asked if it were not true that 'the attitude of the employers towards the unions is one of passive hostility and in some cases of active opposition?' He answered:

> Quite so. While we have the majority with us it will be so, but the moment the employers get the majority it will be the other way. Seeing that in nearly every case we are unionists, at present we have the whip hand . . . I will give you the words of one employer . . . He said: 'I am with you, because you have the majority, but the moment that you are in a minority, I shall be against you'. Those were the words of a very large employer of labour.

The question was followed up: 'The employers now will only take on union men?' 'Yes, in the majority of cases.'[18]

A balance of forces which both sides knew to be precarious was tipped against the union by trends in trade and in technology, and above all by the employers' intent. The new unions were squeezed out of their strong points in London over a period of some years, not, as Clegg and his colleagues were to claim, 'eased out' in twelve months 'with scarcely a ripple of public interest'.[19] The Dockers' Union retained 10,000 docker members in London down to 1891, and 8,500 in 1892.[20]

London Employers Turn the Screw

From November 1890, in their war of attrition, the employers reverted to the old plus system, cancelling the access of workers' representatives to the books by which, since the strike, they had been able to check the bonus for their jobs. The employers also stopped the agreed payment for a half-hour meal break. They reimposed the foremen's choice of workers, and the practice by which a foreman could engage 'outsiders' – his friends, lodgers, men who bought him beer in the pubs – once again became rampant. Royal Commission witnesses, both union officials and working dockers, insisted that this was a deliberate policy: those engaged commonly had no background in the docks and the purpose was the weakening of the union. Ben Tillett confirmed the trend to renege on the 1889 agreement 'in so far that they close the books against us . . . [and] have also ignored the right of the men to choose their associates in working'.[21]

The erosion of the so-called co-operative system had not been uniformly achieved by all employers at the time the Royal Commission took evidence. Tom McCarthy reported that the big shipping companies were operating as follows:

> The system that now obtains is the union placing itself in the position of the middleman and giving work to the men, though it takes no profit, and does not immediately supervise the work. The men themselves elect their own foremen, bosses, and superintendents, and the Union does not interfere except to see generally that they carry out their contract.[22]

A stevedore who ignored his union's decision not to appear before the Commission told yet another story which illustrates the climate during that same year. His union had traditionally enjoyed a closed shop, had entered into only one dispute in twelve years (with the exception of their sympathetic participation in the dockers' great strike) and had enjoyed peaceful bargaining relations with their employers, 'but in the last fifteen or eighteen months we have been continually in hot water.' He ascribed the change, startlingly abrupt, to 'the action of nothing else but the Shipping Federation': after the great strike 'we had a comparatively quiet time till the formation of this Federation'. A major dispute leading to a strike of the 'coalies' (who bunkered steam ships whilst the stevedores were loading the vessels) had prompted the Shipping Federation to introduce free labour to embark the coal: 'They are keeping these men, supporting them in some shed in one of the docks'.[23] In their incompetence, the free labourers dropped coal on and around the stevedores working below them. After an abusive exchange with the stevedores, the coalies began hurling lumps of coal, while the dock police looked on without intervening: the blackleg coalies were seen as privileged and protected *provocateurs*.

The stevedores' problem with the 'federationists' – free labour brought in by the Shipping Federation, and regarded by unionists as 'the riff-raff of the world'[24] – was confined to those operations where the shipowners or brokers undertook loading. Their relations with the dwindling numbers of small master-stevedores remained one of mutual recognition and respect. The other problem they faced in common with the dock labourers was the spreading use of 'permanent' men, engaged on weekly contracts by the employers. It was not an entirely new practice, but in the climate of mass unionization the unions had a much stronger motive for overcoming this division of status within the workforce; and the employer had an equally strong instinct to divide and rule through conferring enhanced security on a minority of the men. We shall examine the operations of the Shipping Federation in detail later, because they affected not only the Port of London, but new unionism throughout provincial docklands. First, it is worth looking at the threat to the unions' near monopoly posed by permanents and other grades of preferred labour under the classification system developed by the London Dock Companies.

The London Classification System

The companies issued a directive to their officials and foremen in September 1890 requiring that men engaged for work should be 'carefully selected, physically strong, and the permanent men are only to be within the years of twenty-three and thirty'.[25] Bills to this effect were fly-posted all over the East End. Obviously they implied a direct challenge to union policies of work-sharing with the old and sick, which persisted down to modern times. The chosen permanents were worked for up to eighty hours a week, and as the 'co-operative' system and union control of hiring outside the dock gate was eroded in this period, it became increasingly difficult for it to police and frustrate this development. Harry Quelch explained the effect of the system to the Royal Commission, and to a bewildered Professor Alfred Marshall, one of the Commissioners. 'Witness after witness', said the Professor, 'has admitted that the rates of pay per hour are so very high, that if tolerably steady employment could be got the condition of the dockers would be thoroughly satisfactory.'[26] Since the weekly wage system improved regularity of earnings, he went on, why on earth did the dockers and their union oppose its extension? Quelch replied:

> It only tends to increase steady employment for a few, and it reduces the number of men employed, because a weekly man has to do anything. A weekly man dare not refuse anything that he is asked to do. A casual man will not do it: a casual man will not work under price . . . being casual men they [say]: 'We do not depend upon you for employment, you can either pay us the extra halfpenny or pay us our money, and we will knock off if you like.'[27]

Quelch went on to argue that a tradesman with a scarce skill might retain a measure of independence whilst working on a weekly engagement, but that the unskilled could not: 'I do not object to casual employment if there were more of it, but it is so exceedingly limited.'[28]

The Dockers' Dilemma

This posed a fundamental dilemma for the new unions in dockland. They sought a union monopoly, which could be achieved in theory either by the widest possible enrolment of all potential, casual labour, or by pursuing the stevedores' road of restricting entry to a smaller, more regularly employed force. In time, the dockers came to learn that the latter was not an option for the mass of non-specialists who comprised the bulk of the Dockers' Union membership.

But the other route to control was frustrated by the employers' recruitment of 'outsiders'. At the retail level, these might be farmworkers or the foreman's friends. Wholesale, far more sinister, collectively and aggressively, they were found by the Shipping Federation's deployment of 'free labour'. The restrictive policy had been tried: Tom Mann issued an instruction to the London docks branches of the new union in 1890, calling on them to cease further enrolments. In the same period, the union advised branches to enrol only able-bodied men who were fit and strong, and to exclude 'weaklings'. This was intended as a conciliatory gesture to the employers, who complained consistently that productivity had collapsed as the power of the union had grown. We have already noted this consequence of the great strike (see chapter 4) and seen how the union had then felt obliged to exhort its members to provide 'a fair day's work for a fair day's pay'.

Harry Quelch's answers to the distinguished economist (who was clearly no sort of sociologist) underlines the problem facing both employers and union. Quelch, though a paid official of a docks union, articulated the rank-and-file response of the older, more sectional docks tradition. The responses to the dilemma from the new, inclusive and potentially general union, seeking to consolidate its precarious hold in dockland by wider recruitment at one stage, and by restricted entry at another, were full of inconsistencies. Some spokesmen at the Royal Commission found themselves advocating the extension of the permanent force, while others wavered, as the Commissioners pressed home the virtue of that system from the labourers' point of view. The dockers' grievance was irregularity of work and earnings: why not then accept the spread of permanent employment? The union recognized the Catch 22 in the question and had no official and consistent answer.

A working docker who testified before the Royal Commission summed up all this ambivalence:

I believe myself that this classification system that they have with the joint committee is for their [the dockers'] benefit, because there is a greater number of men employed now working more regularly than what there were then. But if they were to carry it out in its entirety it would be better: they do not do so. They bring favoured individuals in between the classified men, so that it actually leaves the outsiders, or the remnant, far worse off even than the favoured few. But, of course, there are a greater number of men regularly employed than there used to be.[29]

At this point, a Commissioner, Sir Michael Hicks-Beach, asked: 'Do you consider it, so far as it goes, a good thing or a bad thing?' The docker replied: *'If they could all be employed'* (authors' italics). Hicks-Beach pressed his point: 'But I want you to speak of the actual state of things: do you consider it better in that respect, or worse than it was?' 'For the remnant that is outside, it is far worse, but for those employed it is better, and there are more of them employed now than what there used to be.'[30]

Amongst dock-union officials, the inconsistency of approach to the problem was all too plain. Harry Quelch, as we have seen, came closest to expressing the men's position. 'There is a strong feeling amongst waterside labourers generally against the making of permanent men as they are termed.'[31] Tom McCarthy found himself defending the union against the charge that it had discouraged the spread of permanent employment:

Taking things as they are, do you think that it would be a good step, to start with, to reduce the number of men who are employed at the docks, and to get for those men more regular employment? – I do: always remembering there is a big surplus of unemployed. *Has not the action of the Trades Unions been in the opposite sense?* – I do not think I can say so: so far as I have known, no. If it appears to have been so, it has always been because of having to look after those who could do little work. *Why are you obliged to look after them?* – If I spoke in a bare business-like sense, I would say because they are members of a Trade Union: but generally speaking, because they remember that their own position as workers is unsafe, and that they at any time may become recruits in the ranks of the unemployed . . . *Do you see any reason why the old traditions of the docks should be maintained, and the docks should continue to be a last recourse for those who have been unfortunate elsewhere?* – I do not see why that should not be altered. *And is not the right way to do that to increase the number of permanent men?* – Undoubtedly it is: it is the best means. *But have you not passed a resolution against that?*–Not that I am aware of.[32]

Finally, we may overhear Ben Tillett attempting to cope with similar questions:

is it your opinion that if the dock authorities settle on a certain number of men as available for employment in the docks, that would stop the influx? – It would stop it, or would go a long way towards stopping it. *Men knowing they were not on the staff, so to speak, and could not get a job, would not go there?* – That is so. *Do you think, if by that means you could raise the wages and conditions of a limited number of men, that would be better than having an unlimited number of men who get starvation wages?* – Yes, there would be better organisation. *And would you recommend that?* – I would recommend that. Only in admitting that I would point out that the Dock Companies are not in the position to absolutely guarantee a large number of men work. It is work that is of so fluctuating a character that they may employ 4,000 one day, and require 15,000 the next. So that unless we could make them responsible for the difference between 4,000 and 15,000 it would be an advantage to them, because they could introduce fresh men constantly, and it would be to their benefit to have a drifting number of workmen going to the docks, so that those in will be anxious to keep their place, and those out anxious to get in.[33]

This problem was to live on, albeit in modified forms, until the 1967 decasualization scheme. The reason is evident: the employers' approach to decasualization was always partial. It was in the highest degree convenient to have both a staff of permanent men and a casual pool to call upon when traffic was heavy. A total decasualization, with the maximum coverage, would have represented a heavy economic cost to the industry, and at the same time solved the union's problem, giving it vastly greater power. It is not at all difficult to discern the motivations of the employers in maintaining those conditions, and hence the historical intractability of the issue.

Casualism and Social Reformers

The social reformers Charles Booth, Sydney Buxton, Smith and Nash, however, were continually pressing their nostrums on the employers. The influence of a public opinion which had been awoken by the dock strike became, as the strike receded in time, an asset for this lobby. By invoking the motive of social reform, the employers appealed to humanitarian sentiment. But their purpose was to reimpose control over their labourers, and their reforms were always partial and directed to the unspoken goal. The public view is clearly expressed in the Commissioners' questions to the trade-union witnesses, on the subject of reform of the casual-labour system.

The employers' responses varied. The use of the classification system was confined to the Dock Companies and their Joint Committee. These sought to capitalize on the reforming schemes of Booth, which they could turn to advantage in two ways. They could use them, as we have described, to divide the labour force, and to smash union controls. At the same time, by appealing to the apparent social benefits of such schemes, they could disguise their real motives and assume the mantle of morally responsible reformers. Very soon they were to move decisively in this direction.

On 24 November 1890 the secretary of the Employers' Federation issued a public statement: 'It is the object of my directors to reduce the amount of casual employment at the docks, and secure as far as possible regular work for all classes of labourers in each department. My directors will always be ready to investigate grievances, and redress them whenever they are proved to exist.' The dockers knew only too well that this last sentence was sheer humbug, and that those who complained, or were visible as union activists, were already subject to transparent discrimination at the call-stands. As the companies' use of casuals diminished, their numbers seeking and failing to find work actually expanded, making such victimization all the easier.

Secondary instruments in the companies' struggle to undermine the union monopoly came to hand when, in the aftermath of the great strike, the foremen and permanent hands formed their own unions: the Association of Foremen and Clerks of the Docks, Wharves and Warehouses, and the Permanent Labourers' Mutual Protection Association. Both groups were segregated from the dock communities. The Permanent Labourers' Association was regarded by the dockers as a company union.[34]

The success of the 1889 strike, and the resultant publicity, had allowed the reformers to separate out the 'legitimate' claims of labour from the 'social disease' of casualism, and to define and isolate a destitute stratum, identified by its moral as well as its physical decay. If separated from a stabilized and unionized workforce, this stratum ceased to appear as a political threat and became a social problem, for which Booth's solutions were the formation of 'labour colonies', the poorhouse or prison.[35] Booth's counsel boiled down to three steps: restrict admission to the docks, increase the internal mobility of the workforce and allow the casual element to 'drift away'. According to D. F. Wilson, it was Booth himself who drew up the companies' classification scheme.[36] (Booth's family business was in Liverpool Shipping.) This advice was adopted and followed through persistently, with the result that, by 1904, less than 2 per cent of the Dock Companies' daily employed workforce was made up of casuals. The full record is shown in table 5.4.

Enter the Shipping Federation

The scheme applied, of course, to a dwindling sector of the labour force as the Dock Companies yielded more of their cargo-handling function to the shipowners, who were ready with their own, much blunter, response to new unionism, in the shape of the Shipping Federation, formed in

Table 5.4   *London and India Docks: Percentage of Engagements Given to Weekly and Preference Men, 1887–1904*

	Weekly	Preference
1887	17.0	n.a.
1891	33.5	n.a.
1894	65.6	28.8
1900	62.7	23.8
1904	78.4	19.7

Source: Gordon Phillips and Noel Whiteside, *Casual Labour: The Unemployment Question in the Port Transport Industry, 1880–1970* (Oxford University Press, 1985), p. 50.
(Reproduced by permission of Oxford University Press.)

September 1890. The immediate stimulus to its creation was the setting up of a Union of Shipmasters and Officers, of which Havelock Wilson became 'general manager' with autocratic powers. Wilson's main union – the NSFU – then struck against ships on which, before sailing, the master and officers refused to join the new body, members of which were expected to engage only Seamen's Union members as crew. The Seamen's Union was already applying other pressures at many ports to establish and enforce its closed shop, often with the assistance of dockers and their unions, who became involved in a series of blacking actions against non-union ships in dock.

The objects of the Shipping Federation were formally described to the Royal Commission by its general manager, George Laws, as being:

> for the purpose of maintaining liberty of contract and resisting the new union methods of coercion, more especially the tactics adopted by the National Amalgamated Sailors' and Firemen's Union . . . whose instructions to members are entirely subversive of discipline in the merchant service, and have resulted in a degree of insubordination seriously menacing the security of life and property at sea.[37]

The official historian of the Federation, L. H. Powell, acknowledges the militant spirit of the founders, who regarded it as 'a "permanent battle-axe" . . . against "oppression and abuse" '.[38] 'From the first,' he goes on, 'the Federation was founded as a fighting machine to counter the strike weapon, and it made no secret of the fact.'[39]

Within a month Federation membership, augmented by the adherence of the great liner companies such as the P. & O., represented 6.5 million out of a total of 7.4 million of British merchant tonnage. It set up offices in the principal ports, at which it issued its 'Federation ticket', entitling the holder to preferential engagement in return for a promise to work alongside both union and non-union crew members.

Free Labour and Unfree Unions

As its coverage extended throughout Britain's ports, the Federation organized large mobilizations of strike-breakers, transported and accommodated them, and provided strong-arm protection squads to break the strikes of both seamen and dock workers. The whole operation was systematically planned. Ex-police officers were often engaged as organizers and recruiting agents. Some of their methods were reminiscent of the press-gangs – they were quite capable of taking away by the cartload men whom they had first made drunk.

The Federation had enormous financial resources, raised through a levy on the tonnage owned by the affiliated companies. 'The funds at its disposal . . . could certainly buy up any trade union in England over and over again'.[40]

A series of strikes, involving either seamen or dockers, and frequently both, swept round the country immediately following the Federation's formation. The list of their locations reads like a roll-call of Britain's ports. All concerned the issue of free labour. In most cases, the *casus belli* was the presence of a non-union crew in a ship due to be loaded or unloaded, which was blacked by the dockers. This provoked the importation of more free labour to break the resulting dock strike. In the period between September 1890 and April 1891, there were strikes of this character at Leith (where the shipowner became the first to apply to the Federation, then just three days old, for a supply of free labour, which performed both ship and dock work for him); Bowness (dockers versus a free crew); Grangemouth (a pay strike broken by free labour); Dundee (dockers versus free crew – strike broken); Garston; Barrow (from whence came the 'blacked' ship which provoked the Garston strike); and then, in December, a major conflict in London, to which we shall return below.

Next came a small dispute involving the Federation in Hull, met by imported free labour from Liverpool. The union retreated, but in good order; Hull's great trial of strength was postponed for two more years. The London stevedores failed to carry their members in resistance to free labour in March, whilst in February there had been a major strike of seamen and dockers against the Federation ticket in Aberdeen. Newry dockers struck against the employment of a single free-labour stevedore in March. The list also included a Dublin dockers' strike over the method of discharge and manning of a ship. In that case, free-labour intervention generated a wave of strikes, as lightermen would not handle the corn discharged by the blacklegs, the railwaymen would not touch it either, and finally the millers and the bakers would not grind the corn or bake the flour which reached them from the free-labour vessel. At Bristol, free labour was supplied by the Federation from London in June, and succeeded in breaking a dockers' strike occasioned by the engagement of non-union dockers. This concluded the catalogue proudly presented by George Laws to the Royal Commission.[41]

The Federation responded in every one of these cases with the despatch of free labourers to the point of the dispute; violence was a common consequence and police protection was always afforded to the strike-bearers. Laws's account gives a vivid impression of the extent of the resources available to him, as well as of the vast logistical scale of the operation. Of the Aberdeen strike he reported:

> We had to send men up at considerable expense, and when the dockers saw that, they also came out in what they called a sympathetic strike, and we had to supply dockers. I may say that at that time there was, and at the present there is, any amount of free labour in the country to be had at any time, at any rate, and good labour too. At any rate, the work of the port was done, and the strike after about a fortnight or three weeks collapsed.[42]

He might have been speaking of the supply, quality and price of potatoes.

The London Strike, 1891

We must now retrace our steps to the London strike of December 1891. In 1890 three major shipping lines in the upstream docks made a determined drive to break the Seamen's Union control by shifting the place of hiring from the shipping offices, where union officers could check on union membership, to the ships themselves. At the same time, they insisted on the men's taking up the Shipping Federation ticket, with its commitment to work with non-unionists. The United Labour Council as we have seen (chapter 3) was by no means a representative federation. Nevertheless it called for united action against the Shipping Federation's attack, with the publication of the famous 'Wade's Arms Manifesto', which called on all port workers to strike on the vessels of the shipping lines involved. At first, only the coal-porters responded, the Dockers' Union not having participated in the decision, and only a minority of the stevedores' branches having attended the decisive meeting of the ULC. The Shipping Federation installed free labourers from Kent to do the coaling, housing them in sheds and ships at anchor. Eventually the dockers and stevedores joined the stoppage, and the docks were flooded with free labour, although the dispute never reached the proportions of a port-wide strike.

The powerful, aggressive tactics of the Shipping Federation, coupled with the Dock Companies' breach of the 1889 settlement, brought the Dockers' Union and the SSLPL together into a representative body, the Federation of Trade and Labour Unions connected with the Shipping, Carrying and other Industries, in January 1891. It affiliated twenty-five unions in 1890–1, rising to forty-two in 1895. It appointed Clem Edwards[43] as general secretary, and he had now the assistance of Tom Mann, Tom McCarthy and Thomas Walsh (of the Seamen's Union) in conducting the 'Wade's Arms' dispute and negotiating with the Shipping Federation. The owners' Federation conducted the conflict with total intransigence. Indeed, the contrast with the employers' defensive postures of two years earlier was complete. George Laws ensured an appropriate supply of strike-breaking labour. Moreover, using all the weight of his status, he secured the collaboration of the top Police Commissioner to protect the strike-breakers when the dock police force proved inadequate.[44] Laws, or at least his enthusiastic dockside agents, also appears to have armed strike-breakers with revolvers, some of which were discharged in the mêlées which ensued between pickets and free labourers. Clem Edwards told the Royal Commission of many incidents, including this:

during the dispute in progress at Wapping there was [a] man seen with a revolver. The police refused to interfere with him, and at least in ten or twelve cases men have appeared at loop-holes at the Carron and Hermitage Wharves, have presented revolvers at the pickets outside and have threatened to shoot them. We have approached the police officers in charge, and in every case they have declined to interfere in the matter, saying that they have no right on the wharf, and so on.[45]

The authorities' response to Laws stands in marked contrast:

I . . . saw Sir Edward Bradford and the other Commissioners, and I am bound to say that they quite realised the position. I pointed out that these men should be got into the docks, and on board these ships, in a condition to work . . . the most effective arrangements were made by the police. They adopted our plan . . . and everything was done in the most quiet and orderly way.

After the police withdrew:

a mob of coalies whose places had been taken assembled . . . and commenced to hoot and ill-use and to stone the men in the barges below. We again had to apply to Scotland Yard, the dock police being utterly useless . . . but the Metropolitan police cleared the docks and the work went on. Then we enabled all these vessels to sail.[46]

With these forces at its command, the Shipping Federation's 'negotiation' with the union federation was perfunctory: Edwards and Mann made concession after concession, only to be met with escalating demands, including the full withdrawal of the Wade's Arms Manifesto and the surrender of their whole position on the disputed liners. The strike petered out, and the ship-owners retained the imported free labourers, not only as coalies but also as general dock labourers and as stevedores, engaged by a Federation office on the Albert Dock. The strike, said Laws, was 'utterly defeated'.

This disastrous episode laid the foundation for the subsequent decline of London port unionism for the rest of the decade. The stevedores, still having a (dwindling) enclave of recognition with the small masters, withdrew from further sympathetic actions, having lost much in the Wade's Arms affair through their support for the seamen. The lightermen reacted in similar fashion. The hopes of 1889, that sectionalism might be washed away in the tide of new unionism, were disappointed. The Dockers' Union now moved to alleviate its exposed and weakened position by effecting, in September 1891, a merger of Clem Edwards's federation and the United Labour Council.

An appeal from the dockers for solidarity action in a strike at Wapping wharf followed immediately, but was rebuffed by the stevedores, intent on preserving their closed shop in the upstream part of the port even though their problems at Tilbury, where cement combines forced the master-stevedores to break their traditional relations with the union, came more and more to resemble those of the dockers. Faced with the choice of responding to these trends in either 'open' or 'closed' ways, the stevedores chose to retreat into their laager, even whilst trade continued for the rest of the decade to move away, downstream. In the Royal Docks group, the Dockers' Union maintained its status as the biggest British district in the union until 1900. In 1895 it sought without success to form a new tripartite federation with the South Side Labour Protection League and Sexton's National Union of Dock Labourers. The following year, it had more success in initiating the International Federation of Ship, Dock and River Workers.

None of these initiatives created an effective weapon with which to combat triumphant free labour, and the hegemony established by the Shipping Federation. Instead, the London scene was further clouded by accusations of poaching levelled at the stevedores by Ben Tillett.

Examining Free Labour – Under the Stone

Before turning to review the provincial defeats inflicted on the unions by the Shipping Federation, it is relevant to notice some further features of the free-labour movement. We have noted the Shipping Federation's command of resources – one source suggests that its funds ran to £100 million[47] – its ready access to blackleg labour, its willingness to arm it, and the ease with which it called up weighty police protection.

Further evidence is available on the unscrupulous nature of its operations. A 'crimp' is defined in the Oxford English Dictionary as 'an agent who procures seamen, soldiers, etc., especially by decoying or impressing them'. Crimping houses had long existed in the seaports of Britain and the agents of the Shipping Federation used them to recruit blackleg crews. At the same time, the Federation officially discouraged the use of this source of labour, preferring the crimps to bring their recruits directly to the Federation hiring offices. But this was simply a new, higher form of crimping, since the Federation, not being itself a shipowner, had no more right than the backstreet crimps to issue an engagement to a seaman. Only the *bona fide* servant of an owner had such a right under the Merchant Shipping Act.

When the Federation sacked an agent for practising his crimping unofficially, he left in disgust, asserting that 'the officials of the Federation are as great crimpers as anybody else'.[48] Needless to say, a summons brought in 1908 by the Seamen's Union against the Federation for breach of the crimping section of the Merchant Shipping Act was dismissed.[49]

The Federation's own advice to its members often included the use of the courts to enforce the disciplinary and contractual aspects of the same Act on to their employees. As John Saville has shown, the Federation's militant anti-unionism campaign, directed against the picketing, black-ings and strike methods of new unionism, was reinforced by a wave of hostile judicial findings which came to a climax in the Taff Vale case of 1901.[50]

Nor was the Shipping Federation without imitators. The Engineering Employers followed its lead later in the decade. The Liberty and Property Defence League and the National Free Labour Association emerged at this time to add their choruses of praise for 'freedom of contract' and the virtues of *laissez-faire* – the former from the perspective of High Tory landed and Liberal commercial interests,[51] the latter as the voice of anti-union, right-wing working-class men.[52] *The Times* inveighed persistently and at length against the 'tyranny' of new unionism and its socialist leadership in a sustained campaign consciously aimed at shifting public, judicial and political opinion in favour of all-out war against the unions.

Campaigns for tariff-reform began to win working-class sympathies, and were taken up by the free-labour movement. There was mounting evidence that the great Liberal Party industrialists had turned against trade unionism where it challenged them in their own mills, quarries and waterfronts. Rosebery's administration was no model of competence. In the summer of 1895 it resigned, and the alienated mood of Liberal supporters ensured it had no chance of holding on to office. A Tory government took power: whatever reforms in labour relations might have emerged from the copious inquiries and publications of the Royal Commission on Labour, which completed its string of volumes in 1894, were now stillborn. The only legislation conceded by Salisbury's administration was the weak, voluntaristic Conciliation Act of 1896. In this climate, the mildly corporatist wing of opinion within the Board of Trade, which issued the first of its Reports on Profit Sharing in 1894, went without any real hearing.

Although the Royal Commission produced no results as such, it had afforded to a great coalition of ruling-class forces, political, commercial and academic, a unique insight into the minds of the new unionists and into the links that were established there between unionism and socialism. The ruling classes did not always understand what they heard, but they knew that they did not like it: they knew that it was different from the old unionism with which they were familiar. (Even the Shipping Federation protested that it was not anti-union, only that it required port and seaboard unionism to conform to the 'old model'.)

William Collison and the National Free Labour Association

William Collison formed the National Free Labour Association (NFLA) in May 1893, by which time the Shipping Federation was two and a half years old. He was an East Ender, the son of a policeman, and had drifted into casual labouring work in and around the London docks. He joined the socialist and trade-union agitations of the late 1880s and came to know intimately the principal leaders of that movement. He became a bus-driver and initiated the organization of the passenger-transport workers of London.

In his autobiography, an extraordinary study of a larger-than-life character, he displays a pugilistic, egotistic, yet oddly sensitive personality. In his bid to dominate the meetings of the busmen's union, he clashed with its president, Thomas Sutherst and was expelled from the union's meetings and deprived of office in 1891. The experience undoubtedly led him to revise his pro-union views, though he claimed that his conversion to the cause of free labour came from reading Charles Reade's novel *Put Yourself in his Place* (1870). Collison recounts how, following his humiliation at the hands of Sutherst, he determined to 'escape all thoughts of Trade Unionism, all consideration of the problems of capital and labour, all questions of industrial collectivism and individualism'. In this mood he read the novel, picked up at a second-hand stall. 'The message of that book to me was that the best retreat from Trade Unionism lies in attack. The book said: "Fight the Unions", and from the moment I realized the possibility I saw life anew'.[53] Collison, from this moment, did indeed become a fervent, dogmatic and energetic advocate of all the values and ideology of *laissez-faire*. He was always more than a mere labour agent for capital, though he fulfilled that function readily. His strange personality is illustrated by his account of his last meeting with Eleanor Marx, worth quoting at length:

When I first met Eleanor Marx at the Democratic Club – a place where the people of high ideals and low morals used to congregate in a cellar – she asked me, as she was fond of asking young people, what goal I was aiming for, what end I hoped to attain.

I told her I could not tell. My mind was drifting then. I admitted I was drawn at times to Socialist theories, but always repelled by Socialistic personalities.

Afterwards, about a year before her death, I met her when her face had faded and all the brilliance had died out of her wonderful eyes. In very truth, I think she was dead then, dead in heart and all womanly hope. Many things had happened since we last met. I had found my goal and my mission in life. I knew what I was doing and why I was doing it. I was as fixed in purpose as I am today. The National Free Labour Association had not only been started, but was working with astonishing success. I was doing what I had vowed to do when I felt for the first time in my heart and soul – as I feel now while I am writing – that modern Trade Unionism is an accursed thing, a greater enemy to this country than any foreign power, a greater enemy to you and me than the bitterest individual enemy of ours that exists; I was not only speaking and thinking against it, but I was actively fighting it.

I was breaking strikes.

I knew the heart and spirit of Eleanor Marx, and I knew how unhappy she would have been to know that I had put an unbridgeable eternity between myself and all those 'democratic' forces, no matter what phase or form they took, which she loved so dearly. I was even uncertain as to whether or not she had heard that the young Collison of old had come out, had taken the sword in his hand and was breaking strikes and the strike-makers. So I said little as we stood in the windy twilight at the corner of Chancery Lane, while I noticed the faded beauty of her face and hopeless eyes and the grief inscribed in deep-drawn lines about the mouth. She seemed a little nervous also. She had a fur or a boa, or a clinging scarf of lace round her neck, and she played with it nervously. Then she said presently with her old laugh, and her old infinite grace:

'And what are you going to do now?'

I shook my head.

'I don't know,' I answered.

'But where are you going to? what are you going to be?' she asked again. I thought I would break the news very gently.

'I think I am going to be a Conservative – one day,' I said half humorously.

She looked at me very seriously, even steadfastly.

'Well,' she said, 'you will find a refuge there; it will be very quiet.'

'Not for me, never,' I answered, with my hand in my coat pocket, feeling a ship's rivet that a Trade Union picket had hurled at my head a week before.

Again she looked at me steadfastly – rather pathetically, and nodded at last in a sort of resigned, serious fashion.

'No,' she said at last, 'you are quite right. You will never be quiet, for they will never forgive you; they would forgive others – but not you.'

And her words were prophetic. And I am exceedingly glad. On the day that the Socialists and the Trade Unionists forgive me I will write out my own memorial card with a steady hand, for my part in life will be finished and the time for rest at hand.'[54]

Collison's National Free Labour Association arrived on the scene fortuitously for the Shipping Federation, as well as for employers in many other industries, intent on following its example. The Federation was finding legal and administrative disadvantages in running its own direct supply of blackleg labour through its network of offices. It therefore subsidised Collison's initiative, thus giving itself the option of using the NFLA as a sub-contracting agent.[55] In this capacity, Collison established his own Free Labour Exchanges and offices in the principal centres of industry and trade, employing local agents – often ex-police officers – who maintained a register of workers who had signed the Free Labour pledge, a promise to work with union or non-union workmates.

But Collison did not confine his role to that of strike-breaker, though he relished the physical conflict involved like a professional soldier. His Association became a propagandist for the crude, individualist philosophy, the *laissez-faire* counterrevolution, which rationalized and underpinned its direct intervention in strikes and the labour market.

Amongst other initiatives, the NFLA was an active promoter of the trend towards restrictive legislation aimed at the freedom to picket and against the whole liberal settlement of trade-union law of the 1870s. In both roles, however, Collison was inevitably the servant of big capital. 'In the 'nineties the NFLA was the creature of the Shipping Federation: in the early years of the new century the role of puppet-master was taken over by the Railway Companies'.[56] Although Collison claimed to have engaged in over sixty strike-breaking incidents, his was not the only free-labour association in a period when, said Tillett, 'Trade Union wrecking and strike-breaking became almost a science'.[57] Collison's personal, and wholly eccentric, relish for his apostolic campaign against trade unionism and socialism survives, in his own words, to re-create for us a lost world of absolute certainties, political pugilism and sheer thuggery. In retrospect he wrote:

the very worst of them who live by the sweat of their jaw have shot their last bolt in invective. No words of theirs can harm me now. In the twenty years'

war that has composed the last twenty years of my life, the whole armoury
of abuse has been exhausted against me. Their sweetest phrase is to call
me 'The King of Blacklegs' or 'The Prince of Scabs'. Even in the obituary
notices which the Trade Unionists used to send me to correct before I
died, there was a wealth of fiery phraseology, trying in its warmth perhaps
to acclimatize me to the heat of the Hades to which demagogues, assuming
for the moment the offices of Amateur Destinies, had consigned my soul.
The general reader . . . may find it hard to understand all this bitterness
. . . Remember that for twenty-one years I have stood up against my own
class. I have not argued with Strike leaders, I have broken strikes.[58]

A man of this kind of crazed integrity was an asset to the employers.
Earlier forms of strike-breaking organization, especially in London's
dockland, had plagued Tillett's efforts before 1889 and had re-emerged
in the early days of the Shipping Federation to colour its own efforts with
corruption and criminality. Collison's movement represented a different
phenomenon, and, unlike the villanous gang-masters of what the dockers
called 'bogus' unions, provided valuable and usable copy for *The Times*.

Yet another form of free-labour organization appeared in purely local
initiatives, such as the Free Labour Association in Southampton, which
emerged from the confused and disastrous strike in that port in October
1890.

A Disaster: Southampton

The Dockers' Union in Southampton had enrolled the majority of the
port's labour force in 1889–90, and in August 1890 the employers had
conceded a wage increase. The union nationally was content with that
settlement, but the Southampton men, led by local lay officials, also
demanded full recognition for the union. At the same time, according to
Tom McCarthy, a rumour circulated that the wage increase was to be
withdrawn. A section of the men came out, and on 7 September the
strike spread to the whole port. (Presumably this was just too early for the
Shipping Federation, formed later in the month, to intervene.) In
London the union's national leaders had refused to sanction strike action
only two weeks previously; Tom Mann and John Burns now sent
personal apeals to Southampton for a resumption of work, and their
executive voted by eleven to four to withhold strike pay. Tillett ignored
telegram appeals for support, and Tom McCarthy called for the
maintenance of the executive's authority 'at all hazard'.[59]

Mass meetings at the docks erupted in violence, the Mayor

lost his head, telegraphed to Portsmouth for 250 troops, the fire brigade
was called out, the police in the neighbourhood were called in to help the
Southampton police; people were driven at the point of the bayonet from

the dock gates, telegrams were despatched to us in London that a serious riot had taken place, and that the people were being beaten by the soldiers.[60]

Tom McCarthy was sent by Mann to Southampton, solely to persuade the men to return to work. Shorn of national union support and intimidated by the force used against them, the men ended their resistance, and their local leader, who had been disowned by the national union, got a three-month prison sentence for a common law offence.

The union in Southampton collapsed, in this case not through the actions of strike-breaking free labour but through disenchantment with its national leaders. We have seen that the union did in general adopt a conciliatory policy in the aftermath of the 1889 strike, and also that it was intent on establishing its central authority everywhere. But it behaved in a wholly inconsistent way over the Southampton dispute. It had recently sanctioned a local wharf dispute in London and it was to engage wholeheartedly in arousing support for the Cardiff dockers in their struggle with the Shipping Federation shortly after the Southampton affair. Tom McCarthy told the Royal Commission that the executive simply decided that it was unnecessary to push the Southampton employers on the recognition issue so soon after they had conceded a wage increase.

However the incident is to be explained, the result was that the Southampton men felt betrayed, tore up their union cards and entered – willingly in many cases – into the Southampton Free Labour Association, set up by the local employers immediately after the strike. Its honorary secretary was the president of the Southampton Chamber of Commerce, and it adopted an elaborate, corporatist constitution, with membership sections for both the employers (forty-four of them) and the dockers (2,200 of them).[61] In 1891 it set up an accident fund, a sick fund and a savings bank, all administered by members' committees.[62] A handful of men retained their union membership, but were deterred from active opposition to the Free Labour Association: the employers took on no one who did not carry its ticket. Tom McCarthy, asked if relations between employers and workers had 'been harmonious of late in Southampton', replied, 'Well, there is order in Warsaw. They must be harmonious, the men have no alternative'.[63]

Tom Mann, as a Commissioner, sought to demonstrate the consequences of the triumph of free labour and elicited from McCarthy an adverse comparison between the conditions and wages at Southampton under its free-labour regime and those at all other major ports. Yet McCarthy finally made a damaging admission: that the union is 'entirely broken up', that it was

practically broken up before the Free Labour Bureau was instituted . . . for the reason that the men left it because the executive would not pay strike

pay, contrary to rule. You see the organisation had not taught them: there
had not been sufficient time to show these men what organisation was
properly, and they had not been accustomed to the discipline and order
and rule of a union. [So the] 'chief reason' [for the débacle was] the
quarrel with the executive in London.[64]

The Southampton affair had far-reaching consequences. Within a
month a Plymouth coal-trade dockers' strike had been broken by
blacklegs under heavy police protection and a Free Labour Association
formed, the secretary being the secretary of the Coal Merchants'
Association. It took members away not only from the Dockers' Union but
also from the Bristol and West of England Labourers' Union and the
Gasworkers' Union. There then followed, in February 1891, the Cardiff
strike, the first major engagement of the Shipping Federation with the
Dockers' Union outside London.

Free Labour Goes to Wales

Just as throughout the rest of the country, the fortunes of the new unions
in South Wales depended in large part upon the employers' attitudes,
and these varied from port to port. Capital for port development in South
Wales came from a variety of sources, but was dominated by the wealth
of the land-owning class, swollen by its ownership of mineral rights. The
Bute Dock Company in Cardiff, financed by the Marquis of Bute,
became the principal owner of the port. In 1894, following its diversion
into railways, it changed its name to the Cardiff Railway Company. It
resisted the demand of Tillett's union for recognition, the closed shop, or
union preference, throughout the period under review. It was supported
in this policy by other railway companies which had interests in the docks
– the Rhimney, Taff Vale, and Barry railway companies. It conceded
recognition to the DWRGWU only in 1915. It was more conciliatory
towards the Trimmers' Union.

In Newport the dock had been developed by Sir Charles Morgan,
prominent Glamorgan landowner, for mineral exporting; in the 1890s it
was under the control of the Alexandra Docks and Railway Company.
Swansea was developed by its Harbour Trust, on which sat the Duke of
Beaufort. Colliery-owners built the Barry Dock and its associated railway
as late as 1889. Port Talbot followed this pattern, opening its Railway
and Dock Company in 1898.

These groups of employers and landlords had an obvious mutual
interest in resisting the encroachments of new unionism, but also faced
each other in the competition for export trades in coal, minerals and the
products of the iron and steel industries. Within this competition, unions
sometimes found space to put down roots. Bute and his Cardiff Railway

Company set the example of intransigence, whilst at Newport similar interests conceded a preference for employing union members.[65]

Following the initial recruitment of members by new unionism, these employers collectively formed the Bristol Channel Association, embracing both banks of the estuary, and fought a joint campaign for wage cuts. This Association was almost as strong as the Shipping Federation, consisting chiefly of the dock companies, especially the timber importers. In South Wales, the new unions formed their own Federation of Trades and Labour Unions for mutual defence against the regional employers. As late as 1891 some wage increases were still being won; but a Swansea strike in 1892 against the free-labour office set up by the employers failed to win union support and its officials, led by Harry Orbell, negotiated what amounted to an acceptance of free labour. The strike collapsed after six weeks and the union went into a severe decline. Between 1891 and 1893 the income of its Swansea branches fell from £2,600 to some £300.[66]

Newport avoided any catastrophic industrial war and, although its membership declined by some 50 per cent, it retained recognition from some of the employers. The leadership was relatively content with the situation there, the chief problem of the period being inter-union rivalry and poaching by the National Amalgamated Labourers' Union.

In Cardiff, the Shipping Federation launched a powerful attack against the Seamen's Union, and the dockers struck in sympathy, at the same time advancing grievances of their own against the sub-contracting system. In February 1891 Tillett, Orbell and Clem Edwards were all in the town, organizing and expressing support for the struggle. Tillett interpreted the strike as 'a struggle for our very existence . . . they meant to fight it to the bitter end'.[67] Whilst he and Havelock Wilson predicted sympathy strikes spreading from Cardiff to Hull, Liverpool and London, John Burns strongly advised that the conflict be confined to Wales. Although Burns had little formal status, being only a trustee of the union, his advice carried the day with Tom Mann, and Mann carried the union. Nevertheless, for the seamen and dockers of Cardiff the struggle assumed the proportions of a general strike. Tom Mann appealed in vain for sympathy action from the South Wales miners and railwaymen. He had envisaged that with their participation in a South Wales Labour Federation enough potential power could be mobilized to succeed 'without resorting to the arbitrament of a strike'. Whatever might have happened if regional unity had come about, in its absence the dispute was doomed. Even the coal-trimmers withheld their support. The Dockers' Union was isolated within Cardiff, and though Tillett made three or four speeches a day, predicting that 'there will be a complete reorganisation of labour in South Wales and we shall have a unification in trade unionism', his expectations were no longer realistic, and on 16 March 1891 the strike was called off. 'Tillett then collapsed. Exhausted and ill, he was too weak to lift a spoon to his lips. In the absence of Wilson, who was in jail for "intimidating" free labourers, Mann made the journey to Cardiff to nurse his friend.'[68]

The union was reported as 'moribund' in Cardiff by 1894.[69] In Swansea, making concessions to free labour, the union retained a measure of recognition with some employers and survived, relying heavily on peaceful use of conciliation procedures. The NALU, which had never espoused the methods of new unionism, maintained a relative degree of stability throughout the 1890s, falling from 3,914 members in 1892 to 2,823 in 1895. By the end of the decade, it had recovered to 3,695.[70]

How Tinplatemen Came to the Rescue

The Dockers' Union lost its Welsh membership in copper and gasworks after its defeats in the docks, but its officials made what became a critically important strategic gain, when the South Wales, Monmouthshire and Gloucestershire Tinplate Association dissolved in 1899. This union's demise followed its failure either to resist wage cuts through the slump or to impose effective output restrictions. It had been a closed, skilled craft society, with a hierarchical seniority system similar to the steelworkers' unions. Yet in the inter-union contest to enrol its former members, whilst the Steel Smelters' Union attracted the millmen and some joined the Welsh Artisans' Union (established in 1888), the majority joined the Dockers' Union, after fierce competition from the Gasworkers' Union. Tillett's superior oratory was ascribed a key influence in this success: Will Thorne was no match for him.

Within months of the tinplate union's collapse, the Swansea district of the Dockers' Union claimed 2,500 tinplate members and twenty-four new branches. Tillett proceeded with a scheme to protect these all-important gains. He proposed to the tinplate employers a system of mutual recognition and protection, in which his members would work only for employers who entered into a cartel arrangement to control prices. In return, he sought a closed shop and a wage increase. Although the employers rejected this scheme, they did set up a very advanced form of conciliation board, stabilized wages and agreed to refer disputes to independent arbitration. Four other unions were included in the scheme: the Gasworkers', the Steel Smelters', and the Tin and Sheet Millmen's Unions. (Tillett and Hodge of the Steel Smelters' Union made a demarcation agreement.) Here, in embryo, and before its time, was a model for a Joint Industrial Council.

The significance of the tinplate section in Wales for our unfolding story is hard to exaggerate. Its full import becomes evident only in the first decade of the twentieth century, which we follow in chapter 8. We may anticipate, however, to point to the fact that in 1908 the tinplate members contributed more to the Dockers' Union's income than all other districts combined.

II

The Shipping Federation's Second Offensive

In 1892–3, the Shipping Federation gathered its forces for two crucial onslaughts on the remaining provincial strongholds of the Dockers' Union – Bristol and Hull. At that time, and whilst still surrounded by the aura of success associated with 1889, Tillett joined the political wave of new-union leaders seeking parliamentary advances. His Bradford campaign of 1892 (see chapter 6) is seen by his biographer as 'in one sense, a desperate attempt to break the circle drawn by the Shipping Federation around the Dockers' Union.'[71]

Bristol

The Bristol docks were regarded with special esteem by the union leadership. They had established a closed shop, and the municipal ownership of the port provided a model much celebrated in socialist agitations. The Town Council was not, however, a principal employer of port labour, which remained in the hands of master-stevedores and shipping companies: the municipality simply owned the port and its physical facilities.

It was the timber merchants who provoked the strike of November 1892 by engaging free labour. When the dockers walked off in protest at this breach of their closed shop, the employers rejected recourse to the local Arbitration Board and summoned the Shipping Federation to their aid, declaring at the same time a general lock-out, pending the men's acceptance of the Shipping Federation ticket. The employers' intention to smash the union was obvious.

McCarthy and Tillett both hastened to the town, where street-fights between blacklegs, police and strikers had already erupted. McCarthy sought to conduct the strike (which had been made official) on the lines of the great London strike of 1889, with daily street-processions, some of them at night by torchlight. Tillett's first speeches urged caution, 'sober and prudent conduct'. But the physical conflict escalated (Tillett had no doubt that this was deliberately provoked by the Federation) and troops and cavalry were called in. Still Tillett advocated pacifism: he advised the dockers to go to church to pray for the conversion of the employers to 'nobleness', and advocated the formation of a Labour party. The mood of the strikers was quite contrary to all this: local leaders, addressing mass meetings, recalled the Bristol reform riots of 1831, drawing on the memory to call for 'a second or third revolution if necessary'. At this point Tillett caught the crowd's mood, as he so often did, and launched into incendiary speeches of extremely violent import: 'if it came to guns they could pick them up also.'[72]

The high drama of the strike reached its climax when Tillett led the crowd at a mass meeting in the taking of an oath, which it repeated after him: 'if the necessity demands I will protect my home, my interests, my wages, by means of violent or pacific measures'. Whilst this was in the highest degree inflammatory, the speaker distinguished between individual acts of violence, and concerted action led by himself and the union: 'they should intimidate by the crowd . . . the leaders should organise it'.

Tillett was later prosecuted on a charge of sedition; he was acquitted, but not before further scenes of mass street-warfare had swept through Bristol, as the police and the dragoons broke up one of Tom McCarthy's processions. On that occasion, fifty-seven civilians and fifty-one police were injured. Meanwhile, Tillett himself had moved on from his 'oath' speech to advocate, before another crowd of thousands, that 'they must [make] the workers of Bristol the controllers of Bristol's destiny', and 'It must not finish at trade unionism – it must not finish until the workers of all grades and degrees commanded absolutely the whole machinery of the state, the whole machinery of government, of production, control and distribution'.[73] This was the language of Marxism, of socialist revolution. Edward Aveling stood by Tillett's side in Bristol and himself made a speech. We can account for Tillett's extremism as the product of the fiery mood of the strikers, his emotional identity with the suffering of the people of his own home town, the evident intransigence of the Shipping Federation, and possibly also the strong socialist influence which, as we have already observed (see chapter 4), was a notable feature of new unionism in Bristol in particular.

Whatever the causes of this intransigence, all Tillett's exertions could not prevent the total defeat of the strike. There was one last mass march and demonstration, of heroic proportions, on 4 February 1893. Fifty trades took part, the skilled and unskilled, and men from London and South Wales were amongst the procession of 30,000 people. Thereafter, the strike petered out, weakened by the drain on union finances as, from April, these were diverted to the Hull dockers' struggle, and by the sustained intransigence of the employers. By June, union and 'free' blacklegs were working side by side, and the Shipping Federation's contract with the employers could safely be allowed to expire.

Through the rest of the decade, the story of the Dockers' Union in Bristol is typical. From a peak 1891 membership of 2,500, it declined to 1,250 in 1895, and to possibly no more than 800 in 1905 – these survivors being from the corn-porters, who enjoyed a degree of sectional security. It avoided strikes, and in 1900 made an arbitration agreement at the docks, setting up boards of conciliation, winning a wage increase and obtaining employer recognition. The *Dockers' Record* reported satisfaction with the system.[74]

. . . and Humberside

Hull, Britain's third port, as we saw earlier (chapter 4), had become the jewel in the crown of the Dockers' Union by 1890. The following year the port was still registering record levels of foreign trade. The Dockers' Union held its second annual national conference there, and the National Labour Federation its fifth, both in 1891. The benign influence of the port's largest shipping firm, C. H. and Arthur Wilson, was unique to Hull. It employed only union labour, including its own foremen and shipping clerks, and assisted in the collection of union dues. In January 1891 Tillett proclaimed: 'No town stood higher in the ranks of trade unionism than Hull, for they had not been able to find a blackleg there'.[75]

George Laws, general manager of the Shipping Federation, came to Hull to complain that it was the only port where the dockers persisted in supporting the Seamen's Union's opposition to free labour. He opened a Free Labour Registry on Humber Dock, but it was hardly functional and in time failed. T. Kelly, one of the leading architects of the bogus unions of London, tried his hand at creating a similar organization in Hull, but failed. Tom Mann attended the branch dinner of the foremen's and clerks' branch of his union, a unique occasion. Tillett and Charles Wilson made speeches of mutual admiration at a union dinner.

Pay increases were won on the docks during 1891. The boatmen of the Aire and Calder Navigation Company, members of the union, struck, but they were restrained by Tillett, who negotiated a return to work.

The Hull Trades Council represented 20,000 members in 1891, a gain of 15,000 on its 1889 strength, and was very active in municipal politics, lobbying for free libraries, public parks, standard wages for Corporation contractors, codes for building regulations, and reforms in the Boards of Guardians. Debate between old and new unionists, on the legal eight-hour day and on Independent Labour politics, was fierce. In the building trades, Hull was a 100 per cent union-organized town.

When the Shipping Federation tried to use blacklegs to load a blacked coal ship, it was astonished to find that the Hull Dock Company refused to allow the free labourers to use their cranes!

During 1892, trade in Hull turned seriously downwards and this, together with the countrywide defeats inflicted on the union by the Shipping Federation, led Tillett to speak of caution and restraint in the port, to audiences not at all appreciative of this change of heart. In August 1892 he was loudly heckled by the Hull dockers when he spoke out against strike action to win the Saturday half-holiday. His estrangement from the local leadership may be gauged from a speech by Thomas Chesterfield, secretary of the Hull Dockers' Union, in which he said that 'it was most regrettable that a cloud of distrust had gathered round the name of Ben Tillett'. In this climate, Havelock Wilson mounted a campaign in Hull and throughout the country for a national strike against the Shipping Federation, which was meanwhile exerting severe pressure on the C. H. Wilson shipping company to toe the line of its policy: it organized a boycott of the company by the shipping insurers. Clouds were gathering around the port, which, by early in 1893, represented the bulk of the union's remaining national membership – an asset which Tillett was loath to risk.

The crucial moment came when C. H. and Arthur Wilson joined the Shipping Federation. Charles Wilson claimed that the union's 'dictatorship' could no longer be tolerated: yet after the great struggle which his decision unleashed was over, he stated that 'it had been a fight against the grain with me throughout . . . I may have been compelled to co-operate with those who had some such wish, [to destroy the Dockers' Union] but such co-operation, if it existed, was forced upon me.' This confirms the union view that Wilson was coerced by the Shipping Federation and other local employers. (Wilson was, of course, a prominent Liberal politician and MP in Hull, and this always gave him a strong motive for retaining labour sympathies.)

In March 1893 the Shipping Federation opened its Free Labour Bureau in Hull with a promise of preference of work for those who joined. Wilson's company also ended its practice of deducting union dues from the pay of those dockers who were in arrears, and required its foremen and clerks to leave the union. These combined pressures led Tom Chesterfield, the local docks union secretary, to issue a manifesto entitled: 'Will you walk into my Parlour, said the Spider to the Fly?', warning unionists not to register at the 'Labour Exchange'. Tillett issued a series of statements urging restraint by the men, reinforced by the 'moderate' leader of the Trades Council, W. G. Millington. Havelock Wilson, however, made an inflammatory speech, calling for a general strike of Hull labourers, thus providing the employers with the excuse they needed to import the first 400 free labourers to unload Wilson's ships. Emigrant sheds on the docks were equipped to accommodate them, *The Times* cueing in with a report on the 'splendid sheds' and praising the importation of cooking staff and orderlies to look after the creature comforts of the men. 'Their engagement is for fourteen days certain, with a prospect of permanent employment'. *The Times* failed on this occasion, as it did consistently, to report on the violence of the 'federationists', one of whom fired a revolver at the pickets. On 5 April, more than 100 free labourers returned home after being addressed by union officials.

The national press seized on these opening skirmishes to spotlight the conflict, and the Hull magistrates (some of whom were port employers) called for reinforcements. On 6 April 160 Royal Scots, 90 Dragoons and massive police reinforcements from as far afield as Nottingham arrived in the city, and two Admiralty gunboats appeared in the estuary facing the waterfront. On 11 April the special correspondent of the London *Daily News* referred to 'this preposterous display of force in a town which is as quiet as a Sunday congregation in church.' H. H. Asquith, the Home Secretary, pressed by Keir Hardie in the Commons for an explanation, placed the onus for the authorities' militancy on the City Council and magistrates. The effect was to shift public sympathy towards the strikers, and to augment anti-Liberal, Independent Labour sentiment in the Hull trade-union movement. Above all, it thoroughly alarmed the skilled unionists, including the engineers, who poured large financial contributions into the strike fund. A national response brought over £12,000 to the Hull Trades Council by the second week of the strike, and led Fred Maddison of the Hull Trades Council (a prominent Lib.–Lab. politician) to claim that 'this has certainly been even a more striking rally of the older unions to the aid of the new than was that of 1889'.

The solidarity of the dockers was evident in the results of a ballot announced on 6 April: 3,500 for the strike, with 5 votes against. *The Times* called the result the product of the 'terrorism' practised by the union's officials. In fact, Tillett approached Charles Wilson on 8 April to concede the main point – the ending of the closed shop. He offered an agreement that union men would work with free labour, that clerks and foremen could withdraw from the union and that any disputed items should be referred to arbitration. His only reservation was that free labour should not be given preference of work. Wilson rejected the offer, although what Tillett was conceding was what he had led the men of Cardiff against with such vigour only shortly before. From this point on, the conflict is properly to be regarded as a lock-out. The men had nowhere to go: their backs were firmly pinned to the wall.

Havelock Wilson continued his challenge to Tillett's moderation with a call to 'light the torch at London, Glasgow, Liverpool and Cardiff . . . to prevent them from collecting men to send to Hull'. When he finished speaking, Shipping Federation cards and an effigy of Charles Wilson were burnt. The possibility of the strike's spreading was a real one: Cardiff ship-repairers struck in sympathy, and reports from Middlesbrough, the Hartlepools, the Tyne ports, Swansea and London all suggested willingness to take action on behalf of Hull. It may be that this caused the Shipping Federation to go farther afield for its strike-breakers. Certainly they shipped over free-labour reinforcements from The Netherlands and Sweden: by 11 April they had a force of 1,000 strike-breakers at work.

Tillett began to change his position, joining the speculation about a general strike. Resolutions in support came from seventy-six branches of the shipping trades in London, and from a mass meeting in the London docks. Tillett rushed to Hull on 18 April, fresh from his court acquittal over the Bristol sedition charge, and now spoke in the tones that the dockers wanted to hear:

> That day, right up and down the length and breadth of England, the dockers were preparing for what would be one of the greatest strikes in history. The strike of the London dockers would sink into insignificance by comparison . . . when constitutional methods were useless, they must resort to the fierce arbitrament of a strike, that should be widespread . . . that should shake even the government . . . There was no other way.

Yet behind the scenes, Tillett's old associate John Burns was working hard for a settlement and cautioning against any extension of the strike. He obtained a postponement by proposing, in meetings with Tillett and Havelock Wilson, a national emergency all-union conference, and then prevailed on the leader of the seamen to go with him to meet Charles Wilson and government officials in the House of Commons. Also involved in the mediation was Sir A. K. Rollitt, the Hull Tory MP, who will be remembered as a former patron of Hull's local port unions during their formative period. The ship-owning Wilson, in taking part in these exchanges, was guilty of breaching a week-old resolution of the Shipping Federation that 'no further communications should be held with the union leaders'. Therefore this meeting gave Tillett some hope of a compromise, and he now sought to confine the conflict to Hull. Fund-raising resumed top priority. A national appeal was signed not only by the dockers' leaders, but also by Michael Davitt, John Burns and George Shipton. Always prone to think in military analogies (emulating his early hero, Napoleon), at a May Day rally in Hull Tillett repeated the American Civil War hero General Sherman's famous message: 'Hold the fort, for I am coming.'

At the heart of the conflict, Hull was now a city in rage and turmoil. On 3 May one Hull gunsmith reported that he had sold 200 revolvers in three weeks, as well as large numbers of knuckle-dusters and life-preservers. Each night there was disorder on the streets. Two divisions of cavalry paraded through the town daily. Stone-throwing and police baton-charges were a daily event. Women tore up the paving stones for their men to hurl at the police and military. Railway carriages carrying blacklegs to the Alexandra Dock were stoned. Attempts were made to obstruct trains, and there is evidence that an attempt was made to blow up a bridge carrying the Hull and Barnsley railway line over Beverley Road. Free labourers from Scarborough were met at the railway station and stoned all the way to the docks. The most spectacular event was the great fire of 23 April, visible 20 miles away, which destroyed the Citadel timber yards on the docks. Firemen found their hoses cut when they sought to douse the blaze, and strikers stood around, refusing the fabulous offer of 10s. an hour to help in firefighting. No one has ever established the true cause of the fire. Tillett blamed blacklegs, allowed by the employers to smoke, but arson seems by far the most likely cause.

Agitation by Havelock Wilson for a general strike gained some support from these events, and Tom Mann came close to endorsing it, as did Clem Edwards. Burns, working quietly behind the scenes, had his way when the national conference which he had proposed met on 22 April and rejected the call by forty-five votes to twenty-seven. Burns addressed the conference, speaking 'vigorously against the policy of attempting for so small an issue so great a risk'. Tillett swung round again into line with this decision, but had to exert himself greatly in the next two days, facing spontaneous mass meetings of dockers in London, who denounced it. At one sympathetic walk-out in London's Victoria Dock, Tillett was howled down: after repeated interruptions, ending with a voice shouting 'a strike made you, and if you don't fetch us out the union will be smashed up', the disorder became so great that Tillett, the greatest of mob orators, was forced to abandon his speech before his own London members.

Throughout the strike, no negotiations were possible between the official Strike Committee and the Hull employers. The latter, and particularly Wilson, made several informal attempts in the House of Commons to agree terms. A remarkable and highly significant element in the Hull dispute was that three of the key personalities were at the time Members of Parliament – Charles Wilson represented the Liberal interest for West Hull, Havelock Wilson had been elected in 1892 for Middlesbrough, and at the same time John Burns had won Battersea. Burns, as we have seen, was entrusted by Mann and Tillett with an insider role during the dispute, and was instrumental in arranging the private meeting in the House attended by A. J. Mundella, president of the Board of Trade, C. H. Wilson, J. H. Wilson, Llewellyn Smith (Labour Commissioner), Mr Hopwood (secretary to the Board of Trade), Sir Albert Rollitt, Alderman Woodhouse of Hull and John Burns himself.

The two Wilsons and Burns accepted the terms offered as a basis for settlement. Whilst conceding the entry of free labour to the port, and the severance of the foremen's and clerks' union membership, they stipulated that the free-labour ticket should carry no right to preference. The Shipping Federation rejected the terms, and brought Charles Wilson sharply back into line: he subsequently failed to attend a reconvened meeting of the group of mediators, writing instead to say that 'the York terms were absolutely irrevocable and final'. (York was the venue for the Shipping Federation meetings throughout the dispute.) Other efforts at a settlement were made by Mr Grotrian, a local shipowner and member of the Shipping Federation, in consultation with Tom Mann. To the York terms, which essentially required 'unionists to agree to work with non-unionists', and that 'the British Labour Exchange be kept open, the employers insisting on entire freedom of contract in employing such men as they deem suitable', these two proposed an addition to the last clause. This read: 'But neither registration at the British Labour Exchange nor membership of any union shall in itself carry with it either preference or prejudice, in regard to employment'. By this time, in mid-May, the Borough Justices, the Watch Committee, the Mayor and Council (and behind them the anxious and angry voices of the rate-payers, tradespeople and the local press) were urgently calling for settlement, their pressure being directed solely at the Shipping Federation, which was widely perceived as responsible for the continuance of Hull's distress. The Shipping Federation finally yielded to the point of meeting the Strike Committee and, though dragging its feet for some further days, on 19 May signed an agreement which included the Mann–Grotrian clause. The strike/lock-out had lasted for seven weeks.

The settlement in fact represented a mere tactical shift by the Federation, an adjustment clearly intended to prevent its further isolation as local employers and commercial interests moved away from it. Not only did the Free Labour Exchange remain in being, and the foremen and clerks leave the union (which they themselves did not wish to do), but under the terms of the settlement also dock gatemen, weighers, bookers, gangsmen, berthing masters and assistant berthing masters would sever their connection with the Dockers' Union. No 'external emblem' was to be worn by any member of a union (or of the Labour Exchange) at work or applying for work, and union officials were banned from visiting ships whilst the men were at work. Tom Mann was responsible for accepting these terms, and won much praise for his steadying influence, which was contrasted to Tillett's volatility. Yet the terms were similar to those which Tillett had offered, and seen rejected, weeks earlier.

Fred Maddison put them to a mass meeting of dockers on 14 May. He asked if they would be satisfied with the new clause banning preference for either union or Federation tickets. Greeted with loud cries of 'No!', he then sought to win approval by arguing that, since there would be no preference, the Free Labour Exchange would be redundant, as 95 per cent of the men were trade unionists. He pressed the point: since the Federation had accepted the 'no-preference' clause, the men 'had advanced towards ultimate victory'. This interpretation carried the day, dubious as it was.

It very soon became clear what the settlement had conceded. The Free Labour Exchange remained, and within weeks it was obvious that C. H. Wilson and other firms were indeed giving preference to non-unionists.

Fred Maddison at once asked the Mayor to intervene, but he was powerless. A further strike was proposed, but it was unrealistic: the men were exhausted from their ordeal, and the deceit of the employers, now revealed, only enhanced their demoralization. They rushed to join the Free Labour Exchange: 2,000 had registered by 9 June, although many were unemployed at a time of depressed trade. The Shipping Federation had triumphed.

The last act of violence in a violent conflict was, ironically but tragically, self-inflicted. The Dockers' branch secretary Tom Chesterfield tried to commit suicide by cutting his throat, and was for some time desperately ill. He had loyally gone along with every union concession until the end, even though a 'moderate' like Millington, the Trades Council secretary, had found them unacceptable and withdrawn from the negotiating team at local level.

In retrospect, it seems reasonable to ask whether the leadership's acceptance of the outcome as inevitable was justified. The cynical casuistry of the Federation's concession of 'no preference' must have been apparent to acute and experienced men such as Mann. Against the unbending stance of the Federation was set the matching solidarity of the Hull dockers: there is no evidence of any drift back to work during the whole affair. Could fund-raising have been intensified at a national level? Could the test have been made of a national docks and shipping strike? We have cited some evidence to show that dock workers in many ports were aware of the issues involved, and also that the Federation was becoming increasingly isolated, even in relation to local port employers and perhaps to C. H. Wilson himself. The outcome of a national strike could hardly have been worse than the consequences of the settlement.

Of course, this is to speak with hindsight, in the knowledge of what followed for Hull and for dock unionism generally. The union had already suffered the defeats in Southampton, Cardiff, Bristol and half-a-dozen smaller ports before it confronted the Federation in Hull. The scale of the Shipping Federation's resources, and the ruthlessness with which they were deployed, had been fully demonstrated. And the economic climate was adverse for any prolonged industrial warfare.

The leaders' inner defeatism, from an early stage, seems evident in the influence which Burns was allowed to exert from the distance of the House of Commons. Tillett's biographer has made a nice attempt to understand the relationships, at this critical moment, of the triumvirate which had led the London dockers in 1889:

Tillett's formulation did not represent the softening of Shipping Federation attitudes that he and other advocates of caution had expected. Yet wishful thinking on the part of the Dockers' Executive transformed it into a major concession, and the basis for a settlement. At first Tillett demurred: did he resent the interference of Burns and Tom Mann who

DEFEAT: DEFENCE AND DEFIANCE

also seemed instrumental in arranging the 'new' situation? If so, a sharp note from Burns brought him around. 'Let there be no fooling about the strike and its termination, and don't allow personal feeling to stand in the way of a settlement . . . Settle at once ere disaster awaits you and your men secede'.[76]

Why did Tom Mann conduct the final negotiations in Hull's Guildhall yet leave the signing to Tillett and three local leaders? (Equally, why did Charles Wilson depute his younger brother and junior partner Arthur to sign for his company?) And why did Tom Mann totally ignore the Hull strike in his *Memoirs*, while Tillett in his gave a competely false account, expressing his distaste for the episode and darkly hinting that Havelock Wilson's malign influence was the cause of an 'unnecessary' strike?

The role of Havelock Wilson must indeed be weighed. His was the union originally targeted by the Federation, and it is true that it was reduced to bankruptcy in 1894. But whilst he made the running in militant rhetoric, most notably in the case of Hull, it was the dockers and their union who bore the brunt of the fighting, and their leaders who carried the heavy task of seeking either genuine mass mobilization or a face-saving settlement which might rescue something of their former positions.

The effects of the defeat in Hull were disastrous. Within a few years William Collison could boast of the town as 'a stronghold of free labour',[77] his own National Free Labour Association having more members than the Dockers' Union during most of the rest of the decade. He staged the national annual dinner of the NFLA in Hull in 1899, and spoke of the useful work his Hull branch (3,977 strong) had done on the Clyde, and as far away as Christiania (the former name of the port of Oslo in Norway).[78] Two years later, Hull blacklegs from the NFLA were working for the Taff Vale Railway Company, to whose aid Collison rallied with the enthusiasm of an old campaigner.

The effect of the Hull collapse on the Dockers' Union's finances is some measure of its importance. Income from contributions from Hull fell by £1,000 out of a total income of £4,000. Bristol, despite its own defeat, now became the best organized port for the union.

Tom Mann came to Hull in 1898 to castigate the dockers for their position as 'the worst organised of any of the considerable ports'. Fred Maddison argued in his new magazine the *Trade Unionist* that a new union – he meant a new *local* union – should be formed, a proposal attractive even to George Belt, who had been Tom McCarthy's election agent at the 1895 General Election in Hull (see chapter 6) and was therefore politically quite opposed to Maddison. Tillett came to Hull to head off this idea, and was back the following year, 1899, with Tom McCarthy in the chair, to berate the 'dirty filthy wretches [who] went blacklegging to other ports'.[79]

But the tide turned, and sooner in Hull than elsewhere. In 1900 trade in the port was booming, and the South African war had caused temporary labour shortage on the docks because some dockers were army reservists. Two spontaneous one-day strikes by 'holders-on', joined by 700 grain workers, raised their wages from 5s. to 6s. a day. Just as he had done before, Tillett raced up to Hull and gave a fortnight's notice of strike action. His claim sought to raise the port's daily wage to the national average: Hull at the time lagged 1s. 6d.–2s. behind the rates of 6–8s. paid elsewhere.

Anticipating a trade-union revival, Wilson's company moved quickly to negotiate an acceptable improvement of wages and hours with an unofficial deputation of dockers, cutting the ground from under Tillett's feet whilst he dutifully waited out the fourteen days' notice. Other firms conceded similar gains, thus avoiding recognition of the union. Yet membership of the Dockers' Union advanced in that year to 4,000, a figure which topped the membership of the NFLA. (Free labourers had been a mixed blessing for the employers: in 1894 they successfully struck against Wilson's for an extra half-day's pay!)

Havelock Wilson's union fared no better than the Dockers' Union during the period following the 1893 strike. Nationally, the union was dissolved and reconstituted in 1894. The local Hull Seamen's and Firemen's Amalgamated Association consistently undercut the national union when pay claims were presented in 1898, 1899 and 1900, and Hull was as infamous for supplying blackleg seamen as for providing strike-breaking dockers. Further humiliation was caused by the evolution of Albert Anlaby Bird, one of the founders of the Independent Labour Party (ILP) in Hull in the 1890s. He had been active in the Hull branch of the national Seamen's Union, had become secretary of the Humber Lightermen's Union, but then defected to take a post with the Shipping Federation.[80] More seriously, the Hull coal-porters broke from Tillett's union to form their own, and Hull Trades Council endorsed a move to found a general, separatist docks' union.

Local distrust of the national union centred round the high ratio of working expenses to income. In Grimsby, this feeling was exploited by A. L. Edwards, founder of the Ipswich Mutual Working Men's Independent Federation, who charged that many unions were 'impudent frauds . . . perpetrated upon the working man'.[81] He had founded his Federation in 1893, at the instigation of the Conservatives in East Anglia, to 'get the labourers divided so that they may get a political advantage at the next General Election',[82] and to supply free labour in opposition to George Edwards's genuine Agricultural Labourers' Union. He succeeded in winning the secession of all the Grimsby branches of the Dockers' Union, and in forming a Grimsby General Workers' Friendly and Protective Society. The National Amalgamated Union of Labour also wound up its Grimsby branches, and in Hull the National Labour

Federation collapsed, being replaced with a new Hull and District Labour Federation. The National Federation of Fishermen also disappeared in 1894, and even the more stable Gasworkers' Union had to send Pete Curran, Tom Maguire and others to Hull to boost morale and hold its organization together.

It is clear that the 1893 defeat triggered off a general revulsion towards Tillett's union and the formation of a series of local, non-political, non-militant unions. Clem Edwards was surely whistling in the dark when he suggested that the national impact of the Hull strike was positive, in that it had given a sense 'of "oneness" to the Labour Movement throughout the country'.[83] Later in the decade he himself produced a study of 'free-labour frauds', which listed fifty bogus trade unions – some measure of the underworld offensive against new unionism which flourished in the 1890s.[84]

Beyond the waterfront, the Hull builders' unions, in alliance with the nine Labour councillors who found themselves on the City Council by 1897, developed a remarkably strong position in a growing 'direct-labour' scheme of the corporation. As we shall see in chapter 7, it is in the formation of Independent Labour politics allied to trade unionism that the genuinely positive lessons of the Hull strike were learned.

Sexton and Liverpool

The National Union of Dock Labourers moved its headquarters from Glasgow to Liverpool in 1890: half of its national membership of 25,000 worked on the Mersey. Following the strikes and compromise settlements of 1889–90, the dockers were preoccupied, as in Tillett's union, with the problem of establishing and maintaining union control over labour supply.

At the South End Docks, where the employers were mainly small master-stevedoring firms (and the dockers were mainly Protestant), there was relative harmony. Union labour and the uncontested wearing of the identifying Dockers' Button prevailed. At the North End, dominated by the big shipping companies, and by Catholic–Irish dockers, the employers recruited 'preferred', non-union men, and, led by the Cunard line, banned the wearing of the Button at the call-on. Their campaign succeeded: by 1891 'the public presence of the NUDL virtually disappeared'.[85]

Whilst the Liverpool shipping firms pursued the same objective as the national Shipping Federation, they did so independently of it. A Merseyside Employers' Labour Association was formed in 1890 to fight the new unions and the lightning strikes which took place to defend the Button. It was regarded as ineffective by the large shipowners, who defected to fight their own battles. Nevertheless, the Shipping

Federation did make an arrangement with the ELA to supply blacklegs, and to act as its agent in other ports.

The response of the NUDL was to advance ca'canny as the main plank of resistance – a method now elevated to the status of a panacea. Its other response was to seek local and regional federation, and it succeeded in establishing a Federation of Trades and Labour Unions in connection with the Shipping, Carrying and Other Industries. Fifteen unions from Liverpool and Manchester affiliated on its formation in 1893. It was dissolved in 1899, 'having achieved nothing of consequence'.[86]

The large firms' success in banning the Button, according to George Milligan (who started dock work in 1890 and subsequently became the union's deputy general secretary), rang 'the death knell . . . to the unity of organisation in Liverpool'. Between 1891 and 1911 'the twelve thousand and odd men working for the great companies were in the industrial wilderness'.[87] The union's total membership fell to 8,463 in 1892, stabilizing thereafter at around 10,000.

Although not faced by the acute problem of the Shipping Federation's Free Labour Exchanges, the union's decline drove it in upon itself, and exposed a bitter internecine warfare amongst its branches and against the leadership of McHugh and McGhee. The president, general secretary and vice-president (this last was Michael McKeown, a Birkenhead docker – hence 'the three Macs') were elected along with a lay executive but, unlike the centralized power and funds of Tillett's union, the branches retained large proportions of the subscriptions, as well as a wide autonomy. This reflected the sectional and local 'caste' system of which Sexton complained:

Not the least of our manifold difficulties arose from the prevalence of what I can only describe as the caste system throughout the dockers' fraternity, which led to the creation of almost innumerable small clubs and societies all hostile to each other . . . quite frequently religious and political differences kept these bodies apart, and indeed alive. Thus the coal heavers had one society at the North End, another at the South. The leader of one was a North of Ireland Orangeman, the leader of the other an equally perfervid Irish Home Rule Catholic . . . The only point on which they were united was a mutual objection to mere cargo hands handling coal. Salt heavers took up the same attitude as to the exclusiveness of their job: if you weren't one of them you couldn't touch bulk salt . . . Being what were known in the vernacular of the port as 'good earners', salt and coal heavers alike were greatly desired by the other sex as life partners . . . those whose work was the loading and discharging of railway bars to and from barges and steamers – in which at that time enormous traffic – had their two societies. One was the 'Cabbage Club' . . . the other, the 'Clarence Dock Club', was for men engaged only in the coasting trade . . . in those days, Liverpool had a caste system quite as powerful as India's. The hand busheller of grain – now displaced by the elevator – looked with scorn upon the man who did the donkey work on the quay: the grain carrier who could easily sling a four bushel sack weighing a couple of hundredweights across his back and shoulders, and run along a swinging plank, thought himself the master workman of the ages: the stitcher of the bags used in the bulk salt trade, a veritable artist in his craft, had a most colossal contempt for the man who merely handled bags filled at the salt factory, whilst the tallyman who weighed and checked the bags considered himself the best and most important of all the 'casual dock labourers'.[88]

In this climate, branch corruption flourished, as did intrigue and office-seeking against the leadership of McHugh and McGhee, who had the great disadvantage of never having been dockers. Scandal surrounded them, following accusations in 1890 that they had misappropriated union funds in both Glasgow and Liverpool. In the ensuing libel action, their accuser, a union activist named Kierman, was found guilty, but the jury recommended mercy. McHugh supported this plea. The affair badly damaged the leadership's reputation, and in 1893 McHugh and McGhee jointly resigned, amidst continued rumours of dissension and intrigue. (They both remained devoted and active Georgeites, and McGhee was twice elected to Parliament for Irish constituencies as a Nationalist.)

James Sexton, bone of the bone of the Merseyside dock and labour community, was elected to the general secretaryship on 1 January 1894. He was thirty-seven years old, and his credentials for the post were impeccable. He had abandoned his early Fenianism and revolutionary Irish politics in Merseyside and had become a Home Ruler under the influence of T. P. O'Connor. He had early experience as a trade-union agitator, in the Knights of Labour's Bootle branch, and as a practical docker. The severe accident he had suffered on the docks and the inhumane treatment he had received (see chapter 1) had taught him a bitter lesson about dock employers. His patient, unspectacular administrative abilities and his preference for the legislative path to reform were assets to the NUDL, in dire need of internal reform, regularization of procedure and restoration of propriety. Even Sexton's evident political ambitions chimed with both local and national tendencies, and helped the Merseyside union to overcome an isolation from the mainstream of British affairs. He was a founder member (with just six others) of the Liverpool branch of the ILP, and was its delegate to the Bradford conference of 1893 which established the party nationally. He wrote for the *Clarion*, and was president of the Liverpool Trades Council in 1894. There he clashed with the old guard of skilled Lib.–Lab. unionists, who could not accept his ILP stance. In consequence, he withdrew the NUDL's affiliation to the Trades Council, and did not reaffiliate until 1906. He represented the union at the TUC from 1894, winning a seat on the Parliamentary Committee in 1900.

Whilst pursuing all this extra-mural activity, Sexton was fighting to rid the union of petty corruption and lax discipline. He suspended the Cork branch and sacked the Glasgow secretary for this type of offence. His strict administration, combined with his cautious and conciliatory policies towards the employers, did not make for popularity with his members. Whilst Tillett (and Mann, more consistently) pursued similar goals in the 1890s, seeking consolidation, they kept to a more populist style. For the most part, this held firm their support in the rank and file, at least until after the Hull defeat. Sexton, however, lacked the colour and the platform skills of someone like Tillett, but he was undoubtedly a better administrator and held his union together not by mass appeal but by efficient management. Like the Dockers' Union, the NUDL was in any case in no position to issue major challenges to the employers' ascendancy: its membership had fallen and was relatively stagnant, but recovered from its low point of 1892 to a figure of 14,900 in 1899. There were few disputes to record: industrially the remainder of the decade was without spectacle. An attempt to form a branch in Manchester when the Ship Canal opened in 1894 failed after the collapse of a strike for recognition. (Early in the new century, Tillett was more successful there.)

Shorn of industrial muscle, Sexton and the NUDL pursued a series of political campaigns, backed up by fact-finding and patient lobbying, relating to the problems of industrial accidents, employers' liability and the need for an adequate and knowledgeable inspectorate for the industry. Even in this, Sexton won little popular support, for the dockers, he found, were careless and fatalistic about their own safety – attitudes reinforced by a misguided masculine pride in their 'toughness'. Sexton's campaigns were directed upwards, through the TUC, at the Board of Trade. He won a series of partial advances for his chosen causes. First, the Board issued a directive to dock employers to notify accidents, under the Notice of Accidents Act (1894). In 1895 docks were included for the first time for inspection purposes in the Factory Acts. Yet ships themselves, even when tied up, were still excluded. There were too few inspectors, and the employers found ways to frustrate their orders and instructions. Helped in Parliament by T. P. O'Connor, Sexton won some new regulations – on the fencing of machinery, lighting, gangways, testing and improving of ladders, and similar matters. He complained regularly that the educational qualifications required for the inspectorate prevented knowledgeable but unschooled dockers from becoming inspectors.

He conducted a parallel agitation for improvements in workmen's compensation law. The employers constantly evaded their obligations in this field. They had the resources to fight their cases in the courts, and made full use of the pernicious doctrine of 'common employment', under which an accident occasioned by the negligence of a fellow worker rendered an employer immune from liability. This whole area was a very large issue for new unionism in general, as witness after witness demonstrated before the Royal Commission on Labour. The Workmen's Compensation Act of 1897 went as far as to lay down standard terms of compensation, but prolonged litigation remained a frequent necessity.

Sexton plodded on at this string of reforms, meagre though some of them were, a frequent commuter from Merseyside to Westminster, where he was sometimes received more congenially than he was at the dockside. The men disliked this: often they disliked *him*, and began to call him a 'bosses' man'. But by cultivating a close relationship with the employers and a 'moderate' image, Sexton might perhaps have claimed that he enabled the NUDL to come through both the depression of the early 1890s and the phase of hostility from employers better than other new unions.[89]

Federation? Towards the Greater Unionism, at Home and Abroad

One recurring response to the defensive position into which the new unions were pushed in the 1890s was to seek wider association with each other. This tendency was not new: as we have seen (chapter 1), it reached back to the earliest period of waterside unionism in the 1870s. Port-level federations reappeared in the struggles against the Shipping Federation in London, Hull, South Wales and elsewhere. Clem Edwards's Federation assumed national dimensions, with an affiliated strength of more than forty trade unions. Like most such bodies up to this point, it was essentially a defensive response to an employers' offensive, seeking strength from solidarity. But it also made an early attempt to solve the running problem of inter-union relations through the mutual recognition of union cards amongst the affiliated organizations.[90]

In 1894 Sexton and Tillett brought their two unions together in a joint conference, which resolved that 'an amalgamation of the two unions should be brought about as speedily as possible'.[91] But nothing came of this portentous resolution. Sexton, in particular, may have found it impossible to overcome the sectionalism of which he never ceased to complain.

A more significant and ambitious initiative, attributable, as so many innovations were, to Havelock Wilson and Tom Mann, was the formation in 1896 of the International Federation of Ship, Dock and River Workers. This followed the strategy first practised by Tillett's new union in the immediate aftermath of the 1889 strike, when contacts were established in various northern European ports.[92] The issue of international co-operation surfaced again during a Swedish dock dispute of 1896. Then again, new conflicts broke out in The Netherlands. An appeal was adopted by the British Dockers' Union Conference.

Beginning on domestic ground – 'We of the Dock, Wharf, and Riverside Labourers' Union, in Delegate Meeting assembled, earnestly desire to call the attention of all right minded persons to the conditions under which we, and many thousands of others, are compelled to exist' – it went on to recall the results of the 1889 strike: 'the conditions of labour were improved in many departments of industry'. However:

> many of the conditions then obtained have since been lost, this is in part due to the fact that many of the workers, having been gulled by specious promises of employers and their agents, have acquiesced in conditions that have gone from bad to worse, until now, the conditions in many departments are in every whit as bad as they were seven years ago.

Noting that the wealthy were flaunting even greater extravagances, it linked its call for remedial action quite firmly to international movements:

> Under these circumstances surely it behoves us to take immediate action for a considerable improvement in our conditions . . .
> Let the magnificent stand made by the Rotterdam Dockers serve as an incentive and an example, and remember the blacklegs there went from this country . . . let us at once resolve to formulate our demands, to consult with all kindred Unions, and, if possible, secure common action for the common good. Let us dare to be true to our own manhood, and to have right regard for the women and children.

The resolution ended by authorizing the Executive Council of the union to 'forthwith open up negotiations with other Unions with a view to concerted action'.[93]

The International Federation elected Tom Mann as president and Ben Tillett as secretary. For the next year in the case of Tillett, and the next two years in the case of Mann, this international work occupied much of both leaders' attention. But it was to become more than simply the international arm of the Dockers' Union. Sexton immediately affiliated the NUDL, on the invitation of Havelock Wilson, who also came in.[94]

The short-term objective of the International Federation was to achieve standardization of wages in waterside and shipping employment – in effect a 'levelling-up' of European wages to British standards. In this way the British unions sought to meet a constant complaint levelled at them by the shipowners. Thus, the formal objectives of the International Federation were defined in their rules to include, 'as far as possible, a uniform rate of pay for the same class of work in all ports, and to establish a recognised working day and other regulations in the ports of the world'.

That autumn 19,000 Hamburg dockers struck. They stayed out for nearly three months, and then 'did not win, but they fought splendidly and are now well organised and steadily preparing for another struggle, this time under the auspices of the International [Federation]'.[95] Before, Mann reported, 'they acted independently, and the [International] Federation were not in a position to block vessels loaded by blacklegs . . . The next fight will be . . . scientifically conducted on a scale of unprecedented proportions.'[96]

Rotterdam and Antwerp docks had also been on strike, and had received assistance at the hands of Havelock Wilson from the National Sailors' and Firemen's Union.

In his 1896 Report to the British Dockers' Union, Tom Mann promised 'special attention' to the French ports, including Le Havre, Nantes, Bordeaux, Marseilles, Paris and Dunkirk. Already, he was widening his horizons: 'The French railway workers, who have a splendid Union and are federated with several other countries, are taking a keen interest in the International movement, and ere long we hope the Amalgamated Railway Servants and the General Railway Workers' Union of this country will also join the Federation.'[97]

Quite evidently, both Sexton and Tillett aimed to use the new international body to heal breaches of organization within their own British territories. Mann shared such concerns, but was none the less much more committed to international work for its own sake. At his suggestion, McHugh was enrolled for the task of reviving longshore-men's unionism in New York, using funds from the International Federation; however, he had only a shortlived success there.[98] Mann, Tillett, Sexton and Havelock Wilson, as well as lesser-known figures, visited Hamburg, Antwerp, Rotterdam, Paris, Malmo, Bilbao, Copenhagen, Christiania (Oslo), Bordeaux, Le Havre, Nantes, St-Nazaire and other centres. The bulk of these travels were undertaken by Mann, with a zest and energy which are evident from his later account of the period.[99]

The British leaders addressed mass meetings, and for a time became notorious with the authorities wherever they went. Strikes were generated in several ports, the most important being that already mentioned in Hamburg – a prolonged and ultimately unsuccessful struggle which extended from October 1896 to February 1897. Sympathy action was requested in British ports, but it did not materialize. Tillett, Mann and Sexton were successively arrested and deported, as the continental police in one or another centre sought to prevent them addressing mass meetings. On 24 August 1896, Tillett spent a particularly distressing night in a filthy jail in Antwerp and would have made a diplomatic crisis of the incident had he not been prostrated with illness following the affair.[100] He then departed to convalesce in New Zealand.

Tom Mann was more robust, and clearly enjoyed the cat-and-mouse game which he played with the Paris police in order to address a clandestine gathering of trade unionists and socialists. In 1897, undeterred by the defeat in Hamburg, the International Federation called a conference in London which, although dominated by the British delegates, did bring representatives of the port workers of Antwerp, Rotterdam and Marseilles to confer with them. Tom Mann published his pamphlet, *The Dockers and Sailors in 1897*, in which he elaborated the future goals of the International Federation, particularly the need to combat the common waterfront problem of casual and irregular employment. Yet his personal drive was to substitute for mass participation, and the International Federation did not long survive when he turned his attention to yet another path-breaking movement in Britain: the formation of the Workers' Union.

The International Federation had introduced trade unionism to unorganized continental dockers, and had prepared the way for the next and more durable international organization: the International Transport Workers' Federation, launched in 1908. But it had clearly been too dependent on the British, and on the individual commitment of a few people – particularly Mann, the most genuine internationalist in the leadership. There were two possible responses to unfair foreign competition. International trade-union co-operation was one. The other was xenophobia, protectionism and discrimination. Chauvinism was to emerge at a later stage as a characteristic problem in Britain's ports, not only at rank-and-file level, but sometimes in trade-union leadership.

During all these continental forays, the news for the Federation from Britain had been fairly dismal. In Hull 'a great amount of work yet remains before the Union can exercise a proper influence in the port'; in Bristol 'there is room for improvement'; in Gloucester, likewise; by the time the Dockers' Union Report was prepared for 1896, Bridgwater had just come out of a five-week strike in which 'the men were worsted'. The union had too many officers, and needed a massive recruitment if it was to maintain all its paid officials. None the less, because of the international developments, Mann thought 'that the outlook for Port Workers is brighter than it has ever been before'.

Tillett was still in the Antipodes a year later, so it was again Tom Mann who signed the 1897 Report to the British Dockers. This was not printed until the following year. News on the home front had not improved significantly, although there was some recovery in Middlesbrough and Cardiff, while other districts marked time, and the wound in Hull remained open. In 1897 there was defeat of cataclysmic proportions. The Amalgamated Society of Engineers was locked out by the Engineering Employers' Federation in a contest over trade-union rights. After a long struggle the engineers were forced to submit to a humiliating peace formula which reaffirmed 'management's right to manage', and particularly its right to man new machinery with semi-skilled labour. The employers' victory was an object lesson to other unions. Mann hammered it home:

It behoves all other Unions to seriously consider the reasons that led to such results. Beyond any doubt one of the reasons why the Engineers received such determined opposition from the employers was the fact that the Amalgamated Society was not Federated with any other Union . . . The defeat of the Engineers has stimulated discussions in favour of federation.

The Dockers' Union was already federated with the International Federation of Ship, Dock and River Workers, and 'the Germans, Swedes, Danes and Norwegians are definitely federated with us on a financial basis.'[101] The French and Belgians were poorly organized on the water front, although they remained in 'constant communication'. In Spain there were many women dockers and wages were low, but a nucleus of people was organized. In the United States, McHugh had still been doing his best among longshoremen on the Atlantic coast.

Moving from the universal scene, Mann then retreated to the national dimension:

The Unions of Britain must turn in a more determined fashion to Parliament, and demand therefrom reductions of working hours, extension of Factory Acts to Docks . . . an effective manning scale, adequate accommodation for Sailors, give proper attention to unemployed problem . . . To make this possible all members should endeavour to take a lively interest in political matters, and force on Industrial questions through Parliament.[102]

There is an apparent disjunction here, which reflects the problems arising, not only in choices between different modes of struggle, but also between theatres of action. International co-ordination was to hold a magnetic attraction for transport workers, and for no one more than for seamen and dockers. In co-operation with continental colleagues, it was easy to think that direct action might be raised to a sufficient intensity to defeat recalcitrant employers, whose strike-breakers already ranged freely across frontiers. Such action positively implied the deliberate use of sympathetic strikes. These, however, did not easily fit national structures for bargaining. International action fitted the framework of the international economy, but of itself it offered no direct leverage on political structures, which were all articulated at the level of the nation-state.

The 'battle for democracy', which Marx had long ago established as the first item on the agenda of proletarians, was, therefore, from the beginning a battle for recognition by and representation in national structures. By force of inertia, it would also become Labour's goal to supplant its opponents in those structures, and rule in their stead.

Internationalism was, by contrast, something of an alternative perspective. Since there were no democratic institutions fixed on a global scale, workers could not possess them or subvert them. They would need to develop their own frameworks, starting from scratch, and it was natural for them to attempt such a project from within the industrial space they already occupied. Federation, in these early days, was seen as naturally international. If it worked, it would amount to a radically new approach to democracy. Each alternative strategy generated a proliferation of variant approaches: yet neither could be sundered permanently from the other. These conflicts within the commitment of the waterfront workers were to be amplified on a vast stage, during the ensuing years.

Notes

1   Eric J. Hobsbawm, *Worlds of Labour* (Weidenfeld and Nicolson, 1984), p. 157.
2   Ibid.
3   H. A. Clegg, Alan Fox and A. F. Thompson, *A History of British Trade Unions since 1889*, vol. I: *1889–1910* (Oxford University Press, 1964), p. 83.
4   Basil Mogridge, 'Militancy and Inter-Union Rivalry in British Shipping, 1911–1929', *International Review of Social History*, vol. VI (1961), p. 379.
5   E. L. Taplin, *The Dockers' Union: A Study of the National Union of Dock Labourers, 1889–1922* (Leicester University Press, 1985), pp. 168–9.
6   Arthur Marsh and Victoria Ryan, *Historical Directory of Trade Unions*, vol. III (Gower, 1987), p. 257.
7   Clegg, Fox and Thompson, *History of British Trade Unions*, vol. I, p. 83.
8   Hobsbawm, *Labouring Men* (Weidenfeld and Nicolson, 1963), chapter 8.
9   This was an international debt crisis, triggered by insolvency in Latin America. The public debt of Argentina had risen from £10 million in 1875 to £70 million by 1889. Speculation ran ahead, until, in November 1890, the bubble burst, and as a result 'the great city firm of Baring's went on the rocks'. Its liabilities were more than £21 million. Had it simply sunk, the City itself would have been imperilled. But the Governor of the Bank of England, William Lidderdale, mounted a spectacular rescue with the help of Rothschild's. There was no bank liquidation and Baring's was reborn as a joint-stock company.
10 John Lovell, *Stevedores and Dockers: a Study of Trade Unionism in the Port of London, 1870–1914* (Macmillan, 1969), pp. 28–9 and 38–9.
11 Royal Commission on Labour, Fifth and Final Report, 1894, 581,. p. 31.
12 George Howell, cited in Elie Halevy, *History of the English People in the Nineteenth Century* (Penguin, 1939), book 2, Epilogue: '1895–1905', p. 190.
13 Ibid., p. 192.
14 Llewellyn Smith and Vaughan Nash, *The Story of the Dockers' Strike* (Fisher Unwin, 1890), p. 160.
15 Ibid.
16 Royal Commission on Labour, Minutes of Evidence, Group B, Vol. I, Qs. 2452–60.

17 Ibid., Qs. 2612–14.
18 Ibid., Qs. 2634–6.
19 See Tony Corfield, 'Early Trade Unionism in London', TGWU *Record*, September 1964, p. 36, for a critical commentary on Clegg's account of the union's decline in the Port of London.
20 Ibid.
21 Royal Commission on Labour, Minutes of Evidence, Group B, Vol. I, Q. 3877.
22 Ibid., Q. 526.
23 Ibid., evidence of J. Donovan, Qs. 2452ff.
24 Ibid.
25 Ibid., Q. 3180.
26 Ibid., Qs. 2461–2.
27 Ibid.
28 Ibid., Qs. 2462–4.
29 Ibid., evidence of W. Salter, Q. 2832.
30 Ibid., Qs. 2833–4.
31 Ibid., Q. 2366.
32 Ibid., Qs. 472–7 (authors' italics).
33 Ibid., Qs. 3684–7.
34 Lovell, *Stevedores and Dockers*, pp. 130–1.
35 For a thorough analysis of the positions of employers, labourers and unions on casualism, see Gordon Phillips and Noel Whiteside, *Casual Labour: The Unemployment Question in the Port Transport Industry, 1880–1970* (Oxford University Press, 1985), in particular chapter 2. They express the trade-union problem thus: 'Trade union leaders straddled the two worlds, of reformer and labourer, and displayed an ambivalence on the question of decasualization which was a mark of their frontier existence' (p. 62). On this question see also Gareth Stedman Jones, *Outcast London* (Penguin, 1971), in particular chapter 17.
36 David F. Wilson, *The Dockers: The Impact of Industrial Change* (Fontana, 1972), p. 26.
37 Royal Commission on Labour, Minutes of Evidence, Group B, Vol. I, Q. 4925.
38 L. H. Powell, *The Shipping Federation: a History of the First Sixty Years, 1890–1950* (Shipping Federation, 1950), p. 1.
39 Ibid., p. 5.
40 J. Stafford Ransome, *Master and Man versus Trade Unionism* (London, 1891).
41 Royal Commission on Labour, Minutes of Evidence, Group B, Vol. I, Qs. 4948–57.
42 Ibid.
43 Clem Edwards, 'Labour Federations' (two articles), *Economic Journal*, vol. III (1893), pp. 205–17 and 408–24.
44 Royal Commission on Labour, Minutes of Evidence, Group B, Vol. I, Q. 4954.
45 Ibid., Q. 8640.
46 Ibid., Q. 4953.

47 Jonathan Schneer, *Ben Tillett: Portrait of a Labour Leader* (Croom Helm, 1982), p. 52.
48 Royal Commission on Labour, Minutes of Evidence, Group B, Vol. II, Q. 14491.
49 L. H. Powell, *The Shipping Federation*, p. 20.
50 John Saville, 'Trade Unions and Free Labour: the Background to the Taff Vale Decision', in Asa Briggs and John Saville (eds), *Essays in Labour History, 1886–1923* (Macmillan, 1960), pp. 317–51.
51 N. Soldon, 'Laissez-Faire as Dogma: The Liberty and Property Defence League, 1882–1914', in K. D. Brown (ed.), *Essays in Anti-Labour History* (Macmillan, 1974), pp. 208–23.
52 For the National Free Labour Association, see William Collison, *The Apostle of Free Labour* (Hurst and Blackett, 1913). On right-wing 'labour' organizations generally, see John Saville, 'Trade Unions and Free Labour'.
53 William Collison, *Apostle of Free Labour*, p. 44.
54 Ibid., pp. 83–5.
55 John Saville, 'Trade Unions and Free Labour', p. 336.
56 Ibid., p. 339.
57 Ben Tillett, *Memories and Reflections* (John Long, 1931), p. 176.
58 Collison, *Apostle of Free Labour*, pp. v–vi.
59 Schneer, *Ben Tillett*, pp. 53–4.
60 Tom McCarthy, Royal Commission on Labour, Minutes of Evidence, Group B, Vol. II, Q. 12,276.
61 Ibid., evidence of Thomas Morgan, Q. 12,164.
62 Ibid. for the rules of these bodies, reproduced at appendices LXXVI and LXXVII.
63 Ibid., Q. 12,280.
64 Ibid., Qs. 12,392–6.
65 See Phillip J. Leng, *The Welsh Dockers* (G. W. and A. Hesketh, 1981), *passim*; and Stan Awberry, 'The Story of the South Wales Ports', in the TGWU *Record*, May, June, August and September 1931.
66 Leng, *The Welsh Dockers*, appendix 2, p. 108.
67 Schneer, *Ben Tillett*, p. 54.
68 Ibid., p. 55.
69 Leng, *The Welsh Dockers*, p. 30.
70 Ibid., p. 39.
71 Schneer, *Ben Tillett*, p. 79.
72 Ibid., pp. 81ff.
73 Ibid., pp. 82–5.
74 For Bristol in the 1890s, see Brian Atkinson, *Trade Unions in Bristol* (Bristol Branch, Historical Association, University of Bristol, 1982).
75 The Hull strike has been extensively researched and written about. The quotations used in this account (pp. 156–65) are drawn from: Raymond Brown, *Waterfront Organisation in Hull, 1870–1900* (University of Hull, 1972); Edward Gillett and Kenneth MacMahon, *A History of Hull* (University of Hull, 1980); Clem Edwards, 'The Hull Shipping Dispute', *Economic Journal*, vol. III (1893), pp. 345–57; John Saville, 'Trade Unions

and Free Labour'; Schneer, *Ben Tillett*; and the columns of the *Hull Daily Mail* for 1893.

76 Schneer, *Ben Tillett*, p. 93.
77 Collison, *Apostle of Free Labour*, p. 275.
78 Raymond Brown, *Waterfront Organisation in Hull*, p. 91, recounts that free labour in Hull 'was not always tractable, as may be instanced by their successful strike for an extra half-day's pay in 1894 against Messrs. Wilsons'! He also notes 'a curious feature is that even in the period when Free Labour was strong in Hull the rest of the labour movement always referred to the Free Labour Association with amused contempt, rather than fear and hatred'.
79 Brown, *Waterfront Organisation in Hull*, p. 92.
80 Ibid., p. 94.
81 Ibid., p. 95.
82 Ibid., p. 95n.
83 Clem Edwards, 'The Hull Shipping Dispute', p. 351.
84 Clem Edwards, 'Free Labour Frauds: A Study in Dishonesty', reprinted from the *Critic* (1898), 24 pp.; cited in Saville, 'Trade Unions and Free Labour', pp. 317–57.
85 Taplin, *The Dockers' Union*, p. 40.
86 Ibid., p. 43.
87 TGWU *Record*, June 1923; cited in Taplin, *The Dockers' Union*, p. 43.
88 James Sexton, *Sir James Sexton, Agitator: the Life of the Dockers' MP* (Faber and Faber, 1936), pp. 111–12.
89 Sources for this account of Sexton's union include: Taplin, *The Dockers' Union*; Sexton, *Sir James Sexton, Agitator*; Sexton's evidence to the Royal Commission on Labour; and the NUDL Annual Executive Reports, 1893–9.
90 Clem Edwards, 'Labour Federations', p. 214.
91 Taplin, *The Dockers' Union*, p. 63.
92 Smith and Nash, *The Story of the Dockers' Strike*, p. 161.
93 DWRGWU Annual Delegate Meeting, 1896, Minutes, pp. 37–8.
94 Sexton's autobiography, *Sir James Sexton, Agitator*, pp. 176–80, contains a description of Wilson's role in these events, and of his own adventures. Sexton was imprisoned in Ghent, and deported.
95 DWRGWU Annual Report 1896, p. 7.
96 Ibid.
97 Ibid.
98 Ibid., p. 64.
99 Tom Mann, *Memoirs* (1923; reissued MacGibbon and Kee, 1967), pp. 106–17.
100 He was released after Dilke and Rosebery intervened with Salisbury. Upon his deportation he was informed that he was 'banished from Belgium for seven years'. Tillett, *Memories and Reflections*, p. 181.
101 DWRGWU Annual Report, 1897, p. 6.
102 Ibid., pp. 6–7.

6

Hanging On

Horsemen in General

Some surviving unions in the field of inland transport made steady progress in the 1890s; others were subject to the same destructive forces which visited the new unions in port transport. The Northern Counties Amalgamated Association of Tramway, Hackney Carriage Employees and Horsemen in General (the Tramway and Horsemen here, for short), formed in 1889 with 400 members, had its headquarters in Manchester and branches throughout Lancashire, Yorkshire, the Midlands and South Wales. It recorded 3,799 members in 1894, and closed the century in 1899 with 7,356.[1]

The Tramway and Horsemen's Union's Reports for the 1890s were compiled by a general secretary, George Jackson, who combined cautious Christian sentiment and piety with a deep and consistent sense of outrage at the appalling conditions of work and wages of his members. Nor was he averse to leading vigorous strike action for cuts in working hours and for pay increases, as at Preston in 1894 and Oldham in 1900.

In Preston, carters' hours ranged from 77 to 100 a week (this was quite 'normal' in the industry), for which labour they received from 14s. to 23s. 6d. (from 70p to £1.17). Wages of 2½d.–5d. an hour were common amongst horsemen, but it was the long hours that most moved George Jackson, for they prevented carters

> from giving that care and attention to their children which, as a father, they ought to bestow on them. [Moreover, they are] prevented from taking any part in the welfare of their country . . . are practically disfranchised; and when the wife is debarred of the company of her husband, and her life is made a life of solitude and misery, we say there is a necessity for them to organise in order to free themselves from a life of industrial slavery.[2]

He records the regular appearance of carters before the courts, fined for being asleep whilst in charge of a horse and cart, after starting work at 3.30 in the morning. He told the Royal Commission on Labour that the lack of meal-breaks obliged men to eat with reins in one hand and food on their knees, and that 'when nature calls . . . they cannot obey the call and . . . we find that it affects the men in Manchester very much indeed.'[3]

Although the 1890s were generally a period of weakness for the new unions, Jackson was able to report a series of successful claims for shorter hours, increased wages and recognition, particularly in the tramway industry. Meal-breaks, and in one case three days' annual holiday, were amongst the improvements won by his union. Jackson mirrored new unionism's wider goals in campaigning for the municipalization of tramways and for federation and amalgamation of sectional unions, and customarily wrote of 'the labour movement' as the vehicle for a wider emancipation. During the 1890s he absorbed the Bolton Tramways Union, the Manchester, Salford and District Lurrymen and Carters' Union, the Edinburgh Tramway and Carmen's Union, the Belfast Carters' Union, and the Huddersfield Carters' Union.[4]

Recognition and reduced hours, conceded by the Manchester Carriage and Tramway Company in 1896, gave Jackson particular satisfaction:

> As regards the reduced hours of labour, the men speak very highly of the same. It hardly seems conceivable that such a great change could take place in the conditions of the men in so short a time. From fifteen and a half hours per day to ten hours, exclusive of one hour per day for dinner, is indeed a wonderful record, and sufficient to persuade any man of the advantages of trade unionism.[5]

The following year, the union reported gains of 1s. a week for corporation drivers in Portsmouth, Colne and Birmingham, and reduced hours in Nottingham and Cardiff.

The defeat of the engineering unions in the lock-out of 1897 drew a prescient comment from Jackson, who, on the strength of his surviving Reports, deserves to be recognized as a pioneer campaigner (in an industry then characterized by highly fragmented and sectional unionism) for One Big Union:

> After the failure of such a powerful organisation as the Engineers and Allied Trades, one is bound to admit that some stronger defence is required than many of us can offer in our sectional unions, and that something will have to be done before long in the way of forming a more solid body of trade unionists than we have at present. Whether it shall be federation or amalgamation I am not at this stage prepared to say, but I am strongly of the opinion that all those sectional unions representing kindred trades or occupations should at once be amalgamated into one solid

society, which would go a long way in assisting to bring about an amalgamation or federation of all trade unionists.[6]

Jackson also embraced the co-operative ideals of the anarchist Prince Peter Kropotkin. A full-page report of the Russian's London lecture on 'The Development of Trade Unionism' (at the Memorial Hall in 1897) was included in the union's own proceedings:

> His advice was now to go on steadily with trade unionism and co-operation and . . . to bring into more effective use the municipal powers which already existed, and enlarge them to the possession of buildings, land and machinery. As to 'management' he supposed that English workmen would be quite as capable of managing their own business, if they got the chance, as the old Craft Guilds, which had no capitalists or wealthy directors to guide them.[7]

A final extract from these reports concerns Jackson's appreciation of the connections between urban overcrowding, slum clearance and the rehousing of the working class in more dispersed suburbs, and the resultant need to expand tramways and cheap public transport generally:

> To spread out the community it is necessary that the tramway system should give a cheap, rapid and comprehensive service. In England the uniform fare for long distances as well as short has always been objected to, but it is essential for the extensive use of the system that the uniform fare should be adopted. It is the 'penny all the way' that induces passengers to travel long distances, and to travel in large numbers. The low cost of working electric trams as compared with horses makes it possible to have receipts per car mile and get a much larger profit. The service must be rapid . . . it must be comprehensive . . . so that a working man living in any one part can readily reach another.[8]

Dockers' Leaders in the 1890s

In chapter 5 we followed the story of the Dockers' Union through the shocks it suffered from the attacks of the Shipping Federation. These, as we saw, provoked attempts to respond through wider association by seeking federation, both national and international. Now we must look at the internal government of the Dockers' Union, and at the evolution of its leadership during the 1890s. There are several garbled stories about this in the existing literature, and some of them are generally believed.

Tom Mann's precise role in the union during the 1890s has not been adequately recorded. Tony Corfield, who wrote a series of historical essays for the TGWU *Record* in the early 1960s, did draw attention to it, however. 'It is not widely known', he wrote, 'that [Mann] officially led the Dock, Wharf, Riverside and General Workers' Union during the period

when Tillett was abroad in Australia and New Zealand."⁹ In spite of this
(quite accurate) report, the idea is widely current that Mann had largely
disengaged from the Dockers' affairs when he took up the general
secretaryship of the Independent Labour Party (ILP) in February 1894.
Thus, the Concise version of the *Dictionary of National Biography* says of
him: 'helped in London dock strike, 1889; first president, Dockers'
Union, 1889–93; member of royal commission on labour, 1891–4;
signed minority report; secretary, Independent Labour Party, 1894–7'.

The truth is much more complex. Mann's doings at this time were
very newsworthy indeed. He thought for a brief moment of taking orders,
and discussed the idea with Cosmo Lang, who believed he had netted a
fish of great prize for the Church. No sooner had the idea dawned than it
was the talk of the town. While he nursed the new ILP, he fought for the
leadership of the Engineers' Union, and ran for Parliament in Colne
Valley, Halifax and Aberdeen. All these contests attracted attention. This
was a busy life, and when he spoke about resigning (as he did more than
once) at a Dockers' Union conference, no doubt this would have been
strongly noised about. So, at the time, many people believed Mann had
moved on. Most historians have reflected that belief. Roger Moore,
however, was right when he wrote that Mann was the dockers' president,
'first in the full-time capacity from 1889 to 1892 and then honorary until
1900.'¹⁰ It is worth tracing this evolution, and its interplay with the career
of Tillett.

To those who think of trade-union democracy in twentieth-century
terms, conferences are a matter of mass gatherings of delegates, large
seaside convention halls, television cameras and screeds of (usually
none-too-friendly) coverage in the press. Debates will be closely
structured around resolutions which have been composited into clear
choices from a multitude of proposals received from hundreds of branch
meetings. Discipline will show itself in crisp, short interventions, seldom
taking longer than five minutes and frequently lasting only three.

Things were not quite like that in 1890. The dockers gathered for
their first Annual Delegate Meeting in the Great Assembly Hall in Mile
End Road. Sixty-three people were present, of whom eleven were
officers or executive councillors. Tom Mann presided. He asked his
colleagues to behave in a dignified and calm manner. This, apparently,
they did. The press were to be admitted during the presidential address,
but not for the rest of the proceedings.

John Burns was then introduced, and it was resolved that he be invited
to stay after addressing delegates for a quarter of an hour. Burns too
asked delegates to behave in a 'calm, peaceful and dignified manner'.
After this, the presidential address was pronounced from a printed copy,
already circulated to the press. None of the rest of the deliberations was
to remain so easy to read, since the records were written into a very large
minute-book in a flowing copperplate, which gradually became less and

less calm and dignified, more jagged and, in the end, spidery, as the minute-writer got tired. The meeting itself seems to have remained very orderly, working day by day through all the draft rules and a series of resolutions.

By the time of the second Annual Delegate Meeting in Hull, in late September 1891, participation had diminished to twenty-five delegates plus officers. Four delegates turned up from Hull; Swansea and Bristol were each represented by three; one apiece came from Medway, Cardiff, Newport, Northfleet, Grimsby and Gloucester; and the remainder were from London.

Once again, Tom Mann gave the presidential address, which was described as 'perfectly unique', and which evidently covered a very much wider area than was customary at the time in trade-union orations. Judging by the discussion which was then aroused, Mann's statement covered the question of temperance; Brother Whitehead, of Grimsby, said that there had been a 'wonderful decrease of drunkenness on the part of the men, but a terrible increase on the part of the women'. Mann evidently also spoke about co-operation, since delegates from Swansea and London were moved to comment on co-operative ideas in the speech.

Tantalizingly, as soon as the minutes have recorded agreement on the publication of the president's speech, alongside the general secretary's report, there is an item which reads 'Resignation of President'. Then almost an entire page is left blank, as if the minute-secretary had intended to seek advice on what precisely to record about this matter. In the event, nothing was recorded, and the conference moved on to debate sub-contracting, the inspection of dockside equipment, and the legal eight-hour day. Tom Mann was still signing each day's minutes as a true record right through to the end of the conference.

The third Annual Delegate Meeting brought a couple of dozen delegates to Swansea in September 1892, plus another dozen associates, including officers, executive members and trustees. At an appropriate moment, the delegates left their committee room for a larger hall in order to hear the presidential address, which once again is missing from the ledger which served as a minute book. It was, however, printed in the published record of proceedings, which contains a preface by Ben Tillett, in which he regrets 'that our President has withdrawn from active leadership, although still with us as trustee'.

Tillett's Report to the conference refers to painful internal arguments within the union, and 'the hostile attitude taken up by the districts'. Cliques and factions had emerged. 'In the interest of the union', said Tillett, he had met all this bad blood 'with courage'. There was a special need for an organizational drive in London, where 'revival meetings' were 'imperative'. Other districts 'may be said to be holding their own'.

The printed minutes reproduce Tom Mann's presidential address in full, and show why it again drew many enthusiastic comments. It ranges from a consideration of John Stuart Mill's treatment of the relation between individual initiative and common ownership to an examination of the different roads which were available to secure trade-union goals:

> our ideal is the same as Mill's, viz., 'to unite the greatest individual liberty of action with the common ownership in the raw material of the globe, and an equal participation of all in the benefits of combined labour' – combined labour meaning the organised energy of the workers producing in the most effective fashion – whilst this is our fixed aim, it is a very secondary matter, indeed, as to what precise institution shall be used for its realisation. There is no especial virtue in Trades Union action as against municipal action, or in voluntary co-operative effort as against Parliamentary effort; they are all good when rightly used, and they should all be used to realise the object already set forth. The end is what is required. The means to reach the end must never be treated as the end itself. Thus, given universal co-operation on the voluntary basis, we should then reach the first of our ideals, and there would be but little necessity for Trade Unionism, or given effective action through the municipalities with an effective understanding between each, we should be in the same position, or if as the result of a high level of intelligence it was decided to secure the end in view through the agency of Parliament, the results would still be the same. We must be guided largely by expediency in these matters, and given the temperament of the British people with the existing British institutions it is pretty clear that we must use each and all of the institutions named, but use them all for the purpose declared by Mill.

In following through this diversity of paths, Mann singled out some for special attention:

> The plan proposed by Mr. Mather, M.P., of Manchester, is a bold one and a good one. He proposes to incorporate the trades unions properly representative of their trades, empowering them to deal with the force of law with all matters relative to working hours. But these matters ought not, and must not take the whole of our time; the democratic control of industry in the interests of all is to be brought about, and the principle and practice of co-operation can supplement our trade union work in a splendid fashion. Trade unions enable us as wage earners to secure fair conditions for the time being, but we require to organise also as wage spenders, otherwise it is quite possible to retard trades unionism by neglecting as spenders to see that trades union principles have been complied with as regards the whole of the commodities we obtain by our wages. This can be secured by dealing with the distributive stores which enable us not only to deal exclusively in articles produced under fair conditions, but place a power in the hands of the organised consumers to establish and conduct in their own interests the entire manufacturing departments that are required to supply the distributive stores, and to this

extent we get industry organised under democratic control, and can conduct the same on lines that shall set an example to ordinary capitalistic enterprises.

Many co-operative manufacturing establishments are now working successfully, and during the next ten years we may expect to see a very great spread of the principle . . . In municipal life, also, is to be found many opportunities for spreading the principles we have at heart, and to help on the ideal set forth, a true trades unionist who is also a member of a co-operative society, should not be indifferent to the policy endorsed by his fellow-townsmen.[11]

The printed minutes then diverge from the handwritten ledger account. Some pages of the ledger are not filled, and at least one page has been removed. In moving the vote of thanks, Tillett is reported in the printed minute as reading 'a resolution' (from Bristol) 'begging Mr. Mann not to carry out his intention of retiring from the presidency'.

Clearly Tom Mann had intended his presidential statement to be his swan song among the dockers. It was followed by another long debate on rules revision. After this had continued for a considerable time, Tom Mann

rose and said that it was his fixed determination to comply with the intention already sent out to the delegates. He handed in his resignation [(12 months ago) – this is deleted in the ledger by the minute-secretary, but remains quite legible] at the last annual delegate meeting when it was understood that the governing body would consider the length of time that his notice should expire. He valued the many kind expressions of opinion that had fallen from the lips of several delegates and friends. He could not alter his previous decision; he would not alter it. Whilst however highly appreciating the motives of those who were asking him to reconsider his decision he could not depart from his previous intention.

One delegate after another then spoke, in a chorus of dismay. J. Harrison from Hull was 'sorry that the President had a mind of his own' on this matter. The president had a 'thoroughly democratic, broad, charitable and progressive mind'. Because of this 'he appealed to him from the bottom of his heart to reconsider his decision'. J. Johnson of London said that all his colleagues 'would deeply feel the loss of his splendid services'. Ben Tillett then read out a string of resolutions, from every district in the union, urging the president not to resign. H. G. Spencer from Hull 'animadverted on the work done on behalf of trade unionism and on the dockers in particular by Brother Tom Mann'. J. Morgan from Newport feared that if the president left the union, it would 'break up into sections'.[12] Almost everyone said his piece, and almost all said the same thing.

At the end of the day, exhausted, the conference unanimously carried a motion giving Tom Mann 'until tomorrow morning to reconsider his decision'. But the minute-book then deserts us. It tells us that the 'fourth day's meeting was held on Thursday at 9.30, with the President in the Chair'. And that is all. Three pages are left blank, and we tip straight into yet more debates upon the rules.

The fourth Annual Delegate Meeting met in Bristol for five days in September 1893. It tells us that present was Mr Tom Mann, *Treasurer*. But at the end of the opening address by the Bristol District chairman, Mr Tom Mann 'was unanimously elected to the Chair'.

Ben Tillett reported on the employers' offensive against the union, above all in Hull. John Burns delivered a public oration at a mass meeting on the Grove. It was not until the fourth day that Rule XIX was debated, and Tom Mann was then asked 'whether he would act as Honorary President to the Union'.[13] He asked for time to consider the matter. As the vote was taken on the job descriptions of the various posts listed in the rule, Brothers Frith and Krone (of Hull and London) moved that Tom Mann be 'asked to undertake the position of Honorary President'.[14] After he explained that 'he could not undertake any particular work', Mann accepted. When he left early 'to another engagement', there was a vote of thanks for his efforts during the days he had been present.

The ledger book has blank pages which were presumably intended for the fifth Annual Delegate Meeting; there is, however, a printed record. The dockers gathered in Grimsby Town Hall at the end of May 1894. The fourteen delegates came from London (five), Bridgwater, Newport, Hull (two), Gloucester, Swansea, Bristol (two) and Grimsby. A dozen officers and fraternal observers were also present. Although Tom Mann presided, he declined to give a full-scale presidential speech, saying that 'the time of the meeting was valuable'. But the mood of the time can be caught in the remark 'if their meetings did little to push forward the movement it could not be said they hindered it'.

As if to underline its concern for recognition after the débâcle in Hull, much was made of the hospitality of the Grimsby Council in offering their Town Hall as the seat of the conference. The demonstration, for sure, would have been seen across the estuary! The Lord Mayor then made a welcoming speech. It is easy to read all this, in later times, as formality. But it may be truer to see in it an attempt to recover ground which had been burnt flat by the hired men of the Shipping Federation. Be that as it may, the fifth meeting offers a tantalizing picture of a power-struggle in the working of the union.

Why, asked a London delegate, were two minute-secretaries present? Tom McCarthy had been detailed by the Emergency Committee to take the minutes, 'while Bro A. J. Tomkins was here solely on the authority of the General Secretary'. Tillett defended this decision because Tomkins was aware of all the necessary documentation for the work of the ADM. 'If his action . . . was not confirmed,' he said, 'he would take it as an expression of censure on himself'. There followed a brisk scrap, in which only Swansea came out in support of Tillett. Tom McCarthy, Tillett's close friend, spoke: 'The real question was whether any one man should rule the Union; if this was so there was an end to democratic control'.[15] The present work of the general secretary, he went on, took him so much away from the central office that others constantly had to act in his place. Therefore the decisions of the Emergency Committee 'should be obeyed'.[16] The vote went against Tillett: twelve to nil, with two abstentions. To rub it in, it was then unanimously agreed to send Brother Tomkins back to his desk in London the following day.

The more that his people were moved to criticize Tillett, the more insistently they pressed Mann for his attention. Of course, through all this time he was acting as general secretary of the Independent Labour Party, so that, when he met the demands of the docks with the defensive cry that he was busy, we may very well believe him.

In May 1895 the Annual Delegate Meeting was held in Gloucester, with a dozen representatives, plus three Emergency Committee men and four officers. The following year delegates moved to Newport, and the roster increased by one. Tom Mann presided over both meetings, and delivered an important speech to the earlier one. He also remained in office to chair the seventh meeting: but this, which met in Middlesbrough in May 1899, was the first of a new series of conferences to meet triennially. As a result of this changeover, the detailed affairs of the union are chronicled only in a series of Annual Reports, for the years 1896, 1897, 1898 and 1899.

Tillett was very much a sick man, and largely beaten. In 1897, as we have seen, he was advised by his doctor to take a rest, and he set off for New Zealand. It was to be a long stay. He moved on to Australia in the summer of 1897, and then back to New Zealand. An American interlude was proposed, but the voyage never took place because of illness. It was not until October 1898 that Tillett came home to England. This is how it came about that Tom Mann signed the 1896 and 1897 Reports: 'I have stepped in', he wrote, 'to present the report on behalf of the General Office'.[17]

As we have already seen, the port workers were being heavily intimidated during these years. It showed. 'A general dead level of apathy seemed to characterise the vast majority of Port Workers at the beginning of the year', wrote Mann.[18] It implied efforts to join forces with others in the field, and Mann lost no time in seeking to do just that.

Motions encouraging amalgamation with other unions had been approved in 1893 and 1894. Two Hull delegates had moved two motions on federation in 1893. The first proposed joining up with the American Knights of Labour and other dockworkers' unions internationally. It was amended, to be referred to the TUC. The second motion from Hull urged consideration of the need to federate with the Liverpool dockers and the Miners' Federation.[19] This proposal was reaffirmed in 1894, and it was also reported that overtures had been made to the miners and to the American Federation of Labour, without producing a response.

The Workers' Union

Tom Mann's creative energy had one more moment during this decade: the formation of the Workers' Union in 1898. Its origins lay in the defeat of the engineering unions in the 1897 lock-out, which was attributed – in a widespread debate in the Labour movement – to the sectional, craft structure of the industry's unions. Tom Mann, in calling for the formation of a new union, spoke specifically of the need 'to avenge the engineers' defeat'. In working on the organizational problem, Mann had two models in mind. One, industrial unionism, 'was only just emerging. Scarcely anyone gave serious attention to the matter, as it was felt there was no prospect of success in that direction.'[20] The other, which was also at the time only at an embryonic stage, was an authentically general unionism, and this, in Mann's fertile mind, fitted the need revealed by the structural defects in engineering unionism:

> In the engineering industry, a workman who was on a job for which the recognised union rate was neither paid nor expected was looked upon by the members of the union as an outsider. They made the machine, they would not work the machine, neither would they broaden the basis of their union so that the man who had to work it could be organised in relationship with them. It was the same in every trade, and not more than one-fourth of the adult male population was organised. The proper course, had commonsense prevailed, would have been for the existing unions so to broaden the basis of their organisations as to welcome every worker that came into the industry, and elastic enough for the admission of all. Instead of this, not only was there no provision for an ever-growing number of handy men, which the changing methods made necessary: but between existing unions, each catering for highly-skilled men, there existed an absurd hostility . . . Resolved to face whatever of approval or disapproval it might bring, I determined to attempt at any rate to draft the rules and to prepare the framework of a union that should be open to any section of workers of either sex for whom no proper union already existed.[21]

The objective thus defined by Mann (and it must be stressed that the union was very much his creation from the top down) went far beyond filling the vacuum in the engineering industry. At the founding conference, the object (drafted by Mann) was declared to be: 'The organisation of all sections of the community on an Industrial and Political Basis for the purpose of raising the standard of social life of the

workers, and the ultimate realization of an Industrial Commonwealth'.[22]
These were the terms and the ideology of the Social Democratic
Federation, which had advocated One Big Union for socialist purposes
from the 1880s. But the methods of the Workers' Union were to include
electoral activity more akin to the ILP. Tom Mann, having been general
secretary of the party, had obviously brought over from it not only
contacts, but also the skills he had acquired. The union would 'support
. . . Labour candidates at all Parliamentary, Municipal, School Board,
and other elections'.

To run the provisional machinery of the union, Mann brought in Tom
Chambers, an ILP activist, who was by then the secretary of the
International Federation in Tillett's absence. Mann left Chambers to
organize the central office, whilst he stumped the country to recruit
members and found branches. But his lofty and ambitious hopes were
frustrated. Many in the ILP and in the existing general unions, such as
the National Amalgamated Union of Labour and the Gasworkers'
Union, resented the intrusion of a rival union in their fields, and the
union commenced business with only a few hundred members.
Sustained for a time by Mann's voluntary labours in the field, and by a
short trade boom, it reached over 4,000 members by the end of 1899.
Thereafter, it went into sharp decline in the early years of the new
century, as economic conditions turned downwards again.[23] Its story will
be resumed in subsequent chapters, for it was to play a significant role in
influencing the future shape of the TGWU after it joined the general
union in 1929.

The Workers' Union was not the only response to the defeat of the
engineers. The employers, too, drew their own lessons from that
episode. After their victories over the engineers in 1897 and the Welsh
miners, forced back on the coalowners' terms after a five-month lock-out
in 1898, the Employers' Parliamentary Council was formed on 15
November 1898. This council sought to become a national analogue to
the Trades Union Congress. At its head stood an executive of eleven
people, charged with the monitoring of legislative proposals, and the
organization of appropriate lobbies.

The Long Hunger in the Quarries

The Conservative victory in the General Election of 1895 seemed to the
more intransigent employers to be a licence for heightened aggression
against trade unionism. Lord Penrhyn's slate quarries at Bethesda were
to be chosen as the stage for an exemplary disciplinary sacrifice. The
quarrymen had elected a committee to negotiate with Lord Penrhyn, but
he declined to recognize it. When, in September 1896, the committee
sought an improvement in working conditions, Penrhyn dismissed them.

A strike inevitably followed. It was to last for nearly two years, becoming a *cause célèbre* for trade unionists throughout the kingdom. The *Daily Chronicle* campaigned for the strikers and raised £7,500 for the relief of distress. The Board of Trade made repeated efforts to mediate, but Penrhyn refused any offer of arbitration.

The 1890s had already seen widespread turbulence in the North Wales quarries, but the dispute in Bethesda overshadowed every other strike or lock-out in the region. By January 1897 'more money was coming from outside than from the quarrymen'.[24] Liverpool building workers imposed a levy on themselves and brought their Trades Council into solidarity. The sum of £150 was collected from a teachers' conference. Bethesda choirs went on tour and raised almost £2,500 in collections. Taken together, the strike funds generated almost £20,000.

Lord Penrhyn made four separate attempts to re-open his quarries: in November 1896, and in January, February and April 1897. No local people reported for work, and the only fear that the Bethesda strikers admitted was that outside strike-breakers might be imported. But it was unthinkable that outsiders could be found with any of the requisite skills to produce slates.

The quarry manager, E. A. Young, tried to bring mounted police into the area, and wrote more than once to the chief constable with this aim in view:

> But his evidence was somewhat impressionistic: on a bicycle trip he had noticed that 'some of the men near Bethesda were very sullen', while some strikers . . . had seen fit to shout at him as he rode by. More alarmingly, he reported that when his name had been mentioned at a mass meeting there had been calls of 'shoot him' and 'kill him', while a Welsh newspaper had printed the suggestion that his teeth be knocked out and a knife be stuck in his bowels.[25]

Even without the police, Young's teeth and bowels survived intact through an endless round of completely fruitless negotiations.

Despite the long hunger, the quarrymen remained firm, but their union finally succumbed to political pressures and agreed to settle the strike. The quarrymen's historian tells us that 'it was with some justification . . . that the Bethesda men felt that the agreement had been reached behind their backs.'[26] The manager saw the settlement as 'a complete victory on every point . . . I have no doubt [that] the result of such a beating will be a lesson to have to be content in future when they are well off, but unfortunately, they never seem to realise when they are well off.'[27]

After the return to work, Young set out upon a campaign of victimization and intimidation of the men's leaders. Their chairman was dismissed in December 1898 and the following year another of their spokesmen was victimized. Holidays were annulled by fiat, and a peace offering from the men's committee (in the form of a present for Lord Penrhyn) was peremptorily refused. In these circumstances, it is not altogether surprising that a new leadership began to form among the quarrymen, and that a further round in their long-running struggle with the owners would not long be delayed.

The Foundation of Ruskin College

On the eve of the new century, another development took place which was to bring about important changes in the recruitment of trade-union personnel, and to change the lives of some trade unionists.

Ruskin College was inaugurated in February 1899, John Ruskin's eightieth birthday. Its founder, Walter Vrooman, an American socialist, was inspired by Ruskin's *Unto this Last*, which made a passionate argument for the improvement of the poor through education: 'Either these poor are of a race essentially different from ours, and unredeemable . . . or else by such care as we have ourselves received we may make them as continent and sober as ourselves – wise and dispassionate as we are – models arduous of imitation.'[28]

At the meeting in Oxford City Hall, a considerable crowd included Ben Tillett, James Sexton and Dan Irving of the Social Democrats. Numerous trades councils and co-operative societies were also represented.[29] The new college was to enjoy a tumultuous existence, and some of its graduates were to have an influence on the future conduct of the TGWU.

Adapting – and Reacting – to Adversity

The new unions went through their most severe defeat in the decade under review. In the docks and in shipping they nevertheless survived, wherever they had a national dimension. Local and sectional unions, whether in docks or in inland road transport, often collapsed, except amongst specialist groups such as the London stevedores, and amongst watermen and lightermen generally. Their adaptation to adversity took various forms. They created federations at regional or port level nationally and internationally. These never achieved an adequate degree of mobilization against a ruthless, well-financed and above all national employers' body. In any case, in a time of slump, defensive sectionalism, reinforced by the economic climate, was stronger than the instinct of mutual help. Nevertheless, the experiences of federation went into the pool of inheritance waiting to be analysed and drawn on in future. Clem Edwards made a thoughtful appraisal for this purpose.[30]

The new unionists tried, particularly in the case of the Dockers' Union, to broaden the field of recruitment, but they lacked both the resources and the power to persuade large numbers of potential blacklegs in the fields and pastures of Kent and Lincolnshire to make common cause with urban labourers. In South Wales, where the ports had extensive heavy-industrial hinterlands, they had more success – particularly towards the end of the century – in extending recruitment into manufacturing industry, as well as into general labouring – a development full of meaning for the future general union.

Before the Royal Commission, they argued the case for municipal workshops to absorb the labour surplus which sapped their industrial effectiveness, and for municipal ownership and control of the ports. They put forward embryo schemes of planning and rational use of the ports. They sought to practise and develop local schemes of conciliation and arbitration, and, in Tillett's case, proposed a drastic form of compulsory state arbitration. Most of these strategies would be taken up, with more effect, when the economic and political climate changed in the new century.

But above all, the industrial weakness which they now experienced impelled them to use their own influence in changing the political circumstances in which they worked. To this momentous evolution we must now turn.

Notes

1 Tramway and Horsemen's Half-yearly Reports, 1894 and 1899.
2 Ibid., 1894, p. 3.
3 Royal Commission on Labour, 1892, Q. 17,893; quoted in Arthur Marsh and Victoria Ryan, *Historical Directory of Trade Unions*, vol. III (Gower, 1987), p. 230.
4 Marsh and Ryan, *Historical Directory of Trade Unions*, p. 232.
5 Tramway and Horsemen's Half-yearly Report, 1896, p. 9.
6 Ibid., 1897, p. 10.
7 Ibid., pp. 108–9.
8 Tramway and Horsemen's Half-yearly Report, 1899, p. 127.
9 Tony Corfield, 'The History of the Union: The Metal and Engineering Group', TGWU *Record*, December 1961, p. 37.
10 Roger Moore, *The Emergence of the Labour Party* (Hodder and Stoughton, 1978), p. 45.
11 DWRGWU Annual Delegate Meeting, 1892, Minutes, pp. 18–19. Mather was a liberal employer who actually came to endorse the proposal for the legal eight-hour day; see Henry Pelling, *Social Geography of British Elections* (Macmillan, 1967), pp. 245–6.
12 Ibid., pp. v–31.
13 DWRGWU Annual Delegate Meeting, 1893, Minutes, p. 24.

14   Ibid., p. 25.
15   DWRGWU Annual Delegate Meeting, 1894, Minutes, p. 6.
16   Ibid., p. 7.
17   DWRGWU Annual Report, 1896, p. 5.
18   Ibid.
19   DWRGWU Annual Delegate Meeting, 1893, Minutes, p. 28.
20   Tom Mann, *Memoirs* (1923; reissued McGibbon and Kee, 1967), p. 18.
21   Ibid., pp. 118–19.
22   *Weekly Times and Echo*, 6 February 1898; cited in Richard Hyman, *The Workers' Union* (Oxford University Press, 1971), p. 7.
23   See Hyman, *The Workers' Union*, chapters 1 and 2.
24   R. Merfyn Jones, *The North Wales Quarrymen, 1874–1922* (University of Wales, 1981), p. 188.
25   Ibid., p. 190.
26   Ibid., p. 194.
27   Ibid., p. 195.
28   John Ruskin, *Unto this Last* (Blackfriars, 1862), pp. 111–12.
29   W. W. Craik, *Central Labour College* (Lawrence and Wishart, 1964), p. 35.
30   Clem Edwards, 'Labour Federations', *Economic Journal*, vol. III (September 1893), pp. 408–24.

7

Independent Labour Politics

I

A whole decade was to elapse between the birth of the new unions and the formation of the Labour Party, or, to be more precise, its foreshadowing Labour Representation Committee, in 1900. During that time, as we have seen, the employers mounted a ferocious counteroffensive, which, conjoined with severe unemployment, weakened all unions in some respects and hit some of the newest unions particularly hard. Notwithstanding this fact, overall union membership grew, and the Trades Union Congress, although it was never controlled by new unionism, found itself under relentless pressure, from new and old unions alike, to adopt a more committed political posture.

Government (and Empire) in the 1890s

Most of the first half of the decade saw a weak Liberal government becoming increasingly feeble and beleaguered. During the second half, the Conservatives ruled. The Liberals had regained office in 1892 after careful attempts had been made to attract and hold the Labour vote. In their 'Newcastle Programme', aimed directly at working-class voters, it was pledged that plural voting would be eliminated, and implied that action might be initiated on the question of shorter working hours. Other ameliorative measures were also promised.

In retrospect, the resultant administration of 1892 was often described as 'an interlude' during what would otherwise have been two decades of Conservative hegemony. Gladstone, who resumed the premiership more than halfway through his eighty-third year, was to be haunted from start to finish of his new term by the question of Ireland. Because Liberal Unionists had rebelled and found their own identity, he was now dependent on Irish support. Irish Nationalists numbered eighty-one in the new Parliament. New unionists – or rather spokesmen for new unionists, as distinct from old trade unionists running on a Liberal ticket – had won three seats. Of these, only one was solidly committed to independent Labour action. Gladstone, the Grand Old Man, still towered over rivals, but neither parliamentary arithmetic nor the calendar was on his side. Home Rule dominated his agenda, and he succeeded in completing his Bill, through all stages, only to encounter a resolute veto from the House of Lords.

Having failed to disengage from Ireland, British colonists fanned out on other fronts. Imperialism continued to roll over Africa, assimilating Uganda and following Cecil Rhodes into the Transvaal, Mashonaland and Matabeleland. Machine-gun bullets were traded against diamonds and gold. The Boer War was being prepared, inexorably. As the Liberals were about to fall in 1895, W. T. Stead reported a conversation in which Rhodes told him:

> I was in the East End of London yesterday and attended a meeting of the unemployed. I listened to the wild speeches, which were just a cry for 'bread', 'bread', 'bread', and on my way home I pondered over the scene and I became more than ever convinced of the importance of imperialism . . . My cherished idea is a solution for the social problem . . . to save the 40,000,000 inhabitants of the United Kingdom from a bloody civil war, we colonial statesmen must acquire new lands for settling the surplus population, to provide new markets for the goods produced in the factories and mines. The Empire is a bread and butter question . . . If you want to avoid civil war, you must become imperialists.[1]

This shameless utterance was seized upon by socialist writers and has remained well remembered because it found its way into Lenin's little book on *Imperialism*. But in reality, Rhodes's colonization was an idea most imperfectly realized. To be sure, American immigration was being wound down in response to the economic squeeze: ostensibly it was possible to argue that the British 'surplus population' needed somewhere else to go.[2] But no such large-scale movement of people towards Southern Africa was actually to follow, partly because demographic changes in the home territory eased migratory pressures, but also in large part because the African annexations were not undertaken to deal with population overspill: they were almost entirely the result of greed for mineral resources. By the same token, new markets would be somewhat slow to materialize in this region. Neither of these facts prevented the expression of imperial 'concern' for the relatively few British migrants, and this solicitude was to puff itself up into the provocation of actual war before the end of the decade.

What was really going on was a helter-skelter competition to grab whatever territory was not already taken. Each European power was

1 The youngest
pioneers: the
Match-girls of
Bryant & May,
1888.
*Annie Besant,
An Autobiography*

2 The banner of the Social
Democratic Federation.
*National Museum of Labour
History*

Eleanor Marx

3 Eleanor Marx: unpaid strike secretary. *National Museum of Labour History*

Will Thorne

Ben Tillett

Tom Mann

Harry Orbell

4 Leaders for a Generation: Will Thorne, Ben Tillett, Tom Mann and Harry Orbell in 1889. *National Museum of Labour History*

5 The Coal-heavers' Float: demonstrating for the Dock Strike through the City of London, 1889.

6 John Burns addressing the dockers on Tower Hill, 1889 strike. *National Museum of Labour History.*

7 William Collison: Apostle of Free Labour.

8 Havelock Wilson, an early portrait.

List of Persons willing to speak as advocates of Industrial Syndicalism in their respective districts.

DISTRICT.	NAME.	TRADE UNION.	ADDRESS.
GATESHEAD-ON-TYNE..	NED SCOTT	Railway Servants	3, Fenwick Terrace.
SUNDERLAND	WILLIAM KEY ...	Government Contractor ...	Walworth Street.
MIDDLESBORO	Cr. J. B. DAVIES ...	Dockers Union	97, Commercial Street
HUDDERSFIELD ...	E. J. B. ALLEN ...	Gasworkers	New Street, Honley.
SHEFFIELD	T. J. RING	Cabinet Makers	138, Scotland Street.
OLDHAM	"PIONEER"	Railway Servants	Carr Farm, Diggle.
MANCHESTER	HARRY GREEN ...	Engineers	122, Heald Pl., Rusholme.
Do.	A. A. PURCELL ...	French Polishers	142, Gt. Clowes Street, Broughton.
Do.	F. W. SANDERSON...	Lecturer	26, Boston Street.
LIVERPOOL	FRANK PEARCE ...	Ships' Stewards	6, Spekeland Buildings, 22, Canning Place.
Do.	PETER LARKIN ...	Dockers	36 Gadsby Street.
Do.	F. BOWERS	Stonemasons	11, Ebvey Street
Do.	S. H. MUSTON... ...	Lecturer	266. Smithdown Lane.
NEWPORT (Mon.) ...	GEORGE JACKSON...	Sailors and Firemen ...	31, Ruperra Street.
Do.	ALFRED COX	Dockers' Union	49, Raglan Street.
Do.	GEORGE COX	Do. do.	20, Lewis Street.
SOUTH WALES { MARDY...	NOAH ABLETT ...	South Wales Miners' Fed.	97, Griffith Street.
PORTH	W. F. HAY	Do. do.	28, Mount Pleasant.
YNYSHIR	GEORGE DOLLING ...	Do. do.	11, Upper Gynor Street.
CWMPURE	TOM EVANS	Do. do.	157, Pure Road.
CLYDACH VALE ...	W. H. MAINWARING	Do. do.	3, Llwynceln Terrace.
PONTYPRIDD ...	JAMES RIGG	Brassfounders	20, Brookes Terrace, Tower Street.
PORT TALBOT	Cr. JONAH CHARLES	Dockers' Union	20, Station Road.
LONDON	A. ELSBURY	Tailors	51, Jamaica Street, Stepney, E.
SOUTHAMPTON	R. W. STORRY ...	Ships' Stewards	8, Terminus Terrace
Do.	THOMAS GARNETT	Moulders	39, College Street

9 (above) Advocates of syndicalism: from the first issue of *The Industrial Syndicalist*, July 1910.

10 Strike-breakers and their Protectors. Free labourers and police escort waiting for action on the *Lady Jocelyn* during the Liverpool strike, 1911 (see text, p.244). *Reproduced by permission of the General Council of British Shipping*

11 The Liverpool strikers on 'Bloody Sunday', 13 August 1911, in St George's Square. *Reproduced by permission of the General Council of British Shipping*

12 Police, cavalry and soldiers with fixed bayonets escort a convoy past a strikers' meeting: Liverpool 1911. *Press Association*

13 A Liverpool docker confronts the young soldiers sent to break the strike, 1911. *TGWU*

14 Out in Sympathy: Cardiff coal-trimmers march in support of the dockers, 1911.

chiefly concerned to plant its own claims before the others. In Britain successive governments, of both parties, gave their blessing to this enterprise. While the accompanying noise of jingo patriotism was often deafening, costing them some damage in moral terms, the tangible benefits to the London poor (or indeed to the submerged third of the population in all Britain's major cities) were absolutely negligible. However, no worry on this account emerged to prevent Lord Rosebery, Gladstone's Liberal successor (who took office in March 1894), from embracing the imperial ethos with all possible fervour. In some ways he outdid Cecil Rhodes. On Irish questions this mattered considerably. Rhodes, for all his imperial fervour, had not only endorsed Parnell, but had actually contributed a cheque for £10,000 to his campaign in 1888.[3] Rosebery showed no such weakness. Indeed, this contributed to the short life of his administration, because once the Lords had seen off Gladstone's Irish Bill, Rosebery's studied equivocations about Home Rule brought mutiny among a vital contingent within his majority. In June 1895 he was defeated on a snap vote. The election which followed produced a decisive turn to the Conservatives, and Lord Salisbury became Prime Minister.

The main domestic achievement of the Liberal administrations of 1892–5 had been in the field of local-government reform. The Fowler Act of 1894 established a tier of urban and rural district councils which was to endure until 1974. For the first time a handful of women were actually allowed to vote, and stand for office, in local elections, without any marriage bar. This was to give a notable impulse to the movement for women's suffrage.

Apart from this, the House of Lords killed off an Employers' Liability Bill which had been energetically promoted by Asquith. Death duties were introduced in Harcourt's budget. Nothing much happened about the balance of the Newcastle Programme. Both of the key questions which mattered to Labour, concerning plural voting and shorter hours, were shelved as soon as the votes were in the tin. For all those concerned with the interests of Labour, or with the Irish question, this cumulative record may well have seemed less than inspiring. Only among the miners, whose resistance to a general lock-out in 1893 was strong enough to bring in Rosebery as a government mediator, was there anything to rejoice about.[4] That Lord Rosebery's lucky horses went on to win two successive victories in the Derby, after he had become Prime Minister, probably estranged a greater number of nonconformist voters than those who admired his good fortune with the turf accountants.

Turning to Politics

As we have seen, the industrial luck of the dockers and other waterfront unions did not endure for long. Not only did the employers counterattack with great brutality, but in many places the unions were trodden flat. Some of the most belligerent of the bosses were shipowners and prominent Liberals. Such local tycoons did not scruple to provoke disputes and then call upon their town mayors for full police and military support. Even had they not been predisposed to political action, the dockers' leaders would have been forced into it by the resulting shocks.

Weakened as they were by the loss of membership which we have already reported, these leaders none the less had star quality, not only because each was a remarkable personality, but also as a result of the public impact which their conduct of the great strike had made.

Paul Thompson, the historian of the London socialist movement, recognizes the importance of Burns, Mann and Tillett in the struggle for Labour representation, but believes that their influence 'was reduced by their political inconsistency'. They were socialists, he writes, 'but of a peculiarly individualistic kind. Burns' egotism was already drawing him towards the Liberal Party.' Mann, he sees as being no better at all: 'restless and erratic', indeed, turning 'from the Dockers to the London Trades Council', then agitating for the reform of the Amalgamated Society of Engineers. 'Between 1891 and 1894', continues Thompson, Mann

> worked as a member of the Royal Commission on Labour, at the same time acting as secretary of the L.C.C. Progressive Party organisation. After announcing that he was considering ordination as an Anglican priest, he became secretary of the Independent Labour Party in 1894. Three years later he returned to trade unionism to work for the International Federation of Ship, Dock and River Workers, but this required much time abroad, and after a brief return to politics as secretary of the radical National Democratic League, he set off in 1901 for nine years in Australia and South Africa.

Then there was Tillett, who

> kept to his post of Dockers' secretary, but he too was abroad between 1895 and 1898 on account of ill-health, and proved a somewhat erratic political rebel. He stood as an independent Labour candidate at Bradford in 1892 and soon dropped out of the L.C.C. when he realised its dependence on the progressives. He was 'never a Lib–Lab'. But his socialism was based on confused emotion, and his exhortations in the union's annual reports on 'the ethical conception of duty', and a trades unionism 'not limited to the mere sordid sphere', obscure his protests against the status of the worker as 'a mere wages slave'.

All this, the indictment continues, disrupted the organization at lower levels:

> As a result of this lack of an effective lead from Burns, Tillett and Mann, other leading officials of the Dockers can be found playing somewhat

contradictory political roles. Harry Kay, the union treasurer, after dabbling in Fabianism turned to the I.L.P. and eventually became a Social Democrat. Clem Edwards, an early independent Labour man, became Labour editor of the radical *Sun* in 1893 and stood as a Liberal–Labour candidate for Tottenham in 1895.[5]

The Scope and Limits of Inconsistency

It would of course be difficult, and even pointless, to deny inconsistencies in some of these actions. To seek to impose too much order on this record would be to misrepresent it. But if we examine these events with care, it is arguable that there were fewer contradictions in them than some historians have believed: and that these were far from disabling. First, however, we will look at the element of truth in the indictment.

Tillett's politics in the late 1880s were fluid, as we have already pointed out. In the beginning, he was something of a Lib.–Lab.: but he changed his mind. During this later time, into the 1890s, we might be excused the claim that he had found, for a short but crucial period, a framework of independent Labour action and advocacy which was both resilient and influential. In his later life, Tillett certainly allowed his earlier flamboyance to run unchecked, and he was often wildly unpredictable. Inconsistency, during these convulsions, would come to seem the least of his various vices. His more dramatic twists and turns ensured that he would be right at least some of the time. Now and then the clouds parted, and the sun shone through. What seems very evident is that Tillett's younger days were clearer, and less steamy, than his middle age. Throughout most of the 1890s he followed a relatively steady course, in spite not only of illness but also of the most vigorous assaults from his union's many adversaries. Tillett, like others of his generation, was not only himself self-educated, but was also operating among people who had been denied any chance of instruction and who were prone to respond to all the more crude appeals of demagogy. Continued melodrama sustained a whole generation of leaders who were indeed considerably larger than life. When we come to meet rogues like 'Captain' Tupper, we shall appreciate this: but we need to examine Tillett's contribution before judging it.

As for Burns, his egotism may be recognized, but his move towards the Liberals represented more than personal ambition. The thought of breaking the Lib.–Lab. integument presented real problems for the socialist new unionists. What were men like Burns to do? Their Fabian advisers encouraged them to rely on the goodwill of the younger Liberal radicals, which was not illusory. At the same time, old 'liberal' employers had not the least intention of encouraging their employees to think very actively about their rights. Without independent political organization there could be no change of social direction, but to bring about a new alignment was no simple matter. That this task made it necessary on the Labour side to persuade colleagues in the old organizations to adopt a new style, from the TUC Congress Hall outwards to the branch rooms, meant that dialogue was, for the new leaders, unavoidable. But in the absence of a firm and established centre, the socialist argument needed a more than resilient faith to endure the oppositional pressures to which it would be subjected. Notwithstanding his considerable flair for dramatic action, John Burns lacked the kind of compass which could help him steer through this terrain.

Burns, however, was to end his direct association with the Dockers' Union, if not a lifelong interest in its fate, when he ceased to be its trustee. While no one can deny his part in the events of 1889, his personal engagement thereafter was transitory.

Tillett, by contrast, was to remain general secretary of the Dockers' Union right up to the moment of amalgamation in 1922. Mann became founder of another major organization, the Workers' Union, which was also later to merge with the Transport and General Workers' Union; he also stood in for Tillett when he was forced to convalesce in New Zealand after 1896. If this were not enough, he was again to stand at Tillett's side throughout the formation of the Transport Workers' Federation in 1910, the upheavals of 1911 and the volcanic subsequent reappearance of all the aspirations of 1889. In all the dawn years of independent Labour representation, the big three leaders of the dock strike had a magic appeal: but twenty years on there was still a powerful duo, and their alliance was still enough to shake the complacency of some very powerful people and give heart to all the outcasts living in the margins of the world of labour. Some people will think that there is some consistency within this whole span.

How to Look for Consistency

But we are here concerned with a shorter timescale, and it is in the career of Mann during the initial struggle for Labour representation that we may see the most steadfast continuity, if only we appreciate the task he had in hand. This was precisely to join together the many strands of action and argument which could integrate a new political force. For this reason we are bound to fault the accusation of inconsistency in his case: it makes no sense to present his different fields of work as areas of conflict in his own commitment. His project was one of linkage and persuasion. He had to organize the unorganized, but also to win over his colleagues in the established movement. He had to co-ordinate the most systematic use of the wider franchise and of the extension of local democratic powers. He had to engage with all the currents of thought which moved other social forces in the same direction as that which he had chosen for himself.

It is therefore hardly reasonable to reproach Mann for 'turning from the Dockers to the London Trades Council'. In fact he was the natural spokesman of no fewer than thirty-two of the Dockers' branches which affiliated to the Trades Council in 1890,[6] by which time Mann himself had already been elected to the executive. The decline of the union under the combined weight of recession and the employers' backlash lapsed twenty of these branches in 1893. But it did not lapse Mann, who had already played a major role in reshaping the policy and action of the Council. In doing so, he was making space for a whole generation of new activists. That he coupled this role with his campaign for office in the Amalgamated Society of Engineers speaks of his considerable energy, but betrays no inconsistency at all. The new unionists were seeking to win over the old, and Mann's election organizer among the engineers, George Barnes, was himself to win the general secretaryship only five years later. The dalliance between Mann and the Church followed its active role in the dock strike, but also registered the involvement of concerned young clergymen in the efforts to structure the Dockers' Union.[7] His secretaryship of the Independent Labour Party we shall consider later; it is enough here to say that it gave the new party a decisive push towards the unions, without which the ILP could never have broken from the ghetto surrounding a smallish socialist society into the new milieu of a Labour Party representing the interests and at times shaping the hopes of an entire social class.

The effort to persuade the craftsmen's societies involved the new unionists in active participation in every forum in which they were to be found associated. Inevitably this argued for all-out participation in the work of the Trades Councils and of the TUC. Since so much of Tom Mann's earlier work had hinged around the campaign for a legal eight-hour day, it was unsurprising that the base of the new large-scale associations of dockers and gasworkers should be seen as home ground from which to widen out the attack. The campaign fanned out in a variety of linked assaults. Local agitation, often through Trades Councils, sought to establish the eight-hour day in local-government employment of all kinds. Later, Burns was to add the support of his local-government constituency by monitoring new contracts agreed with the London County Council. At the same time, local campaigning could be linked with national and international issues, first by organizing support for the institution of May Day as a celebration of the worldwide Labour movement for shorter hours, and then by seeking their acceptance of parliamentary and local electoral contests around the same theme. This pattern repeated itself in towns all across the country. In London, Tom Mann went to the Trades Council to form a succession of instruments to help the work forward.

The general platform of this strategy was outlined in the pamphlet on the new unionism which Mann and Tillett had drafted in reply to Shipton, the secretary of the Council: 'Our contention is that at least 500,000 of London's Workers might be organised in bona fide labour organisations, that they might be affiliated to the London Trades Council, and that if this were so, an enormous change for the better might come about.'[8] This 'parliament of London Labour' would give assistance to every union which needed it. It would discharge a series of educational and organizational responsibilities to service all affiliates. Even though efforts to replace Shipton were beaten off from 1890 onwards, until he finally resigned in 1896 with 'a glowing testimonial on vellum and a cheque',[9] the composition of the executive was radically changed. In 1890 a lecture bureau was established to proselytize. Sub-committees to deal with problems in groups of similar trades were set up. Thousands of pounds were collected and distributed in mutual aid for strike and distress funds. Very substantial sums were sent to Australia to support the maritime strikers, in gratitude for their earlier help to the London dockers. As we have already seen, the Council seconded Fred Hammill to help organize the busmen during and after their 1891 dispute.

The Legal Eight-hour Day

The Socialist International had launched the call for the legal eight-hour day at its first Congress of 1889. It was to form the platform of an international demonstration on May Day 1890. Eleanor Marx set about organizing a rally in Hyde Park, and the Trades Council was invited to join. It proposed instead, on Tom Mann's suggestion, to organize the event itself. But the Council favoured only the principle of the shorter working day, 'leaving the precise method to the future', and the Demonstration Committee did not find this acceptable. Consequently there emerged instead a double demonstration, half a million strong, where a series of platforms put the case for the legal eight-hour day, or for shorter hours, according to the convictions of the various organizers:

> Eleanor Marx made one of the most widely reported speeches. 'We have not come to do the work of political parties, but we have come here in the cause of labour, in its own defence, to demand its own rights. I can remember when we came in handfuls of a few dozen to Hyde Park to demand an Eight Hours' Bill, but the dozens have grown to hundreds, and the hundreds to thousands, until we have this magnificent demonstration that fills the park today. We are standing face to face with another demonstration, but I am glad to see that the great masses of the people are on our side. Those of us who have gone through all the worry of the Dock

Strike, and especially the Gasworkers' Strike, and have seen the men, women and children stand round us, have had enough of strikes, and we are determined to secure an eight hours' day by legal enactment; unless we do so, it will be taken from us at the first opportunity. We will only have ourselves to blame if we do not achieve the victory which this great day could so easily give us. There is in the park this afternoon a man whom Mr. Gladstone once imprisoned – Michael Davitt; but Mr. Gladstone is now on the best of terms with him. What do you suppose is the reason for the change? Why has the Liberal Party been so suddenly converted to Home Rule? Simply because the Irish people sent 80 members to the House of Commons to support the Conservatives; in the same way we must kick these Liberal and Radical members out if they refuse to support our programme. I am speaking this afternoon not only as a Trade Unionist, but as a Socialist. Socialists believe that the eight hours' day is the first and most immediate step to be taken, and we aim at a time when there will no longer be one class supporting two others, but the unemployed both at the top and at the bottom of society will be got rid of. This is not the end but only the beginning of the struggle; it is not enough to come here to demonstrate in favour of an eight hours' day. We must not be like some Christians who sin for six days and go to church on the seventh, but we must speak for the cause daily, and make the men, and especially the women that we meet, come into the ranks to help us.

> 'Rise like Lions after slumber
> In unvanquishable number,
> Shake your chains to earth like dew
> Which in sleep had fallen on you –
> Ye are many – they are few.'[10]

'We' were indeed many, and the euphoria of the event convinced Shipton himself that this was 'a brilliant success'.[11] It was brilliant enough to mandate the Council's TUC delegates to abandon their caution about how to approach the goal, and to plump for the legal eight-hour day without reservations. Mann was thus enabled to win a major victory at the Congress, and Broadhurst, the very figurehead of the old guard, resigned from his secretaryship of its Parliamentary Committee.

But the eight-hour-day campaign was not unreservedly popular among casual, low-paid, seasonally employed people. It was reported that members of the Dockers' Union went so far as to vote against it, on the grounds that it was 'not appropriate for dock work', to the great delight of George Howell, who celebrated this decision with a considerable fanfare in the book he wrote to attack the new unions.[12] Even among the gasworkers, Eleanor Marx had to enter a public exchange of letters with George Elleston, a branch secretary of her own union. Elleston wrote:

It seems to me that the legal eight hours' day has emanated from the mechanical class. It will, I think, suit them well. Their wages average from

38s. to £2. 10s. per week. They would save in one week as much as some unskilled labourers earn, our expenses are as great as theirs, the same amount of food and clothing are required for us. There are hundreds of very intelligent men among the unskilled labourers who would not be slow to avail themselves of anything that would tend to better their condition, and it would not be necessary to be continually trying to knock the legal eight hours into their heads. I have not heard one advocate it yet, and until I do, I have not much faith in it. First of all let us, through our organisations, get a sufficient wage to live without working overtime, and then we can see about the legal eight hours.[13]

In reply, Eleanor Marx was disappointingly formal. She showed that indeed the measure was official policy, but she did not give George Elleston an answer to his arguments. There followed a correspondence in the *People's Press* in which other members took Elleston's part, so much so that he himself wrote to express his very good opinion of Eleanor Marx and his pleasure at having provoked a discussion. That his views had wide support was to be shown again the following year, when the London busmen struck for shorter hours, won, and shortly afterwards bartered them away for increases in pay.

Yet many of those dockers, gasworkers and busmen would have been present in the Hyde Park festival of May Day 1890, and most would have been touched by its effect. The political claim for shorter hours was not unpopular, to put it mildly: but it was not easy to realize. The industrial claim for decent minimum earnings was equally difficult to assert, as the economic tides turned against Labour, while strike-breakers were marshalled behind forces armed with truncheons, pistols and bayonets. And it was against this bitter reality that the banners of the new unions regrouped for a counteroffensive aimed at the political powers. The turn to politics, as often happened before, resulted from industrial weakness, not strength.

For this, Tom Mann and Fred Hammill prepared the London Trades Council by establishing in 1891 its own Labour Representation League, with a fund to give it reality. By the 1892 LCC elections, not only were several candidates elected, but factory collections were instituted to maintain them while they performed their new duties. Amongst these duties was the promotion of the eight-hour day.

II

Founding the Independent Labour Party

'The ILP was founded, I think, in 1892. It was founded, or started, by seven men. I believe I was one of the seven; but I am not sure and it does not matter.'[14] Such modesty was not characteristic of everyone who took part in this process, and there is no doubt that Robert Blatchford could afford modesty, because his role could never plausibly be gainsaid. His newspaper, *Clarion*, became far more than a broadsheet. *Clarion* vans and *Clarion* cycling clubs carried the socialist message from town to town, and far out into the villages. Blatchford, however, had perhaps forgotten the date of at least this of his good works, which began in Bradford on 13 and 14 January 1893. Perhaps, of course, he was referring to the foundation during the previous year in Manchester of the local ILP. If we agree that the names of the 'seven' do not matter, it is still very necessary to remember where they came from. Whichever way we look at the question, we find that all the possible candidates were profoundly influenced by the new unions. We also find that the dockers' leaders were in the front rank of these.

It would hardly be an accident if Blatchford's memory tripped him. The year 1892 was indeed the one during which Labour burst in upon Parliament. Previously, Lib.–Lab. members had been elected as part of the Liberal slate, and were therefore subject to an external discipline. But the entry to Parliament of Keir Hardie, John Burns and Havelock Wilson in the General Election of 1892 was something different, and it was instantly symbolized by Hardie's alleged 'cloth cap', when he presented himself in Westminster in what was considered unconventional dress. Myth apart, the election of Burns and Wilson was only a partial discontinuity in the Lib.–Lab. tradition, and the subsequent careers of the two men have persuaded most historians that it was a lesser matter than it seemed at the time. But it is important to recall the circumstances of the early 1890s. Both these men stood as intransigent new unionists, and were seen as having dislodged an avalanche which was to transform the prospects of the Labour movement. As is often the case, however, the real changes lay further below the surface.

Keir Hardie won the seat of West Ham South. No one denies that he, at least, stood for a new beginning. Yet at first 'He was a total stranger with an almost strange programme', wrote Ben Tillett. 'Mann, Thorne, Burns or myself could have been chosen in place of the young Scotsman who was to make political history; but we felt that our work at that time called us to another stage.'[15] During the dock strike Tillett had been approached by the Liberals to contest Battersea, but he had declined. Burns won the nomination, and the seat, in his place.

The New Unions and Local Government

But the spade-work in both constituencies owed much to the organized effort of the new unions. The month after the dock strike, the Gasworkers' Union won two seats on the Barking School Board, and held a torchlight rally of 10,000 people to mark the occasion.[16] Before the end of the year West Ham Council had four new unionists, among whom were Thomas Walsh, the London secretary of the Sailors' and Firemen's Union, and George Lambert, a Canning Town docker who had been supported by the gasworkers. William Athey, of the General Railway Workers' Union, made a third. Three more candidates were elected in 1890, in Kensington North, Camberwell and Mile End. Eleven followed the next year, after Tom Mann joined forces with Will Steadman of the Bargebuilders' Union to promote their political campaign under the sponsorship of the London Trades Council, which, greatly reinforced by new Dockers' and Gasworkers' branches, set up the Labour Representation League to which we have already referred. In November 1891 candidates of this body polled more than 10,000 votes in eleven wards. Nine Labour men followed through on to the London County Council in the election of 1892. Ben Tillett was then co-opted as an alderman.

Parliamentary Campaigning in London

West Ham contained a large population of dockers, gasworkers and Irish people. By 1892 Will Thorne and six other Labour men sat on the Municipal Council. In short, this was one of the few areas where the new unions could make an important difference. Hardie came to it through contact with Burns and with independent radicals like the Christian Socialist Frank Smith.[17] His programme included a strong commitment to the eight-hour day, and his campaign involved a whole series of dock-gate meetings and trade union rallies. At one of these, 'The platform was a full-sized lifeboat, rigged with mast and ropes and gay with streamers and manned by a crew in uniform. I understand it came from the Tidal Basin branch of the Seamen's and Firemen's Union.'[18]

The banners and insignia of the new unions were everywhere during the rallies before polling day, alongside those of the Temperance movement, which also gave its strong support. It is necessary to add that the suicide of the prospective Liberal candidate, Hulme Webster, and the disarray of his local supporters contributed much to Hardie's victory, and that he was careful to tread a conciliatory path during his speeches on the hustings. None the less, alongside him on these platforms stood Thorne and Tillett, who must have struck fear into the hearts of the Liberal 'shopocracy', who had already expressed misgivings because their former candidate had, they thought, given too much support to the dockers only three years before.

John Burns had already been elected to the London County Council before he became the star of the dock strike. He nursed the Battersea constituency carefully, and kept up a constant dialogue with his supporters, reporting back profusely. In 1890 Lord Rosebery, a great power in the LCC, had offered him the Liberal candidature in Bristol.

He declined, as he also declined the Liberal nomination in Battersea itself. He was determined to stand, he said, as a socialist. In the 1892 LCC elections ten Labour candidates were given a free run against the Conservatives, the Liberals having stood down. Seven of these went to the polls with active support from the Liberal organization in their areas. Burns relied instead on his own caucus, the Battersea Labour League.

Whilst this group was solid enough to organize a London election and subsequent victory, it was severely stretched by a parliamentary campaign. Already it carried the burden of raising Burn's weekly salary as a London spokesman, which cost £2 10s. a week. For a national contest, £300 were needed. Burns rejected various offers of Liberal money, but accepted £100 from Champion, having satisfied himself that it was untainted: the 'Tory gold' furnished to socialists in the 1885 contest was still a live stigma, and was to burst into very real flames early in the life of the infant ILP.

Burns's campaign opened in June 1892. It was nothing if not catholic in sponsorship. Messages of endorsement came from Engels, Kautsky and the Marx-Avelings. On the inaugural platform sat the outgoing Liberal Member, O. V. Morgan, alongside George Bernard Shaw and Will Crooks, recently elected as the Woolwich councillor, for Labour. 'Burns's programme was equally mixed. As he told one audience, "in things electoral he was a Radical, in things dealing with Government a Republican, in things social and economic he was a socialist, but in all things he was for Labour night and day".[19] All this scandalized the opposition, and provoked cries of foul play. But the result was a clear and unquestionable victory: a majority of more than 1,500 in an electorate of less than 10,000.

Burns's parliamentary career thus began on 5 August 1892, and was to take him to great heights. But his involvement in the cause of the socialist movement was to become more and more attenuated, and his main radical achievements during the following years were in the fields of local government and the trade unions, notwithstanding his new parliamentary limelight. On the London County Council he pioneered an intervention-ist policy of what would later be called contract-compliance, direct-labour and fair-wages resolutions. Each of these was to have considerable influence in the world of local government during the following years. But the scope for such measures in an overwhelmingly indifferent or hostile Parliament was, to put it mildly, limited. Burns's repeated forays for eight-hours legislation were largely propagandistic, and those concessions he could secure were entirely dependent on the goodwill of sympathetic Liberals. So it was that, while Keir Hardie was moving round the country to recruit an Independent Labour Party, John Burns was invited to a dinner with Gladstone and offered a junior portfolio (which he declined) when Lord Rosebery took over the premiership in 1894.

In this evolution, Burns maintained a cordial and respectful relationship with Havelock Wilson, but became daily more estranged from Keir
Hardie.

In 1890, after repeated urging from his friend and ally Samuel
Plimsoll, the Seamen's Union leader, Havelock Wilson agreed to seek
election to Parliament. Highly articulate shipowners were already
strongly represented, and their immense wealth ensured that they were a
doubly effective lobby. Plimsoll wanted a counterweight in order to press
forward his own campaign for reforming legislation, which was contested
every step of the way. A by-election in East Bristol provided an
opportunity. 'I made what I now look back upon as one of my great
blunders . . .' wrote Wilson. 'The result gave me a first-class shock. The
Radical candidate was returned with about three thousand majority . . .
and I had to be satisfied with six hundred and fifty votes . . . each vote
recorded for me cost about one pound three shillings and sevenpence-
halfpenny'.[20]

From the vantage-point of experience, Plimsoll thought this 'a
magnificent show'. Clearly Wilson was not discouraged, because after
two years he became Member for Middlesbrough: 'Much of my success
. . . was due to the fact that I was sentenced to six weeks' imprisonment,
and I often remarked . . . after, "If you want to get into Parliament get
into gaol first." '[21]

Wilson's imprisonment had followed a strike-breaking attempt by the
Shipping Federation in Cardiff. Sixty-two seamen had been recruited at
North and South Shields on the false prospectus of jobs in Tilbury.
When they entrained they found themselves *en route* for South Wales.
They cabled strike headquarters during the journey, and were met by
more than 1,000 pickets. Almost all of them immediately joined up with
the union men, and paraded the city with Tom Mann, Ben Tillett and
Wilson himself. It was, it seemed, a famous victory. Then Wilson was
charged with unlawful assembly and riot, and subsequently he was sent
to prison. This provoked a general sense of outrage in the Labour
movement, since the charges had no reasonable foundation. Wilson
entered the Middlesbrough contest as hero of the hour.

Militant though he was, however, Havelock Wilson had no socialist
sympathies, even if, at the time, he had many socialist friends. Yet we
should not ignore the fact that he was the only one of the three victorious
Labour independents who actually stood against, and defeated, a Liberal
opponent.

Tillett's Campaign in Bradford

A different story was unfolding in Bradford, where Ben Tillett himself
was standing.

Bradford was quick to feel the influence of the new unions, but although union membership rose sharply under their influence, and notably under the weight of the Gasworkers and General Labourers, headed by Paul Bland, there were other forces leading to the radicalization of the Labour movement:

> Ironically, it was the older crafts which provided substantial support and leadership for the independent movement – and this despite the obvious difficulties and splits within their own ranks. The changing economic circumstances, technological threats, the menace of new industries and new ways of making standard products, and perhaps as important though less explored, the polarisation of the classes achieved in the more stable circumstances of late-nineteenth-century Bradford provided the backdrop to a rapid succession of events.[22]

Already in 1889 a running battle had opened in the Trades Council, in which its more conventional Liberal leaders were acrimoniously challenged. This might have spent itself in a long faction fight but for the effect, in 1890 and afterwards, of the general import taxes imposed by the United States, under President William McKinley, to stimulate its own industry. In Bradford this meant trouble. On 16 December 1890, S. C. Lister and Co. of Manningham Mills announced reductions in wages ranging between 15 per cent and one-third, hitting the silk- and plush-weavers with various degrees of severity.[23] Tariffs notwithstanding, and strikes notwithstanding either, the company was later to pay an 8 per cent dividend to shareholders on the results of that year's work. But the workers, who were completely unorganized at the moment that the cuts took effect, promptly struck and maintained a remarkable strike right through Christmas and on to April 1891. By the time it ended, sympathy action and lock-outs had combined to secure the complete stoppage of all workers at the mills. Over nineteen weeks, more than £11,000 was raised in strike funds by the Trades Council itself, the Yorkshire Miners' Association and trade unions all around the country. Quickly the spokesmen of independent Labour action became acknowledged leaders of the dispute. Their names were to have national impact, in some cases for decades: they included W. H. Drew, F. W. Jowett and Ben Turner. For the most part, the local Liberal establishment rallied closely around the mill-owners, with the result that the conflict involved not only industrialists but also the political leadership of the district, the 'Millocracy'. This was a close-knit and powerful Liberal mafia. Policing was tough, and when the military were called in crowds were driven at bayonet-point down the narrow streets, reminding one witness of 'scenes from the French Revolution'.[24]

At a great protest rally the idea of the Bradford Labour Union came into existence. Even the Power Loom Overlookers' Union, a typical craft organization if ever there was one, subsequently issued a strong formal condemnation of the Town Council for calling in the troops. Charlie Glyde summed up the mood: 'We have had two parties in the past; the can'ts and the won'ts and it's time we had a party that will.'[25]

It was in this heady atmosphere that the *Yorkshire Factory Times*, announcing on May Day 1891 that the strike was over, gave it the warning epitaph: 'Labour has so associated itself that even defeat must be victory'.[26]

The Labour Union formed itself officially on 28 May, and within a little more than a year its supporters had taken over the Trades Council. Ben Tillett was a natural candidate for such a group. But he declined the offer when it first came that May: it had to be pressed home repeatedly before he accepted it three months later.[27]

Initially it was proposed that the dockers' leader should contest Bradford East, where he could have a clear run without Liberal intervention. But his sponsors, and he himself, preferred a challenge and opted instead for a real confrontation with the Liberals in Bradford West, the seat of Alfred Illingworth. Illingworth was not only the party boss; he was also Bradford's largest employer. This contest was, at the local level, to divide the Labour supporters from any lingering Liberal affinities which may have survived the shock of the strike; and nationally it was to cause some embarrassment to those Labour supporters who did not wish to burn their bridges to Liberalism. Sidney Webb wrote to Beatrice to say that he could 'see no alternative' to supporting Tillett.[28] He and Bernard Shaw both made the trip to Bradford in the first months of 1892. So did Tom Mann and Tom McCarthy of the Dockers' Union. But while the Fabians travelled in some apprehension, the new unionists were spoiling for a fight. Thus we find Webb speaking in Bradford about his own membership of the National Liberal Club and a variety of other well-known Liberal organizations, and begging votes for Tillett, whose candidature was best not merely for Labour, 'but for Liberalism itself'. By contrast, Tillett laid about himself with a stout stick: 'Fifty years ago the land owning interest was opposed to the middle class capitalists. The former had either died out or gambled away their wealth . . . The rich capitalist was now replacing the old landlord, and he generally took into possession of the land less conscience . . . There was then no Liberalism or Toryism, but there was capitalism.'[29]

'Cheers,' reported the journalist who transcribed these remarks. Illingworth had little enough to cheer, however. Forced on to the defensive, he had to explain why he did not support the raising of the school-leaving age to twelve, but would compromise by agreeing that children might remain in school until they were eleven. That he was himself a large-scale employer of child labour would have been known to all the members of his audience, although it might have been thought impolite to say so. Tillett, however, was an uninhibited campaigner.

It is not difficult to imagine his joyous response to Illingworth's announced belief that wages were perfectly adequate, but for the demon drink. In opposition to this, Tillett was for a bold legislative programme of reforms:

> He wanted factory legislation. He wanted machinery to be protected, proper sanitary arrangements to be made, the separation of sexes, the appointment of women as inspectors, and an obligation on the part of the employer to supply an exact statement of work given out and the wages paid for it without being asked for it . . . He wanted the people to have the land and the money.[30]

At Bradford, in sum, the cutting edge of the campaign drove in the direction of separating Labour voters from the Liberal influence. Whilst Keir Hardie and John Burns remained unopposed by Liberal candidates, their appeal sought to occlude divisions and to mobilize as many Liberal voters in their cause as possible. In this sense Tillett's defeat – by no great margin (557 votes) – marked an extraordinary breakthrough. 'The light will come', he told rejoicing crowds. 'We shall not be long before we shall . . . shout "Glory Hallelujah" for the Democracy.'[31] The following January, the founding conference of the Independent Labour Party convened in Bradford, not West Ham. And this was hardly an accident . . .

Problems of Independent Labour Organization

The day after his election victory at West Ham, Keir Hardie told the *Daily Chronicle*: 'I hope that we shall soon see the beginning of a new and thoroughly independent Labour Party in the House of Commons. We may be few at first, but we shall attract to us a large number of the new Radicals who have shaken themselves free from laissez-faire Liberalism.'[32]

There were many forces ranged against Keir Hardie's plan, however. Firstly, some new unionists nursed serious hopes of Liberal support for some of their aims, and were by no means ready for a complete breach with the Liberal Party. Thus, John Burns quickly came under the influence of those Fabians who adopted a strategy of 'permeation'. If this sounds uncomfortably like the idea of 'entry' as practised by various left-wing groups in the Labour Party during the 1960s and 1970s, it was none the less defended quite openly by most of the best-known Fabians during the early 1890s. The election of Labour Members of Parliament was seen as a bridgehead to influence within the Liberal Party, rather than as a challenge to the old political alignments.

On the other side, Hardie faced a growing problem with that section of the socialist movement which had, originally, Conservative allegiances and which was now willing to play the old parties off against each other.

He himself had worked closely with H. H. Champion, and merged his newspaper with Champion's *Labour Elector*. Champion was well liked and influential among the dockers, and his organizational talents won him high respect. But he maintained a close liaison with a strange political adventurer, J. Maltman Barry, who had been a Conservative candidate for Banff in 1892. Barry had been an admirer of Karl Marx, and always spoke of him with unbounded enthusiasm. But it is clear that he had also been quite prepared to act as a conduit for Conservative funds, wherever the intervention of Labour candidates might seem likely to damage Liberal electoral prospects. Since Hardie had taken money from Champion during his first contest in Mid-Lanark, he was vulnerable to the charge of receiving 'Tory gold'.

The *Labour Elector* folded in April 1890 and Champion went to Australia – though he was to return in time to conduct a running faction-fight with Hardie during the earliest days of the Independent Labour Party.[33] Meanwhile, on 29 August 1890 Joseph Burgess launched the *Workmen's Times*, which was to play an important role in developing Labour activity, especially in the North.

A third group of adversaries with which Hardie was compelled to contend consisted of the socialist purists, who articulated strong doctrinal objections to co-operation with anyone but themselves. The core constituency of this grouping was, of course, the Social Democratic Federation, but there were some members of that body who were far more tolerant than others.

Crowds and Orators

Among the new unions, the gasworkers undoubtedly had the greatest national reach. But Will Thorne remained loyal to the SDF, and tirelessly exploited its network to build his own union. The dockers had less scope for national recruiting and were more vulnerable to the counterattack of their employers; but in the short term their leaders were the heroes of the great Labour rebellion of 1889. Wherever they went, crowds were attracted. Their speeches were carefully written down by scores of local newsmen, so that their opinions were very widely read and understood. More, they were passionately eloquent, and capable of arousing real fervour among their listeners.

Here, for example, is a gifted journalist's account of one of Tom Mann's flights of oratory:

> To the usual fierceness of his swarthy face, to the habitual menace of his facial gesture, he was led on this occasion to add the airs of a mountebank – shrugging his shoulders, spreading his arms, distorting his mouth and exciting roars of laughter by his whining parody of the Liberal workman.

He laid himself out to split the ears of the groundlings . . . And then he played to the passions of the gallery. He spoke here with terrible method and terrible intention. He knows all the hardship of a labouring life; he knows the discontents and resentments that labour broods over most sullenly; he knows how frequently workmen hate the very ideas of having 'a master'; and in this knowledge he deliberately touched his hearers on the raw, until they bayed with rage in response to the fierce, rancorous, sullen voice that seemed to be giving concentrated utterance to the deepest class-passions of their nature. He spoke of the machine-minder 'afraid to straighten his back lest it should be marked down against him by a man with a watch, employed to follow him up like a sleuth-hound' . . . He denounced nationalism, he denounced the navy; he declared the navy to be an obstacle to the fraternisation of all workers. But Mr. Tom Mann's incendiary invective gradually passed into finer thought and not less effective appeal. In rapid and dark lines he sketched the intolerable fate of an Elswick labourer, whom he called 'a 17s. and 10d. a week man with a small wife and a large family'. He denounced that, he denounced all life on such terms. He called upon his audience to dare to be men; and 'Now young chaps,' he trumpeted, flinging up to the crowded galleries and side elevations an incitant gesture. 'Now young chaps, what are *you* going to live for?' The 'young chaps' were electrified.[34]

Such a powerful performer was in demand all over the country, constantly requested to speak for all the causes, and against all the injustices, to which Labour was prone. Tillett, also, acquired a truly national following. The early conferences of the Dockers' Union became events at which he was lobbied to give his support to a whole variety of campaigns. At the second conference of the Dockers' Union, delegations from Bradford were so insistent in pressing him to accept their parliamentary nomination that the conference formally debated their invitation, which was accepted by twenty-two votes to three.[35]

The Birth of the Independent Labour Party

Tillett's campaign established Bradford as the most propitious centre from which to convene the new Independent Labour Party. Provincial socialists were profoundly wary of London influence, which they saw as prone to elitism and manipulation. Hardie represented a constituency in which he was beholden to the dockers and other new unionists, but he did not have there, or anywhere else in London, the kind of organizational base from which to establish a national network. Burns blew cold on the whole project. Havelock Wilson had entered on a maverick course and was not a volunteer. But the Bradford Labour Union had struck deep roots since the Manningham strike and had no encumbering ties with any part of the political apparatus of either of the two main parties. In 1895, two years after the ILP had been established, Bradford was to provide one-sixth of all the affiliation fees received by the new party. Indeed, it provided one-thirteenth of the entire income of the National Administrative Council during those early days.[36]

Around Bradford, of course, there was strong socialist support in Huddersfield, Dewsbury, Keighley, and the Colne and Holme Valleys. These, too, after an initial pause, made their strong contribution to the new party's organizational base. In a famous passage, E. P. Thompson told us that

> The ILP grew from the bottom up: its birthplaces were in those shadowy parts known as 'the provinces'. It 'was created by the fusing of local elements into one national whole. From the circumference its members came to establish the centre . . .' Its first council seat was won in the Colne Valley: its first authentic parliamentary challenges came in Bradford and Halifax: its first conference showed an overwhelming preponderance of strength in the North of England: its early directories show this strength consolidated. When the two-party political structure began to crack, and a third party with a distinctively socialist character emerged, this event occurred neither in Westminster nor in the offices of Champion's *Labour Elector* but amongst the mills, brickyards, and gasworks of the West Riding.[37]

The element of truth in this contention speaks for itself. But the judgement is rounded out when we examine the organization of the party in areas which were not so successful. John Kelly of the carters' and lurrymen's new union and his colleagues hammered away in Salford, with G. T. Jackson of the tramwaymen and other socialist activists, but the message did not take and the Salford Labour Union would not stick.[38] Instead Salford nourished a strong group of SDF members.

Local leadership is just as necessary to successful organization on the ground as national leadership is to the shaping of overall direction. Without it, grassroots will not grow. Of course, there are many circumstances in which grass is hard to cultivate, even by exemplary gardeners.

On 13 and 14 January, 124 delegates, most of whom came from the industrial North, mustered in Bradford for the ILP's founding conference. More than a third of the delegates came from Yorkshire, while Hardie's Scottish Labour Party provided the core of the eleven delegates from Scotland. Fifteen came from London, representing fourteen different societies. Thirteen Fabians, mostly from the North of England, included George Bernard Shaw. Shaw, however, was equivocal about the idea of an Independent Labour Party and the northern socialists went in terror of his influence.

One of the delegates in Bradford was James Sexton of the Liverpool Branch, soon to become general secretary of the National Union of Dock

Labourers. He had replied to Joseph Burgess's original invitation in the *Workman's Times* to meet to consider the formation of the new party. In his memoirs he describes the trepidation with which Shaw's arrival in Bradford was greeted:

> Both in the press before the Conference, and at the conference itself, he declaimed with all his power against what he called the 'unnecessary and mischievous intervention of a new Party', which was bound, he feared, to queer the pitch for the Fabians and their policy of peaceful penetration of the enemy's ranks . . . Hyndman demanded a scrutiny of credentials and those of GBS were challenged on the ground that he was presumably a self-elected delegate. Thereon it was held that he could take no part in the proceedings . . . But it was no easier then than it is now to make Shaw go the way you want him to go, and though we decided that he was not of us, he certainly remained with us . . . He promptly took up a strong enfilading position in the gallery, from which he bombarded us so violently with his interruptions that on the following day we admitted him to our deliberations in sheer self-defence.[39]

When Sexton came to compose his memoirs in 1935, he sent Shaw a copy of his reminiscences of the Bradford conference. The result was a spicy response, in which Shaw reaffirmed all his old views.[40]

If Shaw was the most famous delegate, the conference included many others who were already well known. Tillett represented Bradford as its former parliamentary candidate. Alongside him was Fred Jowett, later to become a Labour Cabinet Minister. John Mahon and Tom Maguire came from Leeds, Ben Turner from Batley, Robert Smillie from the Scottish Labour Party, and the gasworkers' Peter Curran represented Croydon.[41] Hardie was voted into the chair after the meeting was opened.

The first issue to be resolved concerned the name of the new organization. Two Scottish delegates proposed that it be called the Socialist Labour Party. To this, Ben Tillett was strongly opposed.

> Alderman Ben Tillett could not understand why their friends should apply the term Socialist to their party. One speaker seemed anxious to accord support to their continental brethren, but in practical democratic organisation there was nothing like this old country. It was a lesson to every one of the continental bodies, which although they had so much chatter and blabber, had no real effective detail. For pluck and determination to fight out their details English trade unionism was the best sort of socialism and labourism he knew. He desired to capture the trade organisations of the country, for they were a body of men well organised and were willing to pay their money in order to secure their ends. They were men who were not merely Socialists on the platform but Socialists at their work. They were men who did not advocate blood-red revolution and when it came to a revolution sneak under the first bedpost. (A voice,

'Shame.') These vast organisations of men in this country were working out their own economic salvation, and for work could compare favourably with any of these chatterers. As a trade unionist with a little experience and knowledge of the Labour movement he was glad to say that if there were fifty red revolutionist parties in Germany, he would rather have the solid, progressive, matter-of-fact fighting trade unionist of England, and for that reason he desired that they should keep away from their name any term of socialism. He preferred a man who had spent his life in the Labour movement to three chattering magpies who had neither the courage of their convictions nor the capacity to deal with details of their opinions. He himself was anxious that they should not claim any other power than what they possessed, and he desired that they should respect trade unions. There was not a Socialist party in the world who could show the effective organisation of these men and women in Lancashire. He had become thoroughly sick of people who bore on their foreheads 'socialism' and who were no more Socialist than Bismarck. In conclusion he said that he wanted to keep the organisation out of the hands of the wirepullers, and to keep it in the hands of work-a-day men, work-every-day men, who were anxious to do what was right . . .[42]

Tillett's remarks caused an immediate scandal, which has gone on reverberating through the next century.

His biographer, Jonathan Schneer, rightly reminds us that the Bristol docks were out on strike even while the ILP was gathering for its foundation meeting: 'Tillett wanted, and obtained, from the conference a resolution supporting the strike; but he wanted also hard cash for the strike fund. The fledgling Party was in no position to make such a donation, but the trade union delegates in attendance were.'[43] Be that as it may, the blatant chauvinism of this speech brought about an instant repudiation from Edward Bernstein and was registered as a scandalous affront to the German Social Democratic Party, at the time by far the most impressive detachment of the international socialist movement.[44]

The argument about the title of the party was virtually the only issue confronting the 1893 conference which was finally, and – Tillett notwithstanding – amicably resolved on the spot. The programme of the party was agreed on a consensual formula, supporting every extension of electoral rights and all measures to democratize the system of government. But a fierce dispute broke out over the 'Fourth Clause', which sought to pledge all members of the new organization to refuse votes to all other parties, even where there was no Labour candidate available. Sexton proposed an amendment to devolve this decision on party branches. He was ruled out of order, and the clause was defeated by a majority of almost two to one, to Bernard Shaw's immense satisfaction. (He was to recall this triumph of Fabian realism in his comments on Sexton's autobiography more than forty years later.) But the Fourth Clause would not lie down. Some local groups implemented it in spite of the national decision, and it became a perennial at party conferences, where it was defeated by diminishing majorities year after year. Indeed in 1895 it briefly triumphed, only to be rescinded again just before the election. Finally it faded into irrelevance with the formation of the Labour Representation Committee in 1900.

The new party closed its first deliberations having elected a National Administrative Council. The historian of the ILP, David Howell, describes it as 'very much an ILP second eleven'.[45] In fact it had fifteen members, chosen on a regional basis and therefore packed with local activists lacking any national reputation or experience. Moreover, it lacked money. Consequently it met only twice, costing £48 out of a total income of £130. Factional squabbles were ominously present, and for this reason infrequent meetings were seen by some as a blessing in disguise. At the 1894 conference all this was shaken out. Three members of the old Committee survived: John Lister, the Halifax squire, who was treasurer; Pete Curran of the gasworkers; and George Christie from Nottingham, a veteran of the First International.[46] The newcomers included Ben Tillett, and also Leonard Hall of the Lancashire and Adjacent Counties Labour Amalgamation, another new union. But more significantly, Keir Hardie was elected president and Tom Mann became secretary. The party was preparing itself for the next General Election. This came early, in 1895.

Tom Mann Becomes the Secretary . . .

The circumstances of Tom Mann's election as ILP secretary are not entirely clear. In the discussion after the founding conference, George Bernard Shaw had made much of Mann's absence, claiming that this was a token of weak trade-union support. In January 1894 Russell Smart wrote to the *Workmen's Times* to advocate that Mann should be elected secretary, and later he claimed to have organized a caucus of delegates from Lancashire and Yorkshire to bring about a purge of the National Administrative Council and Mann's appointment.[47] Some recrimination followed, but the decision to field a 'first eleven' was by no means unpopular.

Mann once again applied himself to centralize key powers, while instituting regular monthly circulars to improve membership contact. ILP branches were not keen to surrender power to their national centre, and they were often decidedly reluctant to part with money which they wished to devote to local campaigns. The centralizing pressures were most successful immediately before the 1895 election, and became notably more contentious in succeeding years.

In 1893 and 1894, after the constitution of the ILP, there were by-elections in Halifax, Sheffield Attercliffe and Leicester. In the best of these, John Lister, drawing on his local connections, polled a quarter of the votes in Halifax. But all the results were respectable, given the very slender resources available to the infant party. Joseph Burgess was running against Henry Broadhurst, the scion of Lib.–Lab. conformity, who was teamed with a Liberal capitalist in a two-member constituency. Burgess polled almost 4,500 votes in Leicester, whilst at the same time provoking no small recrimination among the old unionists. Hugh Holmes Gore, an independent with some ILP support, entered the field in a Bristol by-election, following in Havelock Wilson's footsteps. He very nearly won, running his Liberal opponent within 130 votes.

By the 1895 General Election, twenty-eight ILP candidates were in the field. They included Ben Tillett in Bradford, James Sexton in Ashton-under-Lyne and Tom McCarthy, the dockers' organizer, in Hull. They also included Tom Mann in Colne Valley.

Tillett's result fell some considerable distance short of his 1892 performance; he polled only 23.4 per cent of the vote. Thereafter he took a back seat in ILP affairs, dropping out altogether during his convalescence in New Zealand and Australia from 1896 to 1898. But since the dockers' flag was also being carried by others in the 1895 contest, it is interesting to look in closer detail at the campaigns of his two colleagues, Tom Mann and Tom McCarthy.

The parliamentary division of Colne Valley, spread across the Pennines in the West Riding from Huddersfield to Oldham, came into existence in 1885. Its first Liberal Member dissented from Gladstone's policy on Home Rule for Ireland and was again returned, unopposed by the Conservatives, at the next election in 1886. But by 1890 discontent among Liberals had become irresistible, and an orthodox Gladstonian businessman from Leeds was selected. Sir James Kitson then reclaimed the seat in 1892, holding it until after 1906, when he was elevated to the peerage as Lord Airedale. Throughout this time only 59 per cent of adult males possessed the vote nationally. Plural votes included, the proportion in Colne Valley ran to higher levels, and by 1911 they had reached 75.5 per cent,[48] although there is no reason to doubt that the true register enfranchised rather fewer individual electors if duplicate voting were separately identified. In 1895, after the declaration, Mann published an analysis of the result in which he referred to 'six hundred property owners resident in Huddersfield who had helped to swell the Liberal majority, for not one of them had voted for the Labour candidate . . . It would be silly to complain of defeat by such forces.'

. . . and the Candidate

The Colne Valley Labour Union was established on 21 July 1891, and its first meeting, in a Slaithwaite cottage cellar, instructed its secretary to write to Tom Mann to ask him to become their parliamentary candidate.

Mann's first response was cool. In an interview given to a representative of the *Yorkshire Factory Times*, he said:

> I do not concern myself much about Parliamentary parties. My aim is to spread amongst workmen a knowledge of industrial economics, and the channels for the diffusion of this knowledge are the trade union and the co-operative movement, especially the productive branch of co-operation. This knowledge, as it obtains, will soon assert itself in municipal life, and then the workers will take care to put upon local bodies men who are in sympathy with their aims. We want all our energy for these things; by them we shall improve our capability; and until then it is a waste to attempt Parliamentary work. I am, therefore, not anxious to run Labour candidates for Parliament.[49]

None the less, Slaithwaite invited both Tom Mann and Ben Tillett to come up and speak, and a big meeting took place on 24 October, at which Mann repeated his refusal. Continuous representations from all over the area failed to change his mind, although at the time, notwithstanding his responsibilities to the Dockers' Union, he was also a candidate for the office of general secretary of the Amalgamated Society of Engineers. The election of 1892 duly arrived, without a Labour candidate in place. Afterwards, Mann revealed that he had been invited to stand in no less than fourteen constituencies, five of which had guaranteed the necessary funding to finance a campaign. But in the end Yorkshire persistence paid off: the last half of 1892 found Tom Mann delivering monthly speeches in the constituency and finally accepting the task which was pressed upon him.

Colne Valley was not a strong trade-union area. Less than 2 per cent of its population were organized in unions, which ranked it far behind the national average. Even the handful who did hold cards were highly concentrated – in Mossley, right at the seat's western end. If they were excluded from the calculation, in the rest of the division less than 0.5 per cent of the population were trade unionists. This situation was not unique to Colne Valley, but also applied in Bradford and throughout the wool-textile regions. Half-time working was common and child-labour survived, notwithstanding the Education Act or the Factory Acts themselves. E. P. Thompson reports an old lady's reminiscence: 'The mill-owners were very cute in dodging the factory inspectors . . . they had a big whisket handy in the sheds, and when they expected the inspector, we young girls were popped underneath the blankets until he had gone'.[50] Yet the constituency organized itself very competently indeed in its own way. A network of Labour Clubs was created. Extensive social functions raised funds and bonded people together; women played an active part in this. As a result, the constituency elected one of the first Labour county councillors, and began to mount a steady challenge in local elections and for membership of school boards. Nonconformity was a strong and steady influence, and both Mann and Tillett were at the time deeply interested in religion.

None the less, Tom Mann saw trade-union recruitment as the main duty of his long campaign. Early in 1893 he wrote in the *Yorkshire Factory Times*:

> First I have long contended that attention to Parliament is not the first duty of workmen, but that Parliament should receive attention at the hands of those who have already been at work using the agencies that lie ready to hand. Now I am a firm believer in the efficacy of trade unionism, not merely for raising the standard of living of the workers, but for increasing the general industrial prosperity of the country, and I have never yet been able to respect a constituency where the workers clamour for Parliamentary action unless they have made a good show by means of the Trade and Labour organisations. Now the Colne Valley contains some twenty industrial centres where the textile trade is carried on. Have the operatives become identified with their trade unions? No they have not; only a very small proportion have become members, and this proportion is not increasing very rapidly, and unless this changes pretty quickly for the better I shall consider myself at liberty to withdraw my conditional promise.[51]

Had Westminster been his target, he continued, he could have found a compact constituency in London:

> but it does so happen that my attitude towards Parliament today is what it was years ago, when I many times said Parliamentary effort should follow upon, not precede, trade union effort. Now I desire to say that irrespective of cost in time etc, and inconvenience, as Colne Valley is to me a representative manufacturing district, where the operatives are badly paid, I shall have much pleasure in remaining with them and doing all that any one person can to help them up the hill that leads to better conditions, but then they will have to make an effort, and prove to me they make it by their behaviour as trade unionists.[52]

Sir James Kitson was not pleased by all this. On 23 April 1893 he wrote to Herbert Gladstone to decline some preferment or other, acceptance of which might have left the field open to Tom Mann during the subsequent General Election:

> if I am correct in believing that a certain possible appointment might be made having in mind the suggestion that Tom Mann would be an acceptable candidate for the vacancy, and that hereby I should at a future election be placed in a most favourable position in a contest . . . but as I should consider it a calamity if Tom Mann had a direct interest in organising Labour in Leeds for the purpose of combating capitalists, I should not wish to see him in Leeds. My interest, and that of my partners

have suffered by his actions. Today we are almost without work and our men will be without employment. We shall pay £1,000 a week less in wages than a year ago.

I ask you therefore not to consider me in any transactions.[53]

Herbert Gladstone, as Commissioner for Public Works, disposed of some patronage. But while the surviving half of this exchange of letters does not allow us to speculate about what offers had been made to Sir James, it does give rise to the suspicion that the Liberal Party was apprehensive about its prospects if the vote was split.

However, Tom Mann did not confine himself to propaganda and exhortation. While his opponent was biting his nails about the spectre of trade unionism, Mann was using his access to the evidence of the Royal Commission on Labour to compose in 1893 an *Appeal to the Yorkshire Textile Workers*. Within weeks 2,000 copies were sold, all adding specific weight to the general incitement to the people of the West Riding to build the strength of their appropriate unions.

None the less, recruitment remained slow, and by the end of the campaign in 1895 combined union membership was still little more than 1,500.[54] Mann's vote weighed somewhat less, at 1,245, or 13.4 per cent of the electorate.

Tom McCarthy in Hull

Tom McCarthy's campaign was altogether a tougher problem than Tom Mann's. In November 1893 he was selected as ILP candidate for the lion's den – to fight Charles Wilson on his home ground. West Hull, Wilson had said when he first entered the field, had been the favoured spot of the local Tories 'because of the presence in it of large numbers of the upper classes'.[55] There were others, including fishermen and railway workers; but, Henry Pelling tells us, very many people were 'in more comfortable occupations'.[56] The Hull Trades Council balked at Independent Labour representation by a small margin (sixty-four to fifty-two) but two ILPers won local council seats soon afterwards. The editor of the *Railway Review*, Fred Maddison, had fought as a Lib.–Lab. in Central Hull in 1892, and was ferociously engaged to use his extensive influence to prevent the polarization of the Hull unions by an ILP candidature in Wilson's constituency. All the factors which most urgently impelled the Dockers' Union to seek a contest worked equally powerfully against Maddison's powerbroking in the interest of his own chosen political future.[57]

The Trades Council was kept out of the battle under this influence. The Irish National League also stood aside – an especially painful blow to McCarthy, since only two years before they had pressed him to accept a Nationalist nomination. The Social Democratic Federation added their penn'orth of commination, because they did not 'concede . . . the right of choosing a candidate' to the non-socialist ILP.[58]

Little money was available for the election campaign. As late as 5 July 1895 the local press was speculating that McCarthy's nomination might not go ahead for lack of funds, and pointing out that the candidate had 'not yet arrived in Hull'.[59] The Conservatives stood down in favour of Charles Wilson, having warned him off trespass in adjacent constituencies.[60] Wilson attacked union tyranny and beat the drum of foreign competition. He invited those of his employees who had grievances to see him at his office.

When McCarthy did arrive in Hull, he entered immediately on a heated controversy. He was presented as 'a man born amid poverty, a worker since he was eleven years of age' opposing 'a gentleman who owned vast wealth'.[61] The class lines already clear, he then took the platform and announced that 'he was opposing Mr. Wilson because he was the representative of a system which . . . was the cause of poverty, and . . . that while men occupied a position similar to that of Mr. Wilson, there would be poverty, suffering, misery and destitution'. For fifty years, he went on, 'the working men had clamoured for one man one vote, and that reform was still a promise'. The Liberals were resisting the payment of Members 'because it would lead to the complete disruption of the Liberal Party. But they would disrupt it'.[62]

On the plane of real politics, this complaint raised a crucial problem. If the Liberals could resist the widening of the franchise, then it would always remain difficult to get rid of them. We shall return to this question, which needs to be understood if we are to make sense of what happened to the ILP, and to the Labour Party itself in its earliest days. At the more artificial level of the hustings, however, no one needed to organize the 'disruption' of Wilson's campaign. The outraged dockers did that quite spontaneously. Here, for instance, is an account of just one meeting:

Mr. Wilson was received with hisses, cheers, and cries of 'Retire at once'. It was several minutes before Mr. Wilson could make himself heard, and during the greater part of his speech there were frequent interruptions and uproar. He said that at every meeting he had addressed there had been some opposition, but on the whole the opposition had been of a good-natured character. They came to a political meeting for a certain purpose, and ought to behave themselves. They were not there to listen to discordant shouts, which any child or a person wanting in intellect could easily send forth (cries of 'blacklegs'). Now, what did that man mean by that term? He meant a fellow labourer like himself (hear, hear, and uproar). If his platform and views did not agree with those of Mr. McCarthy, they had their remedy in their own hands. Some of them were excited and irritated, because they thought they had a grievance against his firm; or was it against him personally ('No')? Naturally there was still a considerable amount of friction on account of what happened two years ago, and that feeling had, unfortunately, not yet been removed (a Voice: 'It would be if you was to shift Ritson and Knowles'). He had talked the matter over on many occasions, and had come to the conclusion that had there been a little more tact on both sides and a little more listening to reason that strike might have either been quickly ended or prevented. They must always remember that it could not possibly be any advantage to his firm, having all their work to do, to have the men knocking off work and leaving them in the lurch as they did. His own feeling had always been that the strike ought never to have occurred. Whether right or whether wrong, they had got past that state in the history of Hull, and it was now his duty to do all in his power to prevent a recurrence of that deplorable calamity (applause). The duty of all should be to improve the position of the people (a Voice: 'Why don't you do it?'). How was it to be arrived at? Not by quarrelling with themselves. Whether they voted for or against him – (a Voice: 'You will get in') – it would not be because of any ill-feeling on his part (a Voice: 'You'll fly in, Charley'). It occurred to him from what he could see that his party were going to be in a minority . . . What he knew of the [Tory] party was that they would want watching (a Voice: 'You want watching an' all') . . . A Voter: Mr. Wilson, are you in favour of seamen, marine firemen, marine engineers, sea fishermen, and other classes being brought under the Employers' Liability Act (applause). Another Voter: I want you to stop a list of names being sent from your office at the arrival of every ship and a foreman being obliged to start these men and then call to his own men. Another Voter: I wish to ask you if you have the same opinion as you had years ago, for the abolition of the law for distraint for rent. A voter in East Hull desired to ask a question but was not allowed to do so . . .[63]

Earlier, Tillett had written to the *Hull Daily Mail* to denounce the behaviour of the Hull employers after the strike. The settlement, he said, promised absolute freedom to join trade unions, and to withdraw support and recognition from 'any employers' free labour association'. But

not a single condition has been upheld. Messrs. Wilson have organised a staff of clerks to ascertain the name of every trade union man, to pay visits as spies to all labour meetings . . . and have, besides, a paid organiser to blacklist trade unionists. No promise has been kept, and the agreement is not worth the paper it is written on, and has been repudiated by the Union.[64]

On polling day Wilson 'was well supplied with carriages' while Tom McCarthy 'had but a solitary cart to rely on'.[65] West Hull had never been propitious ground for a Labour candidate, but even so, McCarthy polled 1,400, or 17.4 per cent, of the votes.[66]

Tom McCarthy's defeat was shared by Fred Maddison, who lost by a handsome margin to his Conservative opponent. It is at least conceivable that many Hull dockers voted against the Lib.–Lab. precisely in order to register their disgust about a Liberal Party which included the shipowner Charles Wilson on its lists. Be that as it may, historians have considered it 'certainly unusual to find a city where the customary political order of things is reversed, and the working class appears more Conservative than the middle class'.[67]

James Sexton's Campaign

Sexton's campaign had followed the prosecution of some tailors who had been picketing a shop which had been putting work out to Manchester sweat-shops; they were sent to prison for non-payment of fines. Ashton trade unionists were scandalized. Keir Hardie protested in Parliament. The local Trades Council paraded in front of the offending premises with a band playing the Death March. Whilst this issue aroused some sympathy for Sexton's cause, Sam Woods, the miners' leader, stumped the constituency pleading the Liberal cause, and James Mawdsley, the cotton spinners' secretary, campaigned for the Conservatives.[68]

The dockers' leader was thus hemmed in by trade-union opponents. The ILP in Ashton was broke. Sexton's meetings were held on streetcorners. Publicity consisted of chalked slogans on streets or walls. For want of carriages, he sent out bands of ragged children to chant for votes. In the circumstances 415 votes (6.4 per cent) were seen as quite a lot, but the Conservatives walked home with a majority over all opposition candidates combined.

After the dust had settled, Sexton concluded:

> The real lesson of the Election . . . was that the foundation of the movement was insecure. The effort had not got the support of those for whose benefit it was primarily intended. The workers, sectionalised in their trade unions, which themselves were too often embroiled in domestic squabbling, had not realised that their hope and strength lay in their own unity.[69]

Coping with Defeat

For the ILP as a whole, the 1895 election was a fierce setback. Twenty-eight candidates polled less than 50,000 votes. Hardie, in a straight fight with the Conservative, was defeated: a bitter blow to the new party, even if Beatrice Webb told her diary that this might mean that his influence would now diminish – in her opinion, much to the good. Other socialist and Labour candidates went down. The Social Democratic Federation ran four people and of these George Lansbury came out with 203 votes, while Hyndman got 1,498. Lib.–Labs did worse than before. Burns and some of the miners held on, but George Howell lost his seat, in part because of the defection of new-unionist voters following his onslaught against them.[70] Altogether nine Lib.–Labs were elected, five of them miners. By-elections brought in W. C. Steadman at Stepney, Maddison in Sheffield Brightside, and the miners' leader Sam Woods, whom we have already met in Ashton, in Walthamstow. Before the end of the century, then, there were a dozen Lib.–Labs in Parliament, half of whom came from the miners.

Independent Labour representation had been annihilated. Labour members who survived in 1895 were all, still, dependent upon the Liberals. But the Liberals themselves were in a poor way. Gladstone had withdrawn, and with him went a strong commitment to the incorporation of Labour in the Liberal alliance. Engels, had he survived, might have wished to qualify his optimism about the effects of the extension of the franchise, to which we referred in chapter 2. What had become clear was that Labour could win with Liberal support or neutrality, and come near to winning in strong new union territory without such endorsement. This lesson was reinforced by Tom Mann's powerful campaign in Aberdeen North in 1896, to which we shall return shortly. But the new unions were under the hammer. They still had influence, but in many areas they were fading fast.

How had this electoral reverse come about? Tom McCarthy provided the answer during his campaign speech, when he accused the Liberals of inspired tardiness in the extension of the suffrage. During all these years, something like 5 million male workers were denied votes, either because they were lodgers, or paupers, or servants living in, or because, as happened in 1905, they were deprived of the franchise for claiming school meals for their children under a local-government order.[71]

The Politics of the Franchise

Speaking just before the 1867 Reform Bill, Gladstone had revealed the ambiguity of his attitudes quite precisely. Firstly, he accepted that the franchise was too restricted: 'I believe that a smaller portion of working men enjoy the franchise now than enjoyed it thirty years ago after the Reform Bill [1832] was passed.' Yet the working class had been enlarged, it was better off, more educated, and more 'loyal'. 'I must say that proofs of competency such as those ought to have some influence on the spirit of privileged classes, and to induce them . . . with a view of strengthening the laws and institutions of the country, to make some sensible, ay, some liberal, though some safe extension of the franchise'.[72] That same year, he advocated a fair, and liberal, and sensible, though not a sweeping, nor an overwhelming, admission of our brethren of the labouring community to the privilege of the suffrage . . . I should earnestly desire to see an extension . . . not wrung, not extorted as it was in 1832 . . . but given freely . . . in that way which excites confidence and gratitude, instead of engendering something, perhaps even much, of reasoning or even disaffection . . .[73]

At the turn of the century, Gladstone's close friend Alexander Murray, the Master of Elibank, wrote to *The Times* to warn the Liberals to be more accommodating to Labour in case the division between capital and labour should be enlarged to dominate the electoral choices. Gladstone, he thought, 'with his wonderful intuition', whenever labour democracy appeared to be gathering support 'took it by the hand, and led it into gentler paths'.[74]

Max Beer, the socialist historian, noted Gladstone's skill in the management of workers' movements. Gladstone, he pointed out, unlike Disraeli:

had nothing of the social romanticism which lent so much attraction to his great adversary. He perceived with the utmost clearness, in the rise of labour as a class, a danger to the power of the classes. On the one hand therefore, he encouraged the manufacturing, and generally the capitalist, class to allow the wage-earners a larger share in the national income, while, on the other hand, he went warily and acted parsimoniously when it was a matter of granting them political and economic rights. His policy was directed towards their political education . . . it was Gladstone who raised working men to the rank of members of the government; and, whenever he saw labour moving towards political class warfare, he spared no effort to lead it back to middle class paths.[75]

But it was the last Gladstone administration which itself contributed to the calling of this great bluff. Even while efforts were made to 'take by the hand' Lib.–Lab. heirarchs and such new agitators as Burns and Havelock Wilson, the Liberal manufacturers and shipowners began to wage outright battles against their beleagured employees and constituents. A picture in the official history of the Shipping Federation says it all: the depot ship *Lady Jocelyn* 'was the ship most extensively used for housing and accommodating strike breakers, and she was towed round to whatever docks were experiencing trouble'.[76] The picture shows rows of bestriped police officers, resolutely basking in the camera's eye, some reclining on deckchairs while others are more formally seated in postures of controlled dignity. Behind them, bowler-hatted and spruce, as if readying themselves for church, stand the masses of 'free labourers' who are about to be deployed in yet another industrial counterinsurgency. The very fact that these strike-breaking armies were private served to emphasize their political origins. And the fact that the uniformed servants of the state afforded every protection to these strong-arm squads, bashing and battering their way round all the ports of the island, argued the necessity of changes in the state itself.

It has been calculated that as late as 1910 4,665,000 men were excluded from the registers. There were, throughout this time, half a million people with more than one vote. Plural voting was mostly based upon the ownership of property. It produced freak voting registers: 548 per cent of the male population of the City of London had the right to vote there. In Pudsey, 112 per cent could vote. But in the seven parliamentary seats of Tower Hamlets in 1911, an average of 35.7 were enfranchised, and this does not discount the people who had two votes, each of which counted in the total. In Sheffield, Hanley, Stoke, Cardiff, Salford and Manchester less than 60 per cent of men could vote, again without making allowance for plural voting. In Liverpool, the figure for all nine seats was less than 50 per cent. Hull and Birmingham enfranchised 62 per cent of their men. Rural seats did much better, and the seven Lincolnshire seats averaged 84 per cent of all their men enregistered, not allowing for their share of plural voters.

Class voting was to become normal, once nearly everyone could vote after 1918. Before the universal suffrage it was seriously inhibited by tactical considerations. These prevailed throughout the whole period between the 1884 legislation and the First World War, during which time there had been very little improvement indeed in the extension of the franchise, as is clearly shown in table 7.1.

Of course, even these figures exaggerate. It is not difficult to assess the handicaps under which Mann in North Aberdeen, Tillett in Bradford, or Hardie in West Ham were operating. On anything like manhood suffrage, they might have been home and dry; but Labour was not making the rules.

This is not to say that a wider franchise would automatically engender class voting. Duncan Tanner has calculated that many of the voteless men were middle-class lodgers, sometimes from comfortable occupations.[77] Yet, allowing for this, there were certainly many voteless workers and trade unionists. Given access to the ballot, these men and women would need to be persuaded to vote for the Labour Party before it could win. Large numbers of them were not so persuaded even in 1918, and indeed arguments about 'deference' voting were still lustily pressed right into the 1960s.[78]

However, notwithstanding Tanner's elegant reasoning, the core fact is this: the 'social context' of solid Labour voting was, first and foremost, the approach of universal suffrage. Of course, this did not directly entail solid political support for Labour: none the less, without it such political support was far more difficult to achieve. There are strong grounds for offering a formula: trade unionists who could all vote might well be readier to support trade-union candidates, thinking they might win, than

Table 7.1   *Percentage of Adult Males Enfranchised in England and Wales, 1892–1915*

	England and Wales	Counties	Boroughs
1892	66.9	73.2	59.7
1901	63.0	68.1	56.9
1911	65.6	69.9	59.9
1915	68.1	72.8	61.9

'Made up from the 1891, 1901, 1911 census tables, pp. 1893–4 xx.675, which allows comparison of the 1892 electorate with the 1891 population, and pp. 1914–16 lii.596. The England and Wales column includes university voters. The 1915 figure is calculated on the basis of the 1911 census using an adult male percentage of 57%. On the basis of the 1914 male population estimate of Michell and Deane, *Abstract of British Historical Statistics* (1962), p. 10, the England and Wales figure is 66.4% (i.e. below the 1892 figure); no estimates for the 1914 borough and county populations have been found. Because of the rapidly declining birth rate throughout this period, it is important to calculate the *adult* male percentage; comparison on the basis of the all-male population is misleading. The following have been taken as the percentages of males ages 21 and over: 1891, 51.7%, 1901, 54.5%, 1911, 56.0%, 1915, 57.0%, 1921, 59.5%.'
Source: H. C. G. Matthew, R. I. McKibbin and J. A. Kay, 'The Franchise Factor in the Rise of the Labour Party', in J. M. Roberts and G. A. Holmes (eds), *The English Historical Review*, vol. XCI (1976), p. 726.

(Reproduced by permission of the authors and Longman Group.)

they would have been when many of their colleagues were known to be disenfranchised. The fewer they were in the general electorate, the more attractive might tactical voting appear. Of course, the stronger the unions became, the greater the influence which they might expect to exert on their members' thinking, especially when all shared full electoral rights. In this respect, the emergence of the TGWU in 1922 was to represent a great potential advance for Labour: it annulled the ill-effects of fragmentation between the myriad of lesser, often local, trade-union bodies. At the same time it offered powerful encouragement to seek a common political expression.

However, in the 1890s Labour still had far to go before it could ponder these problems of success.

How to Oppose?

Does this mean that John Burns and George Bernard Shaw were right to embrace the doctrine of 'permeation'? Was it necessary to cuddle up to the Liberal machine before Labour could win? Yes and no. Without a Liberal alliance, in practice, Labour representation would be small. But with it, it would tend to irrelevance. Until well into the twentieth century, unless the Liberal boat could be rocked, no beneficial reforms of the electoral law were remotely conceivable. Without some confrontation, nothing would move. With it alone, not much more could be shifted. Insofar as new-union politics were 'inconsistent', this is why: they sought to resolve profound and ample ambiguities in the very narrow space which was open to them. The new unions gave the ILP's activists a real opening. With a trade-union base, it was possible to win some elections, especially at local level. As the new-union presence diminished, a trade-union alliance would involve a more timid orientation, because even where 'new' men had been elected to high office in old unions, the majority of their members had a place in society which was far more comfortable than that of the dockers, carters or general labourers.

Mann's Aberdeen Campaign

Immediately after the dust had settled on the wreckage of Independent Labour hopes in 1895, the party set about its recovery. The opportunity arose in Aberdeen North in 1896. This has been described by David Howell as 'perhaps the most successful of the ILP's Scottish campaigns',[79] and indeed it figures statistically as the party's most successful attempt anywhere.[80] Tom Mann polled 46 per cent of the votes cast, which was 0.4 per cent more than Keir Hardie had drawn in his defeat at West Ham South. It was streets ahead of all the others. Mann was opposing a Liberal in a straight fight, and thus came within 430 of ousting an industrialist who was trespassing in a constituency which was a pillar of the Gladstonian establishment. Mann won the support of the Trades Council at the beginning of his campaign, and was enthusiastically welcomed in the dock areas. He campaigned for dock municipalization and supported the demands of the local fishermen. His election oration was published as a popular pamphlet, and was both rousing and intransigent.[81] David Howell reports that: 'Mann's post-poll euphoric meeting ended with the singing of "Will ye no come back again?"'[82]

He never did. None the less, his candidature achieved that unity of trade-union response which he had sought in vain in Colne Valley, and strengthened the understanding that trade-union support was crucial to Labour success. Within a few years, the dockers of Aberdeen were to be recruited not to Mann's own union, but to the NUDL.

Mann stood again, the following year, in a by-election in Halifax. But he did not repeat his success in Scotland, polling 1,000 fewer votes than 'Squire' Lister had done in 1895. In part this could be explained by Lister's absence; but it was also due to an open squabble with Lib.–Lab. trade unionists. In this way, the lesson of the Aberdeen contest was reinforced by negative example.

The New Unions and Socialist Unity . . .

During these years, active new-unionist participation in the government of the Independent Labour Party gradually fell away. So did the party's overall claims of membership. Tillett did not offer himself for re-election to the ILP leadership in 1895, perhaps in part because of the acrimony caused by his criticisms of the German socialists. Mann had left the secretaryship at the end of 1897. He had been involved in abortive fusion negotiations with the Social Democratic Federation, after a long internal wrangle. Clearly he saw socialist unity as one necessary dimension in the recovery of the political initiative by socialists. It is also clear, from his subsequent actions, that he was willing to conceive a strategy of co-operation with Liberals for at least some specific objectives. If socialist unity had not been a matter of either/or, it is possible that it could have been combined with a new offensive to divide the Liberal forces, thus offering a different perspective from the conformity which marked the earliest days of the Labour Party.

At the ILP Nottingham Conference of 1896, delegates had voted down Hardie's opposition to merger talks with the SDF. His reproach that the SDF had contributed to his defeat in West Ham went unregarded. Talks were in fact stalled when the TUC Parliamentary Committee rejected a tripartite initiative, but the 1897 ILP Conference returned to the agenda of unity and carried a motion for fusion. Hardie, Mann, Ramsay MacDonald and Russell Smart were delegated for the ILP, to meet Hyndman, Quelch, H. W. Lee, George Lansbury and J. T. Barwick of the SDF. The ILP then balloted to accept unity proposals, later in 1897.[83] So did the members of the SDF. Fusion was ditched only in a complex of manoeuvres at the 1898 ILP Conference. These culminated in a declamation by Bruce Glasier, which suffocated all hopes of a united party in a fog of mystical rhetoric:

> Socialism is a very great and a very marvellously pervading and encompassing power. It is the most human spirit that has grown up in the world, and it is the divinest of all things we have ever had vision of with our eyes. We who call ourselves Socialists cannot ourselves comprehend its might or magnitude. We are as reeds shaken in the wind of its coming. We can only receive knowledge of it so far as the space and peculiarities of our minds will allow . . . Is it not, think you, better for a land that there be many pleasant rivers and brooks – yea, and mountain torrents – of socialism . . .[84]

The ILP Executive had commissioned this elegant metaphor in putting up Glasier to offer reasons for reneging on plans for the merger. Such rhapsodies were to become a stock-in-trade of the Independent Labour Party in later years, under the competing influence of Glasier himself, Philip Snowden and Ramsay MacDonald. The effort to straddle a party dependent upon socialist radicals on the one side and craft-union traditionalism on the other called up a remarkable new Muse – demagogic obfuscation.

. . . *and Discord*

But Tom Mann had also encountered unpleasant controversy within the party after the March 1897 Halifax by-election. Acrid comments on his private life had been made by various members of the NAC. A slime of prurient gossip resulted. Pete Curran's defeat in a by-election in Barnsley in October 1897 had been worse than expected. Curran, the gasworkers' leader, was another new-union stalwart, but he came third, after a powerful intervention by Yorkshire miners' leaders on behalf of the Liberals. Mann had also been involved in a sharp exchange with James Sexton, who had backed Fred Maddison in the by-election in Sheffield that August. Maddison, it will be recalled, had been the most vigorous opponent of Tom McCarthy's intervention in West Hull, and his subsequent victory in Sheffield Brightside did not make him any more acceptable to the dockers. That Sexton, a dockers' leader, should be prepared to endorse the dockers' antagonist as 'a pronounced trade unionist . . . instead of the nephew of a duke' seemed to Mann to be 'sheer rebellion'.[85] It in no way wiped away the memory of Charles Wilson's onslaught upon, and destruction of, the Dockers' Union in Hull, and Maddison's ambivalence was seen as willingness to condone strike-breaking and strike-breakers. All of this implied future rivalries over who might win access to organize the Humber again. Sexton was, this time round, admonished by the NAC.

The Lessons of Defeat

If the first reaction of the ILP campaigners was one of dismay at the scale of the 1895 defeat, there were also other important lessons to be drawn from that experience. Liberalism, after all, had been hit even harder than the infant Labour slate. Labour had lost one seat, but the Liberals had lost few short of 100. On the one hand it made sense to see the Labour débâcle as part of the wider swing to the Tories; on the other it was clear that Labour interventions had cost the Liberals very heavily, and that the doctrine of abstention under the Fourth Clause, where it was applied, had also taken its toll:

> The Liberals lost all three seats in Bradford, one seat in Halifax, one seat in Otley, one seat in Shipley, and regained the Huddersfield seat lost at a byelection in 1893. Although there had been a national swing against the

Liberals, it did not go unnoticed that some of the most significant local
losses occurred in areas where the Labour challenge was strong . . .[86]

This perception by a contemporary scholar gives us a remarkable echo
of Ben Tillett's 'victory' oration after his 1895 defeat in Bradford: 'They
set out upon the task of soundly thrashing one of their enemies. They
could not take them both on at once . . . They had not been spreading
their forces for nothing, and if the Liberals did not come to their side,
and fight side by side with them, they would keep them out.'[87]

The National Democratic League

Tom Mann, although he never wavered in his prior commitment to trade
unionism as the base of all Labour organization, clearly drew from these
experiences the related conclusion that changes in the franchise would
be necessary before there could be any parliamentary breakthrough. It
was the South African War which highlighted this question.

Sir Alfred Milner, the British High Commissioner, had demanded a
universal male franchise in the Transvaal for all British immigrants who
had completed five years' residence.[88] Neither blood nor treasure was to
be stinted in this cause, given that its victory would also bring the
Witwatersrand Gold reefs and Johannesburg into the comfortable folds
of the empire. But W. C. Steadman, speaking at the TUC, pointed out
that Her Majesty's domestic subjects, living at a great remove from all
gold mines, were equally or even further distant from the civic rights and
duties which Britain now sought to impose upon the Boers: 'With our
present electoral system not one-half of the million and a quarter
workers whom this Congress represents would have a vote if an election
took place on the morrow.'[89] It was left to the editor of *Reynolds's
Newspaper*, W. M. Thompson, to draw the moral about this widely
detested war: 'It will at least have taught people the great lesson – that
where in any country the franchise is denied, even to foreigners, it is not
only just, but it is an absolute duty to use force to acquire it.'[90]

In order to remedy this deficiency the National Democratic League
was initiated by Thompson, together with Tom Mann, who became its
founding secretary. The new organization involved, among others, David
Lloyd George, John Burns and other radicals, together with Bob Smillie
and Charles Duncan, the secretary of the new Workers' Union. John
Ward of the Navvies' Union also took part.[91] So did stalwart Lib.–Labs
such as George Howell.[92] The platform of the League was that 'a man
should have the right to vote because he was a man, and that it should not
depend upon the house he occupied or the rent he paid'.[93] Besides
universal male suffrage, it demanded payment of MPs and the abolition
of the House of Lords. 'For a time', wrote G. D. H. Cole, the new

organization 'had much more of the limelight than the Labour Representation Committee . . . it gradually lost its importance, but not without playing a highly significant part in the leftward re-orientation of the Liberal Party and thus checking considerably the movement towards Labour independence. It was undoubtedly a factor in the great Liberal victory of 1906'.[94]

The NDL platform launched itself when the Boer War was beginning; it was not to be implemented until the altogether more cosmic mayhem of the First World War made it unavoidable, and Tom Mann's old arguments could still be heard right up until 1918 when the new electoral arrangements were introduced. Then the 'missing men' were finally enfranchised. The vast carnage of young men – many of whom could die for their government but were not allowed to join in electing it – seems to have killed off the argument against giving votes to the soldiers who survived. By that time, a new political order was emerging.

III

International Socialism

We should not leave the story of the transport workers in the ILP without dealing briefly with their international connections. These were to have a certain influence on subsequent happenings.

Unlike many of his colleagues, Tom Mann was to become closely familiar with the French unions, partly because of his experiences in the Socialist International and partly because of his simultaneous efforts to organize the International Federation of Ship, Dock and River Workers.

While he was still responsible for the organization of the Independent Labour Party, as its secretary, Mann found himself in charge of the various arrangements for the housing and administration of the 1896 International Socialist Congress in London. This convened on 27 July and immediately erupted into a famous controversy about the seating of trade-union delegates who were also anarchists, or at any rate anti-parliamentarians. A boiling row between constitutional socialists and anarchists had already broken out in the Zurich Congress of 1893, resulting in the exclusion of a couple of dozen delegates, including the young Rosa Luxemburg.[95]

Anarchism was a frightening concept because it was associated with direct action, which for most trade-union members meant straightforward support for strikes and boycotts: but for that public which was uninformed about the details of labour and socialist organization it invariably implied bomb attacks and senseless terrorism.[96] By 1896 the French trade unions in particular were largely aligned in support of direct action, even though they were obviously far removed from terrorist commitments. As Tom Mann remembered it in his memoirs, fifty-one of the French delegates to the London Congress were of one view about parliamentary methods of work, and the other fifty favoured the other view. He could not remember whether the direct-action school was in the minority or not: but he knew that the majority, whichever way it ran, consisted of one vote only.[97] Partly because the division was so narrow and partly because it was the main force of the trade-union movement in France which was so strongly involved with the allegedly 'anarchist' current, Mann and Keir Hardie voted for the seating of the anti-parliamentary delegates, much to the annoyance of some of the would-be parliamentarians.[98]

In fact there had been five distinct groups, not just two, in the French delegation to London. Parliamentary socialists ranged themselves in two factions, one led by Jules Guesde, Paul Lafargue and M. Deville, and the other by Jean Jaurès and Alexander Millerand. Anti-parliamentarians came from three tendencies: the Blanquists, led by Edouard Vaillant; the followers of Jean Allemane; and the anarchists, grouped around Fernand Pelloutier and the trade-union radicals. Taken together, these trends divided into two broad groups of roughly equal size, as Tom Mann rightly recalled. The contemporary French chronicler A. Hamon gives the syndicalists a majority of two over the parliamentarians.[99]

The three big delegations in London came from England, France and Germany. The Germans were orthodox parliamentarians. The historian of French anarchism, J. Maitron, wrongly records that Tom Mann alone among the English supported the anarchist participation:[100] Mann, of course, was a determined supporter of all trade-union colleagues, regardless of their reported political allegiances – not least because he was busy assembling support for the Transport Workers' International. But Keir Hardie also spoke out alongside his general secretary, against 'state socialism of the German type'.[101]

The two ILP leaders provoked widespread recriminations among supporters of the SDF, who remained sternly opposed to dalliance with anarchism or any other unorthodoxy. From its beginning to its end, the International Congress was an almighty rumpus, which spilt over from the meeting hall into the columns of the London press. The newspapers had a field-day ridiculing the socialist scrimmages. George Bernard Shaw wrote a long apologist essay, making the best of what he clearly saw as a bad job.[102]

The cause of all the aggravation was Pelloutier, the spokesman of the three non-parliamentary caucuses: 'He it was to whom the anarchist mandates had been given at the London Congress; in a word, he was the most conspicuous protagonist of anarchism among the unions'.[103]

Having provoked such paroxysms, Pelloutier was to die within five years, at the age of thirty-four, 'leaving behind an indelible memory of energy, goodness and devotion.'[104] We shall meet his ghost when we come to look at what was to happen in 1910.

IV

Independent Labour and the Trades Union Congress

We have already described the establishment in 1887 of the TUC's Labour Electoral Association, and H. H. Champion's subsequent espousal of its cause. This, however, was to prove shortlived and, as we have seen, Champion's own *Labour Elector* ceased to appear in 1890.

That year saw a set-piece debate on the eight-hours' question at the TUC, and in spite of Hardie's altercations with the old guard during earlier Congresses, the combined weight of new-union affiliations and old-union converts was enough to carry the question. The debate had clearly swept through the old-established organizations. The stonemasons were for the eight-hour day, and repudiated Broadhurst, the TUC secretary, who represented them at Congress. The carpenters and joiners also overruled the strong objections of their secretary. The cautious majority at the AGM of the railway servants in 1889 turned down a proposal to introduce a new class of membership with a weekly contribution of 3*d*. Existing members paid 5*d*. Their reluctance to acknowledge the needs of less-affluent fellow workers produced a speedy reaction. Within two months, the General Railway Workers' Union was founded, and the poorest-paid railwaymen, including porters and platelayers, were swept into its ranks in support of militant new unionism. The new union also recruited amongst van-men and lurrymen, grades neglected by the Amalgamated Society of Railway Servants. Here it could not be accused of poaching. In November it resolved 'that the union shall remain a fighting one and shall not be encumbered by any sick or accident fund.'[105] Both the new General Railway Workers' Union and the old ASRS lined up for shorter hours. The compositors and the ironfounders also joined in.[106]

Broadhurst had had enough, and he stood down as TUC secretary; Charles Fenwick was elected in his place. Even more spectacular was the election of John Burns to the Parliamentary Committee, albeit as runner-up, after not one but two successful though disgruntled Lib.–Labs had withdrawn.

By 1892 the last pockets of resistance to the eight-hours' movement had been brought round by membership revolts in their own unions. Birtwhistle and Mawdsley, of the United Textile Factory Workers' Association, were key cases: 'No trade union leaders reacted more violently' to the 1890 decision than they did,[107] but their joint organization voted by 132 to 21 to join the eight-hours' movement.

In 1891 Congress threw out a scheme for the establishment of a political fund to meet election costs, and to maintain elected members.

But the following year the Parliamentary Committee was mandated to prepare proposals for such a project.

In 1893 Hardie stood against Fenwick for the TUC secretaryship and was defeated. His amendments to the new scheme for Labour representation were accepted, however, committing TUC-sponsored candidates to independence of the established parties, and the public ownership and control of the means of production, distribution and exchange. This, however, was a paper victory, since contributions to the new fund were voluntary. Volunteers were soon found to be wanting.

The year 1894 saw a debate on land and mines nationalization. Hardie, supported by Burns and Mann, put forward an amendment to add the means of production and exchange to this list, and it was overwhelmingly carried, by 219 votes against 61. That year there were three candidates for the secretaryship of Congress: Fenwick, the incumbent; Sam Woods, another miner; and Tom Mann. Woods won on a second ballot, after Mann withdrew, having won one-third of the votes.[108] During that Congress, Mann claimed at least eighty delegates who were supporters of the ILP. Since the dockers were already at a very low ebb, and other new unions were suffering heavy losses, it is quite clear that this tally, and the large support for Independent Labour policies, reflected serious changes of opinion (and personnel) in the established organizations.

The result was a heavy counterblow. In 1895, hot on the adverse election results, Congress was persuaded to accept new standing orders. The block vote was introduced, Trades Councils were henceforth to be excluded, and only those who were working union officers or actively employed at their trade were to be admitted as delegates. Out went Keir Hardie, at whom the blow was aimed. Burns had aligned with Mawdsley in order to bring about the change, but doubtless it was reinforced by the hurt reactions of Lib.–Lab. supporters to the part played by the ILP in their electoral discomfiture. Paradoxically, the bar on Trades Councils was to exclude many Lib.–Lab. centres of influence, as well as the few socialist enclaves. To add to the general sense of rout, Ben Tillett was voted off the Parliamentary Committee, since the Dockers' Union membership was now so diminished.

Tories and Liberals in the Unions

Now Congress seemed almost a fiefdom of two great blocks: the cotton workers and the coalminers. The cotton workers included many traditional Conservative supporters, and the miners were still overwhelmingly Liberal – partly because their geographical concentration meant they could relatively easily drive a hard bargain with the Liberal machine, unlike dockers, for instance; and partly because of a visceral antipathy to landowners, and hence Tories. We have already seen that Rosebery's intervention as a governmental mediator during the miners' lock-out had, in some of the coalfields, done the Liberals no harm at all. Nor did the killing of two miners, shot by soldiers at Featherstone during the same dispute, appear to damage them. The sad intervention of Pete Curran in Barnsley in 1897, which brought about a derisory result for the ILP after powerful intervention by the miners' leaders, only underlined this message. Not only Hardie was out under the new rules: so too was John Burns, for the same reason, but his political position was already secure.

And yet, only four years on, the TUC was to approve its momentous resolution to form the Labour Representation Committee, and at the end of February 1900, 129 delegates were to gather at the Memorial Hall in London to establish it on completely new foundations. How did this come about?

The apparent defeat of the socialists at the 1895 TUC was nothing if not impermanent. The employers' offensive was shaking out older unions, and the lock-out of the engineers served not only to radicalize the activists, but also to make space for Tom Mann's last major initiative of this phase – the Workers' Union. This was much reinforced by new technological developments, which undermined the security of craftsmen and created large bodies of semi-skilled employees. A revolution was brought about in the metal trades with new processes, concentration and mergers, and intensified foreign competition. Upturn or not, 10 per cent of the workers in engineering and shipbuilding were unemployed. The printers and the boot and shoe workers met similar upheavals. Railwaymen were becoming more and more aware of the deterioration in their conditions. Given the continued withholding of recognition, they needed political action. The dockers, in both Tillett's and Sexton's organizations, were no less committed to political action because it proved difficult; and they had gained some real ground in local government. Even more was this true of the gasworkers. By 1898 Keir Hardie claimed that three-fifths of TUC delegates belonged to the ILP. There was certainly a socialist majority, because a motion in favour of support for the 'working class socialist parties' was emphatically carried.

In June 1899 James Mawdsley stood as Conservative candidate in Oldham, and was defeated after heavy Lib.–Lab. intervention. This gave strong support to the notion that independent action was necessary, since Labour would otherwise remain for ever a cat's paw in other people's quarrels. James Sexton was to refer to it, in scathing terms, when seconding the motion at the 1899 TUC for the creation of the Labour Representation Committee. It was necessary, he said, 'to end the present disgraceful confusion in which prominent Labour men . . . opposed each other on separate platforms'.[109]

Taking the Plunge

On 12 October 1899 the South African War broke out. The Liberals were still further divided by it. Liberal imperialism was now compelled to occupy a subaltern role, since the Conservatives were manifestly in charge. Liberal opponents of the war were compelled to run for cover under a literal hail of jingo missiles. That the TUC was already estranged from the established parties was plain from their resolution of the previous year: but now the Liberals offered little credible support to any Labour aspirant, in their obvious confusion and demoralization. Paradoxically, having digested its own experience of the difficulties of independent action, the ILP was much more ready to meet and treat with the Lib.–Labs than at any time in its short history.

The text of the 1899 motion, which it took three hours for the Plymouth Congress to debate, looked a bit like a committee product:

> That this Congress, having regard to its decisions in former years, and with a view to securing a better representation of the interests of Labour in the House of Commons, hereby instructs the Parliamentary Committee to invite the co-operation of all the co-operative, socialistic, trade union, and other working organisations to jointly co-operate on lines mutually agreed upon, in convening a special congress of representatives from such of the above-named organisations as may be willing to take part to devise ways and means for securing the return of an increased number of Labour members to the next Parliament.[110]

One thing, however, was quite clear: while the Parliamentary Committee was to take the first initiative, the new 'congress' would, if it could agree on anything, carry on the baton for the next length. There is some disagreement about how this rather clever formula was evolved. The Webbs report that it was 'drafted in London by the members of the Independent Labour Party'.[111] Henry Pelling doubts this, and tells us that 'It appears rather to have been drafted by Thomas R. Steels, a member of the [Railway] union's Doncaster branch and of the ILP'.[112] Certainly the motion was proposed by the railway servants. Max Beer records that 'in the office of the *Labour Leader*, the organ of the ILP, a resolution was drafted . . . and handed over, through the executive of the Amalgamated Society of Railway Servants, to James Holmes . . . [one] of the delegates'.[113]

James Sexton's memoirs, however, contain a quite explicit account of the matter, which is consonant with both stories once it is realized that there were in fact three motions on the TUC's original order paper: one from the railwaymen, one from the London dockers, and the third from Sexton's own National Union of Dock Labourers. These were composited for debate at an informal meeting in which Keir Hardie participated:

'He, as a visitor, with "Jimmy" Holmes, Ben Tillett and myself, had fashioned the three resolutions of our respective unions into one.'[114] The initiators of the Labour Party, in other words, included two of the most important unions which later founded the Transport and General Workers' Union. They also included the one (in the shape of the NUR) which, later, got away.

The Parliamentary Committee, in its majority, had but small appetite for this decision, even though Congress delegates received its victory with unrestrained jubilation. Four members of the committee were delegated to sup with the socialist devil, in the general supposition that nothing much would come of it. The four people chosen were Sam Woods, W. C. Steadman, Will Thorne and Richard Bell. They represented the miners, the bargebuilders, the gasworkers and the railway servants respectively; but they were also drawn from different allegiances. Woods was a Liberal and rather a progressive one at that; Steadman was a Fabian and a Radical; Thorne a longstanding Social Democrat; and Bell, for the moment, a hostage if not exactly a follower of the ILP. The railway servants would not send him to Parliament unless he stood as an Independent.

Woods it had been who in 1892 had moved the censure of the Parliamentary Committee for failure to act adequately to implement Congress wishes on the legal Eight-Hours' Bill; and it was after this dispute that Woods succeeded Charles Fenwick as secretary of the Parliamentary Committee. Having been defeated as Lib.–Lab. MP for Ince in the landslide of 1895, he had won his way back into Parliament in the 1897 Walthamstow by-election. None the less, his politics were consistently at the Labour edge of the Lib.–Lab. spectrum: he not only campaigned for the legal eight-hour day, but for Irish Home Rule, payment of Members of Parliament, compulsory employers' liability, and nationalization of mining royalties. Like Tom Mann, he was among those who after 1900 joined in the National Democratic League to work for franchise reform. It was useful, to say the least, to have support from such a man, given the general sentiments of the majority of his colleagues among the TUC leadership.

Sexton reported the last act of the Parliamentary Committee in this drama with some wry detachment:

The Special Conference was held in the following year, and was attended by Michael Davitt as a visitor. The Parliamentary Committee . . . gave their report and then left the platform, believing that without their official countenance the whole attempt would fizzle out. No nominally representative body of men can ever have been more totally unable to read the signs of the times or appreciate the mood and spirit of those they were supposed to represent.[115]

So it was that the Trade Union Congress sired the Labour Party, even before the age of artificial insemination, at a distance somewhat greater than an arm's length.

Notes

1 V. I. Lenin, *Imperialism, the Highest Stage of Capitalism*, Selected Works V (Martin Lawrence, 1936), p. 72.

2 See Michael Barratt Brown, *After Imperialism* (Heinemann, 1963), pp. 90ff.

3 R. C. K. Ensor, *England, 1870–1914* (Oxford University Press, 1936), p. 189.

4 R. Page Arnot, *The Miners*, vol. I (Allen and Unwin, 1949), p. 252. It is very likely that this intervention strongly delayed the Liberal decline in the coalfields.

5 Paul Thompson, *Socialists, Liberals and Labour: The Struggle for London, 1885–1914* (Routledge and Kegan Paul, 1967), pp. 52–3. Tom Mann had not, in fact, left trade unionism: this view reflects a general misapprehension about which we wrote in chapter 4.

6 George Tate, *The London Trades Council, 1860–1950: A History* (Lawrence and Wishart, 1950), p. 70.

7 It contributed, as well, to the growth of the quite separate Labour churches. These preached an ethical socialism, of which E. P. Thompson claims, 'It is . . . difficult to describe them as Christian or religious in any sense except that of the broad ethical appeal of the "religion of socialism" whose text was Morris's "Fellowship is Life" ' (E. P. Thompson, 'Homage to Tom Macguire', in Asa Briggs and John Saville (eds), *Essays in Labour History, 1886–1923* (Macmillan, 1960), p. 291.) Without doubting this, Stanley Pierson provides a more detailed account of the Labour church movement, tracing its origins in unitarianism, and following its doctrinal evolution in *Marxism and the Origins of British Socialism* (Cornell University Press, 1973), pp. 226–45.

8 Cf. Tom Mann and Ben Tillett, *The New Trade Unionism* (London, 1890).

9 Tate, *The London Trades Council*, p. 72.

10 Yvonne Kapp, *Eleanor Marx: The Crowded Years, 1884–1898* (Lawrence and Wishart, 1976), pp. 735–6.

11 Tate, *The London Trades Council*, p. 77.

12 Ibid., pp. 201ff.

13 Kapp, *Eleanor Marx*, p. 370.

14 Robert Blatchford, *My Eighty Years* (Cassell, 1931), p. 199.

15 Ben Tillett, *Memories and Reflections* (John Long, 1931), p. 190.

16 Paul Thompson, *Socialists, Liberals and Labour*, p. 101.

17 Kenneth O. Morgan, *Keir Hardie, Radical and Socialist* (Weidenfeld and Nicolson, 1975), pp. 44–9.

18 *Workman's Times*, 25 June 1892; cited in Fred Reid, *Keir Hardie, The Making of a Socialist* (Croom Helm, 1978), p. 130.

19 Kenneth D. Brown, *John Burns* (Royal Historical Society, 1977), p. 65.

20 Havelock Wilson, *My Stormy Voyage Through Life*, vol. I (Co-operative Printing Society, 1925), pp. 202–3.
21 Ibid.
22 J. Reynolds and K. Laybourne, 'The Emergence of the Independent Labour Party in Bradford', *International Review of Social History*, vol. XX (1975), pp. 326–7.
23 See Cyril Pearce, *The Manningham Mills Strike* (University of Hull, 1975).
24 Reynolds and Laybourne, 'The Emergence of the Independent Labour Party in Bradford', p. 329.
25 Ibid., p. 329.
26 Ibid., p. 327.
27 Jonathan Schneer, *Ben Tillett: Portrait of a Labour Leader* (Croom Helm, 1982), pp. 62–3.
28 Sidney and Beatrice Webb, *Letters*, ed. Norman MacKenzie, (Cambridge University Press, 1978), vol. I, pp. 419ff.
29 Schneer, *Ben Tillett*, p. 71.
30 Ibid., p. 72.
31 *Bradford Observer*, 6 July 1892; cited in Schneer, *Ben Tillett*, p. 77.
32 Reid, *Keir Hardie*, p. 134.
33 This and other once-famous squabbles are documented in A. E. P. Duffy, 'Differing Policies and Personal Rivalries in the Origins of the Independent Labour Party', *Victorian Studies*, vol. VI (Indiana University, 1962/3), pp. 43–65.
34 J. L. Garvin, 'A Party with a Future', *Fortnightly Review*, September 1895; cited in Eric J. Hobsbawm, *Labour's Turning Point, 1880–1900*, History in the Making, vol. III (Lawrence and Wishart, 1948), p. 146.
35 David Howell, *British Workers and the Independent Labour Party, 1888–1906* (Manchester University Press, 1983), p. 116.
36 Ibid., p. 17.4
37 E. P. Thompson, 'Homage to Tom Maguire', p. 277.
38 Jeffrey Hill, 'Manchester and Salford Politics and the Early Development of the Independent Labour Party', *International Review of Social History*, vol. XXVI (1981), part 2, pp. 186ff.
39 James Sexton, *Sir James Sexton, Agitator: the Life of the Dockers' MP* (Faber and Faber, 1936), pp. 129–30. Sexton was wrong about Hyndman, who was not present. His recollection of the argument with Shaw is also faulty: the objection to his presence was not based on his 'self-selection' but on his presumed antipathy to Independent politics.
40 Ibid., pp. 135–40.
41 G. D. H. Cole, *British Working Class Politics, 1832–1914* (Labour Book Service, 1941), pp. 138ff.
42 David C. Douglas (ed.), *English Historical Documents*, XII, 2 (Eyre and Spottiswood, 1977), p. 666, Document 172, 'Trade Unions and Socialism'. Douglas uses the report in *The Times*, 14 January 1893.
43 Schneer, *Ben Tillett*, p. 100.
44 Bernstein had many British defenders, and indeed Tillett attracted strong criticism from them. The issue did not go away quickly. (As late as 1965 it became an important part of the indictment of Labour Party provincialism published by Tom Nairn in the New Left broadside *Towards Socialism*.

This sparked a heated exchange among Labour historians: Perry Anderson and Robin Blackburn, *Towards Socialism* (Fontana, 1965), pp. 171ff.; E. P. Thompson, 'The Peculiarities of the English', in Ralph Milliband and John Saville (eds.), *The Socialist Register* (Merlin Press, 1965), pp. 340ff.; Jonathan Schneer, 'Ben Tillett's Conversion to Independent Labour Politics', *Radical History Review*, 24 (fall 1980), pp. 42–65).

There can be no doubt that Tillett's lapse in Bradford was only one of many. Beatrice Webb, in her diary, 27 November 1887, paints a picture of a dockers' meeting in East London, at which Tillett 'ranted against white slavery, sub-contract, and irregular hours'. A stranger entered, and pressed forward to the platform: 'No one knew him except the secretary. He took the seat nearest to me, and asked the chairman to give him the resolution to look at. Then in a stage whisper to the secretary, "I will give you twenty pounds but don't let my name appear. I don't want it to be known. Of course you will support me about foreign immigration"'

No one has been able to show that this donation to his union brought undue influence to bear upon him; but Tillett's condemnation of unrestricted immigration was none the less to be vigorous and outspoken. Thus his pamphlet *The Dock Labourers' Bitter Cry* (London, 1887) argued: 'The influx of continental pauperism aggravates and multiplies the number of ills which press so heavily on us . . . Foreigners come to London in large numbers, herd together in habitations unfit for beasts, the sweating system allowing the more grasping and shrewd a life of comparative ease in superintending the work.'

These and other instances have been documented by W. J. Fishman, *East End Jewish Radicals, 1875–1914* (Duckworth, 1975), pp. 76ff. At the same time, Fishman notes a number of utterances by Tillett which quite contradict these sentiments. Racism and anti-semitism were intricately embroidered on the social fabric of the East End and, says Fishman, 'To most trade unionists, the alien Jew meant sweating'.

45 Howell, *British Workers and the Independent Labour Party*, p. 302.
46 Christie's activities are documented in Peter Wyncoll, *The Nottingham Labour Movement, 1880–1939* (Lawrence and Wishart, 1985), pp. 115–18, 123–5 and 130–5.
47 Howell, *British Workers and the Independent Labour Party*, pp. 306 and 457.
48 David Clark, *Colne Valley, Radicalism to Socialism* (Longman, 1981), pp. 4 and 197.
49 Ibid., p. 30.
50 E. P. Thompson, 'Homage to Tom Macguire', p. 283.
51 Clark, *Colne Valley, Radicalism to Socialism*, p. 39.
52 Ibid., p. 40.
53 Ibid., p. 56.
54 Ibid., p. 89.
55 Henry Pelling, *Social Geography of British Elections* (Macmillan, 1967), p. 294.
56 Ibid.
57 Maddison's biography is to be found in J. M. Bellamy and J. Saville, *Dictionary of Labour Biography*, vol. IV (Macmillan, 1972), pp. 119–22.

58 Statement by F. W. Booth, *Hull Daily Mail*, 10 June 1895.
59 Ibid., 5 July 1895.
60 Ibid., 27 June 1895.
61 Ibid., 12 July 1895.
62 Ibid.
63 Ibid., 16 July 1895.
64 Ibid., 26 June 1895.
65 Ibid., 17 July 1895.
66 Pelling, *Social Geography of British Elections*, p. 295, gives a figure of 10 per cent, but this is of the electorate, not of those voting.
67 Ibid., p. 295.
68 J. Carter, 'The ILP in Ashton-under-Lyne 1893–1900', *Bulletin of North-West Group for the Study of Labour History* (1977), p. 76.
69 Ibid., p. 77; and Sexton, *Sir James Sexton, Agitator*, p. 145.
70 Cf. F. M. Leventhal, *Respectable Radical – George Howell and Victorian Working-Class Politics* (Weidenfeld and Nicolson, 1971), p. 212.
71 H. C. G. Matthew, R. I. McKibbin and J. A. Kay: 'The Franchise Factor in the Rise of the Labour Party', in J. M. Roberts and G. A. Holmes (eds), *The English Historical Review*, volume XCI (Longman, 1976), p. 726.
72 W. E. Gladstone, *Speeches and Addresses Delivered at the Election of 1865*, pp. 47–9; cited in Alan Bullock and Maurice Shock, *The Liberal Tradition* (A. and C. Black, 1956), pp. 143–4.
73 Ibid., p. 145.
74 Max Beer, *Fifty Years of International Socialism* (Allen and Unwin, 1937), p. 140.
75 Ibid., pp. 141–2.
76 L. H. Powell, *The Shipping Federation: A History of the First Sixty Years, 1890–1950* (Shipping Federation, 1950), p. 8.
77 Duncan Tanner, 'The Electoral System and the Rise of Labour', *Bulletin of the Institute of Historical Research* (1983), pp. 205–19.
78 See R. McKenzie and Allan Silver, *Angels in Marble* (Heinemann, 1968), for a convenient account of this phenomenon.
79 Howell, *British Workers and the Independent Labour Party*, p. 169.
80 The figures for all ILP contests are to be found in F. W. S. Craig, *Minor Parties at British Parliamentary Elections, 1885–1974*, pp. 39–40.
81 It has been reprinted in John Laurent (ed.), *Tom Mann –‘Social and Economic Writings* (Spokesman Books, 1988), pp. 63ff.
82 Howell, *British Workers and the Independent Labour Party*, p. 171.
83 David Kynastone, *King Labour: The British Working Class, 1850–1914* (Allen and Unwin, 1976), p. 149.
84 Quoted in E. P. Thompson, *William Morris: Romantic to Revolutionary* (Lawrence and Wishart, 1955), p. 702.
85 Howell, *British Workers and the Independent Labour Party*, p. 121.
86 Keith Laybourn and J. Reynolds, *Liberalism and the Rise of Labour* (Croom Helm, 1984), p. 70.
87 Schneer, *Ben Tillett*, p. 110.
88 G. M. Trevelyan, *British History in the Nineteenth Century and After* (Longman, 1923), p. 420.
89 Henry Pelling, 'British Labour and British Imperialism', in Henry Pelling

(ed.), *Popular Politics in Late Victorian Britain* (Macmillan, 1968), p. 83.
90   Ibid.
91   G. D. H. Cole, 'John Burns', in Michael Katanka, *Radicals, Reformers and Socialists* (Charles Knight, 1973), p. 190.
92   G. D. H. Cole, *The Second International*, part I (Macmillan, 1956), p. 195.
93   Tom Mann, *Memoirs* (1923; reissued McGibbon and Kee, 1967), p. 125.
94   Cole, *The Second International*, part I, pp. 195–6.
95   James Joll, *The Second International* (Routledge and Kegan Paul, 1975), p. 72.
96   It also had other sinister overtones, brilliantly lampooned in G. K. Chesterton's novel *The Man Who Was Thursday* (Arrowsmith, 1908).
97   Mann, *Memoirs*, p. 105.
98   Ibid., p. 104.
99   A. Hamon, *Le Socialisme et le congrès de Londres* (Paris, 1897), p. 124.
100 J. Maitron, *Le Mouvement anarchiste en France* (Maspero, 1975), vol. I, p. 293.
101 Morgan, *Keir Hardie*, p. 88.
102 G. B. Shaw, 'Socialism at the International Congress', *Cosmopolis*, September 1896, III, p. 658.
103 Maitron, *Le Mouvement anarchiste en France*, p. 295.
104 Joll, *The Second International*, p. 61.
105 Philip Bagwell, *The Railwaymen* (Allen and Unwin, 1963), pp. 132–3.
106 A. E. P. Duffy, 'New Unionism in Britain, A Reappraisal', *Economic History Review*, vol. XIV, no. 2 (December 1961), pp. 313–14.
107 Ibid., p. 314.
108 Henry Pelling, *The Origins of the Labour Party* (Oxford University Press, 1966), p. 192.
109 TUC Report, 1899, p. 65.
110 Ibid.
111 Sidney and Beatrice Webb, *The History of Trade Unionism* (1894; WEA edn, 1912), p. 684.
112 Henry Pelling, *Origins of the Labour Party*, p. 205.
113 Max Beer, *History of British Socialism*, vol. II (G. Bell and Sons, 1921), p. 316.
114 Sexton, *Sir James Sexton, Agitator*, p. 194.
115 Ibid., p. 194.

8

In Transition: 1900–1910

I

The Struggle to Survive

When all the bells stopped ringing, and the new century was installed, all the new unions, including those in the 'carrying trades', seemed to have opted for the quiet life. Some had been beaten flat by the mercenaries of the Shipping Federation. Others had survived by adopting the lowest of low profiles. It was to be eleven years before a new 'long hot summer' revived the old hopes on the waterfront.

During those years of apparent torpor, however, the struggle for survival continued. It demanded a high order of courage and commitment, not least because those exposed to its perils were unprotected by wider publicity. The anonymity of trade-union actions during these difficult years has lent superficial credibility to the notion that the 'great unrest' of 1911–14 was a new beginning, rather than a renewal within a continuing process stretching from the 1880s to the 1920s, in which the industrial and political purposes of trade unionism underwent a profound and permanent alteration.[1] We shall return to this academic debate later.

By 1900, in many areas every sign of independence, let alone purposeful protest, had been overwhelmed. This is not to say that all turbulence had evaporated.

Jingo Bells

The year 1900 was that of Mafeking, when Colonel Baden-Powell's beleaguered forces were relieved after an Afrikaner siege of 217 days. This was celebrated in a 'crazy and rather unlovely carnival' throughout

London's streets.[2] 'No one', wrote Gareth Stedman Jones, 'who saw the crowds on Mafeking night ever forgot them'.[3] Bunting and flags and people erupted everywhere in Whitechapel and Bow; more flags sprouted on the trams and buses; the rich threw fivers or sovereigns at the tumult all around them; crowds rejoiced in every street, in song and drink, much of which was distributed free. 'Hundreds of cyclists wearing photographs of Colonel Baden-Powell formed in procession and paraded the principal thoroughfares of Poplar and Stepney', reported *The Times*.[4] Euphoria at the defeat of the Boer set ringing all the jingoistic echoes which dismayed radicals and socialists, but which signalled the presence of a strong patriotic affinity in the East End population. By no means was this attributable to any whiff of prosperity.

In 1902 Jack London, the popular American socialist writer, set out from Stepney Station on his journey of exploration among the London poor. He had originally stopped over *en route* to South Africa. He had a contract to write a book on the Boer War, but after the war ended it was cancelled. He decided instead to record his impressions of London slum life, which became *The People of the Abyss*, his favourite among his own books. Squalor and raw want were still the entire condition of the East End. Jack London began by kitting himself out in second-hand rags, and then dossed his way round all the spikes and Salvation Army hostels of the district. The spirit of Mafeking was, he found, very much abroad: the death of the old Queen had brought in its wake a Coronation, a celebration to unite the nation. So it did, bridging the great social divide with a vast ostentation of artificial pageantry on one side and a wild heave of drunken debauch on the other.

Standing in Trafalgar Square, walled in by a double file of soldiers, and overwhelmed by the sheer power of the well-fed legions of lifeguards, blue-jackets and metropolitan constables, Jack London, visiting from a more democratic world, felt that he could never have understood the stunted toilers of his 'abyss' until he had also seen the strapping Guards in the royal procession 'and come to know that the one must feed and clothe and groom the other'.

> There is cheering down Whitehall; the crowd sways, the double walls of soldiers come to attention, and into view swing the King's watermen, in fantastic medieval garbs of red, for all the world like the van of a circus parade. Then a royal carriage, filled with ladies and gentlemen of the household with powdered footmen and coachmen most gorgeously arrayed. More carriages, lords and chamberlains, viscounts, mistresses of the robes – lackeys all. Then the warriors, a kingly escort, generals, bronzed and worn, from the ends of the earth come up to London Town, volunteer officers, officers of the militia and regular forces . . . there they come, in all the pomp and certitude of power, and still they come, these men of steel, these war lords and world harnessers. Pell-mell, peers and commoners, princes and maharajahs, colonials, lithe and hardy men . . .

and now the Horse Guards, a glimpse of beautiful cream ponies, and a golden panoply, a hurricane of cheers, the crashing of bands – 'The King! the King! God save the King!' Everybody has gone mad. The contagion is sweeping me off my feet – I, too, want to shout, 'The King! God save the King!' Ragged men about me, tears in their eyes, are tossing up their hats, and crying ecstatically, 'Bless 'em! Bless 'em! Bless 'em!' See, there he is, in that wondrous golden coach, the great crown flashing on his head, the woman in white beside him likewise crowned.[5]

A Docker from the Abyss

Leaving the celebrations, Jack London visited the home of a docker, not far from Leman Street in Whitechapel:

It was not a room. Courtesy to the language will no more permit it to be called a room than it will permit a hovel to be called a mansion. It was a den, a lair. Seven feet by eight were its dimensions, and the ceiling was so low as not to give the cubic air space required by a British soldier in barracks. A crazy couch, with ragged coverlets, occupied nearly half the room. A rickety table, a chair and a couple of boxes left little space in which to run round. Five dollars would have purchased everything in sight. The floor was bare, while the walls and ceiling were literally covered with blood marks and splotches. Each mark represented a violent death – of an insect, for the place swarmed with vermin, a plague with which no person could cope single-handed.

The man who had occupied this hole, one Dan Cullen, docker, was dying in hospital. Yet he had impressed his personality on his miserable surroundings sufficiently to give an inkling as to what sort of man he was. On the walls were cheap pictures of Garibaldi, Engels, John Burns, and other labour leaders, while on the table lay one of Walter Besant's novels. He knew his Shakespeare, I was told, and had read history, sociology, and economics. And he was self-educated.

On the table, amidst a wonderful disarray, lay a sheet of paper on which was scrawled: Mr Cullen, please return the large white jug and corkscrew I lent you – articles loaned, during the first stages of his sickness, by a woman neighbour, and demanded back in anticipation of his death. A large white jug and a corkscrew are far too valuable to a creature of the Abyss to permit another creature to die in peace. To the last, Dan Cullen's soul must be harrowed by the sordidness out of which it strove vainly to rise.

It is a brief little story, the story of Dan Cullen, but there is much to read between the lines. He was born lowly, in a city and land where the lines of caste are tightly drawn. All his day he toiled hard with his body; and because he had opened the books, and been caught up by the fires of the spirit, and could 'write a letter like a lawyer', he had been selected by his fellows to toil hard for them with his brain. He became a leader of the fruit-porters, represented the dockers on the London Trades Council, and wrote trenchant articles for the labour journals.

He did not cringe to other men, even though they were his economic masters, and controlled the means whereby he lived, and he spoke his mind freely, and fought the good fight. In the 'Great Dock Strike' he was guilty of taking a leading part. And that was the end of Dan Cullen. From that day he was a marked man, and every day, for ten years and more, he was 'paid-off' for what he had done.[6]

Many parts of the country followed East London into quiescence. Stronger men than Dan Cullen were steamrollered. If the name for such conditions be 'peace', then peace reigned widely while they buried the old century with the old Queen, and installed the new King with his informal but dazzling court of plutocrats and swingers.

But the decade we are considering was not wholly pacifist in its industrial temper. The Homeric qualities of the Penrhyn Quarry strikes in North Wales spread over from the 1890s. The 1907 upheaval in Belfast, which gave James Larkin the impetus to introduce general unionism into Ireland and to invent 'Larkinism', surely prefigured the rising of all the transport workers in 1911. Both disputes fall in this interim period. While Belfast in 1907 anticipated by four years the characteristic militancy of the general labourers in the 'syndicalist' years, the railwaymen also voted by a massive majority for a national strike in 1907: this 'first' was only averted by government intervention to force a conciliation scheme on the reluctant railway companies.[7]

The Roots of Industrial 'Peace'

The general impression of industrial peace is not, however, a false one. In the decade 1890–9 there was an average of 804 strikes per annum. Between 1900 and 1909 the figure almost halved, to 464.[8]

Three reasons may be advanced to account for the relative quiescence of the period. The Taff Vale and other subsequent judgements of the courts in 1901 made serious inroads into the hitherto assumed legality of strike action. Trade-union leaders were certainly constrained to withhold official support for strikes, after heavy financial penalties imposed on the rail union in the Taff Vale case. But this influence could have been operative only for the years 1902–6, after which the incoming Liberal government reversed the judges' rulings in the 1906 Trades Disputes Act (see p. 302). Yet the number of strikes in all industries remained low for the rest of the decade. In any case, the Taff Vale effect, where it operated, served only to reinforce a much longer-held predeliction for peaceful settlements which had been pursued by most new-unionist leaders from the early 1890s onwards – an attitude stemming most obviously from their reduced bargaining, numerical and financial strengths, brought about by economic depression and high unemployment.

We saw in chapter 5 that the long slump ended in the mid-1890s and that an upswing ran through to the turn of the century. Unemployment fell from 7.5 per cent in 1893 to 2 per cent in 1899; but thereafter it rose again to 6 per cent in 1905, fell to 3.6 per cent in 1906, and climbed again to 7.7 per cent in 1909. This perennial instability of the labour market, affecting 'unskilled' and casual labour most acutely, was a constant constraint on new-unionist activities.

The third factor inhibiting union initiatives was the attitude of the employers. The Shipping Federation's onslaught had won the field for its free-labour method of curtailing union power: from the mid-1890s and throughout the 1900s such strikes as occurred on the waterfront were regularly met by the employers with the importation of free labour: it is noticeable how often the reports refer to Hull (Collison's 'stronghold of free labour') as the source of the strike-breakers. In other industries, notably engineering and footwear, strong employers' federations pursued the same methods. In this climate, unions 'kept their heads down', husbanded islands of recognition and existing conciliation procedures, and awaited better times. Equally, most employers, finding themselves in control of the situation, refrained from further union-smashing campaigns, and consequently the unions were not compelled to enter further desperate defensive struggles. Away from the battlefields of the waterfront, Tillett found grounds for satisfaction in 1901, in the tolerance and encouragement offered by those employers who had continued to accept trade unions: 'I am glad to recognise the growing confidence of employers in Trades Unionism, the more practical seeing the need of closer association and discussion with the workers' representatives. This has resulted almost in the abolition of strikes, greatly to the credit of both sides'.[9]

Union Membership

The workers, for their part, had by no means abandoned trade unionism. Membership figures showed a steady, even substantial recovery from the nadir of 1895. In rounded numbers, total membership in Great Britain grew from 1.5 million in 1895 to 2 million in 1900 and to 2.5 million in 1910, only faltering in this trend in the recession of 1904–5. This is an increase of 67 per cent between 1895 and 1910. However, within these totals, the fortunes of transport and general unions varied significantly. 'All-grade' transport unions – the London Carmen, the Amalgamated Carters, the Amalgamated Tram and Vehicle Workers, the Municipal Employees (which had members in municipal transport undertakings) and the NUDL – together registered only a 27 per cent increase in this period. Even that result was beyond the 'general' unions – the London Dockers, the Gasworkers, the NAUL and the NALU – whose combined growth was restricted to a mere 7 per cent. And the 'aristocratic', sectional unions – including the London Stevedores, the Thames Watermen, the Cardiff Trimmers, the Mersey Quay and Rail Carters, and the Winsford Saltmakers – registered no increase at all.[10] This stagnation, most evidently for the London Stevedores and Lightermen, represented an actual retreat, as less formally qualified labour encroached on their territories. We shall see later that this experience contributed significantly to their crucial conversion to the cause of federation at the end of the decade.

Transport Technology

The transport industries continued their technological evolution during this period, largely by substituting steam and electricity for wind- and horse-power. (The full impact of the internal combustion engine came later.) As we have seen (chapters 3 and 5), these changes were hardly ever labour-saving, nor did they enhance the technical sophistication of labour in transport, except where horses were displaced on the roads by electricity, steam and later by the petrol motor. Indeed, in the case of the switch from sail to steam in shipping, the old sailor's old skills in seamanship were displaced, and the ordinary deckhand became more of 'a cleaner and polisher'.[11] However, in the booming passenger-liner trade, a new semi-skilled group emerged, including ships' cooks, butchers, and stewards, with a status superior to the deckies. The number of seamen of all grades increased by 32,000 to 205,000 during the decade.[12] In 1900 the number of sailing ships was still greater by 1,500 than the number of steam ships, but the latter accounted for 7.2 million tons of a total merchant tonnage of 9.3 million. By 1910 sailing ships numbered 9,000, which was then 3,000 fewer than ships under steam power: steamships then accounted for 10.4 million of a total fleet of 11.5 million tons.[13]

On the docks, hydraulic cranes and steam winches had been replacing human lifting power since the 1890s. This change, characteristically, made no impact on the rate of increase of the dock-labour force, which grew by almost 23,000 between 1901 and 1911, to a total of 123,000.[14] This represented a comparable rate of growth to that of the previous twenty years. Similar rates of growth were registered amongst warehousemen, porters and messengers, who totalled 232,000 by 1911.[15] Significantly, watermen and bargemen, having held their numbers at 29,000 for twenty years, lost almost 2,000 between 1901 and 1911 – further evidence of the shrinking base on which their sectional unionism rested.

In road haulage, the decisive displacement of the horse and cart by the motor lorry was still some decades distant (see table 8.1). Road haulage employed a total of 238,001 employees in 1911. Of these, 58 per cent were engaged by haulage contractors; overwhelmingly these were small-scale capitalists. Of the rest, 26 per cent worked on vans and delivery carts in food and drink. Carters were also employed in large numbers by the railway companies, coal merchants and mining companies, brewers, and in local government. The numbers seeking carting work were constantly reinforced by surplus farmworkers, who were well qualified in the management of horses. Booth had calculated that, in 1890, 43 per cent of all heads of families engaged in carting in London were born outside the capital.[16]

Table 8.1   *Commercial Road Vehicles, 1900–1920*
(Nos in 000s)

	1900	1910	1920
Horse-drawn	680	830	430
Motor-driven	2*	50†	142

*1902
†1911

Source: Charles H. Feinstein and Sydney Pollard (eds), *Studies in Capital Formation in the United Kingdom, 1750–1920* (Oxford University Press, 1988), pp. 322 and 326.
(Reproduced by permission of Oxford University Press.)

Horse-drawn buses, mainly developed by large but localized private companies, fulfilled a role in the development of urban passenger transport in the late nineteenth century, but had to compete with trams (which were powered successively by horse, steam and electric power) and later with motor buses. The figures tell the story (see table 8.2).

The dominant era of the electric tram ran from the 1880s to the 1920s. Between the 1870s and 1914, route mileage rose from 100 (or a little over) to over 2,500.[17]

Table 8.2   *Horse-drawn and Motor-powered Omnibuses, 1900–1920 (Nos in 000s)*

	1900	1910	1920
Horse-drawn	35	10	–
Motorized	0*	3†	10

*1902
†1911

Source: Charles H. Feinstein and Sydney Pollard (eds), *Studies in Capital Formation in the United Kingdom, 1750–1920* (Oxford University Press, 1988), pp. 322 and 326.
(Reproduced by permission of Oxford University Press.)

In London the first motor bus began the run from Charing Cross to Victoria before the turn of the century, but its schedule was much disrupted by mechanical hiccups. By 1903 there were thirteen London motor buses, out of a total of 3,636. But six years later more than one-third of London buses had been converted, and General Omnibus sacked its last horse bus in 1911. Others followed more slowly, but the changeover was remorseless, and virtually complete by the middle of the war. Traffic increased proportionately. In 1902 the London buses carried 280 million passengers. By 1913 there were 736 million. After the war there were legions of soldiers who were qualified as drivers, and there followed a big increase in the services run by large companies, together with a mushrooming of little firms run by one or two people. By 1929 London buses carried 1,912 million passengers in the one year.[18]

The overall workforce employed on buses actually declined slightly between 1901 and 1911, from 11,974 to 11,442.[19] The fashionable technology in urban passenger transport at this time was the tram, the first means of transport to exploit recognizable twentieth-century power in the form of electricity. The first decade saw a near-trebling in the value of net capital stock in the industry, from £15 million to £42 million. Thereafter, investment declined, partly through wartime neglect and partly through belated competition from the motor omnibus. In 1920 the tramways' capital stock had fallen to £24 million.[20] The most striking evidence of the tramway 'boom' lies in the numbers employed, which more than doubled in ten years, from 18,244 in 1901 to 42,095 in 1911. (In 1881 there had been a mere 2,650 tramwaymen.) The tram industry was dominated by municipal ownership in the large towns. Municipal 'socialism' was often initiated by local politicians of all colours. It fed local pride. It also made a contribution to the ranks of transport trade unionism.

The changeover from horse-power to the internal combustion engine in the cab trade, whilst in full swing in our period, also climaxed in the following decade (see table 8.3).

The total occupied population grew from 11.2 million in 1881 to 14.3 million in 1901, an increase of 28 per cent. In the same period, the transport trades – that is, all the industries reviewed above – grew by 56 per cent to a total of 817,193. By 1911 the total occupied population had increased to 16.3 million, a gain of 13 per cent for the decade. Transport in 1911 employed 982,344 – a leap of 20 per cent. Between 1881 and 1911 transport employment grew from 4.6 per cent to 6 per cent of the working population.

Table   8.3   *Horse-drawn   Cabs   and   Motor   Taxis,*
            1900–1920 (Nos in 000s)

	1900	1910	1920
Horse-drawn	90	95	50
Motorized	3*	31†	79

*1902
†1911
Source: Charles H. Feinstein and Sydney Pollard (eds), *Studies in Capital Formation in the United Kingdom, 1750–1920* (Oxford University Press, 1988).
            (Reproduced by permission of Oxford University Press.)

'Residual' Labour in Transport and Its Employers

The increase in transport employment fuelled by the Industrial Revolution had generated faster growth than that in manufacturing employment from the mid-nineteenth century onwards. By the beginning of the twentieth century it was by no means over. Almost all transport trades seemed, during the early decades of the 1900s, to have an insatiable appetite for labour. In this they were comparable with the textile-factory trades, mining and metals, during the first stages of industrialization. Thus, although transport was clearly a *group* of industries or services with wide heterogeneities within it, rather than a single industry, its distinct sections had this in common: the workforce was continually reinforced by new recruits as its number expanded. Phillips speaks of it as seeming to be a 'residual' form of employment.[21] (Irish and displaced agricultural labourers made up a large element of the inflow.) This gave to its workers a certain community of outlook, a sense that they were indeed 'general labour', casual, or irregular, or hyper-exploited. Outsiders would characterize them as 'lower', or even 'brutish' classes.[22] Low-level technology prevailed. It is very significant that in the developing struggle towards federation, amalgamation and the ultimate achievement of the unified TGWU, the one branch of transport with an advanced technology – railways – developed a unionism which could not ultimately bring itself to submerge its identity with carters, busmen and dockers. Dislocation of status can be a very painful prospect, and the fear of it must have been a powerful influence.

Matching the complexity of transport labour was the confusion of different kinds of employers. They ranged from the great capitalists of the shipping companies, international in scale, through the large national capitalism of the railway companies – which were taking over more and more dock property (especially in the Humber, the South Wales ports and Southampton) as the new century advanced – to the municipal tramway companies, and the diminutive haulage and cab proprietors. Small capital still held a place in dockland, too, and would continue to do so right down to the Devlin reforms of the 1960s.[23] Whilst there was no simple correlation between scale of ownership and attitudes to unionism, it is true that the shipping magnates and railway-dock owners, together with the major dock companies in London, continued to show the most consistent hostility, whilst small master-stevedoring companies in both London and Liverpool established a much more tolerant relationship with the unions. Private bus companies, notably in London, opposed trade unionism, whilst municipal tramways encouraged it. In carting, the small-scale employers and the larger capitalist brewers shared opposition to recognition, which was not to be overcome until the First World War, and indeed persisted beyond it.

Two Necessities: Recognition and Amalgamation

To grow and prosper, after their setbacks of the 1890s, transport unions (and those general unions which enrolled in the transport trades) needed recognition from the employers. They could compel that recognition against the intransigent sections of the employers only by a show of strength and by the enrolment of a larger proportion of the labour forces. The economic situation was slowly restoring a climate in which such strength might be restored to its 1889 dimensions. But it was borne in upon the trade-union leadership, and ultimately on the membership, that an essential requirement, if their potential strength was to be realized, was to overcome the variety of forms of sectional isolation into which the depression and the Shipping Federation had driven them. Of course, in inland transport, there was no model of previous unity and national organization, such as the dockers inherited from 1889–91. Yet they had their own impulsion, centred round the need to overcome the great regional and local disparities of earnings and conditions which characterized their industry. As with the seamen, their aspirations were directed towards the achievement of national, standard wage-scales. On both the waterfront and the roads, a convergence towards federation and ultimate amalgamation was possible and necessary.

Upstairs, Downstairs

The social condition underlying the great unrest of 1910–14 has commonly been taken to be the decline in real wages which preceded it during the first years of the century. This analysis, nowadays contested, has owed much to the influential work of George Dangerfield, whose book *The Strange Death of Liberal England, 1910–14* was first published in 1935. (It is still a resonant and exciting work.) The Edwardian era was an age in which ostentatious consumption, the crude public display of wealth by a plutocracy growing fat on the profits of imperialism, was given sanction and licence by court circles, and reached levels which positively provoked the proletarian distemper of the great unrest. This was the world of Upstairs, Downstairs.

The case of the millionaire Wilson brothers, shipping magnates of Hull, is characteristic. Already in 1876 they were declaring gross profits of 51 per cent. By the turn of the century they had amassed the largest privately owned merchant fleet in the world, and their business was worth £2.5 million. They monopolized the Baltic trades, driving away potential competitors with notorious ruthlessness. They warred incessantly, and very publicly, with the Hull Dock Company, and also – as we have seen – with the Dockers' Union, after an initial period in which they patronized it. The historians of Hull have written:

> While it had long been the custom of Hull magnates to live in the country, no one had yet displayed the baronial splendour of Charles Wilson, M.P., at Warter Priory, bought from Lord Muncaster, or of Arthur Wilson, his brother and master of fox-hounds, at Tranby Croft. [Charles] married his eldest son to the daughter of a Duke, setting them up in The Cottage, Cottingham (now part of a University Hall of Residence). In 1905, he was ennobled as Lord Nunburnholme . . .[24]

Arthur Wilson was host to a notorious house party at Tranby Croft at which the Prince of Wales (the future King Edward VII) was a guest. A scandal of national proportions arose out of accusations of cheating at baccarat by one of the guests.

Wages Down Below

At the same time, it was believed by a whole generation of historians that the real wage of the working class was actually falling from about 1900 onwards, as the cost of living outpaced money wages. Those price and wage statistics which were available to Dangerfield confirmed this view. The statisticians A. L. Bowley and G. H. Wood produced a series of figures, used subsequently by Layton and Crowther in a study published in 1938.[25] No regular official indices for our period were produced. Bowley's and Wood's work shows that average retail prices rose by some 10 per cent between 1900 and 1910, falling only once in that time, by a single point in 1905–6. During the same period, average money wages fell by 3.3 per cent from 1900 to 1904, recovering only to their 1900 level by 1910. Thus, a fall in real wages of some 10 per cent was demonstrated. Dangerfield accepted this conclusion: 'Society in the last pre-war years grew wildly plutocratic . . . only the workers seemed to be deprived of their share in prosperity: in 1910 the English worker was a poorer man than he was in 1900'.[26]

Sydney Pollard, using more recent statistical research, however, has produced a series showing that the real wage rate rose by 6 per cent between 1900 and 1910.[27] Whilst this may appear to undermine the 'Dangerfield interpretation' of the causation of the great unrest, Pollard has also shown that *wages as a share of national income*, which had held up during the depression, began a decline which took them from 41 per cent in 1896 to 36.6 per cent in 1913 (see fig. 8.1).

E. H. Phelps-Brown, in his examination of industrial relations between 1906 and 1914, relies on Bowley's and Wood's series, but asserts only that 'in several countries, economic forces were *checking the rise* in real wages'.[28] In speculating on why the industrial protest against this trend was so long delayed and confined, when it came, to the 'unskilled', the railways and mining, he reflects: 'One reason may be sheer unawareness of the change. By present standards it was an age of statistical darkness: increasing attention was being given to the cost of living, but if the change in the course of real wages was estimated by one or two specialists, that was as far as knowledge of it had gone.'[29]

Fig. 8.1   Trade Union Membership and Wages, 1870–1912

Source: Sydney Pollard, 'Trade Unions and the Labour Market, 1870–1914', *Yorkshire Bulletin of Economic and Social Research*, vol. 17, no. 1 (May 1965), pp. 101–2. (Reprinted by permission of the Trustees of the *Yorkshire Bulletin of Economic and Social Research*.)

A more recent historian is aware that the statistics involved here were all people, some of whom knew from their own experience what scholars have since had to learn from afar: 'The likelihood is that even had the cost of living remained stable the lower paid would have gradually realised that they were not getting enough. The primary poverty that went with regular wage-earning could hardly be explained away in terms of the 1s. or 2s. in the pound rise in the cost of living'.[30]

The Board of Trade, in response to public concern, reported belatedly on the cost of living for the first time only in 1913, suggesting that it had risen by 14 per cent since 1906. This information clearly came too late to influence pre-war trade-union responses.

But important pioneering work on the distribution of income, and on the statistical evidence of inequality, was emerging in the publications of the Fabians, and in the work of L. G. Chiozza Money, whose *Riches and Poverty* was first published in 1905; it subsequently ran through many editions. He showed that at the income-tax exemption limit of just £160 a year, the national income divided into two equal parts. One-half was shared by 38 million people below the limit, and one-half by just 5 million above it.

Whatever the precise nature of the relative movements of wages and prices, which may remain uncertain, the average movements would, as they always do, conceal from view what was happening to particular groups. Given the expansive growth of their numbers, the frail condition into which their unions had fallen and the absence of negotiating machinery to compel their employers to make standard increases in wages, the general labourers and the transport workers may safely be assumed to have suffered disproportionately from the rise in prices. This combined with the decadent displays of the wealthy, many of whom were directly profiting from the misery of the poor, was the source of the slow build-up to the revolt of the labourers. Alongside it went a degree of disillusionment with the performance of official Labour in Parliament. This was very strong on the political left, and can also be found in more moderate quarters. The Webbs commented in 1912: 'The manual working wage-earner has lost faith in the necessity, let alone the righteousness, of the social arrangements to which he finds himself subjected.'[31]

How general were these sentiments? It is not easy to determine. What is plain is that, whatever people expected from the Labour Party in Parliament, they did not defer to its judgements and would not be restrained by its opinions. The sense of relative deprivation was undoubtedly more consciously experienced at this time, and it combined with the vivid presence of absolute poverty to provide a spur to action.

But first the transport and general unions had to work through a decade of less spectacular recovery and transition, in an economic and social climate which was engendering profound discontent among the mass of the workers. At the same time, trade-union leaders such as Tillett showed evidence in their public utterances and Reports of a mounting apprehension at the growth of trusts, cartels and monopolies: the sheer scale of early twentieth-century capitalism seemed positively to menace labour organization.

II

A Disastrous Strike

In London, the new century opened with further disaster for the Dockers' Union. In a short phase of brisk trade, the dockers at the Royal Docks struck for the stevedores' rate of 8d., with 1s. overtime, at the same time demanding that taking-on be transferred outside the dock gates where they could enforce union control. The union supported the strike, but sought backing from Stevedores' and Lightermen's Unions in vain. The Shipping Federation deployed its tried and trusted method, importing strike-breaking labour. The union was once again humiliated, and lost all influence in the Royal Docks. At the same time, the shift of trade downstream to Tilbury, where the union's presence was marginal, accelerated. The Dockers' Union in London was reduced to minuscule proportions. In 1901, the union's total income from its London districts was £344 11s. 11d., out of a total income for the whole union of £8,033 13s. 9d.[32] Tilbury's two branches returned just £17 10s. 3d.! Little evidence of recovery was forthcoming throughout the decade. In 1910 the Loondon district's income was £551 2s. 1d., out of the national total of £11,391 11s. 0d., with Tilbury hanging on with £25 0s. 11d. In 1891 there were sixty-five branches of the Dockers' Union in London. In 1901 there were only fifteen. At the end of 1910 there were twelve.[33]

Stevedores and Lightermen

The Stevedores' union presided over a shrinking enclave of recognition and security. The cement combine and the large shipping companies were joined by Scruttons', a larger than average stevedoring company, in breaking the union's controls downstream. Yet the union clung to its isolation, refusing participation in the federations initiated by Tillett and Mann in the 1890s. It began to repair links with the wider movement by joining the General Federation of Trade Unions in 1899, it affiliated to the Labour Party and participated in local government. It also held discussions with James Sexton on safety regulations for the industry.[34] But it was belligerently antipathetic to industrial alliances. An undated pamphlet of the Amalgamated Stevedores' Labour Protection League, in which a reformed rule book is proposed, advanced the following Rule 1: 'That there shall be no person enrolled as a member of this Society until occasion demands. That the Transport Workers' Federation be totally ignored'.[35] This attitude, we shall see (chapter 9), was overcome; in the event, the stevedores' joined the National Transport Workers' Federation (NTWF).

Through the decade 1900-10 the isolationists held sway, however, strongly motivated by the memory of their losses in the 1891 conflict with the Shipping Federation. In particular they were estranged from Tillett's union, which had not only encroached on their territories, but had also accused them of blacklegging in the 1900 strike in the Royal Docks.[36] Yet the stevedores' leadership, especially that of James Anderson, its outward-looking secretary, understood that the mere defence of a shrinking specialism could no longer serve as an adequate strategy. Demarcation boundaries had been breached by the major employers, and the union itself had begun to enrol shipboard dockers engaged in discharging, thus abandoning its exclusive concern with loading. The steamship required less finesse in the loading operation, anyway, than had the sailing ship. Since the Dockers' Union was moribund, it could have fallen to the Stevedores' union to initiate any general move to re-create general organization in the port in these new circumstances, which included the acute problem of Tilbury, where employers' dominance was becoming a threat to unions throughout the whole port. Thus, in 1909, Anderson proposed to his executive that 'the necessary steps should be taken to enrol as members all men engaged in the operations of loading and unloading vessels, or handling cargo on dock, wharf, or quay, in the Port of London, and strongly recommends that these steps be taken at the earliest opportunity.'[37] This proposal, had it been implemented, would have transformed the union into an all-grade dockers' body akin to Sexton's union. Powerful, conservative influences in the branches prevented any action to apply it. The logic which had produced it, however, was finally to be acknowledged when the union joined the NTWF.

Similar pressures were impelling the Lightermen's Union to reconsider its exclusivity. The trade's Conciliation Board had collapsed in the 1890s, and it had faced strikes in 1900 and 1909. It opened its membership to non-freemen in 1900, and in 1910 brought in the Medway bargemen, hitherto a grade beneath the watermen's notice. Its relations with increasingly hostile employers were deteriorating, adding further weight to Harry Gosling's long struggle to bring his traditionally aristocratic membership to an acceptance of the need for wider industrial association. In these ways the two sectional, but stable, port unions of London were prepared for the Federal initiatives which were shortly to mature.

Meanwhile, the Dockers' Union stagnated, Tillett's Annual Reports extracting what significance he could from the union's participation in the campaign for government inspection and regulation of safety conditions on the docks, a matter in which Sexton made all the running.

Port Ownership: the Port of London Authority

One structural reform in London might have given dock unionism an opportunity to restore and extend some of its influence. In 1908, the Port of London Act established the Port of London Authority (PLA), a public trust, as the sole owner and manager of all the riverside and docks, though not the wharves. This was part of a general tendency towards sole ownership and management of port installations everywhere. Indeed London had survived longer than other ports as an unplanned, multiple-owned agglomeration of docks and quays. Liverpool and Glasgow had well-established public utility trusts – the Mersey Docks and Harbour Board, and the Clyde Navigation Trust – which had taken over from the civic owners half a century earlier. In Bristol the municipality had acquired sole ownership of the port in 1848. In Southampton, the Humber ports and South Wales the railway companies had financed, and finally acquired control of, port installations over a longer period. In South Wales the Great Western Railway Company completed its regional ports monopoly in 1923, when it took over the Swansea docks from the Swansea Harbour Trust. The Manchester Ship Canal Company raised private capital, and also became a monopoly owner of its docks. The London reform was thus overdue, and followed a series of private mergers which had left all the docks on the North Bank in the hands of a single 'joint docks' committee'.

For the unions, the PLA became a hope frustrated. The idea of public ownership harmonized with their consistent campaigns of the 1890s for municipalization. A public authority such as the PLA might be expected to recognize the status of labour and the unions, and to give its attention to decasualization. But only two labour representatives were initially appointed to the Authority. They were Harry Gosling and James Anderson. (The omission of Tillett from the appointees was in itself a clear indication of his union's condition in the port.) The PLA, far from meeting the union's programmes on labour practices, took over the old Joint Dock Companies' classification system (see chapter 5) and conceded nothing to the unions.[38] Governmental attempts to use legislation to compel the port employers, through the PLA, to plan labour engagement more rationally and to institute daily notifications throughout the port to unemployed dockers, informing them where jobs might be obtained, were totally frustrated by the port's major users of labour – the shipping and merchant interests which dominated the Authority. Only one-third of the port's labour force was in the permanent employment of the PLA: the rest continued as before to fight at the call-stands for the attention of foremen representing the big shippers, stevedoring companies and merchants.[39]

Dockers and Tinplatemen

In the other ports where Tillett's union retained membership, the period was one of modest overall growth (although Bristol doubled its membership) and heavy dependence upon the South Wales (especially the tinplate) districts.

South Wales, as can be seen from table 8.4, saved the Dockers' Union from virtual extinction during the lean years. Much depended on the attitude of the employers. In Newport the dock company and other port employers, largely involved in the expanding coal export trade, recognized and bargained with the union. They established the Newport Coaltipping

Table 8.4 *DWRGWU District Income, 1901–1910*

	1901:£	%		1910:£	%
Bristol	831	(10.3)		1656	(14.5)
Gloucester	727	(9.1)		762	(6.7)
London	334	(4.2)		551	(4.9)
Hull	368	(4.6)		63	(0.6)
North-east*	339	(4.2)		543	(4.8)
Newport[†]	1336	(16.6)		847	(7.4)
Swansea[†]	3989	(49.7)	transit	1850	(16.2)
			tinplate	2198	(19.3)
Barry[†]				739	(6.5)
Cardiff[†]				311	(2.9)
Midlands[‡]				453	(4.0)
Misc.**	107	(1.3)		148	(1.3)
Total:	8033	(100.0)		11391	(100.0)

*Confined to Middlesbrough (dockers) and Teesside.
[†]Swansea was divided into separate transit and tinplate sections in 1907. The tinplate income is incorporated in the 1901 general Swansea total, by which time the tinplate branches of 1910 had already been formed. In 1901, branches in Barry and Cardiff were included in the Newport and Swansea Districts. The combined Welsh contribution to the union's income was 66.3 per cent in 1901, and 52.3 per cent in 1910. Including Bristol, the whole Bristol Channel region contributed 76.6 per cent and 66.8 per cent.
[‡]A miscellaneous group of branches administered by District offices in Stalybridge and Salford, they included the Manchester Ship Canal dockers, and branches in Walsall, Widnes, Wolverhampton, etc.
**Included branches in Arbroath, Ipswich, Bridgwater, Mold, etc., in 1901. Two Southampton branches had reappeared by 1910, one of which dated from 1905.
                                          Source: DWRGWU Annual Reports, 1901–10

and Trimming Conciliation Board, which maintained industrial peace – at least until 1908, when a brief strike was directed against the hiring of Chinese sailors to load general cargo.[40] The National Amalgamated Labourers' Union continued with its attempts to poach the Dockers' members, despite a formal agreement of 1905 between the two unions.

In Swansea, too, employers in the patent fuel and timber trades held to their recognition of the union, and in the docks conciliation was employed to preserve wage levels: a union representative, Tom Merrells, was appointed to the Swansea Harbour Trust. A major strike broke out in 1900, directed against the use of free labour. It spread to Weaver's flour mills nearby, and the Shipping Federation brought in strike-breakers from Hull. Tillett sanctioned the strike and organized a picket on every shop where Weaver's flour was sold. The strike ended with the capitulation of the employers. Elsewhere in Swansea, the union made substantial wage gains in the patent-fuel industry and in the docks between 1900 and 1910. As at Newport, the union clashed with NALU over recruitment rights, in 1908.

In Cardiff the union was faced with opposition from the Cardiff Railway Company, which owned the docks. Deal-runners were defeated in a strike, which again involved the deployment of strike-breakers from Hull. Some union enclaves were created, in iron-ore labouring (1901), pitwood yards (1904) and dry-dock workers (1907). But Cardiff's poor state in 1910 may be seen from table 8.4.

At Barry docks, the union won recognition in 1906 and established a separate district, which also recruited in the flour mills.

Only at Port Talbot did the Dockers' Union prevail against the Cardiff, Barry and Penarth Coal Trimmers, the aristocracy of the waterfront, to recruit this grade of workers.

The NALU preserved its total membership throughout the decade, which it entered with 3,505 members. By 1910 it had retained 3,549.

In the tinplate section, established in the 1890s (see chapter 5), Tillett himself took a special interest and used his influence to ensure that peace and conciliation prevailed, despite several disputes which originated in sectional claims by other unions. No wage gains were pressed, despite the spectacular growth of tinplate exports to Europe, which all but doubled in the decade. The tinplatemen's importance to the union can be seen from table 8.4: their contributions in 1910 were four times as great as the whole of the London district, amounting to almost one-fifth of the union's total income. As well as their own district secretary, the tinplatemen had three representatives on the National Executive in 1910. This representation became a traditional one, and at least one tinplateman was always elected to the General Executive Council of the TGWU until the 1970s. The union's only problem with the tinplatemen arose over politics: it became so involved in promoting Labour Party activity in Swansea and Newport that in the January 1910 General

Election Tillett was selected to fight the Swansea seat against Alfred Mond, the chemical manufacturer, who stood for the Liberals. The tinplate members of Tillett's union backed the Liberals, Mond himself and free trade: they had suffered from the effects of the Americans' McKinley tariff. And their Welsh sabbatarianism was outraged when Tillett held two election meetings on a Sunday. They threatened to leave his union, but were mollified by the result: Tillett lost by a margin of four to one.

The Newport Dispute

In Newport, at the end of the decade, a serious strike erupted, with syndicalist overtones. The shipping firm of Houlder Bros sought to substitute day-wages for the traditional piece-work, giving the men the prospect of reduced earnings and hiring for the day only, instead of for the duration of the job. When the dockers struck against the new system in May 1910, the firm used Shipping Federation strike-breakers from London. This provoked a general dock strike in the port. After fighting between blacklegs and strikers, the 'free' men returned to London. Houlders persisted: the Shipping Federation supplied replacement strike-breakers from its depot ship, the *Lady Jocelyn*, moored in the Bristol Channel. Houlders rejected arbitration and also the negotiated settlement offered by the union's district secretary: the fighting resumed. Frank Houlder demanded, in the most militant and arrogant terms, police and military protection for his labour. The Board of Trade (in the person of Sydney Buxton), the local authority, and the Home Office, turned him down. Sir Edward Troup, Permanent Under-Secretary at the Home Office, was buried in telegrams from the Shipping Federation, the Mayor and Chief Constable of Newport, demanding government reinforcements. He was also subjected to heavy pressure by Houlder himself, as he reported to his political chief, Churchill:

About 10.45 p.m. last night Mr. Houlder called at my house about the Newport disturbances. He seemed to have dined and was much excited . . . [he claimed that] 40 of his men were at that moment being murdered and he demanded that I should instantly take steps to save them. He said that he held the government responsible; that I was the government, and that I should stop it! . . . I said that we were sending 300 police by special train tomorrow. He said that was no use; they must be there tonight and stop the murder . . . He said that in the Argentine they managed things better; they would send artillery and machine guns, and give proper protection to their subjects . . . He had, about this time, been joined by his Secretary, who assumed the same offensive and bullying manner as his chief. They finally left saying that they were going to the Admiralty to demand assistance . . .

In a covering note to Churchill, accompanying this report, Sir Edward commented: 'If Mr. Houlder bullied his stevedores as he tried to bully me, it is no wonder there was a strike!' He also obtained assurances from Newport's Chief Constable that Houlder's report was grossly exaggerated, there being few police and fewer strikers on the dock at the time.

Churchill followed the dispute at some distance, whilst he was on the move: Troup's telegrams were addressed to him successively at Canford Manor, Winborne, Folkestone, Lucerne, Lugana and Venice! The Home Secretary's replies called for restraint in the use of force, condemned the provocative use of free labour by the Federation and Houlder, and urged the deployment of Board of Trade staff to effect an arbitrated settlement.[41] Houlders were forced to accept arbitration, yet promptly won the case, the arbitrator awarding that day-wages might be paid in the port. Tillett insisted on the men's accepting the decision: when they persisted in the strike, he withheld further strike pay.

At this point, the unofficial leadership of Alf Cox, a docker and 'an avid reader of Karl Marx',[42] came to the fore, supported by his brother George, and a following of other dockers and seamen. One of Houlders' ships was diverted to Bristol, despite the availability of labour from the *Lady Jocelyn*. Bristol dockers responded to Cox's personal appeal and blacked the ship, turning down an appeal to work it from the Dockers' Union Bristol district secretary, William Gorman. Eventually he regained control after a port-wide stoppage, and negotiated a return to work. But in Newport the unofficial blacking of Houlders' ships was sustained through the year, following which the dispute was subsumed into the much wider general industrial conflicts of 1911.[43]

In Bristol, the Dockers' Union had entered the new century with a small, hard core of members in the corn-portering section of the docks – only 800 strong. This it protected with an elaborate arbitration agreement, conciliation boards and union recognition. By 1910, when the Houlder dispute ruptured the long peace which had prevailed under this system, the district had doubled its 1901 income. That the dockers of Bristol had not become inured to pacifism in these years is attested by their impressive solidarity in the Houlder affair, when 3,000 dockers struck, unofficially, in a dispute centred around a single ship. The dispute spread to the Avonmouth dock, and the membership boom which accompanied it included the carters, recruited by the branch chairman Ernest Bevin.[44] The Dockers' Union took part in the general revival of membership in 1910 which presaged the unrest of 1911–14, adding 5–6,000 to its total, to end the year with 18,000 members. Tom Mann spearheaded this growth with a nationwide organizing tour.

The Fortunes of Sexton's Union

As we have seen (chapter 5), the NUDL had been reduced from a union with thirty-eight branches at its high point in 1891 to only fourteen by 1895. The principal Irish ports of Belfast and Dublin had been lost to non-unionism, and only in Cork, Drogheda and Londonderry did small struggling branches remain. In Scotland, the principal Glasgow branch was a source of constant complaint in the National Executive reports between 1900 and 1910, arising from its instability, lax administration and fractious, corrupt officials. It was suspended from the union more than once. In Dundee and Aberdeen, the inroads of the Free Labour Association also made for instability and defections. The union made two appointments, in 1904 and 1908, to the post of national organizer, designed to remedy this state of affairs and to advance organization into other major port areas. Sexton clearly aimed to challenge the DWRGWU in Hull from an outpost his union had established in Goole. In 1908 he wrote:

> I must remark that the port of Hull, with its 11,000 dockers, still remains in a complete state of disorganisation, and as such, is a menace to the best interests of us as an organised body, in many ways. If we are not in a position to organise this port, we should insist that those who are in a position to do so either ought to do it, or, if they are unable, to step out and allow someone else an opportunity.[45]

The two new appointments were of James Larkin, a Liverpool Irish dock foreman, and O'Connor Kessack, a Glasgow Scottish labourer and socialist agitator. The NUDL's history in this decade might be written around the contrasting activities of these two men. The union's contribution income was some £4,500 at the beginning of the century. By 1910 it had risen to £6,300, suggesting modest and steady progress.[46] It made the union about half the size of the DWRGWU, but by now most of Tillett's union's membership came from outside the docks. Only in Bristol and South Wales could it make any claim to representative status in the ports.

At the end of the decade, Kessack was called on to make good, as best he might, some of the ravages suffered by the union in Scotland. He struggled once more to restore the union's fortunes in Glasgow and Aberdeen, but found Glasgow 'a heart-break'. The dockers there resolved the problem by declaring their independence in 1911, establishing the Scottish Union of Dock Labourers, which returned to the fold of British docks unionism only when it amalgamated with the TGWU in 1922. Even then, its stay was to prove temporary. Kessack found Dublin equally dispiriting. In Goole and in Preston, twentieth-century branch formation was more successful. Liverpool's branches closed the decade in a weak condition. Sexton wrote in 1910:

> The real reason of the whole unrest in the trade union movement today lies deeper down than the mere bread and butter reason. There is a spirit of revolt against general conditions and against the conspiracy to drive trade unions out of the political arena . . . the sheer force of circumstances . . . are contributing to the revolution in trades unions.[47]

In an important sense, the revolution which Sexton foresaw had been set in train across the Irish Sea by his own national organizer, James Larkin, during his hectic progress between 1905 and 1909. It is to this explosive episode that we now turn.

James Larkin Arrives

In January 1907, Belfast, the most rapidly growing city in the United Kingdom, was the somewhat indifferent host of the Labour Party Conference: 'As the gangplanks went down at the cross-channel quays, just short of the Queen's Bridge . . . unusual visitors could be seen disembarking. Within a few days Keir Hardie, Ramsay MacDonald, Arthur Henderson and others . . . stepped ashore.'[48]

One of the others was James Larkin, delegated by his union to represent it at the conference, but also to seek ways to organize the dockers in the port.

Larkin, a Liverpool Irish man, had a background quite remarkably similar to that of James Sexton. In 1903 he became a foreman dock porter on Liverpool's South End Docks. A socialist since his youth in the 1890s, he was a skilled soap-box preacher. Liverpool was the home of a group of followers of the American Industrial Workers of the World, including Fred Bower, the syndicalist stonemason, a childhood companion of Larkin.[49] The young agitator stayed largely clear of trade-union activism until 1905, when the NUDL became involved in a rearguard battle to defend union recognition against T. and J. Harrison's, where Larkin worked. The firm not only withdrew recognition after an unofficial stoppage, but brought in strike-breakers to defeat the official dispute which inevitably followed. Larkin became involved and established a strong following. He was a dramatic orator and was quickly marked down for victimization. By the same token, he was offered first a temporary and then a permanent job with the union.

That November Larkin ran Sexton's campaign for election to Liverpool Corporation (in which Sexton distinguished himself by his xenophobic remarks about Jewish and Chinese immigration).[50] This was successful, so Larkin was then called upon to organize Labour's forces in

the contest for Parliament, in the West Toxteth division. It was, wrote
Fred Bower (who took on the job of assistant to Larkin), 'a bigoted
orange district', so that Catholic, socialist Sexton was 'perhaps the
worst man we could have selected'.[51] The Conservative candidate,
R. P. Houston, was a millionaire shipowner. He had voted for the
introduction of Chinese labour into South Africa. Now the Chinese issue
had been stood on its head:

> so Chinese Slavery was the battle-cry against him. Larkin had got a glass-
> sided hearse and several cabs. The Labour women had worked all the
> hours they could spare from home ties, in making loose-fitting, over-all
> pants and coats, out of a cheap yellow cloth material. I had cadged a dozen
> picks and a dozen shovels from a friendly contractor in the neighbourhood.
> Some fifty members of the Dockers' Union, who were unemployed, were
> garbed *à la* Chinese. Heralded by a brass band, playing the Dead March in
> Saul, the pseudo Chinamen trailed with their shouldered implements,
> behind the hearse, in which a coffin-shaped box, draped with the Union
> Jack, reposed. And so, on the election eve, the cortege wended its way
> through the main streets of the constituency. It was supposed to represent
> the burial of Freedom. To make it more realistic, Larkin had got hold of
> some decoction which he got the men to put on their faces and hands,
> which gave them a yellow countenance, and he himself had made them
> pigtails, out of oakum, the which they had pinned to their caps.
>   At last they returned from the tour, and were paid off for their three
> hours' work, at trade union pay. But when they came to be paid, the fifty
> had grown to a hundred. Some had only the pigtail to show, some a pick or
> shovel, some a coat or a pair of pants. They had shared the gear with their
> mates, and as no names had been taken, Jim couldn't tell whom he had
> engaged, and whom he hadn't. It was twelve o'clock at night when I left
> them barging, and went home to bed. And there were some two or three
> score of men who didn't dare to go to the docks and look for a job
> unloading Houston's boats, for a week after, when the yellow dye had
> worn off their faces.[52]

Soon Larkin carried the union to Preston, Ardrossan and Aberdeen.[53]
It was perfectly natural to seek to take it to Belfast.

The Belfast Strike

Boom notwithstanding, the condition of the Belfast labourers was dire –
'bordering on starvation', in the words of Thomas Carnduff, a young
Protestant worker from Sandy Row, and at the time an active sectarian
zealot in the Pass Gang, a Belfast Protestant group noted for its
stridency.[54] Respectable official reports were saying much the same
thing, and the historian of the Belfast strike, John Gray, cites damning
evidence to that effect.

There were 3,100 dockers in the city. Larkin started work on his soap-box. By mid-February 1907, he had won 400 to the NUDL. In March he put on a conference about dockers' problems; next month he had 2,000 members and two offices. Police reporters, who had dogged Larkin carefully from the first moment of his arrival, put his score at 2,978 dockers by the end of April, with the 'infection . . . spreading to the 1,500 carters'.[55] Orangemen among the workers welcomed Larkin's departure, in June, to support Pete Curran's by-election campaign in Jarrow, in which he opposed an Irish Nationalist. But Catholics were equally happy about Michael McKeown's appointment as branch secretary for the dockers, since he was a councillor for the United Ireland League.

The first skirmish on the docks followed a (non-union) engineering strike. Kelly's coal quay tried to sack union members, and faced a virtually complete stoppage. This alerted the Shipping Federation, which sent a representative to investigate on 6 May; he was prepared 'to act immediately should the necessity arise'.[56] It would. Meantime, as the warning bells sounded in Northern Ireland, 'thousands of Shipping Federation blacklegs were finishing off a mass strike in Hamburg. Later in the year, the same organisation was to be bloodily engaged on the streets on Antwerp'.[57]

Larkin tried to avoid the next strike, which erupted spontaneously against the Belfast Steamship Company. But the chairman of the company, Gallaher, the 'Tobacco King', was spoiling for a fight, and even after the union had called upon the men to return to work he flatly denied it recognition. Larkin turned the other cheek yet again, and sent the men back regardless. They returned to find themselves locked out, and to discover fifty-three strike-breakers deployed from SS *Caloric*, courtesy of the Shipping Federation. From that point on, things escalated. Altogether 140 Steamship Company dockers joined those locked out. More strike-breakers were imported, and some were set to work at Kelly's coal quay. A pitched battle drove them off, overwhelming the Harbour Police along the way. Talks followed between the union and the blacklegs, some of whom reformed and spoke at dockers' mass meetings. They came from Liverpool, where they had been offered £1 10s. a week, plus 1s. an hour overtime, to cross the Irish Sea and break the strike. Shortly afterwards, all the interlopers agreed to go home, and were seen off by enthusiastic strikers and a flute-and-drum band.

Kelly gave in. A victory parade, led by the Union Jack, sang 'Rule Britannia'. The Orange establishment took fright and offered mayoral arbitration in the remaining dispute, which Larkin accepted. Gallaher refused, and demanded police protection.

At this point, Larkin raised the temperature. Gallaher, he said, was an obscene scoundrel, and if St Patrick had banished the snakes from Ireland, 'there was one he forgot and that was Gallaher – a man who valued neither country, God nor creed'.[58] Later, Larkin returned to this theme with the thought that Gallaher could not be hung 'for no honest rope would do it'. The dockers did not seem to be distressed by this hyperbole.

By now there were 250 strike-breakers on SS *Caloric*, which had to be moored out in Belfast Lough to prevent union approaches to them. A force of up to 300 constables was required to march the blacklegs into work at Donegall Quay. Larkin now sought to recruit Gallaher's tobacco workers to a union, and the employer promptly dismissed seven of them simply for attending the meeting. One thousand women walked out to a mass strike meeting of dockers. The crowds refused to disperse and some windows were broken. The Lord Mayor called in the troops. Two hundred men of the Royal Sussex Regiment now confronted 200 dockers.

Belfast Steamship Company ships were blacked on other docks, and because the police were stretched in defending the Donegall Quay they were unable to prevent the *Caloric*'s being stoned when it tried to disembark strike-breakers elsewhere. In June the coal-heavers on quays other than Kelly's demanded a weekly rise of 2s. and won it. The Dublin Steamship Company also capitulated. More disputes mushroomed all around. To co-ordinate them, on 20 June the NUDL put a claim for £1 7s. 6d. minimum to all the cross-channel shipping companies. Larkin endorsed a claim by the seamen, which won 5s. a month for them. By 26 June 'all the dockers at Heysham, Barrow and Fleetwood berths came out'. The Royal Sussex now sent 500 more soldiers to defend the quays. Fires had already broken out.

Next day the carters began to strike. Blackleg carters were imported from Glasgow; the first cart to venture out under such a driver was followed by 2–3,000 jeering people. That afternoon the Glasgow men asked to go home. On the following day the carters filed a claim for a minimum of £1 6s. a week, with a maximum sixty-hour week. On 4 July the remaining carters joined the strike: 1,000 men employed by sixty companies.

Food began to rot. Quantities had to be destroyed. Polarization was far advanced, and the coal companies now locked out the very workers with whom they had so recently settled. With some apprehension, the strike leaders faced the fact that 12 July was bearing down upon them, with all its potential for sectarian division. A Protestant NUDL delegate to the Trades Council, Walter Savage, wrote an appeal to counter this threat: 'Our fervent prayer is that James Larkin may long be spared, by the help of God, to work for the emancipation of the unskilled workers in his native land.' He claimed that he could 'get 1000 Old Orange Order [union men] to sign this letter'. In the event, both Orange Order processions bristled with pro-strike insignia.

Violent action against strike-breakers was now widespread. The police were impotent. Their commissioners tried to offload the problem on to Dublin Castle, since 'only cavalry' would serve to protect the motor lorries the employers wished to bring in. Traction engines were used, heavily guarded by police, but they were ambushed. One had its cargo discharged into the Connswater river. Another was destroyed by a crowd of 200 in the very centre of Orange loyalism in East Belfast. Sometimes cargoes were destroyed, but sometimes they simply disappeared into people's houses. The strikers were, to say the least of it, undaunted by the prodigious force ranged against them.

It was money, or the want of it, that broke this upsurge. By mid-July 1,000 men needed £400 a week. By the 24th of the month there were 3,500 to be maintained. On the 19th, James Sexton arrived from head office full of good news. 'Every penny' of the NUDL's reserve of £20,000 'should be spent for the benefit of the locked out men', he told them.[59] Other unions would help, too. There was word of '£48,000 by noon on Tuesday next'. In fact, Sexton had brought £200 with him. Worse, he was evidently concerned that Belfast might prove a bottomless pit in which to lose all his union's reserves. He had no wish to explore the possibility. Altogether, John Gray estimates, he spent less than £5,000 on the strike from first to last. Sexton himself claimed it had cost £7,000.[60] The General Federation of Trade Unions, upon whom heavy calls were entirely in order, was even more parsimonious. In all, it spent £1,692 in Belfast. Alarmed at what they saw as a financial burden of unlimited scope, they pressed their Northern Irish affiliates to settle.

Settling was precisely what Sexton had in mind. On 20 July he met the Lord Mayor to seek a 'friendly conference'. With him went Gee and Mitchell of the GFTU. Mitchell then went forward on 25 July to negotiate a 'settlement' of the coal dispute. This proved to be a total disaster: nothing was agreed in writing, and although extravagant and windy promises were made, the coalmen went back to work on a false prospectus. Gee and Mitchell remained in Belfast to 'interpret' their settlement, and consistently ruled in favour of the masters. Although initially Larkin accepted the judgement of his general secretary and the two GFTU spokesmen, within a fortnight he was complaining that the dispute 'had been settled by three Englishmen in his absence, who knew nothing about the situation.'[61]

While the English labour leaders were bending their best efforts to get Belfast's coalmen back to work, the constabulary in that city was bearing the full brunt of the disorders and recalling its own ample grievances. From 10 July to 16 July, and again on the 22nd, an anonymous correspondent, signing himself 'Willing to Strike', began to air police complaints in the *Irish News*. It seemed clear that this correspondent had inside information. Soon others joined in. A delegate conference of policemen was announced for 24 July. This was duly banned by Acting Commissioner Morrell; however, it took place. Two or three hundred men turned up, defying a verbal ban delivered, as it opened, by a head constable. The Acting Commissioner then entered and sought to bully some of the men individually. Fisticuffs ensued. As the meeting was about to form up to march to a protest meeting, Morrell promised to meet a deputation, provided the demonstration did not take place. His offer was accepted, but before the meeting happened the whole story broke in the *Irish News*, and thereafter became sensational copy throughout the province.

Morrell went public, with an 'official' version of events. Constable Barrett, a spokesman for the men, then wrote to the *Irish News* contradicting his chief and confirming every detail in that newspaper's original report. Barrett was promptly suspended. Between 500 and 800 Belfast policemen, out of a total strength of 1,000, then attended an 'illegal meeting' at the Musgrave Street Barracks. Morrell appeared and tried to persuade the men that he would seek permission for a 'legal' gathering if only they would disperse this one. The men shouted him down and called for Barrett. He proposed that written demands be agreed, and that the chiefs be given eight days to respond, during which time police duties would be carried out normally. The loud cheers which greeted agreement on these proposals provoked a press on the gates giving access to the barracks, as hundreds of waiting trade unionists outside pushed forward to hear what was going on. Police and strikers were now intermingled in a stormy enthusiasm, and Barrett was carried in triumph to a mass meeting at Euston House steps, then back to a confrontation at the office of the Commissioner. By now the only 'police' in sight were arm-banded union pickets, who marshalled the crowds impartially, whether they were constables or civilians. Indeed, it was the union officials who finally persuaded the crowds to disperse, as Morrell stalled for time while the Assistant Inspector General voyaged up from Dublin. Even so, many waited. James Sexton spoke to the mixed crowd, urging the formation of a policemen's union. 'You will have fifty Labour men behind you', he told them.

Now the authorities had on their hands a strike and a mutiny. Accordingly, 2,500 soldiers were sent for and emplaced. They were joined by others. By 5 August *The Times* announced that 7,000 troops 'and maxim guns' were deployed in the city.[62] Once they were on the spot, Constable Barrett was summarily dismissed and those other colleagues who had endorsed the men's negotiating agenda were all suspended. 'Almost the entire force' in Belfast was dispersed to country beats in the hinterland.[63] Spectacular meetings and processions of trade unionists followed, and Barrett toured the city to a vast demonstration of solidarity.

But with this firm crackdown, the mutiny was ended. The arrival of so many troops now re-opened the question of national loyalties and the ever-present sectarian schisms which lay not far beneath them. As things were, the pressures of the strike-breakers, the increasing privation and the frustration of all these events combined to trigger an epidemic of riot throughout the Catholic areas. Bayonets were fixed, and deployed. On 11 August troops opened fire in the Falls Road. Two people were killed and many wounded.

In mid-August George Askwith was sent from London by the Board of Trade to mediate, and he has left a controversial account of what happened.[64] After shuttling between Larkin and the men, and the employers, the carters were offered a pay increase, though not the closed shop they demanded, while the dockers were told that settlement might follow a return to work. A meeting was summoned, with the carters in the body of the hall and the dockers in the balcony, to hear this message. Sexton arrived nervously, with not one but two revolvers in his breast pocket. Perhaps they were a testimony to a kind of uneasy conscience.[65] It might be that Sexton feared that his intervention might not be appreciated by his new members. Needless to say, the guns were never used, because Larkin soon had 'the men throwing up their caps and roaring applause.'

Because of their faith in Larkin, the dockers survived the humiliations of what, on most quays, was capitulation. In November 500 coalmen stopped work again, followed by thirty carters and fifty crane-men. Newry coalmen joined in sympathy action. Sexton hurried over and took the dispute out of Larkin's hands. Larkin would have permitted a re-opening of the general, port-wide stoppage, but Sexton foreclosed and ordered everyone back to work.

The predictable result was not long in following. The sense of betrayal which festered was soon to corrode the solidarity which had marked the union's confident beginning. For a brief while, people were willing to be union members first, and Green or Orange afterwards. When James Sexton went home to Liverpool, those days were but a memory of what might have been.

If Sexton was now in a cold fury with Larkin, another political leader – less conspicuous, to be sure – was deeply impressed by the Belfast events. John MacLean, the Scottish socialist, visited Belfast at the beginning of August during a speaking tour. He 'found the situation electrifying', wrote his biographers.[66] Moreover, it upended his previous view of the processes of social change, which had been set in a conventional mould, much influenced by the thinking of Hyndman. Now he addressed audiences of thousands. The labourers were 'mad to join trade unions'. Hitherto, MacLean's perception of trade unionism had been coloured by his experience of the Labour aristocrats of the Clyde: highly skilled, exclusive, cautious. Now he became a partisan of organization among unskilled workers, even while he upheld the primacy of political process.

This distinctive view began to separate MacLean from political orthodoxy, and represents the thin end of an important wedge of Irish influence, or rather of the influence of Irish experience, over in Britain. Particularly in Scotland, this was to carry a long way. The later mixture of the revolt of the labourers with the cause of Irish Nationalism was, perhaps, not inevitable, and it was certainly to inhibit the Belfast workers in later years. But among Irish migrant labourers in Scotland and the British ports, it was undoubtedly an explosive combination. (The first communist MP, Walton Newbold, was later unhesitatingly to attribute his 1922 election victory in Motherwell to this constituency: by then, John MacLean was already dead, after suffering prolonged and brutal imprisonment during the war.) Be that as it may, MacLean's 'conversion' was no small matter, and represents an important achievement by Larkin.

At the time, however, the weight of James Sexton would have seemed heavier than that of an obscure Scottish agitator. This weight was abruptly used.

The Genesis of the Irish Transport and General Workers' Union

Larkin was relegated – sent to spread the NUDL's influence first in Dublin, then in Cork. Whilst happy to bank the new members' subscriptions, the NUDL leader was mainly concerned to box in and limit Larkin's influence. When the Dublin dockers were on the brink of a modest victory in July 1908, Sexton intervened to negotiate a defeat for them. Locked out, they won, with Larkin, arbitration and an agreed return to work. It was Sexton who quite gratuitously conceded that the men would not wear union badges at work. All future disputes were, it was agreed, to be arbitrated nationally, between the employers and Sexton personally.

Clearly, Larkin was on the way out. In short order he was sent on from Cork to Aberdeen. Before he could get to Scotland the Dublin carters struck and Larkin went to them instead. This was seen, in Liverpool, as insubordination.

By 7 December 1908 Sexton had informed his too-able adjutant that he was suspended from office. But Larkin was not disposed to go quietly. He took this disciplinary action to mean that British unions would never represent the true interests of Irish workers, and drew some logical conclusions. Three days after Christmas the Irish Transport and General Workers' banner was raised, and the NUDL had ceded its most exciting prospects over the Irish Sea. The adventures of this new organization are part of another story, of which the great Belfast strike was only a precursor.

A Learning Phase

The first decade of the twentieth century marked a learning phase for dockers' unions of all three types. Tillett's union's harsh experiences demonstrated that dockers needed their own, 'industrial' unity, even though they may be part of a general union. (The tinplatemen might give the union financial security, but had no obvious role in any industrial revival in the ports.) Without the adherence of the specialists – stevedores and lightermen in London, coal-trimmers in Wales, and other specific groups amongst corn-porters and timbermen – their organization would remain partial and vulnerable. The dockers who were enrolled in other general unions were also reaching out for an inclusive dockers' alliance. Such were the gasworkers' docks branches in the North-east and on the Humber, in the National Amalgamated Union of Labour on Tyneside, and in the National Amalgamated Labourers' Union in South Wales. Wherever they were to be found, the dockers, fragmented into a dozen or more unions, were vulnerable to free labour, the infiltration of non-members and inter-union rivalries.

The 'all-grade' dockers' union, exemplified by the NUDL, was faced with the same obstacles to effective progress: but in that case there arose an additional challenge from James Larkin and the special needs of Ireland. Neither type of union was allowed respite from the remorseless and often brutal deployment of strike-breakers from the Shipping Federation and from Collison's free labourers. From Hull, a union 'no-go' area, and to a lesser extent from London, came an endless flow of recruits to break strikes. Evidently nationwide unionism was the only available means to counter this weapon. After all, had not this been the drive behind all previous attempts at federation in the 'carrying trades' in the 1890s?

The specialist unions were also discovering the disadvantages of separatist traditions. The dilution of the special skills of stevedoring and lighterage threatened their established roles in the labour process, and therefore the trade-union method which they had adopted. We have seen that in London adaptation had begun in both these cases. In Cardiff, the Coal-trimmers' Union reached the point at least of affiliating to the new Labour Party, as did the London Cranedrivers. In the North-east, a Trimmers' and Teemers' Association joined a regional federation of shipping and general labour unions, and in Liverpool the North End Coalheavers merged with the NUDL in 1911.[67] These moves are seen by Gordon Phillips, the historian of the National Transport Workers' Federation (NTWF), as the preliminary steps towards a wider association. All were occurring during these formative years.

III

The Seamen

The Seamen's Union, at the receiving end of the Shipping Federation's nationwide free-labour strategy, which had, as we have seen, an international dimension, were natural advocates of waterfront federation. The union recorded growth of membership from 7,000 in 1906 to 12,000 in 1910. It had pioneered the all-grade, national model of port-based unionism, with one exception: it had neglected to organize the growing catering section of the merchant navy. In May 1909 the National Union of Ships' Stewards, Cooks, Butchers and Bakers was formed in Liverpool, where the growth of the passenger-liner business quite obviously underlined the failure of Havelock Wilson's union to meet the needs of people in these occupations. It was led by Joseph Cotter, a ship's cook from Liverpool, a socialist agitator who was an early convert to syndicalism. He was known as 'Explosive Joe'. Four thousand members were enrolled in the new organization.

This nascent division in the ranks of the seamen was to have far-reaching consequences for the future prospects of an inclusive transport unionism. From its foundation in 1887, Wilson had foreseen that the future of his union lay in co-operation with the shipowners. Denied this relationship by the big, anti-union shipping firms, he pursued a policy of national-level militancy, directed to obtaining standard national rates at all ports and the exclusion of non-unionists. 'An alliance with the shipowners remained his ideal, if not his practical policy, for most of the next thirty years.'[68]

Carters

Horse-drawn road-haulage workers, the carters, wherever they had established any organization, were fragmented into local associations, or membership in one of the general unions. The Dockers' Union enrolled them in Bristol and South Wales, the NAUL on the Tyne, and the Gasworkers' Union on the Tyne and the Wear. All these were tiny and scattered minorities. The ports were their main bases of both work and unionism: cartage was a universal requirement between the dockside and the rail terminals. Toiling alongside the dockers meant that some learned the virtues of wider alliance, at least in London, where the Carmen's Union had a tradition of collaboration in union matters.

In Scotland, a future stronghold of 'industrial unionism' in road haulage, the Scottish Carters' Association, formed in 1898, had a former railwayman, John Sampson, as its first general secretary. He had been associated with new unionism in the 1880s and saw the need to organize carters on a national (Scottish) basis, at a time when the English carters' unions were confined to single towns or regions. In 1902 the union sacked Sampson and appointed a Falkirk iron-moulder, Hugh Lyon, to replace him.

> The next ten years are a story of slow recruitment on a narrower basis and the patient organisation of the carters to fight for . . . a standard working day and the limitation of the shocking hours, for trade union recognition, for the right to payment for overtime, for the abolition of unpaid Sunday stable duties, and for improvement of wages, which had shrunk below the levels of 1889.[69]

That programme was common to carters' needs throughout Britain: their organizations would eventually utilize the NTWF to pursue it jointly. At this stage, the appeal to them of federal bodies was limited, and they were in no position to influence the pace or form of federalism.

Road-transport Mergers

Only in the North of England were there signs that the carters were moving out of their localism: the Manchester, Salford and District Lurrymen and Carters' Union, the Huddersfield Carters' Union, and the Edinburgh and District Tramway and Carmen's Union had already, in the 1890s, merged with the Tramway, Hackney Carriage Employees and Horsemen's Association. This was the former Northern Counties Amalgamated Association of Tramway and Hackney Carriage Employees and Horsemen in General, which adopted its new title in 1892. (See p. 178.)

These pioneering mergers prepared the way in the North for the creation in 1901 of the Amalgamated Association of Tramway and Vehicle Workers, which, in a development of great potential, overrode the division between freight and passenger unionism in road transport. In the post-war period this union became known as the 'Blue Button Union', in contrast to its rival, the London and Provincial Union of Licensed Vehicle Workers, the 'Red Button' or militant union, which had pursued a parallel but separate series of mergers to arrive at its form and title in 1913. It had originated as the shortlived Metropolitan Cab Drivers' Trade Union in 1890, reformed in 1894 as the London Cab Drivers' Trade Union, with 3,000 members. In 1911 it merged with the Motor Cab Drivers' Protection Association, which had been formed in 1907. In 1910 the National Union of Carriers was formed to cater for the employees of the removal firm of Carter Paterson.

This whole evolution pointed away from local, sectional road-transport unions, through complex mergers which gradually overcame both their geographical and trade separatism. From the North came the streams which merged into the Amalgamated Association of Tramway and Vehicle Workers in 1901. It could claim a genuinely national status in its tramway section. It had no competitors in that field, and there was no national employers' association to offer resistance. However, that absence also signified that the union was unable to concert wage movements at a national level. In 1910 it was still dominated by its northern membership: six of its executive places were occupied by the northern branches, against only two for the South and Midlands. Its policies were cautious: hence its nickname, 'the Blue'. Inspired by the traditional militancy of the London cabmen, the London and Provincial Union of Licensed Vehicle Workers, like its provincial counterpart, had begun the process of organizing the neglected and newly emergent section of road-passenger transport, the buses, in about 1910.

A further pointer to future trends in this section came in 1908, when the AATVW became a founder affiliate of the General Labourers' National Council.[70]

New Troubles for the Quarrymen

Another, very different, sector entered the century in an embattled state. In mid-October 1900 the Penrhyn quarries entered a new phase of troubles. Fourteen men at Ponc Ffridd were victimized for refusing work in defence of two colleagues. After being suspended, they were told that they would be split up and that their own previous work would be contracted out. Upon his arrival on the site, the contractor was beaten up and thrown out. Another similar incident followed within a few days. Three hundred dragoons were called in, and twenty-six quarrymen were prosecuted.

On Guy Fawkes' Day the case came up at Bangor. All the workmates of those charged struck and marched to court to protest their colleagues' innocence. Twenty of those tried were found not guilty of the affrays, but the entire workforce was suspended for a fortnight. On 19 November the resumption of work was made a pretext for an all-round reassignment of tasks, in which 800 people were not given their places. On 27 November the majority insisted upon the reinstatement of these workers and were told to leave if they were dissatisfied: 2,800 men took up their tools and went. Of these, 1,000 never returned and a further 1,000 were kept out of work until after November 1903.

At Easter 1901 Ben Tillett voyaged up to Bethesda and spoke to a mass meeting on Easter Monday. He pitched into Lord Penrhyn: 'a cross between Pharaoh and Nero', a brute who had ignored people's basic rights; he likened the quarry-owner to Kruger, and his victimized workpeople to 'economic Outlanders'. He told them not to blame the manager of the quarry, who was 'only Lord Penrhyn's jackal'. 'Although he spoke in English, a language "strange" to most of his hearers, his comments were greeted with laughter and applause.'[71] After Tillett had returned to England, those who had condoned his verbal assaults on Lord Penrhyn were subject to continued reprisals. At least one of his Lordship's tenants found himself in trouble for sponsoring the Easter gathering.

As the months wore on, many drifted south in search of jobs in the pits. Some few found work in a co-op quarry which was re-opened by W. J. Parry; but meanwhile Lord Penrhyn's factors made sporadic efforts to inveigle groups of men to return to his own quarry on his own strict terms. In June 1901, 242 succumbed, alongside roughly similar numbers of outside strike-breakers. Violence stewed and brooded beneath the surface, occasionally erupting into open public riot. By July, 200 footsoldiers and 60 cavalrymen were billeted to keep order; 100 more infantrymen and 30 dragoons quickly followed them into place in Bethesda. By September there were more union men up before the courts in Bangor, and by New Year's Eve there were several more affrays and many more soldiers in place.

Peace moves by the County Council failed to take effect, and in 1902 efforts to arbitrate were coolly turned down by both Lord Penrhyn and his manager, the stolid E. A. Young. Hardship clamped down upon the townships. A few more miserable people were tempted back to work. More than 2,000 still stood firm, however, and the lock-out entered its third year. That March, there were impassioned voices raised in Parliament, including that of Lloyd George. The Conservative government was widely criticized for laxity and failure to invoke the 1896 Conciliation Act. But in reality that Act could bring no relief, since its powers of arbitration were restricted to purely voluntary invitations, and Lord Penrhyn was quite determined never, but never, to volunteer. Pleas were made to the Prime Minister, to the new Prince of Wales, to anyone people could think of. Nothing moved. Quarrymen began to emigrate to the United States, and the General Federation of Trade Unions cut off its funding.[72]

'By December the situation in Bethesda was "no work, no union, no fund . . . every fountain has dried up". The traditional Saturday Market closed down; and as the year drew to a close, poverty intensified and fever shut the schools.'[73] The 2,000 were sustained, with their families, by contributions from all over Britain. Their choirs toured the island, raising support wherever they could. At home, comfort came from the chapel. Each mass meeting ended with the hymn 'Rwy'n gweld o bell y dydd yn dod' – 'I see from afar the day that is coming':

> The beautiful light of the dawn,
> From land to land now proclaims,
> That daybreak is at hand;

The tops of the hills rejoice,
As they see the sun draw nearer,
And the night retreat away.[74]

Lord Penrhyn's victory was the result of his power to inflict continuous deprivation upon his workpeople, culminating in their actual starvation. But the North Wales quarrymen had become the living symbol of sheer courage, tenacity and good faith. Their struggle to maintain trade unionism was to continue and, uncannily, even to prosper. As Lord Penrhyn's business declined, the union grew.

The Workers' Union Endures

The historian of the Workers' Union, Richard Hyman, entitles his chapter on these years 'Endurance, 1898–1910'. Founded with ecumenical aims, as we have seen (chapter 6), in this first decade it failed entirely in their realization. Tom Mann had hoped to create for it a leading *political* role, but the formation of the Labour Party in 1900 displaced this possibility completely, and the union, which participated in the foundation of the then Labour Representation Committee, fell into line with its leadership. Industrially, it ebbed and flowed in numbers with the short-term trade cycle, reaching a first peak of 4,172 members in 1899. Thereafter it collapsed in the short recession of 1903–4 to just over 1,000 members. The resumption of the trade revival brought renewed growth by the end of the decade. Later this was to be followed by spectacular expansion.

Tom Mann having departed in 1901 for Australia, and Chambers, the first secretary, leaving to work full time for the Dockers' International, Robert Morley, a skilled iron-moulder from Halifax became president and Charles Duncan, a skilled engineer from Middlesbrough, became secretary. Both were active socialists, Morley for the ILP. These two men dominated the union's policies for the next twelve years. Power gravitated towards them, and to the district full-time officers, as the membership was in the highest degree unstable. In the first eighteen months 3,000 members lapsed and nearly forty branches closed.

The union's recruitment pattern in these years was haphazard. In London, its first base, the 'unattached labourer' proved hard to identify and organize. Membership was established at the Army and Navy Stores, where Duncan's union competed with the Shop Assistants' Union. After an unsuccessful struggle against the employer's opposition, this branch had to close in 1899. The union next formed a branch at Lipton's tea warehouses, where genuine sweated conditions prevailed. These efforts also met with defeat, in 1900, and thereafter the union's membership was predominantly provincial.

A Middlesbrough branch was now its largest outpost, members being drawn from amongst the corporation's workers, but the sacking of unofficial strikers and internal problems led to the branch's closing in 1902. Corporation workers were also recruited in Coventry, with the active assistance of the Trades Council secretary. Again, the branch closed after only a year's existence.

More stability attended the union in West Yorkshire, where there was a mass of unorganized general labour. The union registered its first success when it obtained a wage rise for the workers at the Halifax municipal gasworks. Morley made a personal organizing drive in Manchester, where a branch of 300 existed by 1907. Further successes included the formation of branches in Preston and Halifax, which became the base for the wider organization of welders in the boiler industry, including branches in Derby, Rotherham and Glasgow. In the South Wales iron and steel industry, the union put down early roots and experienced the same swings of fortune as elsewhere. By 1909 it had become one of the union's major centres.

In these early years, the union was active in rural Shropshire: again, initial agitation and organization amongst farm workers were followed by employers' resistance and the closure of branches, all of which had ceased to operate by 1901.

In Birmingham the union found its eventual *métier*, enrolling the machinists in the BSA arms factory, a pioneer site of mass-production techniques. From its base of 600 members here, the union moved on to enrol in the same city's Cadbury's Bourneville factory, amongst the maintenance men. Having attained an engineering membership of 1,000 by 1907, the union was admitted into the local Engineering Workers' Federation, which adopted an official wage-scale for semi-skilled workers. The union had by that time amended its rules to exclude recruitment of workers eligible for membership in the craft unions.[75]

IV

Federation Again

In tracing the chronology of successive attempts to renew the process of federation amongst transport and general unions, we must glance first at the General Federation of Trade Unions, which was formed in 1899, although it did not arise in the transport field. It was born on the initiative of the TUC, as a generalized defensive response to the employers' offensives of the 1890s, especially that of the engineering employers' lock-out of 1897. By 1904 it had affiliated unions with membership totalling 424,000, including both Tillett's union and the NUDL. Its purpose was to provide mutual assistance to unions involved in expensive strikes, through financial supplements to the unions' own dispute benefits. Whilst this might appear to be an incentive to militancy, in practice the GFTU was an extremely cautious body, intent on preserving its funds, and a fervent advocate of conciliation and industrial peace. This is not to say that it shirked the necessity to provide support where this was judged appropriate: it contributed £9,000 to the aid of the Penrhyn strikers, and over £1,000 to the NUDL in the Liverpool strike of 1905. In commending the Federation's work in 1901, Tillett saw it as standing 'for the new development in Trades Unionism, whose evolution has been necessarily slow.' He saw symbolic importance in a body which expressed the unity of purpose of the movement, when faced with the development of capitalism of trusts and cartels.[76]

The GFTU failed to secure the affiliation of several key unions, including the miners and railwaymen. Since it would only admit organizations which were not federal, the miners could not join, and their absence hurt. The GFTU had a limited, insurance function, not adaptable to the development of organizational change and amalgamation, or to the formation of common trade policies. Its message of cautious conciliation was discarded in the turbulent years – from 1911 to 1914 – which lay immediately ahead. Its role became more and more limited as the century advanced.[77]

The need for federal links between unions in the transport and general fields became more urgent as the decade went on. Quite apart from the consistent conviction with which this goal was held by the principal new-union leaders, Mann, Tillett, Sexton and Gosling, pragmatic considerations now pushed the cause to the forefront. These included the growing problem of inter-union rivalries and relations. In municipal employment, the Municipal Employees' Association was involved in a series of poaching disputes with the Gasworkers' and Dockers' Unions, a problem which was instrumental in prompting the formation of the General Labourers' National Council in 1908. Ten affiliates participated in its foundation, including the Dockers' Union, the Gasworkers, the NAUL, the Amalgamated Tramway Workers, and the Workers' Union. The object of the new body was specifically to foster good inter-union relations by arranging for the mutual recognition of cards, transfers of members and spheres of influence. This was a more concrete advance than had hitherto been possible, but it fell short of attempting the co-ordination of industrial and trade policies and movements.

Tillett's union had founded the International Federation of Ship, Dock and River Workers and campaigned all round northern Europe to build it. The decline of dock representation nationally was accompanied by a falling-off of support for the International. But, consistently with their own long-term goals, the dockers reaffiliated to the replacement International Transport Workers' Federation when it emerged in 1908. This timing allowed transport workers to join in the debate on the international workers' movement's response to world crisis on the eve of the First World War.

As the end of the decade approached, a whole series of threats and opportunities pointed forcibly to the need for the greater integration of transport unionism. The GLNC's formation had not catered specifically for transport workers, and had in any case a narrow remit in the general-worker field.

Sounding the Alarm

Tillett interpreted the Houlder dispute in South Wales and Bristol, and the renewed aggression of the Shipping Federation in that affair, as the forerunner of another major assault. Moreover, the NALU in South Wales had been drawn closer to the Dockers' Union by the Houlder dispute. The London stevedores faced the prospect of wage-cutting from non-union labour employed directly by the shipowners. The lightermen on the Thames were still struggling to maintain their agreements against the larger firms which were taking over their industry, and their ancient licensing system was under threat from new powers granted to the PLA. Sexton's union had just lost its major battle against Larkin's breakaway in Belfast and Dublin, and needed allies in the rest of the British trade-union movement.

Havelock Wilson was sounding justifiable alarm bells at the formation of the International Shipping Federation in October 1909. In Amsterdam, Antwerp, Copenhagen, Marseilles, Naples, Paris and Dunkirk, employers' federations on the lines of the British Shipping Federation, founded to do battle with 'workmen's syndicates', had been proposing an international alliance since 1902. In 1907 the British Federation had hosted a London conference of these bodies to discuss 'the maritime labour problem both in England and abroad in all its bearings, more especially with a view to arranging a scheme of co-operation between the various organisations for the mutual support of their members at any time the trade unions should attempt to give effect to their declared intention of themselves concerting attacks upon an international basis.'[78] This conference led to detailed committee planning, and the fully fledged International, complete with plans to maintain employment bureaux 'throughout the world', was ready for business at the end of 1909.

> The newly-formed organisation concentrated . . . upon dealing with strikes both of seafarers and of dock labour – but mostly the latter. Too often in the past, while the national employers in a port might be determined to resist what they considered to be unjustifiable demands, the front was broken – often in ignorance – by a foreign shipmaster anxious to get his ship to sea again.[79]

The Seamen's Union had by now tabled a comprehensive programme of national demands: for a standard wage, new manning scales and an end to the Shipping Federation's ticket of preference. Havelock Wilson presented this to the Shipping Federation in July 1910, but the owners were in no mood to respond. Wilson appealed in vain to the International Transport Federation for an international strike: only the Dutch and the Belgians made positive replies. Sydney Buxton at the Board of Trade was asked by Wilson to persuade the Shipping Federation to accord recognition to his union. It refused. The NSFU was therefore on a collision course at the very moment of formation of the National Transport Workers' Federation, to which it was bound to appeal for support.

The general industrial temper in the transport industry was showing signs of the coming turbulence. Between 1902 and 1905 there were eighty-eight strikes in transport, involving 8,000 workers and occasioning the loss of 146,000 working days. Between 1906 and 1909 these figures rose to 20,000 workers and 242,000 working days.[80]

This was the industrial situation when the Dockers' Union sent their circular inviting unions to a conference on the question of federation. The Dockers' Union had renewed expectations, not just defensive reasons, for its initiative. We have seen that its numbers had improved in the last half of the decade, particularly in the last few months. New groups, such as Bevin's Bristol carters, were joining. The formation of the PLA had also generated an initial optimism. Harry Orbell came to represent the union on its Board: surely here was a return to the status the union had not enjoyed since the early 1890s? At this moment, Tom Mann was to embark on the campaign to spread syndicalism throughout the trade-union world.

Notes

1   H. A. Clegg, Alan Fox and A. F. Thompson, *A History of British Trade Unions since 1889*, vol. I: *1889–1910* (Oxford University Press, 1964), placed much emphasis on the thesis that such a transformation was illusory. They see the upheaval of 1889–91 as having been absorbed and neutralized in the succeeding years, and in the upsurge of 1911–14, therefore, recognize a different phenomenon. The assumption is that the new unionism's intermittent progress proves the superficiality of its 'newness', and that older, less radical, pre-socialist modes of trades unionism provide the underlying, 'real' continuity.

In contrast to this view, Eric Hobsbawm has sketched out a perspective much closer to our own: 'As applied to its period of origin, the 1880s and early 1890s, the term "new unionism" suggests three things to a British labour historian. It suggests, first, a new set of strategies, policies, and forms of organisation for unions, as opposed to those associated with an already existing "old" trade unionism. It suggests, in the second place, a more radical social and political stance of unions in the context of the rise of a socialist labour movement: and in the third place, the creation of new unions of hitherto unorganised or unorganisable workers, as well as the transformation of old unions along the lines suggested by the innovators. Consequently it also suggests an explosive growth of trade-union organisation and membership. The dock strike of 1889 and its aftermath illustrate all these aspects of the "new unionism", and therefore it provides the most popular image of the entire phenomenon. It is interesting that the very similar union upsurge and transformation of 1911–13 has never generated any similar label, though it was quite as innovative and much more radical. This suggests that even at the time it was regarded as a continuation, or a second instalment, of the process initiated in 1889. I believe that this is in fact the best way to see it' (Eric Hobsbawm, *Worlds of Labour* (Weidenfeld and Nicolson, 1984), p. 1,152).

The only qualification which we might make to this judgement is to question why it says '*even* at the time'. Is this intended to imply that those involved were not fully aware of continuity in their struggle? But of course the second wave of new unionists knew perfectly well that in its origins and its nature it was a renewal and further development of their original organizations and long-term purposes. For the most part the same actors were involved, on both sides. In 1911 Mann, Tillett, Sexton, Havelock Wilson on the one hand, and the port employers and the Shipping Federation on the other, renewed conflicts which had been fought to a standstill in the mid-1890s. Then one side was exhausted and the other triumphant. Here we are anticipating the 1911–13 uprising. For the most part, the preceding years were quite different.

2   R. C. K. Ensor, *England, 1870–1914* (Oxford University Press, 1941), p. 255n.

3   Gareth Stedman Jones, 'Working Class Culture and Working Class Politics in London, 1870–1900', *Journal of Social History*, vol. 7, no. 4 (1974), p. 460.

4   *The Times*, 21 May 1900; cited by Jones, 'Working Class Culture', p. 461.

5   Jack London, *The People of the Abyss* (Journeyman, 1977), pp. 62–3.

6   Ibid., p. 68.

7   See Lord Askwith, *Industrial Problems and Disputes* (John Murray, 1920), pp. 115–25.

8   Board of Trade *Abstracts of Labour Statistics*, as digested in Clegg, Fox and Thompson, *History of British Trade Unions*, vol. I, p. 489. The figures for numbers of separate strikes are taken in preference to numbers of working days lost, since the latter can be dramatically inflated by one or two very large and protracted strikes.

9   DWRGWU Annual Report, 1901, p. 4.

10 Eric J. Hobsbawm, *Labouring Men* (Weidenfeld and Nicolson, 1968), p. 180.

11 Gordon A. Phillips, 'The National Transport Workers' Federation, 1910–1927' (unpublished PhD thesis, Oxford University, 1968), pp. 20–1.

12 Ibid., p. 5, table I, based on the 1911 Census figures.

13 B. R. Mitchell and P. Deane, *Abstract of British Historical Statistics* (Cambridge University Press, 1962), pp. 218–19.

14 Phillips, 'The National Transport Workers' Federation', p. 5.
15 Ibid.
16 Cited in Phillips, 'The National Transport Workers' Federation', p. 25.
17 Phillip Bagwell, *The Transport Revolution from 1770* (Batsford, 1974), p. 153.
18 F. Sherwood Taylor, *The Century of Science* (Heinemann, 1942), pp. 44ff.
19 Ibid.
20 Charles H. Feinstein and Sydney Pollard (eds), *Studies in Capital Formation in the United Kingdom, 1750–1920* (Oxford University Press, 1988), p. 330.
21 Phillips, 'The National Transport Workers' Federation', p. 9.
22 Ibid.
23 Just prior to the Devlin reform of the Dock Labour Scheme in 1967, there were 300 registered employers of dock labour in London, and 90 in Hull. A government report in 1956 estimated the UK total at 1,248. See Tony Topham, 'The Dockers', in Ken Coates (ed.), *Can the Workers Run Industry?* (Sphere Books/Institute for Workers' Control, 1968), pp. 157–81.
24 Edward Gillett and Kenneth MacMahon, *A History of Hull* (University of Hull, 1980), pp. 335, 349 and 392.
25 Sir Walter T. Layton and Geoffrey Crowther, *An Introduction to the Study of Prices* (2nd edn, Macmillan, 1935).
26 George Dangerfield, *The Strange Death of Liberal England, 1910–14* (Constable, 1935; reissued Perigree Books, 1980), p. 219.
27 Sidney Pollard, 'Trade Unions and the Labour Market, 1870–1914', *Yorkshire Bulletin of Economic and Social Research*, vol. 17, no. 1 (May 1965), pp. 101–2.
28 E. H. Phelps-Brown, *The Growth of British Industrial Relations: a Study from the Standpoint of 1906–14* (Macmillan, 1960), p. 336.
29 Ibid.
30 Rodger Charles, *The Development of Industrial Relations in Britain, 1911–1939* (Hutchinson, 1973), pp. 46–7n.
31 Sidney and Beatrice Webb, *What Syndicalism Means* (London, 1912).
32 DWRGWU Annual Report, 1901.
33 John Lovell, *Stevedores and Dockers: a Study of Trade Unionism in the Port of London, 1870–1914* (Macmillan, 1969), pp. 219–21; and the DWRGWU Annual Reports, 1901 and 1910.
34 Lovell, *Stevedores and Dockers*, pp. 148–9.
35 *Amalgamated Stevedores' Labour Protection League, Past and Present* (n.d.). The original is in Tim O'Leary's private collection.
36 Lovell, *Stevedores and Dockers*, p. 149.
37 Ibid., p. 152.
38 See Gordon Phillips and Noel Whiteside, *Casual Labour: The Unemployment Question in the Port Transport Industry, 1880–1970* (Oxford University Press, 1985), pp. 64ff., for a study of this episode.
39 Ibid., p. 84.
40 Phillip J. Leng, *The Welsh Dockers* (G. W. and A. Hesketh, 1981), p. 36.
41 Randolph S. Churchill, *Winston S. Churchill*, vol. II (Heinemann, 1969), companion part II, pp. 1,164–75.
42 Leng, *The Welsh Dockers*, p. 50.

43   This account of the Welsh sections of the Dockers' Union is drawn from Leng, *The Welsh Dockers*.

44   This account is based on Brian Atkinson, *Trade Unions in Bristol* (Bristol Branch, Historical Association, University of Bristol, 1982).

45   NUDL Annual Report, 1908.

46   Ibid., 1901 and 1910.

47   Quoted in Eric Taplin, *The Dockers' Union: a Study of the National Union of Dock Labourers, 1889–1922* (Leicester University Press, 1986), p. 79.

48   John Gray, *City in Revolt: James Larkin and the Belfast Dock Strike of 1907* (Blackstaff Press, 1985), pp. 1–2.

49   Bob Holton, 'Syndicalism and Labour on Merseyside', in H. R. Hikins (ed.), *Building the Union: Studies in the Growth of the Workers' Movement, Merseyside, 1756–1967* (Toulouse Press, 1973), p. 133.

50   See P. J. Waller, *Democracy and Sectarianism: A Political and Social History of Liverpool, 1868–1939* (Liverpool University Press, 1981), p. 217.

51   Fred Bower, *Rolling Stonemason* (London, 1936), p. 168.

52   Ibid., pp. 169–70.

53   Emmett Larkin, *James Larkin, Irish Labour Leader, 1876–1947* (Routledge and Kegan Paul, 1965), p. 18.

54   Gray, *City in Revolt*, pp. 13 and 15.

55   Ibid., p. 56.

56   Ibid., p. 59.

57   Ibid., p. 60.

58   Ibid., p. 63.

59   Ibid., p. 100.

60   Clegg, Fox and Thompson, *History of British Trade Unions*, vol. I, p. 451.

61   Gray, *City in Revolt*, p. 107.

62   John McHugh, 'The Belfast Labour Dispute and Riots of 1907', *International Review of Social History*, vol. XXII (1977), p. 10.

63   Emmett Larkin, *James Larkin*, pp. 32ff.; Gray, *City in Revolt*, pp. 111–36. McHugh, 'The Belfast Labour Dispute of 1907', p. 12, cites a report in the *Labour Leader* which speaks of 253 such transfers.

64   Askwith, *Industrial Problems and Disputes*, p. 109; also Gray, *City in Revolt*. pp. 171–3.

65   Askwith, *Industrial Problems and Disputes*, p. 111.

66   B. J. Ripley and J. McHugh, *John MacLean* (Manchester University Press, 1989), pp. 30–3.

67   Phillips, 'The National Transport Workers' Federation', p. 4.

68   Ibid., p. 46.

69   Angela Tuckett, *The Scottish Carter* (Allen and Unwin, 1967), p. 25.

70   This survey of road-transport unions draws on Arthur Marsh and Victoria Ryan, *Historical Directory of Trade Unions*, vol. III (Gower, 1987); Phillips, 'The National Transport Workers' Federation'. See also Part II, Appendix: Profiles of the Unions.

71   Jean Lindsay, *The Great Strike* (David and Charles, 1987), pp. 128–9.

72   The quarrymen had wisely affiliated in May 1899, in time to benefit from GFTU support when Lord Penrhyn struck his blow.

73   R. Merfyn Jones, *The North Wales Quarrymen, 1874–1922* (University of Wales, 1981), p. 215.

74 Ibid., p. 285.
75 This account of the Workers' Union's early years is drawn from Richard Hyman, *The Workers' Union* (Oxford University Press, 1971), pp. 12–35.
76 DWRGWU Annual Report, 1901.
77 See A. Prochaska, *History of the General Federation of Trade Unions, 1889–1980* (Allen and Unwin, 1982).
78 L. H. Powell, *The Shipping Federation: A History of the First Sixty Years, 1890–1950* (Shipping Federation, 1950), p. 109.
79 Ibid., p. 111.
80 Clegg, Fox and Thompson, *History of British Trade Unions*, vol. I, p. 329; source: *Sixteenth Abstract of Labour Statistics*, 1913.

9

The Political Challenge: From Above, or From Below?

I

Transport Workers and the Labour Representation Committee

On 27 February 1900 129 people gathered in the Memorial Hall, in East London's Farringdon Street. They stayed for two days, and at the end of their labours was born the Labour Representation Committee, soon to become the Labour Party. Just over half a million members belonged to the assembled organizations, if their claims can be believed. The three political groups appeared to have exaggerated somewhat: the Independent Labour Party claimed to represent 13,000 members (there were actually 6,084 fee paying members of the ILP in 1900), the Social Democratic Federation claimed 9,000, and the Fabians 861. But the ILP had only 5,000 members the following year. Shrinking though it was, there was no special reason for it to shrink that much in twelve months. But there is good reason to believe that, even with only 5,000 members, it was almost certainly the largest of the socialist groupings. Be that as it may, it was no small achievement that all these different bodies were now sitting down together.

Without the initiative of the two dockers' unions and the railwaymen, none of them would have been there. But the transport workers were now divided and enfeebled. Tillett's union paid its bills only because of the loyal efforts of the South Wales tinplatemen. Along the waterfronts of southern England, the union was at a low ebb. Things were not much, but a little, better in the North. The port workers' memories remained, but it was not possible to organize a political response on memory alone. The clever young men of the ILP needed, and were courting, other trade-union allies, even if they were more staid, better-heeled, less turbulent, than their own founding union fathers. The pioneers were moving on. Burns was now firmly with the Liberals. Tom Mann was soon to leave for Australia. His influence on the dockers would not be replaced, try as Tillett might.

None the less, five waterfront trade unions were represented at the conference, and between them they said they mustered a little over 34,000 members. The representation of the new unions taken together was greater: the Gasworkers and General Labourers claimed 48,000, the Workers' Union clocked in at over 4,000, and a variety of other societies could add something like 10,000 members to the 'new-union' tally. Allowing that problems of definition are intransigent, it is therefore safe to say that approximately one-fifth of the trade unionists represented at Labour's founding conference had been mobilized by the new unions.

The Parliamentary Committee of the Trades Union Congress was not anxious to be dragged into the formation of an independent political body, and it therefore proposed, as a controlling measure, that the trade-union element in the new committee should be represented by – itself. This suggestion was politely declined by Ben Tillett: he thought that to accept their offer would deprive the LRC of 'all its meaning and all its character'. The intention was to create an alliance between the trade unions and a variety of progressive bodies, and he did not believe that the Parliamentary Committee could 'assume a responsibility and an authority it had no right to'.[1] The gasworkers were willing to have the seven representatives of the trade-union movement chosen by the Parliamentary Committee, but a card-vote went with Tillett, and the conference elected representatives of the Lancashire Miners, the Railway Servants, the Gasworkers, the Textile Workers, the Shipwrights, the Steel-smelters and the Vellum Bookbinders to form the trade-union section of the new organization's Executive.

The Options

The political perspectives open to the new party turned around three distinct platforms. The SDF wanted a party organization 'separate from the capitalist parties based upon a recognition of the class war, and having for its ultimate objective the socialisation of the means of production, distribution, and exchange'. The Party, they went on, should 'formulate its own policy for promoting practical legislative measures in the interests of labour, and . . . co-operate with any Party that will support such measures, or . . . assist in opposing measures of an opposite character'.[2]

The shipwrights wanted none of this. A. Wilkie, their delegate, proposed that a Labour Group be formed in Parliament, based on a platform 'composed of, say, four or five planks, embracing questions upon which the vast majority of the workers in the country are in agreement . . .'.[3] Wilkie did not want Labour representatives to be bound to any overall political philosophy, and once they had pledged themselves to promoting Labour's interest, he thought they should be 'left entirely free on all political questions'.[4]

Two dockers' leaders got into an immediate spat on different sides in this confrontation. James Sexton thought that the SDF resolution was 'magnificent, very heroic but . . . not war'. It was divisive, and though he agreed with it he could not vote for it at this conference. Harry Quelch of the SDF denounced Sexton's view as 'humbug', and robustly cast doubt upon all those who proclaimed themselves in favour of a principle which they intended to vote against. Keir Hardie then came through with a third proposal which steered straight down the middle. He wanted a distinct Labour Group in Parliament with its own whips. He chose as many as possible of the words of the SDF motion, including their commitment to the promotion of legislation in the interests of Labour and their opposition to measures 'having an opposite tendency', but carefully filleting out their socialist pronouncements. Hardie received support from Pete Curran of the gasworkers, John Burns and Ben Tillett. His proposal then carried unanimously. Hardie also succeeded in keeping open the question of whether the new group would, or would not, work with the Liberals: 'If he saw anything which Labour had to gain by that, nothing would hinder him from agreeing to it. But every day tended more and more to confirm his belief in the folly of any such a course.'[5]

In reality, the new party was very vulnerable to offers of co-operation with the Liberals, even though its own emergence owed much to the intransigence of local Liberal associations, in refusing to accommodate to electoral change by adopting trade-union-supported candidates. But those Labour men who were elected on a Liberal ticket were still able to bar the road to fully independent action for a number of key trade unions, above all the miners.

Empire and Protection

The General Election of 1900 had confirmed the Conservatives in office, still with a bone-crushing majority. While 334 MPs directly accepted their whip, a further 68 were elected on the allied Liberal–Unionist ticket of Joseph Chamberlain. In opposition there were 184 Liberals and Lib.–Labs; 82 Irish Nationalists; and 2 Labour Representation Committee members, each at odds with the other. Westminster was by now commonly referred to as an 'imperial' Parliament, although it was by no means representative of the subject peoples either abroad or at home. It was still elected on a purely national franchise, excluding all British women – and many British men who happened to be working class – from the right to vote. If it was imperial, it was not as a voice of the peoples of the empire but as the embodiment of authority, the source of the writ which ran around the world. But the old century, and with it the 'Pax Britannica', had really gone.

This peace had been far from absolute, but such as it was, it had

> depended less on Britain's absolute strength than on the absolute weakness of others. This thought was expressed . . . by Ernest Bevin . . . 'What astounds me about the history of the Navy is how cheaply we policed the world for three hundred years. I often think, when I read this history, that it is a good job no-one called our bluff very often . . . the world was policed largely by the British Navy with less than one hundred thousand men'.[6]

In the twentieth century the others' absolute weakness was at an end. Commercial and military competition were already rampant. Imperialism as a British policy was to face a serious political test, which was not at all diminished by the fact that the Conservatives had begun with a notable victory by winning in the so-called Khaki Election, named in honour of the Boer War. The war, which dragged on long after its end had been anticipated, was far from universally popular, but even those who enthused about it were about to be tested by other problems. British industrial supremacy now faced highly effective and sustained challenges from the United States, Germany, France and Japan. Productivity was increasing at double the British rate in each of these countries. Thus, each new recession brought increased unemployment to Britain, and increased the pressure on the poor.

Joseph Chamberlain, from May 1903 the voice of Protectionism, was to be much more than a junior partner in the Conservative administration of Salisbury. As Michael Barratt Brown tells us:

> It is sometimes supposed that his re-entry to the Cabinet as Colonial Secretary was a downgrading. The fact is that he could have chosen any office that he had wanted, and the Prime Minister allowed him 'usually the power of a co-premier and on some rare occasions more'.[7] His choice of the Colonial Office was deliberate, and was central to his plans for a new economic policy for the country.[8]

From this base, Chamberlain eventually developed his proposals for tariff reform, protecting home-based agriculture and industry, but negotiating a system of imperial preferences which would defend British exports and grant privileged access to empire suppliers. Chamberlain did everything he could to win over working-class endorsement of his campaign, but the Labour Representation Committee, under the influence of the doctrines of free trade, moved continuously closer to the Liberals.

Labour and the Liberals

Although the Independent Labour Party had established an impressive support network, capable of damaging the Liberal interest, it had not created a basis for widespread alternative representation. The failure of attempts to unify the two main socialist parties was accompanied by continuous erosion of the ILP. The political intellectuals who supported the ILP felt that a fusion with the SDF would abort any chance of creating a wide alliance with trade unions. Yet, as their own membership declined, they began to seem less than adequate to fulfil the project they had taken on. The departure of Tom Mann, seen by Keir Hardie as 'a strong personality', was accompanied by the rise of Ramsay MacDonald, who was certainly a personality, whether strong or not. With this wordy fellow emerged a style of leadership which was to debilitate the Labour movement for many years. It combined a melodious line in pseudo-millennarian rhetoric with a practical capacity for compromise and short-sighted duplicity, which still has the power to shock when one reads about it at the other end of a century much versed in the finer arts of hypocrisy.

'If I had the power and the authority, I have no doubt that I could come to terms with the leaders of the Labour Party in the course of half a morning,' said Herbert Gladstone, the liberal Chief Whip, in October 1901.[9] Within two years a secret pact had indeed been stitched together. This had been seen as the foundation of the Liberal recovery of 1906, and the simultaneous birth of the Labour Party. But perhaps, had the impact of the issue of Protection been foreseen by Gladstone, he might have been able to think of managing without it.

Back in 1900, eight months after the foundation of the LRC, the railwaymen's leader, Richard Bell, and Keir Hardie gained seats at the General Election. Bell had spent £900 during his campaign in Derby, while Hardie had disposed of £300 to win Merthyr Tydfil. Half of this last sum had been advanced by George Cadbury, the Liberal chocolate king, in opposition to the South African War. Hardie had contested two seats simultaneously, and had not believed that his chances were very good in Merthyr. Accordingly, he campaigned most energetically in Preston, which he failed to win. But one of the two Liberal candidates in Merthyr had been pro-war, and had roundly attacked Hardie as a 'pro-Boer'. It has been alleged that this abusive campaign gave Hardie the seat, so alienated were the South Wales voters by Liberal imperialism. Doubt has been cast on this interpretation. Was the victory simply a reaffirmation of Welsh radicalism? Whatever explanation we choose, the split in Liberal affinities could not have been made plainer.

Fifteen other Labour candidates failed, including Fred Jowett, Ramsay MacDonald, Philip Snowden and Will Thorne. Thorne lost in

West Ham South, where the socialist forces had been doing extremely well in local-government elections. The prospects of the Labour Party were clearly influenced by the Liberal split about the war, and Lib.–Lab. contenders, who still included the miners' MPs, sought to bridle the 'independence' of the LRC by building upon the recognition of this fact. First, they tried to recover lost ground by repeating their attempt to bring all trade-union representatives on the LRC under the control of the TUC's Parliamentary Committee. Beaten in 1902, this ploy was replaced by a variant tactic, seeking affiliation of the National Democratic League, which, as we have seen, had been founded for the purpose of electoral reform by a coalition of Liberals and Socialists, in which Tom Mann had at first played a major role. By this back door, it was thought, all the radical Liberals would enter; the 'independence' of Labour would thus be tidily disposed of.

This initiative was defeated at the 1903 conference of the LRC, and provoked Pete Curran of the gasworkers and James Sexton of the dockers to propose firm measures by which the new LRC might obtain financial independence which could underpin their desire for political autonomy. In 1904 a voluntary levy was agreed and each affiliate was requested to pay a penny per member to a central treasury. In 1905 this levy was made compulsory. All candidates would receive 25 per cent of their election expenses from this new fund, which would also pay Members of Parliament an annual sum of £200. Central funds in 1900 had allowed the expenditure of a princely £33 during the whole election campaign. From now on, however, the LRC would dispose of adequate resources to render the financial blandishments of the Liberals far less influential than heretofore.

Three new Labour MPs arrived in the House of Commons in the by-elections which followed 1900. They were David Shackleton, Will Crooks and Arthur Henderson. Each of the new members, for different reasons, had strong Liberal affinities. Hardie began to weaken in his proclaimed independence. He sought to bring John Burns into the leadership of the Labour faction. In March 1903 he wrote to Burns: 'With your magnificent voice, your rich imagination and attractive personality, you would rouse your fellows as no other man in public life could.' Roger Moore, who has highlighted these events, points out that the 'very fact' that this offer was made 'is indicative of the uncertain future of the Labour Party'.[10]

The Impact of Taff Vale

By 1901 forty-one trade unions with a membership of more than 350,000 had affiliated to the Labour Party. More than 100,000 other trade unionists were additionally affiliated during the following year.

They belonged to 65 separate trade unions. The growth of affiliated membership followed directly on the celebrated (or infamous) Taff Vale case. By 1903, 127 unions with nearly 850,000 members had joined up. In 1905, the total reached 158 unions and 73 Trades Councils. These accounted between them for the lion's share of a total affiliated membership of 900,000.

The Taff Vale strike broke out in the summer of 1900 because John Ewington, a signalman employed by the Taff Vale Railway Company, was victimized. The men were fractious because wages had not risen to meet the rise in prices which resulted from the Boer War. Claims for recognition of their union, the Amalgamated Society of Railway Servants, were rejected. The company blustered, and was accused of dictatorship by the union. When the strike erupted, Ammon Beasley, the railway manager, sent for Collison's free labourers to break it. Two hundred practised blacklegs duly materialized. Beasley went to law to stop the counter-picketing, and was given an injunction against the ASRS. This was quashed in the Appeal Court, but re-established at the House of Lords in July 1901. The Lords further decided that in such a case as this, the union's funds did not enjoy immunity. Given this green light, Beasley pressed ahead to secure damages from the railwaymen and was awarded £23,000 plus costs.

The House of Lords was in a gung-ho mood in 1901, and a couple of weeks after it had ploughed trade-union immunities into the ground, it interdicted boycotts, in the case of *Quinn v. Leathem*. In this case, the Lords sanctioned the principle, first established by the Court of Appeal in the earlier case of *Temperton v. Russell* (1893), that a conspiracy to injure was cause for an action against a union. The government peremptorily rejected Keir Hardie's appeal for legislation to restore protection to union funds.

At the beginning of August, the LRC's secretary, MacDonald, wrote to every union emphasizing the significance of the Taff Vale judgement in particular, which, he said, 'should convince the unions that a Labour Party in Parliament is an immediate necessity.'[11] The LRC agreed to establish a sub-committee to explain the consequences of the Taff Vale judgement; it went to work immediately. As invariably happens during such legal upheavals, union leaders saw the point much quicker than their members. An engineers' ballot on affiliation to the LRC touched only 7,000 members in total. But some leaders took steps to divest themselves of their personal property in order to avoid possible confiscation in subsequent disputes.

Not all full-time officers shared this apprehension. Richard Bell himself actually welcomed the judgement, on the grounds that it would reinforce trade-union discipline and facilitate recognition. It would be 'a useful influence in solidifying the forces of trade unionism', he thought.[12] James Sexton went further along the same line of argument:

'There are those in the Labour Movement sanguine enough to hope that the decision in the Taff Vale case will be a blessing in disguise, and will tend to strengthen executive control and minimise, if not entirely kill, irresponsible action in the localities', he wrote.[13] (Disguised or not, this blessing was to fall well short of the hopes placed in it by the Liverpool dockers' spokesman.) Sexton lost no opportunity to preach this message, and in his 1902 Annual Report he wrote:

> the whole mischief was caused by the first initial step taken being contrary to the rule of the Society itself. Had the action of the men and the Executive been governed by the rules of the Society there would have been no Taff Vale case today, and the Railwaymen's fund would have been richer by £23,000 than it is, while the legal position of trades unions would have remained what it was understood to be previous to the now historic decision. It will, therefore, we hope be fully recognised by our members the absolute necessity of a strict observance of the rules, as any lapsing from them would place us in the same position as the Railwaymen.[14]

Tillett: Arbitration and Recognition

Ben Tillett also saw Taff Vale as an unexpected boost for his policy of compulsory arbitration. Shortly before the House of Lords delivered its judgement, Tillett opined that 'it would do a world of good and stir up those who had got an easy belief in things.'[15] Later, in 1903, he told the TUC that the Taff Vale judgement should stay in place. Of course, he said, the judgement was a threat to Labour; but he could not support the campaign to reverse it. He was strongly critical of the leaders of unions who opposed the judgement and yet paid without demur the legal penalties which were imposed upon them: 'Mr. Bell's society had tamely paid £40,000 or so. If Mr. Bell and his colleague . . . had done six months in prison it would have been better for them all.'[16]

In a more flamboyant mood, speaking to the conference of his own union in 1902, he said that he himself was quite prepared 'to go to the stake, the gallows or jail'. But in spite of his intransigence, Tillett's priority during these years was to establish governmentally regulated binding arbitration. His biographer tells us that he

> began advocating this practice for dockers just as it was falling into general disuse. Tillett could plausibly argue to his own rank and file, for whom trade unionism was a comparatively recent development, that it was a great advance for their representatives merely to appear before an arbiter on equal footing with the employer. The novelty of this sort of equality, however, had long since worn off among craft unionists.[17]

No doubt this is true, but it does not face up to the real meaning of Tillett's policies. Schneer quotes a miners' spokesman: 'He says the capitalist system is wrong. Then why is he creating an Arbitration Court to perpetuate it?'[18]

Schneer believes that Tillett 'no longer seemed interested in replacing capitalism with socialism'. Instead, his disapproval of strikes, and his impulse to maintain the organization of his union, totally dominated his thinking. Schneer is quite right to say that 'probably he was correct in thinking that the Shipping Federation had become too strong for the Union'.[19] But it was not necessary for compulsory arbitration to bring instant success to union claims before it could offer some very real hope to a Labour leader with his back against the wall. What arbitration brought with it was *recognition*, and it was recognition which could reinforce the continuous solidity of class opposition, and therefore the continuity of organization (as we have argued in chapter 3). If a third party, the government, mediated between the forces of labour and capital, whether the decision went ill or well for Labour, all the forces of society were none the less conspiring with Labour to reinforce its self-awareness and its evolving sense of its own identity.

Schneer himself shows how skilfully Tillett argued the case of the Swansea tinplate workers during an arbitration at the beginning of 1904. His cross-examination highlighted all the grievances of the men he represented. He lost his case. But he had persuaded his members of their common cause, at a time when, quite evidently, it was beyond their powers to win their demands in any more direct way.

It is true that Tillett was floundering, because, as we have seen, his union had been gravely weakened in the ports and no longer constituted an important power-base for intervention in the affairs of the rapidly growing Labour Representation Committee. In 1903 he entered into a dubious relationship with Horatio Bottomley, a racketeering business-man with a sleazy reputation, who was seeking to ingratiate himself with Labour leaders as part of his plan to enter Parliament in the Liberal interest in Hackney. Tillett's Annual Reports to the dockers, however, maintained, year by year, a constant flow of class-war commitments.

In 1900, regretting the lack of unity among the waterside unions, he drew a dismal balance sheet of the defeats of the dockers' and lightermen's disputes. Their disunity made it highly unlikely that they could ever force conditions upon the employers.

> For myself, [said Tillett,] I have at all times taken full responsibility for disputes even . . . when these have taken place against my advice . . . I have never thought to save my neck . . . by repudiating the action taken by our members, but have associated myself with them at all times . . .
>
> During the years I have taken an active interest in Labour movements, I have advocated Arbitration and Conciliation; since my visit to the Antipodes, I am convinced that compulsory arbitration is essential to the well being of the worker and the welfare of trade. At present all the law is on the side of the Capitalist who makes as much use of the law as we

should, were we the dominant factor . . . Lord Penrhyn, the great Coal and
Shipping millionaires, Dock Directors, Engineers, and others, have at all
times power to throw industry out of gear without a murmur from the
public, and a public that would go frantic with rage at a dislocation of trade
caused by a dispute of the workmen, the press even siding with the
employers when screwing the wage earners.[20]

This unequal relationship was aggravated by the confusion of the port
industry:

London is the great unmanageable. Here social economy is in confusion,
here government tangled, and even the Port itself is controlled by a
muddled confusion of authorities, its working bungled and costly, while
labour is starved and demoralised instead of being healthy and efficient.
The toilers of London make millionaires by the score, but thousands even
fail to recognise the commercial character of a trade union.[21]

If all this implied the acceptance of arbitration machinery, it also
implied centralized union discipline and the rejection of 'hare-brained'
action. 'Strict adhesion to rule', ballot votes and constitutional behaviour
were to be enforced, 'while the strikes in sympathy should be given a
wide berth.'[22]

All this reorientation was accompanied by a strong statement of
continued loyalty to

the great international movement. Labour must be as international as
capital. The great trusts, the combines, the fact that New York is fast
becoming the successor of London as the money mart of the world,
indicates such a shifting of controlling centres as will make for change in
the humblest industrial calling of the world. Capital speaks all languages;
let labour speak the language of universal brotherhood, and we shall be
able . . . to check the forces which are driving the . . . producer to beggary
and starvation.[23]

There is a confusion here which harks back to the problem of choice
we identified in Tom Mann's words to the Dockers' Union, spoken only
a few years earlier (see chapter 5). International action implies
sympathetic action, which frequently cuts across the rules agreed within
permanent national structures for bargaining. The injunction to eschew
'the strikes in sympathy' was calculated to ease new agreements into
being. International action might ease them out again. National
democratic advance and internationalism might, in theory, be reconcil-
able: but they were certainly not identical processes, and at times one
could conflict with the other.

For the time being, Tillett's main activity was concentrated on a
national stage. He had been elected to the Executive of the Labour
Representation Committee in 1901. His stay there appears to have been

turbulent, and he certainly quarrelled repeatedly with Keir Hardie. By 1903 Hardie thought that 'it would do others of the wavering brotherhood a world of good [if] an example could be made of . . . Tillett'.[24]

Wheeling and Dealing

During all the years in which Tillett was becoming increasingly estranged from the predominant leadership of the LRC, the Committee was growing continuously. (His membership of the Executive was an early casualty of this growth.) The effects of the Taff Vale judgement brought one union after another into the fold. At the same time, efforts to restore direct control by the TUC were recognized as fruitless. In 1904 Richard Bell, now TUC president, and also by now estranged from the LRC, ruled that the Congress had no control over the LRC because it was 'an organisation'. The ILP politicians had thus succeeded in attaching to themselves a growing, and soon to be preponderant, body of trade-union opinion.

Undoubtedly, this was eased by the agreement with the Liberals. Keir Hardie prepared this in a series of appeals to Liberal leaders: first to John Morley, then to Lloyd George. But a secret agreement had been finally concluded between Ramsay MacDonald and Herbert Gladstone, the Liberal's agent, in August 1903. Negotiations had dragged on for several months, with Jesse Herbert representing Gladstone. According to his biographer, MacDonald excelled in these talks:

> He held one or two good cards – notably the Parliamentary Fund – but on the whole his hand was not a strong one. In effect, he was asking the Liberals to allow the L.R.C. to establish itself in Parliament, but he had little to offer in exchange. The L.R.C. had a large affiliated membership, but no one who knew the Labour movement would imagine that the trade unionists affiliated to it could be 'delivered' in a parliamentary election. Many were Liberals already: their votes would go to Liberal candidates without any special arrangement between the Liberals and the L.R.C. Others were Conservative, notably in Lancashire, but it was far from clear that Conservative working-men would vote for Liberal candidates merely because the L.R.C. asked them to. Yet all this was obscured in a tantalizing cloud of promises and threats. The L.R.C., MacDonald claimed, had a membership of a million and a political fund of £5,000 a year. Its candidates were 'in almost every instance earnest Liberals who will support a Liberal Government'. Liberal opposition to these candidates would 'not only lose the possible accession of the erstwhile Tory working man, but will inevitably estrange the hitherto loyal Liberal working man'.[25]

Jesse Herbert received this news impassively, and said nothing very much. But he did ask MacDonald for specific proposals, and he sent post-haste to Gladstone a detailed report which showed that he had missed none of the potential of MacDonald's offer:

'The LRC can directly influence the votes of nearly a million men. They will have a fighting fund of £100,000 . . . Their members are mainly men who have hitherto voted with the Liberal Party. Should they be advised to vote against Liberal candidates, and (as they probably would) should they act as advised the Liberal party would suffer defeat not only in those constituencies where L.R.C. candidates fought, but also in almost every borough, and in many of the Divisions of Lancashire and Yorkshire. This would be the inevitable result of unfriendly action towards the L.R.C. candidates. They would be defeated, but so also should we be defeated.'

Shortly afterwards MacDonald discussed the proposed arrangement with Gladstone and in the next three months he had at least seven further meetings with Herbert.[26]

David Marquand reports an undated note from MacDonald, probably written three years after the event:

Before the General Election of 1906 I saw Mr. Gladstone, the Chief Liberal Whip, twice and his confidential secretary, Mr. Jesse Herbert, several times. There was no bargain struck. I told them what seats we were determined to fight. They were friendly & no doubt expected their friendship to influence our policy. They never asked that it should however. The impression they gave me was that they [agreed] that we should have a fair chance of representation. Their attitude no doubt did influence me in opposing wild-cat candidatures, & in one or two constituencies I told them there would be no Labour candidate because there was no Labour organisation. I repeat, however, that information was not given in any way as a *quid pro quo*. A case in point was Walsall when it was proposed to make Sir Arthur Hayter a peer. I said there would be no Labour candidate. There could have been none.[27]

In the middle of these negotiations, the LRC published a resonant declaration entitled 'Why We Are Independent'. This was dated April 1903 and signed, on behalf of the Committee, by J. Ramsay MacDonald, secretary. It said:

Upon this conflict between Capital and Labour, neither a Liberal nor a Conservative Ministry can be trusted to stand by the workers. The nation is called upon to settle economic and industrial difficulties for which neither of the old political parties offers any definite or satisfactory solution. Would it not, therefore, be futile to commit this new movement to parties which neither understand nor sympathise with its aims?[28]

The document continues with a declaration on 'The Wisdom of Independence', which says:

WE ARE INDEPENDENT, THEN

Because we must unite the democracy;
Because we must have the support of all sections of the Labour movement;
Because if we are Liberal or Conservative, the Trade Union movement cannot unitedly support us;
Because this policy has already secured the support of about 1,000,000 Trade Unionists;
Because we raise new economic and industrial issues, upon which the old political parties speak with an uncertain and hesitating voice;
Because we must be free in Parliament to lay down our Labour policy and adopt the most effective means for vindicating the rights of Labour and improving the social conditions of the people.[29]

For fifty years this declaration was the public face of Labour in Britain. MacDonald's secret accord was effectively blotted out, until it was rescued from Gladstone's archives by Henry Pelling and reprinted by Frank Bealey in 1956.[30]

No one can doubt the electoral significance of this accord. Yet Labour was acting independently in an important sense: campaigns about unemployment, the Poor Law and poverty drew thousands of workers into street demonstrations and made an important impact on public opinion.

Taff Vale Recruits for Labour

And all the while, the shadow of Taff Vale hung over the unions.

On 1 August 1902, David Shackleton, the representative of the United Textile Factory Workers' Association, was elected as Labour member for Clitheroe. His victory brought his union into the Labour Representation Committee the following January. This accession marked a major gain for the Committee; the Textile Workers were its largest affiliate up to that time, and adherents of an 'old' trade union, of a classic type, to boot. No one could doubt the concern of Shackleton's members about Taff Vale, and he was quick to table a very qualified Bill for the restoration of immunities, which would have lifted union liability except, as the Bill had it, 'in cases where the damages were the result of action which had not been authorized by the Union executive'. His measure would also have legalized peaceful pickets. This bill failed, partly on a technicality, and partly as a result of an adverse vote. Subsequently, a Royal Commission was announced, but no trade unionists were appointed to serve on it. Small wonder that unions now flocked to support the LRC, and that their members began a systematic lobby, first of sitting members and then of candidates, to pressure for reform.

The Conservative Split

Chamberlain's criticism of the Balfour government in May 1903 had split the Unionist Party from top to bottom, and in the course of the argument it was 'reduced almost to a rump'.[31] Balfour's administration was already under sustained attack for sanctioning the deployment of Chinese labour in the Rand, under conditions which were very oppressive. The defection of Chamberlain was a fierce blow. It began with a powerful speech in Birmingham, denouncing the continuation of free trade and demanding a system of imperial preferences. It went on to insist upon retaliation against foreign tariffs. The Unionist rank and file responded warmly, but the Cabinet was frigidity itself. Its predominant membership was firmly committed to free trade, while the Prime Minister was concerned to find a compromise and reunify his divided forces. There followed some months of manoeuvre. The Cabinet was reconstructed in order to straddle the issue. Uncertainty grew and grew. The Liberals were overjoyed at their good fortune, finding in the defence of free trade an issue strong enough to dissolve their former divisions on the Boer War. Two popular slogans confronted each other: the Liberals denounced taxes on food, 'The Big Loaf and the Little Loaf'. Chamberlain insisted that 'Tariff Reform Means Work for All'. Balfour got squeezed.

The dockers' unions did not stand on one side in this argument. Sexton, indeed, surpassed himself: the most notable events of the trade-union year, he thought, had been the defeat of the Penrhyn quarrymen, the Taff Vale agitation, and

the protectionist theory raised by 'Joseph and his brethren'. Thanks to the firm attitude taken by the Trade Unionists on this question this attempt to again fool the British workman utterly failed. Joseph himself took flight to the land of the Pharaohs, and returned to find that a host of Pharaohs had arisen that knew not Joseph. It is a source of satisfaction to know that our resolution at the Leicester Trades Union Congress was the means of setting the opposition going in the Trade Union world. A complete answer to the theory of Mr. Chamberlain that protection would find work for everybody is found in the fact of the introduction of cheap Chinese labour into South Africa. Let it not be forgotten that there are hundreds of thousands of persons in this country willing to work but cannot get it, while the country purchased at the cost of many thousand British lives and expenditure of British treasure is now being given over to hordes of Chinamen at 1s.6d. per day. And what can be done in South Africa is also likely to be done here, when under the policy of protection, even were it possible, everybody found work and higher wages.[32]

The General Election of 1906

During the first year of the split in the Unionist forces, unemployment ran high. Had this continued, Chamberlain might have created a bandwaggon of support for his views: but trade picked up subsequently, so that as the country moved towards a General Election the Unionist appeal to public opinion was losing momentum. The election of 1906 decided this argument very clearly. The Conservatives secured the election of 130 Members, and the Liberal Unionists suffered a loss of 40, so that their total was now 28. The Irish Nationalists won 83 seats, with 375 Liberals, 24 Lib.–Labs and 29 candidates of the Labour Representation Committee. One miner joined them after the election.

The twenty-nine now recognized their victory, and assumed the designation of 'the Labour Party'. They had polled 321,663 votes out of a total of 5.6 million.

All shared in the Liberal consensus on free trade. What bonded them as a special group was the commitment to reverse the Taff Vale decision and restore the right to strike. By far the majority of Liberal MPs had pledged themselves in the same sense: but for the Labour Party this was, of course, a core issue. Home Rule remained the banner of the Irish contingent, which Labour supported. Outside Westminster there was a rising clamour of women's voices, demanding admission, and this was to reach deafening volume within a short time. The Labour manifesto had been short, sharp and sweetly compatible with the Liberal ascendancy. It read:

> This election is to decide whether or not Labour is to be fairly represented in Parliament.
>
> The House of Commons is supposed to be the people's House, and yet the people are not there.
>
> Landlords, employers, lawyers, brewers, and financiers are there in force. Why not Labour?
>
> The Trade Unions ask the same liberty as capital enjoys. They are refused.
>
> The aged poor are neglected.
>
> The slums remain; overcrowding continues, whilst the land goes to waste.
>
> Shopkeepers and traders are overburdened with rates and taxation, whilst the increasing land values, which should relieve the ratepayers, go to people who have not earned them.
>
> Wars are fought to make the rich richer, and underfed school children are still neglected.
>
> Chinese Labour is defended because it enriches the mine owners.
>
> The unemployed ask for work, the Government gave them a worthless Act, and now, when you are beginning to understand the causes of your poverty, the red herring of Protection is drawn across your path.

Protection, as experience shows, is no remedy for poverty and unemployment. It serves to keep you from dealing with the land, housing, old age, and other social problems!

You have it in your power to see that Parliament carries out your wishes. The Labour Representation Executive appeals to you in the name of a million Trade Unionists to forget all the political differences which have kept you apart in the past, and vote for . . . . [here was inserted the name of the Labour candidate][33]

Of the twenty-nine Labour candidates who were elected on the LRC ticket, only four had faced official Liberals. Twenty-five had been given a clear field by the Liberal Party, so that they had only to beat the Conservative or Unionist contenders. Keir Hardie faced no Tory opponent, by contrast, but he had to beat one of the two Liberals offering themselves in this two-Member constituency. Twenty-six Labour men failed to secure election, and eighteen of these faced three-cornered contests. The gasworkers' Pete Curran was opposed only by a Liberal and he lost. All others were beaten by Conservatives in straight fights. One of these was James Sexton, who gained 2,592 votes, as opposed to his Conservative opponent's 3,373, in Liverpool West Toxteth. Ben Tillett came third in Eccles. He had been ill and absent, but he also felt that the intellectuals of the ILP were deliberately neglecting to press his case. Among new unionists who were actually elected were J. R. Clynes and Will Thorne of the gasworkers, and Charles Duncan of the Workers' Union. Harry Quelch stood in the two-Member Southampton constituency for the Social Democratic Federation, polling just over 2,000 votes and coming last. Two Liberals were elected there.

There were big regional influences on this representation. Thirteen of the Labour Party's seats were in Lancashire and Cheshire, and all of these resulted from the withdrawal of Liberal candidates. The traditional strength of Conservatism among parts of the working population persuaded the Liberals to be magnanimous in their negotiations with Labour. If they could not expect to win themselves, generosity was a prudent gesture, especially if it might then remove troublesome splits in what they saw as 'their own' votes elsewhere. Yorkshire, by contrast, saw the Liberals in a more secure situation, which made them less flexible. The trade-union movement was weaker there than in the adjacent counties; so there was scant Lib.–Lab. trading. Eight LRC candidates ran, but only three were elected. Jowett won in Bradford against both established parties, building on his own previous campaign and on the earlier trail-blazing contests of Ben Tillett. The other two victorious candidates were the ones who had not been opposed by Liberals.

Taff Vale Reversed, Immunities Established

It was not simply the disposition of candidates and Labour's electoral success, however, that set the framework of the new administration. The TUC had run its own preparatory lobby, to great effect, throughout every constituency, up to polling day itself. Two and a quarter million affiliated members had been asked to withhold votes from every candidate whatsoever who would not pledge himself to work for the complete removal of trade-union liability in disputes. Gone was the caution of Shackleton's defeated Bill. Now Taff Vale was to be totally annulled with the exact restoration of the status quo ante. A number of Conservatives, counting their margins, gave their word. But at least three-fifths of all Liberal candidates signed up in support, and, in contrast to their Tory co-thinkers, a very large proportion of them was elected. Among them was Sir John Walton, who was later entrusted with presentation of the Liberal government's original proposals in the Commons. These were far from satisfactory to the TUC.

After the election, the Conservative-appointed Royal Commission reported, broadly in favour of the 1903 Shackleton halfway-house. The new government moved to legislate accordingly, but by now it was too late for half-measures. The new Labour Members tabled their own Bill for the restoration of full immunity. Premier Sir Henry Campbell-Bannerman gave his support. In the debate in the Commons, Keir Hardie showed that Sir John Walton himself had issued an election poster pledging his unequivocal support for the Trade Union Bill. The heart went out of the campaign for a compromise reform. So it was that there emerged the Trades Disputes Act of 1906, carried through its second reading by 416 affirmative votes to 66 against. Shackleton was given a celebratory banquet by the TUC, the GFTU and the Labour Party.

The Trades Disputes Act of 1906 was an unqualified victory for the trade-union movement. It established that no act done 'in pursuance of an agreement or combination by two or more persons' should be actionable unless it would have been so if done individually. Henceforth it was not open to the courts to regard unions as 'civil conspiracies'. It restored and augmented the rights of peaceful picketing. It brought into force a major concession, legalizing actions 'in restraint of trade' whenever they arose in the course of a trade dispute. And, lastly, it explicitly protected union funds from claims 'in respect of any tortious act'. Some commentators have maintained that this immunity was too far-reaching to be wholly for the good of the unions themselves.[34]

After this 'signal triumph', however, most Labour MPs did not quite know what to do next. The Parliamentary Labour Party, wrote Henry Pelling, 'seemed for a time thereafter to have lost its sense of purpose'.[35]

Different factions pulled in different ways. The party in the country became more restive. There were other lesser gains,[36] most notably an act enabling the provision of school meals (except in Scotland), which, during the depression which followed, brought aid to children in a number of areas with high unemployment. But although the Liberals brought in other measures of reform, they successfully held up or diluted any new proposals from the Labour Party, with the result that criticism mounted as unemployment rose.

Victor Grayson: Voice of the Unemployed

By 1907 there was visible unease, which expressed itself in the election of a young and unendorsed socialist fire-raiser, Victor Grayson, for the division of Colne Valley, which had been contested by Tom Mann in 1895 (see chapter 7). Grayson scandalized his new parliamentary colleagues by a succession of indecorous acts. He ran an open skirmish with Ramsay MacDonald, refused to sign the Labour Party's constitution, and rumpussed continuously about unemployment. As a one-man band, he made more noise than all the Labour MPs put together, and this stimulated some considerable response from people outside Westminster. John Lister of the Halifax ILP summed up the mood of many older socialists in a jingle entitled 'The Lost Party':

> Oh! Where can it be – the old ILP?
>   The party of sinews and brawn?
> Oh! Where is the muscle, that once used to tussle
>   With foes in the days that are gone?
>
> The days that have been – will their like ne'er be seen?
>   When courage and candour stood tall
> Ere we entered the ways – yes the policy ways
>   And hearken to history's warning!
> 'Tis this – that to laike with the old yellow-shirted 'snake'*
>   Is a spree you may rue in the morning.
>
> Anything! Anything! just to get in –
> Any tale! Any tale! so you may win –
> All the false lying spirits unchain,
> Barter your soul man, your voter to claim.[37]

Accountability

All sorts of controversies began during these experiences, and many of them have run on throughout the ninety years which have followed. One

* Alternative version: with Whig or with Liberal to jig

of the most notable concerned the question of who was to call the tune in the new party. The Parliamentary Labour Party which came into existence in 1906 had much to play for along the margin of the Liberal Party, and in fact it made considerable gains within the strategy of covert alliance, the most notable of which was the detachment of the mineworkers from the organizational framework of the Liberals, and the incorporation of the Miners' Federation into the Labour Party's own structure. But the price in conformity was more than many wished to pay.

As early as January 1905 Ben Tillett had moved a motion at the LRC Conference 'That it be an instruction to the Executive of the LRC to enforce the hearty adoption by LRC candidates of all legislative proposals emanating from the Trades Union Congress. In view of the refusal of candidates, that it be the peremptory duty of the Executive to refuse or discontinue support financially and morally.' Tillett was seconded by J. N. Bell of the National Amalgamated Union of Labour, and supported by Harry Quelch, speaking on behalf of London Trades Council. Quelch widened the question, by insisting that the 'Party as a whole' should formulate policy, which the candidates 'would have to accept or stand down'. On a show of hands, Tillett's proposal lost by 148 to 84. A card-vote being called, it was finally defeated by 537 to 245.[38]

James Sexton took the view of the majority, and a year later he reported to the NUDL: 'At the time of the Election this LRC, Labour Party had formulated no official programme. Its first and all-absorbing object is to be – to exist – in independence of all other parties.'[39]

The honeymoon following the victories of 1906 (in the election and then in the enactment of the Trades Disputes Act) did nòt endure long beyond the year. Even at the 1906 Conference, the first to convene under the name of the Labour Party, attempts were made to 'instruct' the parliamentary party on its Trade Union Bill. By 1907 Keir Hardie complained of seventeen separate resolutions containing 'instructions to introduce this and that'.[40] An attempt was made by the National Executive to direct the Standing Orders Committee to rephrase these motions in order to uphold the autonomy of the parliamentary party. It soon became clear that this would not pass the Conference, so a compromise formula was submitted. This left the PLP and the Executive to decide between them the timing of action upon such instructions. Even this was too bitter a pill for some to swallow, although in the end it was accepted.

Unintimidated, Ben Tillett returned to the attack, moving that

The Executive is instructed to secure united and consistent action on the part of its representatives in Parliament. For the aforesaid object the Committee should be sole authority granting the right to back Bills, or support measures, directly or indirectly affecting Labour. The Executive shall organise a Committee within the House of Commons, of Labour

Party Members, to instruct and advise its fellow members on all Parliamentary work.[41]

This uncompromising prescription once again went to a card vote, and lost by 590,000 to 229,000.

Tillett's biographer, Jonathan Schneer, believes that his critique of the Labour Representation Committee had 'so far . . . come from the right'. This hardly fits the evidence. Undoubtedly it is true, as Schneer insists, that personal acrimony between Hardie and MacDonald on the one side, and the dockers' leader on the other, ran at a very high level. In such a scrimmage, people might not worry overmuch about which cudgel to use, in which hand. Neither would they be squeamish about where their blows landed. But although Tillett's dubious friendship with Horatio Bottomley was close enough to permit him to accept financial help to enable him to voyage again to Australia, his overall political commitment had remained very strongly on the left throughout this period. We can see it in the Report to his union in 1905:

> Mr. Charles Booth indicates 4 per cent of the criminal and wastrel class as being voluntary agents of their own downfall by drink, yet a criminal class of less than 1 per cent of the whole population, and only 4 per cent even of this class, are indicated as offering a cause of poverty to the other 99 per cent. It is a pity that so-called leaders of labour subscribe to this mendacity, which only ignorance or wilfulness would ever stoop to make use of.
>
> The restoration to the people of the confiscated thousand millions, the recovery for the community's benefit, of lands, capital, and industrial machinery, will find ample scope for the services of those who claim to serve the country.
>
> Nothing but an economic adjustment can ever suffice as a remedy. I have carefully investigated the services and bonafides of the persons preaching thrift, etc. and without an exception, not one of them has ever done, or even desires to render, service to the community, aiming at least at the abolition of poverty. We ought not to be the victims of time-servers, or permit our sacred cause to be side-tracked by charlatans or incompetents. To create an environment making possible the development of the best types of humanity, with all the aids of civilisation generously at command, and equality of opportunity, with working, sleeping and living conditions, conducing to efficiency; by these means, and these only, can we make for happiness or goodness. There is already a change in thought, and my wish is, that we may have a change in action, in methods making for the acquisition of all the powers ensuring for political and social justice.
>
> Any change in government ought not to act as a soporific, for it is still the same class struggle, whichever party may be in power.[42]

In Australia, Tillett met up again with Tom Mann, and caught some of the feverish *élan* which accompanied his crusade in the Antipodes. He did not return until early 1908.

Abusing and Accusing

Tillett's next onslaught began straight away as an exchange of letters about the need to campaign against unemployment. The Dockers' Union Executive was moved to complain that a number of Labour members had been appearing with Cabinet ministers and prominent Liberals 'on platforms all over the country, in some cases consorting with well known union-smashers'. In particular, the dockers called upon the Executive 'to request explanations of Messrs. Henderson, Shackleton, Richards, Crooks, Duncan, Snowden and others, whose expenses . . . have been met by the Temperance-Liberal party over the last 12 months.'[43]

Shortly afterwards the Willesden Labour Party wrote urging support by the Parliamentary Labour Party for an initiative by Victor Grayson demanding immediate attention to the problem of unemployment. The Oldham Branch of the Social Democratic Party wrote in similar terms. Ramsay MacDonald replied to both letters in a strangely abusive style. To Willesden he said:

> If you understood the methods of getting things done in Parliament you will see that the very last thing to be done in the interest of the unemployed is to adopt your . . . resolution . . . there is nothing more disheartening to our Parliamentary work than the way that well intentioned supporters like yourselves are misled by proposals that appear to be energetic, but which in actual fact are utter rubbish.

In his reply to the Oldham SDP, MacDonald's low threshold of courtesy was lowered even further:

> I am in receipt of yours of the 18th which, knowing as I do the general stupidity of the SDP . . . gives me no surprise. It is perfectly evident that your members, or, at any rate that part of them which voted for the resolution, care nothing for doing anything for the unemployed, but prefer to gas copiously about them . . . The stupid tub-thumpers who compose the SDP glorify an exhibition of weakness and incompetence.

MacDonald wrote in a similar vein to correspondents in a number of other cities, and Tillett gathered some of the replies and published them. They made his point more convincingly than his own arguments, which were equally strident. He also published an abrasive exchange in which, writing on behalf of the union, he accused leading members of the Labour Party in Parliament of giving temperance priority over employment, and strongly hinted that this decision had come about because some Labour leaders had been subsidised by Temperance money.

If MacDonald had been rude in his answers, Tillett was not exactly polite in his accusations. In a pamphlet provocatively entitled *Is the Parliamentary Labour Party a Failure?*, he hit out:

> Why should not the unemployed demand food, the right to live, with vehemence commensurate to the tragedy, and resent with physical violence the callous fate the rich leave them to? There is no argument against the 'right to live', with wealth and production so far advanced as at present. Something must be done to make the rich think over the murderings and starvings under the system which gives them plenty and the wealth-maker nothing at all of the wealth produced.

What forces, he continued, can cope with the increase in unemployment?

> In the House of Commons, flatulent paunches shake under dress waistcoats in laughter at the sally of a Minister utilising some heartless gibe against the Labour Party. On the boards of guardians, hell's own conspiracy is at work to circumvent the law, inadequate though it be. Relief committees spend 80 per cent of their income in expenses, turning out of their mean minds drivel and lies to excuse their wickedness, and damning the poor all round. Political parties edge and shuffle; the Labour Party is not seriously awake to the evils . . .

Echoing Tolstoy, Tillett continued: 'The army of central and local government officials will not get off the backs of the poor, but pile themselves as comfortably as possible with the rest of the thieves.'

From this appreciation he went on in the same vein to denounce Temperance Liberalism as humbug, and to allege that Labour leaders had been suborned by Temperance bribery to forget their true social commitments.

> The duties of the Labour Party should be to look to the purely economic interests of the workers, and avoid as contagion any form of 'red-herring' politics. If liberty be given one section, the movement will be faced with divergent groups of Tariff Reformers, Free Traders, Disestablishers, House of Lords Reformers and Abolitionists, Educational hair-splitters, the while such an important matter as Unemployment is neglected. Poverty is due to the lack of means to live, and as the means of life is the property of capitalists, the Labour Party should exist to combat the system whereby the many are deprived of the means and rights of existence.[44]

Tillett and the SDF

Shortly after the pamphlet was published by the SDF's Twentieth Century Press, Tillett became a regular contributor to Harry Quelch's newspaper, *Justice*. In its columns he continued to berate 'the Temperance bleating martyrs'.

All this helped the majority of the SDF to keep their members out of the Labour Party. The 1908 Labour Party Conference at Hull had carried an ASE motion fixing the party's objects, which included 'the Socialisation of the means of production, distribution and exchange, to be controlled by a democratic State in the interests of the entire community, and the complete emancipation of labour from the domination of capitalism and landlordism'.[45]

Since this declaration of faith precisely mirrored that of the SDF, it is hardly surprising that some of the Federation's members sought to reaffiliate to the party. Dan Irving, of Burnley, was a consistent supporter of affiliation, as well as a great admirer of H. M. Hyndman. In 1908 Hyndman himself came down on the side of rejoining the Labour forces. But the opposition, led by Tillett's friend Quelch, defeated the reunion by a majority of 100 at the Federation's conference.[46] Evidently Tillett's pamphlet caught a mood of intransigence and helped ensure the continued separation of the social democrats.

Hyndman had already embraced Tillett in 1906, when, after the General Election, he travelled to Eccles in an effort to persuade the local Labour movement to re-adopt Tillett as a candidate, following his defeat earlier that year. He had come third, with almost 4,000 votes, in a seat won by a Liberal. The voters of Eccles did not think their Labour candidate was a man of the right, and the local ILP reflected their fear of extreme rhetoric by threatening to withhold support if he were re-adopted. The following year saw the Stuttgart Congress of the Socialist International, which was attended by sixty-one SDF delegates, together with thirty from the ILP and nine from the Labour Party. There were also sixteen Fabians.

When a delegate of the Dockers' Union was debarred from speaking on the question of 'blackleg' labour at Hamburg, 'the British section rose en masse in their seats to protest, Hyndman . . . acting as protestant-in-chief':

Hyndman, with his locks, flowing beard, and waving arms, hurled unparliamentary imprecations at the chair. He shouted out that he and his fellow-British delegates had been supremely self-effacing at the congress, that the German and French speakers had, by their long-winded orations . . . monopolised and dissipated the time of the congress. Cries of 'Order, order! Chair, chair!' in a dozen different languages rose simultaneously in the hall. But Hyndman stood like Casabianca on the burning deck, amidst the flames of Continental wrath, and would not sit down. He was flatly and transparently out of order; he was wildly and shamelessly anarchistic; but the British delegates abetted him in his 'manifestation'.[47, 48]

Tillett's adherence to the SDF was, in the light of these events, not the most unlikely event of the year. Meanwhile, Bruce Glasier wrote that

Tillett 'should be forever disqualified from comradeship in the ranks of self-respecting members of the Party.'[49]

While all this was going on, a new talent was beginning to assert itself.

A New Star Appears

Ben Tillett, thought the historians of the Social Democratic Federation, was not very closely embroiled with the Bristol branch, even though he was born in the city and maintained some family connections; but 'In a later period Ernest Bevin was much more closely associated with the Bristol organisation, and fought his first contest as a candidate for the Bristol City Council in 1909.'[50]

Born in 1881, Ernest Bevin had a hard childhood. He never knew his father, and his mother died when he was eight years old, after which he was cared for by his half-sister and her husband, George Pope, a railwayman. He went to school in Crediton, in Devonshire, and within a year he had reached standard IV and was thus entitled to claim a Labour Certificate and leave; but he stayed on for almost one full additional year, until March 1892. At the age of eleven he started work as a farm boy, living in, with a wage of 6*d*. a week. After moving from one farm to another for a couple of years, he decided to explore the golden streets of Bristol, and at the age of thirteen he went to live with his brother Jack, a butcher. He sold pies, then became a van-boy delivering mineral water. By 1897 he was a tram conductor, and at the turn of the century he was earning 12*s*. a week. When his brother moved, he had to find lodgings, and he also found himself out of work. For two months before the relief of Mafeking he was amongst the unemployed. Then he got work with another mineral-water manufacturer, who also employed his brother Fred. After a year, he had become a permanent driver. By now he was earning 18*s*., plus a commission of 1*d*. a gross on empty bottles. He worked from six in the morning until six at night, after which he groomed the horse. But 'once he had loaded up at the York Street yard . . . he was his own master. The job, in fact, gave him the independence and out-of-doors life which he wanted'.[51]

Alan Bullock tells us about Bevin's tour of the adult-education institutions of Bristol, and his training in nonconformity. But by 1905 he had become a socialist. The Bristol Socialist Society was an outpost of the Social Democratic Federation, and co-existed, at times uneasily, with two branches of the Independent Labour Party. Bevin joined the SDF. To be precise, 'he joined the Bristol Socialist Society, which affiliated to the Federation during 1906'.[52] Bullock reports the reminiscence of Bristol Alderman Milton: 'I think the first time Ernest Bevin spoke was at St. George's Park Gates [an ILP patch] but he did not like the ILP too well. He thought they were social reformers and preferred the Bristol

Socialist Society, who had now become affiliated to the SDF, and who, Ernest thought, had more of the revolutionist spirit.'[53]

Bevin rapidly became a stump-orator. For a time he ran a café and a coffee stall, but by 1908 he was once again working as a carter. This and the following year saw very bad unemployment, and indeed it was at this time that Bevin cut his teeth as a political organizer, as the secretary of a new Right to Work Committee, which lobbied and deputized on behalf of the unemployed. He worked to considerable effect. Very likely he would have used Ben Tillett's new pamphlet on the failure of the Parliamentary Labour Party, precisely inasmuch as it roasted the shortcomings of parliamentarians as agitators for jobs. Because of the skills he showed in this campaign, Bevin was asked to organize a relief fund for the dockers when they came out on strike at Avonmouth in June 1910. At this point he was spotted by Harry Orbell, the Dockers' Union national officer. 'On behalf of the Executive Council', Orbell invited Bevin to become 'delegate for the Carters and Warehousemen of Bristol, and so successful was the appointment that the General Secretary soon called upon him to accept responsibility for much greater efforts than he had anticipated in Southampton, Cardiff, and the whole of the west and other ports of England.'[54]

Bullock describes how members of the ILP had tried to organize the carters into the Workers' Union, and how Bevin outmanoeuvred the opposition to bring them into the Dockers' Union instead. The technical argument concerned whether the Workers' Union was affiliated to the local Trades Council, and it gave Bevin the victory. But we are bound to suspect that here, as in other sectors, there was stiff in-fighting between adherents of the ILP and supporters of the SDP (the Federation changed its name to 'Party' in April 1908). The carmen promptly designated him their first chairman. He was twenty-nine years old.

In short order, Bevin negotiated recognition for his branch, and by March 1911 a Joint Arbitration Board, consisting of seven people from the union and seven employer-representatives, was in place. The union leadership was impressed. That spring Orbell invited Bevin to join the staff of the Dockers' Union on a salary of £2 a week.

Tillett was later to claim that he had 'spotted' Bevin and marked him down for promotion. In the late 1930s he would hold forth in the Trade Union Club about all the victories and traumas of his life, and about the wickedness of Bevin, whom he had 'found and made' and who had 'pushed him to one side'.[55]

A Red Cell?

In truth, Bevin's emergence almost certainly involved a more collective process of 'discovery'. As an effective campaigner in Bristol, he would have met Tillett during his public meetings there. Tillett would have been arguing the cause of the SDP, and his weekly journalism on behalf of the party would certainly have been read by the young activists of the West Country.

But Orbell, too, was an SDP member. George Lansbury, originally from the same school of thought, remembered him as a 'happy, full faced, fresh-coloured man, always cheery, and in the most depressing circumstances quite undismayed and confident that the workers' cause would triumph'. He was, said Lansbury, a 'professional agitator'. Like Lansbury himself, he was a Christian.[56]

As national organizer, Orbell was in a position to ensure that the activists of his small party extended their influence in the Dockers' Union.[57] As Eric Hobsbawm has pointed out, the Gasworkers' Union was 'the nearest thing to a "red" body conceivable before the foundation of Communist Parties . . . virtually all its national and district leaders were Marxian social democrats.'[58] By the time of the great unrest, the nucleus which guided the Dockers' Union was no less 'red'. It joined with Lansbury in promoting the *Daily Herald*. Ernest Bevin's commitment to this long outlasted his apprenticeship to Ben Tillett. We shall examine this a little later in our narrative.

'Meanwhile, the education of the upper strata of the working classes grew apace. Elementary education, continuation schools, debating societies, cheap reprints of some of the best books, socialist propaganda, the classes conducted by the Workers' Educational Association . . . and Ruskin College at Oxford have produced a young generation of working men responsive to the mental currents of the time.'[59] All this led Max Beer to conclude that 'Great Britain possesses now what it never possessed: Labour intellectuals with a healthy desire for the study of economics, social history and science.'[60]

Socialist Agitators and Educators

The election of 1906 had provoked a surge in expectations, and, when these were not met, an outright rebellion. This was soon to rage across the entire economy, and nowhere more violently than in the transport industry. But it began with a mutiny in workers' education, when the students at Ruskin demanded classes in Marxian economics, formed the Plebs League and then broke away, in 1909, to set up a Central Labour College, first in Oxford, then in London.

A considerable effort had developed the thinking of this revolt. The Labour press, especially the newspapers the *Labour Leader*, *Clarion* and *Justice*, underwent a rapid growth. But book publishing also transmuted, with cheap editions of radical classics from the Rationalist Press Association, and Kerr's editions of the writings of Marx and other socialists, imported from Chicago. Hostile witnesses greeted this cultural revolution with dismay:

> At the present time the Socialists are spending between £250,000 and £300,000 every year on organisation and propaganda. In a word, incredible as it may seem, they spend more money, hold more meetings, and circulate more political literature than the Liberal and Conservative parties together. These things could not be done if there were no movement among the people . . . It is estimated that more than a million working-men have been through the branches of the Independent Labour Party and the Social Democratic Party, and assimilated their confiscatory doctrines; and it is certain that fully five or six million others have been influenced by the incessant meetings . . . [61]

No doubt these guesses were far from accurate. But it was not the inflated statistics of revolt which frightened the anti-socialist propagandists so much as the growth of 'extremism' around the fringes of the new movement. The SDF had twice split in the earliest years of the century, to give rise first to the Socialist Party of Great Britain and then to the Socialist Labour Party, based in Scotland but inspired by the doctrines of Daniel De Leon from the United States. 'They are, as a whole, the best-informed Socialists in the Country, and would make incomparable soldiers, or desperate barricadists. As revolutionaries they deserve no mercy: as men they command respect.'[62]

Now they were to be rejoined by two giants, Tom Mann and James Connolly. Both were incorruptibles, both were committed internationalists, and both were to be completely identified with the transport workers, in thought and in deed. And the deeds which followed were to shake the world.

II

Tom Mann Is Back!

On 16 May 1910 the Tom Mann Reception Committee assembled 250 of its supporters and mustered at the dockside to meet their comrade, returning from his long voyages to New Zealand, Australia and South Africa. Ben Tillett and Guy Bowman waited inside a roped enclosure. 'Almost his first words when we met him were: "let's go and see the men of the Direct Action" '.[63]

A fortnight later Mann and Bowman were in Paris, meeting with the leaders of the General Federation of Labour. Within six weeks they had produced the first of a series of penny pamphlets, under the title the *Industrial Syndicalist*. Number 1 was on sale in July, edited by Mann and published by Bowman. Its title was 'Prepare for Action'.[64] Prepared in an especially thin format, designed to fit into an overall pocket, it was a little bomb; in its twenty-four pages Tom Mann distilled his entire experience as a trade-union organizer. Gone were the appeals for arbitration. Experience in Australia and New Zealand had persuaded Mann that state intervention was normally to Labour's detriment, and that only organization, and then better organization, could win for the unions. 'Chief among our faults is our remarkable gullibility. We have been singularly ready to take the word for the deed – and take it with a degree of gratitude and enthusiasm that has gladdened the hearts of the capitalists'.

'Many sops', wrote Mann, 'have been thrown to the snarling Demos. The earliest on record were "bread and circuses". The latest are profit-sharing and Old Age Pensions. But never before have the masters been face to face with a literate and coherent democracy.'

Such a democracy had built trade unionism, powerful co-operatives, and political and municipal organizations. Through these agencies, workers had participated in educational and administrative bodies, and elected, around the world, 'hundreds of members of Parliaments and thousands of municipal councillors'. Too often these representatives had been overcome by the logic of detailed reform, losing sight of the fundamental objectives of the movements which had brought them to office. There had arisen a self-serving discussion on the merits of revolution or evolution, which sought to displace the one by the other. 'You can't', said Mann, 'change the world and yet not change the world. Revolution is the means of, not the alternative to, evolution'. Yet the call of this clarion was carefully composed. It did not refuse political action. What it did was to extol direct industrial action, and organization on the industrial plane.

Here is an example from the first pennyworth:

Direct Action and Syndicalism

. . . what will have to be the essential conditions for . . . success . . .?
That it will be avowedly and clearly Revolutionary in aim and method.

Revolutionary in aim, because it will be out for the abolition of the wages system and for securing to the workers the full fruits of their labour, thereby seeking to change the system of Society from Capitalist to Socialist.

Revolutionary in method, because it will refuse to enter into any long agreements with the masters, whether with legal or State backing, or merely voluntarily . . .

Does this mean that we should become anti-political? Certainly not.

Let the politicians do as much as they can, and the chances are that, once there is an economic fighting force in the country, ready to back them up by action, they will actually be able to do what now would be hopeless for them to attempt to do.

This view of the political process was one that Mann would soon abandon. But he did not abandon his principal commitment to the view that change would come only when working people began to appreciate their own strength:

> The curse of Capitalism consists in this – that a handful of capitalists can compel hundreds of thousands of workers to work in such manner and for such wages as please the capitalists. But this again is solely because of the inability of the workers to agree upon a common plan of action. The hour the workers agree and act they become all-powerful. We can settle the capitalists' strike-breaking power once for all. We shall have no need to plead with Parliamentarians to be good enough to reduce hours – as the workers have been doing for fully twenty years without result. We shall be able to do this ourselves – and there will be no power on earth to stop us so long as we do not fall foul of economic principles . . . Police and Cabinet alike become powerless to enforce the dictates of the bureaucracy when the workers are united.[65]

Was this the classic statement of syndicalism? Tom Mann himself had produced a pamphlet on industrial unionism in Australia in 1909, a few days before he received a copy of James Connolly's fervent pamphlet *Socialism Made Easy: The Industrial and Political Unity of Labour*.

A great deal has been written about the alleged inconsistencies of syndicalist doctrine. In point of fact, there are at least two kinds of inconsistency that can arise within any political doctrine. Its followers may be led, in the test of practical action, to adopt views which are not consonant with their own principles: or, more seriously from the point of view of the logic of the doctrine, contradictory facets may be discovered within the original fabric of thought itself. There were many syndicalists, who drew their ideas from many sources. At one extreme, there were ethical socialists upon whom the main influence came from Christian writers of various kinds, culminating in the modern writings of Chesterton and Belloc, whose *Servile State* (1912) was a warning to many. It expounded the dangers of state socialism, but it could also be read as an indictment of many lesser encroachments of government intervention. Connolly was a Catholic, and had called down on his own head the anathemas of his Church, and the stern admonitions of the leader of his party, the Socialist Labour Party of the United States. Mann, as we have seen, toyed with the ideas of taking orders in the Anglican Church. Another wing of the movement was sternly secular, influenced by Darwin, and to a lesser extent by Marx, and by the numerous rationalist booklets of the time. Rational, it may have proclaimed itself. Tolerant, it was usually not.

The idea of workers' control stimulated men's imaginations, so that they not only began to think and act for themselves but also found that their thoughts and deeds brought them up sharply against widely diverse features of the industrial order to which they were reacting. It would be astonishing if all responded in the same way to these different shocks. A live movement *lives*. As Goethe told us, 'grey is every theory, but green is the living tree of life'.

Some Roots of Syndicalism: Marx

And yet there was a remarkable continuity between the ideas of Tom Mann and those he accepted as his tutors. Marx, for instance, drafted a widely published resolution for the International Working Men's Association:

Trades' Unions. Their Past, Present, and Future
(a) Their past.
Capital is concentrated social force, while the workman has only to dispose of his individual working force. The contract between capital and labour can therefore never be struck on equitable terms, equitable even in the sense of a society which places the ownership of the material means of life and labour on one side and the vital productive energies on the opposite side. The only social power of the workmen is their number. The disunion of the workmen is created and perpetuated by their unavoidable competition amongst themselves.
Trades' Unions originally sprung up from spontaneous attempts of workmen at removing or at least checking that competition in order to conquer such terms of contract as might raise them at least above the condition of mere slaves. The immediate object of Trades' Unions was therefore confined to everyday necessities, to expedients for the obstruction of the incessant encroachments of capital; in one word, to questions of wages and time of labour. This activity of the Trades' Unions is not only legitimate, it is necessary. It cannot be dispensed with so long as the present system of production lasts. On the contrary, it must be generalised by the formation and combination of Trades' Unions throughout all countries. On the other hand, unconsciously to themselves, the Trades' Unions were forming centres of organisation of the working class, as the mediaeval municipalities and communes did for the middle class. If the Trades' Unions are required for the guerilla fights between capital and labour, they are still more important as organised agencies for superseding the very system of wage labour.
(b) Their present.
Too exclusively bent upon the local and immediate struggles with capital, the Trades' Unions have not yet fully understood their power of action against the system of wages slavery itself. They therefore kept too much aloof from general and political movements. Of late, however, they seem to awaken to some sense of their great historical mission, as appears,

for instance, from their participation, in England, in the recent political movement . . .

(c) Their future.

Apart from their original purposes they must now learn to act deliberately as organising centres of the working class in the broad interest of its complete emancipation. They must aid every social and political movement tending in that direction. Considering themselves and acting as the champions and representatives of the whole working class, they cannot fail to enlist the non-society men into their ranks. They must look carefully after the interests of the worst paid trades, such as the agricultural labourers, rendered powerless by exceptional circumstances. They must convince the world at large that their efforts, far from being narrow and selfish, aim at the emancipation of the downtrodden millions.[66]

Annie Besant as an Influence

To a remarkable extent, this view was carried down the years, so that it was still contemporary at the time of the great dock strike. Annie Besant, a staunch Fabian, echoed it the year before she set out to organize the matchgirls:

Why would it be worse to have one's labor controlled by the State than to have it controlled by the individual employer? A workman does not control his labor now; he must sell it for what he can get for it. His labor is controlled by the individual manufacturer, who controls it for his own advantage; whereas the State would control it for the corporate advantage in which the worker would share. But it is, of course, not practicable that the State, as a whole should direct and control the labor of each individual. For what is the State? It is the people, organised as a community. As a whole, the State could not control the labor of each citizen; but when the people are organised in groups of workers, each group can very well control its own labor, and elect its own superintendents, as well as elect such representatives as might be necessary to constitute boards of management to keep group in touch with group. The Trades Unions have in them the germs of the necessary organisation. If every miner were in the Miners' Union, then that union, with its branches in every coal district, would be the body which would immediately control the production of coal in a Socialist state. Can Radicals, who have fostered Trades Unions and urged the workers to combine, oppose a development of them? Can they, who have so preached self-reliance and self-government, maintain that men must always work for masters, and that they are not competent to control their own labor and to regulate their own production?[67]

For Tom Mann, doctrine was always intimately related to practice:

My industrial and political faith is as follows: (1) Industrial solidarity is the real power to effect economic changes. By this I mean that even though resort be had to Parliament it is only effective when the demand is made as the result of intelligent and courageous industrial organisation. It was thus that the Factory Acts were obtained and all other legislation that in any degree is economically advantageous to the workers. (2) The chief economic change must be the reduction of working hours. All through our industrial history nothing stands out more clearly than this, that the reducing of working hours is a genuine method of raising the standard, economically and ethically correct. (3) By a drastic reduction of working hours we can absorb the unemployed. The cure for unemployment is the chief concern of revolutionaries and reformers, and the most natural, most simple, and most effective of all methods is by absorbing them into the ranks of the employed, so apportioning the work to be done over the total number to do it. (4) By removing competition for work we gain the power to get higher wages. (5) It is necessary for every worker to belong to a union, and for every union to unite with every other union in the same industry. (6) Unite to fight, fight to achieve your economic emancipation. (7) Under existing circumstances it is not desirable that membership of an industrial organisation should pledge one to specific political action. (8) Parliamentary action is secondary in importance to industrial action; it is industrial action alone that makes political action effective, but with or without Parliamentary action, industrial solidarity will ensure economic freedom, and therefore the abolition of capitalism and all its accompanying poverty and misery. (9) To ensure industrial solidarity it is necessary that the finances of the unions should be so kept that the Friendly Society benefits should be kept entirely separate from the industrial, so that every union on its industrial side may amalgamate with every other union in the same industry.[68]

None of this said anything about syndicalism.

The French Connection

Tom Mann himself was always at pains to point out that 'syndicalism' was no more than an anglicized version of the French word meaning 'trade unionism'. Even in France, as its historian insists:

Syndicalism was a movement rather than a theory. It was a general trend within the French labour movement, a range of ideas rather than an agreed body of doctrine. Primarily, indeed, it was a way of looking at politics, a temper which was expressed in action, rather than in clearly formulated ideas. The C.G.T. [Confédération Générale du Travail] adopted a number of principles, never a philosophy. Nor did its theorists produce a really unified body of thought. They wrote for the worker rather than the social philosopher. They dealt with issues of the moment. Their ideas were scattered in newspapers, pamphlets and speeches. Nowhere did they attempt to bring these ideas together within the covers of a single book. It would have been difficult for them to do so. Their views changed;

they did not always agree. Even at the level of the printed word, therefore, no integrated system of ideas, certainly no definitive philosophy, was produced by the syndicalists themselves.[69]

Revolutionary syndicalism in France based itself on the ideas of Fernand Pelloutier, and his disciple Émile Pouget. The conditions to which they were responding were different, in a wide range of ways, from those confronting Tom Mann and his colleagues. The French trade unions had polarized in an acrimonious debate about the role of the general strike in their strategy. The first May Day demonstrations, in 1890, had been organized by two separate groups, one favouring the perspective of a revolutionary general strike, the other strongly opposing it. This dual sponsorship persisted, but in 1891 there were serious clashes at some of the demonstrations, and a girl was killed when soldiers fired on a demonstration at Fourmies. In the angry reaction, the militants gathered strength.

In 1892 a new federation was formed – the Bourse du Travail. Pelloutier became the secretary and spokesman of this federation in 1893. English syndicalists were to translate the term 'Bourse du Travail' as 'Trades Council', although this description greatly underrepresented the range of functions undertaken by the French organizations. In origin, they were indeed labour exchanges, as their name implied. They were set up in opposition to the private employment offices which had been established to serve the employers. These private agencies had a dual role: on the one hand they charged applicants for placing them in jobs. On the other, they exercised strong discrimination against trade unionists and maintained lively blacklists. Initially, the Bourses du Travail developed in response to the pressures of the moderate trade unionists, and frequently called upon institutional support from local authorities or the prefectural administrations. But once the Bourses became associated in a national network, the debate on the general strike swept into their forum and carried all before it. It was this commitment which so shocked the parliamentary wing of the Socialist International, back in 1896, when Tom Mann was organizing the London Congress.

Pelloutier began his short political life as a journalist working for Aristide Briand, who, during the early 1890s, was passing through a phase of leftist extremism; later he was to occupy a quite different place in the political spectrum. But Pelloutier was not content with the often demagogic invocation of the general strike. For many of its advocates this was a secular version of the second coming. It would happen spontaneously, of its own accord: and as a result of it, all would be made anew. 'Not at all,' argued Pelloutier. Such a strike would not happen without organized preparation, and even if it did its outcome would be in doubt, unless the workers knew what to do when it happened. It was necessary to have a precise vision of the kind of society which the workers wished to bring into being. For this vision, Pelloutier called upon a rich anarchist tradition in the French Labour movement. He developed the notion of a federation of communes, from a self-regulating community of free individuals to a focus of producer co-ops. Every working collective would be associated in a local syndicat, which would include all the various trades and crafts employed within it. The management would be elected by the producers, who would work for the commune, in which the ownership of the enterprise would be vested. The commune itself would be administered by delegates from all the syndicats within its area. Where more general administrative problems arose, they would be confronted by wider, federated agencies, representing at a higher level, of region or nationality, the primary communes of producers.

All this echoed previous discussions, going back to the days of the First International, founded in 1864. But Pelloutier was completely unambiguous in his blueprint. For him, the heart and soul of the new society was the local trade-union organization. Within the framework of workers' control, all the conventional tasks of trade unionism could be subsumed. Unions must control hiring and firing, apprenticeships, training and promotion. To discharge these functions, and thus monopolize labour supply, they must take on profound educational functions. Managers must be educated from within a trade-union academy. Every Bourse would thus maintain its workers' college, library and educational circles.

Anarchist Overtones

Pelloutier died in 1901 at the age of thirty-four. His book on the history of the labour exchanges was published the following year. Far more widely read was a popular tract, half novel, half programmatic statement, by his followers Émile Pataud and Émile Pouget. This was translated into English under the title: *Syndicalism and the Co-operative Common-wealth (How We Shall Bring About the Revolution)*.[70] It appeared in Britain in 1913 with a foreword by Tom Mann, a preface by the Russian anarchist Prince Peter Kropotkin, and a series of striking cartoons by Will Dyson. In so far as British workers came under the direct influence of French syndicalists, this book was undoubtedly a main source. Most British activists, however, were responding to a message from sources nearer to home.

The French syndicalists were far more consistently hostile to political, or parliamentary, forms of action than was Tom Mann in 1910. One of his first actions then was to join up with the SDP, alongside his comrade Tillett. Later he left the organization, and he was to become more distinctly reserved about parliamentary politics; during the war he was actively hostile to the Labour Party for this reason. But his judgements on parliamentary politics throughout this period seem to have been more tactical than strategic. For the French, political sociology argued a more fixed course:

> the proletariat did not form a majority of the electorate in France at the turn of the century. The socialist party must therefore make electoral agreements: the class enemy becomes the friend of the polls. The same thing necessarily occurs in parliament. The socialists' only hope of ministerial office lay in collaboration with bourgeois parties. Policy degenerates into bargaining, concessions and ultimately a betrayal of the working class. The parliamentary milieu is itself bourgeois and thus a further corrupting influence.[71]

This coloured a series of consequent attitudes:

> Whatever benefits may be gained for the working class as a result of compromise, they cannot compensate for its dangers. Democracy is a system designed by the bourgeoisie for bourgeois domination. It is a façade to hide the real nature of social conflict; its ideology – universal franchise, equality before the law – distracts from the real economic inequality that it protects. The parliamentary game is, in the last analysis, but a means of diverting the energy of the proletariat into harmless channels.
> Social legislation is part of this attempt to stifle the class war. Reforms do not alter the fundamental property relations and concede nothing of real importance. They do, however, undermine the class struggle by creating an impression of benevolence and social harmony. They are the crumbs the rich man throws from his table to satisfy the hunger of a proletariat that would otherwise be driven to revolt. Genuine concessions are never achieved through parliamentary action but only through the direct action of the workers themselves.[72]

For this reason, French syndicalists identified with their unions, not with parties. Bowman was more 'French' than Mann about this, but less able to draw support from British unions, so that, within a year or so, the two men were to find themselves at odds. What is clear is that if Mann had simply sought to become the evangelist of a cross-Channel creed, his impact would not have been at all comparable to what it actually was. Bowman's influence, by contrast, is a matter for the footnotes.

Connolly Comes Home

While Tom Mann was arranging the publication of his monthly letters on syndicalism in 1910, another wanderer was coming home, this time from the United States. On 26 July, James Connolly arrived in Derry. His mission was to superintend the publication of his journal the *Harp*, recently transferred from America to Dublin. The Irish edition was to have been edited by James Larkin; however, Connolly disembarked in time to find that his colleague was otherwise engaged. To see him it was necessary to go to Mountjoy gaol: he had been sentenced to one year's imprisonment with hard labour on a baseless charge of fraud. Meanwhile, his new union, the Irish Transport and General Workers' Union, was being hammered by employers on the one side and obstructed by some of the related English unions on the other.

James Connolly was born in Edinburgh in 1868, the third son of Irish immigrants. His father was a manure carter, working for the Edinburgh Corporation. James himself became a compositor's labourer on the *Edinburgh Evening News* after his tenth birthday. Since even the factory inspector thought this was too early for the boy to be employed, the discovery of his age led to his dismissal. He then found work in a bakery, and later in a tiling factory, until at the age of fourteen he enlisted in the King's Liverpool Regiment.

This regiment was heavily infiltrated by Fenians, so much so that it had been disarmed during the Fenian uprising for fear that it might take its weapons and join the rebels. Its guns were likewise confiscated and locked away during the Land League troubles of 1881: but by the following year the trouble was deemed to be under control, and when his battalion was sent to Ireland that year James Connolly paid his first visit to his family's homeland. It was a long tour of duty, lasting until the beginning of 1889.

At the same time that Connolly's regiment was recalled to Aldershot, his father was injured at work and consequently dismissed. Deeply worried, James deserted from the army and went to Scotland. Within a few months he had married and had become a socialist. He started to write for *Justice*, the journal of the social democrats, and began to speak at meetings of the Scottish Socialist Federation, of which his brother John became the secretary. By 1894 he was a candidate in the Edinburgh Municipal Elections. Then he was victimized. Without work, and with three daughters to care for, he was greatly relieved when in May 1896 the Dublin Socialist Club offered him a position of paid organizer.

In Dublin he formed the Irish Socialist Republic Party and began a programme of writing which was to have an enduring influence on the Irish Labour movement. The salary of Ireland's socialist organizer proved intermittent, and to eke it out Connolly did labouring jobs, found employment in the shipyard and became a publisher's proofreader. Even so, money was short and the family found the way to the pawn shop often enough.

Under such dire conditions were published the first essays which were to become *Labour in Irish History*. But although Connolly was from the beginning deeply involved in the movement for Irish independence, he was also, from the beginning, a committed internationalist. He became a correspondent for the American socialist *Weekly People*, the journal of the aggressively doctrinaire Daniel De Leon. In 1898 Connolly spent weeks in County Kerry reporting on the famine for this newspaper, and later the same year he was to launch a newspaper, *The Workers' Republic*, in Ireland.

All this agitation brought on the pronounced dissatisfaction of the Roman Catholic Church, which did not approve of socialism. When Connolly stood for election to the Dublin Municipal Council in 1901, priests told their flocks that no Catholic should vote for him, under pain of excommunication. After lecture tours in England and the United States, the hardship of life in Dublin became too much, and Connolly decided to emigrate to the United States. Here it was that he met the Industrial Workers of the World (IWW), the apostles of One Big Union for workers' control.

The American Experience

Daniel De Leon expressed the original idea of the IWW in a pamphlet entitled *The Socialist Reconstruction of Society* which first appeared in 1905.

> Political power is reached through the ballot-box. But the ballot-box is not an open field; it is a veritable defile. The defile is held by the agents of the Capitalist Class. The election inspectors and returning boards are capitalist appointees; they are veritable garrisons with which the Capitalist Class holds the defile. To imagine that these capitalist garrisons of the election defiles will complacently allow the candidate of the Revolution, whose programme is the dismantling of the political burg of capitalism, peacefully to file through, is to indulge in a mooncalf's vision. The revolutionary ballot of Labour is counted out now; it has been counted out from the first day of its appearance; it will be counted out even more extensively in the future. This fact is taken by some as a sufficient ground from which to conclude that the political Movement is utterly useless. Those who arrive at that conclusion fall into the error of failing to realise that correct conclusions never flow from single premises. They can be arrived at only by considering all the premises in the case . . .
>
> Without political organisation, the Labour Movement cannot triumph; without economic organisation, the day of its political triumph would be the day of its defeat.
>
> Industrialism means Might. Craft Unionism means impotence. All the plants of production, aye, even the vast wealth for consumption, is today in the keeping of the Working Class. It is workingmen who are in charge of the factories, the railroads, the mines; in short, all the land and machinery of production, and it is they also who sit as watch-dogs before the pantries, the cellars, and the safe deposit vaults of the capitalist class; aye, it is they who carry the guns to the armies.[73]

One Big Union

Connolly shared this view, and indeed never diverged from it. But De Leon's concept of politics was rigidly intolerant, and in 1908, while Connolly was still in the USA working with the IWW and the Socialist Party of Eugene Debs, it resulted in one of those resoundingly acrimonious splits for which the American Labor movement was to become so famous. Connolly drew the conclusion

> that since the political party was not to accomplish the revolution but only to lead the attack upon the political citadel of Capitalism, there no longer existed the same danger in the unclearness of its membership, nor compelling necessity for insisting upon its purification . . . it is our belief there will evolve . . .
> One Socialist party, embracing all shades and conceptions of Socialist political thought.
> One Socialist industrial organisation drilling the working class for the supreme mission of their class – the establishment of the Workers' Republic.[74]

In *Socialism Made Easy*, first published in Chicago after the dispute in the De Leonite ranks (and, as we have seen, coming into the hands of Tom Mann while he was still in Australia), Connolly set out his vision with limpid clarity:

> social democracy, as its name implies, is the application to industry, or to the social life of the nation, of the fundamental principles of democracy. Such application will necessarily have to begin in the workshop, and proceed logically and consecutively upwards through all the grades of industrial organization until it reaches the culminating point of national executive power and direction. In other words social democracy must proceed *from the bottom upward*, whereas capitalist political society is organized *from above downward*.
> Social democracy will be administered by a committee of experts elected from the industries and professions of the land;
> capitalist society is governed by representatives elected from districts, and is based upon territorial division.
> The local and national governing, or rather administrative, bodies of Socialists will approach every question with impartial minds, armed with the fullest expert knowledge born of experience; the governing bodies of capitalist society have to call in an expensive professional expert to instruct them on every technical question, and know that the impartiality of said expert varies with, and depends upon the size of his fee.

This conception of socialism, thought Connolly, 'destroys at one blow all the fears of a bureaucratic State, ruling and ordering the lives of every individual from above.' It would ensure that 'the social order of the future will be an extension of the freedom of the individual, and not the suppression of it.' Connolly continued:

> To focus the idea properly in your mind, you have but to realize how industry today transcends all limitations of territory and leaps across rivers, mountains and continents; then you can understand how impossible it would be to apply to such far-reaching intricate enterprises the principle of democratic control by the workers through the medium of political territorial divisions.
>
> Under Socialism, States, territories, or provinces will exist only as geographical expressions, and have no existence as sources of govern- mental power, though they may be seats of administrative bodies.
>
> Now, having grasped the idea that the administrative force of the Socialist republic of the future will function through unions industrially organized, that the principle of democratic control will operate through the workers correctly organized in such industrial unions, and that the political territorial State of capitalist society will have no place or function under Socialism, you will at once grasp the full truth embodied in the words of this member of the Socialist Party whom I have just quoted, that '*only the industrial form of organization offers us even a theoretical constructive Socialist programme*'.[75]

Syndicalism: Cause, Effect or Catalyst?

One historian after another has told us that such notions as these were 'an effect rather than a cause' of the great unrest, which was so shortly to follow.[76] Tom Mann, wrote Dangerfield, 'was one of the most successful and intelligent agitators in British Labour history', but for all that he could not shape his times. No one will deny that the syndicalists failed to reach their ultimate objectives. But their influence was direct and immediate, and men and events followed and reflected their counsel far more closely than is generally appreciated.

While their impact on the state and the social–economic order was contained, their interaction with the trade unions produced a result which was anything but neutral. Connolly played his part in the development of the Irish Transport and General Workers' Union, and this is the subject of our chapter 13; but he found himself learning from the members he led, and the mistakes of American industrial unionism were largely avoided in this process. The historians of the IWW tell us that 'For nearly a decade the IWW made little headway in organising basic industry. Landmark strikes in scattered geographic areas did little more than establish an IWW presence and style. Even the momentous 1912 victory at Lawrence failed to lead to permanent mass organisations in textiles.'[77]

Revolutionary unionism often sits uneasily with recognition, representation and the to-and-fro of collective bargaining. Strikes explode, organizers arrive to help them win, members are recruited and the agitators move on. Maybe more agitators are recruited, and maybe they move on. It is difficult enough to establish a stable, self-governing, continuous organization, even when you are trying to do so. To succeed without trying calls for a truly exceptional amount of luck.

Tom Mann always tried. That is why, however he changed his strategic view about the role of the state, and however the shifting power-balance moved to the combines, or to the workers, he always eschewed dual unionism.

For him, if workers were not strong enough to maintain control of their unions, they would never recover control of anything else. Breakaways might be quick, but they were always likely to prove brittle. To penetrate Tom Mann's thinking, it is always necessary to go to specifics. For him such universal ideas as he would embrace must always reveal themselves in particular, real, practical experience.

One Big Port Union?

The second penny number of the *Industrial Syndicalist* appeared in August 1910. It was entirely devoted to the transport industry. No other country had so large a proportion of its workforce engaged in this sector as Britain, wrote Mann. This resulted from British pre-eminence in shipping, carrying half the world's oceanic trade, and from a dominant position in export trade. As a result, Britain was surrounded by ports, with easy access to all sea-lanes. 'I was brought into close contact with the men in the carrying trades', he went on,

> when, as a social-democrat in the years 1885–8, I did my share of propaganda work among these men, but it was not until the London Dock Strike of 1889 that I became really intimate with . . . [their] conditions. And when I once grasped the full meaning of 'casual' labour . . . it gave me revolutionary stimulus . . . to do all that could be done to abolish such a system.

Now, twenty years on, it was time to take stock. In London the number of permanent men had increased and wages were a little higher. But the conditions of work had deteriorated with speed-up, while casualism was still the rule. 'The conditions of the *pre*-strike days obtain at present.' The cutting of the size of work-gangs had once again become the rule:

> Since the '89 period many changes have taken place in the method of unloading vessels. In the discharge of grain in bulk, for instance, which

prior to '89 in all the London docks except Millwall was done by hand; since that time the suction elevator or else the cup elevator, have been in general use, which has added enormously to the unemployed. A very moderate statement is that two men out of every three formerly employed in the discharge of grain are now dispensed with, i.e. thrown into the ranks of the unemployed. The system now resorted to is to have as few handlings of cargo as possible, and as little storage as possible. Thus at the Victoria Docks there are two flour mills. The grain is hauled in at one side of the mill from the vessel or lighter, and it goes through all the necessary processes almost without the aid of man. It is then lowered as flour from the other side of the mill into the barge ready for delivery; and every time an improved method of handling is resorted to, it means more profit for the Capitalists and more starvation for the Workmen.

In the discharge of bags of flour from a ship's hold, formerly there would be nine men in a gang in the hold, four men on each side of the boat and one man to hook on the sling. Now the pace is set so keenly that there are only three men on each side, that is, seven men instead of nine, to do the same work. This is when working under the crane. When working under the winch, less powerful than the crane, formerly they had six men in a gang, now only four, but there is the same amount of work to be done.

The same slave-driving was general in the discharge of cargoes of American flour. Mann gave a wealth of detail on working practices:

To sum up, on the average there are twenty thousand employed each day in the Port of London; but there are quite 40,000 more left out. It does not mean that 20,000 get regular work. It means that it is shared in an uneven way between the 60,000, only the permanent men getting regular employment.

It should not be necessary to urge that these conditions should be altered without delay.

Then comes the question 'who is to alter them?' And to that there is only one reply: The men themselves must do it. Ah, but How? There is only one way: viz. by proper Industrial Organisation.

'Now,' he continued, 'it is necessary to ask if the workers are properly organised.' The answer could only be 'No.'

one is compelled to admit that organisation is very far from being efficient.

The Dockers Union, with headquarters in London, has a membership in London and provinces of 14,000; and in the Bristol Channel ports many of the men are receiving 25 per cent, better conditions than before they were organised. But improved methods of doing the work are constantly being employed, resulting in more profits and less wages, and this is universally operative.

In the country generally, there are some twenty different Unions connected with the Transport or carrying Trades.

The Dockers Union, with headquarters at Liverpool, has also about 14,000 members, but as yet there is no real working arrangement between these two, or between these and either of the other Unions in the Transport Industry. The effects of this sectional unionism can be seen by what has just happened in the Welsh ports.

Here, Tom Mann drew the lessons of the struggle among trimmers and tippers for a half-day on Saturdays. The workers were in four separate unions, two being London-based, one being situated in Cardiff and another in Swansea:

I propose giving a few details in connection with this matter, because it serves well to illustrate the impossibility of effective action with the multiplicity of Unions, working each independent of the other; and in doing so I have one object only, and that is to bring to a head what I am sure is the desire of all the better men in each of these Unions, viz. the unifying of these respective organisations so that they shall become powerful for good, instead of being powerless as they are at present.

The ports where the men desired to get the Saturday half-holiday were Cardiff, Barry, Penarth, Swansea, Port Talbot and Newport.

Now to show the complexity of the situation:

In Cardiff, the Trimmers belong to the Coal Trimmers Union, but the Tippers belong to the A.S.R.S. In Newport, the Trimmers and Tippers belong to the Dockers Union. In Barry, the Trimmers belong to the C.T.U., but the Tippers belong to the A.S.R.S. In Port Talbot, the Trimmers and Tippers belong to the Dockers Union. In Penarth, the Trimmers belong to the C.T.U., but the Tippers belong to the A.S.R.S. In Swansea, the Trimmers and Tippers belong to the N.A.U.

Several Conferences were held between the delegates of these respective Unions, and it was agreed that notices should be given in as a preliminary to action to obtain the Saturday half-holiday. Then it transpired that one of the Unions was not prepared to give in notices. Another Conference was held and then it was found that another of the Unions was not prepared to take any action beyond informing the Shipowners and Brokers they would like to have the half-holiday; by which time the owners on their side, knowing perfectly well the sectional nature of the men's organisations, rode the high horse and declared that such a claim as that put forth for Coal Trimmers and Tippers to finish the week on Saturdays at 1 o'clock could not be entertained. If vessels needed coals the men must work till 5 o'clock, and if it was a case of getting the boat out by next tide, they must work till 8 o'clock on a Saturday; and so the matter is supposed to be settled.

This has just happened, the Owners had no reason to advance other than that the corresponding men in the North of England, at Hull, Shields, etc., worked these hours, and, therefore, they must continue so to work in Bristol Channel ports.

Now the Saturday half-day has been established over 40 years in many occupations, and there is no reason why men connected with coal loading should not have this condition as well as others. Ships are loaded now in half the time they were a few years ago, and there is no reason why Saturday afternoon should be worked any more than Sunday . . .[78]

Founding the National Transport Workers' Federation

Only sectional divisions, and the chaotic proliferation of unions, gave the employers the initiative. If the unions could work together, they would win: 'It is not necessary to dwell at greater length upon the necessity for unity. It is self-evident to every thoughtful person'.[79]

Ben Tillett was one such thoughtful person. He engaged with the doctrine immediately, above all for its advocacy of larger union unity for fighting purposes – whether in the form of industrial or general unionism. Tom Mann recorded his historic intervention without sensation. But in truth it was a momentous event:

Having been invited to attend an executive meeting of the Dockers' Union by the general secretary, my old colleague, Ben Tillett, I submitted a proposal urging that invitation be sent to the various Transport Workers' Unions with a view to forming a 'National Transport Workers' Federation'. This was done, and a conference, held in London, achieved the object.[80]

The invitation sent in the name of the Dockers' Union, July 1910, read:

The conditions of port workers in the United Kingdom, in common with all other workers, leave very much to be desired . . . In common with others we of the Dockers' Union desire to do all that is possible to bring about changes for the better: and we are glad to know that other unions are wishful to be at the work also . . .

We are of the opinion that there is urgent need for a genuine federation of all unions connected with the carrying trades and that this should be attempted without delay. The Executive of the Dockers' Union therefore respectfully make this overture to each of the other unions in the transport industry, and ask: – Will your organisation take part in a conference having in view the unifying of the transport workers' organisations in a genuine federation, for the purpose of taking such action as may be necessary for improving the standard of the workers in the transport industry, and to enable us to ally ourselves with all other industrial organisations for fighting purposes?[81]

Fifteen unions sent delegates to the founding conference, held in the Compositors' Hall, London, from 22 to 23 September 1910. They resolved to form a federation for the purposes of 'controlling and conducting disputes in the trades covered', preventing 'unwarrantable competition between unions for members, and . . . the overlapping of unions'.[82] They also agreed upon an immediate, combined, recruiting campaign. In November, seventeen unions took part in appointing a Rules Committee; in December the committee drafted a constitution; and fourteen unions attended the inaugural conference in March 1911.

Twelve unions sent delegates to the first General Council held three months later in Liverpool's Engineers' Hall. By June 1911 the following unions had affiliated: the Amalgamated Society of Watermen, Lightermen and Bargemen (2,244 members); the National Union of Dock Labourers (12,000); the National Sailors' and Firemen's Union (10,000); the National Union of Ships' Cooks, etc. (3,000); the Amalgamated Stevedores' Labour Protection League (4,000); the Upper Mersey Watermen and Porters (986); the Dock, Wharf, Riverside and General Labourers' Union (8,000); the National Union of Enginemen, Firemen, etc. (2,000); the National Union of Gasworkers and General Labourers (5,000); the London Carmen's Trade Union (4,000); the National Amalgamated Labourers' Union (2,096); and the South Side Labour Protection League (1,390).

Amongst unions withdrawing from the negotiations between November 1910 and June 1911 were the Amalgamated Society of Railway Servants, the General Railway Workers' Union, the National Amalgamated Union of Labourers, the Workers' Union, the London Cab Drivers, and the National Coal Porters. The Irish Transport and General Workers' Union attended the March conference, but was refused permission to affiliate on the grounds that it originated in a breakaway from the NUDL; the NUDL had submitted an objection to its membership and, at the June council meeting, it was resolved 'that the entrance fee of the Irish Transport Workers' Union be returned', Joseph Cotter and Frank Pearce, the delegates of the Ships' Cooks' Union, dissenting from the decision.

We shall have cause to review the affiliations again at later stages of the NTWF's history. At this stage we should note the absence of the largest inland transport unions: the Amalgamated Tramwaymen did not enter until 1918, following the lead of the London and Provincial Licensed Vehicle Workers, who joined in 1916. The road-passenger unions' initial judgement was that the Federation was weak in substance and potential; the rail unions came to similar conclusions.

Thus the NTWF in its initial form was overwhelmingly based on the waterfront unions. It was this which prompted the gasworkers and NALU to affiliate only their dock memberships in order to protect them from poaching. A rule declared: 'Where in any industrial undertaking there is a union already catering for men and having a branch or branches in existence for enrolling such men as members, no other affiliated union shall attempt to cater for members of that undertaking.'[83]

The NAUL, significantly, later affiliated only its London and Liverpool members, not its Newcastle dockers, 'who were unlikely to desert it',[84] since neither the Dockers' Union or the NUDL had a presence in the North-east. Rule XIII, moreover, stipulated that a member of a union with 'a controlling interest' in an area should have preference of employment, followed by members of other affiliated unions. This rule embodied the dockers' aim to deny the mass of general labour access to port employment. It resisted strongly, throughout the NTWF's existence, the idea of the single 'Federation ticket'. The general unions, on the other hand, were strong advocates of the ticket.

Harry Gosling, general secretary of the lightermen, was elected as the NTWF's first (and as it transpired, its only) president. The first secretary was James Anderson of the stevedores. These appointments emphasize the critical importance of the 'craft' unions' conversion to the cause of federation. It is certainly true to claim that 'without the adhesion of the Stevedores and Lightermen, the National Transport Workers' Federation could never have got off the ground in London'.[85] Yet Gosling later, with characteristic modesty and generosity, gave the credit for the NTWF's birth to Ben Tillett, who, he said, 'had long been urging closer union between the many organizations catering for transport workers'.[86] Tillett's understanding of the need for the goodwill of the specialist London unions is evident in his move to nominate Gosling for the presidency, and in stepping aside from the secretaryship to allow Anderson of the stevedores to take that post. Clearly, in its origins the NTWF was dominated by the London waterfront, the main outside lever being of course the Mersey-based NUDL, which had taken no part in the preliminary gatherings. (Sexton does not mention the 1910 meetings in his Annual Report for that year, nor does he refer to the NTWF in his memoirs.)

It remains to emphasize that, whilst the concept of the NTWF came from Tom Mann, and the organs and conferences of the Syndicalist League gave every encouragement to its formation, the NTWF was not 'a syndicalist artifact'.[87] It was formed for pragmatic reasons by trade-union leaders seeking solutions to both immediate and long-term problems of organization and effectiveness. Yet would it have been formed so soon if Tom Mann had stayed in Australia? With his encouragement, it was born on the eve of the greatest upheaval that the labouring people had ever created: and the fortunes of the NTWF were, for the next four years, intimately bound up with the elemental flux of militancy associated with the syndicalist spirit.

None the less, the NTWF's first contemplation of militancy – over the gathering crisis in the shipping industry – was quickly set aside. At the June Council meeting, the delegates 'regretted' the attitude of the International Shipping Federation towards the request of the seamen's two unions to the establishment of a Conciliation Board. The motion containing this regret concluded that 'All unions affiliated to this Federation are hereby requested to do their utmost to assist the National Seamen's and Firemen's Union, and the National Union of Ships' Stewards, Cooks, Butchers and Bakers.'[88] This sentence was deleted from the motion, on an amendment! It was too early to risk a test of the new body's cohesion in a pending industrial conflict.

But, if the leaders were rightly apprehensive about going too far in front of their men, who, after all, had two decades of endurance and quiescence behind them, this condition was not to last long. Soon they would have to run to catch up with a workforce intent upon action, action and more action.

And what of the syndicalists? They were not about to topple the throne. Nor, for sure, would they overthrow the plutocracy that surrounded it. They could not even persuade trade unions to do many of the things that would have prepared them better to look after themselves in a still profoundly unfriendly world. But they were forming close and even brotherly alliances with other trade unionists, embracing old adversaries, and in the process bringing new courage to formerly defeated men and great hope to a completely new generation. As the time came near, the image of what was to happen is clear in the deeds of two men. Havelock Wilson, hero of an older Lib.–Lab. age and villain of an age to come, is laying the fuse. And it is Tom Mann who brings the spark.

Notes

1   LRC Report on the Conference on Labour Representation, 27 February 1900, p. 11.
2   Ibid.
3   Ibid., p. 12.
4   Ibid., pp. 11–12.
5   Ibid., p. 16.
6   L. C. B. Seamen, *Post-Victorian Britain, 1902–1951* (Methuen, 1966), p. 3.
7   W. Scovell Adams, *Edwardian Heritage* (Frederick Muller, 1946), p. 83.
8   Michael Barratt Brown, *Global Imperialism: 1870–1914* (Mimeo, 1989), p. 13.
9   Frank Bealey and Henry Pelling, *Labour and Politics, 1900–1906* (Macmillan, 1958), p. 131.
10 Roger Moore, *The Emergence of the Labour Party, 1880–1924* (Hodder and Stoughton, 1978), p. 84.
11 Ibid., p. 87.
12 Mark Stephens, *Roots of Power* (SPA Books, 1986), p. 65.
13 Ibid.
14 NUDL Annual Report, 1902, p. 10.
15 Jonathan Schneer, *Ben Tillett: Portrait of a Labour Leader* (Croom Helm, 1982), p. 125, from the TUC Annual Report, 1903, p. 69.
16 Ibid.
17 Schneer, *Ben Tillett*, p. 122.
18 TUC Annual Report, 1901.
19 Ibid.
20 DWRGWU Annual Report, 1900, p. 5.
21 Ibid., p. 6.

22 Ibid.
23 Ibid., p. 9.
24 Schneer, *Ben Tillett*, p. 127.
25 David Marquand, *Ramsay MacDonald* (Jonathan Cape, 1977), p. 79. For the full text of Jesse Herbert's memorandum, see Keith Laybourn, *The Labour Party 1881–1951: A Reader in History* (Alan Sutton, 1988), pp. 61–2.
26 Marquand, *Ramsay MacDonald*, p. 79.
27 Ibid., p. 80.
28 Laybourn, *The Labour Party 1881–1951*, p. 60.
29 Ibid., pp. 60–1.
30 Henry Pelling, *The Origins of the Labour Party* (Oxford University Press, 1954), p. 227. Cf. *Bulletin of the Institute for Historical Research*, 1956; cf. also Bealey and Pelling, *Labour and Politics, 1900–1906*.
31 R. C. K. Ensor, *England 1870–1914* (Oxford University Press, 1936), p. 355.
32 NUDL Annual Report, 1903, pp. 15–16.
33 F. W. S. Craig, *British General Election Manifestos, 1900–1974* (Macmillan, 1975), pp. 9–10.
34 Sidney and Beatrice Webb, *The History of Trade Unionism* (1894; WEA edn, 1912), p. 606, wrote that this was 'an extraordinary and unlimited immunity, however great may be the damage caused and however unwarranted the act, which most lawyers, as well as all employers, regard as nothing less than monstrous.'
35 Henry Pelling, *A History of British Trade Unionism* (Penguin, 1963), p. 126.
36 G. D. H. Cole, *British Working Class Politics, 1832–1914* (Labour Book Service, 1941), p. 191.
37 Keith Laybourn, *The Labour Party 1881–1951*, p. 64.
38 LRC Conference Minutes, 1905, p. 52.
39 NUDL Annual Report, 1905, p. 14.
40 R. T. McKenzie, *British Political Parties* (Heinemann, 1955), p. 392.
41 Labour Party Annual Conference Report, 1907, p. 58.
42 DWRGWU Annual Report, 1905, p. 6.
43 Ibid., 1908.
44 Ben Tillett, *Is the Parliamentary Labour Party a Failure?* (London, 1908).
45 London Municipal Society, *The Case Against Socialism* (George Allen and Sons, 1908), p. 38.
46 Walter Kendall, *The Revolutionary Movement in Britain* (Weidenfeld and Nicolson, 1969), p. 31.
47 *Labour Leader*, 30 August 1907.
48 Chushichi Tsuzuki, *Hyndman and British Socialism* (Oxford University Press, 1961), p. 165.
49 Schneer, *Ben Tillett*, p. 131.
50 H. W. Lee and E. Archbold, *Social Democracy in Britain* (Social Democratic Federation, 1935), p. 92.
51 Alan Bullock, *The Life and Times of Ernest Bevin* (Heinemann, 1960), vol. 1: *Trade Union Leader: 1881–1941*, p. 8.
52 A. L. Morton and G. Tate, *The British Labour Movement, 1770–1920* (Lawrence and Wishart, 1956), p. 225.

53 Bullock, *The Life and Times of Ernest Bevin*, vol. I, p. 15.
54 DWRGWU Triennial Delegate Meeting, Official Souvenir, 17–21 May 1920, p. 16.
55 Schneer, *Ben Tillett*, p. 218.
56 George Lansbury, *Looking Backwards – and Forwards* (Blackie and Son, 1935), pp. 191–3.
57 At a municipal binge given by William Devenay on the occasion of his selection as first Labour Mayor of West Ham, in 1919, Tillett, Bevin, Thompson, Kay and other dockers' leaders all took part in the conviviality. The dockers' *Record* (November 1919, p. 4) reports that the proceedings were enlivened by songs from the Mayor's daughter, and the general secretary, 'who gave us "cockles and mussels"'. A good many toasts were drunk, and the 'Labour movement' was toasted on the proposal of Mr W. J. Barwick. 'He said he looked back with a certain amount of pride on being one of the earliest members of the old SDF, with which were associated many members who were also associated with the Dockers' Union. He recalled such stalwarts as Tom McCarthy, Jack Williams, Pete Curran and Harry Orbell.'
58 Eric J. Hobsbawm, *Labouring Men* (Weidenfeld and Nicolson, 1968), p. 327.
59 Max Beer, *History of British Socialism*, vol. II (G. Bell and Sons, 1921), p. 352.
60 Ibid.
61 W. Lawler Wilson, *The Menace of Socialism* (Grant Richards, 1909), pp. 315–16.
62 Ibid.
63 Guy Bowman, Foreword to Tom Mann, *From Single Tax to Syndicalism* (Guy Bowman, 1913).
64 Reprinted with a Foreword by Geoff Brown (Spokesman Books, 1974).
65 *Industrial Syndicalist*, Documents in Socialist History, no. 3 (Spokesman Books, 1974), pp. 19–20.
66 *Documents of the First International* (Progress Publishers, Moscow, n.d.), vol. III, pp. 290–2.
67 Anne Besant, *Essays on Socialism* (Freethought Publishing, 1887), p. 16.
68 J. H. Harley, *Syndicalism* (T. C. and E. C. Black, 1912), pp. 44–5.
69 Ridley, *Revolutionary Syndicalism in France* (Cambridge University Press, 1970), p. 170.
70 A modern edition was published in 1989 by Pluto Press.
71 Ridley, *Revolutionary Syndicalism in France*, p. 172.
72 Ibid.
73 Daniel De Leon, *The Socialist Reconstruction of Society* (Socialist Labour Press, n.d.), pp. 27–9.
74 Cited in Bernard Ransom, *Connolly's Marxism* (Pluto Press, 1980), p. 58.
75 Peter Berresford Ellis (ed.), *James Connolly – Selected Writings* (Penguin, 1973), pp. 151–2.
76 George Dangerfield, *The Strange Death of Liberal England, 1910–1914* (Constable, 1935; reissued Perigree Books, 1980), p. 232.
77 Stewart Bird, Dan Georgakis and Deborah Shaffer, *Solidarity Forever* (Lake View Press, 1985), p. 8.

78 *Industrial Syndicalist*, pp. 58–66.
79 Ibid.
80 Tom Mann, *Memoirs* (1923; reissued McGibbon and Kee, 1967), p. 207.
81 Letter from Ben Tillett, DWRGWU, 7 July 1910; NTWF Inaugural Conference Minutes, 1911.
82 Ibid., 22 and 23 September 1910, Agenda.
83 NTWF Annual General Council Report, June 1911.
84 Gordan A. Phillips, 'The National Transport Workers' Federation, 1910–1927' (unpublished PhD thesis, Oxford University, 1968), p. 71.
85 John Lovell, *Stevedores and Dockers: a Study of Trade Unionism in the Port of London, 1870–1914* (Macmillan, 1969), p. 150.
86 Harry Gosling, *Up and Down Stream* (Methuen, 1927), p. 147.
87 Phillips, 'The National Transport Workers' Federation', p. 57.
88 NTWF Annual General Council Report, June 1911.

1911: Big Bang

I

Spontaneous Combustion?

Ignition was planned for 14 June 1911. But Southampton seamen stopped work on 9 June, five days in advance of the chosen date for the national strike. Others followed. Suddenly all around were involved. Seamen inspired seamen, and together they fired the dockers. Dockers provoked carters. In almost no time, and in every major port, nothing could move.

Those who live or holiday in the Mediterranean and Adriatic regions will know that in the 1980s a series of summers hotter and dryer than usual produced devastating outbreaks of forest and brush fires. They erupted without warning in areas far apart from one another, each within days of the other. Every fire was a separate event, not contiguous with the others. Emergency after emergency, each demanded its own mobilization of services, firefighters, ambulances. Yet no one supposed that all these fires broke out at the same time by coincidence, or through divine intervention. We all knew that the same climatic conditions, the same sun, prepared the tinder-dry conditions in which any carelessly discarded match, bottle or cigarette could ignite the trees in their distinct and distant habitats.

So it was in the British ports in 1911. Decades of pain and intimidation were, in an instant, overcome. Now, unbelievably, the workers in this abused and impoverished world had the initiative, and in that initiative the power to turn all things upside down. The upsurge of 1889 had been the pride of the unskilled trades of East London; but now the entire subjected kingdom stood tall at the same time. Historians took their revenge upon the insubordination of the oppressed by describing these events as an 'unrest'. But its sheer scope was so awe inspiring that it is even now remembered as the *Great* Unrest.

What provoked this elemental uprising?

Economic and Social Conditions, 1911

The spreading fires of the transport strikes in 1911 were part of an even wider conflagration covering the years 1911–14 which burst out at the juncture of very powerful social and economic pressures. We have already discussed some of these (see chapter 8, pp. 252–6) in our survey of the first ten years of the new century. We must now resume these themes.

From about 1900, real wages stagnated while prices rose easily and continuously, and money wages staggered feebly after them. This rising cost-of-living curve (see fig. 8.1, p. 254) coincided with a time of high and flaunted fashion. The Edwardian rich threw off the constraints of Victorian respectability to indulge a new taste for open, and often crass, ostentation. The combination of decadent waste and struggling poverty served to provoke an unprecedented sense of social injustice among working people.

Then, crucially, the short slump of 1908–9 suddenly gave way to a trade boom the following year. Unemployment fell, confirming the general upward trend of the economy.

The number without work fell to 4.7 per cent of the working population in 1910. The figure stayed low throughout the years of unrest down to the outbreak of war in 1914. Might Labour once again ride the back of such a boom to make real wage gains, as it had done twenty-one years earlier? Several key leaders of the general workers were certainly astute enough to entertain the thought. Yet, although 1911 heralded a true renewal of new unionism, the port workers' strikes of that year were not at all a carbon copy of 1889. Then, orderly processions, well marshalled and peaceful, had presented the main face of the strike. The middle classes were sympathetic, and the press reflected that sympathy. Now there was to break out a passion amounting to rage, which bewildered many commentators, and indeed many participants. Surely this wild outburst must require explanations other than economic rationality? Some later historians have reflected this feeling. One who emphasized an instinctive element of revolt in the movement was the influential French observer Elie Halevy, whose studies were first published in English in the 1930s.

Disillusion and Injustice

Halevy charts the disillusion with the social-reform programme of the Liberal government between 1906 and 1910, which had won the well-behaved support of the new Labour Party in Parliament. But 'Ramsay MacDonald was not the man to give the impression . . . that the advent of the Labour Party meant the birth of a new world'.[1] Moreover, he points out, largess, in the form of new administrative and official jobs, was now sufficiently obtainable to influence the behaviour of numbers of people. Under the Trades Boards Act, in the new labour exchanges and under the National Insurance Act, many relatively secure and well-paid posts became available. These were systematically distributed among hundreds of trade-union officials. The introduction of salaries for MPs pointed in the same direction, towards the incorporation of the new political and industrial forces in an arrangement which was not open to the mass of workers.[2] To a growing sense of exclusion was added resentment against conspicuous upper-class over-indulgence. This stimulated commentary from all sides, not least from apprehensive Labour leaders, fearful of the alienation of their followers in a revolt against the still fragile political structures which they had helped to create, in a toil which had cost two decades of intensive effort. Writing on the eve of the strikes, Phillip Snowden said:

In 1910 . . . with stationary wages, the real condition of the workers is one of diminishing power to satisfy desires . . . With the spread of education, with the display of wealth and luxury of the rich, it is certain that the workers will not be content. It is the duty of statesmanship to acknowledge the justice of the desire of the workers for a more humane and cultured life, and to satisfy this unrest by concessions of reform. If employers and politicians are so unwise as to ignore the demands of labour, then what might be done by safe and constitutional methods will, by great suffering and loss, be accomplished by industrial strife, and through social anarchy . . . The year upon which we have just entered is likely to be a momentous one for Labour. There is trouble brewing in a number of trades which may break out into open hostilities. Labour has become aggressive, and is not merely opposing attack, but is determined upon advances.[3]

Snowden's fellow parliamentarian, Ramsay MacDonald, made a characteristically muddled attempt to understand the revolt of labour in an essay published in 1913. A brief extract is enough: 'The education and experience of the workman had led him to discover many economic flaws in society, and he challenged it. But there was something more that was wrong. Society was not merely a poor inefficient thing, it was an irritatingly vicious thing.'[4]

Tom Mann at Work

Tom Mann carefully nourished this growing awareness of injustice in all his eager audiences. He railed against all forms of subordination and supplication. In the face of avarice and neglect by capital and the legislature, he called for revolt, and nothing less than revolt. In 1889 John Burns and Ben Tillett had held the spotlights on themselves. They were the orators of the great dock strike, while Mann was the officer in charge of organization, even if this task ensured that he was not to be without his own share of platform time. But now, in the Great Unrest, it was Mann's voice which gave tongue to the entire mute mass. His technique was direct and simple. Jack Jones has given 'a youngster's impression' of Mann's oratorical style, recalled from the inter-war years:

> Tom Mann, first of all, was a good powerful speaker, but he also had a bit of acting ability. He was the sort of man who would walk up and down the stage declaiming and then would suddenly sit down – 'Come up and have a cup of tea, don't bother about it!' In other words, he was denouncing those who wanted to stay at home and have a cup of tea, and not do anything about reforming the world.[5]

Another eye-witness of Mann's meetings has told of the same element in his speeches. He would berate the members of his audience for their meekness before the parliamentarians: 'You petition them for pensions . . . for jobs . . . for food . . . for houses . . .', and at each item in his list of pleas he would literally grovel, kneeling on the stage, hands together, eyes raised in prayerful supplication. In peroration, as he swung over into the opposing message of self-help through direct action, he would raise himself and stand upright and four-square.[6] In an age of mass politics governed by more professional and, it must be said, less honest forms of public television 'performance', the impact of Mann's speeches, no less than that of his organizing and writing, is hard to recapture. But it cannot be lightly dismissed.

'Sectional Unionism Is Our Curse!'

There are many other witnesses to Tom Mann's eloquence. But it was *what* he said, not how he said it, which ran in front of him around the ports, and through all the arteries of trade within the kingdom.

'Sectional unionism is our curse', he trumpeted to all the members of every little provincial section:

> The ability to act trade by trade, occupation by occupation, each independent of the other, may have been of some service a couple of generations ago. But it is no use now! Let us see!

Miners are organised in a given district. Engine drivers at the hauling engines are organised. Miners have trouble with the Masters. They strike. They ask the Engine drivers to help them by refusing to lower blacklegs into the mines, or to haul any stuff whatever that is detrimental to the Miners' interests. The Engine drivers take a vote of their members. They decide it is not their quarrel – why should they risk good jobs? A big majority against the miners decides the latter's fate . . .

The Shipping Federation systematically supplies British workmen as 'scabs to order' in this or any other country. It is no use objecting that these miserable wretches ought not to be called British Workmen. The facts are too palpable. And these blacklegs, with all their necessary food, liquor, bedding . . . are shipped and conveyed over hundreds of miles by rail and road, as well as water, by other Union men. The drivers of locomotives, conveying them in batches of a hundred to the port, carry their Union card. The Engineers on the boat belong either to the Marine Engineers' Union or the Amalgamated Engineers. The carman, carrying food stuffs for the scabs, is a member of his Union. The carpenters who make to order the fittings to house them, are Unionists.

It is these Union men, and not the capitalists, who beat the other Unionists trying to resist reduction or obtain increases. And so it must continue until we can organise by Industries and not merely by Trades. Until we can unify the Industrial Movement into one compact fighting force.

Comrades, we have got to face the fact that Sectional Unionism is played out.[7]

Quiescent Port Unions . . .

Sectional or not, trade unionism was not played out. Overall trade-union membership had already registered substantial growth in the years 1906 and 1907, increasing by half a million its long-fixed total of approximately 2 million. The rise was checked in the short recession which followed, but resumed, with a further gain of 4 per cent, in 1910. Was the prescience of the syndicalists, who had sharpened up their doctrine before the Great Unrest came to demonstrate its power, based on an apprehension of the effects of the boom in trade?

In the ports, however, there was no immediate rush to join this surge of membership, despite Tom Mann and the NTWF's recruitment drive, even though the trade-cycle upturn was, as always, to show itself in a new burst of traffic. London's port unionism remained moribund, and elsewhere the DWRGWU was simply hanging on. Ben Tillett's Annual Report for 1910 (in which he celebrated his return to work 'after my last protracted illness'[8]) contained no hint of what was to come: it was preoccupied with parliamentary matters, with the Osborne Judgement of 1909 (in which the Law Lords had ruled that trade unions must not spend their funds on political activity), with old-age pensions, labour exchanges, increased taxation, the increased cost of living, invalidity and unemployment insurance. Tillett did express himself sceptically about the efficacy of the reforms, and shared the mood of syndicalist rejection. The NUDL, though more prudently administered, lay similarly flat. Sexton, in that same year, wrote simply. 'We do not propose to labour the report this year for more than one reason, but the main one is to let those who have had the actual experience in the various localities speak for themselves.'[9] (The regional reports which follow this cryptic introduction, sent in by loyalist and aggrieved officials, make very plain that Sexton's reticence had much to do with his sense of injury over the 'Larkin affair'.)

. . . Elsewhere, Portents

In 1908 the number of strikers doubled over 1907. There was a pause in the following year. Then, in 1910, the number of workers involved in strikes more than doubled again over those of 1909 (see table 10.1). The trend of strike figures is also evident in the number of stoppages, rising from 346 in 1904 to 521 in 1910, and in the totals of working days involved, growing from 1.5 million in 1904 to 9.9 million in 1910. In all these series, the same escalation is visible, interrupted alike in 1908–9 by a downturn in the trade cycle, during which unemployment temporarily doubled, from 3.7 per cent in 1907 to 7.8 per cent in 1908 and 1909. But the number of strikers in 1910 was the highest since the great defensive struggles of 1893. In that year, the *casus belli* had been the defence of trade-union membership against free labour. It is highly significant that in 1910 the Board of Trade Report remarked that 30 per cent of those who struck work had come out in protest at the engagement of non-union labour. In that year, too, the troops fired on the miners of

Table 10.1   *Number of Workers*
Directly Involved in Strikes,
1904–1910

1904	56,380
1905	67,653
1906	157,872
1907	100,728
1908	223,909
1909	170,258
1910	385,085

Source: Labour Department of the Board of Trade, *Reports on Strikes and Lock-outs.*

Tonypandy, engaged in the great Cambrian coal strike in South Wales, killing one striker. In the ensuing riots, over 500 were injured. The ostensible cause of the strike was a disputed wage rate for coal-getting in a new seam which the Cambrian Coal Combine had opened in the Rhondda Valley. But the whole industry was tinder dry for revolt, with the possibility of an industry-wide stoppage never far from men's minds.

Tireless, busy everywhere, Tom Mann was present. The ebullient and combative Home Secretary, Winston Churchill, followed up this act of class warfare in South Wales two months later by personally supervising, in London, the direction of rifle and cannon fire against two Russian anarchists at the 'siege' of Sydney Street. Tom Mann's journal, the *Industrial Syndicalist*, saw this in a symbolic light: it offered a 2-guinea prize for an essay of 3,000 words on the question: 'If two men can keep two thousand men employed and hold them at bay on one street, how many men would be required to defeat two or three million men, spread over the area of Great Britain?'[10] No one knew the answer to that question.

The new spirit of rebellion, fostered and expressed by young men in the coalfields, in cotton and elsewhere, was lovingly nurtured by the syndicalist agitation. Tom Mann's tours and publications took him everywhere. The worker-students and Marxist tutors of the newly formed Central Labour College had already touched the dockers in South Wales in 1910 (see chapter 8, pp. 261–2). In that dispute, at Houlders' ship in Newport, the sight of the blacklegs brought in from London to break the strike provoked a violent cry from one of the strikers: 'You bloody bastards . . . Are we going to let them take the bread out of our mouths? Let's go for them!'[11] The offensive flavour of the language, captured for history in the Arbitration Board's Report, should not obscure for us the rage of that man, expressing the dockers' long years of humiliation at the hands of free labour. Tom Mann, as we saw in chapter 8, had preached his message in the South Wales ports just prior to the Houlders' dispute. Amongst the converts who came to him was the strikers' unofficial leader, Alf Cox. He represented a new generation, touched by the influence of the syndicalist spirit. At the height of the unrest to come, a shipowner remarked to Lord Askwith, 'The dockers . . . had new leaders, men unknown before; the employers did not know how to deal with them'.[12]

Tom Mann's evangelizing tour of the ports followed the formation of the National Transport Workers' Federation; but it was also co-ordinated with Havelock Wilson's campaign to revive the Seamen's Union and to prepare for a major strike. Alone amongst the affiliates of the NTWF, the NSFU had adopted a programme of demands, intended for national and even international application. A team of NSFU speakers, led by Wilson, canvassed the idea of an international seamen's strike right across the trading world, from New York to Norway.

As applied to British owners, the union's demands were comprehensive:

> The claim was for a conciliation board, a national minimum rate of wages, a manning scale for stokehold, deck, and galley, the abolition of medical examinations by doctors privately appointed by the Shipping Federation, abolition of engagement of seamen at Shipping Federation offices, the right of seamen to a portion of their wages while in port and to have a representative present while signing on, the fixing of working hours and overtime rates and improved forecastle accommodation.[13]

Behind this impressive shopping list, of course, and crucial in all that followed, lay the demand for recognition, which was anathema to the anti-union moguls of the Shipping Federation. This recognition was pursued at *national* level, for standard national, if not yet international, terms and conditions. It was ambitious beyond the dreams of the more sectionalized and localized, and, be it said, more timid, leaders of the dockers, carters, tram and bus workers enrolled in the NTWF. But out of the turmoil to come, it was recognition, even more than wage increases, which ultimately emerged as the dominant objective of those occupations, inspiring them, and belatedly their official representatives, to follow the seamen's lead.

The Role of Havelock Wilson

It has been said that the strike wave of 1911 was largely leaderless, or (more plausibly) that its leaders were local men, not the national union hierarchs. There is some truth in this. But clearly there is another figure, besides Tom Mann himself, who provided a vigorous national lead. Havelock Wilson has been remembered in Labour and trade-union lore as the author of various betrayals and some degree of corruption, and it is clear that his union suffered during decades of his autocratic rule. In 1911, however, this evolution could scarcely have been predicted, and even in retrospect Tom Mann (admittedly ever generous) paid his own very real tribute to him. Speaking of the events of 1911, Mann writes:

> the shipowners, over a period of many years, with the aid of clever lawyers, did their utmost to make Havelock Wilson a bankrupt. In the whole history of the trade-union movement of Britain, there is no case of such persistent, systematic, and venemous persecution of a union official as that to which Havelock Wilson was subjected by the shipowners of this country.
>
> In ultimate ideals and objectives, Havelock Wilson and I have nothing in common, but I have had occasion to work in close relationship with him in trade-union affairs, and we have been colleagues in many industrial disputes. I have always found him a straightforward, honourable and loyal

comrade. Moreover, he was always at his post early in the day, tackling the most difficult tasks with the utmost readiness. I take the opportunity of saying this because there is considerable feeling against Wilson for certain of his activities. I like to dwell upon other phases, and especially upon what happened in 1911, in the industrial arena of Britain, and particularly in connection with the transport industry . . .

Tom Mann's remarkable nose for action had undoubtedly helped him to identify the scent of trouble brewing:

I had faith in Wilson's ability to seize the opportune time for vigorous action, knowing that he was in deadly earnest and above all anxious to make no mistake when the right time came. I was informed of conferences held quietly in the chief ports. Wilson told me he was convinced that the summer of 1911 would be the time . . .
  I readily agreed to identify myself with the intended effort, for I shared Wilson's hopes and beliefs, though all the time eager for a broader and bigger outlook to prevail . . .

The great strike of miners in South Wales had already impressed port workers all round the Principality:

in the ports, solidarity with the miners had been earnestly advocated. Some union officials, however, positively refused to participate in the effort, which they regarded as untimely. In some cases they went further and tried to stultify the movement. In May 1911 it became evident that the time for action was at hand. We decided to approach the shipowners through the Shipping Federation . . . The reply . . . was of that haughty type characteristic of dominant Capitalism. This left us no alternative but drastic action. The Sailors' and Firemen's Union therefore had another conference, and decided to call a strike for the middle of June.[14]

When the call came, the International Transport Workers' Federation failed to evoke the planned international action. German, Danish and Norwegian shipowners quickly made concessions to their seamen, and international solidarity as quickly collapsed.[15] Nearer home, the NTWF wavered.

'Suspicion Brooded Melancholy'

The first Annual General Council Meeting of the NTWF was held only two weeks before the seamen's strike call, yet it side-stepped a direct call for federal support for the looming conflict. James Anderson, the NTWF secretary, expressed his anxiety about Wilson's 'bull and rush' mood. Harry Gosling recalled: 'Havelock Wilson's task was no easy one, but in spite of his growing physical disabilities he conducted it with amazing energy. The blaze spread rapidly . . . though at one moment we were all saying more or less volubly that he could not possibly succeed, the next we found ourselves travelling along behind him.'[16] Robert Williams said of the NSFU and their 1911 strike: 'It certainly appeared to those who knew that this Union's fortunes were at a very low ebb, that this proposed international strike was a gambler's last chance.'[17] The NSFU was reported to owe its bank £6 13s. in 1911.[18]

Ben Tillett reported, of the founding of the NTWF: 'Following the trend of the general working class moving towards solidarity, the Transport Workers themselves, encouraged by the movements initiated in other directions, came together almost stealthily with much caution and with much fear. Suspicion brooded melancholy over the most optimistic anticipations.'[19] But, says Tillett, it was Havelock Wilson, 'although crippled with rheumatics, sick and enfeebled', who 'struggled bravely to the middle of the summer'.[20] Gosling says quite precisely: 'It was J. Havelock Wilson who actually set fire to the heather.'[21]

The Mystery Explained

The heat generated in that fire was more than metaphorical: the English summer of 1911 was the hottest for forty-three years. Under a remorseless sun, one by one, the ports burst into flames. And this is not simply a metaphor; all too often the fires were real ones, not moral upsurges. In the immediately preceding months, militant – even riotous – strikes, which were widely reported and debated, had set the scene in the coalfields and in the cotton towns. In Ireland (all of which was still a province of Great Britain), a convulsive industrial struggle in Belfast and a colourful revolutionary trade-union leader, James Larkin, had already given a premonition of all of these trends and had shaken the staid leaders of the National Union of Dock Labourers. In 1911 'the transport workers disturbed, emotionally and physically, not just their industry, but society at large.'[22] A leading Labour politician told Askwith, 'I don't know what has come over the country. Everyone seems to have lost their heads.'[23]

In that summer of 1911, then, trade was booming, there was a rising sense of social and political injustice among the workers, there was syndicalist agitation, a rising tide of militancy was already apparent, and there was a conscious plan for a national seamen's action. Finally, and if we are to give due weight to the remarkable testimony of Tom Mann himself (who speaks consistently of 'we' and 'us' in his memoirs, in recalling the joint planning of the seamen's campaign by Wilson and himself), there were two highly experienced men giving practised and dedicated leadership and coherence to the movement in the ports.

In short: opportunity, provocation, incitement, example and leadership. Some historians have felt that the uprising of the ports in 1911 remains mysterious.[24] The only mystery is why it took so long for this convergence to generate itself. Now at last, action against the long-standing abuse of human beings in the ports was not only possible, but real. After years of privation and oppression the seamen, dockers and carters left their work in droves and together took to the streets. The all-powerful Shipping Federation and its Free Labour Battalions were rendered impotent. So forceful was the revolt that all opposition was lightly brushed aside.

II

Jumping the Gun

A short strike by the Southampton coal trimmers, supported by the Dockers' Union, provoked the stoppage by seamen in that port, which, as we have seen, anticipated the official national seamen's strike.

> Meanwhile, amongst the transport workers solidarity was being earnestly advocated in all ports, and for all sections, but not by any means by all Union officials; on the contrary, some of these declined to be identified with the effort, declaring it to be 'altogether untimely,' etc., etc.
>
> The deciding factor that fixed June as the best month in the year for the struggle was that trade was exceptionally busy, that the Coronation [of George V] would take place in that month, and that an exceptional number of over-sea visitors would be making their way to this country. June was therefore beyond question the best month in the year for the struggle, and at the conference of sailors, the 14th June was ultimately decided upon as the particular day on which to commence hostilities.
>
> The largest ocean liner ever built up to that date was lying in Southampton, and making ready for her maiden voyage across the Atlantic; it was the SS *Olympic*. The first shots were fired by the coalies who refused to load the vessel except under improved conditions. It looked as though there would be a serious delay in the departure of the big boat, but the public generally little thought that the vessel would be absolutely tied up, especially as she was to bring back a special contingent of American millionaires to join in the Coronation junketings. But so it was; the *Olympic* could not get away, and on the 14th war was declared in all the chief ports of the country, and the men responded in magnificent style.
>
> Even now the Capitalist press was utterly unable to calculate the forces at work, and tried to laugh down what they called 'the wicked and insane attempts to hold up the shipping'. In three days' time it dawned upon them that something quite out of the ordinary had taken place; they saw that every vessel, as it came into port, had to remain there, and that there was a strong indication on the part of dockers and others to make common cause.

The experience was unique in industrial battles. Shipowners who had absolutely refused to have anything to do with the workmen, now earnestly wrote to get a conference. The Shipping Federation proved utterly incapable of helping its clients, and after having dictated conditions for over twenty years they had in a single day lost all power whatsoever. The workmen simply folded arms, saying that they were 'quite willing to return to work when their demands were granted, and not before'. Shipowners begged of Union officials to 'instruct the men to take out the mail boats and others,' on the assurance that they would meet in conference without delay, and discuss all points desired. But it was too late to discuss; the situation had now reached a point when discussion was out of the question, and the actual granting of the demands should be complied with'.[25]

The Seamen's Demands Conceded

We have already itemized the official programme of seamen's demands (p. 342). It was a truly formidable claim, but, 'to the surprise of everyone,' concluded Tom Mann, 'all these demands were complied with in a few days'.

The seamen, although summoned to the contest nationally, on a national programme, fought and negotiated port by port. This was inevitable, since the Shipping Federation had rejected any kind of formal bargaining relationship with the unions. The settlements forced out of local groups of shipping companies reflected this: Cardiff seamen won a 30s. increase, but in Hull only 5s. were conceded.[26] The same was true of the strikes by dockers and carters. Having received no national call, either from their unions or the NTWF, the local unions formed *ad hoc* strike committees in attempts to focus and express the initially inchoate demands of the strikers. The National Transport Workers' Federation role was marginal: it lent its name and some shape to the Strike Committee in Liverpool and – later in the summer – much more substantially in the London strike. In the Humber and the Bristol Channel, its existence may have helped local co-ordination.[27] Nowhere in the provincial settlements of 1911 did the employers recognize the NTWF as a bargaining agent. In London things were different. Consequently, the dockers and carters also came out of the strikes with a wide variety of wage increases – though some were very substantial, in the range from 30 to 40 per cent.

One consistent demand was presented everywhere: for union recognition, and preference of employment for union members. And one consistent and permanent result of the strikes was the flood of new recruits who flocked to join – or rejoin – the waterside unions. The events of 1911 permanently transformed the fortunes of the new unions in transport. Though they were to face declining numbers in the 1920s, there was never, after 1911, any equivalent setback to match that of the 1890s. No counterattack by the employers ever again reduced the general union and its associated organizations in transport and general trades to the impotence of 1893–1910.

Liverpool Epic

The Liverpool strikes were an epic complete in themselves. They reached into the imagination of the age. Indeed, long afterwards their dramatic overtones moved Trevor Griffiths to make them the subject of a major television script. This was commissioned in 1971 by the BBC as one of a series on *The Edwardians*; but it proved too raw for the modern age, student demonstrations and UCS work-ins notwithstanding, and it was filleted out of the series by the Corporation's controllers. By 1990 it had still never been seen. Fortunately, British publishing has until recently been largely free of such self-censorship and the drama of Tom Mann's impact on the Liverpool scene of 1911 can at least be read.[28]

On 13 June Mann arrived at the Liverpool Exchange Station by train. He had come to help the seamen. Although the NTWF gave belated support to the ensuing stoppage, Mann held no national office in that body. He was given a district responsibility. Yet he was immediately elected chairman of the Joint Strike Committee, presiding over the officials of the unions of seamen, dockers (James Sexton himself), ships' stewards and Liverpool carters, whose vice-president, Billal Quilliam, was a local solicitor.[29] Of these leaders, Sexton was of course the general secretary of a national union, and the Ships' Stewards' Union also had its national headquarters in Liverpool. Its two representatives on the committee, Frank Pearce and Joe Cotter, were both syndicalists. Was there perhaps some flicker of doubt in Sexton's mind over the propriety of these arrangements? What were the apprehensions of a moderate and financially prudent leader, confronted with the national spokesman of the syndicalists surrounded by his strong supporters? And such a fire-eater given the authority of the chair . . . ? If these questions troubled him, they never showed in Sexton's public role during the strikes. He and Mann negotiated jointly, and spoke unanimously on the public stage – a remarkable partnership of opposites.

The committee concentrated its first attentions on the big, independent passenger-liner companies at the Liverpool North End Docks, rightly judging them most vulnerable. Cargo-shipping, controlled by smaller firms affiliated to the intransigent Shipping Federation, was less vulnerable. Imperishable cargoes, at least, could await shipment or discharge for a time, but passengers who had booked an expensive transatlantic crossing could not. The liner firms faced severe international competition and, in addition, had mail contracts to fulfil. Several such sailings were scheduled, and were duly stopped by the strike on 14 June. Mann instantly translated the theory of class solidarity into action, calling 'upon all departments of the transport trade – the dock labourers, the carters, the coal porters, the bargemen and the railwaymen . . . to rally to the support of the seamen . . . the object aimed at . . . was to unite the transport workers on the sea with those on the land.'[30]

Within days, and following the capitulation of the Blue Funnel line, in succession the White Star, Canadian Pacific, Cunard and Booth lines had ceded. Breathtaking victories, these, to the strikers. All grades of seamen won an increase of 10s. a week, the abolition of the company medical examination, no victimization, and recognition of their appropriate union. The long contraband union badges could now be worn in public, and union officials could board company ships. The unions' demand for a Conciliation Board was waived for the moment. The NSFU and the Stewards' Union were promptly flooded by thousands of new members.

The local press identified the decisive factor in the astonishing breakthrough: 'for the first time in the history of the port of Liverpool, yesterday saw "all hands" throwing sectionalism to the wind and joining hand in hand for the furtherance of a common cause. It was a remarkable – even an historic – event in trade union progress.'[31] Up to this point, the dockers' and the carters' unions had held back from direct action on behalf of their own causes, although some unofficial dockers' action in sympathy with the seamen had already occurred.

But Mann judged that the smaller cargo firms, buttressed by the Shipping Federation, would require a more general mobilization to ensure a comparable success. He issued 50,000 copies of a manifesto calling a seamen's and catering-staff strike in these firms for Monday, 25 June, at the same time calling on all dockers and other cargo-handlers to black the goods of the firms. 'All eyes are now turned upon Liverpool men, anxiously watching whether they will exhibit solidarity or whether the evils of sectionalism shall curse our movement once more'.[32]

On the day before the strike, between 3,000 and 4,000 workers attended a mass meeting at St George's Plateau. It resolved on support for the seamen. Blacking was then endorsed by the NUDL and the Carters' Union. The dispute became, in effect, a total stoppage, since no cargo was to be moved in or out of ships which had been tied up, and no ship could move. In the face of this action, the dockers were prompted to remember their own grievances and assert their own demands: for union rates of pay and recognition of the NUDL. Hitherto such a mutiny would have been an unthinkable affront to bosses who were affiliates of the Shipping Federation. But, faced with such solidarity, the employers caved in, again one after another. During a single day Mann and Sexton went together to the offices of four cargo-shipping companies, obtaining union recognition in every case. As they emerged from each office, they made impromptu speeches to crowds of cheering dockers. 'Tell your readers,' said Tom Mann to a local journalist, 'that never in the course of my career have I seen so successful a fight for labour accomplished in one day. We have given wonderful proof of the unity existing between all the affected unions. We have broken the back of the opposition to trade unionism along the line of docks'.[33] Sexton was, characteristically, more laconic: 'It has been a good day, a very good day. I am satisfied with it'.[34]

The demand for union recognition now spread to the dockers working for the large liner companies. Seamen began to give thanks for the solidarity shown to them by striking in sympathy with the dockers. Two thousand coal-heavers downed shovels to join the union and the movement. Boiler-scalers and cold-storage men in turn came out to join the strikes. The South End men joined with the North Enders in common cause, after all those years of separation. Sexton and Mann negotiated union recognition from Cunard on behalf of all the Liverpool liner firms. The union badge was to be worn once again. When Mann and Sexton accepted the companies' wish to defer implementation of the union's port-working rules, including payment of union rates, the men revolted against their own leader. George Milligan, secretary of No. 12 Branch and an active member of the NUDL who at the time shared the dockers' old suspicions about Sexton, led the protest. At the men's insistence, Milligan was co-opted on to the Joint Strike Committee, which was now in danger of losing control of the strike.

The big firms gave varied and equivocal answers to the men's demands, submitted to them by Mann, Sexton, Cotter and now Milligan. When presenting compromise settlements for acceptance by mass meetings, Mann was heckled, even though Milligan supported his plea for a return to work. Cotter tried his persuasive powers, as did Sexton, who told strikers: 'If you don't take our advice today, I can do no more for you'. But the recommendations were rejected. The Strike Committee then offered the following resolution to the men:

we, the joint committee advise those employed at the firms mentioned on the White List [i.e. those firms who had agreed to the recognition of all unions] to return to work at once pending the Dockers' Union port rules being granted during the coming month, and pledge ourselves that, should the north end not receive the full recognition of union rules at the end of the month we shall fully support their activity to obtain such.[35]

Mann addressed mass meetings to win support for this advice. Despite Milligan's and other local leaders' support, the vote was evenly split. The union threatened the expulsion of members for defying what was now an instruction to return to work. Union officials toured the docks to persuade the men, who finally conformed to their pressures: union discipline had prevailed.

The tugboat men now struck, winning a wage gain in a few days. And though the dock strikes were now apparently over, the men's truculent responses to foremen who failed to implement all the details of the settlement led to daily walk-outs, at which Milligan appeared as the over-worked troubleshooter. The union preached order, discipline, loyalty, and Milligan became a firm supporter of Sexton and his policies. Soon he was appointed deputy general secretary of the NUDL. (In 1922 he became the first area secretary of the TGWU for Area No. 12 on Merseyside.)[36]

After many meetings, on 4 August the conference of shipowners and unions signed the White Book Agreement. All the major employers of port labour signed. For the men outside the NUDL, the separate coal-heavers' unions of North and South Ends signed for their dockers. The settlement provided for the union button to be worn at the call, agreed that employers would not discriminate in favour of non-union labour, and established a Conciliation Board. In practice, preference for union labour was decisively imposed, in return for a union commitment to maintain work in any dispute whilst it was before the Board. This was the constitutional settlement of which Sexton had dreamed, and he set himself thereafter to deliver the union side of the deal.

He and the employers expected that the agreement signalled the end of the dock strikes. But on 7 August the railway-goods porters struck for reduced hours and increased pay. Although the ASRS condemned the strike, Mann's Strike Committee supported it, co-opted local officials of the ASRS and the General Railway Workers' Union, and called on all transport workers to black goods moving to or from rail depots and stations. This, of course, reactivated the dockers. The shipowners were outraged and threatened a port lock-out unless the NUDL prevailed on its members to work normally. But other forces were propelling the city towards a general transport strike. Some sporadic violence and arson had already occurred and the authorities mobilized extra police and the military on the very day that the Strike Committee summoned 80,000 people to a demonstration at St George's Plateau in support of the railwaymen.

Joe Byrne, later to be a branch official of the TGWU on Liverpool docks, had childhood memories of that day:

> We lived at Seaforth (it's all docks now, but then it was sands and the townies would flock down there at the weekend). Nearby was a barracks for the Scots Greys and one Sunday I saw the Scots Greys mounted with lances and flags ride past the end of the road. Some women came to my mother and asked 'Has Patrick gone to the meeting in town?' She said he had. 'Oh God', they said, 'I hope he won't get hurt.'
>
> Tom Mann had come to be Number One speaker that day. There had been religious trouble and Tom Mann marched up William Brown Street

with a green and orange sash to the Plateau to symbolise Liverpool united, Protestant and Catholic.[37]

This picture of Tom Mann sporting the colours of both communities, striding out to heal sectarian divisions, inspired 'Nemo', who is better remembered as Robert Blatchford, to write an imaginary dialogue between Order and Conscience:

The Old Order:– Surely, we as reasonable men cannot be governed by this fellow, Tom Mann. Who is he? Is he not a discredited agitator, expelled from England, from Australia, who must inevitably be found out?

The New Conscience:– Tom Mann was loved and honoured by Cardinal Manning, the greatest Christian since the time of Francis of Assisi. He was admired and loved by Archbishop Benson, one of the greatest Churchmen of the Church of England, who offered him Orders without the preliminary examination. He had the hearts of the workmen of London and of Broken Hill, just as he has the hearts of the workpeople of Liverpool. He voices the voiceless wrath of the wretched, and their unlearned discontent. Say he is another Attila, who styled himself the Scourge of God. Could Attila have ravaged Europe unless his warriors believed in him? Could Mann hold up the port of Liverpool unless the docker, the carter, the seaman and fireman, the cook and steward, the coal-heaver, the tramwayman, believe that through the solidarity of whose mighty wave he is the crest, that they will be able to get an extra slice of bread for their children, an extra hour's leisure for their wives, even if it is expressed only through an increase of wages?

The Old Order:– The men could have had all this gradually. Why couldn't they agitate resonably?

The New Conscience:– Do you mean by that they should have waited for their claims to be settled by arbitration?

The Old Order:– Certainly. It takes time for all claims to be settled. They cannot be adjusted in ten minutes.

The New Conscience:– It does not take much time for men to starve. The Conciliation Board took an average of sixteen months to settle claims. A man can die of hunger in three days.'[38]

Sectarian violence was always a possible risk. But the forces which drew blood in Liverpool were entirely secular, as Joe Byrne recalled many years later:

The police were waiting inside Lime Street Station, and my Dad who was on the Plateau said to Tom 'Looks as though there's going to be trouble'. There were thousands out, it was like a Sunday outing, all in their straw hats.

The mounted police sailed out of the station and drove them right off the Plateau so they ran into the troops coming up Dale Street. The fighting went on all Sunday night and the best part of Monday. Wherever people gathered they attacked them.

Years later, I was asked to chair a meeting for Tom Mann . . . I'll never forget it: the place was packed with women in shawls, sitting on the window sills. When I introduced Tom Mann, they got off their seats and hugged and kissed him. When I got home, my Dad told me all about 1911 and Bloody Sunday: that's what they called it. Those women remembered all about it and Tom Mann leading the men.[39]

The police and the troops between them put over 350 people in hospital on Bloody Sunday. Two thousand more soldiers were brought to the city, and the shipowners did close the docks, putting 15,000 out of work. The Strike Committee promptly called for a general strike, and 66,000 responded. Military escorts were needed for any movement of goods, which the Strike Committee sanctioned by issuing permits; only bread and milk received such permits. At this point, the railway strike had become national, but was resolved in just three days, when the railway companies – which had traditionally opposed union recognition with the same vehemence as the Shipping Federation – agreed to meet the unions.

In Liverpool, violence continued. Troops shot and killed a dock labourer and a carter during an obscure tumult involving a prison van on a dockland street. On 17 August the city tramwaymen, power-station workers and dustmen all struck. The Corporation dismissed the tramwaymen, and only a threat by the Strike Committee to renew the general strike secured the promise of reinstatement. (In the event, this was long delayed.) Finally, on 25 August, the NUDL and the shipowners agreed terms for a return to work at the docks. The great strikes were over. All sections had made advances except the tramwaymen.

Conflagration in Hull

For the first time, during the 1911 strikes the NUDL became deeply involved in the Humberside ports. As we have seen it had established a branch at Goole as early as 1902, and had chafed at the failure of the DWRGWU to take back into its fold the 11,000 Hull dockers who lapsed their union membership after its collapse in 1893. The Goole men were the first to strike on 14 June, in harmony with the seamen, although only one-third of them held union cards before the strike. In Hull, too, despite the almost complete absence of organization, the dockers' sympathy action with the seamen was total. The NUDL sought to solidify the strike into a permanent association and its national organizer, O'Connor Kessack, hastened from Leith to the Humber, where he was active in both Goole and Hull during the strike.

As elsewhere, the seamen's strike in Hull had been well prepared.[40] The NSFU had appointed John Bell as its Humber organizer in 1910.

Planning meetings began in February 1911 and the NTWF seems to have played an active role in promoting them. They were addressed by Tom Mann, Ben Tillett, Havelock Wilson and his extraordinary organizer, the 'sky-pilot' Rev. A. B. Hopkins.[41]

Throughout the spring new members flocked into the unions: fish-dock workers, grain workers, checkers and weighters. The DWRGWU began its own recruitment drive in May. This came just too late to prevent a formation which ever after impaired the monopoly of the TGWU in the port: the Fish Dock Workers' Protection Society was supported by the Gasworkers' Union in its struggle with the trawler-owners, and this paved the way to their eventual merger into what became the General and Municipal Workers' Union, which retained the membership of the fish 'bobbers' down to modern times.

Madame Sorgue, the French syndicalist leader, made appearances in Hull in the build-up to the strike. On 14 June a crowd of 4,000 gathered in Paragon Square to hear the strike declared by John Bell. A rocket-flare confirmed the decision that evening at 8.30. (This signal was used to start the strike in other ports too.)

Initially, the success of the strike was not guaranteed. Hull, of course, was a stronghold of Collison's Free Labour Association, which had some success in bringing strike-breakers from Europe, Wales and Lancashire. And a long-established local seamen's union, the Hull Seamen's and Marine Firemen's Amalgamated Association, was strongly represented in the port, with 800 members. Its secretary, J. Butcher, was a 'moderate' who valued his intimate relations with the shipowners; the NSFU organizer called him 'a tool of the Federation'. Butcher railed at the 'agitators' who had 'warped' his members into a strike mood, but when they walked out and joined the stoppage it became clear that he had lost control. (The Hull seamen merged with the national union only in 1922.)

The battle between pickets and free labourers in transit to and from their depot ship, moored in the Humber, was reminiscent of the 1890s. It was no less bloody. A striker was shot and seriously wounded by gunfire from a strike-breaking cargo ship as she put to sea. Its captain was arrested when he docked in Rotterdam. Hamburg dockers sent a telegram to report that they were refusing to unload ships from Hull. Far from being intimidated, the resolve of the seamen was strengthened. It spread when the dockers made their first gesture of solidarity with a one-day strike at the Alexandra Dock. This prompted Tillett to send a telegram: 'No instructions from the Dockers' Executive to Hull dockers to cease work.' But in fact 90 per cent of them were non-unionists, and they went right on to extend their strike. Tillett's message did, however, register. As a result the Hull dockers denied a platform at their mass meetings to the local dockers' secretary and took their lead instead from a young, hitherto obscure docker, John Burn, a non-unionist who nevertheless, reported the local press, 'had always believed that the salvation of the working classes did not lie in politics, but in their industrial organisation, by means of which they could obtain anything they liked'.[42]

This strongly suggests a young man under the influence of the months of syndicalist advocacy. He rapidly assumed the chairmanship of the Joint Strike Committee, which included Kessack, representing the Goole dockers for the NUDL. Significantly, Burn proposed that a regional committee of the NTWF be formed, independent of other bodies. This was taken to be a rebuff to Tillett's union, as well as to the Hull Trades Council, whose response to the strike had been cool. That Burn seized on the idea that the NTWF should be strike co-ordinator suggests that its role was seen much more in 'syndicalist' terms in the provincial ports than at the centre, where it remained low-key, if not exactly inert, until August and the London strike.

For a time the shipping lines, including C. H. and Arthur Wilson's, were able to get some ships away, with the aid of non-English-speaking and untrained crews. Even so, this usually meant defiance of Board of Trade regulations. Clerks and warehousemen continued to break the strike of the dockers. The Shipping Federation adopted postures and issued statements strongly reminiscent of 1893, and began to incur criticism from the press and from local traders. The owners claimed that, since the strike leaders were unofficial, no meeting with or recognition of them was possible.

Want and hunger amongst the strikers and their families became a threat to the solidarity of the strike: except in the seamen's case, no union strike-benefit was available to allay it. To aggravate matters, food prices rose, as supplies, most of which arrived by sea, were cut off. Charities made some contribution and the *Hull Daily Mail* ran a fund to relieve the suffering. The Strike Committee now sought to extend the strike, to increase pressure on the owners. One thousand lightermen came out and the railwaymen acted outside their union's authority to take sympathy action. Picketing was increased and became more effective. The scent of perishable cargoes rose over the port and flattened out on the city in the summer heat. It was estimated that some 300,000 pounds of rotting produce was held up by the strike.

Other ports throughout the country were settling: the absence of any gesture of conciliation from the shipowners in Hull led the Strike Committee – and the strikers spontaneously – to press for a general strike of the whole city. On 27 June thousands of strikers stormed a ship which was being unloaded by female stewards. Evidently the new Liverpool-based Ships' Stewards' Union had established no presence in Hull. From that moment the action became more directly violent and intimidatory. The strikers compelled a shut-down at Reckitt's factory, and flying pickets then quickly brought out the flour-millers, the timber-porters and the boiler-scalers at the Fish Dock. Daily police baton-charges became ritual. The constables were very busy: all traffic had to be escorted. This was not enough for the shipowners, who pressed the government to be more assiduous in its efforts at repression. The Home Office responded: 'Mr. Churchill is in telegraphic communication with the Mayor of Hull and has reminded him that it is his duty to maintain order and take adequate measures to secure the landing of perishable cargoes.'[43]

The Board of Trade finally stirred itself to break the impasse: George Askwith, the chief conciliator, set off for Hull armed with a concession from the Shipping Federation nationally. Some 'moderate' advance in wages, they now admitted, might be justified, although they would not concede recognition of the unions.

The scene which met him almost unnerved him: 'There was no doubt about the upheaval. Employers were greatly surprised by the developments. The strike-leaders were men unknown to them, the violence unexpected, and the strait-jacket attitude of the Shipping Federation rendered them quite inadequate to the task.'[44]

Askwith was able to achieve a series of concessions immediately. In the case of the seamen, whose strike was official and who had a national programme of demands to work to, wage increases were granted, the 'Federation ticket' was withdrawn, the medical examination modified and an arbitration procedure agreed. But no settlement was attempted in the whole complex of claims which had been voiced by the 'sympathy strikers' on and around the docks. In spite of this the Strike Committee endorsed the settlement. Askwith reported that the violence and desperation of the dock communities, aggravated by near-starvation, had petrified the local leadership of the committee. Yet it was surely predictable that violence might be provoked, rather than discouraged, when the shore-workers' grievances were denied a settlement. Failure to agree was announced to a crowd of 40,000 outside the Royal Station Hotel, where Askwith was staying.[45] The strike leaders' performance verged on the irresponsible. Kessack told the angry crowd to go back to work because the town's tradesmen faced ruin. He then begged them to think of the welfare of the country. Burn said that, as most strikers were unorganized, his committee could not advise them. Askwith wrote a classic report which many historians have chosen to symbolize the temper of the Great Unrest:

It was estimated that there were fifteen thousand people there when the leaders began their statement. They announced a settlement; and before my turn came, an angry roar of 'No!' rang out; and 'Let's fire the docks!' from the outskirts where men ran off. The crowd surged against the platform in a space below the hotel; women who had come to see the show shrieked with alarm . . . I heard a town councillor remark that he had been in Paris during the Commune and had never seen anything like this: the women were worse than anything he had ever seen, and he had not known there were such people in Hull – women with hair streaming and half nude, reeling through the streets, smashing and destroying.[46]

Although the docks were not fired that night, 2,000 dockers rampaged through them, wrecking the offices of Wilson's line, and the depot of the British Free Labour Association. They used paving slabs, wood, even gravestones; 1,300 policemen were mustered in baton-charges. The following day the shops were shuttered, the town crouched in fear. Five hundred men of the Metropolitan Police arrived, and more troops were deployed. In fact, as *The Times* reported, 'Hull is in far greater danger of famine than of mass violence'.[47] In comparison with the wild abandon of the police in Liverpool, the Hull authority's action was almost benign: only seventeen people received hospital treatment.

After a weekend's pause (Askwith sought peace at the seaside: he went to Bridlington), the Strike Committee and the conciliator did what they should have done initially: they held sectional negotiations for all groups on strike, and exacted concessions. First among these was a wage increase of a halfpenny an hour for the dockers. Work was then resumed on Tuesday, 4 July.

Although Askwith's famous account of events has been used to exemplify the general mood of the working class in 1911, there were in reality very specific causes for the frustrations and rage of the Hull dockers. On the employers' side, there was the embattled posture of the old warriors of the Shipping Federation, blind even to their own long-term interest. The vestiges of free-labour strength were particularly strong in Hull, whose union structures and loyalties had been so vitally enfeebled in the dismal years since the 1890s. Local disillusion with Tillett was particularly strong. Conciliatory unions had filled the vacuum for almost two decades. When the strike broke out, Mann was tied up in Liverpool and Tillett offered no leadership at all. On the contrary, he actually sought to discourage action. He was personally preoccupied with the pending London strike. In their absence, leadership devolved on inexperienced men who had organized relationships with neither the strikers nor with the national offices. At the crisis of the movement, these spokesmen lost their nerve. The only officer involved who had any experience of national union affairs was O'Connor Kessack, and he took after James Sexton rather than Tom Mann.

The Hull dockers were, in short, not well served by the unions or their leaders, and they won their own victory unaided by either. Skilled strategic and tactical leadership did not prevent violence in Liverpool, but there it was visited on a peaceful rally by an unprovoked police charge. In Hull, it was the workers who initiated the violence, in sheer frustration and despair. Belatedly, it won them a settlement which they could accept. Tillett's neglect of Hull came home to his union when, after the strike, John Burn was able with Kessack's help to form branches of the NUDL, in direct opposition to the DWRGWU. The lightermen, too, went their own way by forming a branch of the NSFU. Harry Orbell and James Anderson, for the NTWF, finally came to Hull, and worked to re-form Tillett's union and a regional federation. The DWRGWU benefited to the tune of 1,000 new members enrolled in July 1911, but the majority were now in the NUDL. Rivalry between them found a morbid expression outside the TUC conference hall that autumn, when Tillett and Kessack exchanged blows![48]

Apart from the NUDL, the other beneficiary of Tillett's weakness in Hull was the Gasworkers' and General Labourers' Union. It had, of course, held a position there since the 1880s. Its membership was always more stable, and it had not suffered catastrophic rout in the 1890s. At the beginning of the 1911 strikes, on 17 June, Will Thorne had spoken in Hull and offered mature counsel on the real possibilities for concerted action of the kind then under way in Liverpool: 'He spoke at length about the "mechanics" of a general strike of all transport workers, stressing the need for scientific organisation. It was this lack of organisation and permanence he said, which had made the Shipping Federation reluctant to negotiate . . . but now all workers must unite.'[49]

We have already seen that the gasworkers won over the specialist Hull fish-dockers, the 'bobbers', in the spring of 1911. Through July and August, coal-heavers, timber workers, cement workers and flour-millers, all of whom had been brought into the Hull strikes by the dockers' picketing, were represented not by the Dockers' Union but by local officials of the gasworkers. Their Hull district secretary, Councillor R. H. Farrah, had established himself on the City Council in the 1890s as a member of the 'progressive group' sponsored by the Trades Council. He won union recognition and a wage increase for each of these groups, despite the autocratic opposition of Joseph Rank, the largest mill-owner in the town.

What was at work in this complex process, of course, was a competition between separate new unions to recruit membership among the hitherto unorganized strikers. In Hull, Tillett's union was poorly placed, because of its past defeats and recent abstentionism. Its failing image was reinforced by the absence of its leaders at the critical time. Little progress came its way. The NTWF had, in principle, been formed to police the process of recruitment. A similar role was envisaged for the General Labourers' National Council. At this stage neither body was effective in preventing fragmentation. Enclaves of membership were thus built almost at random, and these perpetuated the divisions of the future general unions. The split between the NUDL and the DWRGWU was, of course, to be healed in 1922; but the seeds of distrust of national dockers' leaderships, so powerful in later twentieth-century history, were sown in part by the Hull dockers' experiences from 1893 to 1911.

Strikes and Conciliation in Manchester

Lord Askwith had barely finished his work in Hull when he was summoned to Manchester. Here, the seamen's strike had also called down a dockers' stoppage on 27 June, which closed the Manchester Ship Canal docks. On 3 July all the city's carters had struck, not only those employed by the carting contractors but also those who worked for the railway companies. Manchester was thus gripped by a total transport strike. Eighteen unions were involved, and each was pledged not to return to work until the demands of all had been satisfied. Police were drafted in from Birmingham and troops were stationed in Salford. The Lord Mayor organized a vast conciliation operation, using every room in the Town Hall. Lord Askwith described the process:

> In every room . . . different trades were closeted, employers and employed, debating, discussing, and almost fighting. Hour by hour, and day by day, it was only possible to go from one to the other, get a dispute upon apparent lines of possible settlement, and then answer a hurried summons to another room to prevent a conference breaking up. For five days, for all the days and nearly all the nights these conferences proceeded, until at last, on Sunday night (July 9), all the trades had come to agreements except two, which would require the acceptance by the seamen of an arrangement slightly modified from one which the men had refused but their leaders seemed inclined to accept, and the consent of the Great Northern Railway Carters to go back to work without any change.[50]

By dint of persuasion, and the attrition tactics of an all-night session behind locked doors, Askwith won the consent of these two groups, and on 10 July the Manchester strikes were over.

They left behind a series of problems, some of which were spelt out by Will Hughes in Tom Mann's new Liverpool-based broadsheet, the *Transport Worker*. Assuming a regular magazine format, this represented great progress beyond the pocket-sized pamphlets of the *Industrial Syndicalist*. The front page bore two legends: 'Circulation 20,000' on one side, and, in capital letters, 'NON-POLITICAL' on the other. Non-political or not, the same front page of the first issue reported on a 'great French Labour Demonstration' under the title 'War Against War'. Unbelievably, Tom Mann had run over to Paris in the middle of the strike to participate in, and give his account of, an anti-war rally of the Confédération Générale du Travail. 'If the Transport Workers on land and sea actually refuse to carry or handle any material,' he wrote, 'government could no longer play at War.'

On Manchester affairs, its reports were severely practical: the United Carters' Union had gained 1,500 members and were exploring amalgamation with the Mersey Quay and Bolton Carters' Associations;

railway allegiances among carters and crane-drivers were complicating the task of rationalization of union structures; the dockers were

> going strong, they have increased their membership by over 100 per cent, making a membership of something like 3,500. This is extraordinary considering the short time since organising was started on a proper basis, viz., at the latter end of last October. Irma Dock is organised to a man. A new Branch has been opened for the Dry Dock Workers, and is doing well. Branches have been opened for Grain Workers and other allied industries.
>
> Practically every man has tumbled into the Branch for the Coal Tippers at Gartington; this, by the way is one of the sections of workers whose grievances were not tabulated in time for discussion before the settlement, but a definite promise has been made by the Ship Canal Company that these demands will be favourably dealt with under present negotiations. The Sailors and Firemen's Unions continue to make good progress.[51]

All this organizing, on the strength of the Manchester victories,

> has put new hopes for the future in the hearts of all the workers, including even the Foreman and Stevedore. Every man appears to be assuming the actions of a man, and now walks erect, I shouldn't wonder if the Death Rates are not reduced 25 per cent during the coming year, owing to the improved physique of the workers' walking attitude. They have at least realised that they have the right to live, and are becoming more determined to live by demanding the necessaries for giving that life.[52]

The Most Dangerous Man . . .

Leaving Manchester in this high euphoria, Askwith managed to fit in an emergency dash to Leeds to settle – again at 2 a.m. – a strike of the city's tramwaymen, before hurrying on down to London to conciliate in the dock strike there. During that year he was here, there and everywhere. Ben Tillett has left a shrewd and perceptive picture of the man and his role, as observed in the London strike.

> Sir George Askwith, the patient plodding man, with pigeon-holes in his brains; who listened without sign of being bored or absorbed, who concealed his mind like a Chinaman. Emotionless, except that he would peer through his glasses at someone making a statement of moment, never raising his diplomatic voice, or appearing to hurry over anything; guiding without falter or apparent effort the disputants however heated they may be, himself the inscrutable, patient listener. And such patience! It was more than dour in its persistence and calmness; it compelled by its coldness, and saved us from bickerings on occasions when the wisest become puny and spiteful.

He is the most dangerous man in the country. His diplomacy is and will be worse than war. Unless it absolutely succeeds in forcing industrial combatants to appreciate the human oneness of the community it will be a danger, inasmuch as it will make with its great genius for a peace that after all will be artificial.

There is no real peace for the toilers so long as the wage system exists. Men like Askwith might make the more supine and ignorant believe there can be peace without paying the price of war.[53]

Harry Gosling also recalled Askwith's methods: 'He always seemed to be waiting until nobody could think of another word to say and then he would come in . . . but he never decided for you. You always found you had decided for yourselves and he had merely counter-signed your own decision.'[54]

Askwith also seems to have been the originator of the 'smoke-filled room': 'he was more responsible than any other man', said Gosling, 'for introducing smoking at gatherings of this kind.'[55]

South Wales Catches On

The strikes which erupted in the complex of the South Wales ports were also detonated by the seamen's strike. In common with other ports, they received no coherent and official directives from either the NTWF or the DWRGWU. As a result, their responses were conditioned entirely by local trade-union resources, and by local leadership. The strikes which developed in the Cardiff docks exemplify the problems involved in a proliferation of sectional unions. This debility was never more evident than now, at a moment when port-wide solidarity was essential to success. When would it ever be more reasonable to call for sympathetic actions?

In Cardiff, the port's trade was dominated by coal, exports of which were booming. Two grades of dock workers, the tippers and the trimmers, constituted the key groupings in this trade. Each generated powerful loyalties and traditions. In the initial surge of new unionism during 1889–91, we saw that the trimmers had founded their own, exclusive union, based on tight control of labour supply and a closed, craft outlook (see chapter 4). By 1911, this attitude had become so rigid that the union did not even seek membership of the NTWF. Its leadership was essentially 'moderate', greatly valuing its close relationships with the port employers and also with the coal-owners. A mutual dependence had come into being. The coal-tippers, less skilled than the trimmers but still an exclusive, elite band when compared with the general dock labourers, had originally joined the DWRGLU in 1890. But in 1898 they had broken away to join the ASRS, in an effort to win closer relations with the Cardiff Railway Company and to improve their security and status as regular workers. The railway owned the port and was also a principal port employer. The defection of the tippers left the Dockers' Union greatly weakened. Henceforth it had no members in strategically placed occupations, and organized only the general cargo-handlers. In addition, dock membership was shared with the NALU, a purely regional union (despite its title), which had an old-style rule book and upheld the customs of an earlier age.

When the seamen stopped work in Cardiff on 14 June 1911, these divisions on the waterfront threatened them with isolation. Not only was there no call from the NTWF for dock workers' sympathy strikes, but even if such an appeal had been made, both tippers and trimmers were outside its membership. Tillett was far from enthused about the prospects of a wider strike, viewing his base in South Wales in a proprietorial and defensive light. Soon he was sending instructions to his members in the region – for example in Swansea, where the dockers had struck on 23 June – for an immediate return to work. This was of a pattern with his response to the Hull strike. Both decisions reflected a preoccupation with the pending strike in the Port of London.

The chemistry in the provinces and principalities was powerful, however. In South Wales the same yeast was working as in all the other ports around the kingdom. Syndicalist evangelists were hard at work, especially encouraged in Wales by the response they had aroused in the Cambrian coal strike and the success of Houlder dock strike of the previous year. The *Industrial Syndicalist*'s 'List of Persons willing to speak as advocates of Industrial Syndicalism in their respective districts' included George Jackson of the Seamen's and Firemen's Union, as well as Alfred Cox and George Cox, both of the Dockers' Union, and all of Newport. Six persons from the South Wales Miners' Federation, including Noah Ablett, appeared in the same list, as well as Councillor Jonah Charles, of the Dockers' Union in Port Talbot (see plate 9).[56] Madame Sorgue made a tour of South Wales in June 1911 to reinforce local supporters; and Tom Mann was a recent visitor too, rounding the coast from port to port in preparation for the seamen's strike.

But as the seamen began their strike in Cardiff, the coal-tippers and trimmers continued working. Their action was a restraint, holding back any surge of solidarity action which might have flowed from the example of the sailors. Liverpool and Hull were not, it seemed, to be imitated. At one point, it seemed possible that the tippers would break loose of their own accord, in response to their own grievances. They had sought the same status as railwaymen, but their inclusion in the Conciliation Board established in 1907 had not been confirmed; moreover, they now entered a claim for a shorter working week. On the very verge of a strike which would have given the seamen their first backing, Jimmy Thomas hastened to Cardiff for the ASRS, obtained the tippers' admittance to the Conciliation Board and a concession over their hours. He succeeded in his goal of defusing their grievance. And, 'with the tippers apparently bought off, was it likely that those notorious moderates the trimmers would come out?'[57]

Captain Bombast

One man who knew that drastic action was urgently needed, and was highly qualified by temperament to provoke it, was 'Captain' Edward Tupper, an extraordinary combination of bombast, flamboyance, racialism and alcoholism. He was the Seamen's Union organizer and moved from port to port throughout the year. He had been enrolled, a vigorous thirty-nine-year old, by the fifty-nine-year old, arthritic Havelock Wilson in 1910, specifically to assist in the planned strike and to act as Wilson's emissary. (He had a vague record as a speaker on Liberal Party platforms.)[58]

In early July 1911, Captain Tupper was hopping with frustration and anxiety because the Cardiff dockers' sympathy action had failed to materialize. He later recalled: 'I was getting desperate. Coal was thundering down hour after hour from the coal tips, into ships' holds and bunkers.'[59] On 3 July he proclaimed a general strike of the Bristol Channel ports, but nobody came out. Undaunted, he sustained the work of provocation.

At his union meetings in Bute Street, Cardiff, he wore a morning coat and a silk top hat, drank large quantities of 'Bass', and frequently challenged Shipping Federation toughs and employers to box against him at the Neptune Park, Cardiff. On 17th July, Tupper issued a challenge to Mr. E. Handcock, a Cardiff tug-boat owner, to fight him for £50, and at the head of a large procession he marched to Handcock's office. The demonstration got out of hand, and coal and jack-knives were thrown through the company's windows. Tupper was arrested, served with sixteen summonses, and appeared at the City Hall the next day.

His presence in court had a considerable effect upon industrial relations at Cardiff. Local members of the Dockers' Union, who until then had declined to strike . . . left work and were joined by workers from all sections of the port. The strikers also armed themselves, and soon many of them 'carried sticks and bludgeons; clubs with knife-blades and cut-throat razor blades set in the end, rope coshes with nails sticking out from the knots and plenty of weapons'. When the court decided to remand Tupper in custody, dockers and seamen stormed the City Hall, but were beaten back by large numbers of mounted and foot police. They retreated to the docks, stole barrels of stout and bottles of whisky from ships and warehouses, set fire to the Dublin and Liverpool warehouse, attacked the Glagow warehouse, and pushed a lorry into the dock. Further damage was prevented only by a fierce baton charge by the Cardiff constabulary. During this riot Tupper was in the cells at the City Hall . . . [he] was released the next day on bail; according to him, the magistrates realised that he was the only person who could prevent more disorder.[60]

Tupper's incitement included blatant racism, as he attacked the Chinese labour which was being used to man one ship. Recalling this episode, Tupper himself was to write:

That same night Liverpool Chinamen were taken from a train in the village of Marshfield and put into cabs. We knew all about it, and ship's rope was stretched across the Newport road. I had strictly commanded that there was to be no violence, and there wasn't: but those Chinks, on their knees in the road, thought their last hour had come.

'No goee blackee-leg! Wanchee go Livelpool – one time! No goee blackee-leg! Bad men makee talk, send Chinamen in tlain allee-same on piecee. No can do!' There was a terrible screeching, all trying to appeal to me, the 'Serang' – the boss. 'Cardiffi-side no good. Wanchee go back Livelpool! Can do? I solly, solly, solly! Bad men makee talk . . .' We sent them back to Liverpool.[61]

Thus wrote the self-proclaimed 'King of the Bristol Channel', future acting general secretary of the Seamen's Union. This 'leadership' provoked racial attacks on Chinese laundries and shops in Cardiff, and the terrorized Chinese workers required police escorts to go about their business.

One eye-witness, Pat Murphy, a rank-and-file seamen's leader, recorded that

In Cardiff, there were seven ships needing crews but there was no response from the unemployed seamen crowding the street at the Merchant Shipping Office, most of whom were coloured. Captain Tupper, one of the leaders of the union, made a fighting speech appealing for determination, but he made some very nasty remarks about Chinese and Arabs, who had really stood firm with British seafarers . . . Tupper's racialist speech inflamed some men and caused bitter quarrels among the seamen, and agents spread rumours to inflame disunity.[62]

Racial prejudice was a weapon deployed not only by Captain Tupper: it was manifest in the speeches of Havelock Wilson.

After these 'Tupper Riots' the Cardiff dockers, trimmers and tippers now all came out in sympathy action. The last trimmers left work on 20 July, led by Tupper himself, flamboyant to the last, perched in front of the march-out on a bicycle, from which vantage-point he brandished a trimmer's outsize shovel like an emblem of battle. All were then joined by the tippers and trimmers in Barry and Port Talbot.

But there remained serious divisions between the dockers themselves at the different Welsh ports. At Swansea the dockers' unofficial strike in June had won a wage increase, and now they rejected the call for sympathy action with the seamen. The Cardiff seamen won major gains, and the Joint Strike Committee in the port accepted them as a settlement of the whole dispute, just as they had in Hull. This committee included in its ranks the railwaymen's Jimmy Thomas, representing those tippers who were members of the ASRS, and also Ernest Bevin, newly appointed as a Dockers' Union official in Bristol and now seconded to represent the dock labourers' cause in Cardiff. He chaired a meeting of 40,000 in the city. Tupper represented the seamen, and there were representatives of the coal trimmers and of NALU. Bevin was the only member to oppose both the settlement and the return to work; his members had gained nothing from the Cardiff Railway Company. The seamen won a new, fixed port rate, union recognition and a Conciliation Board. These gains were undoubtedly attributable to the support finally given by the dock workers. The Strike Committee had initially resolved: 'That we recommend the men now on strike at Cardiff to remain out until settlement is arrived at affecting every section of workers involved . . . the full settlement to be submitted to a full conference for confirmation. Any section violating this will be repudiated.'[63]

Following the seamen's triumph, the Strike Committee had presented the employers with the dockers' demands – union recognition, no victimization and a prompt meeting to negotiate their grievances. The Cardiff Railway Company set its face against recognition of the Dockers' Union and promised the tippers no more than that they would be treated like other 'railway servants'. The seamen had settled; and the committee, despite Bevin's strong objections, ended the strike on these terms. The Dockers' Union received no reciprocal sympathy support to help break the hostility of the Cardiff Railway Company.

A second, unofficial strike against the Railway Company took place in August, but again failed in its object to win recognition or a bargain over wages. Dockers employed by other companies in the ports, however, won recognition in the July settlement, together with preference of employment. On this base, the union was able to re-establish itself in the port, although no standard port rate was achievable against the intransigence of the Railway Company. Divided rule in the Strike Committee, and the reassertion of sectional interests, produced an untidy and debilitating settlement. Bevin replied to his members' criticisms: 'He denied absolutely that he was a guilty person in bringing about that particularly unsatisfactory settlement. His last appeal in the conference room was to hold out for the sake of his men . . . but he found that he did not succeed so he shut up.'[64] For the young and aspiring Bevin, it was a salutary lesson on the evils of sectionalism.

The fragmentation of the workforce was perpetuated down to the First World War. Tippers had been embraced in the Railways' Conciliation machinery, and remained in the ASRS; the trimmers returned to their isolation, rejecting the renewed overtures of the NTWF. The Dockers'

Union had re-established a presence in the port, but faced the sustained opposition of the Railway Company. Much more could have been won with a united leadership. Less opportunism would have been a welcome asset, too. The dockers clearly felt that they had been exploited by the seamen. It is difficult not to hold Tupper personally responsible for this result.

The union in Newport was stronger, even before the events of 1911. It had a more radical tradition, and had been blooded in the Houlders dispute of 1910, which was still festering. However, Newport men faced employers of a less hostile temper than the Cardiff Railway Company. The strikers looked to the whole Bristol Channel to hold out for an estuarial agreement. They rounded on the Cardiff men's unilateral settlement, which 'sold their neighbours',[65] and they resolved to fight on alone. On 31 July, the Newport Employers' Committee concluded a settlement which gave preference to union workers and substantial wage gains. A comparison of the wages of different grades of docker at the three main South Wales ports after all the settlements shows that at Cardiff, rates were consistently 2–3s. per week less than at Swansea and Newport.[66]

As a final act, the Newport dockers sought to use their strength to resolve the long-standing dispute with Houlder, and to compel him to revert to the piece-work system. A blacking campaign, significantly supported by the NTWF, extracted a wage increase and other concessions from the company, which satisfied both the NTWF and the Newport Strike Committee. But the dockers were appalled by the company's insistence that its long-serving blacklegs should be allowed into their union, with the same rights of preference, as part of the settlement. Alf Cox, who had been up in Belfast, was summoned by the men to resume his unofficial leadership of the conflict. The Executive of the NTWF condemned the men and withdrew all further support. Cox summoned a mass meeting and formed an Emergency Advisory Committee. Among his colleagues and helpmeets was the seaman and fellow syndicalist Percy Knight. Their renewed leadership over the men was to be sorely tested in the following year.

Action in Bristol . . .

In Bristol, as we have seen, the dockers' exercise of rank-and-file solidarity in the 1910 Houlders dispute had anticipated the great unrest by a year. In that conflict, conducted on behalf of the Newport men, the Bristol dockers had demonstrated great solidarity. They had been backed up by rail and engineering grades in the port. Tillett had sought to restrain the men, and this highlighted the fact that 'there had long been an under-current of rank-and-file discontent with the moderation of the

Dockers' leadership'.[67] The strike of 1910 had already stimulated union growth in other sections of Bristol labour, notably amongst the carters, whose branch chairman was Ernest Bevin.

The initial impact of the seamen's dispute on the Bristol dockers was minimal: the few Bristol-based shipping companies made early settlements in June 1911, and the limited solidarity actions by dockers on their behalf, and in support of a carters' agreement, were shortlived. A spark from a different source fired an explosive strike of Bristol dockers in August. Without union endorsement, they struck solidly in support of the railwaymen, at first in connection with a local dispute and then in sympathy with the national rail strike. The dockers, following the pattern almost everywhere, then drew up their own programme of demands and called out the carters for good measure. Soon 6,000 men were on strike, in addition to the railmen. Some factories, and even two adjacent collieries, downed tools against union advice. The army appeared (what a familiar scene this had become in Britain's ports by August!) and fired over a crowd's heads to disperse them.

The railway strike was settled in days, however, and the dockers returned to work in comparative peace and good order to await the terms of a Joint Conciliation Committee. Union recognition was accorded to the Dockers' Union, victimization was ruled out and wage rates were increased by a halfpenny, to 7d. an hour, with night rates up a penny to 10d. Uncomplicated by association with the seamen's strike, which was resolved before they acted, or by serious inter-union differences or fragmentation, the Bristol dockers and carters had a relatively straight furrow to plough through the year: their victory 'marked the high water mark of the Dockers' achievements in [pre-war] Bristol.'[68] By 1914 their union had established a virtual monopoly of all port labour and was organizing in brickyards and widening its appeal to the carters. In contrast to Hull, the Dockers' Union moved into these new fields at a moment when the Gasworkers' Union in Bristol was dwindling to 'a pale shadow of the Dockers'.[69]

. . . and in Glasgow

In Glasgow, the seamen appealed to the Trades Council for assistance as soon as their strike got under way on 14 June. A young, militant Co-operative mill-worker (he found the work very dull) was sent by the Council to render support on the Clyde waterfront.[70] In this way, Emanuel Shinwell enters the story of transport unionism for the first, but by no means the last, time. To begin with, he worked voluntarily for the strikers, in the evenings and for two holiday weeks. The Clyde, he reminds us, along with Southampton and Liverpool, was one of the centres of the passenger-liner trade, shipping out thousands of emigrants to Australia, Canada and the USA. Seamen earned £4 a month, firemen £4 10s. They now demanded an increase of £1 a month for both grades. The dockers, by now organized in the Scottish Union of Dock Labourers, their breakaway from the NUDL (see chapter 4), came out in sympathy. Shinwell became involved with them too, addressing their meetings not only on the Clyde but in Leith and Dundee besides.

According to Shinwell, the Glasgow liner companies included amongst their directors some powerful figures who were prepared to be conciliatory, and the sums demanded by the NSFU locally were soon conceded. But Havelock Wilson had made an accord with the Shipping Federation accepting 10s. less, in return for a union monopoly of labour supply. This account is not unique.[71] Wilson's sights were set on winning recognition, and he was prepared to pay the price, in terms both of moderation in wage settlements and in transforming his union into an agent of industrial discipline. In Southampton this had already led to the breakaway of the NSFU branch to form the British Seafarers' Union, an episode which was to cast a long shadow, darkening Ernest Bevin's desk at Transport House in the early years of the TGWU (see vol. II). There is further evidence available of the evolution of Wilson's methods away from militancy and towards a material intimacy with the shipowners: several of the most prominent magnates were present at the union's annual dinner after the 1911 strikes. Captain Tupper tells the story of this bizarre change in his fortunes with evident satisfaction:

> Many of the leading shipowners were invited to the annual dinner of the union, held at the Holborn Restaurant. Havelock Wilson, of course, was in the chair, and amongst us of the Union was the Rev. Father Hopkins, that famous Calcutta Seamen's padre, who had fought valiantly in the fight just won. Havelock Wilson said that the Union did not desire unnecessary trouble in any direction. He declared that, after his experience of the mercantile marine, he would say that he did not believe shipowners had had real value for the money they had paid out – that over twenty-five per cent of the men in the mercantile marine, Asiatics of all kinds, were not fit for the job . . . In replying to the toast of 'The Shipping Industry', Sir Walter Runciman . . . said they had just emerged from one of the most bitter fights – a well-conducted one – that had taken place in his time . . . he did not believe that there was a shipowner present or absent who was not glad of the rise in wages.[72]

The arrangement of such convivial encounters set in thereafter as a standard practice.[73]

In the Glasgow episode, two of Wilson's assistants arrived with the intention of closing down the seamen's branch because it had obtained the higher rate of wage increase. The two were none other than Richard McGhee, now a Nationalist MP for an Irish constituency, and Captain Tupper. Here was a supreme irony: the veteran co-founder of the NUDL in harness with the demagogue of Cardiff, invested with the task of negotiating a wage reduction and the closure of a union branch! The seamen responded by forming the Scottish Seamen's Union, and in 1912 this breakaway merged with its Southampton counterpart to form the British Seafarers' Union.

Meanwhile, the dockers of Glasgow, who had won a wage increase after striking for only eight days, solicited Shinwell's services as their secretary, a post which he declined in favour of the secretaryship of the new seamen's union. This appointment was no sinecure. Neither was it free from hazard. In recalling the temper of this period on the Clyde, Shinwell claims that he was once fired on at a meeting by one of Wilson's hired men, 'with the result that the person standing next to me was killed'.[74] The Scottish Union of Dock Labourers put an end to its own isolation from the rest of dockland by affiliating to the NTWF in February 1912.

. . . and London Follows On

It is time to turn to the drama on the Thames, where there had been no immediate mass dock strike upon the declaration of the seamen's strike in June. This pause gave Tillett and the other leaders of the NTWF, whose National Executive was dominated by the London waterfront unions, the opportunity to work out a strategy for the coming movement and to present agreed common demands, in the name of the NTWF, to the London employers. In this way they were assured of the leadership of the new upsurge. A public meeting in April in Canning Town had already pledged all port unions to support the simple and long-cherished demand for a 'port rate' of 8d. an hour, 1s. overtime and regular call-times. At the end of June these demands were presented by the NTWF to the PLA, the shipowners and the wharfingers.

Of course, by this time the provincial strikes were well under way (despite Tillett's various efforts at discouragement) and some had even been favourably settled. Tillett claimed that the period of restraint in London was attributable to union and NTWF discipline. This seems a bold claim when set against the fact that, at the outset of the unrest, less than 50 per cent of all types of waterfront workers on the Thames were trade-union members, Tillett's own union being, as we already know, particularly weak. The level of organization had not been greatly improved by the recruitment drive in the months since the formation of the NTWF. When it came, the London dockers' militancy and solidarity were as formidable as elsewhere. The tardiness of their action is nevertheless curious. Tillett himself, although in 1911 wholly engaged with the cause of London, admitted that 'it may be said with safety and due regard to truth that there would not have been a London movement but for the provincial Transport Workers' agitation . . . In nearly all the important ports the movement had progressed with great strides, forcing recognition of trade unions, better conditions of labour, improved rates of pay, and a healthier outlook.'[75] In using capital letters to designate the transport workers in that passage, Tillett was claiming for the NTWF an initiating role which it did not in fact play. (Tillett himself was, we have seen, actually discouraging provincial strikes.) On 27 June it had threatened 'drastic action'. At its executive meeting on 3 July it decided against any kind of national call and, as we know, each port followed its own methods in responding to wave after wave of unco-ordinated strikes.

In London the sequence of events was quite different, with the initiative for a crucial early period in the hands of Tillett. He used it, on the day after the NTWF ultimatum, to dispatch the concerted London demands to the PLA, the shipowners, the wharfingers and the granary-keepers. Uncertain, despite abundant evidence from the provinces, of the temper of his own men, he together with Gosling, the NTWF chairman, and the rest of the Joint Committee nevertheless set a deadline for an employers' response: 3 July, the date chosen by the NTWF for its call for national sympathy action. The Lightermen's Society put in a separate claim, so seamen, dockers and lightermen converged in claims on the London employers. At this point, the employers undoubtedly contributed to the men's decision to hold their hand when, in an unprecedented response, they offered to meet the NTWF committee and discuss its claims. The employers were clearly alarmed by the mass strikes in the provinces. The NTWF then cancelled its plans for a sympathy strike – evidence that its preoccupation was with London. The provincial dockers, whose actions had clearly prompted the London employers' unprecedented readiness to deal, were left without a framework of national support.

For all that, the negotiations in London between the groups of employers led by the PLA, and the NTWF, were the first occasion when something like modern collective bargaining took place in the port, unaccompanied by mediators from outside the industry. In London at least, the NTWF was working. Apart from the PLA, the employers' side included at first the Shipping Federation, the Wharfingers', the Granary Keepers', the Master-Lightermen's, and the Short-Sea Traders' Unions. However, the short-sea traders withdrew from the negotiations, and this had important effects on the course of the subsequent strike and settlements. In their absence it was impossible fully to achieve the goal of a single port rate. Nevertheless, the two sides concluded the Devonport Agreement, named after Lord Devonport, chairman of the PLA. Under its terms, those dockers on 6d. and 8d. got an increase of 1d. an hour on both normal and overtime rates, whilst those already on 7d. and 9d. were to receive 8d. and 1s. Clearly the 'port rate' had not been achieved, and several grades of dockers, including those in the short-sea trades, won nothing. Yet to the negotiators it must have seemed incredible: a wage increase had been negotiated without a strike, after twenty-odd years of trade-union stagnation. The conduct of the negotiations, as recorded by Tillett, had some of the hallmarks of today's collective bargaining, with the unions deploying arguments based on productivity improvements, manning scales and the cost of living. But although they had won some wage increases, no progress was made on union control of hiring, or on the wage claims of many specialist groups, including tugboatmen and coalies.

Now, however, Tillett, Gosling and Will Thorne were to be ambushed by unambiguous evidence of the temper of the men: at a mass meeting on 28 June, their presentation of the Devonport terms was howled down. Tillett recorded that 'Only respect for the Chair and platform prevented a violent antagonism.'[76]

Tillett claimed that the negotiators would not have settled for the Devonport Agreement 'had that spontaneous outburst been given a month earlier [for] it would have been of incalculable value to us. Although we battled with all the courage, persistence, and brains we were capable of, we realized the apparent weakness of our own side'.[77] The contrast between Havelock Wilson's frontal attack – adventurous, officially led from the centre – and the caution of Tillett (and Gosling) could not be sharper. Of course Wilson's militancy, whilst fierce and even unscrupulous, was highly ambiguous. It enabled him first to control his union and then to lead it into the uniquely compromised relationship with the shipping magnates which we have described above. The challenge to Wilson's leadership came only at the edges, in Glasgow and Southampton. Here on the docks the NTWF leaders were given no such latitude. They were ignominiously sent back from the mass meeting, and told to negotiate better terms with Lord Devonport's committee. But the employers would not amend a line of the agreement. Now at last, six weeks behind the provinces, a general port stoppage was inevitable.

The coalies, excluded from the deal, began it on 29 July. Others whose claims were unsettled followed: they were absolutely not prepared to await the results of the proffered arbitration. Gosling and Orbell made one last effort to restrain them, but on 2 August, at a further mass meeting, the leadership caved in, accepting the plain fact that the Devonport 'agreement' was not enough and was not going to be 'agreed'. An official port strike was called. Immediately the lightermen came in with their own demand for a ten-hour day. On 3 August the Port of London stopped. An awe-inspiring collision, this was 1889 revisited, and Tillett did a rapid about-face to claim the leadership of the conflict. The employers were indignant: how was collective bargaining to be conducted in good faith with such a leader? Why, had he not sanctioned the strike's commencement for the very day that Sir Albert Rollitt had been due to perform his official function as arbitrator over the key issue of the port rate, referred to him under the Devonport Agreement?[78] Tillett had displayed great caution, and evidently wished to establish stable permanent-bargaining structures, but the men were urging him to wage intransigent battle instead. He heard them. And he went with them.

The strike had all the colour of its great forerunner, with its marches, rallies and mass meetings on Tower Hill and in Trafalgar Square. But it had a momentum of its own, not determined by leaders but driven forward from demand to demand by the force of the strikers themselves, and by their will that no section should be deserted before a settlement was reached for all of them.

The 1911 strike was different also in that each grade and group acted on its own behalf, and in tune with its separate unions' aspirations, whilst consenting to federal presentation of their case in negotiations. In addition to dock labourers, the lightermen, tugboatmen, ship repairers, sail-bargemen, coalies, carters and stevedores all entered the struggle, wave after wave, each union with its own demands. For the leaders and negotiators, this made a moving and constantly changing picture; consequently, as they sought agreement for one group and at one level of compromise, they found that the impetus had moved on, or that the minimum acceptable terms had increased.

This shifting pattern brought out the contradictory sides of Tillett's leadership and personality. On the one hand, he sought pacific, negotiated settlement. On the other, as always, he was caught up in the mood of the men and driven by his always passionate engagement with the deprivation and suffering of the dock community. He was also excited by the demonstration of the enormous, if negative, power which this overwhelming refusal of labour services meant for London. The capital ran short of food. Perishable cargoes turned rancid, green with mould or infested with flies and vermin in the hot-houses which warehouses and ships became in the heat of the summer. Ice could not be produced to cool the unmoveable wares, as no coal was carried to drive refrigeration plant. As in other ports, the Strike Committee issued permits to ensure essential supplies to hospitals and orphanages. Without such protection, nothing else moved. The general effect was dramatic, and Tillett basked in that drama, enjoying every nuance of its symbolism:

> The number of meetings was increasing, the enthusiasm was spreading, excitement was rising high, there were skirmishes with the police; frantic, panic-stricken officialdom bungling their functions and powers. The Transport Workers' fingers were for the time being on the throat of trade. What a contrast between the squealing, struggling capitalist and well-to-do class, who squirmed and shrieked as they shouted 'Famine!' 'Famine!' and the year-round silent suffering of the 52 per cent of our number who are more or less constantly fighting and facing the grim devils of hunger, misery and death. For a moment the great British public had brains and conscience, not that it cared so much for the hundreds of thousands of our

class, who had endured for months and years and decades and generations, but the public's stomach was being pinched, and there was a wolf-howl as it snarled its hate of possible hunger.[79]

And Tillett undoubtedly meant to preach this lesson more widely to workers who, for so long, had incurred his displeasure for their passivity and fecklessness: 'I want to say that the workers should for ever remember that their hands are on the throat of trade and industry at all times . . . they have only to use their power . . . to bring the whole activities of civilisation to an abrupt standstill'.[80]

The condition of the carmen moved him more than most: at the end, their massive strike, which was the making of carters' unionism in London, won the magnificent victory of a ten-hour reduction in their working week – to a new standard week of seventy-two hours!

In the midst of this turbulence fell the decision of the Rollitt arbitration. He awarded the full claim of 8d. and 1s. to the dockers employed by overseas shipowners and contractors. Nothing moved, none the less. The strike rolled on: the NTWF told all to stay out until every sectional claim was satisfied. The strikes of carmen actually gathered force after the Rollitt award, paralysing all street traffic. Other specialist dock grades joined in even at this late stage. In all, the Strike Committee, assisted by the tireless and dispassionate Askwith as conciliator, made nine separate agreements. Some were so complex that their final details were still being settled in September, long after the dispute was over. Askwith recalled one such agreement, for the sail-barge crews of the Thames, Medway, Sittingbourne and Faversham. The men had gone back to work on the understanding that the new rates would be back-dated to 21 August, the date their strike was called off. The new rates had to cover every class of cargo: 'The completed list contained about 600 items, with rates for cement, lime, bricks, clay, coal, coke, corn and grain, ballast, timber, wood-pulp, manure, flints, oil, and a number of miscellaneous items.'[81] Such were the minutiae, essential matters for the bargemen concerned, of the great upheaval in the Thames.

Around this tortuous and exhausting process of meetings, the lobbying and political pressures swung to and fro. Winston Churchill at the Home Office resisted the mounting demands of merchants, anxious for their cargoes and their businesses, and of the West End, anxious for its stomach, to put soldiers in to move the cargoes. (There was no need to send them in to break picket lines, as there were none. There were no strike-breakers on hand to be dissuaded.) John Burns, as the minister responsible for local government in this Liberal government, met and dealt with his old comrade of 1889. Tillett was not hostile: 'Although the dock agitator was now a Cabinet Minister, he really forgot that at times.'[82]

As the strike extended in scope and duration, so did its organizational reach. By mid-August the London membership of the Dockers' Union

had risen from 2,000 to 22,000, and its branches from 14 to 49. The
Stevedores' Union grew from 4,000 to 8,000.[83]

The main sectional deals were completed in four hectic days at the
Board of Trade, between 8 and 11 August. They covered lightermen,
sail-bargemen, carmen, coal-porters. The NTWF and the employers'
associations were the signatories. The lightermen alone signed as a
separate union. Askwith countersigned them all.

It might have been expected that, following these agreements, which
all conceded much on wages, hours and conditions, the strike would at
last be over. But in fact no return to work was possible. The PLA refused
reinstatement to 3,000 labourers, and the NTWF supported a renewed
protest strike of the PLA men, who were also incensed by a second
grievance: the PLA alone would not concede the mealtime payment
which had been negotiated. (These irritants can be seen in hindsight as
portents of Lord Devonport's intransigent behaviour in 1912.) A second
set of problems attended the return to work, for the men now eagerly
sought to impose union control over hiring. They struck again at the
Royal Docks when the call-on continued inside the dock gates, where
the union could not control it. Again the NTWF endorsed the men's
spontaneous strike – it is noticeable how much more readily the
leadership responded to rank-and-file initiative as the year's experience
changed its perceptions of what was possible and what was prudent.

The government viewed the prospects in mid-August with renewed
alarm. The upheaval in the Port of London had defied every concession
and still raged on; Liverpool had now erupted in a general strike, and a
national rail strike was in the offing. Whilst the government was
prevailing on the railway companies to conciliate, the Home Office also
leant on the London port employers: the shipowners were to concede
that the call-on should take place outside the dock gates, although the
master-lightermen refused an equivalent concession. The men at the
short-sea trades had also been excluded from previous settlements, and
the variations in the rates they earned from different groups of employers
was a classic example of the general case for a port rate for all dockers. In
a final effort to achieve a total resumption of work, short-sea-trade men
with this outstanding grievance were induced to go back whilst an
arbitrator dealt with their case. When he did, in October, he found
against the men. The strike, which came to an end for this group only on
31 August, could not be immediately revived; but the decision added
provocation to the untidy muddle of sectional settlements which
complicated port wage structures. It was to mark a pause in, not a
resolution of, the pre-war struggles of the London dockers.

III

The Effect of the Transport Strikes

What was the sum effect of the 1911 strikes in transport? How did it influence the argument for amalgamation? The scale of the unrest was enormous; the number of workers involved in stoppages during the year was almost 1 million, and the number of working days lost more than 10 million. Nothing remotely like this had happened since 1893. Now, as then, the majority of strikers were port and transport workers. (As many as 80,000 workers were involved in a series of shipbuilding and engineering strikes, and 4 million days were lost in the coal industry.) Excluding the railway strikers, some 120,000 transport workers – seamen, dockers and carters – had been involved in the stoppages.

The effect on union membership was dramatic and immediate (see table 10.2). The main port unions' figures doubled or trebled, compared with an increase – spectacular enough itself – for all trade unions in the same year of 22 per cent, from 2,565,000 in 1910 to 3,139,000 in 1911.

Table 10.2   *Membership of Waterfront Unions, 1911–1912*

	NSFU	DWRGWU	NUDL	Stevedores (London)	Lightermen (London)
1911	20,000	20,000	12,000	4,000	3,000
1912	60,000	50,000	24,000	8,000	6,761

Source: TUC Reports

The annual accounts of the NUDL tell of the impact of the year. Contribution income doubled to £2,475. Expenditure on strike pay had been reported as only £921 in 1907, the year of the Belfast strike, even though James Sexton had claimed in the union's Annual Report to have spent £7,000. It fell to £565 in 1908, £147 in 1909 and a mere 12s. in 1910. But it was £10,886 in 1911. At the same time, the union increased its expenditure on officers' salaries by £1,300 to £3,915. Although his finances were modestly improved by the merger with the Liverpool North End Coal Heavers' Society, which brought £536 9s. 9d. into the coffers, the parsimonious Sexton actually ran down the capital account by £4,462 to finance the strikes.

The real membership of the union at the year end is in some doubt. In table 10.2 we have used the figures of membership affiliated to the TUC, but the union's Annual Report gives its membership at the year end as 'something like 50,000'.[84] Of Liverpool, Sexton writes: 'Suddenly, like a bolt from the blue came the dispute of last July . . . with the result that before the end of August, it might be truly said that there was scarcely a man, either seeking work or employed at the Docks, who was not a member of our organisation.'[85] And he confesses, 'We entered upon that dispute with a feeling of anything but hope, owing to past experience . . . We were very soon convinced . . . that our analysis of the new spirit was not the right one . . . The change, when we come to consider it, is simply marvellous.'[86] Thomas Hutchcroft, branch secretary in Goole, reported that, although the maximum number of dockers did not exceed 1,200, the union ended the year with 1,550 members, the balance being made up of gasworkers and general labourers, who came in after the strike. In Ireland the union 'still seems to lag behind . . . At the present time we occupy the same position only as last year'.[87]

After the strike, Sexton set about establishing greater central control over the funds, attacking the 'out-of-date method of all branches maintaining their own funds'.[88] At the same time, he sought to generalize the new practice in Scotland and Hull of creating District Committees.

Tillett's Annual Report also records the advances of the year, but is less than comprehensive in its accounts of the strikes. Whilst it celebrates the great gains of the London dispute, it refers only to 'a very prolonged lock-out of the dry dock workers in Barry and Cardiff', amongst all the other provincial strikes. Bristol increased its income by £2,000, Cardiff by four times to £1,244, and London from £554 to £6,753. All round the southern and eastern districts, the Report records the renewal of union membership and life, from East Anglia to Plymouth. All districts, except Barry, Hull and Workington, had comfortable excesses of income over expenditure. Of Hull we learn that 'against many difficulties, we succeeded in increasing income . . . from £64 2s. 3d. to £298 0s. 3d. The expenditure was £457 11s. 10d., being £159 11s. 7d. in excess of the income'.[89]

In total, the DWRGWU spent £3,643 on dispute pay. Of this sum, no less than £1,474 was expended in supporting the locked-out members in the Barry dry-dock. (This was an obscure affair, but a lock-out no doubt left Tillett with no option but to finance his members.) In London the union dispensed a mere £656 on strike pay, in Port Talbot £590, in Swansea £511, in Hull £136, in Bristol £66 and in Cardiff £3 10s.

Tillett, despite his ostensible militancy, by refusing to sanction so many of the provincial disputes had spent less than one-third of the sum laid out by his rival, the prudent Sexton. The NUDL's active role in the Humber ports that summer cost Tillett the bulk of those dock members who might have been expected to return to him, as Hull's old hero of 1889–90. Memories proved shorter, going back only to the sad manoeuvres and retreats of 1893. In any event, it was not the record of olden times, but the impact of present activities which brought Hull dockers home to a different union.

The carters in the main ports all took part in the upsurge of trade unionism. Following their participation in the strikes, many flocked to enrol themselves on the union books. Some substantial improvements in terms and conditions were gained. At this time, carters were principally organized in their own specialized unions, the main exception being Bristol, where Bevin brought them into the Dockers' Union. The principal unions present in the ports in 1911 were: the Mersey Quay and Railway Carters' Union in Liverpool; the Amalgamated Carters' and Motormen's Association in Manchester; the London Carmen's Trade Union in London; and the Scottish Horse and Motormen's Association in Glasgow. Their membership performance at this time is shown in table 10.3.

Table 10.3   *Membership of Road Transport Unions, 1911–1913*

	1911	1912	1913
Carters and Lurrymen (Bolton)*	3,000	3,000	3,000
London Carmen's Union†	4,980	8,000	4,000
United Carters' Association (Manchester)‡	3,000	5,000	5,000
Amalgamated Association of Tramway and Vehicle Workers (Manchester)**	18,000	21,000	21,000

*Joined the NTWF in 1917 and the TGWU in 1922.
†Changed its name from London Carmen's Union to National Union of Vehicle Workers in 1913. Sam March continued as its secretary. Joined TGWU in 1922.
‡Became the United Road Transport Union (URTU).
**Though Manchester-based, took over the London Tramway Employees' Association in 1904 and so had national status. Affiliated to NTWF in 1916. In 1919 joined with the London and Provincial Licensed Vehicle Workers' Union to form the United Vehicle Workers' Union, which joined the TGWU in 1922.
Source: TUC Annual Reports, 1911–13.

Hugh Clegg rightly concludes that the actions in which these bodies became engaged were 'a series of organisation strikes, such as had also occurred in 1871–4' and again in 1889, and were to break out yet again in the United States and France during the 1930s. 'Such a series', he writes,

> begins either with rapid recruitment into trade unions in industries where unions have hitherto been weak and unrecognised, or with spontaneous strikes leading to union recruitment . . . The employers are taken by surprise. Some concede quickly. Others resist, but they are ill-prepared . . . Most eventually yield. The new union members are confirmed in their support of their unions, and further recruits flock in. Other ill-organised groups . . . rally . . . and so on.[90]

All these unions benefited from their association with the wider transport strikes. They fitted easily into the strike committees and eventually into the NTWF's structures, being for the most part new and 'open' unions with strongly centralized constitutions, dominated by the full-time officers.[91]

We have acknowledged already the crucial role of the Seamen's Union in precipitating the strike-wave. Its own fortunes improved sharply. Membership, as well as the level of wages, increased proportionately. Militant action paid off. But we have also noted the roles of two distinctly shady characters, Hopkins and Tupper, in these battles: both were unscrupulous adventurers personally deployed by Wilson. At the same time, new patterns of collaboration were for the first time brought into being in Glasgow, Southampton and Manchester. We have noted evidence of the 'deal' which Wilson made at some point in the strikes, to settle for less than the official claim in return for closer relations with the shipowners. Similar reportage suggests dissent at this tactic also amongst the seamen of Goole.[92] Formal relations were quickly established. Before the year was out, Wilson was entertaining Sir Walter Runciman, an archetypal Edwardian Liberal, shipowner and member of the Shipping Federation. Runciman became president of the Board of Education, with a seat in the Cabinet, in 1908, at the same time that Winston Churchill joined him as president of the Board of Trade. Seeds of later bitter conflicts between Wilson and his contemporaries in the NTWF and the wider trade-union movement were sown, albeit discreetly, in the flush of the success which was due to his initial combativeness.

If these were the main components of the waterfront struggles, this port-by-port survey has drawn our attention to many smaller, local, sectional unions. The overwhelming evidence, at least as obvious to contemporaries as to historians, is that these divisions seriously impaired the process of bargaining, co-ordination of strikes and the achievements – in wages, conditions and union recognition – won in the settlements. Of course, 'it takes two to tango', and the other side of this coin is the evident fragmentation, or the complete absence of, employer organization capable of conducting mature, binding and constructive negotiations with the unions.

The Role of the National Transport Workers' Federation

The young NTWF was intended to solve the problem of fragmentation on the union side. Undoubtedly, it had in this respect stepped out in front of the employers: contrary to some views of the evolution of British industrial relations, a study of the history of transport unionism strongly suggests that the innovators in collective bargaining were the unions. But in 1911 the NTWF was untried, and was top-heavy with London unions. Moreover, it had no regional structures. On top of this it was led by men who commonly looked back in apprehension to the 1890s, while they freely confessed that they had failed to read the mood of the men of 1911 correctly. The result of these impediments was that the NTWF's role in the strikes was minimal – with the important exception of London, where it assumed an advanced role not only as strike initiator and co-ordinator, but as a bargaining agent and signatory of agreements.

Impressed with their own achievements in the capital, NTWF leaders tended thereafter to claim far too much for the federal role in 1911. Gosling wrote:

> The 1911 transport workers' strike was the biggest, sharpest, and most successful dispute that had ever been known. The men had been absolutely loyal, which made it possible for us to get on with the negotiations without unnecessary distractions. The settlement was one quite without precedent, inasmuch as every section involved had obtained at least some concession . . . Of course the secret of it all was the federation ticket, which had cemented the men together as never before. It was their first real taste of solidarity . . .[93]

This claim may have substance in the case which Gosling is describing, the London strike. Elsewhere, however, solidarity actions were the order of the day, and the NTWF often played little part in them.

Nevertheless, the NTWF benefited greatly, both in reputation and in membership, from the actions of the year. In June 1911 it had an affiliated membership of 54,716. By April 1912 this had become 220,000. Up to February 1912, eleven new affiliations had been made.[94]

Railwaymen and Dockers

The railwaymen touched the dock strikes at many places in 1911. In the ports of South Wales, the Humber and in Southampton, railway companies, as owners or part-owners of the quays, the cranes and the rail links to the dockside, employed many grades of dock labour. They ran carting services to and from the docks, and so were big employers of the carters. Frequently the railway companies offered a form of permanent, as opposed to casual, employment to their 'servants' in the ports. They practised the same paternalism as on the railways proper, and applied similar standards of discipline. The dockside railworkers were consequently induced to join railway unions, such as the ASRS and the Railway Clerks' Association. In Cardiff, we saw that the coal-tippers' membership of the ASRS told against their solidarity with the general-strike movement in that port. The ASRS, and from 1913 the NUR, never did enter the NTWF. Its chosen path was that of the 'one union, one industry' model. That industry was to be the railways, narrowly defined: not the transport industry seen inclusively. Regularly employed rail-company dock porters, carters, crane-men, maintenance-men, and lock-gate keepers, potentially key grades in a strike, were embarked on roads which diverged from those chosen by the general dock labourers. Shipping clerks, many of whom were unionized for the first time in 1911, joined the Railway Clerks' Association in the railway-owned ports but formed their own union in London. Later this was to adhere to the TGWU. The resultant divisions survived in the ports down to modern times.

Yet in 1911 the railmen's intimacy with docks and dockers was still strong enough to generate widespread sympathetic participation, unofficially, in a common struggle. The national rail strike itself had its origins in Liverpool, where Tom Mann's Strike Committee brought the city to a standstill on their behalf. Elsewhere, solidarity actions linking railwaymen with port workers were common – almost as frequent as joint action between seamen and dockers. The chosen method of industrial unionism of the railways had not at that time frozen into rigid forms. Participation by the rail unions in the NTWF, and later the TGWU, was widely anticipated and would have enabled waterfront railway employees to build on the links made in 1911, just as the road transport men eventually did. This is one of many 'ifs' on the road to the general union's formation; similar speculation is provoked by the case of the seamen's unions. Road-, rail- and water-transport workers all focused their efforts around the dockside. In 1911 they made common cause in their actions, but they did not press forward to develop a common organization.

Developing the NTWF

If the railwaymen stayed clear of the NTWF, those who had already moved to join forces in it did derive great benefit; and, indeed, they quickly learned from the experience.

In 1911, however, the leadership drew the appropriate lesson. Gosling told the TUC in September: 'I think it has now been made clear that we must now abandon every form of sectional strike and get the men into much larger federations. In this particular case [the London strike], we were able to drop the individual unions, and speak of the whole of the trades as a federation'.[95]

The Federation embarked on internal reforms. The provincial unions sought to end the London domination on the Executive and, in an

important move, District Councils were set up, with financial assistance
from the centre. This was a natural development arising from the
experience of the *ad hoc* Joint Strike Committees of the summer, and
indeed some DCs had been formed before the NEC's decision that they
be established. Well designed for the co-ordination of industrial
movements, such councils were also much better placed than the centre
to adjudicate in poaching disputes and to issue a Federation ticket. They
developed considerable autonomy, being enjoined only to 'consult' the
NEC in any dispute which was 'likely to cause a national stoppage'.[96] It is
significant that, of the present-day regional offices of the TGWU, five of
the eleven – in Hull, Bristol, Liverpool, Glasgow and London – were
chosen in 1911–12 as locations for Federation district headquarters.

Bargaining, Conciliation and the State

The impact of the strikes on the development of collective bargaining
was most advanced in Liverpool and London, where the White Book
Agreement in the first case, and the Devonport Agreement in the
second, represented the results of genuine bilateral bargains, the first of
their kind. Even in these cases, however, the degree of union recognition
involved and the permanence of the relationship were uncertain.
Elsewhere (and in the later stages of the London dispute) the
intervention of conciliators was often necessary to bring the antagonists
to the bargaining table. For the port employers were reluctant, and
nowhere more so than in London, to acknowledge that the days of free
labour and the depot ship were almost over. In this respect, the changed
attitude of the state was critical. The readiness of the administrations of
the 1890s to smash picket lines and protect strike-breaking labour with
police and troops was replaced by a new caution in the face of massed
strikers. This undoubtedly had a profound effect on the outcome. In
place of the cavalry – or in some cases, admittedly, in addition to the
cavalry – the new response was: send George Askwith! The records of
the Shipping Federation are revealing. Writing of the situation at the
commencement of the 1911 strikes, its historian relates:

> Although the Federation was in a position to obtain the services of large
> bodies of men to replace strikers, the necessary protection for them could
> not be obtained.
>
> As an instance of 'the entire helplessness of the authorities', the
> Federation reported at the time that during the strikes in London the
> Federation's depot ship *Lady Jocelyn* lay in the Thames for some days with
> men on board ready to discharge cargo. Bodies of men were at the same
> time standing by in various parts of the country in readiness to proceed to
> London to work where required. The Home Office and police authorities,
> however, declined to allow the vessel to enter the docks, or to permit the

men who had been engaged to be brought into London. The machinery of the Federation for the supply of dock labour was thus rendered virtually inoperative . . . The records of the Federation at this period dwell repeatedly on the question of picketing. The outstanding feature of the strikes, it is reported, was undoubtedly 'the licence which from the commencement took the form of gross intimidation, which was assumed by union pickets under the Trades Disputes Act', coupled with the attitude of the central authorities which 'appeared to proceed upon the assumption that any attempt to replace men on strike must be regarded as a provocative act – practically justifying intimidation'.[97]

The Shipping Federation sent a deputation to Winston Churchill at the Home Office. He told them that the Trades Disputes Act 'did not directly countenance violence'. He said that he believed that pickets should be limited in number to those sufficient to convey information, and that they should wear a distinguishing badge. He sent a circular to police authorities affirming these points. Churchill, of course, had received a lot of adverse publicity following the action of the troops in Tonypandy, and he was clearly reluctant to add to this stigma by letting loose another bout of repression. Given that Sir Walter Runciman of the Federation was a Cabinet colleague, and that Lord Devonport, before his elevation to the peerage, had, as H. E. Kearley, been a government whip, this mild response to its protests must have shocked the die-hards of the Shipping Federation. John Burns's status in the government was an additional indication of the administration's adjustment to new realities. All this must have had something to do with the presence, after the settlement of the strike, of Walter Runciman at the union's dinner.

Askwith was himself more than just a pioneer of state conciliation. He had, with his evidence to a Select Committee, swung opinion round to the feasibility of the Trades Board system which Churchill, then at the Board of Trade, had introduced in 1909.[98] Further evidence of new forces and new faces at work on labour reforms is the introduction of William Beveridge, again by Churchill, to prepare plans for labour exchanges, aimed to tackle the problem of casual labour. Beveridge, who came from Toynbee Hall (a generation after Llewellyn Smith), was himself highly placed in the Board of Trade as Permanent Secretary. The Board's policy, shaped by these influences but also confirmed by the veritable avalanche of case material it dislodged in this period, was to promote union recognition and collective bargaining. Although they denied it, the 'practical', the pragmatic Smith, Askwith and the rest had clear departmental opinions, and in this represented a new engagement in Whitehall, alien to its older tradition of amateur, gentlemanly detachment. Right-wing Tories and industrial magnates regarded these officials as promoters of socialistic tendencies, while the left saw them as designing bureaucrats who were set upon seduction of the trade unions into a cosy, neutered relationship. The 'servile state' was much criticized not only in literary magazines but also among Labour activists. Trade-union leaders might share this suspicion but, given their own goals, could hardly afford to reject whatever help and support might be forthcoming from this quarter.[99] At the least, the days of thoroughgoing state support for unmitigated capitalist individualism were gone, not to return until the Conservative administrations of the 1980s.

Employers emerged from the experience of 1911 with varied reactions. In Liverpool, far-sighted big capitalists led the way in granting union recognition and control of labour supply. But they won, in return, commitments from the Dockers' Union, and from Sexton personally, to exert a new disciplinary control over the membership and to abide by collective agreements and agreed procedures. The pages of Sexton's Annual Reports in succeeding years are full of exhortation to this end:

> we are gradually getting back to the old spirit of discipline, with the new spirit of vigorous activity to help us on. For our one grave danger was to know how to use the NEW POWER we had gained by the enormous addition to our ranks. A Trades Union is the workman's industrial army, and no army can hope to enter upon a campaign with divided counsel. Its army regulations are the rules of the organisation, and are of such a democratic character that every member of the organisation can participate in the framing of them. But, having done so, they must be administered . . . by legitimately elected officers and committees . . .[100]

In other ports, resistance to change amongst employers was often stronger than in Liverpool, amongst both great employers, like the railway companies, and small. But even the carters' unions obtained three separate formal collective agreements during the year.

New Leaders

The unions benefited not only from an influx of mass membership, but also from the emergence of a new generation of capable younger leaders. Some, like John Burn in Hull, were unknown before the strike, and held no office at all. Many such volunteers were needed quite quickly to fill new official posts. Others, like Bevin in Bristol and Milligan in Liverpool, through their intense participation in the 1911 struggles rose from voluntary positions as branch officials to become full-time officers and major influences at regional level. Others again, like the Cox brothers in South Wales, took up no formal appointments but continued as goads to local militancy and voices of discontent.

Ben Tillett, in his history of the strike, paid generous tribute to the activists in London. They included many of his own generation, together with important new faces. Amongst these he numbered J. B. Ruark, whose father had been 'one of the great characters of the 1889 strike', from the Stevedores' Union; Sam March, general secretary of the London Carmen's Union; George Grisley, representing the Cranemen and Enginemen, 'young, experienced, strong of limb, lung, and voice . . . one feels glad that men as young as Grisley are to the front and helping to make history'; Frank Stillwell, financial clerk of the Dockers' Union, 'among the useful younger men'.[101] Two others selected for Tillett's praises were Bob Merry and John Davenport, the older and younger representatives of the United Order of General Labourers. Clearly a federal, all-union strike leadership had been achieved. And there was Fred Knee, the 'mighty atom', who along with Harry Quelch rendered help from the London Trades Council. Both of them, of course, were political comrades of Tillett's in the Social Democratic Federation and the British Socialist Party.

In 1911 the NSFU also threw up its new generation of leaders, two of whom we have already described as rather dubious members of the new wave. Set against them was the young, pugilistic Manny Shinwell. Joe Cotter, secretary of the new Ships' Cooks and Stewards Union, and Frank Pearce, the union's treasurer, were both syndicalists, and both sat on the Liverpool Strike Committee. (Pearce was shortly to abscond with the union's funds; Cotter evolved, after a post-war period of intense conflict, towards an intimate relationship with Havelock Wilson and much later took office in the Seamen's Union. Adventurism and defection do seem to have been endemic in the history of seafarers' trades unionism. We shall return to this problem.)

Another syndicalist on the Liverpool Strike Committee was James Murphy of the Liverpool Trades Council. With Tom Mann in the chair, it is clear that the doctrine was well represented there. But Mann was the opposite of sectarian in his conduct of the dispute and the Liverpool strike was by far the best directed of the whole series: 'Mann's syndicalism was limited in the short-term to the creation of "industrial solidarity". This was intended as the first step towards fuller industrial unionism, committed to revolutionary industrial rather than Parliamentary methods.'[102]

Outside Liverpool, where local syndicalist propagandists like Peter Larkin (James Larkin's brother) were especially active, syndicalists also came forward as strike leaders in Hull, Manchester and in South Wales. But, as in Mann's case, they were concerned to stay inside the limits set by the strikers themselves and by their local trade unions. The essential advice which they gave was to strive constantly to overcome sectionalism, and to learn unity in action. It was an important message.[103]

IV

The Growth of the Workers' Union

The Workers' Union had spent its earliest years in struggle with an unfriendly environment. It found progress and expansion most difficult to achieve. By 1910 its membership of 4,500 was little more than it had been at the turn of the century, when it had been only two years old. But all of a sudden, its luck turned: the next four years saw a transformation. Its membership growth was spectacular: entering the Great Unrest in 1911 with 18,000, the figure reached 143,000 in 1914.[104] Now it was to exercise real influence on the growth and potential of general unionism.

This last figure ran the union close up against the gasworkers, then the largest general union. Upon the outbreak of the First World War, the Workers' Union had become the fifth largest in the country. Recruitment on this scale fed further success.

From the first, the union had built its strength from the top down, relying on the appointment of full-time officers who were put to work in the field to bring trade unionism to hitherto wholly neglected areas, industries and occupations. This rather haphazard, but necessary, method now received a huge filip; as the union's contributions income grew, so it ploughed it back in the creation of many more full-time recruiting and organizing officers. In 1910 the union had six officers in the field, plus president and secretary. In 1914 it had more than forty; at that time the gasworkers, slightly larger in numbers, had only fourteen.

These four years saw more than continued random growth. Now there emerged a clear industrial and geographical pattern. Whilst the union had shared to some extent in the catch-as-catch-can expansion of the other general unions in the great revival of unionism, it also acquired its most significant industrial and occupational focus: as a mass organization of the semi-skilled grades in the engineering industry, and as a regional focus in the West Midlands.

Early 'Fordism'

Three factors, two specific to engineering, helped to define its role. The first was the nature of the Workers' Union; as a general union, willing and eager to expand wherever opportunity offered, it was tailor-made for the chance which now opened before it. Engineering unionism was dominated by the craft societies, and especially by the ASE, the original mid-Victorian 'new model' union. The engineering craftsmen had evolved a successful formula of closed, apprentice-based recruitment, based on the twin pillars of yesterday's labour aristocracy, fitters and turners. (Other crafts, the blacksmiths, the boilermakers, the pattern-makers, plumbers and carpenters, followed similar methods in the single-craft unions which abounded in such industries as engineering, vehicle building, construction and shipbuilding.) The craftsmen had no interest in the unionization of the 'unskilled', who were regarded as a sub-class.

Tight craft control on labour supply depended upon two things: the apprenticeship system and the indispensability of particular skills. But in consequence of a profound, transforming technological change, these controls were becoming daily more difficult to uphold. The turner and the fitter used handtools, on the lathe and at the workbench. But more and more automatic, power-driven machines were being invented to do the turner's work without handtools, so that his function, essentially the shaping of revolving metal components, could be performed by a machine-minder, whilst the lathe itself became more versatile. Training for the machine-minders' work was far less exacting than it had to be for the craftsmen. Similar advances were made in automatic, repetitive assembly processes, which undermined the indispensability of the craft fitter. The final element of change was the increasing size and specialization of engineering companies, which enabled small-batch and one-off jobs to be replaced by long runs of standardized products, at which point mass production, and the assembly line, became economic; the requisite inventions were naturally further stimulated by this. Management methods adapted in turn to this evolution. In place of the autonomy of the craftsman came rigid supervision, the elevation of the foreman's discipline, and detailed planning and control of the worker's every move. His speeds were increasingly determined by the machine which he 'minded'.

This change did not happen overnight. As it matured it came to dominate production industry with an all-pervasive engineers' culture, 'scientific management' and 'Fordism'. (The term 'Fordism' refers to the system of mass production – usually based on the assembly-line method of factory layout – in which the operatives' skills are reduced to a minimum, and he/she is required to perform endless, minute, repetitive tasks. It was first developed by Henry Ford at his Model T factory in Detroit, USA, in 1908. The term is now used more generally to denote the whole era of twentieth-century, labour-intensive, mass-production methods, which are now, at the end of the century, being superseded by automated, robotized and computer-controlled factories – hence the concept 'post-Fordism'. We shall deal at length with the 'Fordist' phase of the TGWU story in a subsequent volume.) The Workers' Union was in almost at the start of this profound process and, as its adoption spread further, the union could frequently run ahead of managers who were themselves learning as they went along. By successfully organizing this new, soon-to-be dominant assembly-worker grade in engineering, the

Workers' Union helped to ensure its eventual incorporation into general unionism, as the Dockers' and Gasworkers' Unions did for workers in many other rising mass-production industries such as chemicals, rubber, paint, oil-refining, brewing, flour-milling, food-processing, brick and cement production, and so on. In engineering, both these unions had some presence amongst the purely labouring groups, but it was the Workers' Union which pinpointed the needs of the semi-skilled workers, at the very moment that they were becoming part of a recognizable grade, with its own particular needs in the bargaining and wages structures of the industry.

Skilled Men and Labourers

The ASE could, of course, have forestalled the rise of the Workers' Union by opening its ranks to the recruitment of non-apprenticed workers. Indeed, it was urged to do so by both Tom Mann, and by Charles Duncan (the union's first president after Mann accepted the honorary title of vice-president. Duncan later became General Secretary). Both men came from the skilled ranks of the ASE themselves, and both had worked together on reform projects within it. Not only did the ASE fail to take their advice, but it also failed in the attempt to prevent the employers from displacing the traditional skills by the use of new methods. Semi-skilled employment grew apace. The 'machine question' lay behind the great national lock-out of 1897–8, and the resultant defeat of the ASE culminated in the employers' reassertion of their managerial prerogative 'to select, train, and employ those whom they consider best adapted to the various operations carried out in their workshops, and . . . pay them according to their ability as workmen'.[105]

Although by 1914 machine-minders made up one-fifth of the industry's labour force, the ASE's reluctance, at branch level, to admit them even after the union modified its entry qualifications, left them with nowhere to go – until the Workers' Union, which had not embarked on this course initially, recognized their needs and swept them into mass membership.

The union's first major advance in the industry was at the Birmingham Small Arms (BSA) factory. From this base, where mass-production methods were already in place, the union's growth was predominantly in engineering, with the result that by 1914 half of the union's hundred largest branches were almost exclusively composed of engineers. They set themselves to promote the claims of the semi-skilled in a wage structure which had at that time little coherence and no national standards, outside the craft rate. As a highly centralized union, seeking to promote the interest of a new grade, it was always likely that it would be a force tending to promote general, standard wage claims over as wide an area as possible. This is exactly what happened in the great Midlands engineering strikes of 1913.

Already in 1911, a significant strike at BSA Birmingham set the pattern for what was to follow. The semi-skilled had followed the craftsmen into a strike with demands of their own, and emerged with much improved relative wages. They made particular gains for the piece-workers. Beginning the strike mainly as non-unionists, their lack of funds and consequent destitution won publicity and public sympathy. It also taught its own lesson, for recruitment enjoyed an immediate stimulus. More WU organizers were appointed, including Julia Varley, the first woman officer, because female labour was common in the Birmingham engineering industry.[106] Of course, the ASE did not admit women members. In 1913 the union raised the banner of its demand for a standard 23s. a week minimum in engineering, with a minimum 12s. for women!

The Black Country Strikes

The scene was set for the Black Country Strike – a struggle which rivals in significance the more famous epics of the labour movement. The Black Country Strike began as a series of unconnected disputes and culminated in a vast wave of industrial action. There were three main phases. First there was a movement, largely successful, to win the 23/- minimum at the major engineering firms in Birmingham, Smethwick, and West Bromwich. Then came strikes in Smethwick and the Black Country which caused a chain reaction. Finally the strike fever turned into an epidemic, and for six weeks around 40,000 workers were affected.[107]

Avery's weighing-machine factory was the first to yield a new minimum of 21s., union recognition and separate negotiations for the extra 2s. In West Bromwich, United Hinges' women strikers spread their stoppage to neighbouring factories, and John Beard and Julia Varley formulated precise claims. (Beard, a former farm worker, and now a union organizer, was soon to replace Robert Morley as the union's president.) Most of the women earned less than 10s. a week, and the demand was made for a 12s. minimum, for enhanced piece-rates and shift premia. In two weeks the firms affected conceded the bulk of this programme. BSA and the huge Metropolitan Carriage and Wagon Company in Saltley conceded the 23s., and by the end of April most firms had followed suit. As a result, 10,000 workers gained an increase of 2s. a week.

In the next phase, a prolonged strike originated in the Birmingham Carriage Company; as elsewhere, the strikers entered the dispute as non-unionists and were ineligible for strike pay. A massive community effort went into providing relief, with charity shows at theatres, tradesmen donating food, and the Town Council of Smethwick feeding children at school. Varley summoned up the strikers' wives to lend support. They were being sustained, by these means, by only 1–5s. a week.

Wolverhampton Trades Council now led a new agitation for the minimum wage. Its secretary, Harry Bagley, later became a Workers' Union organizer. Women workers again took a prominent part in the town's campaign. Strikes spread throughout the district. In May, tube workers in Wednesbury and Walsall struck for the 23s. Their battle mirrored those that had inspired it: first the strike of non-unionists with vague but strong discontents, then the arrival of the WU organizers and the adoption of the union's programme of demands, then the mobilization of neighbouring factories and of public support. By the end of May, this wave of action involved some 10,000 workers.

At the end of May, the Smethwick carriage strikers, still in deadlock, made a renewed surge towards victory by spreading their struggle to Oldbury and Wednesbury, where the company's workers joined the strike after receiving 1,500 marchers from Smethwick. The tube strikers copied this method, marching from Wolverhampton through Great Bridge, West Bromwich, to Halesowen, where workers at Stewart and Lloyd joined in. The movement was so general that Beard set up, as a co-ordinating body, a Minimum Wage Council, which drew up a more elaborate set of common demands.

During June, strikers numbered between 30,000 and 40,000. As some firms conceded the 23s. and work was restored, new disputes broke out to take their place. The 3,000 workers at GEC, a firm with notoriously bad conditions, made a specially large addition to the total. The union had, until this point, supported every new outbreak; it never initiated claims, but followed them round, articulated the demands and won thousands of members in this process. Now it began to discourage further strikes, but without much effect. Public relief funds raised locally were becoming clearly inadequate; a national appeal produced a good response, but not sufficient to prevent the first deaths from starvation in early June. Strikers now had resort to Poor Law relief. The employers, who had been in retreat since the first wave of strikes, began to show intransigence; they formed a Midland Employers' Federation to stiffen their opposition to the union. In mid-June they conceded some part of the union's claims, but insisted on a differential of 2s. between Birmingham's minimum of 23s. and the Black Country rate. At this point, hunger marchers were dispatched to raise funds countrywide, and more firms conceded when the ASE's craftsmen threatened sympathy action. Other firms sought to break the strike, some trying to reopen with anti-union labour. The levels of violence, stone-throwing and street collisions with police notably increased.

George Askwith Arrives . . .

The pattern of 1911 in the port strikes, already evident in the recurrent surges of stoppages, was completed when George Askwith appeared on the scene and almost immediately succeeded in opening the process of conciliation. The Midland Employers' Federation accepted his role, and conceded 23s. immediately for Birmingham, Oldbury and Smethwick. Elsewhere the rate went up to 22s., with the last shilling forthcoming in six months' time. Women won a general 12s. minimum. Permanent conciliation machinery was agreed. The MEF was converted to collective bargaining, and Askwith recorded his satisfaction at improved industrial relations in the Midlands following the settlement.

The Midlands strikes embraced boiler and bridge works, metal-rolling firms, tube works, railway-carriage and wagon works, nut-and-bolt works and many related trades. In their midst, a serious but separate dispute occurred in the Midlands firebrick-making industry, and a Wages Board was created as a result. Askwith's role was crucial: the speed with which state conciliation effected settlement was astonishing, given the tough stance adopted by the employers up to the moment of his intervention. He arrived to find the two sides, the MEF and the Birmingham and Allied Trades Societies' Federation, holed up in different hotels. Within three days the conciliation was accomplished, and a disputes procedure was agreed which recognized the union. It 'involved stages of exhaustive discussion, speedy examination of claims, and no stoppage of work while negotiations were pending, together with avoidance of stoppage or suspension of work on account of outside disputes, while at the same time the right to strike or lockout was maintained.'[108]

After the great port strikes of 1911–12, a Birmingham manufacturer had said to Askwith that he just could not understand what had got into port workers. But by 1913 he and his fellows had their explanation. There was, as Askwith recognized, a clear connection: the dock strikes had their demonstration effect on the previously non-union men and women of the Midlands.

The dispute in the Midlands was a sequel to the economic disputes of 1911 and 1912, but it must not be supposed that any of these disputes failed to leave a mark. They indicated to labour the value of organisation, which was being actively pressed throughout the country, and the value of propaganda, which more and more made its force felt; they increased the cohesion of labour, particularly among semi-skilled and unskilled labour; they educated both leaders and rank and file on things to be done and things to be avoided in the course of a strike.[109]

Beard summed up the gain in the union's stature: 'In the Midlands, we can hold our own against craft and sectional prejudice, and we are able to declare that the Workers' Union stands for class as against craft.'[110]

The union continued its progress, across trades and industries, territories and counties, until the First World War. Even a partial catalogue of its conquests makes astonishing reading. In the core Midland towns, membership rose twenty-eightfold. In Coventry, in a highly significant development, a three-day strike brought the cycle and motor-vehicle trade into organization, recognition and a minimum wage of 26s. 6d. The Employers' Federation signed an agreement on Provisions for Avoiding Disputes; amongst the signatories were Daimler and Humber cars. In Swadlincote among the clay and pipe workers, in Burton at the breweries, in Stoke, in Nottingham, in Gloucester and Swindon, the union gained many members and considerable victories. Many of these sectors remained within the TGWU, after the absorption of the Workers' Union into the amalgamation, on into the 1990s.

Teaching by Example

In Manchester, Cheshire, Preston and North Wales, new groups were organized and wage gains won. In Yorkshire, engineers, foundry and boiler workers, gas, road and other council workers, builders' labourers, brickmakers and quarrymen, textile labourers and maintenance-men, brewery and metal workers came in from Halifax and the Calder Valley to Sheffield and Doncaster.

In South Wales, steel workers joined, struck and won a minimum day-wage. Smelter workers struck for nine weeks and obtained extra Sunday pay, although they did not win alleviation in their working hours, which increased the risks of lead-poisoning. In Cardiff the flour-millers and others formed a regional membership of 12,000.

In Cornwall, an embittered struggle against the clay-pit owners of St Austell resulted in much police violence. Beard was kicked and punched when he appeared on the picket line. Julia Varley was also injured. Eventually, after a year of conflict, even here the union won recognition, wage increases and complete organization amongst the clay workers.

In Glasgow, foundry and building labourers, the herring-barrel coopers, railway shopmen and brewers were organized.

In the South, there was renewal in London and much success in Essex, where Colchester became a major centre for the WU, which also organized a ball-bearing factory in Chelmsford. In Braintree, Courtaulds workers were organized, and in Bedford and Oxford so were the Witney blanket mills.

Such widespread progress was possible because of the boom in trade.

But it was helped by the discovery of 'workers' power' through trade-union success, by new technologies which were grouping new grades of workers together in mass production, and of course because much of the union's drive was directed to non-union, virgin territory.

Inter-union Rivalries

But not always. Such a rapid progress inevitably gave rise to inter-union problems, and brought the Workers' Union to the heart of the debate on the federation and amalgamation of general workers' unions. Its very success made it suspect in the eyes of some other unions. Inevitably, it was accused of poaching – by, amongst others, the main steel union. Its application to affiliate to the TUC was rejected. Even so, it does not seem to have had a worse-than-average record as a predator among older unions. Doubtless it was also resented because, although it recruited previously unorganized workers, it often seemed to be invading territories which others regarded as theirs. Was it felt to harbour 'ecumenical ambitions' to be itself the 'One Big Union'?

In practice, however, it never sought to invade the area of the great craft societies, and always insisted that it was a union of the semi-skilled. In agriculture, where it genuinely was the industrial union, and in engineering, where it systematically recruited the machine-minders, it had a status and role which were unique. It was in engineering, nevertheless, that for the WU inter-union friction was most intense. Its aim – to represent the semi-skilled in the industry's hierarchy of wage movements – was resented and frequently frustrated by the ASE.

How the union understood its proper place in the whole structure was shown when it took part in the 1902 attempt at amalgamation of the general unions, and when it joined the General Labourers' National Council in 1908. A ballot of its own members in 1911 showed a large majority in favour of the merger of all general unions. Subsequently, it took part in the major debate on amalgamation of both general and transport unions in 1914, a subject to which we shall return in chapter 15.

V

The Children Join In

Reverting to 1911, as if to provide a final note to that incredible year, in September, when all the actions were over, the schoolchildren ended their summer holidays and promptly struck school. It had been a holiday during which they had witnessed their fathers joining in massive actions to change their conditions – conditions which their families, young and old, shared. Teachers, parents and the public at large were astonished when, in town after town (at least sixty major urban areas, including all the ports, were affected), school after school broke out of its classrooms at the start of the new term. 'Some of the [press] reports speak of hundreds of children parading through the streets and at Dundee and Hull thousands of pupils defied the school authorities, but it is not possible to give the actual numbers of children who left their classrooms.'[111] But with every major city in the land included in the list of places where *some* children struck – London, Birmingham, Glasgow, Coventry, Newcastle, Nottingham, Manchester, Sheffield and Southampton amongst them – we are faced with something on the scale of a junior General Strike!

The children organized pickets, bands and marches, stoned school windows, intimidated 'blacklegs' and went from school to school calling out their fellow pupils. Their marching song was 'Fall In and Follow Me'. For sure, the slum schools which engendered these rebellions were grim enough 'work-places', mirroring the harsh environment of adult work which surrounded them. If head teachers were not always sadistic bullies, the teaching was often repetitious and boring. The children invented appropriate demands. Their banners demanded 'No More Stick', 'Payment for Monitors', 'Half-day Holidays'.[112]

These poor, undernourished, undersized children had caught the mood of revolt. They were starting a serious but immensely spirited game: it was played out to the end when the parents, especially the mothers, recovered from the shock and broke the strikes by delivering up their charges to retribution at the school gates. It is an intriguing question: how many of those children, eleven years later, were to constitute part of the first generation of TGWU members?

Notes

1 Elie Halevy, *A History of the English People in the Nineteenth Century*, vol. VI: *The Rule of Democracy, 1905–14* (Ernest Benn, 1934), book II, p. 445.
2 Ibid., pp. 446–7.
3 Quoted in Lord Askwith, *Industrial Problems and Disputes* (John Murray, 1920), pp. 146–7.
4 J. Ramsay MacDonald, *The Social Unrest* (T. Foulis, 1913), p. 35.
5 Jack Jones, 'A Liverpool Socialist Education', *History Workshop Journal*, issue 18 (1984), p. 4.
6 Recalled by Jim Roche, a veteran militant from the Leeds clothing workers' union. Jim Roche, who was close enough to Tom Mann to be a pall-bearer at his funeral, also recalled that the old man, who ended his days as a publican in Yorkshire (he died in 1940), used to say that there was more sense talked in his bar-parlour in one evening than in a year of parliamentary debate!

7   The *Industrial Syndicalist*, Documents in Society History, no. 3 (Spokes-man Books, 1974), pp. 39–40 and 41–2.
8   We have reported several of Tillett's previous bouts of ill-heath, which alternated throughout his career with phases of intense activity, in a discernible pattern. His biographer has summarized this process: 'When healthy, Tillett would work at a feverish, indeed manic, pace. Letters, pamphlets, proclamations and articles would flow from his pen; he would embark upon ambitious speaking and organising tours, he would take up with great energy the cause of the moment, all the while carrying on the multitude of administrative tasks which fell to him as general secretary of a major union. His activities would reach their climax: a strike would be won or lost, a political manoeuvre succeed or fail. Immediately afterwards Tillett's health would break, he would be out of commission for months at a time, his illness real but accompanied by psychosomatic symptoms and depression amounting on more than one occasion to complete nervous breakdown' (Jonathan Schneer, *Ben Tillett: Portrait of a Labour Leader* (Croom Helm, 1982), p. 114).
9   NUDL Annual Report, 1910, p. 2.
10   The *Industrial Syndicalist*, vol. I, no. 6, p. 48.
11   Phillip J. Leng, *The Welsh Dockers* (G. W. and A. Hesketh, 1981), p. 49.
12   Askwith, *Industrial Problems and Disputes*. p. 149.
13   Arthur Marsh and Victoria Ryan, *The Seamen: A History of the National Union of Seamen* (Malthouse, 1989), p. 54.
14   Tom Mann, *Memoirs* (1923; reissued McGibbon and Kee, 1967), pp. 207–9.
15   M. J. Daunton, 'Inter-Union Relations on the Waterfront: Cardiff, 1888–1914', *International Review of Social History*, vol. XXII (1977), p. 368, and L. H. Powell, *The Shipping Federation: A History of the First Sixty Years, 1890–1950* (Shipping Federation, 1950), p. 21.
16   Harry Gosling, *Up and Down Stream* (Methuen, 1927), pp. 147–8.
17   Report of the International Transport Federation, Berlin, 1913; quoted in Basil Mogridge, 'Militancy and Inter-Union Rivalry in British Shipping, 1911–1929', *International Review of Social History*, vol. VI (1961), p. 381. Williams's comment was made in retrospect, for he succeeded James Anderson as General Secretary of the NTWF only in June 1912, at the age of thirty-one. He had been a cardiff coal-trimmer, President of the NALU, and a local councillor. He will occupy centre stage throughout Part II of this volume, and continued in his post with the Federation until 1925.
18   Powell, *The Shipping Federation*, p. 24.
19   Ben Tillett, *History of the London Transport Strike of 1911* (National Transport Workers' Federation, 1912), foreword, p. x.
20   Ibid.
21   Gosling, *Up and Down Stream*, p. 147.
22   Gordon Phillips, 'The National Transport Workers' Federation, 1910–1927' (unpublished PhD thesis, Oxford University, 1968), p. 84.
23   Askwith, *Industrial Problems and Disputes*, p. 149.
24   G. A. Phillips, 'The National Transport Workers' Federation', p. 78, says: 'The events of 1911 are still, in large part, inexplicable. To union leaders

they remained as mysterious as they were unexpected. And historians have not come much nearer to establishing their origins.' It is interesting to note that H. A. Clegg, Alan Fox and A. F. Thompson, *A History of British Trade Unions since 1889*, vol. I: *1889–1910* (Oxford University Press, 1964), p. 55, open their account of the great 1889 precursor of 1911 with a similar sense of mystery: 'The "new unionism" stands out as one of the most colourful and baffling phenomena in British trade union history'.

25   Tom Mann, *From Single Tax to Syndicalism* (Guy Bowman, 1913), pp. 68–70.

26   Phillips, 'The National Transport Workers' Federation', p. 95.

27   Ibid., p. 97.

28   Trevor Griffiths, *Through the Night and Such Impossibilities: Two Plays for Television* (Faber and Faber, 1977). The other programmes in the series, all of them screened, were on E. Nesbit, the Countess of Warwick, Marie Lloyd, Baden-Powell, Conan Doyle, Horatio Bottomley, Rolls-Royce, and Lloyd George. As Trevor Griffiths puts it in his foreword to the volume, 'Tom Mann might well have roughed the series up a bit, but it's arguable he might have also done something towards redressing its "balance" too.'

29   The Liverpool carters' chairman was a prominent local Tory. The union was strongly 'Orange' in its image and influence.

30   *Liverpool Daily Post and Mercury*, 15 June 1911; quoted in E. L. Taplin, *The Dockers' Union: A Study of the National Union of Dock Labourers, 1889–1922* (Leicester University Press, 1986), p. 85.

31   Ibid., 21 June 1911; p. 86.

32   Ibid., 26 June 1911; p. 87.

33   Ibid., pp. 89–90.

34   Ibid., 28 June 1911; pp. 89–90.

35   Ibid., 3 July 1911; pp. 91–2.

36   George Millington's obituary notice, TGWU *Record*, June 1925, p. 244.

37   R. A. Leeson (ed.), *Strike: A Live History, 1887–1971* (Allen and Unwin, 1973), pp. 41–2.

38   *The Transport Worker*, vol. I, no. 1 (1911), p. 46.

39   Leeson, *Strike: A Live History*, pp. 40–2.

40   The following passage draws on the account by Keith Brooker, *The Hull Strikes of 1911* (East Yorkshire Local History Society, 1979).

41   Father Hopkins had been the cathedral organist and chaplain in Rangoon, and in Arakan and Calcutta was the founder and Superior-General of the Anglican Order of St Paul. He appeared at Liverpool, South Wales and in London during the 1911 strikes, as well as in Hull. He became a trustee of the union and a strong supporter of Havelock Wilson on its Executive.

42   Brooker, *The Hull Strikes of 1911*, p. 12.

43   Ibid., p. 17.

44   Askwith, *Industrial Problems and Disputes*, p. 149.

45   This is the figure given in Taplin, *The Dockers' Union*, p. 85. Askwith, *Industrial Problems and Disputes*, gives 15,000 and Brooker, *The Hull Strikes of 1911*, gives 'several thousand'.

46   Askwith, *Industrial Problems and Disputes*, p. 150.

47   Brooker, *The Hull Strikes of 1911*, p. 20.

48   The fight is reported in Brooker, *The Hull Strikes of 1911*.
      Taplin, *The Dockers' Union*, p. 84, cites an official NTWF source, which reported diplomatically on the inter-union relationship in Hull a year later: 'the two unions have worked as one for the benefit of the Hull dockers . . . and there are over 10,000 dockers enrolled in the two unions' (Humberside Transport Workers' *Gazette and Monthly Record*, 16 February 1912). Tillett's union had a district office and two branches, and the NUDL had a district office and four branches. In 1912 the NUDL's Liverpool branches' contribution income totalled £10,660, and Hull's £2,284. The Hull branches of Tillett's union returned only £438 in the same year. For the NUDL, the figure for 1911 had been £1,112 and for the DWRGWU, £298 (*source:* Annual Reports of the two unions).
49   Quoted in Brooker, *The Hull Strikes of 1911*, p. 11.
50   Askwith, *Industrial Problems and Disputes*, p. 152.
51   *The Transport Worker*, vol. 1, no. 1 (1911), p. 3.
52   Ibid.
53   Ben Tillett, *Memories and Reflections* (John Long, 1931), p. 30.
54   Gosling, *Up and Down Stream*, p. 153.
55   Ibid.
56   *The Industrial Syndicalist*, vol. 1, no. 10 (April 1911).
57   M. J. Daunton, 'Inter-Union Relations on the Waterfront', p. 370.
58   Tupper wrote his memoirs, *The Seamen's Torch* (Hutchinson, 1938), in which, whilst revealing nothing of his life before 1910, he hints at an adventurist past: 'my doings in half the countries of the globe would make a passable book'. His claims to naval or military rank were almost certainly spurious, as was his entitlement to the VC. Basil Mogridge describes him as 'a bankrupt company promoter turned private detective' (*International Review of Social History*, vol. VI (1961), p. 401n.). After his prosecution for incitement to riot, when the Crown was represented by F. E. Smith (Lord Birkenhead), he revelled in Smith's having designated him 'the most dangerous man in Europe'. He was as proud of his strike-breaking activities in the inter-war shipping industry, as Havelock Wilson's principal assistant, as he was of his agitator's role in 1911. In his last years he became an agent for the government's spy system, helping to identify 'bolsheviks' amongst his own members. Yet in 1911 he succeeded in smuggling a pro-union cook on board the Shipping Federation's depot ship, the *Lady Jocelyn*, who then poisoned the strike-breakers and their crew. In addition to his exploits in Cardiff that year, he showed similar intransigence in Liverpool, where on 'bloody Sunday' he appeared on the rostrum with Tom Mann, the Rev. Hopkins and the Strike Committee. In the police-charge that day, he received a truncheon blow on the head from a constable as he joined the fleeing crowd. He survived to participate in a wide range of colourful events, living on until 1942. Four years later, 'his ashes were consigned to the deep from the *Queen Mary* in the presence of the British delegation – Government representatives, shipowners, and seafarers – on their way to the Seattle Conference in 1946. It would no doubt have pleased Captain Tupper, who all his life was a valiant fighter for the cause he had adopted, to have known that even at the last he had the final word; some of his ashes were blown back over the delegates!' (Powell, *The Shipping Federation*, p. 25). See also vol. II.

59   Tupper, *The Seamen's Torch*, pp. 39–40.
60   Leng, *The Welsh Dockers*, pp. 57–8.
61   Tupper, *The Seamen's Torch*, p. 34.
62   Leeson, *Strike: A Live History*, pp. 42–3.
63   Daunton, 'Inter-Union Relations on the Waterfront', p. 372.
64   Ibid., p. 374.
65   Leng, *The Welsh Dockers*, p. 61.
66   Ibid., p. 62.
67   Brian Atkinson, *Trade Unions in Bristol* (Bristol Branch, Historical Association, University of Bristol, 1982), p. 17.
68   Ibid., p. 20.
69   Ibid., p. 21.
70   Emanuel Shinwell, *Lead with the Left: My First Ninety-six Years* (Cassell, 1981), pp. 45ff.
71   Pat Murphy's recorded notes (Leeson, *Strike: A Live History*, p. 43), in a section on the shipping strike in Goole, relate that 'Havelock Wilson issued a manifesto declaring that if the shipowners recognised the union he was prepared to concede more favourable terms, and threatened his members with fines for questioning his actions'.
72   Tupper, *The Seamen's Torch*, p. 63.
73   Mogridge, 'Militancy and Inter-Union Rivalry in British Shipping', pp. 384–5.
74   Shinwell, *Lead with the Left*, p. 49.
75   Tillett, *Memories and Reflections*, p. 4.
76   Ibid., p. 14.
77   Ibid., p. 13.
78   This is the same Albert Rollitt whom we met in chapter 1, when he was Tory MP for Hull and a patron of the earliest Hull dockers' union, and later in chapter 5, mediating in the 1893 Hull lock-out.
79   Tillett, *Memories and Reflections*, p. 69.
80   Ibid., p. 20.
81   Askwith, *Industrial Problems and Disputes*, p. 158.
82   Tillett, *Memories and Reflections*, p. 36.
83   John Lovell, *Stevedores and Dockers: a Study of Trade Unionism in the Port of London, 1870–1914* (Macmillan, 1969), p. 173.
84   NUDL *Annual Report, 1911*, p. 4.
85   Ibid.
86   Ibid.
87   Ibid.
88   Ibid., p. 7.
89   DWRGWU Annual Report, 1911, p. 8.
90   H. A. Clegg, *A History of British Trade Unions since 1889*, vol. II: *1911–1933* (Oxford University Press, 1985), p. 40.
91   Paul Smith, 'The Process of Unionisation in the Road Haulage Industry' (unpublished PhD thesis, Warwick University, 1988), p. 68.
92   See note 71.
93   Gosling, *Up and Down Stream*, p. 157. Robert Williams made a similar claim in his report to the ITF in 1912: 'The phenomenal success of the mass movements of 1911 was due to the existence of the Federation and

the vague recognition or their identity of interest shown by all transport workers'; quoted in Phillips, 'The National Transport Workers' Federation', chapter 2, p. 98.

94 See Phillips, 'The National Transport Workers' Federation', pp. 579–80. The eleven new affiliations were: the Amalgamated General and Warehouse Workers' Union, the Amalgamated Protective Society of Engine and Crane Men, the Boiler Firemen and Wire Rope Makers, the Hull Seamen and Marine Firemen's Association, the Liverpool South End Coalheavers' Association, the Mersey Quay and Railway Carters' Union, the United Carters' Association of England, the United Order of General Labourers of London, the Weaver Watermen's Association, the National Amalgamated Union of Labour, and the Scottish Union of Dock Labourers.

95 Ibid., quoted p. 99.
96 Ibid., chapter 3, contains this discussion.
97 Powell, *The Shipping Federation*, p. 22.
98 Eric Wigham, *Strikes and the Government, 1893–1974* (Macmillan, 1976), p. 22.
99 See Alan Fox, *History and the Heritage: The Social Origins of the British Industrial Relations System* (Allen and Unwin, 1985), pp. 248–9; and Keith Middlemas, *Politics in Industrial Society: The Experience of the British System since 1911* (André Deutsch, 1979), pp. 29–31.
100 NUDL Annual Report, 1912, pp. 4–5.
101 Tillett, *History of the London Transport Strike of 1911*, p. 56.
102 R. J. Holton, 'Syndicalism and Labour on Merseyside, 1906–14', in H. R. Hikins (ed.), *Building the Union: Studies in the Growth of the Workers' Movement, Merseyside, 1756–1967* (Toulouse Press, 1973), p. 139.
103 P. Lloyd has sought to trace 'The Influence of Syndicalism in the Dock Strikes in Hull and Manchester in 1911' (unpublished MA thesis, Warwick University, 1972). He concludes that 'Syndicalism in both Hull and Manchester was only contributory in a secondary and indirect way to the tactical conduct of the Dock Strikes of 1911.' In Hull, only Burn of the dockers and Bell of the seamen, can be found uttering syndicalist sentiment, and though in Manchester there is slightly more evidence of 'institutionalized' syndicalist presences, 'how strong these were is difficult to assess'. Syndicalism never became "institutionalized", but its grapevine, its informal networks, were important contributors to the spirit of independence and militancy which inspired the strikes.
104 In these pages, we have drawn freely on Richard Hyman, *The Workers' Union* (Oxford University Press, 1971), chapter 3; on Askwith, *Industrial Problems and Disputes*, chapter XXV: 'The Midlands, 1913'; and on Clegg, *History of British Trade Unions since 1889*, vol. II, pp. 58–60.
105 Hyman, *The Workers' Union*, p. 41.
106 When the union merged into the TGWU in 1929, Julia Varley, together with Florence Hancock and Ellen McCullough came with it to become successive TGWU National Women's Officers.
107 Hyman, *The Workers' Union*, pp. 50–1.
108 Lord Askwith, *Industrial Problems and Disputes*, p. 257.
109 Ibid.

110   Hyman, *The Workers' Union*, p.60.

111   Dave Marson, *Children's Strikes in 1911*, History Workshop Pamphlets no. 9 (History Workshop, 1973).

112   The historian of the children's strikes, Dave Marson, was – appropriately – a Hull docker, who attended a day-release course taught by Tony Topham, went on to Ruskin College and there researched and wrote his pamphlet (see previous note). He then used the material, with Billy Colville, as the basis of a play, *Fall In and Follow Me*, which was successfully performed at the Half Moon Theatre in Whitechapel, 10–27 July 1973. The script was published as History Workshop Pamphlet no. 13.

Index